lonely planet

New York & the Mid-Atlantic

New York State
p103

Pennsylvania
p220

New York City
p48

Philadelphia
p175

New Jersey
p150

Maryland
p317

Delaware
p298

West Virginia
p387

WASHINGTON, DC
p251

Virginia
p344

Ray Bartlett, Jule
John Garry, Michae
Marisa Pa

CONTENTS

Plan Your Trip

The Journey Begins Here	4
New York and the Mid-Atlantic Map	8
Our Picks	10
Regions & Cities	24
Itineraries	26
When to Go	34
Get Prepared	36
The Food Scene	38
The Outdoors	42

The Guide

New York City 48
Find Your Way 50
Plan Your Days 52
Financial District & Lower Manhattan 54
SoHo, Chinatown, Nolita & Little Italy 63
East Village & the Lower East Side 68
West Village & Chelsea 73
Midtown 80
Upper East Side 86
Upper West Side 92
Brooklyn 97
Places We Love To Stay 101

New York State 103
Find Your Way 104
Plan Your Time 106
Montauk 108
Beacon 116
Woodstock 122
Lake George 129
Ithaca 136
Buffalo & Niagara Falls 142
Places We Love To Stay 149

New Jersey 150
Find Your Way 152
Plan Your Days 153
Princeton 154
Beyond Princeton 156
Cape May 160
Beyond Cape May 163
Places We Love To Stay 173

Philadelphia 175
Find Your Way 176
Plan Your Days 177
Old City & Society Hill 178
Chinatown & the Gayborhood 185
Rittenhouse Square & Center City West 192
Logan Square & Fairmont 196
Fishtown & Northern Liberties 199
South Philadelphia 204
University City & West Philadelphia 208
Beyond Philadelphia 214
Places We Love To Stay 219

Pennsylvania 220
Find Your Way 222
Plan Your Time 223

Cape May (p160)

Pittsburgh 224
Beyond Pittsburgh 230
PA Wilds 235
The Poconos 239
Lancaster & PA Dutch Country 243
Gettysburg 247
Places We Love To Stay 249

Washington, DC 251
Find Your Way 252
Plan Your Days 254
The White House & Foggy Bottom 256
National Mall 261
Penn Quarter & Chinatown 266
Southwest 269
Capitol Hill 273
Northeast 279
Adams Morgan & the U Street Corridor 282
Downtown & Dupont Circle 288
Georgetown 292
Places We Love To Stay 297

Delaware 298
Find Your Way 300
Plan Your Time 301
Wilmington 302
Dover 307
Rehoboth 310
Places We Love To Stay 315

Brooklyn Bridge (p55)

Annapolis (p320)

Maryland	317
Find Your Way	318
Plan Your Time	319
Annapolis	320
Beyond Annapolis	323
Eastern Shore	325
Ocean City	329
Baltimore	331
Frederick	336
Western Maryland	340
Places We Love To Stay	343

Virginia	344
Find Your Way	346
Plan Your Time	347
Richmond	348
Williamsburg	353
Charlottesville	359
Roanoke	362
Harrisonburg	366
Virginia Beach	369
Beyond Virginia Beach	371
Arlington	373
Fredericksburg	376
Alexandria	380
Places We Love To Stay	385

West Virginia	387
Find Your Way	388
Plan Your Time	389
Charleston	390
Beyond Charleston	394
Morgantown	398
Beyond Morgantown	400
Places We Love To Stay	405

Toolkit

Arriving	408
Getting Around	409
Money	410
Accommodations	411
Family Travel	412
Health & Safe Travel	413
Food, Drink & Nightlife	414
Responsible Travel	416
LGBTIQ+ Travelers	418
Accessible Travel	419
Nuts & Bolts	421

Storybook

A History of New York & the Mid-Atlantic in 15 Places	424
Meet the East Coasters	428
The Birth of America's Summer Vacation	430
Mid-Atlantic Wines	433

Storm King Art Center (p118)

NEW YORK & THE MID-ATLANTIC
THE JOURNEY BEGINS HERE

The Mid-Atlantic is a region caught in between. There's southern charm and northern chutzpah, eastern beaches and western mountains. In New York, you'll find the nation's most populous city and the contiguous USA's largest protected park. Growing up in the rural Catskills, I thought I had to choose: country or cosmopolitan. But what I love most about living here now is that compromise isn't required. When done right, life can be an everything bagel, sprinkled with all the spice cabinet's flavors. Take the train a couple of hours from NYC and you can trade steel towers for rocky summits. Ride the ferry and all of a sudden you're on the Jersey Shore. The nation's founding practically happened underfoot and history gets made daily in DC. World-class museums? We got 'em. Exceptional farm-to-table food? Check. Local vineyards? Overflowing. Then there are the seasons – ever-changing and always ready with a colorful palette of new adventures.

John Garry
@garryjohnfrancis

John Garry is a writer, teacher, urban wanderer, mountain hiker and avid museum-goer who probably eats out too much in Brooklyn.

My favourite experience is hiking between sculptures at **Storm King Art Center** (p118), an alfresco Hudson Valley museum that blends handcrafted beauty with natural wonder – it's exceptional around peak leaf-peeping season.

WHO GOES WHERE

Our writers and experts choose the places that, for them, define the Mid-Atlantic.

Philadelphia is so full of great districts it's hard to recommend just one, but **Center City** (p192) is the most versatile. It's got the City Hall building and the statue of William Penn atop it. At Penn's feet are the city's best restaurants, delightful museums, and historic sites, all within 30 minutes' walk.

Ray Bartlett
@kaisoradotcom

Ray has worked on more than 100 Lonely Planet projects.

Maryland (p317) is lovely around its edges, with the Eastern Shore a highlight. Secluded coves shelter waterside towns, quiet marshlands echo with the calls of ospreys, brilliant sunsets and unique traditions endure. When you cross the Bay Bridge, you feel slower-paced rhythms taking over.

Mary Fitzpatrick
@MaryFitzTravel

Mary is an Africa-based writer and author with long roots in Maryland.

The **Delaware River** (p235) and its tributaries cut through a swathe of rural Pennsylvania and New Jersey. Whether white-water rafting, canoeing or tubing, you're floating along a river that has played an integral role in the area's and the nation's history.

Michael Grosberg
likelocal.io

Michael is longtime Lonely Planet writer based in Philadelphia and co-founder of travel start-up LikeLocal.

Washington, DC (p251) is a beautiful, creative city that's both full of nature and has an extensive calendar of interesting intellectual, artistic and cultural offerings. And while it may seem like everyone has an opinion (and they're happy to tell you about it), they're also happy to tell you about their favorite restaurant, pottery class or even to take you out for a drink. For all the political charge in the city, Washingtonians are friendly and exceptionally accepting.

Marisa Megan Paska
@_marisamegan

Marisa is a travel journalist with a passion for cultural preservation, remote travel and the ocean.

Fredericksburg's (p376) main drags – Caroline and William Sts – are literally the crossroads of Virginia's historic, edgy and undeniably Southern-charmed worlds. The brick sidewalks. The hip art shop with graffiti-draped skateboards. The corner coffee shop with latte art pizzazz. The bank that's morphed into a farm-to-table destination. To think George Washington apparently threw a coin across the Rappahannock River around the corner, too.

Jesse Scott
@jesserobertscott

Jesse is a native Virginian who writes about travel, entertainment, food and real estate worldwide.

As a sailing enthusiast, I had been trying forever to glimpse the tall ship Kalmar Nyckel, a replica of the Swedish vessel that arrived in 1638 and a reminder of Wilmington's seafaring history. A **Copeland Maritime Center** (p303) staff member told me that the ship would pull in toward closing time, so I stuck around and saw the majestic vessel come in after a sail. One day in the near future, I plan to join a sail in Wilmington or Lewes.

Julekha Dash

@foodtravelart

Julekha is a writer who covers art, restaurants, real estate and travel, specializing in the Mid-Atlantic region.

I love riding a bike along the **Monongahela River** (p399). The rail trail here cuts such a perfect cross-section through Monongalia County and a cyclist could spend days exploring the roads and paths that branch off it. West Virginia is famous for its epic mountain biking, but this trail is suitable for cyclists of almost any age or experience – and there's no better way to finish a ride than with a meal and a pint on Morgantown's High St.

Robert Isenberg

robertisenberg.net

Robert is a writer and filmmaker based in Rhode Island. His most recent book is Mile Markers: Essays on Cycling.

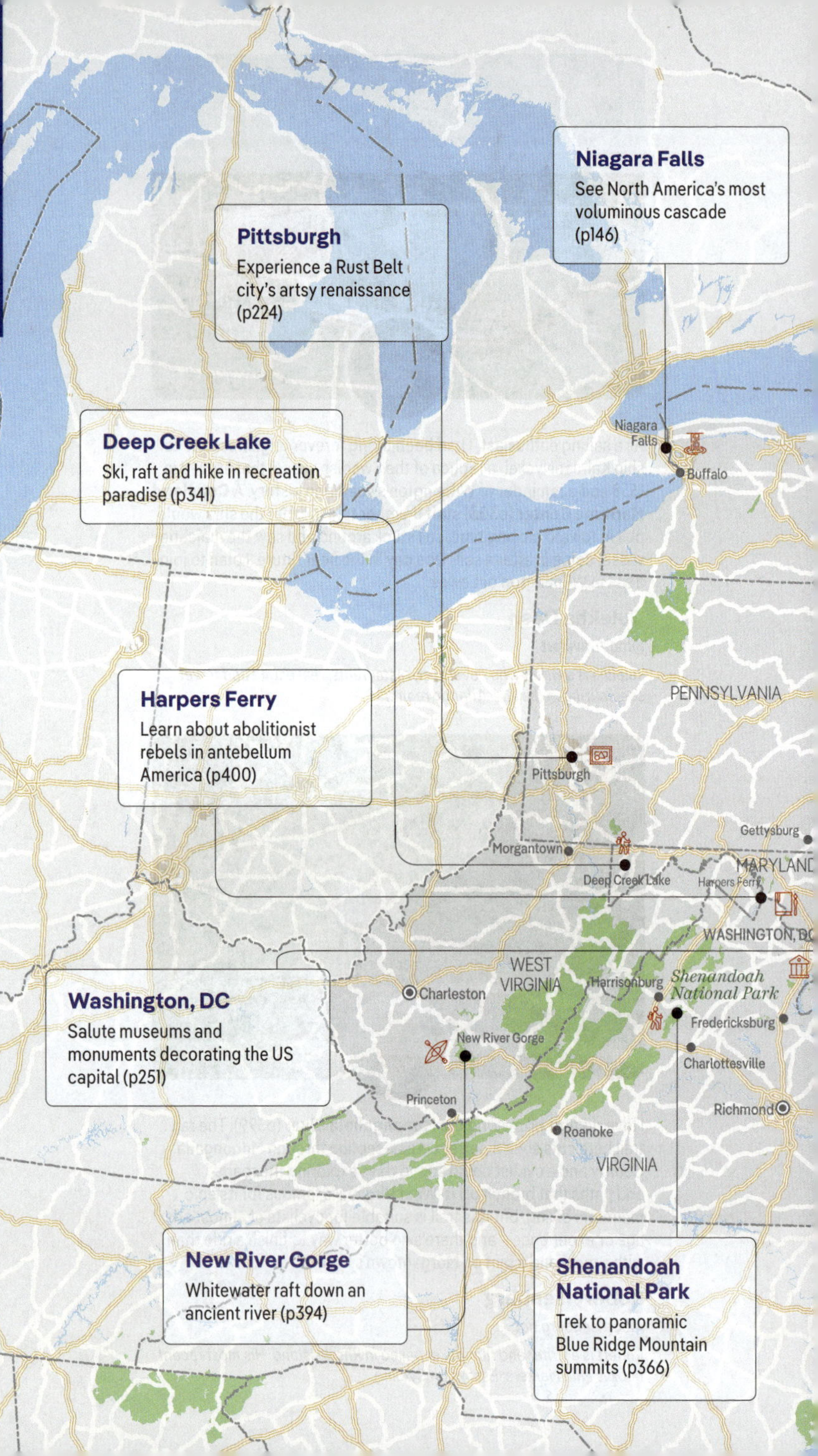

PLAN YOUR TRIP

Niagara Falls
See North America's most voluminous cascade (p146)

Pittsburgh
Experience a Rust Belt city's artsy renaissance (p224)

Deep Creek Lake
Ski, raft and hike in recreation paradise (p341)

Harpers Ferry
Learn about abolitionist rebels in antebellum America (p400)

Washington, DC
Salute museums and monuments decorating the US capital (p251)

New River Gorge
Whitewater raft down an ancient river (p394)

Shenandoah National Park
Trek to panoramic Blue Ridge Mountain summits (p366)

Niagara Falls

Buffalo

PENNSYLVANIA

Pittsburgh

Gettysburg

Morgantown

MARYLAND

Deep Creek Lake

Harpers Ferry

WASHINGTON, DC

WEST VIRGINIA

Charleston

Harrisonburg

Shenandoah National Park

New River Gorge

Fredericksburg

Charlottesville

Princeton

Richmond

Roanoke

VIRGINIA

8

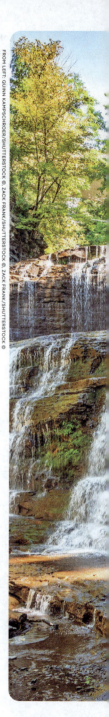

HIGHLIGHTS OF HISTORY

America's origin story starts here – among waterways linking Europe to America and at cultural crossroads carved by the Mason-Dixon line. This is where America's forefathers raged against Great Britain and brothers battled during the Civil War, where every US President called the shots and where social movements found their voice. The region's bones archive dramas diving even deeper – into ancient seas and Paleo-Indian communities, with its secrets hiding among glacier-carved lakes, mountain caves and memorialized in magnificent museums.

Indigenous Beginnings

Native groups thrived here long before colonists arrived: archaeologists have found evidence of life dating back at least 10,000 years in Pennsylvania's **Pocono** mountains (p233).

Let Freedom Ring

Philadelphia (p175), dubbed the 'cradle of liberty,' planted seeds for the American Revolution (1775–83) and provides insight into the pivotal war at dozens of local sites.

Engaging Exhibitions

Many of DC's 17 free-to-visit **Smithsonian museums** (p264) offer a US history intensive, with galleries dedicated to things such as American politics, African American culture and nature.

Cascadilla Gorge (p137)

BEST HISTORY EXPERIENCES

Wind through Ithaca's ❶ **gorge trails** (p136), lined with sedimentary rocks deposited 400 million years ago when the area was an inland ocean.

Find your sea legs in Historic St Mary's City aboard the ❷ **Dove** (p323), a replica of the British ship that startled Maryland's indigenous Yaocomico community in 1634.

Visit the Trenton site where ❸ **George Washington crossed the Delaware** (p155), leading the Continental Army to its first major Revolutionary War victory.

Imagine 'bombs bursting in air' at Baltimore's ❹ **Fort McHenry** (p335), where Francis Scott Key penned verses that became the national anthem.

Step inside ❺ **John Brown's Fort** (p 400), the Harpers Ferry engine house where abolitionist John Brown faced off against US Marines, sparking the Civil War.

MAJESTIC MOUNTAINS

If you soared above the Mid-Atlantic as a broad-winged bald eagle, you'd see the Appalachian Mountains and its many subranges spiking along the East Coast like a giant dinosaur spine. This 2000-mile mountain chain rolls through nearly every Mid-Atlantic state, with deciduous forests, spring-fed lakes and rivers fit for outdoor adventures. New York's Adirondacks are also imposing and, like the Appalachians, invite all-season exploration: there's summer hiking, autumn leaf peeping, winter skiing and wildlife watching in spring.

Appalachian Trail

More than 3000 people attempt to hike the 2190-plus-mile **Appalachian Trail** (p241) between Georgia and Maine annually; only a quarter of those conquer the entire course.

Rocky Connections

The Appalachians' 33-plus subranges include New York's **Catskill Mountains** (p121) and the **Blue Ridge Mountains** (p366), which pass through Maryland, Pennsylvania, West Virginia, Virginia and four other states.

Into the Wild

Adirondack Park (p129) is the largest reserve in the contiguous US, spread across six million acres – roughly the size of New York's neighbor, Vermont.

Catoctin Mountain Park (p337)

BEST MOUNTAIN EXPERIENCES

Bask in the glow of ❶ **Mill Mountain Star** (p364), the illuminated icon shining above Roanoke on Virginia's Blue Ridge.

Choose between 100 miles of paths at ❷ **New River Gorge National Park and Preserve** (p394), designed for day hikes to rocky crags and a canyon.

Summit ❸ **Buck Mountain** (p107) for sweeping Adirondack Mountain views, then jump into Lake George to cool off on a summer's day.

Fall in love with Maryland's ❹ **Catoctin Mountain Park** (p337) in autumn, when the views from Chimney Rock showcase forests painted auburn and gold.

Gaze high into the heavens at ❺ **Cherry Springs State Park** (p236), a sensational stargazing summit lit only by the Milky Way.

OUR PICKS | PLAN YOUR TRIP

URBAN ADVENTURES

The East Coast is home to the USA's oldest cities, with densely packed streets that tell centuries-old stories. But even in the most historic metropolises, reinvention ensures things never get stale. New cloud-piercing architecture redraws NYC's skyline as fast as new Michelin stars decorate its restaurants. Waves of politicians and immigrants continually shake up the flavor in Washington, DC. No matter the city, there's art, nightlife, shopping and more surprises to satiate voracious culture vultures.

Heads of State

Nine US cities have served as the nation's capital, and all of them are in the Mid-Atlantic. Aside from DC, NYC and Philadelphia held the title longest.

Rust-belt Revitalization

Industrial towns such as Pittsburgh and Buffalo saw economic collapse in the 20th century, but the dark days are done. Don't overlook these refined enclaves on the upswing.

No Car Necessary

Leave the car behind in NYC, Philadelphia and DC. You can explore these cities on foot, bike or public transportation – and travel between them on trains.

FROM LEFT: IGOR LINK/SHUTTERSTOCK ©, SEAN PAVONE/SHUTTERSTOCK ©, FRANCOIS ROUX/SHUTTERSTOCK ©

Brooklyn (p97)

BEST CITY EXPERIENCES

Hop between ❶ **Brooklyn's best nightlife venues** (p100) for a taste of what NYC's artsy crowd is cooking up: craft cocktails, burlesque, drag performances and cutting-edge music.

Skip or cycle down ❷ **Virginia Beach's 3-mile boardwalk** (p369), popping into ocean-view restaurants for a refreshing orange crush.

Learn about Pittsburgh's boom, bust and beautification on a ❸ **Rivers of Steel tour** (p221), showcasing how graffiti writers reimagined post-industrialization.

Explore international cultures by attending a culinary festival or musical performance at one of the 178 foreign embassies around ❹ **Washington, DC** (p251).

Roam the charming streets of Philadelphia's ❺ **Old City** (p178), where historic landmarks are as common as trendy boutiques.

ON THE ROAD

Buckle up and put the pedal to the metal: one of the best ways to see the Mid-Atlantic's diverse landscapes is through a windshield. Around 400 national and state scenic byways zip the region together, zooming from sparkling cities to coastal highways, over forested mountains and through one-stoplight towns plucked from Edward Hopper paintings. Cyclists roll along miles of bike paths, too, following back roads, rail trails and towpaths into the region's green heart.

Choose the Season

Between December and March, snow and black ice can make driving through northern states and high elevations dicey. Fall is most magical, with forests sporting an autumnal ombré.

Cruise the Blue Ridge Parkway

This 469-mile parkway is America's longest linear park, linking Virginia's Shenandoah National Park to North Carolina's Great Smoky Mountains. The best part? No traffic lights.

Refuel Your Car

Gas stations are ubiquitous and EV charging stations are increasingly common, usually peppered near populated areas. You can't pump your own gas in New Jersey: it's illegal.

Great Allegheny Passage (p340)

BEST ROAD-TRIP EXPERIENCES

Uncover uplifting abolitionist history on the 125-mile ❶ **Harriet Tubman Underground Railroad Byway** (p326), with 45 stops connecting Dorchester to Philadelphia.

Coast through West Virginia's ❷ **Northern Panhandle** (p402) to see 2000-year-old indigenous burial grounds, a haunted penitentiary and a peacock-packed Hare Krishna enclave.

Cruise around New York's ❸ **Western Catskills** (p128), sprinkled with charming main streets showcasing boutiques, breweries and Delaware River views.

Cycle the 185-mile C&O Canal Towpath from DC to Cumberland, then pedal 150 miles more on the ❹ **Great Allegheny Passage** (p340) to Pittsburgh.

Beware the mythical Richmond Vampire while biking along the ❺ **James River** (p352), streaming past a Civil War prison camp and distinguished cemetery.

WATERFRONT FUN

Nearly all the Mid-Atlantic's most beloved cities and towns share one defining trait: they're waterfront communities. Before roads and railways stitched the nation together, waterways served as natural highways. Today, these spots offer opportunities to splash, paddle and cruise. Get amusement-park thrills on a seaside boardwalk, kayak along rambling rivers or jump in the spring-fed waters of mountain lakes. There's also 11,443 miles of Atlantic coastline. Bring a beach towel and dive in.

Fabulous Freshwater

New York has more than 7600 lakes, ponds and reservoirs – the most of any Mid-Atlantic state. For a summertime soak, visit the Adirondacks or Finger Lakes.

Shark Tales

More than 50 shark species call the Atlantic home, but encounters with swimmers are extremely rare – despite horrors evoked by *Jaws*, set in a fictitious Long Island town.

Cruise Control

Kick back on a boat tour. Sightseeing rides around cities and lake towns can be a fantastic way to appreciate architecture and dive into local history.

Coney Island (p99)

BEST WATERFRONT EXPERIENCES

Stroll ❶ **Coney Island**'s (p99) Riegelmann Boardwalk, where sugar-sand beaches and kitschy roller coasters compete for attention.

Road trip down the Jersey Shore from Sandy Hook to ❷ **Cape May** (p160), exploring untamed shorelines and bustling boardwalks.

Spend a day ambling along the mile-long boardwalk at ❸ **Rehoboth Beach** (p310), dubbed the 'Nation's Summer Capital' due to the seasonal influx of DC residents.

Feel the force of ❹ **Niagara Falls** (p160), North America's most powerful waterfall, while braving the super-soaked Cave of the Winds.

Prepare to get drenched on the rapids of Pennsylvania's Youghiogheny River as you raft through ❺ **Ohiopyle State Park** (p233).

PLAN YOUR TRIP OUR PICKS

WINTER WONDERLAND

Snow and ice transform the Mid-Atlantic into a frosted paradise from December to March. Downhill daredevils hit ski slopes around Adirondack Park and West Virginia's mountains, skaters glide across city rinks and, with a pair of crampons or snowshoes, it's possible to scale hiking trails in the Catskills and Poconos. Indoor activities are equally delightful: holiday festivities pack December's social calendar, quaint cabins invite fireside snuggling and there's no better time to visit museums.

Embrace the Cold

Although most ski resorts open around Thanksgiving, warm weather can prevent Mid-Atlantic slopes, especially those between Pennsylvania and Virginia, from being fully operational until January. Plan accordingly.

See the Snowscape

If you're searching for snowy landscapes, head to the Finger Lakes and Buffalo: roughly 90 inches of white powder can pack Central and Western New York each season.

Olympic Legends

Adirondacks town **Lake Placid** (p135) hosted the Winter Olympics in 1932 and 1980. Between an associated museum and athletic training centers, it's possible to celebrate winter sports year-round.

Snowshoe Mountain (p403)

BEST WINTER EXPERIENCES

Fly down ❶ **Whiteface Mountain**'s (p135) – a 3430ft vertical drop on snow skis, or inside a gondola overlooking the frozen Adirondacks.

Lace up ice skates to spin around Tinseltown – a holiday lights festival glowing in Philadelphia's ❷ **FDR Park** (p207).

Spend a cozy weekend at Scribner's Catskill Lodge, a retreat in the shadow of ❸ **Hunter Mountain** (p124), with its 67 skiing and snowboarding trails.

Head to Maryland's ❹ **Deep Creek Lake** (p341) to tube down Wisp Resort's 750ft-long snow chute or cross-country ski along Herrington Manor's paths.

Pummel the powder on West Virginia's ❺ **Snowshoe Mountain** (p403) before clinking hot toddies at an après-ski event.

OUR PICKS | PLAN YOUR TRIP

FARM TO FORK

Experience the Mid-Atlantic's riches on your taste buds. More than 160,000 farms root themselves across the region, and there's plenty of fresh fish straight from the sea. Bite into Pennsylvania apples, dip into Adirondack goat cheese, sip Long Island rosé and chew Chesapeake Bay oysters. Whether at farmers markets or fine dining, indulging in local-grown ingredients is a must.

Amish Country

Pennsylvania boasts around 49,000 farms – the most in the Mid-Atlantic – including Amish-run estates where ranchers rely on traditional planting methods and avoid pesticides.

Agrotourism Abounds

Many farmsteads aren't only food producers – they're memory makers. Keep an eye out for cow-milking lessons, you-pick produce programs, harvest festivals and more year-round activities.

FROM LEFT: HUTCH PHOTOGRAPHY/SHUTTERSTOCK ©, ZACCHIO/SHUTTERSTOCK ©, CAROLINA WOJTASIK/BLOOMBERG/GETTY IMAGES ©

22

Fishkill Farms (p120)

BEST FARM EXPERIENCES

Fill bags with autumn apples at ❶ **Fishkill Farms** (p120) before enjoying local cider made from ingredients foraged on site.

Meet the animals at Amish-run ❷ **Old Windmill Farm** (p244), where you can learn to make butter from fresh cow cream.

Taste local meats, veggies, seafood and beer in ❸ **Frederick** (p336), Maryland, where kitchens prize their regional bounty.

Cruise along Rte 25 in ❹ **Long Island's wine country** (p114), with vineyards and seasonal farm stands tempting visitors at every mile.

Head to ❺ **DuPont Circle's Sunday farmers market** (p290) to pick your own produce, sample local spirits and nosh on artisanal baked goods.

REGIONS & CITIES

Find the places that tick all your boxes.

New York State

FORESTS, FARMSTEADS AND CULTURED ENCLAVES

The Empire State is home to America's largest park and the continent's most powerful waterfall. Miles of mountains challenge experienced hikers, glorious gorges grace towns around Ithaca and wave-bashed beaches delight on Long Island. Then there's the art scene – bountiful near Beacon – and locavore restaurants primed for discerning palates. **p103**

New York City

AMERICA'S NON-STOP CULTURAL CAPITAL

NYC constantly redraws its map with cutting-edge restaurants, splashy Broadway musicals, engaging art exhibits, skyscraping architecture and a revolving door of trendsetting boutiques. It's also anchored by plenty of history. From Lady Liberty's torch to art deco towers and an Egyptian temple at the Met, this city is spoiled with surprises. **p48**

New Jersey

SHORE LIFE, OUTDOORS & HISTORY

Cape May is for the birds, Atlantic City is for the boardwalk, and the Hudson River bank serves stunning NYC views. Ivy Leaguers roam Princeton, the mythic Jersey Devil stalks the Pine Barrens's cedar bogs and artsy crowds congregate at Asbury Park in summer. From ocean shore to cities, Jersey delivers. **p150**

Pennsylvania

FORESTED PARKS, LIVING HISTORY & RIVER TOWNS

It takes approximately six hours to drive across Pennsylvania. The journey passes from whitewater rivers ruled by bald eagles to rural 'Pennsyltucky' with its horse-and-buggy Amish towns, highland forests and battlefields where the Civil War seethed. It ends in steel-stacked Pittsburgh, an industrial urban canvas for artistic innovation and culinary quirks. **p220**

Delaware

BEACHES, ART & HISTORY

The second-smallest state in the US packs a serious amount of tax-free fun into nearly 2000 square miles. Wilmington, the state's largest city, offers top-notch restaurants, a recreation-packed waterfront and intriguing museums. The Brandywine Valley dazzles with mansions and gardens, while the gold-sand coast attracts summertime sojourns. **p298**

New York State
p103

Pennsylvania
p220

New York City
p48

Philadelphia ◉
p175

West Virginia

**THE ENDURING
HEART OF APPALACHIA**

Spread across the Appalachians, the Mountain State is a wild wonderland where hikers, bikers and whitewater desperados whet their adventurous appetites in six national parks. There's also a fascinating history of rebellion. If these rolling hills could talk, they'd spin yarns of daring abolitionists, hard-laboring coal miners and bloody family feuds. **p387**

New Jersey
p150

Maryland
p317

Delaware
p298

West Virginia
p387

★
WASHINGTON, DC
p251

Philadelphia

**HISTORY, CULTURE, ART &
INCREDIBLE FOOD**

Philly's cultural tapestry is sewn together by stripes of cobblestone streets where Founding Fathers stood and stately museums with world-class art. Its eclectic neighborhoods shine like stars: the rainbow-splashed Gayborhood, funky-flavored Fishtown, collegiate University City and luxury-laden Rittenhouse Square. It might be an underdog city – unpretentious, gritty – but there's plenty of prestige. **p175**

Virginia
p344

Virginia

**A TIME-TESTED,
EVER-EVOLVING 'OLD DOMINION'**

Ever since the British planted permanent roots along the James River in 1607, Virginia has been central to the American saga. Wander homes of former presidents and cross Civil War battlefields. Construct sandcastles on beaches or cruise the Blue Ridge Parkway through magnificent mountains. Shuck the oysters, drink the wine: Virginia is for lovers. **p344**

Washington, DC

THE CAPITAL OF THE USA

'DC' is America's political powerhouse, adorned with iconic monuments and leafy parks celebrating American presidents, social leaders and war heroes. An impressive collection of museums speaks to the city's academic ideals, and while the politics of the White House change every few years, the city remains a creative, liberal stronghold. **p251**

Maryland

AMERICA IN MINIATURE

The East Coast's midpoint sits at the crossroads of southern refinement and northern efficiency – at the place where salty eastern seashores connect to wooded western mountains. Bike among dunes where wild ponies roam, explore the streets of edgy Baltimore and roll along the historic Underground Railroad. Diversity makes life here blue-crab-meat sweet. **p317**

Washington Monument (p262)

ITINERARIES

Bright Lights, Big Cities

Allow: 7 days **Distance:** 230 miles

No car? No problem. Travel between all these cities on Amtrak trains and explore their coolest corners on foot. Driving this route allows for detours to quaint rural areas, but there's plenty in each metropole to keep train travelers pleased: art, food, local culture infused with international sensibility and centuries of US history.

❶ NEW YORK CITY ⏱ 2 DAYS

Stick to Manhattan for a quick trip to **NYC** (p42). Follow immigrant footsteps on **Ellis Island** (p58), glimpse New York's colonial past in **FiDi** (p62) and order global cuisine around **Chinatown** (p65) and the **East Village** (p68). Day two is about culture: see art collections at magnificent museums, amble along **Hudson River Park** (p77), applaud a **Broadway** (p81) show, or treat yourself to a Michelin-star meal.

❷ PHILADELPHIA ⏱ 1 DAY

Choose from colonial history, world-class art and culture on a **Philly** (p175) overnight. Walk hallowed halls of **Independence National Historical Park** (p182), peer at the **Barnes Foundation**'s (p197) impressionist paintings, applaud **Gayborhood** (p185) drag performers and praise **Fishtown** (p199) chefs.

Detour: Spot the horse-and-buggy brigade in Amish town of **Lancaster** (p237). ⏱ Half a day. 🚗 1.5 hours

❸ WILMINGTON ⏱ 1 DAY

Pass through or pass out at the **Quoin Hotel** (p315) – just don't pass over **Delaware's largest city** (p302). Wilmington's **Christina River** (p302) waterfront is great for biking, strolling and grazing. Uncover stories about indigenous tribes and Black communities at the **Delaware History Museum and Mitchell Center for African American Heritage** (p305), then dine at **Bardea Food & Drink** (p305).

④
BALTIMORE ⏱ 1 DAY

Some call it DC's scrappy little sister, but **Baltimore** (p331) wasn't nicknamed Charm City for nothing. Watch playful puffins splash around one of the nation's top-ranked aquariums, step aboard a 19th-century warship, then set sail to **Fort McHenry** (p334), where Francis Scott Key wrote verses that eventually became the national anthem. Don't leave without gobbling a meaty Maryland-style crab cake, perhaps from **Faidley Seafood** (p334).

⑤
WASHINGTON, DC ⏱ 2 DAYS

The nation's sophisticated Capital (p251) is inundated with enough **National Mall** (p261) monuments, art exhibits and science centers to keep crowds endlessly entertained. There's also **Dupont Circle**'s (p288) boutiques and restaurants, the **U Street Corridor**'s (p282) Black heritage and immigrant enclaves all over. Not everything here is politics.

🚗 *Detour:* Get a glimpse into the life of first US President George Washington at his former **Mount Vernon** (p381) home. ⏱ 4 hours. 🚗 40 mins

Hudson Valley (p116)

ITINERARIES

Untamed New York

Allow: 8 days   **Distance:** 530 miles

Drive north of NYC for a week of woodland escapades that scale mountains, splash in rivers and visit some of the most magnificent waterfalls around. Refuel at local farms, breweries and vineyards, and make a point to visit a few museums. You'll find some of the region's best contemporary art hidden in unassuming hamlets.

❶ BEACON ⏱ 1 DAY

Begin by reaching **Mt Beacon**'s (p118) summit to survey rolling mountains surrounding this **river town** (p116), accessible by car or train. Spend the rest of the day ambling along Main St's collection of boutiques, restaurants and bars, or see what the art scene is cooking up. Don't miss Dia Beacon's minimalist collection and Storm's King's outdoor sculptures.

❷ HUDSON ⏱ 1 DAY

Stop at Olana, an art-packed mountaintop mansion with manicured meadows, while driving to trendy **Hudson** (p119), then spend the afternoon searching Warren St for fine antiques and local art while eating your way through town.

Detour: Choose an easy or challenging trail to **Kaaterskill Falls** (p122), New York's tallest two-tiered cascade, which pours into a clove of the Catskill Mountains. ⏱ 3 hours. 🚗 40 mins

❸ LAKE GEORGE ⏱ 2 DAYS

It's all about the outdoors in wild **Adirondack Park** (p129). Go high-octane on the hiking trail to **Buck Mountain** and **Indian Head** (p132), sail across **Lake George** (p129) on a historic steamboat cruise or tube down the **Hudson River** (p132). With more time to spare, drive to picturesque **Lake Placid** (p135), where you can ride the gondola on Whiteface Mountain.

④ ITHACA ⏱ 2 DAYS

Central New York's hippie **college town** (p136) gets an A+ for gorges and gastro tourism. The state's tallest single-drop waterfall cuts a path through **Taughannock Falls State Park** (p136), and if you're dying for a dip, follow gorge trails in several state parks to falls-fed swimming holes. Eat farm-to-table around Ithaca's Commons and Trumansburg, then salute the **Finger Lakes** (p136) while sipping wine at a waterfront vineyard.

⑤ BUFFALO ⏱ 2 DAYS

If Taughannock Falls left you gobsmacked, stop at **Letchworth State Park** (p145) while driving to **Buffalo** (p142), where three giant waterfalls splash through the 'Grand Canyon of the East.' Once in Buffalo, it's all about architecture, including prairie-style homes by Frank Lloyd Wright.

🚗 *Detour:* After a week of seeing captivating cascades, cap it off with a trip to **Niagara Falls** (p146), the undisputed star of North American waterworks. ⏱ Half a day. 🚗 20 mins

ITINERARIES

Appalachian Wilds

Allow: 8 days
Distance: 480 miles

Appalachia, a region comprising farming communities and coal-mining towns, links southern New York to northern Georgia along hills alive with bluegrass music. This road trip explores its rural roads, snaking from Pennsylvania through West Virginia and into the Blue Ridge Mountains, searching for natural splendor.

Fayette Station (p395)

① PITTSBURGH ⏱ 2 DAYS

Get your culture fix around the steep hillsides of **Steel City** (p224) before venturing into Appalachia. Celebrate 'Burgh-born Andy Warhol at his pop-art museum, dig into Pittsburgh's past at the **Heinz History Center** (p228), munch on monster-sized sandwiches on the Strip and take a River of Steel industrial tour.

🚗 *Detour:* Survey Fallingwater (p230), Frank Lloyd Wright's 1935 ode to organic architecture in Pennsylvania's Laurel Highlands. ⏱ 3 hours. 🚗 1hr 15mins

② MORGANTOWN ⏱ 1 DAY

Spend a night in this former coal capital turned **college town** (pictured, p398), where life centers around High St, a strip streaming with undergrads who skip between bars, restaurants and the the **Monongalia Arts Center** (p398). Between spring and fall, rent kayaks to paddle the Monongahela River town, or choose between cycling and strolling the Mon River Trail.

③ NEW RIVER GORGE NATIONAL PARK & PRESERVE ⏱ 2 DAYS

Pitch a tent or stay in an Amish-style lodge to explore one of the newest additions to the **national park roster** (p394). Stop by the visitor center for views of the western hemisphere's longest single-span arch bridge, then tick off all the outdoor activities possible: hiking, climbing, skiing, whitewater rafting and, if it's October, BASE jumping.

④
ROANOKE ⏱ 1 DAY

The '**Star City of the South**' (p362) shines bright – literally: the 10,000lb Mill Mountain Star illuminates Roanoke with 2000 feet of neon tubing. Flashy decor aside, Roanoke glimmers with recreation opportunities: cycle to views and brews on an e-bike tour, hike to the Roanoke River Overlook (an easy trek along the bucolic Blue Ridge Parkway), then refuel with gravy-smothered, Southern-style biscuits.

⑤
HARRISONBURG ⏱ 2 DAYS

Finish this trip strong by trekking through **Shenandoah National Park** (pictured, p366), or the Blue Ridge Mountains near **Harrisonburg** (p366). You'll need an entire day to hike up Old Rag Mountain – a 9-mile loop with rocky scrambles and 360-degree views that glow burnt sienna in autumn.

➤ *Detour: With extra time, tour the vineyards around* ***Charlottesville*** *(p359) and view Monticello, Thomas Jefferson's mountaintop home.* ⏱ *Half a day.* 🚗 *1hr 15mins*

ITINERARIES

Coastal Treasures

Allow: 9 days **Distance:** 475 miles

Save this Virginia-to-New York road trip for summer, when Atlantic waters warm and oceanfront boardwalks teem with activity. There will be plenty of traffic, especially on weekends, but at the end of every highway, salty water awaits. Surfers, kayakers, birdwatchers, party people and cotton-candy pundits – everyone will find their groove.

Cape May (p160)

① VIRGINIA BEACH ⓢ 2 DAYS

The 3-mile boardwalk is the place to be in this **seaside city** (p369). Surrender to life's simple pleasures – seafood, orange crushes and waves rolling in. There's nautical history in nearby **Norfolk** (p371) and a colorful array of residents at the Virginia Aquarium.

Detour: Walk through the 18th-century streets of **Colonial Williamsburg** (p353) and ponder the impact of Jamestown. ⓢ Half a day. 🚗 1hr 15mins

② OCEAN CITY ⓢ 2 DAYS

Gear up for family fun around this summer **resort town** (pictured, p329), where amusement-park rides blink along the boardwalk and there's always another ice-cream cone within reach. Nearby towns such as Berlin, offer quieter retreats.

Detour: Run wild with the ponies of **Assateague Island** (p329), a tranquil camping and recreation escape. ⓢ Half a day. 🚗 20mins

③ CAPE MAY ⓢ 2 DAYS

As one of the nation's oldest vacation destinations, New Jersey's southernmost point knows how to make everyone's shoulders drop – with sunrises and sunsets along sandy beaches, exceptional birding trails and the highest concentration of Victorian homes outside of San Francisco.

Detour: Stop in at **Atlantic City** (p160) to experience blinking casinos along America's first boardwalk. ⓢ 3 hours. 🚗 50mins

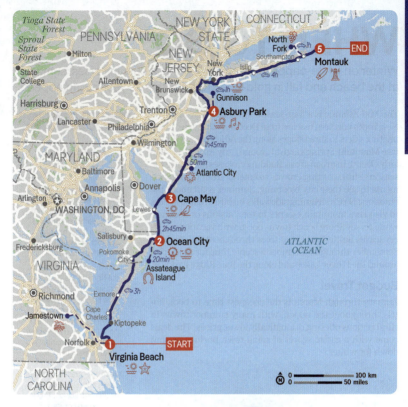

④ ASBURY PARK ⏱ 1 DAY

The Jersey Shore's artsiest, edgiest **enclave** (p170). Traipse down a mile-long boardwalk sprinkled with carnival-style sweet treats, new-wave restaurants, cocktail lounges, beaux arts architecture and a vintage pinball arcade. Hear rock bands jam at the Stone Pony. Join the LGBTIQ+ crowd at beach-adjacent bars. Jump in the ocean. Do it all again.

↪ *Detour:* Sick of swimwear? Let it all hang out at **Gunnison Beach** (p171), Sandy Hook's clothing-optional beach.
⏱ 3 hours. 🚗 40mins

⑤ MONTAUK ⏱ 2 DAYS

After braving summer traffic to reach New York's **easternmost edge** (p108), you may decide to lay in the sand at Kirk Park Beach and never leave. But then you'd miss the surfers at Ditch Plains, the state's oldest lighthouse, the bougie crowds eating shellfish at Duryea's and the can't-be-beat sunsets at Montauket.

↪ *Detour:* Go wine tasting on Long Island's **North Fork** (pp114), where more than 60 vineyards celebrate the local terroir. ⏱ Half a day. 🚗 1hr

WHEN TO GO

Winter on white-capped mountains, spring in bustling cities, summer at the beach and fall in gold-hued forests: there's year-round appeal.

The Mid-Atlantic is a four-season fantasia. Snow blankets New York's northern reaches from December through March, inviting skiers to shred slopes along the Adirondacks' Whiteface Mountain. Spring's arrival around early April is particularly electric in urban areas. Budding crocuses announce the season's shift, coaxing crowds to emerge from their apartments to see their city blooming. Summer is all about the outdoors: NYC's steaming sidewalks inspire urban dwellers to visit cool mountain escapes in the Catskills or Poconos, while Jersey Shore beach towns boom with vacationers. Fiery leaves ignite East Coast trees throughout fall, making September through November a scenic time for road trips around the Finger Lakes and along the Blue Ridge Parkway.

Budget Travel

January through March is the cheapest time to book hotels throughout the region, with many summer towns in rural regions offering dramatically lower prices. The deals come with a catch: scores of small-town businesses shut down for winter.

⊗ I LIVE HERE

MAN FOR ALL SEASONS

Garrett Miller co-founded Finger Lakes Cider House, a cidery, restaurant and farm, summer concerts and a farm, hosting summer harvest festival. @flxciderhouse

Something unique about the Northeast is its striking seasonality. I love settling into summer's groove by swimming in Cayuga Lake. I love how temperatures cool for fall. After harvesting pumpkins and apples, I look forward to winter's dark months. We call spring 'green up' – grass is growing, calves and lambs are born, the orchard blooms. There's a burst of life.

WHERE'S THE WARM WATER?

The Atlantic Ocean remains icy most of the year, but swimmers deadset on diving into waves will appreciate August. Temperatures around Jersey Shore destinations peak around 75°F, and things get even warmer in Virginia, where temperatures sometimes hit the low 80s.

Belmar (p165), New Jersey

Weather through the Year in New York City

JANUARY	FEBRUARY	MARCH	APRIL	MAY	JUNE
Avg. daytime max: 39°F	Avg. daytime max: 42°F	Avg. daytime max: 50°F	Avg. daytime max: 60°F	Avg. daytime max: 71°F	Avg. daytime max: 79°F
Days of rainfall: 11	Days of rainfall: 10	Days of rainfall: 11	Days of rainfall: 11	Avg. rainfall: 12	Avg. rainfall: 11

S'NOWHERE TO BE FOUND

Snow in NYC movies like *Miracle on 34th Street* is a blast from an unfamiliar past. Between 2022 and 2024, New York experienced a 702-day dry spell with no serious accumulation of fluffy stuff. Four of the city's five warmest winters have occurred after 2000.

Big Annual Events

Pride (p75) NYC rolls out the rainbow carpet with gatherings that range from family-friendly to bedazzled debauchery, all culminating at the NYC Pride March, the Mid-Atlantic's largest LGBTIQ+ celebration. **June**

Independence Day Fireworks erupt throughout the Mid-Atlantic on July 4, including notable festivals in Philly and Colonial Williamsburg, but Washington, DC, pulls out all the stops. Marching bands parade down Constitution Ave, and the National Symphony Orchestra booms before the Capitol. **July**

Halloween Skeletons and spiderwebs decorate stoops from NYC's West Village to Cobble Hill throughout fall – a prelude to All Hallows Eve (October 31), when New Yorkers get sartorially spooky for the Village Halloween Parade. **October**

Thanksgiving The US president pardons a turkey in DC days before Philadelphia kicks off this traditional tryptophan food fest with the nation's oldest Thanksgiving Day parade. **November**

Wacky & Wonderful Festivals

Groundhog Day Will roly-poly groundhog Punxsutawney Phil spot his shadow upon emerging from his Pennsylvania den? The rest of winter's weather hinges on the answer to this question. **February**

Dyngus Day (p106) Visitors in Buffalo might get swept up in a polka, flirtatiously tapped with a pussy willow or stuffed like a pierogi with borscht and beer during this post-Lent party packed with Polish pride. **April**

Mermaid Parade Artsy crowds don nautical costumes to flip their fins down Coney Island's (p99) Surf Ave during this silly, seedy and sexy summer-solstice celebration. **June**

Chincoteague Pony Penning 'Saltwater Cowboys' herd a horde of semi-feral swimming ponies into Virginia's Assateague Channel, then auction the foals on Chincoteague Island (p372). Onlookers coo over the cloppers' manes, bobbing above the water. **July**

🛈 I LIVE HERE

WEST VIRGINIA WINTER

Eve West has spent 30 years working in US national parks. New River Gorge is one of her favorites. @newrivernps

Spring's wildflowers are gorgeous, summers are so pleasant and fall sees migrating warblers pass through, but my favorite season in the park is winter. Without foliage, you can spot historic ruins from industrial towns, and nothing blocks the view while driving along the New River.

New River Gorge (394)

LEAF PEEP LIKE AN EXPERT

Fall's arboreal color fest starts in September and lasts through early November, with leaves turning red, orange and yellow. I LOVE NY *(iloveny.com)* issues weekly foliage reports, compiling observations from on-location 'leaf spotters', helping travelers know when peak leaf-peeping season arrives.

JULY	AUGUST	SEPTEMBER	OCTOBER	NOVEMBER	DECEMBER
Avg. daytime max: **85°F**	Avg. daytime max: **83°F**	Avg. daytime max: **76°F**	Avg. daytime max: **65°F**	Avg. daytime max: **54°F**	Avg. daytime max: **44°F**
Days of rainfall: **10**	Days of rainfall: **9**	Days of rainfall: **9**	Days of rainfall: **10**	Days of rainfall: **9**	Days of rainfall: **11**

Central Park (p94)

GET PREPARED FOR NEW YORK & THE MID-ATLANTIC

Useful things to load in your bag, your ears and your brain

Clothes

Casual Clothes Many rural establishments cater to jeans-and-tee crowds, particularly in West Virginia, western Pennsylvania and northern New York.

Smart, upscale attire NYC style leans toward looser silhouettes, while DC tends toward buttoned-up sophistication. Either way, a well-tailored outfit always fits in with sartorially savvy East Coast fashionistas.

Layers Bring options no matter the season. Winter weather snaps from bone-chilling to balmy; spring and fall are temperamental; summer days might start sweaty but can finish brisk.

Sneakers Forget heels for urban outings. After slogging around sidewalks, up and down subway steps and around miles of museums, your feet will thank you.

> ### Manners
>
> **Talking to strangers** Keep to yourself on city streets (NYC especially). Expect a friendly 'hello' in small towns.
>
> **Walking on sidewalks** Cities use them for commuting, not wandering. Traffic sticks to the right. Need to pause? Step to the side.
>
> **Public transit** Give elderly, disabled and pregnant passengers priority seating. Allow passengers to exit before entering. Asking for directions is fine: be direct and brief.

Hiking shoes Sneakers are fine for many outdoor adventures, but serious mountain trails from Shenandoah to the Adirondacks require waterproof boots ready to tackle all terrain.

📖 READ

Age of Innocence (Edith Wharton; 1920) Pulitzer Prize-winning portrait of Gilded Age scandal among NYC socialites, and a 1993 Scorsese film.

Demon Copperhead (Barbara Kingsolver; 2022) Retelling of David Copperfield set in opioid-addicted corners of Appalachia.

Heartburn (Nora Ephron; 1983) Ephron's roman-à-clef revenge against ex-husband Carl Bernstein, doused with DC politics and New York neuroticism.

Vanishing New York (Jeremiah Moss; 2017) Nonfiction exploration of socioeconomic forces and gentrification in NYC's historic neighborhoods.

Words

Bodega Technical definition: an NYC store with no more than two cash registers that sells milk and mostly food. Spiritual definition: neighborhood lifeline for groceries, beer, cleaning supplies, lottery tickets, ATMs and the beloved BEC (bacon, egg and cheese).

The City If anyone in New York State tells you they're going to 'the city,' they're not talking about Buffalo or Albany – they're talking about NYC. If you're in NYC, they're probably talking about Manhattan.

Crick A stiffness in your neck, possibly, or a small brook (the little sibling of a creek) in Western Pennsylvania and parts of Appalachia.

DMV For locals around DC, it's the 'DC-Maryland-Virginia' area – not the Department of Motor Vehicles.

Jagoff Derogatory Pittsburghese slang for someone stupid or irritating.

MTA Metropolitan Transit Authority – the company responsible for NYC's subways and buses.

POTUS Acronym meaning President of the United States, likely seen or heard while exploring DC's political arena.

Schmear A Yiddish word referring to a spread. At Jewish delis, you might hear 'bagel and a schmear,' which means a bagel with cream cheese.

Yankee Used by the Confederate South to demonize Union soldiers during the Civil War. Today, a regional epithet occasionally heard in Virginia, referencing New Englanders and East Coasters from places like New York and Pennsylvania. Also NYC's baseball team.

Yinz (or yunz) Western Pennsylvania's plural 'you', akin to 'y'all,' which you may hear used in the American South.

🎬 WATCH

Dirty Dancing (Emile Ardolino; 1987, pictured) A sizzling summer romance dances through the Catskills at a 1960s Borscht Belt resort.

Angels in America (Mike Nichols; 2003) Miniseries version of Tony Kushner's Broadway masterpiece about AIDS in 1980s Manhattan.

Fences (Denzel Washington; 2016) Struggles of a 1950s African American family, documenting Black life in Pittsburgh.

Lincoln (Steven Spielberg; 2012) Biopic following Abraham Lincoln as he attempts to abolish slavery.

Rocky (John G Avildsen; 1976) Philadelphia underdog boxes to the top. Listen to 'The Statue' podcast – a fantastic companion piece.

🎧 LISTEN

Bowery Boys (Greg Young and Tom Meyers; 2007–present) Pithy history podcast diving deep down the back alleys of NYC's past.

Hamilton (Lin Manuel Miranda; 2015) America's forefathers rap for democracy through the hip-hoppified lens of musical theater.

Lady Sings the Blues (Billie Holiday; 1956) Riveting recording featuring iconic jazz vocalist Holiday – born in Philly, raised in Baltimore, discovered in Harlem.

Woodstock: Music From the Original Soundtrack and More (Various artists; 1971) Rock out to performances from Bethel's 1969 hippie fest.

PLAN YOUR TRIP — GET PREPARED

People sharing a New York slice of pizza

THE FOOD SCENE

International plates attract epicurious eaters. Seafood and farm fare appease devout locavores. Mom-and-pop or Michelin-starred, there's something for all.

The Mid-Atlantic can be a thrill ride for foodies. One day, you're chowing cheap street eats that taste like a million bucks; the next, you're savoring a 10-course meal by an award-winning chef. You might slurp down oysters from a nearby bay, or sip wine produced at a local vineyard. In some cities, you can walk a block to dine around the world. There are rural towns where you'll meet the entire community at the local diner.

Differences in regional menus highlight the Mid-Atlantic's cultural crossroads. Virginia bakes Southern-style biscuits. New York serves New England–style lobster rolls. Generations of immigrants have influenced port-city diets, and you can trace the movement of communities by following their foodstuffs: Jewish populations took their bagels from NYC to Jersey; Germans brought their pork-forward diets to Pennsylvania. New waves of immigrants ensure the Mid-Atlantic remains culinarily eclectic, but at its best, you'll always find hyper-local flavors. Bud-to-bottle, bay-to-tray and farm-to-table – these are true East Coast palate pleasers.

NYC-Style

The Big Apple serves a global array of tastes at more than 25,000 restaurants across five boroughs. In the East Village alone, there's Burmese, Korean, Moroccan, Punjabi and more foreign flavors than you'll find at the United Nations – get a taste on p72. In 2016, native New Yorker Andy Doro

---

Eat it by Hand

BAGEL
Shiny exterior, slightly gooey interior. Slather on cream cheese.

BEC
Bacon, egg and cheese – an on-the-go NYC bodega breakfast.

BISCUIT
Fluffy, buttery flour treats, Southern-style – possibly served with gravy, ham or jam.

CHEESESTEAK
Philly favorite: grilled steak, onions and gooey cheese on a roll.

(everycountryfoodnyc.com) started documenting the amount of international cuisines he could eat around the city; he's now tried food from more than 150 countries.

Though quenching a cultural thirst is easy, scoring a table at top restaurants is tough. Make advance reservations for popular restaurants when possible (sometimes a month beforehand), especially if they have a Michelin star or James Beard Award nomination. If you can't grab a seat, show up at opening to try to secure a table. Luckily, no other city is as cutthroat for diners. Still, it never hurts to book ahead.

Fun on the Farm

Forget the club. The hottest place to hang in rural areas might be with the crops. It started decades ago with kid-friendly fare like petting zoos and autumnal pumpkin-patch traditions. But in recent years, a new generation of growers started harnessing their farmsteads' rural-chic aesthetics to attract city dwellers seeking photogenic red-barn charm. You'll find cider tasting rooms, occasional concerts and immersive experiences throughout the region. Chaseholm Farm in Pine Plains, NY, throws a drag show out of its dairy barn in June; **Finger Lakes Cider House** (p134) near Ithaca goes full-on Burning Man, setting an 'Apple Man' aflame during harvest season. Dozens of farms have a 'you-pick-produce' program, where visitors pluck summer berries and savor the fruits of their labor. Can't make it to a farm? There's always a farmers market within egg-tossing distance.

Glorious Gluten

The East Coast is obsessed with handheld dough delights. NYC practically runs on

FOOD FESTIVALS

Thurman Maple Days (p133; visitthurman.com; March weekends) Drive between Adirondacks maple farms to learn how sugar-makers turn sap into syrup.

Feast of San Gennaro (p66; sangennaronyc.org; September) Italians paint NYC's Mulberry St in red sauce for this 11-day festival with zeppoles, meatballs and pizza.

Roadkill Cook-off (pccocwv.com; late September) See who makes the tastiest meal out of animals often found dead along Marlinton, West Virginia's roadside: squirrel gravy, rabbit stew etc.

National Apple Harvest Festival (p248; appleharvest.com; early October) Apples, apple cider, apple guacamole, apple pie and an Apple Queen: you'll find it all in Biglerville, PA.

Maryland Crab Cake Festival (p339; carrollcountyfarmmuseum.org; late October) Savor all the sweet crab-meat cakes you can, then see which one is crowned the state's best.

Finger Lakes Cider House (p140)

Mulberry St (p66), New York City

PASTRAMI SANDWICH	PIZZA SLICE	PRIMANTI BROS SANDWICH	LOBSTER ROLL
Brined, smoked, steamed beef stacked on rye with cheese and mustard.	Thin triangular-cut pie crust bubbling with cheese and sauce: New York-style.	Two Italian bread slices stuffed with grilled goodies, coleslaw and fries.	Sandwich of meaty crustacean chunks with melted butter or mayonnaise.

DINER DEMOCRACY

The diner is a chrome-covered bastion of Americana – an affordable, egalitarian 'greasy spoon' serving all-day breakfast alongside sandwiches, fries, pies, wings and sides. Menus are novels. Coffees are bottomless. They're immortalized in Edward Hopper's *Nighthawks* painting (inspired by a Greenwich Village diner in NYC) and Suzanne Vega's song *Tom's Diner* (still open on NYC's Upper West Side). Roughly 450 of these swivel-stool sanctuaries call New Jersey home – more than any other US state – making it the world's diner capital. In the past decade, however, many nostalgia-stuffed restaurants shuttered – victims of rising expenses and changing tastes. But the diner isn't done – it's adapting to the times. New additions to the scene incorporate international flavors, such as NYC's *Golden Diner*; others celebrate locavore movements, like *Phoenicia Diner* in the Catskills. While menus might differ, each diner holds this truth to be self-evident: all sides of coleslaw are created equal.

bagels and pizza. Philly has its cheesesteaks. Pittsburgh has **Primanti Bros** (p224).

Most of these staples come from working-class traditions. Bagels arrived in NYC around the 19th century, boiled by Jewish Polish immigrants living in the Lower East Side's cramped tenement buildings. Italian immigrants brought pizza – cheap to make, easy to eat. The Primanti Bros sandwich started during the Great Depression. With fries and coleslaw stuffed into the heavyweight hangover cure, truck drivers could eat their lunch with one hand while steering with the other.

In some ways, these affordable food items are a lot like Mid-Atlantic urbanites – direct, practical, largely democratic. When it comes to comparing favorites, everyone's a critic. Be it Philly's cheesesteak or Manhattan's pizza, locals debate preferences like they're at a congressional showdown in DC.

Straight from the Sea

Coastal dwellers go coo-coo for crustaceans and mollusks. In Maryland, it's all about blue crabs, harvested in Chesapeake Bay. Their scientific name, *Callinectes sapidus*, translates to 'beautiful savory swimmer,' and Marylanders savor them indeed. In summer, hungry hordes salivate over piles of steamed pinchers at an abundance of waterfront crab houses. Picking sweet meat from crabs is a seasonal sport requiring patience, precision and sometimes a hammer (see p326).

Oysters are equally admired throughout the Mid-Atlantic, with connoisseurs slurping these aphrodisiac appetizers like fine wine. The flavor profile – sometimes briny, nutty, buttery, vegetal – hits the palate like a wave, its singular seasoning imparted by the ocean.

Beer, Wine & Whiskey

Fermentation aficionados keep East Coast imbibers satiated with a bevy of locally made beverages. New York and Pennsylvania have the second– and third–most craft breweries in the US, with more than 500 hop houses in each state. Virginia is the 'birthplace of American wine,' and New York's wine scene is underrated no more, thanks to Long Island's grape-gleaming North Fork (p114) and Finger Lakes (p140). Pennsylvania claims birth rights to American whiskey. Today, roughly 70 distillers fill barrels with brown libations. When in doubt, try something local – it's likely delicious.

Vineyard, Blue Ridge Mountains (p360)

Cuisine Across Cultures

Jewish Deli Food

Blintz Crepe-style wrap, often stuffed with a sweetened cheese such as ricotta, topped with fruit compote or possibly sour cream.
Knish Dough pockets plumped with something savory or sweet such as potatoes, spinach or perhaps blueberry cheese.
Lox Technically the thinly sliced, salt-cured fatty belly portion of a salmon, but really any cold smoked salmon tossed atop a bagel.
Matzo ball soup Tender eggy dumplings made with ground *matzo* (unleavened bread), dunked in steamy chicken broth, usually garnished with celery, fresh dill and possibly carrots.

Pennsylvania Dutch Delicacies

Apple butter Highly concentrated caramel-brown apple sauce spiced with cloves. Smooth or lumpy; delicious as a spread.
Lebanon bologna Salami's Pennsylvania cousin: dried, smoked, sweet-and-sour beef.
Scrapple Loaf of pig-part mush bound with cornmeal and flour – often sliced, fried and served between bread.

Chicken and matzo ball soup

Shoofly pie Uber-rich, molasses-packed, crumb-dusted pie to satisfy any sugar craving.

Find it in Chinatown

Dim sum Meaning' touch the heart' in Chinese, these small, shareable plates feature an assortment of dumplings, buns and rice rolls stuffed with seafood, meat, veggies and sweets.
Hot pot Restaurants with 'hot pots' offer communal eating experiences: gather around a simmering, seasoned bowl of broth and cook raw ingredients (meats, noodles, veggies) to your liking.

MEALS OF A LIFETIME

Thai Diner (p65) Slide into a booth for this Bangkok-meets–Big Apple mash-up, an edible example of NYC's melting pot.
Elwood (p201) Each plate at this meat-forward Philly restaurant is an homage to locally sourced Pennsylvania Dutch flavors, served with a side of local history.
Pineapple & Pearls (p274) Balloons aren't the only things decorating this champagne-popping, Studio 54–inspired DC restaurant – it's also got two Michelin stars.
Moosewood (p139) Join veggie devotees dining on farm-to-table fare at Ithaca's plant-based pioneer, making tofu fashionable since 1973.
One Coastal (p314) Dine on delicacies plucked from Delaware farms and the Atlantic Ocean at Fenwick Island's culinary king.

THE YEAR IN FOOD

SPRING

Easter means stores are chock-full of chocolate, but spring is best for garlicky ramps (related to leeks) along with sweet strawberries. Fly-fishers catch trout in the Catskills and crabs show up on Chesapeake Bay plates.

SUMMER

The scent of grilled burgers announces three months of outdoor barbecues. Expect lobster rolls, sea bass and clams by the ocean. July is best for blueberries and cherries; August delivers juicy peaches and corn on the cob.

FALL

Apples hang heavy, waiting to be picked, while patches of pumpkins get carved up for pies. Hunting season brings venison and turkey to tables, and beer-clinking festivals celebrate the harvest season with Oktoberfest oom-pah-pah.

WINTER

As temperatures cool, crack open big-bodied red wines from Long Island vineyards, paired well with meaty main dishes and root vegetables such as sweet potatoes. The holidays invite decadence: prepare for hearty meals.

Whiteface Mountain (p135)

THE OUTDOORS

Salt-swept shores splash east; rugged mountains rise west. There's winter skiing, summer swimming and cities to explore on foot year-round. No matter where you go, get ready to wear out those walking shoes.

More than 11,000 miles of tidal-tapped coastline reach toward forests flowering across millions of acres. Five major river systems cut through the landscape – and that doesn't count creeks pouring through the Adirondacks and mighty Appalachians, with its many subranges and craggy climbs. Two Great Lakes tickle New York and Pennsylvania, and thousands more pools dot the way down to Virginia. Add in paved spaces where city folks strut and the Mid-Atlantic becomes one vast amusement park. Swim, cycle, kayak, skate: in every location, adventure awaits.

Hike & Stroll

Ditch the car: the best way to reach the region's wild heart is by hoofing it. Hardcore hikers can trek through most Mid-Atlantic states (save Delaware) on 980 miles of the **Appalachian Trail**. More challenging climbs top the **Adirondacks** (p225), with 46 peaks reaching beyond 3800ft above sea level. Seaside promenades around **Assateague Island** (p329) inspire solemn strolling, while wheelchair-friendly options such as **Walkway Over the Hudson** (p119) ensure accessibility.

Added bonus? Hiking trails are usually free, aside from occasional park fees. Most routes are well maintained and easily navigable, though downloadable maps on apps such as AllTrails always come in handy.

Conditions for woodland hikes are best from May to October. Winter brings ice and snow, requiring crampons or snowshoes on high-

---

Adrenaline Rush

BIRDING
Aim binoculars skyward above **Cape May** (p160) as 400 avian species flap along the Atlantic Flyway throughout autumn's migration season.

FLY FISHING
Cast a line in creeks around Livingston Manor and **Roscoe** (p127), dubbed 'Trout Town USA' and the birthplace of American fly fishing.

ICE SKATING
Glide through an NYC winter by slipping on skates at **Wollman Skating Rink** (p94), lit by twinkling skyscrapers above Central Park.

FAMILY ADVENTURES

Count rainbows while sailing aboard the **Maid of the Mist** (p147), a sopping-wet thrill ride at Niagara Falls State Park.

Pretend you're pioneers while riding a horse-drawn wagon around **Pine Creek Gorge** (p235), dubbed Pennsylvania's Grand Canyon.

Spend quality time with friendly cows at **Sunset View Creamery** (p137), a Finger Lakes dairy farm with calves more cuddly than labradors.

Stroll the easy 1.25-mile track to **Muddy Creek Falls** (p342), Maryland's tallest waterfall – a gorgeous gusher near Deep Creek Lake.

Escape Manhattan's mayhem on car-free **Governors Island** (p54), zooming down the city's tallest slide and cycling the park's scenic perimeter.

Take a break from sandcastles to savor ice-cream or shout on amusement-park rides along **Ocean City's boardwalk** (p329).

---

elevation trails in the Catskills and Adirondacks. Spring melt creates muddy conditions, though waterfalls gush with gusto.

In urban areas, it's a pedestrian party all year – just ensure to dress for the weather. The average NYC resident walks more than 2.5 miles daily – easily accomplished while wandering the romantic West Village or skipping through one of Frederick Law Olmsted's splendid urban parks. More bipedal beauty awaits around DC's cobblestoned Georgetown and Philadelphia's Old City.

Swim & Paddle

Nautical recreation abounds between May and September, when bracing waters become ideal for dunking. Freshwater lakes and rivers reach top temps in July and August – spectacular times to jump in Ithaca's **swimming holes** (p136) or tube down Fredericksburg's **Rappahannock River** (p376). The coast is another summertime magnet. On holiday weekends like July 4, expect to jockey for space along popular shorelines.

Paddling pleasures await in every state. Kayak through **Blackwater National Wildlife Refuge**'s (p326) brackish waters, or glide down the NY-PA border on the lazy **Delaware River** (p124). Hop in a kayak around **DC** (p295) or **Buffalo** (p145) to see city skylines from a cormorant's point of view.

Cycle

Consider trading public trains for pedals in DC, NYC or Philadelphia. Thanks to ever-expanding bikeshare programs, it's easy to find wheels throughout each city, and an acceleration in e-bike usage means riders can go faster and farther without breaking a sweat. Bike paths outside big cities offer more eco-friendly ways to explore. Roll between DC and Pittsburgh by following the **C&O Canal towpath** (p402) and **Great Allegheny Passage** (p340) for 333 miles, fly down West Virginia's **Snowshoe Mountain** (p403) on mountain-bike trails, or discover Delaware on Wilmington's **Markell Trail** (p302).

> **ACTION AREAS**
> See p44 for more activities

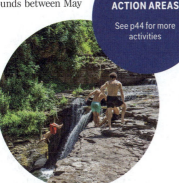

Ithaca (p136)

ZIP LINING
Soar over Harpers Ferry on a 1200ft-long course – West Virginia's fastest high-speed, all-steel **zip line** (p402).

SKIING
Rip down the East Coast's largest vertical drop on **Whiteface Mountain** (p135), the snowy Adirondacks slopes where Olympians raced.

SURFING
Walk the nose at Montauk's **Ditch Plains Beach** (p108), where consistent waves attract serious surf crowds throughout the year.

WHITE-WATER RAFTING
Thrash down frothy, white-capped, class I–V rapids raging through **New River Gorge National Park & Preserve** (p394).

NEW YORK & THE MID-ATLANTIC

THE GUIDE

New York State
p103

Pennsylvania
p220

New York City
p48

Philadelphia
p175

New Jersey
p150

Maryland
p317

Delaware
p298

West Virginia
p387

WASHINGTON, DC
p251

Virginia
p344

Chapters in this section are organised by hubs and their surrounding areas. We see the hub as your base in the destination, where you'll find unique experiences, local insights, insider tips and expert recommendations. It's also your gateway to the surrounding area, where you'll see what and how much you can do from there.

New River Gorge (394)
WANDERLUSTER/GETTY IMAGES ©

47

New York City

AMERICA'S NON-STOP CULTURAL CAPITAL

Skyscraper canyons. Honking cabs. Rattling trains. Massive museums. Michelin-starred restaurants. The bright lights of Broadway. The list doesn't stop; New York doesn't either.

NYC is a superlative city. It's the most populous metropolis in the United States, with 8.3 million residents. You'll find more subway stations here than in any other city worldwide, and you might hear 800 languages – New York the most linguistically diverse destination on Earth. This modern-day Babel boasts biblically tall towers, including One World Trade Center, the Western hemisphere's highest building. There are 170-plus museums, 2300 green spaces and more than 20,000 restaurants spread across five boroughs. Take a bite of the Big Apple and you'll barely scratch the surface. Spend a lifetime here and you'll still find yourself surprised.

Change is New York City's only constant. Initially the indigenous Lenape's stomping ground, the island they called 'Manahatta' saw its first shady real-estate transaction when the Dutch purchased the area in 1626 and dubbed it New Amsterdam. The British barged in next, renamed it New York and vacated after losing the Revolutionary War. There was good reason to fight for the land – with its superior port and eventual river link to the Great Lakes, New York became the United States'

financial and industrial powerhouse, built on the waves of American ambition. Immigrants followed, lured by the promise of prosperity, and between 1800 and 1900, New York's population ballooned from 60,000 to 3.4 million.

The burgeoning populace became a progressive pressure cooker, transforming New York into the creative center it is today. But the path to contemporary times was plagued with potholes: epidemics, economic crises, political corruption, riots, terrorist attacks and aging infrastructure have all threatened to level the city. Through it all, locals remained resilient – a testament to their tenacity and willingness to adapt. Despite its knack for reinvention, NYC is generally easily navigable, thanks to the city grid on which it was built. This regimented map of measured blocks defines local life. There's no definitive city center but a mosaic of cultural focal points – each block a mini-universe linked to the greater urban galaxy. No wonder NYC is called 'the city that never sleeps.' With something new around every corner, why waste time snoozing?

SERGII FIGURNYI/SHUTTERSTOCK ©

THE MAIN AREAS

FINANCIAL DISTRICT & LOWER MANHATTAN	SOHO, CHINATOWN, NOLITA & LITTLE ITALY	EAST VILLAGE & THE LOWER EAST SIDE	WEST VILLAGE & CHELSEA
Soaring skyscrapers and colonial relics. **p54**	Delicious dumplings and fashionable duds. **p63**	Edgy style and immigrant history. **p68**	Architecture, art and urban parks. **p73**

Left: Statue of Liberty (p58); Above: The New York skyline

MIDTOWN	**UPPER EAST SIDE**	**UPPER WEST SIDE**	**BROOKLYN**
Bright lights and Broadway.	Magnificent museums and old-money airs.	Sprawling green spaces and culture.	Waterfront wonders and post-industrial panache.
p80	**p86**	**p92**	**p97**

Find Your Way

Transportation here is more than yellow cabs and subway cars, though both are icons of urban commuting. Appreciate the city's shifting landscape while zipping by on bikes, or play a role in the sidewalk ballet by hoofing it block-by-block. It might initially seem like chaos, but NYC's choreography is precise.

FROM THE AIRPORT

Most visitors arrive in NYC via one of three airports – John F. Kennedy (JFK), LaGuardia (LGA) or Newark (EWR). Public transit from all airports to Midtown generally takes one to 1½ hours. Cabs may be faster outside of rush hour, but cost significantly more.

WALK & BIKE

NYC is a pedestrian town, and strolling is a fantastic way to see the sites – as long as you follow the unspoken city sidewalk rules: keep right, walk no more than two people across and don't stop abruptly. Prefer speed? Cycle the city's 1500 miles of interconnected bike lanes.

NEW YORK CITY

THE GUIDE

Brooklyn p97

East Village & the Lower East Side p68

Tenement Museum

West Village & Chelsea p73

Whitney Museum of American Art

High Line

Hudson River Park

SoHo, Chinatown, Nolita & Little Italy p63

Brooklyn Bridge

Financial District & Lower Manhattan p54

Ellis Island

Statue of Liberty

Governors Island

Liberty State Park

Upper New York Bay

Red Hook Recreational Area

Prospect Park

Prospect Park Lake

JFK Airport (10m)

Coney Island (3.5m)

Newark Bay

Passaic River

0 — 2 miles
0 — 4 km

TAXI & RIDESHARES
Yellow cabs are synonymous with NYC. To hail a cab, step off the curb and throw your arm in the air. When the number on a taxi's top light is lit, it's available. Ridesharing apps Uber and Lyft also work, though taxis are usually cheaper.

SUBWAY
NYC's subway system is the biggest and busiest in North America, with 1.4 million daily passengers chugging between 462 stations spread across 665 miles of track. It's cheap, efficient, operates 24/7 and provides a dynamic snapshot of New York's diverse population.

51

Plan Your Days

New York is enormous. It's impossible to see everything in a few days; even a lifetime would be tricky. Use this guide to focus your time on essential experiences.

Chinatown (p65)

Day 1

Morning
● Begin with a local history crash course at the **Museum of the City of New York** (p87), then saunter down to the **Metropolitan Museum of Art** (p88). After admiring Egyptian and European masterpieces, ramble across Central Park via the **Jacqueline Kennedy Onassis Reservoir** (p95).

Afternoon
● Nosh an Upper West Side staple for lunch (try **Absolute Bagels** (p96) or **Mama's TOO!** (p96) before stepping into the 19th-century townhouse of the **Nicholas Roerich Museum** (p96).

Evening
● Nab tickets to a Broadway musical, then process the show over food and drinks at **Bar Centrale** (p81). Finish the day dazzled by **Times Square's** (p84) lights.

You'll Also Want to...

See the city's greatest hits, then get off the beaten path to feel the pulse of local life in art galleries, boutiques and restaurants.

EYE EXCEPTIONAL ART

Go contemporary at **MoMA** (p83), or spend an afternoon wandering around far-west Chelsea's free-to-visit **art galleries** (p79).

EXPLORE GREEN SPACES

Lean into island time on car-free **Governors Island** (p54) and find serenity among the sculptures at **Elizabeth St Garden** (p66).

SAMPLE GLOBAL CUISINE

Immigrants have trained NYC's taste buds to enjoy international flavors, best experienced at the East Village's glut of **global restaurants** (p72).

Day 2

Morning
● Stretch your legs while admiring architecture along the **High Line** (p75), with detours to food-filled **Chelsea Market** (p75) and **Hudson River Park** (p77).

Afternoon
● Beeline to the **Whitney Museum of American Art**, (p73) with its permanent collection packed with American art masters. The West Village's picturesque maze begs to be explored next. Snatch one of **St Jardim's** (p76) street-side tables to sip espresso while savoring the scene.

Evening
● Plan for a late night in Brooklyn. Start with a memorable meal at **Lilia** (p99), then continue east for a rowdy night at **House of Yes** (p100) or a concert at **Elsewhere** (p100).

Day 3

Morning
● Sail to the **Statue of Liberty** (p58) to consider how the green goddess's ideals compare to America's realities. Follow it up by exploring **Ellis Island's** (p58) immigration museum.

Afternoon
● Eat your way through **Chinatown** (p65) en route to the Lower East Side. Pop into shops along **Orchard St** (p69), or join a guided **Tenement Museum** (p68) tour for more insight into the immigrant experience.

Evening
● For dinner, sample **Thai Diner's** (p65) Bangkok-meets–Big Apple menu before catching an avant-garde cabaret at **Joe's Pub** (p66). Cap it off by quaffing cocktails at a renowned speakeasy-style bar such as **Attaboy** (p69) or **PDT** (p72).

SHOP AT UNIQUE BOUTIQUES
Look past the big-name brands in **SoHo and Nolita** (p63), where fashionistas hunt for one-of-a-kind statement pieces.

UNCOVER NYC HISTORY
Follow the footsteps of American revolutionaries in **Lower Manhattan** (p62) and ride a century-old thrill ride at **Coney Island** (p99).

ADMIRE THE ARCHITECTURE
Spot styles spanning centuries, from the Gilded Age's Gothic **Brooklyn Bridge** (p55) to the modern observation deck at **Hudson Yards** (p80).

SEE A LIVE SHOW
Go classical at the **Metropolitan Opera** (p96), or contemporary with **Comedy Cellar** (p76) stand-ups: NYC's performers are among the world's best.

Financial District & Lower Manhattan

NYC HISTORY, SCULPTED IN STEEL

GETTING AROUND

FiDi is well serviced by subway trains. Main hub Fulton connects the A/C, J/Z, 2/3 and 4/5 lines, which stop near the World Trade Center site. For access to the Brooklyn Bridge, take the 4/5/6 to Brooklyn Bridge-City Hall. If you're hopping on a boat, take the 1 to South Ferry. Governors Island ferries depart from the Battery Maritime Building. For ferry service to Staten Island, use the Whitehall Terminal. For the Statue of Liberty, board in Battery Park. Be sure to explore this neighborhood on foot: skyscrapers form impressive steel canyons on FiDi's narrow streets.

Business first – Lower Manhattan encompasses the Financial District ('FiDi') and Tribeca. Pleasure second – it's home to sites such as the Statue of Liberty and the Brooklyn Bridge, along with colonial relics, magnificent museums and a collection of elegant parks and piers. Lower Manhattan is much like the stock market: prone to ups and downs. With waterfront access and plenty of ports, the area became a powerful 19th-century trading hub and global financial center, and today Wall Street remains a key player in global economics. Despite its many fortunes, there's been plenty of pain, including economic collapses, natural disasters and terrorist attacks, but still the neighborhood's steely resilience shines. New skyscrapers soar as testaments to New York's tenacity, Tribeca is having an art-gallery boom and, after years of pollution, the waterfront is cleaning up its act. Wander cobblestone streets, eye cloud-piercing architecture and remember to ride a ferry – this city isn't only cement.

Sail Away to Governors Island

Escape the city's incessant buzz

Car-free, glamp-ready and laced with paths for strolling and cycling, **Governors Island** might be a five-minute ferry ride from Manhattan's southern tip, but it's energetically worlds away. Choose your own adventure on this 172-acre pleasure pad, which is shaped like an ice-cream cone and sprinkled with activities for all palates.

To see the sites quickly, cycle the island's 7 miles of trails for panoramas of Lower Manhattan's skyline. Rent wheels from **Blazing Saddles** ($30 a day), or use one of three Citi Bike stations around the island.

Art enthusiasts can spend an afternoon admiring mammoth outdoor sculptures, such as the indigenous fruit trees populating the living *Open Orchard* earthwork. Kids can get a thrill zooming down the city's longest slide, a 57ft screamer on aptly named **Slide Hill**. When hunger calls, head to

Liggett Tce's food trucks or a waterfront restaurant with New York Harbor views. To decompress, book a session at **QC NY's** Roman-style spa (starting at $98), where guests unwind in saunas and steam rooms, and soak up city views from a heated outdoor infinity pool.

Governors Island has seen tremendous transformations since native tribes fished here in the 1500s. It's now 100 acres larger, having been bulked up in 1912 with debris from the Lexington Ave subway excavation, and decorated with architectural remnants from two centuries as a military stronghold. **Fort Jay** and **Castle Williams**, completed in the early 19th century, are the most impressive – both served as prisons for Confederate soldiers during the Civil War. In 2023, one of the island's last parcels of undeveloped land went to Stony Brook University, which plans to build a campus focused on researching climate-change solutions, expected to open in 2028.

Ferries depart from Lower Manhattan's **Battery Maritime Building** daily. Adult tickets cost $4; on weekends, all passengers ride free until noon.

Stroll the Brooklyn Bridge

Architectural icon with breeze-buffeted views

When this marvel of modern engineering opened in 1883, it was the world's first steel suspension **bridge** and the first land link between Manhattan and Brooklyn, spanning 1596ft across the East River. Longer NYC bridges have since snatched the spotlight, but this 1-mile-plus journey still inspires awe. Its elevated pedestrian path is like an open-air cathedral, with granite stones forming neo-Gothic arches that point toward the heavens, while at sunset, the latticework of steel-wire cables seems like stained glass. Reach the bridge's apex for picture-perfect frames of Manhattan's skyscrapers and Brooklyn's waterfront.

For a soul-stirring jaunt to Brooklyn, start at the bridge entrance at Manhattan's City Hall Park. The Brooklyn side has two exits. The first leads to Dumbo, with easy access to Brooklyn Bridge Park (p97), while the second ends where leafy Brooklyn Heights meets gritty Downtown Brooklyn. Expect large crowds from late morning to early evening, particularly in good weather.

Constructing the Brooklyn Bridge was no walk in the park. An estimated 27 people died during the 14-year process, including designer John Roebling, who contracted tetanus after his foot was crushed at Fulton Landing in the early stages of work. His son, Washington Roebling, took the baton, only to become bedridden with the bends (decompression sickness) after toiling away in underwater caissons used to excavate the riverbed for the bridge's towers. His wife, Emily, supervised most of the construction and became the first person to cross the bridge in a carriage, holding a rooster as a sign of victory.

CHOOSE YOUR RIDE

Citi Bike, NYC's ubiquitous bikeshare program, offers day passes ($19 for unlimited 30-minute rides) that allow users to unlock bikes at one station and drop them off at any other station around the city. This option is most convenient for short, quick trips. Finding a station to dock your bike can occasionally be a hassle, particularly on summer weekends in popular neighborhoods, when it's hard to find parking spaces. You can purchase day passes at station kiosks, but download the Citi Bike app for a better user experience. **Blazing Saddles**, a rental company with a South Street Seaport outpost, offers one-hour ($10) and full-day bike rentals ($28). A rental is best for longer rides where you plan to stop and explore at leisure.

☑ TOP TIP

If you plan on visiting favorites such as the Statue of Liberty, One World Observatory and the National September 11th Memorial and Museum, expect crowds. Purchase tickets online in advance. For a free activity, ride the ferry to Staten Island.

FINANCIAL DISTRICT & LOWER MANHATTAN

TOP SIGHTS
1. Brooklyn Bridge

SIGHTS
2. African Burial Ground National Monument
3. Battery Park
4. Lovelace Tavern foundation
5. National Museum of the American Indian
6. National September 11 Memorial
7. National September 11 Memorial Museum
8. Oculus Center
9. One World Trade Center
10. Slave Market Historical Marker
11. South Street Seaport Museum
12. Stone Street
13. Trinity Church

SLEEPING
14. Beekman
15. Greenwich Hotel

EATING
16. Brookfield Place
17. Fraunces Tavern
18. Frenchette
19. Le District
20. Manhatta
21. Tin Building
22. Tiny's & the Bar Upstairs

DRINKING & NIGHTLIFE
23. Dead Rabbit
24. Overstory
25. Smith & Mills
26. Split Eights

TRANSPORT
27. Battery Maritime Building
28. Blazing Saddles
29. Whitehall Terminal

THE GUIDE

NEW YORK CITY FINANCIAL DISTRICT & LOWER MANHATTAN

PRACTICALITIES

Scan this QR code for ticket prices and opening hours.

TOP SIGHT

Statue of Liberty & Ellis Island

'Lady Liberty' is New York's most enduring icon, her torch shining high above the harbor since 1886. A one-woman welcoming committee for millions of immigrants, 'Liberty Enlightening the World' (her official name) is an international symbol of freedom, justice and opportunity. Nearby is Ellis Island, America's immigration epicenter from 1892 to 1924, from where 40% of the US population can trace their ancestry.

DID YOU KNOW?

Lady Liberty was intended as an icon of emancipation, not immigration – Ellis Island didn't open its 'golden door' until six years after it was unveiled. The original idea was replaced by the sentiment of Emma Lazarus' 1883 poem 'The New Colossus', on the pedestal, which welcomes 'huddled masses yearning to breathe free.'

Ride the Ferry

Start your journey beside Battery Park's **Castle Clinton**, where crowds congregate for the 15-minute ferry ride to Liberty Island. Expect airport-style security screenings at the boarding station, with 30- to 90-minute lines during summer's high season. Grab a seat by the lower-level windows or on the upper-level railings for views of **Governors Island** (p54), the Verrazzano-Narrows Bridge and Manhattan's jagged skyline.

Visit the Museum

Step into Liberty Island's free museum – a 26,000-sq-ft complex completed in 2019 – for a riveting introduction. The statue's original torch, removed in 1984, is the visual pièce de résistance, while the most engaging exhibit digs into the statue's hypocrisy. In 1886, 'universal liberty' was a dream deferred for many Americans – women didn't have the right to vote and African Americans suffered through racist government policies during post-Civil War reconstruction. Even today, America maintains a complicated relationship with Lady Liberty's ideals.

Gaze at the Goddess

While staring at Lady Liberty's sea-green copper sheen, consider the fantastic feats it took to bring her to America. Designer Frédéric-Auguste Bartholdi's 450,000lb giantess was constructed in Paris between 1881 and 1884, with help from French engineer Alexandre Gustave Eiffel (of the eponymous tower), using 300 copper sheets, each about 7.8ft wide. She was transported to New York across the treacherous Atlantic in 214 crates, reassembled from 350 pieces over four months, then placed on a granite pedestal designed by architect Richard Morris Hunt, bringing her total height to 305ft.

Sail to Ellis Island

Traveling to Ellis Island begins as it did for roughly 12 million immigrants – on the water. The 27.5-acre plot of land is only accessible by ferry, which leaves from Liberty Island, sailing for 15 minutes to the National Immigration Museum. Get your camera ready: the trip from Liberty Island is particularly scenic.

Understand the United States

Immerse yourself in the complex tapestry of US immigration prior to Ellis Island's debut around the Main Building's 1st-floor museum. *Journeys: The Peopling of America, 1550–1890*, traces the movement of people to and through the US as they built the blocks of the nation's foundation. Stories of displaced Native Americans, enslaved Africans and optimistic immigrants illuminate America's ongoing struggles with identity.

See an Immigrant's Point of View

On the Main Building's 2nd floor, you can visit *Through America's Gate*, an exhibition chronicling the step-by-step process for newly arrived immigrants on Ellis Island. Begin in the 338ft-long Registry Room, where thousands of hopefuls once gathered daily to wade through the tape of US bureaucracy. From here, wander through halls to learn about medical and legal inspections necessary to gain admittance to the US, including the 29 questions that would determine a person's future. While 98% of immigrants eventually made it into the country, 2% of people faced the personal and financial pain of rejection – which could account for more than 1000 people per month. Take a moment to examine pieces of salvaged walls, scrawled on by immigrants desperate to make their mark.

OYSTERS TO ELLIS

Native Americans called Ellis Island 'Kioshk' (Gull Island). The Dutch called it Oyster Island for its mollusks. It was then dubbed Gibbet Island when criminals were hanged here in the 1760s. Today's name comes from Samuel Ellis, who took ownership in the 1770s. He unsuccessfully tried to rid himself of the property while alive. Now his name is famous.

TOP TIPS

- Statue Cruises is the only company that sells tickets to Liberty and Ellis islands; the box office operates inside Castle Clinton and New Jersey's Liberty State Park. Book online to avoid queues.
- If you want to see the Statue of Liberty and Ellis Island in one day, hop on a ferry before 2pm.
- Liberty Island's food is expensive and mediocre. Pack lunch or snacks to enjoy on site instead.
- Head to Ellis Island's lobby to check the schedule for free tours, screenings of the 35-minute film *Island of Hope, Island of Tears,* and to pick up a free audio guide.

VIEWS FROM NEW YORK HARBOR

Captain Jonathan Boulware, president and CEO of South Street Seaport Museum. *@seaportmuseum*

New York is a maritime town. It was a port before it was a city, and its identity as a global destination is rooted in its port-ness. Until the middle of the 20th century, when people arrived here, their first sight of New York was from the harbor, looking at the lower end of Manhattan. It's possible to see that historic vista from two **South Street Seaport Museum** vessels: the 1885 *Pioneer* schooner and the last surviving New York–built wooden tugboat, *WO Decker*. Trips last a couple of hours, starting at Pier 16, and usually cruise toward the Brooklyn Bridge and Statue of Liberty.

The Battery

Bike Around Manhattan's Tip
Pedal through an outdoor museum

Thanks to 1500-plus miles of bike lanes, cycling is one of the fastest and most efficient ways to navigate NYC – and in Lower Manhattan, a 3-mile stretch tracing the island's southern tip also happens to be exceptionally scenic. You can zoom along this path in less than 30 minutes, but add in stops for food, shopping and views and this can quickly turn into a half-day affair. Before hitting the bike path, fuel up at the **Tin Building**, a two-floor food hall hocking picnic-ready treats. From here, a two-way bike lane glides beneath FDR Dve. Follow the path south along the East River toward the **Whitehall Ferry Terminal**, then curve west to reach the **Battery**, a serene spot to pause and appreciate waterfront views and manicured gardens. As the trail swerves north, it connects with the Hudson River Greenway – a picturesque 13-mile paved ribbon that links to Inwood. Park your bike around **Brookfield Place**, a posh retail-and-food palace, to grab snacks (perhaps French pastries from **Le District**) and explore the nearby One World Trade Center site on foot.

EATING IN LOWER MANHATTAN: BEST MEALS

Tin Building: Jean-Georges Vongerichten attracts crowds to this South Street Seaport spot with 53,000 sq ft of food counters. *8am-10pm* **$$**

Manhatta: Splurge on the tasting menu or sip a cocktail bar-side – what's most important are the 60th-floor views. *hours vary.* **$$$**

Frenchette: This French bistro is more Left Bank Paris than West Side Manhattan. *noon-10pm Mon-Fri, from 11am Sat, 11am-9:30pm Sun.* **$$$**

Tiny's & the Bar Upstairs: American classics get doused with modern pizzazz at this pretty-in-pink 1810 townhouse. *hours vary* **$$$**

See NYC from One World Observatory

Soar to great heights

The World Trade Center site's 16-acre campus is a symbol of NYC's resilience. There's the **National September 11 Memorial** and a connected **museum**, a somber tribute honoring victims of the deadliest terror attack on US soil, alongside amazing modern architecture, including Santiago Calatrava's gleaming cream **Oculus**. The greatest testament to the city's recovery from 9/11 is **One World Trade Center** (aka Freedom Tower), which soars 1776ft above the plaza like a phoenix, claiming the title of tallest building in the Western Hemisphere.

The shimmering 104-floor spectacle is impressive from below, but wait until you reach the observation decks on levels 100 to 102. Floor-to-ceiling windows showcase a 360-degree panorama of all five boroughs and three adjoining states. If you need help identifying landmarks, interactive mobile tablets programmed in multiple languages are available, included in a combo ticket for a well-spent extra $10.

Purchase tickets online (oneworldobservatory.com/tickets) to avoid long queues and consider arriving early to beat the crowds (sunsets on clear days are particularly busy). The experience is more 'theme-park glam' than 'NYC grit,' but if you can stomach snaking security lines and wide-eyed visitors, it's worth the trip.

WHO HEARTS NY?

NYC fell on tough times in the 1970s, and to save New York's tourism industry, graphic designer Milton Glaser was tasked with designing an inviting logo. While bumping along in the back of a cab, he scribbled an idea on an envelope. It read 'I Love NY,' with a rosy-red heart (spoiler alert: it caught on). Since then, the design has been updated in moments of local duress. There was Glaser's 'I love NY more than ever' after 9/11, then 'I can't afford to love NY,' which has appeared as graffiti in the last decade, mocking rising rents. Most recently, the city introduced 'We Love NYC' as a post-pandemic panacea – much to the chagrin of the original's fans.

TALL TOWERS & SWEEPING VIEWS

Manhattan's skyscraper forests loom largest over Lower Manhattan and Midtown. To appreciate more cloud-piercing architecture, zoom to the top of the **Empire State Building** (p81) or the **Edge** (p80) at Hudson Yards.

DRINKING IN LOWER MANHATTAN: BEST COCKTAILS & COFFEE

Overstory: This lounge on the 64th floor is best for marveling at the city's lights. Reserve an outdoor table ($75 minimum spend). *5.45pm-midnight*

Dead Rabbit: It's tough beating this three-floor bar named after a 19th-century Irish-American gang – the Irish coffee is a knockout. *11am-2am, to 3am Fri & Sat*

Split Eights: Let the bartender decide what you should imbibe at this moody hang where buttoned-up crowds let loose. *4.30pm-2am*

Smith & Mills: Ex-carriage house turned cocktail bar and restaurant. Don't leave without seeing the loo, inside a 1902 cage elevator. *4-11pm Sun & Mon, to 1am Tue-Sat*

UNCOVER NEW YORK'S COLONIAL PAST

In a city known for its relentless drive to be 'New,' a trove of old-world history hides in plain sight. Take this 2-mile walk to see ghostly remnants of Manhattan's yesteryear. Start at the ❶ **Battery**'s (p60) waterfront, facing Lady Liberty, to consider how her lofty ideals compare with the city's complicated origins. Before Henry Hudson arrived in 1609, the Lenape paddled here in wood-carved canoes. Stop by the ❷ **National Museum of the American Indian** on the park's eastern side to learn about 'Turtle Island' land before European takeover. Trace the park to ❸ **Pearl St**, the city's original shoreline before landfill expanded it outward, and jog east to ❹ **Fraunces Tavern**, where George Washington famously threw back a few pints. Across the street, look for the bones of ❺ **Lovelace Tavern's foundation**, buried beneath the sidewalk. Built in 1670 and burned down in 1706, the site wasn't rediscovered until 1979. Next stop is ❻ **Stone St**, which became the city's first cobblestone-paved passage in the 17th century. Three blocks northeast is a plaque marking the site of New York's ❼ **slave market**, opened in 1711. Slavery was introduced to the city in 1626; by 1730, 42% of the population owned enslaved people. Walk west on ❽ **Wall St** (an actual defence wall in the 17th century) toward ❾ **Trinity Church** (resting place of Alexander Hamilton) and north along ❿ **Broadway** (built on an old Lenape route). End at the ⓫ **African Burial Ground National Monument**, a memorial and museum honoring the estimated 15,000 African souls interred on site. Unearthed in 1991 during construction of an office building, the mass grave is a reminder of the backs on which New York was built.

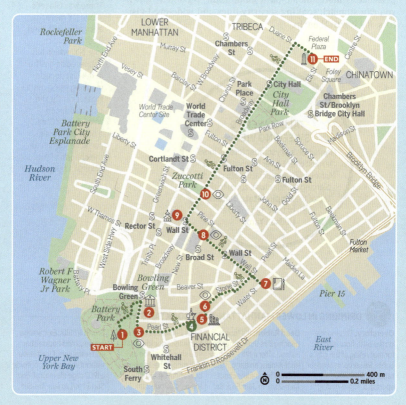

SoHo, Chinatown, Nolita & Little Italy

DELICIOUS DUMPLINGS, FASHIONABLE DUDS AND ART

SoHo (South of Houston) and Nolita (North of Little Italy) dominate as Manhattan's trendsetting epicenters, home to boutiques, bars and eateries that appear to pop from the pages of *Vogue*. Chinatown and Little Italy simmer with the nostalgia of far-off homelands – two idiosyncratic cultures cohabitating side by side.

Walk among SoHo's ornate cast-iron facades, which resulted from Gilded Age development when the neighborhood was a popular 19-century commerce hub. Despite appearances, the area didn't remain favorable for long. By the early 20th century, it was called Hell's Hundred Acres, and by the late 1950s, urban planner Robert Moses attempted to run a highway through it. Luckily, his plans fell flat. Similarly, Chinatown was once the site of Five Points, a 19th-century slum known for crime and vice – eventually wiped off the map. Throughout its ups and downs, artists and immigrants have served as proud stewards, transforming these streets into pedestrian playgrounds.

See SoHo's Artsy Side
Free galleries and sidewalk surprises

Fashionistas lust over SoaHo's flagship stores today, but in the 1960s, many New Yorkers considered the area a wasteland – unless they were among the artists living and working in its industrial loft spaces. By the 1980s, these creative crowds turned the neighborhood into NYC's arty epicenter. Look beyond the storefronts for a couple of hours to spot SoHo's stylish origins.

Begin at the **Leslie-Lohman Museum of Art**, the world's first museum dedicated to LGBTIQ+ themes. Charles Leslie and the late Fritz Lohman started showcasing their gay-centric art collection from a SoHo loft in 1969 – an assemblage that rapidly expanded as they rescued works by dying artists during the 1980s AIDS pandemic. Nearby, you'll find the **Drawing Center**, a nonprofit institute focused solely on

GETTING AROUND

Traffic often gets congested. Stick to the sidewalk and the subway; avoid cabs and buses. In terms of navigation, SoHo is bound north to south by Houston and Canal Sts and east to west by Lafayette St and 6th Ave. Nolita stretches east to Bowery. Chinatown bleeds into the surrounding neighborhoods, but is generally bound east to west by Allen St and Broadway. Canal St is the main artery separating SoHo and Chinatown; it's serviced east to west by the J/Z, 6, N/Q/R, A/C/E and 1 trains.

☑ TOP TIP

If you're dining in SoHo between Friday and Sunday, reserve a table in advance. Trendy restaurants book up quickly, which can make snatching a table for dinner seem impossible. Alternatively, visit Chinatown's many grab-and-go food stands.

SOHO, CHINATOWN, NOLITA & LITTLE ITALY

SIGHTS
1. Basilica of St Patrick's Old Cathedral
2. Chinatown Fair Family Fun Center
3. Columbus Park
4. Drawing Center
5. Elizabeth Street Garden
6. Judd Foundation
7. Leslie-Lohman Museum of Art
8. New York City Fire Museum
9. New York Earth Room

SLEEPING
10. Crosby Street Hotel
11. ModernHaus SoHo

EATING
12. Golden Steamer
13. Lombardi's
14. Mei Lai Wah
15. Raoul's
16. Rubirosa
17. Thai Diner
18. Yi Ji Shi Mo

DRINKING & NIGHTLIFE
19. Cafe Integral
20. Ear Inn
21. Fanelli Cafe
22. Felix Roasting Company
23. Jimmy

SHOPPING
24. Alexis Bittar
25. Bloomingdale's
26. Canal St Market
27. Corridor
28. IF Boutique
29. Olfactory NYC
30. oo35mm
31. Oroboro
32. R Swiader

THE GUIDE — NEW YORK CITY

64

drawings. Founded in 1977 as SoHo's art scene took shape, the free-to-visit museum is now a neighborhood fixture that's featured everyone from Michelangelo to Richard Serra.

Continue to the 2nd floor of 141 Wooster St to see the work of artist Walter de Maria – a room filled with 280,000lb of dirt. This is the **New York Earth Room**, on view since 1980 – it's a heady experience, open noon to 3pm and 3:30pm to 6pm Wednesday to Sunday. Finally, watch where you step while walking over the northwest corner of Prince St and Broadway (outside Prada) and you'll spot the work of sculptor Ken Hiratsuka, who carved roughly 40 sidewalks after moving to NYC in 1982. This design took about five hours of actual work, though its completion took two years (1983–84), as police patrols often disrupted Hirasuka's illegal chiseling.

Eat Everything in Chinatown
Dumplings, rolls, buns and bao

The most rewarding way to visit Chinatown is through your taste buds. Follow this 1-mile food tour past dangling duck roasts, paper lanterns and simple storefronts where food is the main attraction. Begin inside the East Broadway Mall, a largely abandoned shopping center beneath the Manhattan Bridge. Look past the grungy vestibules and let your nose lead you downstairs to **Fu Zhou Wei Zhong Wei Jia Xiang Feng Wei**, which roughly translates to 'the tastiest Fuzhou hometown -flavor restaurant.' Order the dumplings and decide if the food lives up to the name. Next stop is **Mei Lai Wah**, famous for pineapple buns with roast pork. There's often a line snaking

MORE CONTEMPORARY ART

If you love SoHo's museums, spend an hour or two hopping around Chelsea's free-to-visit **galleries** (p63), which showcase up-and-coming creatives alongside some of the biggest names in the business.

SNAKE DOWN DOYERS ST

In a city dominated by an orderly grid, Doyers St – a curved block in Chinatown – refuses to conform. Named after Hendrick Doyer, an 18th-century Dutch immigrant who owned a distillery here, Doyers became the epicenter of Chinatown as it took shape in the late 1800s. By the end of the century, the street earned new monikers, including the 'Bloody Angle' – a reference to criminal activity. Throughout the early 20th century, warring *tongs* (Chinese gangs) attacked rivals by hiding behind the street's sharp bend – a cause for concern for anyone visiting nearby tenement buildings packed with gambling parlors and opium dens. Today, it's a peaceful pedestrian promenade. Instead of blood stains, a mural decorates the block.

 EATING IN SOHO & CHINATOWN: BEST MEALS

| **Thai Diner:** Classic NY-diner style retooled with Southeast Asian flavors. $$ | **Raoul's:** Cool kids started lining up for Raoul's French-bistro in 1975. Order the peppercorn-crusted burger. $$$ | **Lombardi's:** Opened in 1905, this Neapolitan-style parlor claims to be America's first pizzeria. $$ | **Golden Diner:** Trek to this Manhattan Bridge haunt for surprising takes on greasy-spoon grub, including Asian influences. $$ |

WHEN LITTLE ITALY WAS BIG

Mulberry St, named after the mulberry trees that once lined its sidewalks, became synonymous with Italy in the late 19th and early 20th centuries as millions of Italian immigrants funneled into the country. By 1910, roughly 10,000 Italian Americans crammed themselves into a 2-mile radius of tenement buildings that Jacob Riis called the 'foul core of New York's slums.' After WWII, the community began a mass exodus and, as Chinatown expanded, Little Italy went from a brash boot to a slim sandal. But wiping out the Italian heritage is impossible: restaurants such as **Rubirosa** ensure Mulberry St remains soaked in red sauce, and September's 11-day Feast of San Gennaro festival revives its red-white-and-green glory.

Elizabeth St Garden

outside this tiny shop. Once it's your turn, place an order at the digital kiosk inside and watch the kitchen staff prep to-go bags for ravenous hordes. Give your belly a break from the food frenzy in **Columbus Park**, once a part of Five Points – NYC's first tenement slums. Today, entering the leafy oasis is like a trip to Shanghai: spy spirited mah-jongg meisters, slow-motion tai-chi practitioners and aunties gossiping over homemade dumplings. Continue to Elizabeth St's **Yi Ji Shi Mo**, a tiny, unassuming counter famous for rice rolls. End your food tour with Chinatown's tastiest *bao* (steamed buns) at **Golden Steamer**. Order the pumpkin – if they haven't already run out.

Expect Great Performances at the Public
Off-Broadway theater and cabaret

Broadway isn't the only place to see great theater. See what's playing at the **Public** (publictheater.org), a legendary Off-Broadway house founded in 1954 that launched some of New York's biggest hits, including *Hamilton* in 2015. Today, you'll find a lineup of new works and reimagined classics, with Shakespeare on heavy rotation.

Next door is **Joe's Pub**, named for Public Theater founder Joseph Papp. Part bar, part cabaret venue, the intimate space serves up top-shelf entertainers, ranging from downtown icon Joey Arias to Broadway's biggest divas and heavy hitters (Adele even sang here). Take a chance on lesser-known names. Who knows? They might be New York's next big thing.

Find Solitude in a Secret Garden
Nolita's hidden public park
Cement-smacked SoHo and Nolita are largely devoid of green space, save for **Elizabeth St Garden** (11am-6pm), a hidden oasis between Prince and Spring Sts. It started in 1991, when an antiques dealer leased the abandoned lot from the city, added landscaping and sprinkled its acre with outdoor sculptures. This whimsical spot is now a serene refuge for shop-weary New Yorkers. Grab a coffee from nearby **Café Integral** to sip in the shade of garden trees. Visit while you can – the city has spent years battling the garden's grass-roots community to pave paradise and put up an apartment building.

Shop Til You Drop
Pop into unique boutiques
Soho and its surrounds burst at the seams with sartorial splendor. Spend an afternoon following NYC's style fiends to the neighborhood's trendiest shops. Start by strutting down Broadway for global chains from Adidas to Zara and everything in between – including **Bloomingdale's**, a department store beloved by big spenders. Zigzag west toward West Broadway to try on designer labels at spots like **IF Boutique**, a SoHo fashion stalwart since 1978.

In Nolita, jewel-box boutiques sell unique threads, kicks and fragrances. Don't miss **Oroboro** (upscale-casual womenswear), **R Swiader** (gender-optional clothes plus a salon) and **Corridor** (thick-knit plaids for gents). For fantastic street vendors, skip to the stands on Prince St (between Mulberry and Mott) to see handmade jewelry and art. Searching for scents? Stop by **Olfactory NYC**. Dewy-skin serums? Try **oo35mm**. For statement bling, gawk at **Alexis Bittar's** collection. He started selling Lucite jewelry on SoHo's streets in the 1980s; now he's a household name.

You don't need to be a fashionista to enjoy the consumer circus. Bookstores such as **McNally Jackson** cater to literati, and you can choose between shopping and eating at **Canal Street Market**.

Serious shopaholics should consult the city's in-the-know retail blogs before arriving – there's always a 'sample sale' going on. Try thestylishcity.com to see what's hot.

TOP SPOTS FOR DOWNTOWN NOSTALGIA

Basilica of St Patrick's Old Cathedral: Descend into the catacombs on a guided tour of the Gothic Revival basilica, a 19th-century Irish Catholic stronghold.

Merchant's House Museum: Tour this red-brick mansion from 1832 for an authentic look at 19th-century life.

Judd Foundation: Admire minimalist artist Donald Judd's five-story, cast-iron home, purchased in 1968 for a now-unthinkable $68,000.

Chinatown Fair Family Fun Center: This Mott St arcade has been going strong since 1940, delivering childhood sentimentality with games such as Ms. Pac-Man.

New York City Fire Museum: Visit this 1904 firehouse to see historic equipment such as a horse-drawn fire-fighting carriage.

 DRINKING IN SOHO: BEST BARS & CAFES

Ear Inn: See how SoHo looked before fashionistas took over at this 18th-century house-turned-drinking-den.

Jimmy: Tipsy patrons spill onto the open deck at this sky-high hangout atop ModernHaus SoHo.

Fanelli Cafe: A saloon from 1847, Fanelli bridges SoHo's past and present. The table looking down Prince and Mercer Sts is the envy of TikTok.

Felix Roasting Company: Contemporary cafe culture meets Gilded Age at the Greenwich St branch of this java chain fit for an Astor.

East Village & the Lower East Side

IMMIGRANTS, PUNKS, ARTISTS AND GOURMANDS

GETTING AROUND

Houston St (pronounced 'How-ston') is the neighborhood dividing line: East Village is above Houston; Lower East Side (LES) is below it. For subway travel to the East Village, take the L to First or Third Aves, the 6 to Astor Pl or the F to Second Ave. For the Lower East Side, take the B/D to Grand St or the F or J/M/Z to Delancey-Essex Sts. If you prefer the bus, the M14, M21 and B39 routes run along 14th, Houston and Delancey Sts.

☑ TOP TIP

The Lower East Side's epicenter is Orchard St, a strip with boutiques and restaurants leading to Dimes Sq, Manhattan's unofficial cool-kid corner. The East Village's heart is St Marks Pl, packed with food counters, tattoo parlors and bars. Walk down either for a sense of their character.

These neighborhoods are integral to NYC's multicultural melting pot as home to successive waves of immigrant communities, remnants of which linger around every corner. This is also where all the cool stuff happened – it's where the Beat Generation gravitated in the 1950s, the hippies came in the '60s, and CBGB kick-started the careers of punk and new-wave musicians such as the Ramones, Blondie and Television in the '70s. The Velvet Underground was the house band at Andy Warhol's Electric Circus extravaganza. In a nutshell, things got sketchy and it came to a head in the late 1980s with riots in Tompkins Square Park. The neighborhoods continued changing, for better and for worse, but they remain Manhattan's most eclectic, creative and funky places to be. New restaurants, cocktail bars and fashion boutiques seem to open weekly, all vying for attention amid the old-school delis and dives that still garner attention from downtown's latest trendsetters.

Explore the Tenement Life of Immigrants

Big stories, tiny apartments, tasty sandwiches

Stand in one of the tenement apartments alongside eight or 10 fellow visitors on the popular tours at the **Tenement Museum** and you'll get an idea of what it was like living in these cramped quarters. Depending on which tour you choose, a docent will lead you through various rooms of the historically restored buildings and tell you the stories of people who lived there in the 19th and 20th centuries – including stories of Jewish immigrants, along with expats from Germany, Puerto Rico, Italy and China, among other places. Tours are the only way to experience the museum and they sell out daily, so book tickets in advance.

For a post-museum taste of historic Jewish cuisine, stop by kosher **Katz's Delicatessen** (established 1888). This kosher-style deli has all the trappings: neon signs out front, table seating, gruff but kind-hearted staff and usually a line out the door. You might be surprised by the prices, but the sandwiches are huge and best shared, along with fries and a pickle. For something sweet, try **Yonah Schimmel Knish Bakery**, which started selling its namesake Jewish dough pockets from a Coney Island pushcart in the 1890s.

Pop into Storefronts along Orchard Street
Shopping and strolling

In the early 1700s, there was actually an orchard on Orchard St, but in the late 1800s this became the Lower East Side's main shopping street, with garment workers packed into tenement buildings and storefronts selling textiles. Nowadays, Orchard St is the hippest part of the neighborhood, especially the stretch between Houston and Canal Sts, which is lined with indie boutiques, happening restaurants such as **Scarr's Pizza** and upstart art galleries. Wander this seven-block strip and you'll still find some yesteryear holdouts, including **Orchard Corset**, which opened in 1968 and caters to everyone from Orthodox Jews to trans women – all with the aspirations of Victorian silhouettes.

Sweat it Out at the Russian & Turkish Baths
Spa day in a townhouse basement

Locals have been schvitzing at this slightly cramped downtown **spa** since 1892. These days, it draws an eclectic mix of actors, students, couples, singles, Russian regulars and old-school locals. Everyone strips down to their skivvies or bathing suits (towels, cotton shorts and sandals are provided) and moves between steam rooms, saunas, an ice-cold plunge pool, the sun deck and the restaurant. Most hours are coed (clothing required), but there are blocks of men- and women-only hours (clothing optional). Massages, scrubs and Russian oak-leaf treatments are available, too. The cafe serves specials such as Polish sausage and blinis.

Go to the Movies at Metrograph
Classic cinema and indie features

Serious cinephiles should consider devoting a few hours to this **indie movie house**, equipped with state-of-the-art digital projectors and an old 35mm reel-to-reel. Check the schedule for a wonderfully eclectic mix of premieres, classic oldies and rare archival films, as well as interviews with directors and filmmakers. The whole vibe is a love letter to great American movie theaters of the 1920s. Stop by the on-site Commissary for cocktails and food pre or post-show, and grab upscale candy and chocolate from the snack stand.

EDGY ART, MUSIC & CINEMA

New Museum: Work by emerging and established contemporary artists inside a seven-story fortress that looks like a series of off-kilter building blocks.

Hole: Art openings attract rowdy crowds at this bi-coastal gallery known for performances and special events.

Bowery Ballroom: Audiences adore this concert venue for its intimate feel and great sound system. Head downstairs for drinks and mingling.

International Center of Photography: Rotating exhibits celebrate the vast humanitarian and political documentary work of world-class photographers.

Slipper Room: Squeeze in tight for hit-or-miss shows featuring comics, magicians, burlesque dancers and circus performers, often worth the gamble.

 DRINKING IN THE VILLAGE & LOWER EAST SIDE: COCKTAIL & WINE BARS

Attaboy: Speakeasy vibes – tell the barkeep what you like and they'll whip up the concoction of your dreams.	**Amor y Amargo:** 'Love and Bitters' is a cocktail chemistry lab showcasing its namesake amaro selection.	**Accidental Bar:** The sake sommeliers behind this Japanese juice joint with a hilariously descriptive menu.	**Ruffian:** If you're into orange wines, try this joint to taste Eastern European grapes and vegetarian fare.

Sip Cocktails by Expert Mixologists
Take a cocktail tour

NYC's craft-cocktail revolution technically began behind the bar of Midtown's Rainbow Room, where chief bartender Dale DeGroff became 'daddy' of the 1990s mixologist craze. But the trend exploded thanks to cutting-edge drinking destinations that bubbled up around the East Village and Lower East Side in the early 2000s and never left. For a taste of liquid magic, start at **Death & Co**, where classy bartenders have been mixing bespoke beverages with exotic liquors, fresh juices and artisanal garnishes since it opened on New Year's Eve 2006. It doesn't take reservations, so line up before opening to secure a seat. **PDT** (short for Please Don't Tell) is still here, too – it opened in 2007 and became famous for combining speakeasy-style digs with creative concoctions. Make a reservation, then enter through the telephone booth inside Crif Dogs. You'll also find enough new cocktail bars to make you dizzy, while the Lower East Side's **Double Chicken Please** was named 2023's Best Bar in the US by the World's 50 Best organization.

Taste NYC's Melting Pot
Gorge on global cuisine

The diversity of worldwide cuisines in the East Village is jaw-dropping. Find what tickles your taste buds, then tour the world through food. **Nowon** is a favorite for American-Korean 'drinking food,' and some people say the northern-style pho at **Hanoi House** is better than anything in Vietnam. Nibble Nordic delicacies at **Smør** and its adjoining bakery, try Burmese specialties at **Little Myanmar**, and if you like spicy Thai food, go to **Soothr** (pronounced 'sood'). Meanwhile, **Cafe Mogador** has been turning out Moroccan favorites since 1983, **Takahachi** has been a stalwart for sushi and Japanese noodles since 1991 and **Awash** has been serving Ethiopian injera since 1994. For quick, cheap eats, follow the cab drivers to **Punjabi Grocery & Deli** for delectable vegetarian fare.

NYC'S HIPPEST MICRO-HOOD?

Is Dimes Sq the hippest new micro-hood in NYC? Does it even exist? Media coverage has debated whether this small Lower East Side corner around Division and Canal Sts is a publicity joke or a real thing, and talking about it has brought it into being. What we know for sure: **Dimes** restaurant was an immediate hotspot for cool downtown kids when it opened in 2013. We're still happy to hang out there if we can get a table. Dine elsewhere with the in-crowd at one of the area's fashionable bars and restaurants, including the chic **Lobby Lounge** inside Nine Orchard Hotel. It might be a media-made gimmick, but it's cool – like the rest of the Lower East Side.

EATING IN EAST VILLAGE & LOWER EAST SIDE

Superiority Burger: The best veggie burger in town, plus mouthwatering pies and flavor-packed sides. $$

Veselka: This vestige of the area's Ukrainian past has been serving handmade *varenyky* (pierogi), borscht and goulash since 1954. $$

Rosella: Sustainably minded sushi earns this restaurant an A+. The menu has locally caught fish, all approved by Seafood Watch or NOAA. $$$

Yellow Rose: Flour tortillas give Tex-Mex taquerias their north-of-the-border flair at this far-north-of-Texas outpost. $$

Abraço: Sip espresso while inhaling the dangerously addictive olive-oil cake inside this ground-level cafe. $

Supermoon Bakehouse: Lines of laminated pastries, including cruffins, look like designer jewelry at this shop where flavors change weekly. $

Russ & Daughters: Feast on bagels and the city's best smoked salmon at this diner extension of a long-running Jewish delicatessen. $$

Librae Bakery: Middle Eastern ingredients combined with Danish baking techniques result in concoctions like pistachio rose croissants. $

West Village & Chelsea

INDUSTRIAL PARKS, ART AND LGBTIQ+ HISTORY

Yes, it's as pretty as it looks in the movies. The West Village brims with trees, cobblestone streets and brownstones, and though it's among Manhattan's most expensive neighborhoods, it's not hard to discover traces of a grittier past. Once hunting grounds for the Lenape and fields for Dutch farmers, these blocks later sprouted townhouses for immigrants drawn to jobs by the bustling docks and factories nearby. Artists and free thinkers settled here in the 20th century, and as an outgrowth of their spirit, the Village became an LGBTIQ+ hub and site of the 1969 Stonewall Uprising, which sparked a fight for LGBTIQ+ rights worldwide. The adjacent Meatpacking District stayed grimy through the 20th century, but butchers and sex workers eventually gave way to swanky stores fed by the High Line's pedestrian runway. Further north, Chelsea is chock-full of art galleries, restaurants and tech offices.

Admire the Whitney Museum's Permanent Collection

America's modern art masters

The **Whitney Museum of American Art** opened as a showcase for home-grown artists in a W 8th St townhouse in 1930. After successive expansions north, including a stint at Madison Ave's Marcel Breuer–designed concrete colossus, the modern marvel returned downtown in 2015. It now anchors the southern reaches of the High Line (p75) in a glass-and-cement building by Renzo Piano, suggesting a giant cruise ship. Outdoor decks – uh, terraces – lead to a smattering of sculptures and exceptional skyline views. If you're short on time, beeline to the 7th floor's permanent collection, packed with American all-stars such as Edward Hopper, Jasper Johns, Georgia O'Keeffe and Andy Warhol.

GETTING AROUND

Chelsea lies between Sixth Ave and the Hudson River from 34th to 14th Sts. The West Village and Meatpacking District are south, west of Sixth Ave and Hudson St, and best walked. Greenwich Village, to the east, is bound east to west by Fourth and Sixth Aves and north to south from 14th to Houston Sts. If you're riding the subway, take the A/C/E or 1/2/3 lines to stops between 23rd and 14th St for Chelsea. Head further south to West 4th St (on the A/C/E) or Christopher St (on the 1) for the Village.

☑ TOP TIP

It's possible to take the M14 or M8 bus to the West Village, but it's a shame to see this labyrinth of streets from a vehicle. This postcard-perfect neighborhood is ideal for strolling. Just remember to arm yourself with a map (or GPS).

73

WEST VILLAGE & CHELSEA

TOP SIGHTS
1. High Line
2. Hudson River Park
3. Whitney Museum of American Art

SIGHTS
4. 520 West 28th Street
5. Dia Chelsea
6. Gagosian
7. Gansevoort Peninsula
8. High Line Nine
9. Hudson Yards
10. Little Island
11. Pace Gallery
12. Paula Cooper Gallery
13. Pier 45
14. Pier 57
15. Stonewall National Monument
16. Union Square
17. Washington Square Park

SLEEPING
18. Hotel Chelsea
19. Jane Hotel

EATING
20. Anixi
21. JeJu Noodle Bar
22. NY Dosas
23. Semma
24. Shukette

DRINKING & NIGHTLIFE
25. 124 Old Rabbit Club
26. Cubbyhole
27. Eagle NYC
28. Employees Only
29. Julius'
30. Marie's Crisis
31. St Jardim
32. Stonewall Inn
33. Té Company

ENTERTAINMENT
34. Atlantic Theater Company
35. Comedy Cellar
36. Lucille Lortel Theatre
37. Smalls
38. Village Vanguard

SHOPPING
39. Chelsea Market
40. Cueva
41. Goods for the Study
42. Printed Matter, Inc
43. Screaming Mimis
44. Union Square Greenmarket
45. Zuri

Raise a Glass to LGBTIQ+ History
Epicenter of a global movement

No neighborhood captures the queer imagination quite like the West Village, its crooked streets daring to defy Manhattan's grid. At the center of this nonconformist nabe stands the **Stonewall Inn**, where an infamous police raid on June 28, 1969 sparked an uprising that changed the course of LGBTIQ+ liberation. Fed up with never-ending discrimination and persecution, the bar's lesbian, gay and transgender patrons decided to stop playing nice with bigoted authorities and fought back. The event was a watershed moment for LGBTIQ+ rights worldwide, turning the Village into a place of queer pilgrimage. Raise a glass to the brave pioneers with a pint at today's Stonewall (next door to the 1969 incarnation), part of the **Stonewall National Monument**, designated in 2016. A visitor center set to open in 2024 will share in-depth info on the bar and the movement it came to symbolize.

Find Artisanal Treats at Chelsea Market
Industrial setting for food and fashion

This urban bazaar, open since 1997, has spawned many imitators but belongs in a class of its own. **Chelsea Market** occupies a block-long building where Nabisco once used to manufacture cookies in army-size quantities. Today, it's where visitors peruse independent, small-batch delicacies catering to foodies, fashion hounds and more. The architecture leans into the site's manufacturing past, with huge cast-iron pipes and serrated blocks of granite. Over three dozen vendors ply their temptations throughout, including **Miznon** (Israeli street food), the **Lobster Place** (good luck resisting its rolls), **Fat Witch Bakery** (brownies and other decadent hits) and **Los Tacos No. 1** (authentic Mexican tacos). Head to the covered sidewalk tables for outdoor seating. Once you've had your fill, check out **Artists & Fleas**, a small market where local artists sell their wares. It makes a great pit stop while wandering the **High Line**.

Skip Down the High Line
Chelsea's elevated train-track park

Snaking between the Meatpacking District to Hudson Yards, 30ft above street level, the **High Line** is a fabulous example of industrial reuse. Once a 20th-century freight line linking slaughterhouses along the Hudson River, it's now

GLOBAL FASHION, JOURNALS & ZINES

Screaming Mimis: This funtastic shop carries an excellent selection of vintage, designer and flamboyant costume threads.

Cueva: A streetside sandwich board showcases the eclectic designs represented by this seasonally curated international menswear collection.

Zuri: Colorful racks of one-style-fits-all dresses. Derived from the Swahili word for 'good,' Zuri lives up to its name with ethically sourced clothes from Kenya.

Goods for the Study: Hardcore journalers and sketch-pad savants go ga-ga for this assortment of paper and writing utensils.

Printed Matter, Inc: Trim shelves hide thousands of ideas packed into strange zines and artist monographs.

DRINKING IN THE WEST VILLAGE: LGBTIQ+ HANGOUTS

Julius': One of NYC's longest-running gay joints, this cozy dive, famous for a 1966 civil rights 'Sip In,' is refreshingly unpretentious.	**Cubbyhole:** Femme-forward crowds have been cramming into this snug spot since 1994.	**Eagle NYC:** Leather fetishists and himbos cruise this three-level sleaze palace while dancing and drinking.	**Marie's Crisis:** The show tunes never stop at this all-are-welcome basement piano bar near Stonewall.

APPLAUD PERFORMING ARTS

Village Vanguard: Turn a quiet Monday night into a big-band jamboree by seeing the Vanguard Jazz Orchestra at this prestigious jazz club.

Comedy Cellar: Talented regulars, including up-and-coming TV writers and personalities, have tested new material inside this chuckle den since the 1980s.

Atlantic Theater Company: This Off-Broadway house knows how to pick 'em: numerous shows here went on to win Best Musical Tony Awards.

Lucille Lortel Theatre: Clock the sidewalk stars in front of this Off-Broadway playhouse, including theater wordsmiths such as Neil LaBute and Charles Busch.

Smalls: Intimate basement jazz den that winks at Prohibition-era speakeasies.

MEET THOSE DANCIN' FEET
Consider yourself a theater buff? Grab drinks alongside chorus kids at some of their favorite **Midtown haunts** (p81) and don't miss the **Museum of Broadway** (p81), a love letter to NYC show business.

an art-strewn pedestrian ribbon running between galleries, modern high-rises and swanky shopping centers. The High Line's story began in the early 20th century, when the west side's booming industrial enterprises were served by perilous street-level tracks, earning Tenth Ave the nickname 'Death Avenue.' A two-story-high railway became the expensive solution, and the 'West Side Elevated Line' ran its first train in 1933. It wasn't long before the train line became a money pit and fell into disuse; in the 1990s, demolition was mooted. Enter the Friends of the High Line, with a vision of an elegant park. Years of activism resulted in the jewel we enjoy today: a pedestrian catwalk, planted with 500-plus native species, wending its way above former factories and plenty of top-dollar real estate.

Begin your one- or two-hour journey near Hudson Yards (p80) (enter at 30th or 34th Sts), with super-tall skyscrapers shining eastward. Plant-packed railroad tracks evoke the industrial wilderness that preceded the park's creation. As the path narrows, you'll see tons of contemporary constructions, including starchitect Zaha Hadid's futuristic glass-and-metal apartment complex at **520 W 28th St**.

For a bird's-eye view of Tenth Ave, sit on the amphitheater-style seats at 17th or 26th Sts and watch as cabs whiz by. If you prefer serene scenery, snag a train-wheel-tracked chaise longue on the **Diller-von Furstenberg Sundeck** – named

 DRINKING IN THE VILLAGE: BEST BARS & CAFES

Employees Only: This speakeasy-style bar ushered in a new era of mixology when it served its first egg-white cocktail in 2004.

St Jardim: Perched on a lively Village side street, this all-day cafe and natural wine bar is perfect for people-watching.

124 Old Rabbit Club: The reward for finding this craft-beer haunt ...rare brews and local ales.

Té Company: Teas from Taiwanese farmers served alongside sweets so pretty they belong in a Wes Anderson film.

Little Island

after fashion queen Diane von Furstenberg and her billionaire husband Barry Diller, the pockets behind this entire project.

The High Line ends at the foot of the Whitney Museum (p73) and near a few other noteworthy areas, including Hudson River Park and the West Village's winding streets.

Head to Hudson River Park
The west side's green ribbon

Hudson River Park is the 550-acre shining star of Manhattan's modern green spaces, and its most popular sections hug the Village and Chelsea. Spend a sunny afternoon roaming around the waterfront.

Start at **Pier 45** (also called Christopher St Pier and beloved by queer crowds), where Speedo-clad gaggles gather to worship the sun – and each other. Walking north, there's **Gansevoort Peninsula**, completed in 2023 and billed as Manhattan's first public beach. Lounge in Adirondack chairs and admire David Hammons' ghostly *Day's End*, a skeletal art installation evoking the docks that once populated the riverfront.

Up next is **Little Island** (littleisland.org), which appeared like a surrealist dream in 2021: 132 concrete pods shoot from the water like tulips, crowned by undulating green hills. Stroll the 2.4-acre folly's footpaths to enjoy gentle breezes and expansive views, or check the seasonal event schedule for live performances.

A VILLAGE THEORY

The Village's compact, winding streets are chockablock with charm. To find out why this neighborhood beguiles, read *The Death and Life of Great American Cities*, a 1961 tome by urban-planning guru Jane Jacobs. Inspired by Greenwich Village, Jacobs was the first to expound ideas that are now commonplace: that density spurs commerce and community; and that city life takes place outdoors in a 'sidewalk ballet.' Her greatest adversary was urban planner Robert Moses, a political Goliath who fought to build a highway through Jacobs' beloved neighborhood. You can see who won the battle: the late Jacobs is immortalized with a plaque at 555 Hudson St ('Jane Jacobs Way') – it's a charming chunk of street, hardly a highway.

 EATING IN THE VILLAGE: RESERVATIONS RECOMMENDED

| **Semma:** Experience summer in South India with the spicy chutneys and sauces on Michelin-starred Semma's menu (if you can snag a reservation). **$$$** | **Shukette:** The fluffy pita is an enticing teaser for what's to come – bites of delicious, shareable Middle Eastern delicacies. **$$** | **Anixi:** This faux-meat fortress is dressed to impress, with velvet curtains and chandeliers as fancy as its Mediterranean-inspired menu. **$$** | **Je Ju Noodle Bar:** Don't be fooled by the 'Nighthawks' awning. No Edward Hopper paintings here – just Michelin-starred Korean ramen. **$$$** |

QUEER PIER PAST

Ken Lustbader, co-founder and co-director of the NYC LGBT Historic Sites Project, explores the Greenwich Village waterfront's 20th-century history. *@nyclgbtsites*

This was one of the country's busiest ports, comprised of piers and beaux-arts-style shipping terminals. Eventually, those piers were abandoned and became urban ruins, which were appropriated by men who had sex with men, as well as gay artists who used the decrepit, deteriorating pier structures for public artwork and open-air sexual experimentation. Artist David Wojnarowicz was at the piers regularly, taking photographs, and even said, 'This is the real MoMA.' If you go there now, it's a sanitized version of a waterfront, without any of this history discernible in the current landscape.

Pier 57 rounds out the park with its range of offerings: **City Winery's** live music, **Market 57's** James Beard Foundation–curated food vendors and a rooftop park great for picnics and panoramas.

Meet the Locals in Washington Square Park
A slice of Village life

Grab a seat in Greenwich Village's unofficial **town square** and you'll see it all: NYU students scurrying between classes, street vendors selling handmade clothes, fearless squirrels, socializing canines, speed-chess pros, brassy buskers, barefoot children splashing around the fountain – and possibly ghosts.

Centuries ago, this site was a marshy area crossed by Minetta Creek. Dutch colonists granted land rights (for a price) to settlers of African descent, who created a community known as Little Africa. Later, the plot became a public cemetery for the unidentified deceased. When the burial grounds turned into a space for military parades in the 1830s, real-estate developers followed and some of the city's toniest homes sprouted on the park's north border. Today, the park is dominated by the Stanford White–designed **Washington Square Arch** – 73ft of gleaming white Tuckahoe marble. Originally made of wood to celebrate the centennial of George Washington's inauguration in 1889, it proved so popular that it was replaced with stone six years later.

Head to the park's northwest corner to see an English elm considered one of Manhattan's oldest trees. Known as **Hangman's Elm,** its branches were used (according to legend)

DO MORE DIA
Dig Dia Chelsea's minimalist style? Consider a day trip to **Dia Beacon**, where works by Richard Serra and other magnificent modern artists breathe new life into a former Nabisco factory on the Hudson.

Washington Square Park

to hang traitors during the American Revolution. If hunger calls, grab food from **NY Dosas**, Sri Lanka–born Thiru Kumar's South Indian pushcart near the dog run (11am to 3pm Monday to Saturday). Chow down while taking in the scene.

Ogle Art at Chelsea's Galleries
DIY contemporary-art crawl

Zigzagging through far-west Chelsea is like visiting a free contemporary-art museum. The area is home to NYC's densest concentration of galleries; most are open to the public from 10am to 6pm Tuesday to Saturday. Spend a couple of hours seeing what's on view. A perfect starting point is **High Line Nine** (507 W 27th St). This thin strip mall linking 27th and 28th Sts is a gallery space where collectors spot up-and-coming artists. The eight floors of the **Pace Gallery** (540 W 25th St) showcase work by leading contemporary artists. Don't miss its smaller 4000-sq-ft space at 510 W 25th St – inside one of the many auto garages that once populated the area. Seeing exhibits at global chain **Gagosian** (555 W 24th St) is akin to spinning around the Guggenheim – except everything is for sale. Check the website to see what's showing – perhaps Jeff Koons or Nam June Paik. The massive pieces inside the 20,000-sq-ft **Dia Chelsea** (537 W 22nd St) would dwarf most jewel-box Manhattan galleries. Marvel at their size before perusing the picture-perfect art bookshop. End at **Paula Cooper Gallery** (534 W 21st St), the eponymous founder of which started SoHo's gallery explosion in 1968, then moved to Chelsea in the 1990s before it became cool.

NEIGHBORHOOD NEXUS

Union Sq, a public park atop a busy train hub east of Chelsea, attracts a frenetic melange of chess players, Hare Krishnas, protesters, university students and old-money New Yorkers. The Union name, while fitting for the local conglomeration, comes from the early 19th century, denoting the nexus of two major Manhattan roads – Bloomingdale (now Broadway) and Bowery (now Fourth Ave). In the following decades, social and political protest became central to Union Sq's identity, but today, the main attraction is produce. Every Monday, Wednesday, Friday and Saturday, more than 100 vendors assemble for the **Union Square Greenmarket**, selling veggies, cheeses, baked goods and crafts to roughly 60,000 shoppers in peak season.

Midtown

NEON LIGHTS, BUSTLING STREETS AND BROADWAY

GETTING AROUND

Midtown is accessible from nearly all subway lines. For Midtown West, take the 1/2/3, 7, A/C/E or N/Q/R/W to Times Sq-42nd St. For Midtown East, take the 4/5/6 to Grand Central-42nd St. The S (Shuttle) travels between both stations. The B/D/F and M takes you to Rockefeller Center. The 1/2/3 and A/C/E gets you to Madison Square Garden at 34th St. For train travel outside of NYC, head to Grand Central for Metro-North and the Long Island Railroad (LIRR). The Amtrak, LIRR and NJ Transit serve Penn Station.

Long mythologized as the 'Crossroads of the World,' Times Square is what non–New Yorkers often picture as its emblem: commerce, crowds and around-the-clock entertainment. Give in to the gravitational pull of bright lights shining around 42nd St and Broadway, but don't skip areas to the east and west, such as food-packed Koreatown, LGBTIQ+-haunt Hell's Kitchen and green-pocket Bryant Park. Slices of Midtown have taken many monikers, such as the 'Tenderloin' for its dicy 19th-century years, the 'Garment District' for early 20th-century clothing manufacturing and the 'Diamond District,' known for its gems and jewelers. Times Square became smut central around the 1960s, but a clean-up project in the mid-'90s led to its Disneyfication. Still, Midtown isn't exactly Main Street America. Gritty holdouts from previous eras link to shiny new skyscrapers around Hudson Yards and Billionaires' Row. It's chaotic, sure, but it's also colorful, illustrating NYC's chameleon-like instinct to change with the times.

Compare Skyline Views

Climb higher than King Kong

For adrenaline-pumping perspectives on Midtown's urban forestry, jet to some of its highest observation decks.

Hudson Yards' skyscrapers look like mini Dubai. The tallest of the bunch, the **Edge**, adds adrenaline boosters such as slanted-glass fencing, where you can lean out to peer at taxis 100 floors below. Serious thrill seekers can don a helmet and harness to climb outside for the world's highest open-air building ascent ($185, minus deck entry price).

The **Top of the Rock**, crowning 30 Rockefeller Plaza, has three levels of blockbuster perspectives, including a 360-degree panorama from the 70th floor. It's 850ft up, without glass barriers, making it perfect for pictures. For an additional $25, you can shoot above the scene on a steel beam for 90 seconds, recreating the famous 1932 photo *Lunch Atop a Skyscraper*.

Times Square

Then there's the **Empire State Building** – King Kong's pick for most climb-worthy tower. Built in a frenzied 410 days, this steel-framed, limestone-and-granite-clad art deco emblem opened in 1931 as the world's tallest building. Although its local title has since been stolen by One World Trade Center, the ESB reigns as NYC's queen.

The main observation deck on the 86th floor is outdoors. There's also a tiny room with floor-to-ceiling windows on the 102nd floor ($35 extra). While on the 86th floor, train binoculars on the nearby Chrysler Building to admire its deco details. Admission grants access to exhibitions on the 2nd and 80th floors, which include the history of the ESB's construction and its place in pop culture. If you like cinema shtick, snag a photo with King Kong's giant paw, giving your best impression of Ann Darrow (the unfortunate woman caught in his grip). Reserve timed online tickets in advance for all.

Rub Shoulders with Broadway Babies
Destinations beloved by theater folk

Aside from office work, seeing a show on Broadway is what brings many locals to Midtown. For a taste of old-school insider Broadway, stop by **Sardi's**, a restaurant with walls covered in caricatures of famous patrons. You might spot actors clinking glasses post-performance at **Bar Centrale** and **Joe Allen**, or singing at **Don't Tell Mama**, all on 46th St's Restaurant Row. You'll definitely rub elbows with theater cognoscenti searching for scripts at the **Drama Book Shop**, designed by *Hamilton's* scenic designer. Can't make it to a show? The interactive **Museum of Broadway** is worth a visit, especially for theater kids. You'll see costumes, artifacts and paraphernalia from Broadway's most iconic productions, such as *Oklahoma*, *Cats*, *The Producers* and *Wicked*.

THEATER TICKET DISCOUNTS

Broadway tickets often have three-digit prices, but there are ways to score fabulous seats at a fraction of the cost. For the most options, visit the Theatre Development Fund's **TKTS booth** under the red steps in Times Square's Father Duffy Sq, offering up to 50% off same-day shows and next-day matinees (lines can be long). Most shows hold lotteries, allowing select winners to purchase choice seats at bargain prices. Many productions also have rush tickets, slashing seat prices on a first-come, first-served basis. The TodayTix app offers discounted pricing in all forms, including digital lotteries – the most convenient way to grab tickets before arriving in NYC.

☑ **TOP TIP**

Finding public bathrooms in Midtown can be tough. When nature calls, your best bets for restrooms are train hubs such as Grand Central and Penn Station, along with major department stores like Macy's. Bryant Park's restrooms are particularly fancy and worth a peek, even if you don't need to freshen up.

MIDTOWN NEW YORK CITY

TOP SIGHTS
1. Grand Central Terminal
2. Museum of Modern Art
3. Times Square

SIGHTS
4. AKC Museum of the Dog
5. Bryant Park
6. Curry Hill
7. Edge
8. Flower District
9. Garment District
10. Hudson Yards
11. Intrepid Sea, Air & Space Museum
12. Koreatown
 - see 5 Le Carrousel
13. Museum of Broadway
14. Radio City Music Hall
15. Top of the Rock
16. United Nations

ACTIVITIES, COURSES & TOURS
17. Circle Line Boat Tours
18. Don't Tell Mama
19. Empire State Building
20. Manhattan Community Boathouse
21. Manhattan Kayak Co

SLEEPING
22. Moxy Times Square
23. Romer

EATING
24. Ace's Pizza
25. Barbetta
 - see 5 Bryant Park Grill
 - see 1 Grand Central Oyster Bar & Restaurant
26. HanGawi
27. Joe Allen
28. Le Bernardin
29. Mercado Little Spain
30. Sardi's

DRINKING & NIGHTLIFE
31. As Is
32. Bryant Park Cafe
 - see 27 Bar Centrale
33. Dickens
 - see 1 Grand Central City Winery
 - see 15 Pebble Bar
34. Tomi Jazz
35. Turntable LP Bar

ENTERTAINMENT
36. Madison Square Garden
37. Playwrights Horizons

SHOPPING
38. Drama Book Shop
39. Grand Central Market

INFORMATION
40. TKTS Booth

Time Travel at the Museum of Modern Art
Admire the art world's stars

Name a notable artist from the 19th century onward – Van Gogh, Matisse, Picasso, Kahlo, Rothko, Warhol, Bourgeois – and **MoMA** (moma.org) probably shows some of their best work among its 200,000-piece collection. For aesthetes, it's an encounter with the sublime; for the uninitiated, a cultural crash course. Attempting to see everything in MoMA's 630,000 sq-ft space could take half a day or more – a surefire way to experience museum fatigue. Instead, go through the collection chronologically, ensuring a glimpse of the big names on display. Pieces rotate through the galleries at least once a year, which means first-timers might miss some famous works, but repeat visitors will get a fresh experience.

Work your way down: **Floor 5** covers the 1880s–1940s. Count on seeing Van Gogh's swirling *Starry Night*, Monet's Impressionist water lilies and, if you're lucky, Frida Kahlo's gender-bending *Self Portrait with Cropped Hair*. **Floor 4** tackles the 1940s–70s, with Jackson Pollock and Andy Warhol leading the charge. Don't miss Faith Ringgold's 1967 response to Picasso's *Guernica* in the shocking *American People Series #20: Die*. **On floor 2** (1970s–present), there's Richard Serra's *Equal*, composed of 80-ton steel stacks, and works by NYC painter Jean-Michel Basquiat.

Recharge from the gallery grind by stepping outside into the **Abby Aldrich Rockefeller Sculpture Garden**, with works by greats such as Giacometti and Picasso. (It's free to the public from 9am to 10:15am.) Timed tickets are required to guarantee museum entry; book online in advance.

Slow Down at Grand Central Terminal
Relive the railroad's golden age

Don't rush through this 1913 beaux-arts station hall like Metro North's commuters. **Grand Central Terminal** evokes the romance of rail travel and it's worth spending at least an hour falling in love with its treasures. Start by strolling across the marble-trimmed concourse to gaze at the vaulted aquamarine ceiling depicting the night sky's constellations. The starry wonder isn't original – it's a 1944 copy covering water damage in the first fresco designed by French painter Paul Cesar Helleu. A 1990s renovation added twinkling lights (part of Helleu's plan) and cleaned the ceiling. Follow Cancer's claws to the northwest corner to a tiny black rectangle: an original patch of soot, approximately nine-by-five inches, caused by decades of air pollutants. While admiring the work, examine the layout. The zodiac is actually backwards. After its unveiling, railroad officials swatted away critics, saying it was painted from the perspective of God. For more hidden wonders, head to the **'Whispering Gallery'** between the Main Concourse and Vanderbilt Hall, where an acoustic quirk allows people to stand on opposite gallery corners and carry a conversation sotto voce. There's plenty to eat and drink, too – try **Grand Central Market** (fast casual), **Grand Central**

PERFORMANCES, TOURS & QUIRKY MUSEUMS

Playwrights Horizons: Boundary-breaking Off-Broadway institution known for new works by up-and-coming American writers.

Radio City Music Hall: Join the 60-minute Stage Door Tour for the inside scoop on the famous performance complex and meet a working member of the Rockettes.

Madison Square Garden: Can't make it to a Knicks NBA or Rangers NHL game? Tour the complex instead.

AKC Museum of the Dog: The airy 1st-floor galleries contain paintings of dogs, and an upstairs library carries books on every breed.

United Nations: Enter international territory on a guided tour through Le Corbusier and Oscar Niemeyer's mid-century masterpiece.

Grand Central Terminal

TIMES SQUARE'S EVOLUTION

Facades are the faces of most New York neighborhoods, but in **Times Square**, it's all about the ads. Building exteriors are de facto canvases for products, and many feature digital billboards running nonstop videos. But being seen in this neighborhood wasn't always admirable. Starting in the 1960s, Times Square became a pit for peep shows, porn theaters and three-card monte scammers – in 1981, *Rolling Stone* dubbed 42nd St the 'sleaziest block in America.' All that changed in the mid-1990s when city mandates downgraded the area's X-rating to a G (Naked Cowboy not included). Now, roughly 360,000 people pass through Times Square every day.

Oyster Bar & Restaurant (fine dining), **Grand Central City Winery** and the **Campbell**, which features live jazz on weekend evenings.

Take a Break in Bryant Park

Eat, shop, skate and stroll

European coffee kiosks, alfresco chess games and outdoor events for the whole family make leafy, Parisian-style **Bryant Park** *(bryantpark.org)* a whimsical break from Midtown's mayhem. Office workers stream in at lunchtime, competing for tables with skyscraper views. There's also **Bryant Park Grill**, with a patio ideal for twilight cocktails, and neighboring **Bryant Park Cafe**, an alfresco hang from mid-April to November. Ping-pong, played on the northern side, can be intensely competitive. Kids whirl around on **Le Carrousel's** 14 painted ponies. The scene is particularly popular in summer, when you can watch cinema by starlight at one of Bryant Park's free movie nights (bring a blanket and a picnic for thorough enjoyment). The park is great in cold weather, too: find unique gifts at the holiday market, open between Thanksgiving and Christmas, or ice skate all winter long on the city's largest free-admission rink. It's hard to believe this was a crime-ridden hellscape in the 1970s. Check the park website for events.

 EATING IN MIDTOWN: BEST RESTAURANTS

Le Bernardin: Eric Ripert has spent decades steering this restaurant to deceptively simple seafood heaven. Michelin agrees. Book ahead. **$$$**

Barbetta: Linger at this gorgeous Restaurant Row time warp for Piedmontese specialties such as gnocchi and risotto. **$$$**

Mercado Little Spain: Chef José Andrés brings the Iberian peninsula to the Hudson Yards mall, where kiosks and sit-downs serve Spanish cuisine. **$$**

Ace's Pizza: When hunger strikes around Rockefeller Center, head here for rectangular Detroit-style pizza slices. **$**

Set Sail in Midtown West
Tours, cruises and kayaks

Midtown's most notable coastal assets are almost entirely on the west side. The **Intrepid Sea, Air & Space Museum**, a hulking aircraft carrier that survived both a WWII bomb and kamikaze attacks, houses an impressive interactive military museum with videos, historical artifacts and frozen-in-time living quarters. The flight deck fewatures fighter planes and military helicopters, which might inspire you to try the museum's high-tech flight simulators. On a pier just to the Intrepid's south, board a **Circle Line** tour for a floating perspective of the city's profile. The 90-minute Landmarks cruise is one of those one-time-musts for New Yorkers eager to see the skyline from afar. Next door to Circle Line, on Pier 94 (at 44th St), **Manhattan Kayak Co** offers a variety of kayaking and stand-up paddleboarding classes and tours. To try out kayaking on the Hudson for free, in a more limited area, head north to Pier 96 (at 55th St) and the **Manhattan Community Boathouse**.

MIDTOWN'S MICRO NEIGHBORHOODS

Midtown is massive, but tourists generally keep to its midsection. Worth exploring is Curry Hill, a stretch of Lexington Ave between 26th and 30th Sts with around two dozen Indian restaurants. There's also Koreatown, with Korean restaurants stretching along 32nd St between Madison and Sixth Aves. (Grab a floor cushion for veggie Korean at **HanGawi** or belt karaoke at **Turntable LP Bar**.) The fragrant Flower District, basically a block of shops on 28th St between Sixth and Seventh Aves, offers a kaleidoscopic array of flora. Don't forget the historically significant Garment District between 34th and 42nd Sts and Sixth and Eighth Aves – this is where most Broadway costumes get made.

MORE AMAZING ART

Art history buffs: wander along Fifth Ave as it skirts Central Park. It's dubbed Museum Mile and is home to the **Metropolitan Museum of Art** (p88), showcasing centuries of creative genius.

DRINKING IN MIDTOWN: BEST BARS

Pebble Bar: This bar has done the unthinkable – create a cool cocktail scene in Rockefeller Center.

Tomi Jazz: Stumble into this Japanese jazz den after 6pm, when whiskey flows as freely as an improvised sax solo.

As Is: Hell's Kitchen's beer heads agree – this hops den is tops, with 20 beers on tap.

Dickens: Dine and drink inside this posh four-floor LGBTIQ+ palace, an elevated answer to Hell's Kitchen cramped gay dens.

Upper East Side

MAGNIFICENT MUSEUMS AND OLD-MONEY AIRS

GETTING AROUND

The 4/5/6 trains travel along Lexington Ave; the Q runs up Second Ave to 72nd, 86th and 96th Sts; the F stops at 63rd St and Lexington Ave. The bus is best for traveling west. Crosstown buses at 66th, 72nd, 79th, 86th and 96th Sts head through Central Park to the Upper West Side. M1, M2 and M4 buses run down Fifth and Madison Aves between the Village and Harlem. Walking up Fifth Ave is sensational, particularly for architecture buffs who love Gilded Age opulence. Stroll on the street's east side, along Central Park, to appreciate the details from a distance.

The Upper East Side (UES) is a swath of old-school elegance sloping from Central Park to the East River. Synonymous with NYC's blue bloods, this is where the Vanderbilts once threw extravagant balls and where septuagenarian socialites still hold court inside lavish prewar apartment buildings. From the west, there's Fifth Ave, designated 'Museum Mile' from 82nd St to the top of the park. Madison Ave is the go-to strip for high-end clothing boutiques and ritzy restaurants frequented by 'ladies who lunch.' Nearing the East River, middle-class families and young professionals reign supreme – when 5pm hits, a symphony of their clinking glasses spills from Second Ave's bars. Unlike neighborhoods that embrace change, the affluent Upper East Side appears preserved in amber. You won't find the city's cutting edge here, but you'll unearth something greater – a slice of NYC tradition, served by locals who love their neighborhood too much to change it.

Visit Austria at the Neue Galerie
Art and food with Viennese flair

Austrian and German art from 1890–1940 takes center stage inside this **1914 mansion** designed by Carrère and Hastings (the architects behind New York Public Library and the Frick). The museum's most prized collection is a series of sketches and paintings by Gustav Klimt, including his gold-flecked 1907 *Portrait of Adele Bloch-Bauer 1*, acquired for a cool $135 million by cosmetics magnate and museum founder Ronald Lauder. (The 2015 film *Woman in Gold* recounts the painting's fascinating history, which includes looting Nazis, a feisty Bloch-Bauer heir and the obstinate Austrian government.) A connected bookstore is a museum unto itself, decorated with artist monographs and coffee-table books.

TOP SIGHTS
1. Metropolitan Museum of Art

SIGHTS
2. Asia Society & Museum
3. Carl Schurz Park
4. Frick Collection
5. Jacqueline Kennedy Onassis Reservoir
6. Jewish Museum
7. Museum of the City of New York
8. Neue Galerie
9. Solomon R Guggenheim Museum

SLEEPING
10. Carlyle
11. Graduate

EATING
12. Café Sabarsky
  see 18 Heidelberg
13. JG Melon
14. Lexington Candy Shop
  see 18 Schaller's Stube Sausage Bar

DRINKING & NIGHTLIFE
15. 2nd Floor Bar & Essen
16. Bemelmans Bar

ENTERTAINMENT
17. Park Avenue Armory

SHOPPING
18. Schaller & Weber

For an immersive Austrian experience, reserve a table at Vienna-style **Café Sabarsky**. With dishes such as goulash soup, roasted bratwurst and *topfentorte* (quark cheesecake), you might mistake the Upper East Side for Europe's Eastern Alps.

Cover Centuries of NYC History
Museum dedicated to local stories

The **Museum of the City of New York**, housed in a Georgian Colonial Revival–style building near the top of Central Park, artfully illustrates the past, present and future of this ever-evolving city. At a minimum, spare 28 minutes to watch *Timescapes*, a multiscreen documentary that chronicles NYC's past 400 years from tiny Dutch trading center to international powerhouse. Other permanent exhibits explore centuries of social activism and feature notable New Yorkers such as poet Walt Whitman and urbanist Jane Jacobs. Icing on the cake: admission is pay-what-you-wish.

☑ TOP TIP

Fifth Ave's Central Park proximity makes it a practical place to start exploring Manhattan's green heart. For city panoramas, enter at 90th St and walk north around the **Jacqueline Kennedy Onassis Reservoir** (p95). If you prefer solitude, venture around the Conservatory Garden's fountains and flower beds at 105th St.

87

Interior, Metropolitan Museum of Art

PRACTICALITIES

Scan this QR code for ticket prices and opening hours.

TOP SIGHT

Metropolitan Museum of Art

This stately, two-million-sq-ft museum, founded in 1870, is an encyclopedic bastion of world-class art, celebrating 5000 years of human creativity. The Met's one-million-plus objects cover all corners of the globe with artifacts, paintings, sculptures, textiles and even an Egyptian tomb guarded by a moat. It's the Western Hemisphere's largest museum, overflowing with must-see treasures. Dive in.

DON'T MISS

Temple of Dendur, Gallery 131

Leon Levy and Shelby White Roman Sculpture Court, Gallery 162

Van Gogh's *White Field with Cypresses*, Gallery 822

Temple of Dendur, Gallery 131

Egyptian Art

Time-travel through Egypt's history in 39 galleries covering the Paleolithic to Roman eras (c 300,000 BCE to 400 CE). Start at the **Tomb of Perneb**, a limestone burial chamber with intricately painted reliefs (Gallery 100). Next, after walking past pyramid pieces and funerary statues, pause at Gallery 136's mysterious *Fragment of a Queen's Face* (c 1390–36 BCE) to appreciate the sculptor's laser-like precision. If you only see one thing, make it the **Temple of Dendur** (Gallery 131). This is the Western Hemisphere's only complete Egyptian temple, built over 2000 years ago on the banks of the Nile.

Greek & Roman Art

With more than 30,000 individual pieces, this is North America's most comprehensive assemblage of toga-wearing trophies. Start south of the **Great Hall** to gape at chiseled gods preening under a vaulted beaux-arts ceiling. All this eye

Fifth Avenue entrance

candy might inspire staying put, but even greater treasures await in the sunlit **Leon Levy and Shelby White Roman Sculpture Court** (Gallery 162). Bonus points for spotting the headless **Three Graces of Greek** mythology – Beauty, Mirth and Abundance.

European Paintings

From Giotto to Gauguin, the Met has it all: religious iconography from the 13th century, every Dutch master you can name and a sweeping selection of 19th-century French Impressionists. Unlike *Starry Night* at **MoMA** (p83), you won't contend with crowds to see Vincent Van Gogh's paintings here. Stand before his *White Field with Cypresses* (Gallery 822) to imagine a blustery day in Saint-Rémy-de-Provence. Don't leave without viewing self-taught artist Henri Rousseau's *The Repast of the Lion* (Gallery 825).

Islamic Art

Objects sacred and secular fill these 15 galleries dedicated to the Arabian Peninsula, Turkey and Central and South Asia. The glazed-tile **mihrab** (prayer niche; Gallery 455) is a vision in blue, framed by the five pillars of Islam, written in Kufic. If you're a fan of interiors, stop by Gallery 461 to wow over gold-leaf embellishments in the 18th-century **Damascus Room**.

American Wing

This two-floor collection in the museum's northwest corner covers everything from colonial times to the early 20th century, including Emanuel Luetze's iconic *Washington Crossing the Delaware*, which looms large over Gallery 760. If you need a pick-me-up, stop by the American Wing Cafe in the **Charles**

TOP TIPS

- Beat the Great Hall's snaking ticket line by entering at 81st St.
- Don't try to see everything in one visit. Pick a few galleries or a handful of pieces and immerse yourself.
- Upon entering, join the virtual queue via QR code for temporary exhibits. These artist retrospectives and cultural deep-dives are often some of the city's most fantastic museum shows.
- Stream the Met's free audio guide, which includes a Highlights Tour – an exceptional resource available on your smartphone. Visit metmuseum.org/audio-guide.
- Docents offer free guided tours of specific galleries. Check the website or information desk for details.

DON'T MISS

Damascus Room, Gallery 461

Leutze's *Washington Crossing the Delaware*, Gallery 760

Charles Engelhard Court

Benton's *America Today*, Gallery 909

Cantor Rooftop Garden Bar

Engelhard Court – a glass garden filled with American-made sculptures and framed by a marble facade that once graced Wall St. Visit on Friday or Saturday for Date Night (5pm to 9pm), when live music sets a romantic scene.

Modern & Contemporary Art

Georgia O'Keefe, Edward Hopper, Pollock, Dalí – the museum's southwestern corner is a who's who of art-world titans from the late 19th century onward. Particularly impressive is Thomas Hart Benton's *America Today* (Gallery 909), a room-sized mural depicting the US at the Great Depression's onset.

Cantor Rooftop Garden Bar

Float above Central Park's tree canopy for unobstructed views of Billionaires' Row in Midtown, spiked with super-tall skyscrapers. Art installations grace the rooftop space, which you can peruse with a refreshing post-museum cocktail. Plan your visit for sunset, when the sky improvises a scene that competes with the artwork.

The rooftop of the Metropolitan Museum of Art

Carl Schurz Park

Taste Yorkville's German Past

Bratwurst and beer

At the end of the 19th century, NYC had the world's third-largest German-speaking population after Berlin and Vienna. Yorkville – sandwiched by East 79th St, 96th St, Third Ave and the East River – was better known as Germantown, and East 86th St was called Sauerkraut Boulevard. Today, it's still possible to hear the sounds of oom-pah-pah on Second Ave between 85th and 86th Sts. Begin at **Heidelberg** (open since 1936) to feast on classics such as Bavarian beer and *schweinshaxe* (pork shank). Peek into **Schaller & Weber**, a sausage stalwart since 1937, to load your bag with brats and, if you're wild for wiener, stop at **Schaller's Stube Sausage Bar** next door, with international twists on to-go sausages. End by skipping to **Carl Schurz Park**, named after the first German-American elected to the US Senate.

MAGNIFICENT UES MUSEUMS

Guggenheim Museum: Architect Frank Lloyd Wright's iconic inverted ziggurat spirals up from Fifth Ave like a steady crescendo, overshadowing the artwork inside.

Frick Collection: Walk through this Gilded Age jewel box to find gilt-framed masterpieces by Rembrandt, Vermeer and more.

Jewish Museum: Housed in a 1908 French Gothic chateau, this 30,000-piece collection spans 4000 years of Jewish culture.

Park Avenue Armory: This Gothic Revival behemoth features a 55,000-sq-ft performance space, plus designs by the likes of Stanford White.

Asia Society & Museum: One of America's preeminent institutions for pan-Asian art: Chola-period Indian bronzes, modern Japanese paintings etc.

 EATING & DRINKING ON THE UES: OUR PICKS

JG Melon: No-frills, cash-only pub serving one of NYC's best burgers since 1972. Wash it down with a beefy Bloody Mary. $	**Lexington Candy Shop:** Order an egg cream at New York's oldest family-run luncheonette, serving since 1925. $	**Bemelmans Bar:** Sip Manhattans and admire murals by *Madeleine* illustrator Ludwig Bemelmans as pianists tickle the ivories.	**2nd Floor Bar & Essen:** Down drinks and shtetl-style bar bites in this speakeasy above a kosher deli.

Upper West Side

SPRAWLING GREEN SPACES AND CULTURE

GETTING AROUND

Take the 1/2/3 train for easy access to destinations between Broadway and Riverside Park. The B and C are best for areas east of Broadway, including Central Park. The A and D trains run express from 59th St-Columbus Circle to 125th St in Harlem. For bus travel, the M104 runs along Broadway between Midtown and Harlem. The M110 runs along Central Park West. Crosstown routes at 66th, 72nd, 79th, 86th and 96th Sts head to the Upper East Side. If you're daring enough to bike, follow Central Park West's path uptown and Columbus Ave while cycling downtown.

☑ TOP TIP

Many tourists – and even New Yorkers – stick to Central Park's lower half, from roughly 86th St and below. If you want to escape the crowds, dare to explore north of the Jacqueline Kennedy Onassis Reservoir.

The Upper West Side (UWS) is a storied residential district defined by the bucolic pleasures of its bookends, Central and Riverside Parks. When Central Park opened in the late 19th century, it spawned a frenzy of property development, with the Gothic-style Dakota (1884) ushering in an era of high-end urban living. The elegant apartments of Broadway and the dazzling art deco towers of Central Park West remain some of the city's swankiest digs, yet even amid such luxury, this neighborhood represents New York's diverse crossroads – largely thanks to stretches of affordable-housing developments that keep the neighborhood's attitude in check. Join the area's artists, intellectuals and progressives by skipping between brownstone-lined streets to diners, delis and cultural mainstays such as Lincoln Center. Head east to lose yourself in one of the city's greatest green spaces. Zip west to toe the Hudson River's banks. Soulful Harlem sits north of Central Park.

Geek Out at the American Museum of Natural History

NYC's greatest science museum

You could spend a lifetime (or at least a couple of hours) exploring this **cutting-edge science center** and can't-miss hit for kids. From the main entrance on Central Park West, enter the soaring **Theodore Roosevelt Rotunda** to spot skeletons of a barosaurus and allosaurus frozen in combat. The always-astounding **Milstein Family Hall of Ocean Life** contains interactive lessons about marine food chains – all under a suspended, 94ft-long replica of a blue whale. Budding entomologists should beeline for the **David Family Butterfly Vivarium** in the new Gilder Center, where fluttering specimens land on outstretched arms. Armchair astronauts will appreciate the **Rose Center for Earth & Space**, its spherical theater transporting visitors to faraway galaxies. And don't forget the hundreds of dinosaur fossils – they're on the top floor.

TOP SIGHTS
1 Central Park

SIGHTS
2 American Folk Art Museum
3 American Museum of Natural History
4 Bethesda Fountain
5 Central Park Zoo
6 Dakota Building
7 Jacqueline Kennedy Onassis Reservoir
8 Lincoln Center
9 New-York Historical Society
10 Nicholas Roerich Museum
11 North Woods
12 Ramble
13 Riverside Park
14 Strawberry Fields
15 The Ansonia
16 The Apthorp
17 The Beresford
18 The San Remo

ACTIVITIES, COURSES & TOURS
19 Sheep Meadow
20 Wollman Skating Rink

SLEEPING
21 HI New York City Hostel

EATING
22 Absolute Bagels
23 Cafe Luxembourg
24 Ellington in the Park
25 Le Pain Quotidien
26 Mama's TOO!
27 Tatiana

SHOPPING
28 Zabar's

TRANSPORT
29 Central Park Bike Tours

Sheep Meadow

PRACTICALITIES

Scan this QR code for ticket prices and opening hours.

TOP SIGHT

Central Park

With 843 acres of meadows, ponds and woodlands, Central Park seems like Manhattan in its raw state. But every inch was built by human hands. And thank goodness it was: the merger of nature and art provides a welcome respite from urban jungle living. Spend half a day getting lost on its curving pathways – designed as a break from Manhattan's grid.

DON'T MISS

Central Park Zoo

Sheep Meadow

Strawberry Fields

Bethesda Fountain

Ramble

Jacqueline Kennedy Onassis Reservoir

North Woods

Central Park Conservancy's guided tours

A Grand Project

In the early 1850s, this area of Manhattan was occupied by pig farms, a garbage dump, a bone-boiling operation and Seneca Village, the largest community of African American property owners in pre–Civil War New York. All that changed in 1858, when plans created by landscape designer Frederick Law Olmstead and architect Calvert Vaux began taking shape. Today, this people's park has over 18,000 trees, 136 acres of woodland, 21 playgrounds, seven bodies of water and more than 40 million visitors a year.

Tour the South End

Most visitors enter Central Park from its southern edge at W59th St. Walk along the **Pond** at the southeast corner to spot ducks and geese flapping in the blue. In winter, crowds ice skate at **Wollman Skating Rink**, where Midtown's soaring skyscrapers provide a dramatic backdrop.

Continue northeast to the small-but-mighty **Central Park Zoo** (near E 64th St; admission fee required), the pavilions of which house penguins, grizzly bears, tropical birds and even a snow leopard. Kids (and most adults) will love petting goats in the children's area and watching sea lions sing for their supper.

Perhaps most popular in this part of the park is **Sheep Meadow** (near W 67th St), a 15-acre lawn where thousands picnic, toss Frisbees and bare their skin in summer. Spending a few hours people-watching here is a quintessential city experience.

A skip north is **Strawberry Fields** (near W 72nd St), a tear-shaped garden and moving memorial for John Lennon, assassinated in front of his home at the Dakota (p96) in 1980. It contains a grove of stately elms and a tiled mosaic that says simply, 'Imagine.'

Amble around Mid Park

Work your way east to **Bethesda Fountain**, then cross picture-perfect **Bow Bridge** to enter one of the park's most transporting sections. The **Ramble**, a 36-acre forest, features waterfalls, rocky outcroppings and unpaved paths through thickets of trees. Don't be surprised to see people pointing binoculars at nearby branches: this is a beloved birding destination. Central Park, located along the Atlantic Flyway (an important route for migrating birds), acts as a resting pad for weary winged travelers. Twitchers can spot more than 200 avian species resting among the leaves in spring and autumn. Continue north and you'll arrive at the **Jacqueline Kennedy Onassis Reservoir**, stretching between 86th and 96th Sts. The 1.6-mile gravel path along its perimeter is the domain of runners, who navigate the loop in a strictly clockwise direction. Exercise deference if you walk the loop to snap a pic of skyscrapers reflected on the water's glassy surface.

Wind through the North End

Crowds thin out as you head uptown, making a wander through the **North Woods** particularly magical. This 40-acre arcadia on the upper reaches of Central Park feels more like the Adirondacks than the heart of Manhattan. Amble along the waterfall-linked **Loch**, a gentle tree-hugged stream (accessible via the Glen Span Arch near W 103rd St), to spot scampering chipmunks and the occasional raccoon. If you wander deep enough, skyscrapers disappear and traffic becomes but a murmur.

EXPERT GUIDES

If navigating the park alone seems Sisyphean, join a tour led by the Central Park Conservancy. Guided walks cover everything from ecology to little-known park histories and iconic landmarks. Most tours (aside from low-cost, family-geared offerings) start around 10am, cost $25 and last roughly 1½ hours. Check the website for schedules and pricing; booking is required.

TOP TIPS

● Speed through the park by cycling its 6.1-mile loop. For rentals, try Central Park Bike Tours. There's also Citi Bike, though the docking system makes it difficult to park and explore.

● If you didn't pack a picnic, dine alfresco near Sheep Meadow at casual **Le Pain Quotidien**, or stop by a food cart for snacks and drinks (be prepared with cash).

● Turned around? Check the numbers at the base of park lamp posts. The first two digits indicate nearby cross streets; the second two note if you're east or west (even numbers mean you're on the park's east side).

MORE UWS CULTURE

Lincoln Center: This travertine complex is home to renowned performance venues such as the Metropolitan Opera and New York City Ballet.

Nicholas Roerich Museum: Free townhouse-turned-art temple featuring rich Tibetan landscape paintings by Russian-born Roerich (1874–1947).

Zabar's: Cheese, meats and fresh-from-the-oven knishes: a bastion of gourmet kosher foodie-ism since 1934.

New-York Historical Society: NYC's oldest museum (1804) showcases 60,000-plus quirky and fascinating objects covering all eras of Gotham's development.

American Folk Art Museum: Kaleidoscopic quilts, hand-carved decoy ducks and other art celebrates homegrown, self-taught makers.

Ogle Elaborate (& Exclusive) Real Estate
Architecture tour of famous buildings

The Upper West Side's imposing facades have set the standard for refined 'apartment' living for over a century. While these buildings are off-limits to visitors, a few have impressive exteriors that merit a look. Spend an hour admiring their details.

Start at the **Ansonia** (73 St & Broadway), a beaux-arts confection from 1904. In the 1970s, Bette Midler belted it out at the Continental Baths, a gay bathhouse that once occupied the basement. Next up is the **Apthorp** (78th St & Broadway), subject of screenwriter Nora Ephron's 2006 essay 'Moving On, A Love Story,' written about the Italian Renaissance Revival complex she called home for 24 years. The **Dakota** (72nd St & Central Park West) is the neighborhood's most famous coop. Leonard Bernstein, John Lennon and Yoko Ono have all called this chateauesque fortress home. Continue north to see two limestone stunners by architect Emory Roth – the twin-towered **San Remo** (74th/75th Sts) and the **Beresford** (81st/82nd Sts), both revivals of Renaissance style.

Catch the Light in Riverside Park
Sunset on the west side

The **five-mile green expanse** stringing 59th St to 155th St might get overshadowed by nearby Central Park, but as the sun starts setting, nothing beats the spectacular light show from its triple-tiered paths. You'll find some of the best views at **Ellington in the Park** (open April to November), a casual outdoor restaurant overlooking the Hudson River. Arrive before twilight and snag an upper-level picnic table to soak in the sun as it dips behind New Jersey.

EATING ON THE UWS: CHEAP EATS & FINE DINING

Absolute Bagels: Bagels made by Thai immigrants might make connoisseurs uneasy, but there's usually a line down the block for a reason. $	**Mama's TOO!:** You'll understand why people crowd outside this pizza shop after tearing into a slab of hot honey-drizzled pepperoni. $	**Tatiana:** Good luck getting a table at this Afro-Caribbean-inspired restaurant in David Geffen Hall. $$$	**Cafe Luxembourg:** Upper-crust locals have been knocking back cocktails and nibbling steak tartare at this French bistro since the 1980s. $$$

Brooklyn

INDUSTRIAL-CHIC TRENDSETTERS AND WATERFRONT WONDERS

Brooklyn has come a long way since its 17th-century days as a Dutch farming settlement known as Breuckelen. It's now the city's most populous borough, with 2.6 million people at last estimate, and a trendsetting destination at home and abroad. Its image as the global epicenter of 'cool' is most apparent in Williamsburg, with blocks of buzzy bars, restaurants and boutiques that spill north into neighboring Greenpoint. Head east for Bushwick, an industrial neighborhood dipped in street art and colonized by a cutting-edge crew. Once up-and-coming, both neighborhoods have undoubtedly arrived. But everything here isn't artsy-fartsy hipsterdom: Brooklyn is immigrant-grown and diverse, packed with green parks, historic architecture and carnival-style Coney Island. While many people cross the Brooklyn Bridge to see Manhattan's skyline from river-flanked Dumbo, dare to explore deeper. You could come for the day or spend an entire trip in Kings County. It's a universe unto itself.

Spend an Afternoon on Brooklyn's Waterfront

See NYC from Brooklyn Bridge Park

Jaw-dropping views and recreational activities, plus restaurants, stores and performance spaces: **Brooklyn Bridge Park** is a one-stop shop for urban leisure. Devote a few hours to this 85-acre green space hugging the East River.

For a breezy introduction to Brooklyn's historic waterfront, hop on a Manhattan ferry at Midtown's 34th St or Fidi's Pier 11, sailing across the river like writer Walt Whitman in the 19th century. You'll land at **Fulton Ferry Landing**, where lines from his 1856 poem 'Crossing the Brooklyn Ferry' are engraved on the guard rails.

Like so much of NYC, this landscape differs greatly from the time when Whitman wrote '...Brooklyn of ample hills was

GETTING AROUND

The L and J/M/Z trains serve Williamsburg and Bushwick. The G train connects South Brooklyn to Queens, crossing through Williamsburg to Downtown Brooklyn and beyond. For Dumbo and Brooklyn Heights, take the A/C, F or 2/3 trains. To reach Coney Island, take the D/F or N/Q to Coney Island-Stillwell Ave – the last stop on the line. The ferry is a delightful alternative. The East River route links Manhattan, Dumbo, Williamsburg and more. Check ferry. nyc for routes. There's also a two-way bike path from Greenpoint and Dumbo.

☑ TOP TIP

Brooklyn is big – you can't see it all in 24 hours. Williamsburg and Bushwick can be explored in a day. Brooklyn Bridge Park and Dumbo can be done in a couple of hours. Coney Island deserves half a day.

TOP SIGHTS
1. Coney Island

SIGHTS
2. Brooklyn Bridge Park
3. City Reliquary
4. Empire Stores

ACTIVITIES, COURSES & TOURS
5. Deno's Wonder Wheel Park
6. Jane's Carousel

7. Luna Park

SLEEPING
8. Ace Hotel Brooklyn
9. Pod Brooklyn
10. Wythe Hotel

EATING
11. Bonnie's
12. Fornino at Pier 6
13. Laser Wolf
14. Lilia

15. Nathan's Famous

DRINKING & NIGHTLIFE
16. 3 Dollar Bill
17. Brooklyn Brewery
18. Grimm Artisanal Ales
19. Long Island Bar
20. Maison Premiere
21. Mood Ring
22. Pilot
23. SEY Coffee

24. Talea

ENTERTAINMENT
25. Avant Gardner
26. Elsewhere
27. House of Yes
28. Théâtre XIV

TRANSPORT
29. Fulton Ferry Landing

mine.' In the following decades, the Brooklyn and Manhattan Bridges became Big Apple landlines. Red-brick buildings shot up along the waterfront, home to companies that manufactured goods such as cardboard boxes and Brillo pads. Commercial production didn't last long: by the 1970s, businesses left and the waterfront became a wasteland. Industrial facades, cobblestone streets and antique railroad tracks remain today, but the waterfront is otherwise transformed in a triumph of urban renewal.

Venture north of Fulton Ferry to soak in an East River panorama. For 360-degree views, spin around **Jane's Carousel**, a vintage 1922 treasure housed in a Pritzker Prize-winning acrylic box. Behind the carousel is **Empire Stores**, which houses the **Time Out Market** (a collection of bustling food stalls and bars) plus a selection of retail chains.

Crowds thin out south of Fulton Ferry. If you're willing to hoof it, stop by Pier 6 for alfresco eating options, including **Fornino** (unfussy wood-fired pizza) and **Pilot** (oysters and cocktails on a wooden schooner, May–October).

Time Out Market

Feast Your Eyes on Quirky Relics
Williamsburg's kooky mini-museum
Walk through an antique subway turnstile into **City Reliquary**, a tiny museum dedicated to Big Apple ephemera. The three-room collection contains an oddball mix of memorabilia: Lady Liberty figurines, Second Ave Deli signage and a shrine honoring Brooklyn Dodgers star Jackie Robinson. Seeing the jam-packed space takes 20 to 30 minutes tops – a bit steep for the $10 ticket, but worth it if you like marching to the offbeat. Check its online event calendar to catch occasional readings, burlesque shows and junk craft classes in the art-filled backyard.

Get Topsy Turvy at Coney Island
Amusement rides on Brooklyn's 'riviera'
Tattooed mermaids, vintage roller coasters and greasy-food stands await at this gritty-glamorous escape along the Brooklyn waterfront. A one-hour trip from Midtown, **Coney Island** became a democratized day-tripper destination in turn-of-the-20th-century New York, promising sugar-sand beaches and cotton-candy clouds. Spend half a day admiring its charms.

BROOKLYN'S HEADY HISTORY

Brooklyn is no stranger to beer. As German immigrants flooded New York in the 19th century, breweries sprang up around the borough, turning Kings County into Lager Elysium. By the turn of the 20th century, Brooklyn was home to nearly 50 breweries, and a 12-block stretch linking Williamsburg and Bushhwick earned the nickname 'Brewer's Row' thanks to its near-dozen suds-focused establishments. But as the decades marched on, business dried up. By 1976, all of Brooklyn's beer makers were gone. It took more than a decade to turn the tap back on and now Brooklyn is once again the leader of NYC's pint-sized revolution. Sample various styles at **Brooklyn Brewery** (the OG), **Talea** (fruit-forward) and **Grimm Artisanal Ales** (funky flavors).

EATING IN WILLIAMSBURG: OUR PICKS

Lilia: Pasta restaurant in a former auto shop, cranking out some of the best noodles in town. Getting reservations is notoriously tough. **$$$**

Laser Wolf: Everything here is a feast – mezze appetizers, Israeli-style skewers and views of Manhattan from the Hoxton Hotel's terrace. **$$$**

Bonnie's: A Cantonese-American marriage of flavors, plus a rowdy party scene, especially if you're drinking the Long Island iced tea pot. **$$**

Smorgasburg: Every Saturday from April to October, foodies file into Marsha P Johnson State Park to sample treats at this culinary bazaar. **$$**

WILLIAMSBURG'S BEST NIGHTLIFE & PERFORMANCE VENUES

Elsewhere: Rap, rock and rave music are just a few styles you'll hear inside this furniture factory–turned-concert venue in East Williamsburg.

Avant Gardner: Dust off your dance shoes before seeing a show at East Williamsburg's 80,000-sq-ft EDM palace.

3 Dollar Bill: Brooklyn's biggest queer bar packs its 10,000-sq-ft space with fantastic performances and a colorful crowd.

House of Yes: Burlesque performers, drag artists and circus acts set the stage at this all-inclusive warehouse club with Burning Man flair.

Théâtre XIV: Deliriously bawdy takes on well-worn tales, each infused with ballet, burlesque, circus and cabaret.

Coney Island

The official season for this summer escape is Memorial Day to Labor Day, when you can expect big weekend crowds. Start by skipping down **Riegelmann Boardwalk**, a 2.5-mile waterfront promenade from 1923, to pass a sea of colorful characters, along with whirling carnival rides.

Fancy getting flung into the air at 90mph? The **Sling Shot** awaits at **Luna Park**. Perhaps the 56mph race around the 2233ft-long **Thunderbolt** is more your speed. Or you can go old-school – New Yorkers started shrieking down the wooden **Cyclone's** 85ft plunge in 1927, and the drop still thrills riders.

At **Deno's Wonder Wheel Park**, you can hop on the **Wonder Wheel**. Around since 1920, Coney Island's oldest ride is also its most romantic: sweeping views from 150ft above ground are bound to make your heart pitter-pat.

If your stomach survives the thrills and spills, get a taste of tradition by biting into one of **Nathan's Famous** hotdogs. The beefy frank, snuggled in a toasted bun, has been a Coney classic since 1916.

 DRINKING IN BROOKLYN: BEST BARS & CAFES

Maison Premiere: Visiting the green fairy at this absinthe-forward oyster-and-cocktail bar is like traveling to 19th-century New Orleans.

Mood Ring: Tattooed 20-somethings with a zeal for the zodiac get sweaty at this ultra-inclusive astrology-themed club.

Long Island Bar: Retro 1951 juice joint always abuzz with cool-cat clientele, sipping cocktails crafted by Cosmo inventor Toby Cecchini.

SEY Coffee: A mad-scientist attention to detail ensures this Nordic-style coffee roaster produces impeccable brews.

Places We Love to Stay

$ Budget $$ Midrange $$$ Top End

Lower Manhattan MAP p56

Greenwich Hotel $$$ Robert de Niro's Tribeca hotel is understated luxury: leather chairs, marble counters, handcrafted mattresses. Bonus points: the on-site spa and LocandaVerde, serving Italian downstairs.

Beekman $$$ Come for the 19th-century architecture and impressive lobby skylight; stay for chef Tom Colicchio's Temple Court restaurant and in-room products by local scentologist DS & Durga.

SoHo MAP p64

ModernHaus SoHo $$$ Expect Bauhaus German design, including geometrically precise finishes and paintings by Deutsche darlings. Rooftop bar Jimmy is a summertime scene.

Crosby Street Hotel $$$ Vibrant patterns and colorful splashes adorn every room, making this serene hotel seem like it was plucked from a glossy fashion magazine.

Lower East Side MAP p70

CitizenM Bowery $ Itty-bitty modular rooms with picture windows; upper floors boast fantastic skyline views. The location (bordering Nolita) is ideal for downtown exploring.

Public Hotel $$ Studio 54's disco days are over, but you can still stay up all night in the neon glow of club co-founder Ian Schrager's slick, minimalist digs.

Nine Orchard $$$ Housed in a 1912 beaux-arts bank, this Dimes Sq hotel seems fit for a modern Vanderbilt. Non-guests: sip cocktails in the grand Lobby Bar.

West Village & Chelsea MAP p74

Jane Hotel $ Ship-cabin-sized rooms were initially constructed for sailors in 1908; Titanic survivors stayed here in 1912. Now it's a haunt for out-of-town hipsters.

Hotel Chelsea $$$ This iconic bohemian hang for big-name artists (Hendrix, Mapplethorpe, Madonna) got a plush 2022 revamp. Raise a glass to their ghosts in the Lobby Bar.

Midtown & Beyond MAP p80

Freehand $ Arty, affordable and located in Flatiron (close to Midtown and Chelsea). Save bucks by bunking four to a room, or spread out with a king.

Romer $$ It's a skip to Broadway, Central Park and Ninth Ave's glut of international restaurants. The best part: sage-green rooms provide a tranquil escape from Midtown mayhem.

Moxy Times Square $$ The rooms might be tiny, but you'll be spending your time in the buzzy communal spaces, including the rooftop amusement park.

Upper East Side & Beyond MAP p86

Graduate $$ Escape NYC's hustle on Roosevelt Island's only hotel, where you can get drunk on city skyline views from the 18th-floor Panorama Bar.

Carlyle $$$ Resting pad? More like regal institution. This sophisticated 1930 stalwart has pampered greats from JFK to Princess Diana. Also home to **Bemelmans Bar** (p91).

Upper West Side & Beyond MAP p92

Harlem Flophouse $ Old-school style works its charm inside this Victorian brownstone, 15 minutes' walk north of Central Park. Most rooms share a bathroom, complete with antique claw-foot tubs.

HI New York City Hostel $ Bare bones isn't bad at this clean, congenial dorm, perfect for young upstarts looking for Big Apple buddies.

Brooklyn MAP p97

Pod Brooklyn $ The perfect Williamsburg crash pad after a Brooklyn all-nighter.

Ace Hotel Brooklyn $$ Downtown Brooklyn's stylish spot to catch zs doubles as a hang for cool crowds from Fort Greene, Dumbo and beyond, thanks to special events and public workspaces.

Wythe Hotel $$$ With fab on-site French brasserie Le Crocodile, Williamsburg's factory-turned-upscale-hotel brings Parisian elegance to an industrial space.

Above: Niagara Falls (146); Right: Montauk Point Lighthouse (p110)

THE MAIN AREAS

MONTAUK
Long Island's
summertime surf haven.
p108

BEACON
Art museums
and mountain hikes.
p116

WOODSTOCK
Woodland bohemia
in the Catskills.
p122

New York State

FORESTS, FARMSTEADS AND CULTURED ENCLAVES

Patchworks of woodland and tilled terrain link mountain towns and waterfront villages. It's a far cry from the hustle and bustle of city life.

New York is more than its eponymous metropole. Though NYC is the state's megawatt attraction, accounting for roughly 40% of the population, it covers less than 1% of the state's area. Over half the state is covered in forests – a wild universe lit by constellations of charming villages and midsize cities, with 180 state parks framing salty beaches, freshwater lakes, rambling rivers and three major mountain ranges. It's a jungle out there.

If you ask residents from NYC, anything north of Manhattan is considered 'upstate' – a distinction hotly contested by everyone else. Follow the Hudson River north and you're in the Hudson Valley, a network of arty towns and rural farmland easily accessible from Manhattan. The Catskill Mountains rise west of the Hudson, with eccentric communities of outdoor enthusiasts hidden along snaking backroads. Jet northeast to the Hudson River's source and you're in the Adirondacks, home to the largest publicly protected park in the contiguous United States. Central New York sparkles with the Finger Lakes, cross-hatched by gorges and cultivated by farmers. Western New York draws crowds thanks to Niagara Falls, which neighbors Buffalo, the state's second most populous city. Definitively downstate and east of NYC is Long Island, stretching into the Atlantic Ocean like a 120-mile-long fish. Suburban sprawl gives way to vineyards and ritzy summer escapes built atop former whaling villages perched perilously close to the sea.

VADIM 777/SHUTTERSTOCK ©

LAKE GEORGE
Pristine lakes dot
the untamed Adirondacks.
p129

ITHACA
Lakeside vineyards
and gorges galore.
p136

BUFFALO & NIAGARA FALLS
Urban renewal and
spectacular waterfalls.
p142

Find Your Way

New York spans 54,554 square miles. While buses and trains travel throughout large swaths of the state, covering a land mass this size requires a car, especially when accessing serene mountain towns and state parks.

Ithaca, p136
College kids lend a youthful glow to this city on Cayuga Lake's southern tip, surrounded by scenic vineyards and cut by a series of gorges.

Buffalo & Niagara Falls, p142
Industrial relics from Buffalo's manufacturing heyday are kicking off their rust and getting revamped 20 miles south of New York's most dramatic cascades.

CAR
Renting wheels is cheaper outside of NYC, so take a train elsewhere to pick up a vehicle. Watch for tiny-town speed traps and wild animals while driving, particularly around the Catskills and Adirondacks. Expect wintry conditions such as ice and snow between December and March.

TRAIN
If NYC is your home base, visiting Beacon and Montauk is possible via Metro North and Long Island Rail Road. Metro North trips along the Hudson River are splendid in fall, chugging past crayon-colored woodlands. Amtrak serves Buffalo, where rideshares are easy to find upon arrival.

Lake George, p129

Centuries of turbulent American history splash along these shores, now a summer escape for campers and a gateway to the rugged Adirondack Mountains.

Woodstock, p122

This Catskill Mountains artist magnet sits at the doorstep of outdoor adventures that scale gentle mountains and cross lazy rivers dotted with hippie havens.

Beacon, p116

Riverfront main streets compete for attention with art museums and mountain hikes around the Hudson Valley, all pretty as a Thomas Cole landscape painting.

Montauk, p108

Surfers crowd waves at Ditch Plains year-round, but the real party starts in summer when city slickers and well-heeled Hamptonites flock to Long Island's eastern tip.

105

Plan Your Time

The Empire State's size can be overwhelming. Stick to a geographic region based on your interests – perhaps Long Island's beach towns or the Adirondacks' mountainscapes – or explore it all on a whirlwind road trip.

Ditch Plains Beach (p108)

A Long Island Weekend

● Venture to New York's easternmost edge for two days of seaside pleasures. Wake up with coffee from Montauk's **Bird on the Roof** (p110) before driving to **Montauk Point Lighthouse** (p110), an 18th-century beacon for sailors and now a museum for history buffs. In the afternoon, book a surf lesson with Sunset Surf Shack to ride waves at **Ditch Plains Beach** (p108), then reward yourself with sunset cocktails at **Montauket** (p109).

● On day two, snag breakfast from **Amber Waves Farm** (p112) before driving to **Sag Harbor** (p112), where Main St is lined with independently owned stores. Take the ferry to Greenport, gateway to **North Fork vineyards** (p114).

Seasonal Highlights

Many towns hibernate until summer, and fall makes for great road trips. Winter's snow inspires curling up indoors or skiing.

APRIL
Buffalonians celebrate spring with **Dyngus Day**, a traditional Polish festival with pierogies and polka dancing in the historic Polonia district.

MAY
Eastern Long Island kicks off summer with four days of live performances at the **Montauk Music Festival**.

JUNE
Livingston Manor gets fishy for the annual **Trout Parade** (p127), honoring upstream swimmers and anglers who love them.

Five Days in the Hudson Valley & Catskills

- Devote a day to expansive Hudson Valley museums, including sculpture park **Storm King** (p118) and minimalist sanctum **Dia Beacon** (p116), followed by artisanal ales from **Hudson Valley Brewery** (p119). On day two, climb panoramic **Mt Beacon** (p118) or head to **Hudson's Warren St** (p119), a strip of antique stores and art galleries.

- Cross the Hudson River to explore the Catskill Mountains. After skipping down Woodstock's Tinker St, behold the two-tiered **Kaaterskill Falls** (p122). With extra time, sample greasy-spoon favorites from **Phoenicia Diner** (p124) en route to appealing Western Catskills towns such as **Livingston Manor** (p128).

A Week-long Upstate Road Trip

- Spend a few days immersing yourself in the Adirondacks: zoom to **mountain peaks** (p129), rent a kayak to paddle around **Lake George** (p129) and drive to **Lake Placid** (p135), where Olympic history looms as large as Whiteface Mountain.

- Next stop is Ithaca, graced with gorge trails at **Robert H Treman State Park** (p136) and **Watkins Glen State Park** (p136). After days of athletic adventures, kick back on a Finger Lakes winery tour or snuggle with **Sunset View Creamery's** (p137) cows.

- For a rousing finish, devote a day to **Niagara Falls** (p146), a series of breathtaking cascades at the heart of the nation's oldest state park.

THE GUIDE

NEW YORK STATE

JULY	AUGUST	SEPTEMBER	OCTOBER
Oenophiles fill their glasses with vino from more than 80 vineyards while listening to live music at the **Finger Lakes Wine Festival**.	The **Hudson Valley Shakespeare Festival** presents adaptations of classics by the Bard in an open-air tent throughout summer.	Catskill Mountains artists, farmers, food makers and musicians draw crowds to **Bethel Woods** for Harvest Festival weekends.	Leaf peepers fawn over fall's fiery forests statewide, but nothing burns brighter than the Hudson Valley's **Great Jack O'Lantern Blaze**.

Montauk

SAND | SURF | MARITIME TALES

GETTING AROUND

A car is necessary to explore beyond Montauk's downtown, including the Hamptons (roughly 40 minutes away) and the North Fork (roughly 1½ hours away). Get ready for traffic: torrents of NYC weekenders clog the roads in summer. If you hit rush hour, the three-hour pleasure cruise from Manhattan becomes a four- to six-hour ordeal. Prefer the back seat? Hop on the **Hampton Jitney**, an express bus from NYC to the heart of Montauk, with beaches, restaurants and bars in walking distance. The **Long Island Rail Road** also provides service from NYC to **Montauk Station**. Ubers and taxis (try Pink Tuna) pick up passengers from the train station.

Montauk sizzles like a summer romance, burning hot and heavy from Memorial Day to Labor Day, then cooling off as winter's population shrinks from 40,000 to 4000. Falling in love with this Long Island escape is easy: the peninsula is kissed by breezy beaches and wrapped with six leafy state parks. It's New York's easternmost point – nicknamed 'The End' – and the state's last stop before jumping into the Atlantic, far from NYC's towers and beyond the South Fork's tony Hamptons.

The hamlet has seen its fair share of suitors, starting with the Indigenous Montaukett, followed by English colonizers, fisherfolk and eventually Carl G Fisher, who tried turning Montauk into the 'Miami Beach of the North' in the 1920s. Although his plan failed, future generations succeeded. Some 20th-century tackle shops and dive bars beloved by sun-bleached surfers remain, but most are now fine-dining fish huts and cocktail joints serving summer's moneyed masses.

Hang Ten in Montauk
Surf with the pros

Montauk is the holy land of East Coast surfing, and catching waves at **Ditch Plains Beach** is akin to attending church. Unlike typical Atlantic Ocean waves that break quickly over sandy shores, Ditch Plains waves cascade over cobblestones, offering surfers minute-long rides to fine-tune their surfing skills. Seasonal variations add to the allure: summer brings gentle waves, while fall and winter unveil majestic swells fit for serious board disciples. There's a blend of clean and consistent surf, making it paradise for both beginners and experts. As a result, Montauk teems with seasoned surfers – and knowledgeable teachers – who genuflect before their boards year-round.

If you're eager to join this spiritual communion, **Sunset Surf Shack** (*sunsetsurfshack.com*) offers hour-long lessons starting at $100, complete with wetsuit, surfboard and instructor. Bring a towel, some water and a can-do attitude:

TOP SIGHTS
1. Montauk Point Lighthouse

SIGHTS
2. Amsterdam Beach Trailhead
3. Camp Hero State Park
4. Kirk Park Beach
5. Montauk Point State Park
6. Shadmoor State Park
7. South Edison Beach

ACTIVITIES, COURSES & TOURS
8. Ditch Plains Beach
9. Sunset Surf Shack

SLEEPING
10. Breakers
11. Daunt's Albatross Motel

EATING
12. Bird on the Roof
13. Ditch Witch
14. Duryea's
15. El Taco Ole
16. Naturally Good
17. Seaside House Bar

DRINKING & NIGHTLIFE
18. Montauk Brewing Co
19. Montauket
20. Surf Lodge

TRANSPORT
21. Hampton Jitney & Ambassador

hanging ten can be tough, but the promise of a wave-riding revelation can't be beaten.

Montauk is spoiled with spectacular beaches, and though they're all open to the public, parking is usually restricted to permits issued by the Town of East Hampton. This includes beloved Ditch Plains. Permits for non-residents cost $500 – a steep price for a weekend getaway – though some beaches have reasonable day passes, such as **Kirk Park Beach** ($35) and **Hither Hills State Park** ($10). Don't defy local laws – cops sniff out illegally parked cars like sharks smelling blood. Prefer free parking? Consider booking a hotel near popular

✓ TOP TIP

If you like laid-back towns and juicy wines, visit Greenport, anchoring Long Island's vineyard-laced North Fork. The most scenic way to travel from Montauk is by ferry: take the **South Ferry** from Sag Harbor to Shelter Island, then hop on the **North Ferry** to Greenport.

 DRINKING IN MONTAUK: OUR PICKS

Montauket: Ideal for soaking up sunsets with seafaring locals. Come early for window-facing seats. Seafood served in summer.

Montauk Brewing Co: Red-barn bastion for beer, founded by three local buds. Chill vibes.

Surf Lodge: Summer's go-to hotel club. Tough to get in, potentially worth waiting. Renowned musical artists perform for see-and-be-seen crowds.

Naturally Good: Organic juice, smoothies, wellness shots and coffee served alongside feel-good breakfasts inside a health-food store.

109

IDEAL SURF DAY

Craig Leider, co-owner of Sunset Surf Shack and MTK Surf Shop. @sunset_surf_shack

When we wake up, my whole family piles in the car and goes to Ditch Plains. It's the beginning of June, right before Montauk gets crazy with crowds. The waves are really good this time of year. We surf for three hours. When we leave, we stop at **Ditch Witch**, a food cart at the beach. My kids get cinnamon rolls; my wife and I get coffee. Then we go home and hang our suits up so they're dry for later. The evening sessions are magic – the sun is setting and we can surf until almost 8pm. We always see tons of friends – and possibly whales.

South Edison Beach so you can walk to the seashore (try **Daunt's Albatross Motel** (p149)), or hike the easy 1.5-mile trail to **Amsterdam Beach**.

Stand on Long Island's Tip
Views from Montauk Point Lighthouse

New York's **first lighthouse** is the exclamation point on Long's Island's eastern edge, standing 110ft above the sea-battered coast since 1796. Originally commissioned by President George Washington to warn sailors of the rocks below, it's now the photogenic heart of **Montauk Point State Park**, an 862-acre expanse of wooded trails and bluff-backed beaches. A small museum, located in the keeper's house from 1860, provides historical insight, and climbing the tower's 137 iron steps leads to 360-degree views. Stop by around sunrise or sunset (outside of museum hours) when the candy-colored tower gets painted burnt sienna by the light. For exquisite views from afar, head to **Camp Hero State Park** and hike east along the seaside bluffs – the lighthouse shines as a distant maritime beacon. Look over the bluffs to see a series of 'hoodoos' – precarious clay-and-sand castles sculpted by the wind and ocean.

Skip through Sag Harbor
Whaling past to wealthy present

The 'un-Hampton' – until a decade ago, that's how locals fancied Sag Harbor. While well-heeled Manhattanites colonized towns such as East Hampton with status-symbol shops (Gucci, Rolex etc), Sag Harbor maintained its charm with locally owned boutiques and a dedication to historic preservation. Although some of the magic is waning (everything here is expensive), stroll down Main St to see why Sag Harbor remains a South Fork standout. Start at the **Sag Harbor Whaling and Historical Museum**, erected in 1845 for a whaling tycoon. Whale blubber, used to make oil, earned locals big bucks throughout the 1830s and '40s, but the rush was brief. By the 1850s, overfishing sank the whale-oil market just as kerosene and petroleum gained popularity. Continue north to Main St's three-block shopping center and you'll see that money found its way back to town. Stop for slices at **Sag Pizza**, snap a picture of art deco **Sag Harbor Cinema** and pop into **Sag Harbor Books** to leaf through *Moby Dick* (author Herman Melville gives the village a shout-out). Sag Harbor's **marina** punctuates Main St's history. In summer, mansion-sized yachts line the docks – a nod to Sag's seafaring origins and recent wealthy upswing.

 EATING IN MONTAUK: BEST RESTAURANTS

Bird on the Roof: Aussie-inspired brunch transitions to American-style dinner with pastas, curries, fish and inventive cocktails. **$$**

Duryea's: Seasonal spot to catch the sunset while slurping oysters and sipping rosé. Connected to a market and boutique. **$$$**

Seaside House Bar: It's actually roadside, but the sushi tastes straight from the sea. Poke bowls round out the menu. **$$**

El Taco Ole: Tacos and burritos bring Baja flavor to beach bums at the seashore, five minutes away by foot. **$$**

AROUND MONTAUK

THE GUIDE

NEW YORK STATE MONTAUK

See Montauk map p109

Block Island Sound

Fort Pond Bay

Ditch Plains

Montauk

Napeague Bay

Gardiner's Island

Gardiners Bay

Plum Island

Devon

Amagansett

Gerard Park

Springs

East Hampton

New York/ New Jersey Bight

Orient

East Marion

Greenport

Shelter Island Heights

Shelter Island

Little Noyack Bay

Southold

Noyack

Channing Daughters

Bridgehampton

Sag Harbor

Mecox Bay

Water Mill

Southampton

Sparkling Pointe

Long Island Sound

Cutchogue

New Suffolk

Robins Island

North Sea

Shinnecock Hills

Shinnecock Bay

Mattituck

Laurel

Jamesport

Great Peconic Bay

Hampton Bays

Northville

Riverhead

Flanders

East Quogue

Quogue

Quiogue

0   10 miles

0   20 km

TOP SIGHTS
1 Channing Daughters
2 Sparkling Pointe

SIGHTS
3 Bedell Cellars
4 Big Duck
5 Borghese Vineyard
6 Dia Bridgehampton
7 Elizabeth A Morton National Wildlife Refuge
8 Hither Hills State Park
9 LongHouse Reserve
10 McCall Wines
11 Old Field Vineyards
12 Paumanok Vineyards
13 Pindar Vineyards
14 Pollock-Krasner House
15 Sag Harbor Village Marina
16 Sag Harbor Whaling & Historical Museum
17 Wölffer Estate

SLEEPING
18 Hotel Moraine
19 Roundtree

EATING
20 Almond
21 Amber Waves Farm
22 Claudio's
23 Doubles
24 Frisky Oyster
25 Sag Pizza
26 Sen

DRINKING & NIGHTLIFE
27 Brix and Rye
28 Greenport Harbor Brewing Co

ENTERTAINMENT
29 Sag Harbor Cinema

SHOPPING
30 Sag Harbor Books

TRANSPORT
31 East End Bike Tours
32 Montauk Station
33 North Ferry
34 South Ferry Company

SPECTACULAR SIGHTS IN THE HAMPTONS

Shadmoor State Park:
Montauk trails thick with black cherry trees lead to WWII bunkers and oceanside bluffs.

Pollock-Krasner House:
Explore the paint-splattered studio and home of husband-and-wife abstract expressionists Jackson Pollock and Lee Krasner. Open May-October; reservations required.

Dia Bridgehampton:
This 1908 house has served as fire station, Baptist church and, now, exhibition space for minimalist Dan Flavin's fluorescent artwork. Free.

Big Duck:
Quirky detour where the North and South Forks split. Step inside the 20ft-tall Pekin duck from 1931.

LongHouse Reserve:
More than 60 sculptures, including works by Yoko Ono and Willem de Kooning, sprout from this 16-acre garden.

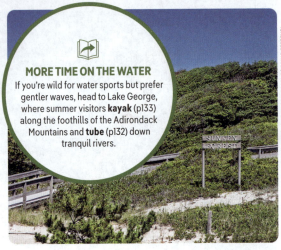

MORE TIME ON THE WATER
If you're wild for water sports but prefer gentler waves, head to Lake George, where summer visitors **kayak** (p133) along the foothills of the Adirondack Mountains and **tube** (p132) down tranquil rivers.

Sunken Forest

Birdwatch on the Bay
Twitcher paradise in Sag Harbor

Birders, get your binoculars ready. Sag Harbor's **Elizabeth A Morton National Wildlife Refuge**, which juts into Noyack and Little Peconic Bays, presents a veritable avian odyssey spread across a 187-acre sanctuary. Even in winter, you're guaranteed to spot some feathered friends. The best way to see them is along the **Wild Birds Nature Trail**, a 1.2-mile loop through woodland and marshes. You'll likely run into rafters of wild turkeys year-round, and in spring the forest becomes a chorus of migrating songbirds. At **Jessup's Neck**, a rocky beach-rimmed peninsula, you might spot ospreys hunting for prey, black ducks floating in the blue and piping plovers flitting along the seashore. White-tailed deer, chipmunks, painted turtles and green frogs also frequent the trails. With a bit of patience, you might see them all.

Although these animals may seem friendly, don't offer them food. A long-standing practice of feeding birds at the refuge has had the unintended consequence of threatening endangered species by luring predators such as raccoons to vulnerable nests. Enjoy the flapping wonders from a safe distance, and keep the snacks to yourself. Parking costs $4; enjoying the wildlife is free.

 EATING IN THE HAMPTONS: MARKETS & RESTAURANTS

Amber Waves Farm: (p106) Charming roadside cafe and market on a farm in Amagansett. Great for kids. **$$**

Almond: Bridgehampton's boisterous French-style bistro, where white-collar crowds dine on roast chicken and raw bar delicacies. **$$$**

Doubles: Amagansett's outpost for Caribbean-influenced food, including doubles (fried dough topped with a curried chickpea concoction). **$$**

Sen: Sag Harbor's casual sushi-bar staple, going strong on Main St for three decades. **$$$**

Find Freedom on Fire Island
Long Island's LGBTIQ+ summer escape

Muscular architecture, maritime forests and sweeping dunes lapped by the Atlantic: there are myriad reasons to board the **Sayville ferry** for a day trip to Fire Island, a slender sandbar off Long Island's coast. But the main draw? LGBTIQ+ crowds. Between May and September, queer travelers cast off their mainland drag to don Speedos around car-free **Cherry Grove** and neighboring **Fire Island Pines**.

Cherry Grove became 'America's first gay and lesbian town' around the 1930s and 1940s. Pay your respects at the **Cherry Grove Community House and Theater**, where openly LGBTIQ+ residents played important roles in civic life decades before the US elected queer politicians to office. Summer evenings center around the **Ice Palace**, a club and performance space graced by the likes of Liza Minelli, Patti LuPone and scantily clad men who come for Friday night's Underwear Party. If you prefer low-key to late night, take a detour to the **Sunken Forest**. A 1.5-mile boardwalk loops through its 300-year-old collection of American holly trees, sassafras and juneberry, 'sunken' beneath protective dunes.

While Cherry Grove welcomes mixed LGBTIQ+ crowds, including a strong sapphic contingency, the Pines is predominantly gay. Join the boys strutting its boardwalks to ogle eye-candy architecture. Many of the modernist homes were designed by architect Horace Gifford in the '60s and '70s, using cedar and glass to complement the natural surroundings. The facade of **252 Bay Walk** looks like a proscenium arch for a seductive stage play; **482 Tarpon** boasts a deck that hovers above its neighbors – a voyeur's delight.

All boardwalks here eventually lead to the **Blue Whale**, where gaggles gather around 5pm to babble over cocktails at 'Low Tea.' At 8pm, crowds flow to the adjacent pool deck for 'High Tea.' The final stop is **Sip-n-Twirl**, where music pulses until dawn. Don't feel beholden to these hedonistic affairs – a perfect Pines day can be spent on the beach, poring over Jack Partlett's historical memoir, *Fire Island: A Century in the Life of an American Paradise*.

LONG ISLAND OR ATLANTIS?

In the 18th century, **Montauk Point Lighthouse** (p110) stood 400ft from the sea. Due to erosion, it's now only 100ft away. A $44-million coastal resiliency project, completed in 2023, fortified the bluffs against encroaching waters, but extreme storms and rising sea levels persist as formidable adversaries. Nearby Fire Island benefited from similar beach-fortification efforts in 2019, when a $1.7-billion project dropped 2.3 million cubic yards of sand along its shores. It only took four years for the top-dollar beaches to disappear. As climate change evolves and the ocean's onslaught continues, difficult decisions remain: continue to pump money into a nonstop battle with nature, or let these magnificent sites become the East Coast's Atlantis.

EATING & DRINKING AROUND THE NORTH FORK: OUR PICKS

Claudio's: Three dockside venues serving ocean catches to big crowds – an alfresco hang, historic dining room and pizza parlor. $$

Frisky Oyster: The oysters 'friskafella' (briny, garlicky) are mythical sirens, calling you to this sea-to-spoon restaurant. $$$

Brix and Rye: Lively watering hole with cocktails and brick-oven pies from neighboring 1943 Pizza Bar; shuffleboard on the ground level.

Greenport Harbor Brewing Co: Head to the expansive Peconic location for its beer garden, live music, brewery tours and food (sandwiches, ramen).

HELP ME PICK:

North Fork Vineyards

When Louisa and Alex Hargrave planted wine-centric vines on a North Fork potato farm in 1973, locals called it a silly fad. Half a century later, Long Island has transformed from scrappy grape-juice upstart to established oenophile, with more than 60 vineyards covering 3000 acres. Expect elegant cabernet francs and merlots – products of the region's Bordeaux-style terroir. Some notable South Fork growers please palates, but the North Fork reigns as viticulture king. Take a sip.

Where to sip if you love...

Sweet & fizzy whites

Sparkling Pointe Chandeliers glittering above the tasting room hint at what's to come: a bubbly ballet of sparkling wines produced through the méthode champenoise (champagne method). This is Long Island's only winery with a dozen effervescent, zesty zingers.

Paumanok Vineyards Walt Whitman evokes Paumanok, Long Island's Indigenous name, in a *Leaves of Grass* poem, honoring the land's 'sweet brooks of drinking water.' Winemakers here make Whitman proud with their award-winning, late-harvest sauvignon blanc – sweet as a sugar cube.

Elegant Reds

Borghese Vineyard Long Island's pioneering winery opened as Hargrave Vineyard over 50 years ago, producing old-world wines (try the merlot). The tradition continues under Borghese, beloved by laid-back grape gurus. Expect a greeting from Herb (short for 'Herbaceous'), the furry, four-legged welcoming committee. No party buses allowed.

Bedell Cellars The tuxedo of North Fork wineries: a black-and-white tasting room where rich reds steal the show. Sample the silky cabernet franc and sultry malbec.

Rustic-barn Ambience

McCall Wines Farm tools from the 1900s hang on slat-wood walls around this low-key tasting room, formerly a potato barn. The earthy pinot noir, with its tobacco undertones and fruit-forward finish, adds to the agricultural sensibility.

Old Field Vineyards Drinking wine here feels like imbibing at your kooky aunt's house – if your aunt has a peep of clucking chickens and knows how to make a sauvignon blanc that's juicier than fresh-picked pears.

Exuberant Crowds

Pindar Vineyards Long Island's largest vineyard turns up the volume on festivities with live music throughout the weekend. The menu features plenty of varieties sure to suit all tastes.

Vineyards in the Hamptons

Channing Daughters The South Fork's most inventive boutique winery serves flights patio-side, overlooking 33 acres of vine-wrapped trellises. Try the Meditazione (Italian for 'meditation' an orange wine with chamomile-tea undertones) and the plummy rosato syrah (rosé). Passionate staff members provide insight.

Wölffer Estate Most folks come here to drink pink, pretty stuff – namely, the Summer in a Bottle rosé (affordable, Instagrammable) – but the sleeper hit is the cabernet franc. Join picture-happy hordes in the tasting room, which is a mishmash of European influences.

Scan this QR code for a full list of wineries

Borghese Vineyard

HOW TO

When to go Vineyards see big crowds on sunny summer and fall weekends. During the week, there's more time to schmooze with sommeliers. Winter tends to be slow.

Booking ahead Most wineries require reservations, especially for tours, though some are first-come-first-served. Check before you go.

Budget considerations Wine flights cost roughly $30 to $40; small, single samples, if offered, run around $6 to $8. Expect vineyard tours to cost under $50.

Finding food Many tasting rooms serve overpriced cheese and charcuterie; some allow outside picnics. Your best bet – fill up on organic goodies from roadside farm stands throughout the North Fork.

Getting Around

For flexibility, nothing beats flitting between farmsteads in a personal car. You can improvise as you go, zigzagging to different vineyards and stopping at farm stands to pick up snacks. Most vineyards dot Routes 25 and 48 between Riverhead and Greenport, and it's possible to cruise down either road and stop whenever the mood strikes. The only downside: you'll likely need a designated driver. If everyone in your group decides to imbibe, call Main Street Drivers or North Fork Designated Driver ($48 to $50 per hour, four-hour minimum) – hired chauffeurs from either company will drive your car for the day.

If you prefer seeing the landscape at a slower pace, try East End Bike Tours, located in Mattituck. Guided backroad romps lead to fields of vines and tiny produce farms (starting at $117). You can also rent bikes to follow a preplanned route or create a solo, DIY excursion (starting at $65).

Limos and party buses might be attractive for large groups (call North Fork Wine Tours; packages start at $130), but many North Fork vineyards deny entry to these services, limiting choices for tastings.

The cheapest option is public transportation. The S92 bus, which runs along Route 25 ($2.25 a ride), stops near vineyards such as Pindar and Paumanok, but you'll have to hoof it from the bus stop and stick to the transit schedule.

Beacon

RIVER TOWNS | ART | HIKING

Bohemian Beacon's unofficial nickname is 'Brooklyn North' – a nod to the influx of ex-urbanites who've spent two decades transforming it into King's County's scrappy upstate cousin. Walk down Main St and the comparisons are clear. All the Brooklyn-as-brand signifiers are present: artisanal boutiques, small-batch breweries, avant-garde art galleries and farm-to-table restaurants. But Beacon, located in the mid-Hudson Valley region, is more than NYC's facsimile. Sandwiched between the Hudson River and Hudson Highlands, it's a jump-off point for outdoor adventures, including a collection of heart-pumping mountain hikes.

Beacon became America's second-largest hat manufacturer between the late 19th and early 20th centuries. When factories shuttered around the mid-20th century, the city fell on hard times, like many Hudson Valley towns. The 2003 arrival of Dia Beacon, a minimalist art museum, marked the city's rebirth as Brooklyn's rural outpost, now a go-to for urbanites raring to break in their hiking boots.

Lose Yourself in Steel Canyons
Dia Beacon's mega-sized minimalist art

Manhattan day-trippers arrive via Metro North to drool over NYC's most sought-after commodity: space, superabundant at contemporary-art institution **Dia Beacon**. Roughly 300,000 sq ft of this former Nabisco box-printing factory devotes itself to minimalist paintings and mammoth sculptures that wouldn't fit through an NYC doorway. The most transportive works feel less 'contemporary art museum' and more 'aesthete's playground.' Winding through Richard Serra's rust-red *Torqued Ellipses* feels like hiking Arizona's Antelope Canyon, the sweet scent of Meg Webster's 8ft-tall *Wall of Beeswax* recalls a buzzy honey farm, and barbed-wire walls by Melvin Edwards add a tinge of danger while walking about. Free guided

GETTING AROUND

Beacon is 60 miles north of NYC – a 1½-hour train ride from Grand Central via Metro North and a similarly long drive from Midtown Manhattan. Driving isn't necessary if you plan on sticking around Beacon's Main St. The **train station** is a 15-minute walk away, while the **Beacon Free Loop** bus travels from the station down Main St (Monday through Saturday). Nearby attractions, including Storm King, sometimes cater to car-free travelers with shuttle services. If driving from Manhattan, follow routes 9 and 9A to zip through scenic river towns.

☑ TOP TIP

Hudson, an elegant river town one hour north of Beacon by car and accessible by train, also makes a fantastic home base while exploring the region.

THE GUIDE

NEW YORK STATE BEACON

TOP SIGHTS
1. Dia Beacon
2. Mt Beacon

SIGHTS
3. Boscobel House & Gardens
4. KuBe Art Center
5. Madam Brett Park
6. Magazzino Italian Art
7. Pete and Toshi Seeger Riverfront Park

ACTIVITIES, COURSES & TOURS
8. Breakneck Ridge Trailhead
9. Bull Hill Trailhead
10. Madam Brett Park Trailhead
11. Storm King Mountain Trailhead

SLEEPING
12. Beacon Bed and Breakfast
13. Roundhouse

EATING
14. Homespun Foods
15. Kitchen & Coffee
16. Noble Pies
- see 13 Roundhouse

DRINKING & NIGHTLIFE
17. Big Mouth Coffee Roasters
18. Denning's Point Distillery
19. Hudson Valley Brewery

TRANSPORT
20. Beacon Free Loop
21. Beacon Train Station

117

GREAT MUSEUMS & GALLERIES

Boscobel House and Gardens:
This 19th-century Federalist home, overlooking the Hudson River, showcases how the fledgling US remained tethered to British influence.

Art Omi:
Wander 120 acres of outdoor sculptures among fields and forests in Ghent.

Magazzino Italian Art:
Bold postwar Italian art fills this beautiful brutalist space (Magazzino means 'warehouse' in Italian). Wave to the museum's 14 Sardinian donkeys.

KuBe Art Center:
Edgy 'Kunsthalle Beacon' transforms a former high school into an art gallery with cheeky rotating exhibits. Tours available on weekends.

Kykuit:
Four generations of oil-rich Rockefellers inhabited this Gilded Age mansion atop historic Sleepy Hollow.

tours take place on Saturday and Sunday at noon and 1:30pm, though it's best to experience the museum at your own pace. Gliding through the galleries, lit by 34,000 sq ft of skylights, is a meditative experience. An on-site cafe serves treats from **Homespun Foods**, one of Beacon's best Main St restaurants.

Peep Leaves & Art at Storm King
Cornwall's outdoor sculpture park

Storm King Art Center marries what the Hudson Valley does best – nature and art. Hike around this pastoral park's 500 acres, open from April to November, and you might wonder where one ends and the other begins. Colossal pieces sprout from manicured lawns and pop among the woodlands. Site-specific works also mimic the landscape, such as Maya Lin's *Storm King Wavefield*, an 11-acre earthwork undulating like a miniature Hudson Highlands.

Budget a few hours to adequately explore. Start by trekking around the North Woods, then walk counterclockwise, stopping by Menashe Kadishman's gravity-defying *Suspended* on your way to the top of Museum Hill, the park's highest point. Here you'll find the museum's shop and gallery space, housed in a Normandy-style chateau. Finish by meandering among native grasslands, creeks and allées, where you might spot white-tailed deer, box turtles and cottontail rabbits crawling around works by Roy Lichtenstein, Alexander Calder and Mark di Suvero.

If you want to zip through the park quickly, rent a bicycle ($20 to $30) or hop on the wheelchair-accessible tram loop. Getting here is easiest by car (25 minutes from Beacon), though it's possible to take a free museum shuttle from Beacon's train station (summer only) or catch a Coach bus from Manhattan. Plan a trip around leaf-peeping season (mid-September to early November), when trees put on an arboreal art show rivaling the sculptures.

Reach Mt Beacon's Fire Tower
The Hudson Highlands' highest peak

Scale **Mt Beacon's** 1600ft summit to reap big rewards. The 4-mile out-and-back journey leads to breathtaking views of the Hudson Highlands, Catskills and Shawangunks – on clear days, you might even spot Manhattan's distant skyline. The trail is usually less crowded than routes such as Breakneck Ridge and Bull Hill, plus it's packed with local history.

Mt Beacon's pyrotechnic past began during the Revolutionary War, when the Continental Army built fire signals (or

EATING IN BEACON: BEST RESTAURANTS & BAKERIES

Homespun Foods: Sit in the colorful retro kitchen or on the outdoor patio for flavorful takes on brunch-and-lunch classics. **$$**

Roundhouse: Seasonal fare served inside this hat factory–turned-hotel is just an appetizer for the views of a gushing Fishkill Creek waterfall. **$$$**

Noble Pies: The Hudson Valley apple pie is a salute to Americana, served with other sweet and savory selections at this regional chain. **$**

Kitchen & Coffee: Salads, sandwiches and vegan treats. Need something decadent? Grab a donut from Peaceful Provisions across the street. **$**

'beacons') across Hudson Highlands peaks to alert forces of British advancement. The mountain ignited intrigue again in 1902 when the Mt Beacon Railway opened, becoming the world's steepest passenger funicular. Guests came from afar to ride the rails, which led to a casino and eventually a hotel being constructed. Disaster struck in 1927 when both buildings burned, and though they were rebuilt, the Great Depression cemented their fate. The funicular chugged along until 1978 – several years after its closure, another fire destroyed its remnants. Today, only skeletal foundations from Beacon's 20th-century heyday remain, along with one ironic survivor: the mountain's fire tower.

Think of the trail in two separate sections. The first mile, starting at 788 Wolcott Ave (the parking lot), scales a 200-step staircase and rocky path, tracing the now-defunct railway to the casino's ruins, where views of Beacon spill out below. From here, the route ascends through a deciduous forest thick with maple, birch and oak trees before scrambling across a rocky ridge to the fire tower. Climb to the tower's top for a spectacular panorama. Bring plenty of water and snacks, best enjoyed at the summit. The hike takes roughly three hours.

Wander Down Warren Street

Hudson's trendy heart

Uber-hip Hudson is beloved by NYC weekenders, who travel by car or train to cruise Warren St's antique stores, boutiques, galleries and restaurants. Join the crowds for a one-mile stroll.

Start with a breakfast sandwich at **Kitty's** near the train station, snack on a sourdough croissant from **Mel the Bakery**, or rev up your engine with java from **MOTO Coffee Machine**, a coffee-and-motorcycle shop. You'll spot more than 10 art galleries along Warren St, including **Carrie Haddad's** collection of notable locals. (Peep the hidden upstairs hallway dedicated to Mark Beard's athletic nudes.) There's an eclectic collection of upcycled decor at **LikeMindedObjects**, vintage home furnishings at well-curated **FINCH Hudson** and high fashion with an outdoorsy edge at **Meridian**. The antiques game is strong here, too. Pop into **Red Chair on Warren** for Swiss, Belgian and French finds from the 17th, 18th and 19th centuries. At **Spotty Dog Books & Ale**, you can thumb through novels while sipping beer.

Throughout the journey, admire Hudson's beautiful bones. Warren St is chockablock with 19th-century architecture, including Federal, Queen Anne and Victorian homes.

TOP HUDSON VALLEY HIKES

Bull Hill:
Trek past scenic overlooks and mysterious ruins on this 5.4-mile loop trail near Beacon.

Breakneck Ridge:
Brace yourself for rocky scrambles and steep ascents on this short-but-strenuous 3.2-mile hike, accessible on summer weekends via Metro North.

Storm King Mountain:
Circle the crown of this 1300ft peak on a 2.4-mile trail, different from the same-named art park.

Madam Brett Park:
Follow Fishkill Creek past an abandoned hat factory towards birder-friendly Dennings Point on an easy 1-mile-plus path.

Walkway Over the Hudson:
Stroll or roll across the world's longest elevated pedestrian bridge, a 1.3-mile link between Poughkeepsie and Highland.

 DRINKING IN BEACON: BEST BEER, COFFEE & SPIRITS

Hudson Valley Brewery:	Big Mouth Coffee Roasters:	Factory at Sloop Brewing:	Denning's Point Distillery:
Lavender, dandelions and sour candy are a few flavors found in these funky ales – arguably Beacon's best.	First-rate third-wave coffee, with art-adorned walls (for sale), ample seating and on-site bean roasting.	Pizza, burgers and arcade games keep hopheads happy at East Fishkill's beer palace.	Tasting room pouring artisanal spirits made from locally sourced grains and fruits. Friday happy hour.

SEEGER'S DIRTY STREAM

Folk singer and activist Pete Seeger (listen to *My Dirty Stream*) built a cabin on a Beacon hillside in 1949, where he observed the steady degradation of the Hudson River below. As sludge from manufacturing plants such as General Electric turned the once-pristine waterway into a toxic sewer, Seeger sailed into action. In the late 1960s, he raised money to build a 106ft sloop and cruised the river, singing his message of preservation all the way to Washington, DC, where he lobbied for the Clean Water Act of 1972. The boat (clearwater.org) still tours the Hudson, while a river swimming pool, floating along Beacon's **Pete and Toshi Seeger Riverfront Park**, accentuates his success.

Look closely at each storefront and you might also spot artwork by the late Earl Swanigan, a local folk artist who painted quirky anthropomorphized animals on found materials and sold them streetside. His work, hanging nearly everywhere, is a lot like Hudson: colorful, scrappy and oozing charm.

Pick Fruit at Fishkill Farms
Organic goods from local grounds

Throughout summer and fall, farms around the Hudson Valley invite visitors to pick their own produce while enjoying the landscape. **Fishkill Farms** (fishkillfarms.com), stretching over 270 acres, is particularly Edenic. It's also one of the Hudson Valley's oldest working apple orchards, founded by the Morgenthau family in 1913. Expect strawberries and snap peas in June, cherries in July and peaches in late August. It's all about apples from mid-September to mid-October, with more than a dozen varieties hanging from trees like precious gems. A weekend **Harvest Festival** features live music and hay rides throughout the season. If you want to pick fruit, book a time slot – reservations usually open a few days in advance, pending crop availability. If picking produce isn't your passion, try the on-site **Cider Bar**, a bud-to-bottle operation where you can sample hard cider flights along with beer, wine and kombucha. Don't leave without perusing the farm's shop, either, with its assortment of artisanal home goods, fresh-baked donuts and homemade pies.

Does Anyone Still Wear a Hat?
Fishkill Creek's former most popular export

Before Fishkill Creek became Beacon's prized recreational ribbon, it was the powerhouse behind the city's most popular export – hats. Matteawan Manufacturing Company started the trend in 1864, shipping out thousands of wool caps to adorn American heads. Tioronda Hat Works followed in 1879, along with nearly 50 more companies, turning Beacon into the nation's second-largest hat producer. Most set up shop along the creek, using its water to clean and dye wool. The Great Depression and cheap imports decimated the industry, with most companies abandoning their brick factories in the 20th century. Some, such as Matteawan, have found new life (it's now the Roundhouse (p118) hotel-restaurant), while Tioronda's ruins recall the hat-making empire's fall in Madam Brett Park (p119).

 EATING IN HUDSON: BEST RESTAURANTS

| **Lil' Deb's Oasis:** Home to Hudson's avant garde, who gobble trendy takes on Mexican food while sipping from goblets of wine. **$$** | **BackBar:** Pack into a picnic table at this relaxed indoor-outdoor hangout for Southeast Asian plates and cocktails. **$$** | **Rivertown Lodge:** Wake up with weekend brunch at this Warren St hotel. Order the ricotta-maple Dutch baby. **$$$** | **Feast & Floret:** Tuscan-inspired farm-to-table fare in a 19th-century townhouse. From food to decor, everything is cozy. **$$$** |

Visit the Homes of Hudson River School Artists
America's first major art movement

Rapid industrialization and westward expansion captured the imaginations of most 19th-century Americans. But painter Thomas Cole (1801–48), an émigré from soot-smothered England, saw power in preservation. His prescient viewpoint became the canvas for America's first significant artistic fraternity – the Hudson River School, coined in the 1870s to classify a group of landscape artists who depicted the country's wild frontier as sublime. The Hudson Valley and Catskills served as Cole's local muses, and paintings of places such as **Kaaterskill Falls** became his artistic form of proto-environmentalism. Visit his art-filled property in Catskill – the **Thomas Cole National Historic Site** (thomascole.org), a 10-minute drive from Hudson. The three-building compound showcases Cole's work inside his Federal-style home, framing distant mountains. Strolling the grounds is free; guided tours cost $20.

After seeing Cole's work, drive across the Rip Van Winkle Bridge to **Olana** (olana.org), a Gothic-Moorish mansion owned by Cole's protégé, Frederic Edwin Church (1826–1900). Church studied with Cole from 1844 to 46 before making a name for himself with romantic landscapes of the Andes Mountains, icebergs and more distant landscapes most New Yorkers would never see in real life. Paintings aside, Church's standout work is this fairy-tale castle (completed in 1872), which he designed in collaboration with Central Park architect Calvert Vaux. Wandering the 250-acre estate, free and open to the public daily from 8am to sunset, is like stepping into one of his oil paintings. More than 5 miles of carriage roads roll from meadows to an artificial lake and on to expansive views of the Hudson River and Catskill Mountains. The home is even more impressive, with exterior brickwork and ceramic tiles nodding to the international curios displayed inside. Tours of the landscape ($12), house interior ($20), or a combo of the two ($40) enhance the experience. Book tickets in advance.

AMERICAN MYTHOLOGY

If you know the supernatural stories *Rip Van Winkle* (the Catskills man who hit a 20-year snooze button) or *The Legend of Sleepy Hollow* (Ichabod Crane's ill-fated meet-up with the Headless Horseman), you know Washington Irving, America's first celebrated wordsmith. Both tales, published in 1819, feature one of his favorite locations – the Hudson Valley – where he bought a stone Dutch house, transforming it with eclectic architectural styles. The property, **Sunnyside**, is tour-worthy, as is the nearby town of Sleepy Hollow, renamed in 1996 to capitalize on his ghoulish account, now sewn into American mythology and celebrated in pop culture. Watch Tim Burton's same-named film around Halloween – it's a spooky-season treat.

DRINKING IN HUDSON: BEER, COFFEE & JUICE

Quinnie's: Equal parts coffee shop, bakery, specialty market, sandwich shop and cocktail bar inside a 1700s farmhouse on six acres.

Suarez Family Brewery: Pilsners, saisons and pale ales – this small-batch mom-and-pop brewery makes some of the state's best low-ABV beers.

Half Moon: One-stop shop for last call (local beer), late-night munchies (pizza) and the occasional concert.

Maker Lounge: Imbibe inside a 19th-century carriage house retooled as a low-lit cocktail parlor within the Maker Hotel.

Woodstock

WOODLAND WONDER | OFFBEAT ART | CHARMING VILLAGES

GETTING AROUND

It's possible to reach Woodstock by **bus** (try Trailways), but a car is necessary when exploring anywhere off Tinker St. Scenic byways throughout the Catskills make driving cinematic, including portions of trips from Woodstock to Hunter, along the Mountain Cloves Scenic Byway, and to Phoenicia, along the Catskill Mountains Scenic Byway. Phone reception is spotty in the Catskills, particularly on back roads. When using smartphone GPS, connect to wifi and input directions before driving off.

✅ TOP TIP

Woodstock is 15 minutes' drive from historic Kingston and an hour from hip Livingston Manor, closer to the Delaware. While driving around, tune into Kaatscast, an inquisitive podcast that dives into Catskill Mountains art, culture and history.

No, not that Woodstock. The 'three days of peace and music' that rocked America's psyche in 1969 copied the name before bringing the concert to Bethel, 60 miles west. Woodstock, which grew around an art colony from 1902, still brims with the free-love ethos that made the festival legendary, though the actual town skews more 'bougie hipster' than 'thrifty hippie.' Wander along Tinker St for a taste – galleries, tchotchke shops and inventive restaurants bring in creative crowds, often dressed in their outdoor best, ready to scale nearby peaks.

Woodstock's creek-crossed downtown sits in the Catskill Mountains – a vast wilderness of rolling plateaus, including 600,000-acre Catskill Park, sculpted by trout-packed streams, cobalt lakes and forests. The Hudson and Delaware Rivers frame the landscape, speckled with sleepy main streets where a cultural renaissance is underway, steadily moving westward across the region with rustic-chic resorts and a formidable art scene that attracts Manhattanites searching for solitude.

Stand in Awe at Kaaterskill Falls
Choose-your-trail waterfall hike

New York's **tallest cascade** – a two-tiered stunner 90ft higher than Niagara Falls (p146) – has inspired artists for centuries. Washington Irving described its 'feathery foam' in *Rip Van Winkle*, and poet William Cullen Bryant evoked its 'palace of ice' in wintertime. In Thomas Cole's paintings, fall leaves frame the shale-and-sandstone amphitheater like stage curtains. Today, 100,000-plus annual visitors attempt to capture the 260ft local icon on camera. Follow their lead: if you only take one hike in the Catskills, this should be it.

Start at the Laurel House Rd parking lot and choose from routes catering to novices and experienced hikers alike. Take the easy 1000yd round-trip trail to the **Falls Viewing Platform** to see

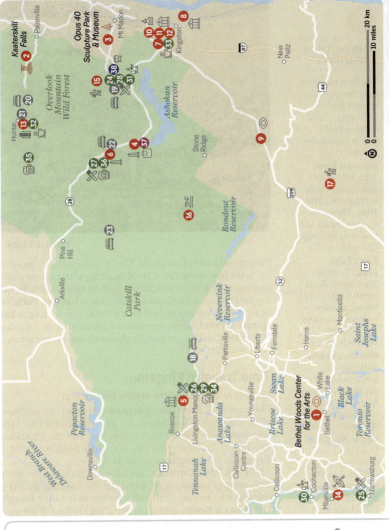

THE GUIDE
NEW YORK STATE WOODSTOCK

TOP SIGHTS
1. Bethel Woods Center for the Arts
2. Kaaterskill Falls
3. Opus 40 Sculpture Park & Museum

SIGHTS
4. Brunel Sculpture Garden
5. Catskill Fly Fishing Center & Museum
6. Emerson Kaleidoscope
7. Four Corners
8. Hudson River Maritime Museum
9. Kelder's Farm
10. Old Dutch Church
11. Senate House State Historic Site
12. Ulster County Courthouse

ACTIVITIES, COURSES & TOURS
13. Hunter Mountain
14. Lander's River Trips
15. Overlook Mountain
16. Peekamoose Blue Hole
17. Sam's Point Area of Minnewaska State Park Preserve

SLEEPING
18. DeBruce
19. Henwood Inn
20. Hotel Lilien
21. Scribner's Catskill Lodge
22. The Pines
23. Urban Cowboy Lodge

EATING
24. Good Night
25. Heron
26. Katskeller
27. Phoenicia Diner
28. Silvia

DRINKING & NIGHTLIFE
29. Catskill Brewery
30. Cochecton Fire Station
31. Early Terrible
32. Fellow Mountain Cafe
33. Rough Draft Bar & Books
34. Upward Brewing Company
35. West Kill Brewing
36. Woodstock Brewing

SHOPPING
37. Fabulous Furniture

TRANSPORT
38. Woodstock Bus Station

123

MORE OUTDOOR ADVENTURES

Overlook Mountain: Pass the charred remains of a 19th-century hotel on this 4.6-mile hike to views above Woodstock.

Delaware River: Tube, raft or kayak down gentle rapids with **Lander's River Trips**, offering multiple launch-and-land sites, including Narrowsburg.

Sam's Point Area: Climb the Shawangunk Ridge on this 7-mile trek to panoramic overlooks, ice caves and 187ft-high Verkeerderkill Falls.

Peekamoose Blue Hole: Cool off during summer's dog days by braving Roundout Creek's icy, Caribbean-blue water ($10 permit required).

Hunter Mountain: Shred slopes from late November to early April on 67 trails spread across 320 acres of skiable (though often icy) terrain.

Kaaterskill Falls

the glorious gusher from above. The 1.4-mile round-trip jaunt to the lower falls will get your blood pumping with its steep staircase (unsuitable in icy conditions). Tack on an extra mile by following the Kaatskills Creek downstream to **Bastion Falls**, or head to the Escarpment Trail for a 4.8-mile loop leading to **Inspiration Point**, where you can see Kaaterskill Clove, a slender cleft in the Catskills sculpted by glaciation and the persistence of Kaaterskill Creek.

Time Travel in Kingston
Historic relics around the state's first capital

The streets of Kingston's **Stockade District**, 15 minutes' drive southeast of Woodstock, are an architectural time capsule from New York's Dutch beginnings and the American Revolution. Amble around the eight-block neighborhood for a snapshot of old-fashioned New York.

Start at **Four Corners**, the only US intersection with 18th-century homes on all four sides, to imagine the city's colonial streetscape. Grab coffee for the walk inside **Rough Draft Bar & Books**, located in one of the old stone buildings. Dutch colonizers first moved to this area in 1658 due to skirmishes with the nearby Indigenous Esopus tribe. The director-general of the New Netherland Colony, Peter Stuyvesant, ordered the establishment of this settlement, surrounded by a 14ft-high stockade fence, for its safety. Bloody fights with

EATING AROUND WOODSTOCK: BEST DINERS & RESTAURANTS

Phoenicia Diner: Greasy-spoon aesthetics and creative Catskills takes on classics, like po'boys with cornmeal-crusted trout. **$$**

Good Night: Slide into a plush velvet banquette for upscale Southeast Asian–inspired plates with plenty of crunch, spice and tang. *hours vary* **$$$**

Silvia: Unpretentious take on farm-to-fine dining. Start with the horseradish-spiced mushroom lentil pâté; finish with a wood-smoked pork chop. **$$$**

The Pines: Like many Catskills hotels, the restaurant is a destination unto itself. Comfort food and occasional live music. **$$**

the Esopus continued, eventually pushing the tribe off their land. Continue west on Crown St, where contemporary street murals juxtapose the old limestone houses, then hook a right on Front St, lined with vintage shops. You'll eventually spot the **Senate House State Historic Site**, where New Yorkers formed a new state government in the summer of 1777, several months before British forces set Kingston ablaze during the Revolutionary War. Join a tour of the house, built between 1676 and the 18th century, from mid-April through October.

Next, follow Fair St to the **Old Dutch Church**, founded in 1659 and constructed in 1852. A plaque outside commemorates George Washington's 1782 visit, a year before the US won sovereignty from Great Britain. Nearby on Wall St is the **Ulster County Courthouse**, where, in 1818, abolitionist Sojourner Truth sued and won her son's freedom from slavery in Alabama.

For more tales of yesteryear, drive 10 minutes to the **Hudson River Maritime Museum**. The exhibits, including an impressive flotilla of mini-boat models, present an exhaustive history of all things Hudson River–related. From May to October, visitors can sign up for solar-powered boat tours that motor around the Hudson River to a 1915 lighthouse ($35).

Stop by Kooky Roadside Attractions

Americana kitsch and artsy inventions

Whoever said 'everything's bigger in Texas' didn't drive around the Catskills. A 4-mile stretch of Route 28 features oversized roadside attractions worth pumping the brakes to see. First up is the world's largest kaleidoscope (the **Emerson Kaleidoscope**) in Mt Tremper. Pay $5 to enter a 60ft-tall grain silo from the 19th century, lean against the sloping boards and gaze towards the cosmos. The 10-minute psychedelic light show is out of this world. Don't miss the connected shop's trippy collection of handheld prismatic pieces.

Next, drive south to **Brunel Sculpture Garden**, where French artist Emile Brunel constructed concrete totem poles and sculptures between 1929 and 1941. Current property owners Cynthia and Evgyney Nikitin act as stewards for the art, which is all dedicated to Indigenous culture – some weigh 20 tons. Finally, there's Steve Heller's **Fabulous Furniture**, a gallery and sculpture garden with an extraterrestrial edge. Walk around his lawn, packed with enormous metal-welded aliens, oil-can elephants, golf-iron monsters and more Frankensteined junkyard inventions. Still not impressed? **Kelder's Farm**, a 30-minute drive away, is home to 'Gnome Chomsky',

REMEMBER THE BORSCHT BELT

Early 20th-century summers in NYC were synonymous with sweltering sidewalks and stuffy tenements. For Jewish immigrants on the Lower East Side, the Catskills became an escape hatch. Over the coming decades, roughly 1000 bungalow colonies, camps and hotels sprang up to cater to the community, including sprawling resorts where up-and-coming comedians (Joan Rivers and Sid Caesar among them) cut their teeth in front of cultured crowds. In the 1970s, changes in travel (airplanes, anti-discrimination laws, air conditioning) put the kibosh on the Catskills, and by the early 21st century, all the resorts were shuttered. Watch *Dirty Dancing* to remember when the Catskills were colloquially known as the 'Borscht Belt.'

 DRINKING AROUND WOODSTOCK: OUR PICKS

Early Terrible: This cocktail lounge makes farmhouse decor sexy. A yard connects to Mud Club (bagels, pizza), with fire pits aglow.	**West Kill Brewing:** Sip beer made with locally grown and foraged ingredients on a historic 127-acre farm. Cinematic scenery.	**Fellow Mountain Cafe:** Victorian farmhouse with a wraparound porch serving coffee and pastries near Hunter Mountain.	**Woodstock Brewing:** Bare-bones interior, so the important things shine – craft IPAs and sours – at this Phoenicia brewery.

WHERE THE WILD THINGS ARE

They often appear around dawn or dusk. White-tailed deer dash roadside – and whenever you see one, expect five more nearby. Bald eagles soar above the Delaware River with turkey vultures – their red heads and jagged wings a common sight while cruising country highways. Squirrels and chipmunks scurry among woodlands, accompanied by the occasional porcupine, which considers the bark of hemlock trees a delicacy. Chevron-skinned timber rattlesnakes (New York's largest venomous serpent) sometimes sun on rocks along rugged hiking trails, and snapping turtles (the official state reptile) enjoy fishing along quiet creeks and marshes. Roughly 1800 black bears call the Catskills home but, similar to the region's bobcats and coyotes, they're elusive – encounters are unlikely.

MORE WONDERFUL WATERFALLS

If you love chasing waterfalls, head to Ithaca, a Finger Lakes city graced with more than 100 gushing cataracts, including the East Coast's tallest single-drop waterfall, **Taughannock Falls** (p136).

the world's third-largest gnome, standing 13.5ft tall. Between spring and fall, the farm invites guests to pick produce (come for apples and pumpkins in fall), all under the watchful eye of the jolly-faced giant.

Sing the Praises of Opus 40

America's Stonehenge

Quarrying bluestone was a profitable enterprise in the 19th-century Catskills. Cities from Albany to NYC used the durable, slate-blue sandstone for sidewalks until the 20th century, when cement took over. Many quarrying companies folded as a result, leaving square-cut scars across the landscape. Self-taught sculptor Harvey Fite turned some of those scars into the Catskills' most captivating artwork. After purchasing property surrounded by abandoned quarries, Fite started a 37-year project: **Opus 40** (1939–76), a whimsical 6.5-acre handcrafted earthwork, visible on his property-turned-sculpture-park from late March through late December. Fite adapted Mayan stone-working techniques to create his serpentine structure – an open-air monument to Indigenous design and the majestic Catskill Mountains.

EATING & DRINKING IN THE WESTERN CATSKILLS: OUR PICKS

Heron: Nearby farms provide most ingredients at this Narrowsburg spot for southern-inspired American fare. Sublime outdoor-terrace views. $$

Cochecton Fire Station: Former pyro police pad turned contemporary cocktail joint with wood-fired pub grub.

Katskeller: Sit at outdoor picnic tables to savor Neapolitan pizza and sides in Livingston Manor. Try the brook trout rillettes, a local creek delicacy. $$

Catskill Brewery: This Livingston Manor hang is famous for the pinewood finish of its Devil's Path IPA.

Woodstock concert grounds

Feel Woodstock's Beat in Bethel
Rock legends and live concerts

In the summer of 1969, America was at war. Nixon commanded the Oval Office, LGBTIQ+ patrons revolted against police brutality at Stonewall and soldiers lost their lives in Vietnam. But on Max Yasgur's dairy farm, nearly half a million people found peace – unless they tripped on the bad acid supposedly going around. This was the Woodstock Music and Art Fair, a three-day hippie happening that took the sleepy town of Bethel by surprise. Rock legends including Janis Joplin, the Grateful Dead and Santana electrified crowds. Jimi Hendrix riled audiences with a rousing rendition of *The Star Spangled Banner*, turning the national anthem into a guitar hero's protest.

Though the crowds have long gone – save a few white-haired hippies who never left – the spirit lingers. Yasgur's farm is now **Bethel Woods Center for the Arts** (p107; bethelwoodscenter.org), where you can revive Woodstock's memory at outdoor summer concerts. There's also a seasonal museum (April–December) bursting with music and images from Woodstock. For the full summer of '69 experience, consider booking a campsite during one of the shows. (Unlike Woodstock, where visitors camped for free on mud-slick farmland, this sanitized and markedly grassier version starts at $172 a night.) There's also a weekend harvest festival throughout September and October, with plenty of artisans, food trucks and live music on display.

If you can't attend a summer concert, drive by to pay your respects. While lingering before the coffin-shaped monument near the field where history sang, commiserate with Joni Mitchell by listening to her wail 'Woodstock'. She missed the cultural capstone, too.

TROUT TOWN, USA

When spring blossoms erupt around the Catskills, fly-fishers pull out their poles to catch trout. Fly-fishing is a local tradition dating back to the 1890s, thanks to Theodore Gordon – 'Father of American Dry Fly Fishing' – who revolutionized the sport with new techniques (dubbed 'Catskill style') in rivers and creeks around Roscoe and Livingston Manor. Today, both towns wear their fishy history with pride. Roscoe calls itself 'Trout Town, USA,' and Livingston Manor celebrates local legends at the **Catskill Fly Fishing Center and Museum**. Things get extra fishy in June, when Livingston Manor dons its best river drag for the wacky and wonderful **Trout Parade**, led by marching bands and giant trout puppets.

TOUR THE WESTERN CATSKILLS' CUTEST TOWNS

The Catskills' recent revival as 'hickster' haven is most apparent in small towns near the Delaware River, where birch trees and bald eagles give way to walkable main streets peppered with boutiques and breweries. Driving between destinations, you follow a portion of the Upper Delaware Scenic Byway (Route 97) as it snakes along Pennsylvania's border. The trip takes 45 minutes without stopping, but plan a whole day to enjoy each town's offerings. Begin on Main St in ❶ **Narrowsburg**, perched on a bluff above the Delaware. Breakfast sandwiches from Tusten Cup fuel some light shopping: there's River Gallery (landscape paintings), Narrowsburg Proper (market snacks) and One Grand Books (lit hand-picked by famous creatives). In summer, swimmers jump into the river from rocks below the sea-green Narrowsburg–Darbytown Bridge. For a gentler swim, head to Skinners Falls, 10 minutes north, where giant boulders create serene river pools. Next is ❷ **Callicoon**, derived from the Dutch 'Kollikoonkill,' meaning 'Wild Turkey Creek' – still fitting for a town resembling the set for a cowboy flick. Sample whiskey at distiller Catskill Provisions and peek inside Farmhouse Project, an artisan shop and cocktail parlor exuding Victorian elegance. The town seems to quadruple in population for Sunday's farmers' market (11am to 2pm), where local vendors hock honey, jam, baked goods, pottery and piles of organic fruit and vegetables. ❸ **Livingston Manor**, unfurling along Willowemoc Creek, is the liveliest town of the bunch. Walk Main St to peruse shops and grab food (eye Homstedt's cabin-core collection; gobble biscuits from the Walk In), then drive to ❹ **Upward Brewing Company** to sip craft beer on its 120 acres, complete with ski-mountain-inspired chalet. Cap off the day by hiking to the property's peak, aptly named Beer Mountain.

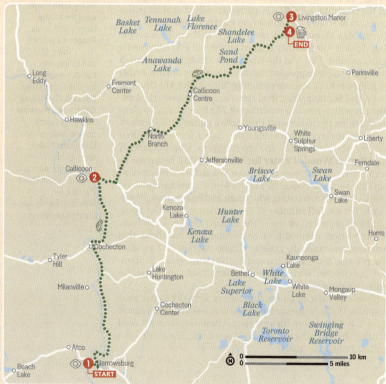

Lake George

UNTAMED MOUNTAINSCAPES | OUTDOOR SPORTS | AMERICANA

Crowned by pine-packed peaks and bejeweled with over 170 islands, Lake George, dubbed the 'Queen of American Lakes,' is royal indeed. Humans have spent centuries admiring the 32-mile-long, spring-fed stunner. The Indigenous Haudenosaunee (or Iroquois Confederacy) and Mohicans came first and called it 'Andia-ta-roc-te' (lake that shuts itself in); they were followed by the French, who were pushed out by the British, who renamed it after King George II in 1755. Gilded Age travelers built grand cabins here throughout the 19th century, and these days, armies of summertime tourists descend upon the lake between Memorial and Labor Days.

Along the queen's southern shores sits the village of Lake George – a seasonal pitstop for retro putt-putt courses and chintzy gift shops. It's also the gateway to Adirondack Park – a six-million-acre preserve dotted with 3,000 lakes and ponds, 30,000 miles of rivers and streams, and 46 mountains stretching over 4,000ft high. Go wild.

Climb Every Mountain

Hike or drive to viewpoints

Over 2000 miles of hiking trails weave their way through the Adirondacks, with options for all levels of outdoor enthusiasm.

Experienced hikers in the Lake George area will appreciate the 6.5-mile out-and-back route to Buck Mountain (p107), which shoots 2000ft above Lake George's eastern banks. Crawl across granite slopes knotted with tree roots, littered with boulders and cut by gentle creeks to a spectacular view of the island-dotted lake below. Bonus points if you can spot the Sagamore Resort, a historic horseshoe-shaped hotel on the edge of Green Island.

Novice nature lovers can take in more lake views from **Up Yonda Farm** ($5 parking fee), a family-friendly environmental education center with well-marked trails and informative signposts, plus a dedicated birding corner and summertime butterfly exhibit.

Continued on page 132

GETTING AROUND

To reach the Lake George region, take an Amtrak train to Fort Edward (30 miles south), fly into Albany International Airport (50 miles south) or **bus** in on Adirondack Trailways or Greyhound. In summer, red trolleys run by the Greater Glens Falls Transit System usher visitors around the village of Lake George, Bolton Landing (10 miles north) and Glens Falls (10 miles south), but if you want to explore Adirondack Park's greatest offerings, it's necessary to have a car. Cell service is spotty – download directions before hitting the highway.

☑ TOP TIP

Explore scenic lakes and villages north of Lake George. Schroon Lake and its tiny main drag are quiet Lake George alternatives, Keene is peppered with cute shops and hiking trails, and Lake Placid's historic Winter Olympic village is a doorway to outdoor adventures suitable in any season.

LAKE GEORGE NEW YORK STATE

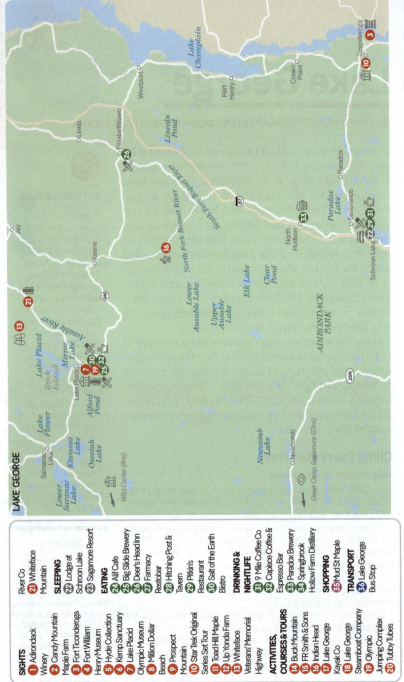

SIGHTS
1. Adirondack Winery
2. Candy Mountain Maple Farm
3. Fort Ticonderoga
4. Fort William Henry Museum
5. Hyde Collection
6. Kemp Sanctuary
7. Lake Placid
8. Million Dollar Beach
9. Prospect Mountain
10. Star Trek Original Series Set Tour
11. Toad Hill Maple
12. Up Yonda Farm
13. Whiteface Veterans' Memorial Highway
21. Whiteface Mountain

ACTIVITIES, COURSES & TOURS
14. Buck Mountain
15. FR Smith & Sons
16. Indian Head
17. Lake George Kayak Co
18. Lake George Steamboat Company
19. Olympic Jumping Complex
20. Tubby Tubes River Co

SLEEPING
22. Lodge at Schroon Lake
23. Sagamore Resort

EATING
24. Alif Cafe
25. Big Slide Brewery
26. Deer's Head Inn
27. Farmacy Restobar
28. Hitching Post & Tavern
29. Piton's Restaurant
30. Salt of the Earth Bistro

DRINKING & NIGHTLIFE
31. 9 Mile Coffee Co
32. Capisce Coffee & Espresso Bar
33. Paradox Brewery
34. Springbrook Hollow Farm Distillery

SHOPPING
35. Mud St Maple

TRANSPORT
36. Lake George Bus Stop

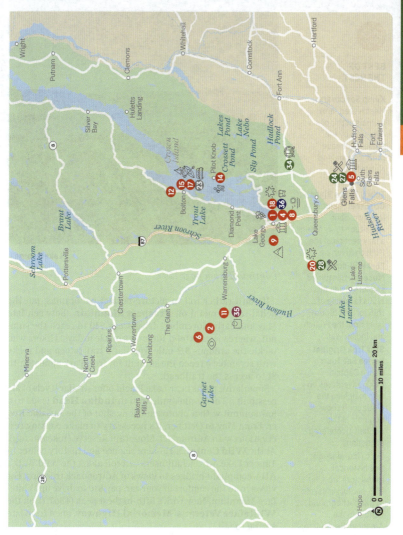

BEST OF THE REST

Kemp Sanctuary: Meet retired farm animals at this oasis overseen by the artisanal cheese producers behind Nettle Meadow Farms.

Tubby Tubes River Co: Expert guides lead two-hour inner-tube tours along a lazy section of the Hudson River.

Fort William Henry Museum: Costumed soldiers inside this 1950s facsimile of a 1755 fort tell bloody tales from the French and Indian War.

Star Trek Original Series Set Tour: Relive Captain Kirk's adventures on sets matching the 1960s sci-fi show originals at this oddball Ticonderoga attraction.

Fort Ticonderoga: See historical reenactors fire 18th-century muskets at this battleground central to the American Revolution.

Lake George

Continued from page 129

If you'd rather roll to picture-perfect panoramas, put the pedal to the metal on **Prospect Mountain**. Between late May and early November, drivers pay $10 to reach the summit, where views extend 100 miles on clear days. Hikers who tackle the arduous 3.2-mile woodland trail (steep and rocky with scrambles) reach the summit for free. Park along Smith St to access the trailhead.

Superlative paths near Lake Placid offer similar levels of accessibility. The 10-plus-mile trail to **Indian Head** leads to a low summit with a photogenic long shot of the Ausable River. From May to October, it's necessary to make parking reservations with Adirondack Mountain Reserve (hikeamr.org). At the **Wild Center**, a 115-acre science and history center in Tupper Lake, wheelchair users can roll along the Wild Walk's ADA-compliant bridges to views of Adirondack treetops. For views from the comfort of your car, pay $10 to drive up Whiteface Mountain, New York's fifth-highest peak (4867ft), on the **Whiteface Veterans' Memorial Highway**, open from late spring to fall.

Be prepared to contend with ice and snow while hiking outside of summer. Most trails require crampons or snowshoes in winter.

EATING AROUND LAKE GEORGE: BEST RESTAURANTS

Farmacy Restobar: Snag a chef's-table seat to watch food chemists prepare small, flavor-packed plates in Glens Falls. $$$

Hitching Post & Tavern: It's all about cheese at this restaurant and market run by Nettle Meadow Farms, a purveyor of fantastic goat *fromage*. $$

Alif Cafe: Muhammad Saud's all-day Glens Falls cafe serves South Asian–inspired street food – butter chicken, samosa *chaat*, cardamom coffee. $

Pitkin's Restaurant: A Schroon Lake staple since 1907 with all the feel-good, no-frills greasy-spoon goodies you can handle. $

Swim, Kayak & Cruise
A day on Lake George

While touring the Adirondacks in 1791, Thomas Jefferson wrote, 'Lake George is without comparison, the most beautiful water I ever saw.' Spend a few hours floating around the lake and it's hard to disagree. In summer, join families on the 51-acre **Million Dollar Beach** ($10 parking) and wade into crystal-clear waters under the protective eye of a lifeguard. Water tends to reach 70°F to 75°F, with peak temperatures around late July and August.

If you'd rather explore the lake's wild shores without crowds, rent a kayak, canoe or stand-up paddleboard from **Lake George Kayak Co** (p107) ($30/70 per hour/half-day). There are tons of boat-rental companies around the lake, too, though not all are reputable and costs can be prohibitive. At **FR Smith & Sons** in Bolton Landing, a full-day affair on a four-person boat costs $467 – a price worth the pleasure of speeding off to a private cove. For a uniquely Lake George experience, see the sights from one of **Lake George Steamboat Company's** historic cruise vessels, docked along the lake's south side. The most adorable of the bunch is *Minnie-Ha-Ha*, one of America's last steam paddle-wheel ships, which toot-toots along the lake during an informative, family-friendly, one-hour tour (adult $24, May–October). A calliope – the boat's 32-whistle steam organ – belts classic tunes between journeys from the top deck.

Satisfy Your Sweet Tooth in Thurman
Maple-flavored fun

Adirondacks farmers tap into an Indigenous tradition between February and April, transforming sugar maple tree sap into syrup. Roughly 2000 sugar makers across the state practice the ancient alchemy, producing more than 800,000 gallons of the liquid gold annually – the second-largest US producer next to Vermont. To sop up exceptional sweet stuff, head to Thurman, a rural town self-dubbed the 'Maple Capital of Warren County.' Throughout March, farmers gear up for **Thurman Maple Days**, leading tours of 'sugar bushes' (groups of trees tapped for sap) and 'sugar shacks' (tiny cabins where the sap-to-syrup magic happens). Farms remain open to visitors year-round, selling products to satisfy any sweet tooth: maple-infused creams, candies, nuts, teas, coffees, BBQ sauce and a seemingly endless syrup supply. The most impressive operation is **Toad Hill Maple** *(518-623-4744)*, run by husband-and-wife team Randy and Jill Galusha. Step in-

ISLAND CAMPING

Lakeside campfires, yodeling loons, blinking fireflies and no outlets to recharge your phone – roughing it isn't for everyone, but for those who don't mind scurrying to an outhouse when nature calls, camping on one of the islands dotting Lake George, Saranac Lake and Indian Lake can be a serene, inexpensive way to experience the Adirondack Park's wild side ($33 a night and under). Snatching the perfect campsite gets competitive: bookings (reserveamerica.com) open nine months before reservation dates, and popular spots disappear within seconds, especially around Lake George. After snagging a spot, secure your mode of transport. Reaching these private slices of paradise requires a motorboat or canoe, available for rent on all three lakes.

DRINKING AROUND LAKE GEORGE: OUR PICKS

| **Paradox Brewery:** Sample craft beer made with pristine water from Adirondack Park's granite bedrock. | **Springbrook Hollow Farm Distillery:** Order flights with something sweet (limoncello), energizing (coffee-infused vodka) and smoky (bourbon). | **Adirondack Winery:** Swirl rieslings, fruit-infused wines and ciders at this vintner's Lake George tasting room. | **9 Mile Coffee Co:** Coffee at this Schroon Lake java joint is just a vehicle for washing down cinnamon rolls. |

ADIRONDACK ARCHITECTURE

Timber-frame homes, stone chimneys and bark-covered banisters with decorative twigs... step inside enough Adirondacks establishments and you'll eventually see a theme emerge – even in architecture, nature is the main character. This classic style – a hodgepodge of Swiss chalet and American Craftsman, often dressed with taxidermy – traces its roots to William West Durant. Durant elevated the common cabin to Gilded Age glamor in the 1870s, after designing the rustically resplendent Camp Pine Knot (now Camp Huntington). The luxury lakefront estates that followed became known as Great Camps. For more insight into these 19th-century summer escapes, sign up for a tour of **Great Camp Sagamore** (sagamore.org), built for the Vanderbilt family in 1897.

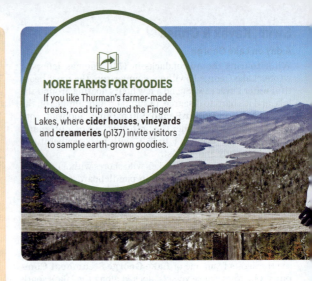

MORE FARMS FOR FOODIES
If you like Thurman's farmer-made treats, road trip around the Finger Lakes, where **cider houses**, **vineyards** and **creameries** (p137) invite visitors to sample earth-grown goodies.

side their white-pine production facility to see the stainless-steel evaporator, responsible for turning watery sap into thick maple syrup; call ahead for an informal tour. Make it a road trip by stopping at nearby **Candy Mountain Maple Farm** and **Mud St Maple** (bring cash – owners here use the honor system to purchase products, sold inside a wooden shack). Download a map of local farms at visitthurman.com.

Eye the Hyde Art Collection

6000 years of art, one jewel-box collection

Charlotte and Louis Hyde had seriously good taste – just step inside the **Hyde Collection**, their 1912 Renaissance Revival home in Glens Falls, for proof. Over a roughly 50-year period until Charlotte's death in 1963, the house became a gallery for some of the best American and European artists around. There's a Rembrandt casually hanging in the wood-paneled library and a Picasso in Charlotte's understated bedroom. Renoir, Rubens, Seurat, Degas, Botticelli and Cézanne surprise around every corner. Even the furniture deserves mention, spanning five centuries. (The Hydes were apparently coocoo for 18th-century rococo.) It's connected to a modern museum that shares the growing collection's newer acquisitions, with New York notables such as Haring and Hopper included.

 EATING & DRINKING AROUND LAKE PLACID: OUR PICKS

Salt of the Earth Bistro: Step inside a cozy century-old home for seasonal meats and veggies along with local beer, wine and cider. **$$$**

Capisce Coffee & Espresso Bar: Strong brews, sandwiches and a small selection of local art and vintage clothes.

Deer's Head Inn: The Adirondacks' oldest tavern (1808) serves classics utilizing local ingredients, modernized with international zest. **$$$**

Big Slide Brewery: Sip brews while admiring beer-filled fermentation tanks. Try the pale ale, whispered with hot pepper spice.

Lake Placid

Go for Gold in Lake Placid
Olympic history in the Adirondacks

Lake Placid, two-time host of the Winter Olympics, doesn't need snow to celebrate seasonal sports – the alpine village wears its athletic heritage like a badge of honor year-round. Spend a day following in the ski tracks of global champions at sites in and around town. Start at the **Lake Placid Olympic Museum**, a small-but-mighty look at the 1932 and 1980 Games. The museum holds a little something for everyone: plenty of history, graphic and fashion designs from Olympics past and a riveting video chronicling one of the most legendary Olympic upsets – the underdog US ice-hockey team's 1980 victory over the Soviet Union. There's also an interactive section where visitors can hop into a bobsled for a virtual thrill ride. Adrenaline junkies who prefer a real-life rush should soar to the **Olympic Jumping Complex**, where ski jumpers zoom down steep ramps before taking flight. Take a similar (and safer) journey on the high-speed **Sky Flyer Zipline** ($45). Your final stop is **Whiteface Mountain**, where Olympic slalom stars raced for gold in 1980. Between the end of November and mid-April, visitors can purchase a day pass ($105) and rent equipment ($71) to test their skills on the East Coast's biggest vertical drop (3430ft). Ski shy? Take the 15-minute **Cloudsplitter** gondola ride to the top of Little White Face ($25, open year-round), gliding above the ski trails to a majestic view of Lake Placid and nearby Lake Champlain.

MEMORIES OF THE MOHICANS

Heather Bruegl, Indigenous historian and first-line descendant of the Adirondacks' original Stockbridge-Munsee (or Mohican) inhabitants, shares her thoughts on Indigenous narratives prevalent throughout the region. @heathermbruegl

There's a lot of romanticized Indigenous history around Lake George, particularly around James Fenimore Cooper's *The Last of the Mohicans*.

The 19th-century novel's title implies we all died off, an idea perpetuated throughout history, along with Indigenous imagery and inspired objects around Lake George that often lack context. There were shady land deals and land was forcibly taken, but we didn't disappear. We were moved to different areas of what is now called the USA and our traditions continued. But the land still remembers who we are – and we still remember the land.

Ithaca

WATERFALLS | WINE | FARM-FRAMED LAKES

GETTING AROUND

To get to Ithaca, take a bus (Coach USA or Greyhound) to **downtown** or fly (Delta or United Airlines) from NYC to **Ithaca Tompkins International Airport**. Upon arrival, a car is the key to exploration. Driving around Cayuga Lake takes roughly two hours without stopping – an easy day trip passing through Trumansburg, **Taughannock Falls State Park**, Seneca Falls, Aurora and dozens of vineyards. Watkins Glen and its namesake state park are 30 minutes' drive west. Corning and its must-see museums are 50 minutes south. Driving here is delightful, with rural roads rolling around lakes, farms and forests.

Look at a map of Central New York and you'll see 11 spindly bodies of water splayed out like a mythical giant's hands. These are the glacier-gouged Finger Lakes, adorned with bucolic farmsteads and tiny towns. At the bottom of 39-mile-long Cayuga Lake, the hand's longest appendage, sits hippie-dippie Ithaca, bookended by Cornell University and Ithaca College. The city's academic underpinnings make it a magnet for free-spirit thinkers and wizened hippies who dine and drink around the Commons, Ithaca's pedestrian strip below Cornell's campus.

The city's ubiquitous green-and-white tourism slogan since the 1970s, 'Ithaca is Gorges,' plays on the region's abundance of geological showstoppers: narrow canyons carved by creeks and lashed by some of the East Coast's most magnificent waterfalls. Drive between these sites to find their supporting players – cider houses, creameries and vineyards supporting a root-to-restaurant food scene, plus novel museums and historic villages, all pretty as a postcard.

Gawk at Waterfalls
Trails to powerful plunges

More than 150 waterfalls grace gorges in a 10-mile radius around Ithaca, with more gushers dazzling further afield. The most wow-worthy of the bunch is **Taughannock Falls**, the East Coast's tallest single-drop waterfall, shooting 215ft into a canyon of gun-metal-gray shale. Follow the well-groomed and largely flat 1.8-mile out-and-back Gorge Trail to feel its power from below, then drive to the Taughannock Park Rd viewing platform to appreciate the landscape from above.

For spectacular gorge trails, **Watkins Glen State Park** sets the gold standard. This 3-mile out-and-back trail climbs 832 stone steps to 19 cascades that appear plucked from the pages of a Tolkien tale. Closer to Ithaca, there's **Robert H Treman State Park**, which has a dozen cascades on its 4.5-mile Gorge and Rim Trail loop. **Buttermilk Falls State Park** packs 10

Watkins Glen State Park

> ☑ **TOP TIP**
>
> Get a taste of local flare at the **Ithaca Farmers Market** every Saturday and Sunday morning (hours vary seasonally). Between April and December, nearly everyone in the city seems to gather under twinkling fairy lights inside the bazaar's open-air pavilion to sample artisanal products while noshing on breakfast food.

waterfalls into a similar 1.6-mile loop. Both showcase natural swimming holes at the base of frothy cataracts – perfect for a refreshing post-hike dip in summer.

In downtown Ithaca, you can drive by **Ithaca Falls**, a 150ft-tall, 175ft-wide powerhouse visible from Lake St and popular with fly-fishers, or hike through **Cascadilla Gorge**, passing six feathery falls on a 1.2-mile round-trip path linked to Cornell.

The strength of each waterfall depends on the season. Winter's icescapes melt into muscular spring streams, and summer's green-framed falls become leaf-littered trickles by fall. To hike all the gorge trails, visit between late May and October. Taughannock Falls remains open year-round, but many paths close between winter and spring.

Cuddle with Cows

Farm adventures for all ages

Live out your 4-H fantasies at **Sunset View Creamery** (sunsetviewcreamery.com), an artisanal cheese farm spread across 348 acres, 10 minutes' drive south of Watkins Glen. Sheep dogs, insistent on playing catch, guide visitors on free DIY property tours, while farmers lead one-hour milking lessons ($99). The beautiful bovines are exceptionally friendly, and guests moved to make their acquaintance can sign up for 30 minutes of 'cow cuddling' ($15) – a spooning session with three to four gentle calves inside a hay-covered pen (wear farm-ready footwear). They're basically big puppies: curious, snuggly, obsessed with chin scratches and known for giving tongue baths. Once you've hugged your fair share of farm animals, head to the on-site shop to sample farm-fresh cheese and learn about the cheese-making process from staff members. Book spots in advance; up to six guests can join the petting party at a time.

ITHACA

TOP SIGHTS
1. Taughannock Falls State Park
2. Watkins Glen State Park

SIGHTS
3. Buttermilk Falls State Park
4. Cascadilla Gorge
5. Corning Museum of Glass
6. Dr Konstantin Frank Winery
7. Forge Cellars
8. Heart & Hands Wine Co
9. Ithaca Falls
10. Lakewood Vineyards
11. Robert H Treman State Park
12. Rockwell Museum of Western Art
13. Six Eighty Cellars
14. Sunset View Creamery
15. Women's Rights National Historical Park

ACTIVITIES, COURSES & TOURS
16. Keuka Lake Outlet Trail

SLEEPING
17. Firelight Camps
18. Inns of Aurora

EATING
- see 18 Aurora Cooks
19. Cayuga Lake Creamery
20. Creekside Cafe
21. Graft Wine + Cider Bar
- see 20 Hazelnut Kitchen
22. Moosewood
23. Rook
24. Skaneateles Bakery

DRINKING & NIGHTLIFE
25. Bar Argos

26. Finger Lakes Cider House
- see 20 Gimme Coffee!
27. Ithaca Beer Co
28. Personal Best Brewing
29. Press Cafe

SHOPPING
30. Ithaca Farmers Market

TRANSPORT
31. Ithaca Bus Station
32. Ithaca Tompkins International Airport

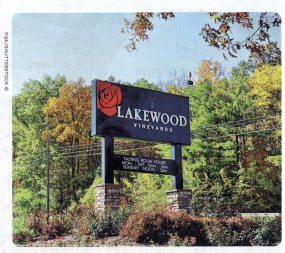

Lakewood Vineyards

Unwind at Verdant Vineyards
Tour top wineries

Drive the pastoral perimeter of Cayuga and Seneca Lakes, decorated with neat rows of grape vines. Nearly 150 winemakers call the Finger Lakes home – a tradition that flowered in the 1960s when Ukrainian refugee Dr Konstantin Frank successfully planted vinifera grapes near Keuka Lake. While the region is best known for German-style rieslings, plucky vintners have recently shown potential for cultivating reds such as cabernet franc and pinot noir. Quality here varies drastically, so instead of hopping on one of the area's touted wine trails for an improvised tour, choose your stops judiciously. **Six Eighty Cellars** (p134) is Cayuga Lake's west-coast-cool kid, with knowledgeable staff espousing the virtues of bubbly pét nats and smoky chardonnays. Tastings come with a charcuterie board, which you can enjoy in the light-filled, whitewashed tasting room or in an outdoor Adirondack chair overlooking Cayuga Lake. At **Forge Cellars**, located on a steep hill with heavenly Seneca Lake views, it's all about the local terroir. Sample rieslings that differ in only one way – the site upon which the grapes were grown. A map of local growing sites accompanies flights. **Lakewood Vineyards** is best for budgets, with $5 flights – choose between samples of sweet or dry wines. Don't sleep on **Heart & Hands Wine Co**

GORGEOUS GORGES

Josh Teeter, New York State Parks environmental educator in the Finger Lakes, explains why 'Ithaca is Gorges.' @nystateparks

So many creeks flow into Ithaca, and over thousands of years all the gorges they carved and all the stone that came out of them filled in the southern end of Cayuga Lake. So the city of Ithaca is literally built on gorges. One of my favorites is at Robert H Treman State Park. The most spectacular part, **Lucifer Falls**, is a newer gorge that's 10,000 to-12,000 years old. Right after the falls, you see the gorge open way up – a section that formed around 100,000 years ago. The swimming area is also beautiful – there's a diving board next to a 40ft waterfall.

 EATING AROUND ITHACA: BEST RESTAURANTS

Moosewood: America's longest-running vegetarian restaurant planted seeds for a farm-to-table revolution in 1973 and remains top tier. **$$**

Rook: Sizzling kitchen pans and soft indie jams serve as the soundtrack at this cozy nook for contemporary twists on comfort classics. **$$**

Hazelnut Kitchen: Regional ingredients get dressed to impress, but this dining room in Trumansburg remains casual and quaint. **$$$**

Aurora Cooks: Join adventurous eaters behind the chef's counter for a four-course meal paired with local wine and beer. **$$$**

CELEBRATE REVOLUTIONARY WOMEN

In 1848, the US government denied women the right to vote, own property, attend college or work anything but low-status, underpaid jobs. Cady Elizabeth Stanton, along with a cohort of confidants, decided to do something about it. On July 19 and 20, they gathered more than 300 people inside Seneca Falls' Wesleyan Methodist Chapel for the First Women's Rights Convention, birthing a gender-equality movement that continues evolving today. The women of Seneca Falls owe this vision of an egalitarian future to their Indigenous Haudenosaunee neighbors, who modeled girl power with a long lineage of power-wielding matriarchs. Visit the **Women's Rights National Historical Park** in Seneca Falls (one hour from Ithaca) to honor the mothers of modern feminism.

MORE GREAT GORGES

Drive two hours west of Ithaca to **Letchworth State Park**, with its breathtaking canyon and collection of waterfalls. Further west is **Niagara Falls** (p146), flowing into the glorious gorge between New York and Canada.

(pinot noir) and **Dr Konstantin Frank Winery** (riesling), either. Need a chauffeur to usher you between vineyards? Hire a ride through **Main St Drivers** (mainstreetdrivers.com; $48 per hour, four-hour minimum).

See Corning's Spectacular Museums

Glass blowing and America's Wild West

You'll never look at a chandelier the same way after visiting Corning, 50 minutes' drive southwest of Ithaca. As America developed a taste for luxury glass in the late 19th and early 20th century, Corning became the epicenter of production. Business really lit up around 1879, when inventor Thomas Edison commissioned Corning Glass Works to create an encasement for a carbonized cotton thread filament, giving

DRINKING AROUND ITHACA: OUR PICKS

| **Finger Lakes Cider House:** Swill ciders on a hillside farm with expansive views, or take a tour to learn about bud-to-bottle production. | **Personal Best Brewing:** Come to this industrial, brewhouse for hop-forward suds; stay for the full-sized shuffleboard courts and board games. | **Ithaca Beer Co:** Flower Power IPAs grace taps in 15 states, but you'll only find kegs of its experimental ales here. | **Bar Argos:** While Cornell's party crowds down shots around the Commons, sophisticated sippers head to Argos Inn's Victorian-style lobby. |

Corning Museum of Glass

birth to the lightbulb. In the coming years, Corning became known as Crystal City. Spend half a day seeing the city's edifying museums.

The **Corning Museum of Glass** celebrates 35 centuries of glass making, showcasing everything from ancient Egyptian decorative arts to swirling contemporary creations by Dale Chihuly. Live demonstrations with glass blowers are especially captivating, with artists discussing the act of creation while working over open flames.

Unrelated, but also impressive, is Corning's **Rockwell Museum of Western Art**, a few minutes away by car. The three-floor collection romanticizes the American West with a small-but-mighty collection of paintings and objects. The best works – Indigenous artifacts and majestic landscapes by the likes of Albert Bierstadt – await on the top floor.

VILLAGES WORTH VISITING

Trumansburg: Skip down creek-crossed Main St for delicious dining options 12 miles north of Ithaca.

Aurora: Century-old mansions line a manicured 2-mile strip along Cayuga Lake. Grab a walking tour brochure from Inns of Aurora (378 Main St).

Watkins Glen: Seneca Lake's southern tip is graced with this village's pretty eponymous park. Make a post-hike reservation at **Graft Wine + Cider Bar**.

Skaneateles: Grab a whoopie pie from **Skaneateles Bakery** while roaming this picturesque town on Skaneateles Lake's northern shores.

Penn Yan: Watch for horse-drawn buggies driven by the Amish en route to the scenic **Keuka Lake Outlet Trail**.

EATING & DRINKING AROUND ITHACA: BREAKFAST, COFFEE & SWEETS

Press Cafe: Ithaca's coffee-fueled undergraduate digerati clack away on keyboards inside this two-room cafe showcasing local art.

Creekside Cafe: Snug, low-key operation for breakfast sandwiches and sweets, located at the heart of Trumansburg's Main St.

Gimme Coffee!: Sip *cortados* on the patio of this hip worker-owned coffee co-op as the Trumansburg Creek rushes by.

Cayuga Lake Creamery: Divert from vineyards for homemade ice-cream flavors such as jalapeño popper, apple-cider sorbet and maple bacon. **$**

Buffalo & Niagara Falls

ARCHITECTURE | CASCADES | URBAN RENEWAL

GETTING AROUND

Visitors who arrive by plane at **Buffalo Niagara International Airport** or Amtrak train at the **Exchange Street Station** have several options for transportation upon arrival. Rideshares (Uber, Lyft) are available, and the Buffalo Metro Rail offers limited service along a 6.4-mile strip, mostly down Main St. Public transit's better option is the NFTA bus system. Still, a car is best for getting around, particularly if you plan on exploring Niagara Falls (30 minutes north) or the suburbs.

☑ TOP TIP

Buffalo isn't a walkable city, but you can park in several neighborhoods and stroll. For bars, cafes, restaurants and shops, head to the Elmwood or Allentown. For museums and mansions, try Delaware Park. Canalside is best for waterfront activities.

Its winters may be harsh, but Buffalo is a city in spring. After economic turmoil in the late 20th century, artists, preservationists and a squad of local cheerleaders are planting the seeds for Western New York's Rust Belt revitalization.

Buffalo, incorporated in 1832, owes its origins to the Erie Canal. When the artificial waterway opened in 1825, the city overflowed with riches and became an industrial boomtown. By 1901, it boasted more millionaires per capita than any American metropole – a fact reflected in the city's architecture, much of which stands as a testament to Gilded Age ambition. But after WWII, industries vanished, leaving behind their brick-and-cement skeletons. These bones are now the bedrock of Buffalo's rebirth, with visionaries turning abandoned buildings into breweries, museums, restaurants and parks. There's still plenty of grit, though recent population growth ensures the dark days are done for Lake Erie's urban garden.

Tour Historic Architecture

Styles spanning two centuries

Buffalo's architectural landscape glimmers with riches from its industrial past. From the 19th century, there's **Delaware Park**, designed by Frederick Law Olmsted (of Central Park and Niagara Falls fame) and the neighboring **Richardson Olmsted Campus**, featuring the Romanesque Revival Buffalo State Asylum for the Insane, now a boutique hotel. Artsy **Allentown** pops with Queen Ann homes painted like Lisa Frank fever dreams and downtown enchants with the **Old Erie County Hall**'s Romanesque resplendence (1870). There's also **Buffalo City Hall** (1931): after enjoying its art deco details from Niagara Sq, take an elevator to the 25th floor and walk up three flights for panoramic city views.

Thanks to local preservationists, Buffalo is also the greatest sanctuary, outside of Chicago, for Frank Lloyd Wright's organic architecture. The Prairie-style **Martin House**

Buffalo City Hall

(1903–06, commissioned by self-made millionaire Darwin Martin) is most magnificent – even Wright called it 'a well-nigh perfect composition.' Book a guided tour to see interiors on the 30,000-sq-ft grounds (75-minute tours cover the main structures, two-hour tours enter all six). Exploring the building's Roman brick exterior and gardens is free, though a $15 audio tour enhances the experience. The **Graycliff Estate** (1926–31), constructed as a Lake Erie summer home for the Martin family, awaits 30 minutes' drive south in Derby, NY. Standard one-hour tours examine the property, or make it a six-hour affair by signing up for the Martin House/Graycliff Experience ($125), with tours of both estates and lunch included.

More worthy Wright structures in Buffalo didn't see the light of day until after his death, including the granite **Blue Sky Mausoleum**, commissioned by the Martin family but left undone after the family lost its fortune in the Great Depression. The structure, constructed posthumously in 2004, memorializes America's groundbreaking architect and the man who heralded his work.

Wander the Waterfront

Industrial history and outdoor fun

Efforts to rinse off Buffalo's Rust Belt image are most apparent throughout **Canalside**, a district transformed from bustling Erie Canal terminus to late-20th-century wasteland and

MORE MUSEUMS & TOURS

Buffalo AKG Art Museum: America's sixth-oldest museum houses modern and contemporary art inside a 1905 neoclassical temple, 1962 modernist addition and 2023 glass-walled wing.

Burchfield Penney Art Center: Admire dreamy landscapes by local watercolorist Charles Ephraim Burchfield (1893–1967).

Buffalo History Museum: Cover 12,000 years of local history inside a 1901 palace built for Buffalo's Pan-American Exposition.

Silo City Ground and Vertical Tours: Explore Buffalo (explorebuffalo.org) leads seasonal 1½-hour explorations of abandoned and repurposed grain silos.

Buffalo Transportation Pierce-Arrow Museum: Western New York's automotive history revs up motorheads with its collection of vintage vehicles and local history.

EATING IN BUFFALO: OUR PICKS

West Side Bazaar: Immigrant and refugee chefs show off their skills at this food hall featuring Congolese, Jamaican, Korean and more. **$**

Dapper Goose: The goose is debonair indeed, with smart takes on shareable American plates and meaty mains served under pressed-tin ceilings. **$$$**

Gabriel's Gate: The city's spicy, deep-fried Buffalo wings were invented at Anchor Bar (1964) but perfected here. **$$**

Butter Block: Glance through the floor-to-ceiling kitchen window inside this patisserie to see chefs prepping delicate, doughy French delights. **$**

BUFFALO

TOP SIGHTS
1. Buffalo AKG Art Museum
2. Buffalo City Hall
3. Martin House

SIGHTS
4. Blue Sky Mausoleum
5. Buffalo Heritage Carousel
6. Buffalo History Museum
7. Buffalo Transportation Pierce-Arrow Museum
8. Burchfield Penney Art Center
9. Canalside
10. Colored Musicians Club
11. Delaware Park
12. Freedom Park
13. Old Erie County Hall
14. Outer Harbor
15. Richardson Olmsted Campus
16. Shark Girl

ACTIVITIES, COURSES & TOURS
17. BFLO Harbor Kayak
18. Ice at Canalside
19. Spirit of Buffalo

SLEEPING
20. Hotel at the Lafayette
21. Richardson Hotel

EATING
22. Brothers
23. Butter Block
24. Dapper Goose
25. Gabriel's Gate
26. West Side Bazaar

DRINKING & NIGHTLIFE
27. Lucky Day Whiskey Bar
28. Public Espresso
29. Resurgence Brewing Co

TRANSPORT
30. Queen City Bike Ferry

now a recreation-packed park. Spend an hour exploring the area, or plan an adventure that lasts half a day.

Roaming around is half the fun: historical placards provide Erie Canal insight and **Shark Girl**, the 'fish out of water' statue by Casey Riordan, begs passersby to snap a selfie. Throughout summer, visitors can paddle around Elevator Alley (a stretch of river flanked by towering grain elevators) with rentals from **BFLO Harbor Kayak** ($25 per hour) or hop on the **Queen City Bike Ferry** for access to Lake Erie's serene **Outer Harbor** ($1). Ride the **Buffalo Heritage Carousel** from 1924, skate around winter's **Ice at Canalside** (New York's largest outdoor rink), or cruise Lake Erie on a two-hour **Spirit of Buffalo** schooner tour. From this point of view, Buffalo's renaissance has arrived.

Gaze into the Grand Canyon of the East
Breathtaking geology

The Genesee River has spent thousands of years carving Letchworth Gorge – the shale-and-sandstone centerpiece of 17-mile-long **Letchworth State Park** (p140), dubbed the 'Grand Canyon of the East', one hour's drive from Buffalo. While the comparison to Arizona's stony celebrity is flattering, it belies the singular beauty on view here: 600ft-high cliffs topped by woodlands thick with hemlock, oak and sugar maple trees – a spectacular sight in fall. There are also three major cascades – the Upper, Middle (most magnificent) and Lower Falls. Though not as powerful as Niagara Falls, the park is less crowded and more wild, making it a worthwhile Buffalo detour.

To experience the park on foot, follow the 14-mile out-and-back **Gorge Trail**. Don't be alarmed by the mileage – this is more of a steady stroll than a heart-pounding hike, following the gorge's scenic western rim.

The park also prioritizes accessibility. Parking lots and pull-outs for cars are near all the top sights, and the **Autism Nature Trail**, a one-mile route with eight sensory-friendly stations, provides autistic individuals a safe space to experience the great outdoors.

BUFFALO'S BLACK HERITAGE

Saladin Allah, director of community engagement at the **Niagara Falls Underground Railroad Heritage Center**, shares highlights of Buffalo's Black legacy. *@niagarafallsugrr*

Something beautiful about this area is the Black community's history of resistance and agency, and the places dedicated to sharing their stories. In the **African American Heritage Corridor**, the **Colored Musicians Club** chronicles Buffalo's contributions to jazz music at home and abroad, starting in the 20th century. **Brothers** is a Black-owned soul-food restaurant showcasing how the community thrives today. There's also **Freedom Park**, renamed in 2023 for Buffalo's Underground Railroad history. This is where my ancestor, Josiah Henson, and so many others crossed the Niagara River to find freedom from slavery in Canada.

 DRINKING IN BUFFALO: OUR PICKS

duende: Grain silos and gardens surround this industrial indoor-outdoor bar pouring drinks inside a 1940s American Malting Company office building.

Lucky Day Whiskey Bar: Choose from an encyclopedic list of brown libations inside a 1904 Masonic lodge.

Resurgence Brewing Co: Sip ales around the beer garden and tasting room – a revamped manufacturing workshop from 1910.

Public Espresso: Plush banquets, potent brews and decent breakfasts attract downtown's worker bees to this spacious cafe in the Hotel at the Lafayette.

TOP SIGHT

Niagara Falls

Prepare to be mystified: North America's most powerful falls dump roughly 700,000 gallons of water over three distinct cascades every second, plunging into the Niagara Gorge at 25mph. Their immensity is hypnotic, attracting conservationists, industrialists and thrill-seekers to the boundary between the US and Canada for centuries. Join thousands of onlookers, electrified by nature's spectacle each day.

PRACTICALITIES

Scan this QR code for tickets and event info.

DON'T MISS

Maid of the Mist

Prospect Point Observation Tower

Luna Island

Three Sisters Islands

Goat Island

Cave of the Winds

Niagara Falls Underground Railroad Heritage Center

Celebrate Niagara's Sculptors

Begin your journey at **Prospect Point**, overlooking the crest of the American Falls. More than 12,000 years in the making, Niagara's story begins with receding glaciers from the last ice age, which carved the Great Lakes, unleashed a deluge of melting ice and formed the Niagara River linking Lake Erie and Lake Ontario.

The verdant crown atop the park owes its existence to the Free Niagara movement, a cadre of 19th-century environmentalists appalled by industrial abuse of the natural wonder. Their fiery advocacy culminated in the establishment of Niagara Falls as the nation's first state park in 1885. Follow the park's sinuous pathways, designed by Calvert Vaux and Frederick Law Olmsted, to experience the falls for free.

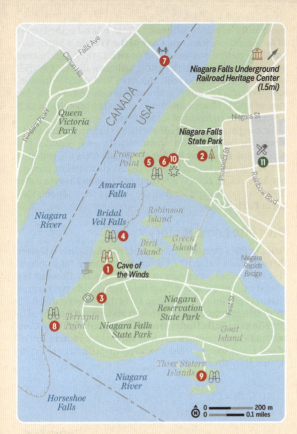

TOP SIGHTS
1. Cave of the Winds
2. Niagara Falls State Park

SIGHTS
3. Goat Island
4. Luna Island
5. Prospect Point
6. Prospect Point Observation Tower
7. Rainbow Bridge
8. Terrapin Point
9. Three Sisters Islands

ACTIVITIES, COURSES & TOURS
10. Maid of the Mist

EATING
11. Savor

TOP TIPS

- Arrive early to snag parking near Prospect Point ($10 Monday to Thursday, $15 Friday to Sunday) or on Goat Island.
- If walking isn't your thing, hop on the Niagara Scenic Trolley – a vintage hop-on, hop-off bus that cruises around the park April to December ($2 to $3).
- Cycle around Niagara Falls using the bikeshare Reddy program or Sight See Rentals.
- Food sold around the park is mediocre and overpriced. Bring snacks or hold out for a meal at Savor, prepared by Niagara Falls Culinary Institute students.
- Purchase timed-entry tickets for Cave of the Winds in advance.
- Wear shoes you can get wet – waterproof is best.

Feel the Powerful Falls

Though walking above the falls is pretty, sailing into the thundering cascades is the best way to appreciate their force. On the **Maid of the Mist** boat tour, operating since 1846, visitors brave the water's icy embrace on a half-hour ride ($28.25; enter at Prospect Point). Despite the experience's theme-park trappings (long entrance lines; exit through a gift shop), the ride provides heart-pumping, must-see perspectives. Be sure to don the blue ponchos provided and store your phone somewhere safe – floating near Horseshoe Falls, the largest waterfall, can be like cruising into a tempest. Tickets include access to the **Prospect Point Observation Tower** ($1.25 when sold separately, but a sensible post-ride pitstop), which extends over the gorge for panoramic views.

Find Your Favorite Viewpoint

From Prospect Point, follow Goat Island Rd to an archipelago above the gorge. On tiny **Luna Island**, peer over railings to gasp at the brink of Bridal Veil Falls. **Three Sisters Islands** offers a glimpse of the park's untamed origins, spread across

147

> **DAREDEVIL DAMSEL**
>
> Annie Edson Taylor celebrated her 63rd birthday in 1901 by climbing into a barrel and plunging over Niagara Falls. She became the first person to survive the death-wish journey, escaping with but a cut on her head. The stunt, she hoped, would solve her financial woes. It didn't, and her fame lasted as long as the ride – just over 15 minutes.

rocky tufts lapped by whitecaps. **Goat Island** is the largest of the collection, featuring **Cave of the Winds**, a hurricane-worthy waterfall encounter 175ft down into the gorge. Instead of a cave (it collapsed in the 1950s), visitors walk along a series of wooden boardwalks built 20ft from Bridal Veil Falls' non-stop torrents. The entire boardwalk is only installed during summer ($21), though thousands of nesting seagulls make it a worthwhile sight out of season ($14).

You can partially admire Horseshoe Falls from Goat Island's **Terrapin Point**, but for unobstructed views, consider traversing the **Rainbow Bridge** to Canada (cars $5, pedestrians $1 – passports required; check ezbordercrossing.com for border-crossing tips). While parts of Canada's Niagara suffer from over-commercialization, the scenery from **Queen Victoria Park** is tops.

Dive into Local History

Niagara Falls' proximity to Canada, which abolished slavery three decades before the US, made it a haven for freedom-seeking African Americans in the 19th century. Crossing the Niagara Gorge became a promising path to liberty, turning Niagara Falls into a crucial stop along the Underground Railroad. To learn more about the town's abolitionist past, head to the **Niagara Falls Underground Railroad Heritage Center** (p145) (five minutes north by car), which centers stories of self-emancipating freedom seekers in its immersive exhibit, *One More River to Cross*.

Terrapin Point

Places We Love to Stay

$ Budget $$ Midrange $$$ Top End

Montauk & Long Island MAP p108

Daunt's Albatross Motel $$
Spartan but stylish: slate-gray floors, sea-green tiles and blonde wood like fine sand, designed to match Montauk's South Edison Beach two blocks away. Fantastic value.

Breakers $$ Whitewashed walls seem sun-bleached, just like the surrounding landscape as it spills into the ocean. Private cottages give 'summer camp' vibes. Walkable to Montauk restaurants.

Hotel Moraine $$$
Contemporary Scandinavian take on a motel, with Long Island Sound views and a private beach. Close to Greenport's downtown and numerous vineyards.

Roundtree $$$ High-end boutique hotel in a classic Hamptons shingle-sided abode on Amagansett's main strip. Book a private cottage to cosplay as a local.

Beacon & the Hudson Valley MAP p116

Nest Hudson $ Rooms inside this 1920s craftsman building are tiny, but you'll likely spend your time strolling around Hudson's main drag, two blocks away.

Beacon Bed and Breakfast $$ No need for a car at this snug getaway, within walking distance of the train station, Main St and Beacon's best hikes.

Gather Greene $$ Glamp-style cabins with landscape-framing windows are the region's hottest hotel trend; this collection is one of the best, price included.

Roundhouse $$$ With minimalist rooms overlooking Fishkill Creek and Beacon's Main St, it's hard to believe this serene space once whirred with 19th-century manufacturing equipment.

Maker Hotel $$$ Much like Hudson's Warren St shops, everything in this bohemian lodge feels like an upscale antique.

Woodstock & the Catskills MAP p122

Urban Cowboy Lodge $$
Step inside a Pendleton ad at this creekside lodge with a hearty on-site restaurant, forest footpath, wood sauna and antlers galore.

Hotel Lilien $$ Initially built in the 1890s as a summer refuge for the Lilienthal clan; now a fashionable boutique lodge near Kaaterskill Falls where guests are family.

Herwood Inn $$ All four rooms in this cheery lodge pay tribute to iconic female musicians (Joni Mitchell, Stevie Nicks etc); 15-minute stroll from Woodstock's epicenter.

DeBruce $$$ It's hard to choose between Foster Supply Hospitality's five idyllic western Catskills retreats, each catering to various budgets. Plus points here: exceptional food and Livingston Manor proximity.

Scribner's Catskill Lodge $$$
Swiss-chalet vibes on Hunter Mountain: perfect for après-ski or hike. Book a yurt-style Rounds cabin for maximum seclusion.

Lake George & the Adirondacks MAP p129

Lodge at Schroon Lake $$
Hotel rooms, private chalets and glamp sites nod to the region's 19th-century Great Camps above this lesser-known, no-less-stunning Adirondacks lake.

Sagamore Resort $$$ An icon of Lake George luxury since 1883, comprising a Colonial Revival mansion and multi-unit lodges perched on Green Island.

Ithaca & the Finger Lakes MAP p136

Firelight Camps $$ Glamp on the edge of Buttermilk Falls State Park in safari-style tents with plush bedding, balconies and electric heaters for cool nights.

Inns of Aurora $$$ This campus of historic homes revamped as cozy, museum-worthy accommodations is the pearl of Cayuga Lake; serene spa and top-tier restaurants included.

Buffalo MAP p142

Hotel at the Lafayette $
Louise Blanchard Bethune, America's first female architect, was the brains behind this 1904 hotel's French Renaissance aesthetics.

Richardson Hotel $$ Don't worry about ghosts inside this Gothic fortress, originally built as a 19th-century insane asylum – contemporary comforts ensure everyone sleeps soundly.

149

THE GUIDE

NEW JERSEY

New Jersey

SHORE LIFE, OUTDOORS AND HISTORY

From neon-lit Ferris wheels on super-sized boardwalks to refined tranquility, the Jersey Shore has a beach for every pleasure. Elsewhere, escape to historic towns and rural locales.

When temperatures soar in July and August, everyone goes 'down the shore' (as locals say) and New Jersey's 127 miles of Atlantic Ocean coastline smell of fried dough, sausage, pepper and onions, and, for those raised on the traditional migration as a rite of passage, like childhood. Much of the state is flatter than the proverbial pancake, with the Skylands near the northwestern corner a startling contrast. New York City's skyscraper-heavy profile comes into view when you're deep in New Jersey's own epic urban sprawl, a labyrinth of bridges and highways and densely developed suburbia that for some is the dominant image of the state.

But the variety of ecosystems would surprise many, as would the volume, diversity and ease of spotting migrating wildlife.

The legacy of the state's earliest inhabitants, the Lenape, lives on primarily in place names. Its colonial-era, pre–Revolutionary War history and architecture are preserved in picturesque townships. After the American Revolutionary War in the 18th century, New Jersey became the third state in the Union, and Cape May on the shore was the first seaside resort in the US. Post-war New Jersey was a destination for African Americans moving north, industrial cities like the 'big six' – Camden, Trenton, Newark, Elizabeth, Paterson and Jersey City – helped drive the country's economy, and newer waves of immigrants have shaped neighborhoods like Newark's Ironbound.

ALEXANDERPHOTO7/SHUTTERSTOCK ©

THE MAIN AREAS

PRINCETON	**LAMBERTVILLE**	**NEWARK**	**HOBOKEN & JERSEY CITY**	**CAPE MAY**
Idyllic college town. **p154**	Antiquing and cycling canal towpath. **p157**	District of great food and cafes. **p157**	NYC skyline views and Hudson River trips. **p158**	Refined and peaceful end to the Shore. **p160**

150

THE GUIDE

NEW JERSEY

Left: Atlantic City (p165); Above: View of Manhattan from Hoboken (p158)

FRANCOIS ROUX/SHUTTERSTOCK ©

WILDWOOD	**ATLANTIC CITY**	**LONG BEACH ISLAND**	**ASBURY PARK**	**PINE BARRENS**
'Big kahuna' of Jersey boardwalks. **p163**	Casino resorts and classic boardwalk kitsch. **p165**	Show tunes, boating and idyllic beaches. **p169**	Retro vibes and music venues. **p170**	Forested refuge with hiking and kayaking. **p171**

151

Find Your Way

The Jersey Shore shouldn't be missed, but pick a base and settle in. Other beaches are short drives away. Central Jersey, only 55 miles at its widest, is a maze of turnpikes and highways that can be challenging to navigate.

THE GUIDE

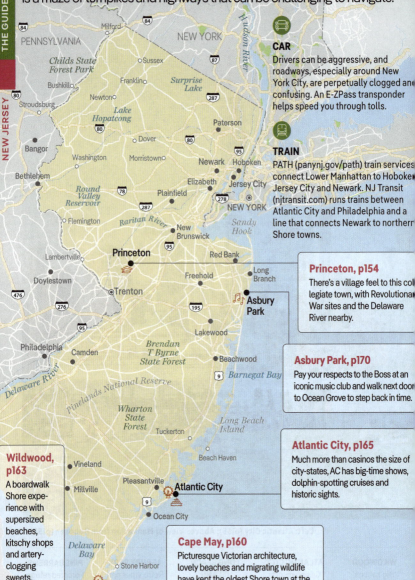

CAR
Drivers can be aggressive, and roadways, especially around New York City, are perpetually clogged and confusing. An E-ZPass transponder helps speed you through tolls.

TRAIN
PATH (panynj.gov/path) train services connect Lower Manhattan to Hoboken, Jersey City and Newark. NJ Transit (njtransit.com) runs trains between Atlantic City and Philadelphia and a line that connects Newark to northern Shore towns.

Princeton, p154
There's a village feel to this collegiate town, with Revolutionary War sites and the Delaware River nearby.

Asbury Park, p170
Pay your respects to the Boss at an iconic music club and walk next door to Ocean Grove to step back in time.

Atlantic City, p165
Much more than casinos the size of city-states, AC has big-time shows, dolphin-spotting cruises and historic sights.

Wildwood, p163
A boardwalk Shore experience with supersized beaches, kitschy shops and artery-clogging sweets.

Cape May, p160
Picturesque Victorian architecture, lovely beaches and migrating wildlife have kept the oldest Shore town at the top of many people's list.

152

Princeton (p154)

Plan Your Time

During warm weather, head 'down the shore' (mid-week is best to avoid crowds), or to a Delaware River town or forested park to beat the crowds. NYC-based travelers can head to Newark for the feel of a trip abroad.

Shore Time

● This can be done in a long weekend or a week. Book a B&B at **Cape May** (p160) or a motel in **Wildwood** (p163). Go wine tasting, go bird-spotting, climb the lighthouse and take in the architecture in Cape May. Stroll Wildwood's boardwalk and hit Morey's Piers for rides and waterpark fun. Then head to **Atlantic City** (p165) for a dolphin-watching cruise and organ recital.

Two-Day Central Sample

● Begin in **Asbury Park** (p170) with lunch, then head to **Ocean Grove** (p170) to the Great Auditorium. Then northwest, navigate roads surrounded by forest to reach the Delaware River and **Lambertville** (p157) and **Washington Crossing State Park** (p157). Overnight in Lambertville and then take off for historic **Princeton** (p154).

SEASONAL HIGHLIGHTS

SPRING
Kayaking on the Delaware; birdwatching and biking in Cape May. This might be the time to nab a bargain hotel.

SUMMER
Everyone goes 'down the shore.' If crowded beaches aren't a bother, there's no denying the fun.

FALL
Harvest celebrations at wineries, apple and pumpkin picking and warm enough weather for a Shore stay.

WINTER
Shop at Lambertville's thrift stores. The majority of businesses shut, but those that stay open offer deals.

Princeton

ART | FOOD | WALKS

GETTING AROUND

Express buses 100 and 600 with Coach USA (coachusa.com) run frequently between Manhattan and Princeton (1½ hours). NJ Transit (njtransit.com) trains run frequently from New York Penn Station to Princeton Junction train station (one to 1½ hours). The 'Dinky' shuttle will then run you to Princeton campus ($4.50, five minutes).

Settled by an English Quaker missionary, this tiny, perfectly coiffed town is filled with lovely architecture and several noteworthy sites, number one of which is its top-tier Ivy League university. Built in the mid-1700s, Princeton became one of the largest structures in the early colonies, and ever so briefly the capital of the country when the Continental Congress met in Princeton in 1783. Like most seats of learning, there are brewpubs, an indie cinema and top-flight bookstore, but for a college town, it's more upper-crust than collegiate, with preppie boutiques edging central Palmer Sq. There's also more than its fair share of haute cuisine dining, popular with visiting parents, compared to places catering to budget-minded students. Just over a mile from the campus and town, however, you can escape to the bucolic Institute Woods, a 600-acre forested retreat.

In Washington's & Einstein's Footsteps
Revolutionary War site and wooded park

There isn't much to see at **Princeton Battlefield State Park**. There's mostly just a grassy field, some plaques and a historic house. It takes a leap of imagination to picture the fighting that occurred, some of the Revolutionary War's fiercest. But it was here, on January 3, 1777, where George Washington and his ill-equipped troops won their first victory against British regulars, then the world's most powerful army.

Sharing the same parking lot and adjoining Princeton's Institute for Advanced Study is the nearly 600 acres of **Institute Woods**, a bucolic slice of forested countryside that connects with the Delaware and Raritan Canal, a popular kayaking spot. The soft, loamy pathways are good for long strolls and birders (it's an important stop for warblers during spring migration).

Washington and his troops marched through here before the battle. Later, Robert Oppenheimer, Albert Einstein and John Nash, to name a few intellectual luminaries, found the woods a beneficial refuge for contemplation.

☑ TOP TIP

Princeton is a lovely town to walk around. However, it's also blessed with several nearby parks and gardens. **Sourland Mountain Preserve** has a network of trails, including one through a boulder field, the leftovers of a glacier. **Grounds for Sculpture** is a bucolic park with over 270 works of contemporary art.

SIGHTS
① Princeton University Art Museum

ACTIVITIES, COURSES & TOURS
② Princeton University

SLEEPING
③ Nassau Inn

EATING
④ Chuck's Spring Street Cafe
⑤ Little Chef Pastry Shop
⑥ Mistral
⑦ Winberie's Restaurant & Bar

SHOPPING
⑧ Labyrinth Books
⑨ Princeton Record Exchange

Town & Gown

Tour Princeton's campus and shops

You can stroll around **Princeton's campus** on your own or take a student-led tour through its various immaculately landscaped quads. Its **art museum** is a sort of miniature version of NYC's Metropolitan Museum of Art, with world-class galleries ranging from European and modern art to Asian works, antiquities and photography.

Just across the street from the entrance to the university, Palmer Sq and surrounding streets are pleasant to walk. For those who still have a CD player, and especially vinyl lovers with a turntable, stop by the **Princeton Record Exchange** to browse over 100,000 musical selections (but who's counting?) – many for sale for just a few bucks. And bibliophiles and more casual readers can make like a college student and wander the two floors of **Labyrinth Books**.

'TEN CRUCIAL DAYS'

Ten days before the battle at Princeton, on Christmas night, 1776, Washington led his army across the Delaware River. That vital crossing was forever immortalized in Emanuel Leutze's painting on view at the MET in NYC. After the crossing, Washington was victorious in a surprise attack in Trenton, NJ on December 26. Trenton's battle is remembered at the **Old Barracks Museum** (barracks.org), and every December reenactments are held.

EATING IN PRINCETON: OUR PICKS

Chuck's Spring Street Cafe: Wings are the thing at Chuck's – you can order up to 100 of these twice-cooked tangy buffalo-style ones at a time. $

Little Chef Pastry Shop: The Haitian-born pastry chef at the helm here has been spinning out croissants, napoleons and eclairs for years. $

Winberie's Restaurant & Bar: Aka 'the Princeton Pub,' this Palmer Sq staple has the town's best fried chicken, as well as other upscale comfort food. $

Mistral: This place serves three- to four-course brunches and dinners, with flavors ranging from the Caribbean to Scandinavia. $$$

Beyond Princeton

Experience the Jersey (sub)urban jungle, a continuation of NYC's sprawl. Or go south and west for smaller towns and more refreshing Delaware River landscapes

Places
Robbinsville p156
Lambertville p157
Newark p157
Hoboken p158

Central New Jersey is known for its bedroom communities, many upscale, for those commuting into New York City. It's not uncharitable to say that post–September 11 and due to NYC's astronomical housing costs there have been waves of development, which haven't abated entirely, in Hoboken and Jersey City especially; the latter's waterfront, with awesome views of Manhattan, is lined with generally generic-looking skyscrapers.

Once away from the Meadowlands, where sports stadiums were built over an industrial-wasteland swamp ('disappeared' Teamster leader Jimmy Hoffa was allegedly buried in stadium concrete), you can explore more of the locales that justify NJ's 'Garden State' moniker, including charming Lambertville, right on the 60-mile D&R Canal towpath.

Robbinsville
TIME FROM PRINCETON: **15 MINS**

BAPS Shri Swaminarayan Mandir

Central New Jersey might seem like an anomalous location for one of the largest and most elaborately and exquisitely designed religious sites in the US. And on first seeing the 49ft-tall golden bronze statue outside at the entrance of **BAPS Shri Swaminarayan Akshardham** (usa.akshardham.org), it can seem like an otherworldly apparition. The statue depicts a yoga pose that Neelkanth Varni, later known as Swaminarayan, the founder of this Hindu denomination with an estimated one million congregants worldwide (and New Jersey has one of the largest Hindu populations in the US), is said to have held for 2½ months in a Himalayan winter. Born in 1781, Varni left his home in northwestern India at the age of 11 and traveled solo for seven years before attaining enlightenment, according to followers.

'Akshardham' refers to a divine abode, essentially a place where god lives, and the largest mandir (place of worship) on the campus, whose profile's spires resemble the shape of mountains, is made from weather-resistant limestone, and the inside of marble from Turkey and Greece. Inside, throughout, there are intricately detailed carvings depicting important moments in Swaminarayan's life, from birth to death. Other Hindu deities have their own altars and according to the

GETTING AROUND

The PATH system connects Newark, Hoboken and Jersey City to NYC (with stops in Midtown and Lower Manhattan). The AirTrain connects to Newark Liberty International Airport.

New York Waterway (nywaterway.com) ferries run up the Hudson River, and from the NJ Transit train station in Hoboken to the World Financial Center in Lower Manhattan.

scriptures and principles, they're fed, clothed and 'put to rest' several times daily.

Remarkably, there's another mandir on the campus, this one dedicated to worship and no less a remarkable work of art, basically covered by a modern-looking building because its own exterior marble is vulnerable to the elements.

All faiths are welcome – in fact, it's an extremely visitor-friendly experience, already welcoming busloads of non-worshipping tourists on incredibly informative guided tours (daily, except Tuesday, from 9am to 7:30pm; reservations required on weekends and holidays) that begin with a short, explanatory film on the creation of the temple. Wearing of shirts, shorts or sleeveless tops is not permitted (sarongs are provided if needed).

The very large **Shayona Café** (11am to 8pm) serves excellent vegetarian Indian fare and a small **grocery** sells sweets, staples and other delicacies.

Lambertville

TIME FROM PRINCETON: 30 MINS

Antiquing

At the **Golden Nugget Antique Flea Market** 2 miles south of Lambertville on Rte 29, haggle to your heart's content amid this collection of vendors, who hawk furniture, books and a thousand other collectibles. Browse the outdoor tables and 20-plus specialist stores inside, which are a sort of haphazard cornucopia of potential future *Antiques Roadshow* treasures. It's by far the biggest and oldest operation, first opening in 1967, though there's at least another half dozen top-quality specialty antique shops in town, as well as an equal number of art galleries and home-furnishing stores, with an emphasis on mid-century modern. Walk the bridge over the Delaware River (don't drive; the traffic can be awful) to Pennsylvania and the lively cafe- and restaurant-filled town of New Hope (p248).

Cycling the Towpath

The 70-mile **D&R Canal** trail follows the old canal and is relatively easy on the lungs. A convenient entry point is just before the bridge that crosses into New Hope. Stop by **Pure Energy Cycling & Java House** to rent bikes. History and cycling buffs can tour some pivotal points in American history, including **Washington Crossing State Park**, located seven miles south of Lambertville on the towpath. Soak up the history and wander around the grounds, recouping with a snack before heading further south or returning to Lambertville.

Newark

TIME FROM PRINCETON: 1 HR 10 MINS

Eating in the Ironbound

Many NYC-bound travelers fly into Newark Liberty International Airport. Few stick around. One of the country's oldest cities, first settled in the mid-1600s, Newark, and especially the Ironbound neighborhood (so named for the ubiquity of railroad tracks in the area), has seen wave after wave

BEST STATE FORESTS & PARKS

High Point State Park: The state's highest point (1803ft), with views of the Delaware River and surroundings; great for camping and hiking.

Norvin Green State Forest: Awesomely isolated 5000-acre forest near New York border; trails from moderate to difficult, with spectacular views.

Cheesequake State Park: A blend of pine barrens, salt- and fresh-water swamps and forest with four easy-to-moderate trails, swimming and kayaking.

Kittatinny Valley State Park: Home to lakes with campsites, hiking and cycling paths. Part of the Appalachian Trail runs along the ridge.

Wharton State Forest: New Jersey's largest single tract of parkland forest in the Pine Barrens (see p171).

BEST FESTIVALS

Red, White & Blueberry Festival: Hammonton, the birthplace of the American blueberry, celebrates in style, including with a massive pancake breakfast to begin the day.

Atlantic City Air Show: Mid-August weekend that brings a half million people to AC. Come on warm-up day before to avoid the throngs.

Mutzfest: Fill up with mozzarella at Hoboken's most famous festival. If you have room, there are pastries too.

Barefoot Country Music Festival: Wildwoods' relatively new biggie books A-listers for beachfront performances on the third weekend in June.

Shadfest: Lambertville's celebration of fishing for shad (the largest in the herring family), with music, food and fun for non-shad lovers.

of working-class immigration, from Italian, Polish, German and Jewish communities to Portuguese fleeing their country's dictatorship in the late 1960s and early '70s. More recent arrivals are Brazilians, Ecuadoreans, Salvadoreans, Mexicans and Uruguayans, as well as Nigerians, Ghanaians and Hasidic Jews.

Walking on Ferry St, the major commercial thoroughfare that bisects the Ironbound, the smell of garlic and burning charcoal, Spanish and Portuguese voices and signage can make you feel as if you've simultaneously traveled to another country and back in time. The area explodes with life during the city's Portugal Day festivities and on soccer-match days at nearby **Red Bull Arena**.

The best way to experience the neighborhood is by downing some sangria and seafood paella at one of the Brazilian, Portuguese or Spanish restaurants or grabbing an empanada at an Ecuadorean cafe (there are as many varieties as there are countries and regions represented), or a *paleta* (popsicle) at a Mexican bakery. Family-owned **Casa d'Paco** features tapas with a traditional Galician influence and has flamenco dancing on the last Thursday evening of every month; **Mompou** does innovative, Barcelona-style tapas (there are also flamenco performances, check their website for the schedule); **Casa Vasca** features old-school Basque cooking; and **Sabor Unido** serves sophisticated new-wave Brazilian and Portuguese.

Hoboken

TIME FROM PRINCETON: **1 HR 20 MINS**

On the Water(front)

Wandering the length of Hoboken's Washington St, past trendy cafes, restaurants, bars and boutiques or down its lovely, brownstone-laden side streets, and you'd think you were in a fashionable Brooklyn neighborhood. Undoubtedly it's appealing as a slightly less expensive though still very pricey alternative to NYC living, and crowds line up at spots

Hudson River, Hoboken

like **Carlo's Bakery**, of TV renown, for cakes, cupcakes and breakfast croissants, and **Vito's & Son** for football-sized sandwiches with 'mutz' (mozzarella). But visitors should come to get out on the Hudson River for a different perspective on the city. The **Hoboken Cove Community Boathouse**, operating for around two decades, runs free one- to two-hour kayaking trips on Sundays (from the end of May to mid-September; reservations required; 2 miles round-trip). The unobstructed views of Midtown are spectacular. On Tuesdays, Thursdays and Saturdays you can kayak or stand-up paddleboard (SUP) in the cove (no reservations needed). The club also runs a Hawaiian-style outrigger-canoe team that newbies can try out on weekends.

Nearby, **Resilience Paddle Sports** can get you paddling out on the river as well; sunset and nighttime trips, when NYC is illuminated by millions of sparkling lights, are most recommended. And if you want to add some environmental education to your cruising experience, from May until October, **Hackensack Riverkeeper**, an activist environmental organization, runs 'ecocruises' on canoes, kayaks and pontoon boats several times monthly through the Meadowlands, a huge wetlands ecosystem known for its ecological diversity as well as being a dumping ground for every waste product you can imagine during the 19th and 20th centuries.

THE LENAPE

New Jersey was originally settled by the indigenous Lenape, a matrilineal tribe whom subsequent European settlers dubbed the Delaware. They lived in groups of 25 to 50 people, in modern-day Pennsylvania, near the Delaware River, and throughout New Jersey and into New York. Italian explorer Giovanni da Verrazzano met the Lenape in 1524 near Sandy Hook. As Europeans came to dominate the region, conflict over territory and raw materials led to hostilities, while introduced diseases like smallpox further decimated the population. The Lenape were forcibly resettled during the 19th century in the Oklahoma Territory, and most Lenape now live in Oklahoma or Canada. Their place names survive in towns and cities like Manasquan, Mantoloking and even Manhattan.

 EATING IN DINERS BEYOND PRINCETON: OUR PICKS

White Mana Diner: At this pioneer of the fast-food hamburger, sitting at the circular linoleum counter is still a rite of passage for Jersey City kids. $

Tick Tock Diner: Aka 'The Tick,' this legendary diner in Clifton serves classics like disco fries covered in mozzarella and brown gravy. $

Shut Up and Eat!: This Tom's River spot adds a dose of Jersey attitude with pajama-clad waitresses, snappy repartee and kitsch. $

Summit Diner: Grab a counter swivel stool and chow down on diner breakfasts and sandwiches at this railroad-car-designed diner. $

Cape May

BEACHES | ARCHITECTURE | FOOD

GETTING AROUND

Cape May is the end of the line, Shore-wise. The Cape May–Lewes car ferry crosses the bay in 1½ hours to Lewes, Delaware, near Rehoboth Beach. NJ Transit (njtransit.com) buses serve a variety of Shore towns from Philadelphia (3½ to four hours) and NYC (three to five hours). If flying American Airlines out of Philadelphia International Airport, you can book your flight as if you're flying out of Atlantic City's airport. However, the AC–Philly leg is aboard a comfortable bus. You check your bags and go through TSA screening in AC (long-term parking is cheap here) and are transported directly to your gate in Philly.

Cape May, at the far southern tip of New Jersey and the only place in the state where the sun both rises and sets over the water, is something of a Shore outlier. Originally established as a village for the whaling industry in the late 1600s, it later evolved into one of the country's first seaside resorts. Meticulously landscaped gardens front stately Victorian homes, many now housing B&Bs. There's more order, more serenity and yes there are sweeping beaches, but there's also outstanding wildlife viewing and historic tours, not to mention a handful of wineries, distilleries and breweries.

Perhaps the best place to get a handle on Cape May's lush and dramatic geography is with a bird's-eye view at the top of the 199 steps of the circa 1859 Cape May Lighthouse. Situated in Cape May Point State Park's wetlands, here you can see for miles out to sea and know you've reached the end of your shoreline journey.

Victorians by the Shore
Tour the town's architecture

The Victorian era never looked so good. Sure, men and women bathed separately (red and white flags marked their respective areas of the beach), the upper crust built conspicuous bathroom additions to mark their ascendance to indoor plumbing, and the lack of air conditioning meant, well, it's hard to imagine how uncomfortable being formally dressed in summer was. But those pastel-colored gingerbread homes with their wraparound porches and filigreed trim are the antithesis of generic, contemporary condos seen elsewhere on the Shore. Take a **trolley tour** (capemaymac.org) for an overview of Cape May's Victorian architectural legacy. The guide points out Italianate, Queen Anne towers, shingled mansard roofs and the distinctive Victorian colors, with scripted and improvisational comedic asides about the town's history and

SIGHTS
1. Cape May Bird Observatory
2. Cape May Point State Park
3. Emlen Physick Estate
4. John Hand Black & White House

SLEEPING
5. Congress Hall
6. The Hugh Inn

EATING
7. Lobster House
8. Mad Batter
9. Taco Caballito
10. Uncle Bill's Pancake House

important figures. Cape May's oldest house, circa 1690, is the **John Hand Black & White House**, built by a group of Mayflower settlers.

Cape May's preeminent Victorian mansion is the whimsically designed 1879 **Emlen Physick Estate**, where 45-minute guided tours by often witty, salty-tongued volunteers provide a close-up view of how the towns' upper class once lived. The 14½-acre estate once ran all the way to the beach.

Migratory Patterns

Spotting birds and marine life

We're not referring to Philadelphians and Jerseyites who head 'down the shore' en masse after Labor Day. Rather, the birds, butterflies, dolphins and whales that travel to the area, and further north, for its salubrious climes. The diversity and numbers of birdlife makes the county the premier birding spot in the state. **Cape May Bird Observatory's** mile-long loop trail is a good place to start; there's plenty of books, binoculars and birding bric-a-brac in the bookstore.

The area is considered the best place to see peregrine falcons, with one of the largest populations after the Florida Keys. These predatory birds, the fastest animals in the world, move in big numbers diurnally, with the September and

✓ TOP TIP

Many Jersey Shore communities charge a beach-access fee, issuing a badge/tag for the day. From Long Beach Island north to near Sandy Hook, all have a fee; the southern Shore, Atlantic City and the Wildwoods are free. It might be worthwhile investing in a weekly badge, although some hotels provide them.

BIRDING ALONG THE SHORE

Jesse Amesbury, naturalist. @j_amesburyphotos

Besides Cape May, other top birding spots are Edwin B Forsythe National Wildlife Refuge near Atlantic City; Sandy Hook; and Celery Farm in Bergen County, northern New Jersey. Anywhere you have a green patch near lots of development is a good spot for birders; Central Park in NYC is a good example.

The New Jersey Audubon Society's World Species of Birding (in Delaware it's called the Birdathon) is held annually on the Saturday of Mother's Day weekend. Teams have 24 hours to work their way around the state and log their sightings. In 2024 the winning team logged 213 species. They typically start the morning in the Delaware Water Gap and work their way to the coastline.

October the best months for viewing, and **Cape May Point State Park** the best spot.

The most iconic of New Jersey's endangered bird species is the piping plover (the American goldfinch, a bright yellow species, is the state bird). The piping plover was put on the endangered species list in the 1990s and its numbers have remained largely the same since; only a couple thousand are left. It's the poster child for habitat loss in the state; it needs sandy beaches with few disturbances, so basically beaches closed to humans. Some areas have 'symbolic fencing', with information signs indicating good habitat for these birds.

You can also spot thousands of monarch butterflies (in the last half of September and beginning of October), which undertake an incredible journey between northern Mexico and Canada every year, the longest migration of any butterfly species. Parts of Cape May can look like snow globes of butterflies. It takes four generations to complete the trip, with each of the first four living only a month on the trip north. The fifth generation does the entire return flight south to Mexico, living six to eight months; a 'switch' in DNA is triggered by the angle of the sun and daylight.

Cape May also has some of highest density of Atlantic bottlenose dolphins, migrating whales (especially in March and April) and massive populations of horseshoe crabs that spawn every springtime. Several companies run dolphin- and whale-watching cruises out of the marina here.

A Drop of Jersey Vino

Indulge in a growing wine industry

New Jersey's wine industry, youthful and growing, can trace its origins to Cape May's farmlands, blessed as they are with a long, frost-free growing season. But it was the 1981 New Jersey Wine Act, which stamped out restrictive Prohibition-era rules about winemaking, that allowed the industry to grow. The New Jersey Wine Growers Association (newjerseywines.com) provides a wine 'passport' you can get stamped at some three dozen stops.

One of the seven wineries in Cape May County worth visiting is brothers-run **Hawk Haven**. They began growing grapes on their grandparents' farmland where lima beans once grew, experimenting and figuring out what the grapes wanted to do There's a food truck out back and live music on Friday nights in summer.

 EATING IN CAPE MAY: OUR PICKS

Uncle Bill's Pancake House: With the decor of a 1950s high-school cafeteria, Uncle Bill's has been drawing crowds for 50 years. $

Taco Caballito: Open-air beachfront *tequileria* and tacos – we like the short-rib banh mi – with especially good service. $

Mad Batter: Tucked away in a Victorian B&B and beloved for brunch, including oat pancakes and rich clam chowder. Live music nightly. $$

Lobster House: Classic waterfront experience. Order from the raw bar or takeout window or grab a wharfside table for a full-blown lobster. $$$

Beyond Cape May

With the area studded with resort towns from classy to tacky, you'll start wondering how to make the Shore part of your own annual migration

Every Shore town is different like every snowflake. And everyone has strong opinions as to which is best. You'll find as many kids building sand castles as partying 20-somethings à la MTV's reality show *Jersey Shore*. Summer weekends are mobbed, but you could be wonderfully alone on the sand come early fall.

Atlantic City's gargantuan casino resorts line the country's longest boardwalk and the one in the city of Wildwood delivers oversized classic summer fun. Whether it's Long Beach Island's deep-sea fishing, Asbury Park's music legacy or surfing breaks throughout, there's always more to experience than simply sunny beaches. And the Pine Barrens' trails, meandering bogs, wetlands and pygmy forests couldn't feel further away from the urbanized eastern seaboard.

Places
Wildwood p163
Atlantic City p165
Long Beach Island p169
Asbury Park p170
Ocean Grove p170
Sandy Hook p171
Pine Barrens p171

Wildwood
TIME FROM CAPE MAY: **20 MINS**

Nostalgia in Wildwood Crest
You know them as 'oldies but goodies.' Chubby Checker and Frankie Valli, The Coasters, The Drifters, The Platters. Songs from the '50s and '60s that you can't help singing along to, referred to as 'doo-wop'. Wildwood was integral to its popularization. Bobby Rydell even wrote a song called 'Wildwood Days.' Dick Clark hosted *American Bandstand* from the Starlight Ballroom and Chubby Checker introduced 'The Twist' in the Rainbow Room – both places are long gone. But the doo-wop architectural style that came of age at the same time (also referred to as 'googie' and 'popularize') survived, and more recently come roaring back in Wildwood Crest, the southernmost part of the Wildwoods, with angled roofs, bright colors, bold signage and exotic-sounding property names. The origins of these buildings, which appear 'Jetsonian', are wrapped up in post-WWII American socioeconomic dynamics: returning GIs with discretionary income, many who rotated through Hawaii and other Pacific locales, built beachside hotels with names that alluded to faraway places, even outer space. A few meticulously restored and updated quintessential examples featuring plastic palm trees (an American signifier of the exotic) are the lime-green **Caribbean Motel**, the **Starlux** and the Shalimar Hotel. Even McDonald's and Walgreens have signage in classic doo-wop fashion. Walk, cycle or drive along Atlantic

GETTING AROUND

Rte 206 is the main thoroughfare connecting most everything in this remote region. If you head off into the Pine Barrens, be sure to bring a GPS, although service can be spotty. Amtrak has a sparsely attended station (there's no waiting area or ticket office) in Atco, near Rte 30.

QUICK GUIDE TO OTHER SHORE SPOTS

Ocean City:
There are plentiful hotels here but because it's a 'dry town,' with several kid-centric amusement areas, it's more of a family destination.

Point Pleasant:
Jenkinson's Boardwalk has food and fun; elsewhere there are idiosyncratic beachfront homes and seafood restaurants in marinas along the Manasquan River.

Seaside Heights:
Boardwalk bars make Seaside Heights a party spot for twenty-somethings, and the narrow beach means quiet and space are hard to find. The sky ride, a cable car above the boardwalk, is worth a visit.

Long Beach Island:
This beautiful tidal island offers fishing and wildlife. Of the 10 miles of relatively untouched beach, swimming is good in areas marked with flags by lifeguards. The bay side is good for kayaking.

Ave in the Crest to ogle at the neon, and stop by the **Doo Wop Experience**, a small 'museum' overflowing with neon signage and furnishings from Wildwood's 1950s heyday. That sound you hear? Neon bulbs flickering. Out front, the 'neon-sign garden' shows off relics from buildings long gone. On Tuesday and Thursday nights in summer, a **trolley tour** departs from here, passing the most colorful landmarks.

'The Crest' is dry, if that matters to you. Of course, there's no shortage of bars nearby.

The Big Daddy of Boardwalks

This is summer on steroids. The boardwalk of your fantasies. Or dystopian nightmares if you seek peace and quiet. With gargantuan beaches to match. Wildwoods are as wide as two football fields, so wide in fact that a proposal to ferry beachgoers across the sands on camels was once floated, but voted down (North Wildwood's beach is significantly narrower, so much so it's frequently undergoing replenishment). **Morey's Piers**, probably the best and biggest of the Shore parks, takes up huge chunks of boardwalk real estate, with three amusement piers and two water parks (all-day passes can be purchased to access every property). Locals debate who has the better slice

EATING IN WILDWOOD: OUR PICKS

Maui's Dog House: Since 1999 they have served up dogs from Hoffman's, the nation's oldest wiener maker – more than 20 varieties in all. **$**

Bandanas Mexican Grille: A family-owned and family-friendly place, with far-above-average tacos and burritos, as well as more innovative street fare. **$**

Surfing Pig: The menu here combines burgers, fresh fish and a raw bar. There's live music and an upstairs wine bar. **$$**

Jersey Girl: This place offers a wide-ranging menu, including a raw bar, tacos, poke bowls and a hearty brunch. **$$**

Wildwood

of pizza on the beach: **Sam's** thin crust or **Mack's** doughy? **Wildwood's Honky Tonk**, a huge country bar with live music, is housed in a former boardwalk arcade. And since 1949 a miniature rubber-tired **tram** runs the length of the boardwalk, intermittently chirping 'Watch the tram car, please.' Cycling can be fun too – one of New Jersey's longest bike paths runs for 12 miles along the oceanfront. Some hotels let you use their wheels for free and there are rental shops as well.

For those interested in more quiet, head to the beach access at **Rambler Rd** just south of the southern end of the boardwalk. There's free street parking nearby and clean bathrooms. And for even more tranquility, visit the **Hereford Lighthouse** (pronounced 'heh-ford'), circa 1874, situated at the very northern end of North Wildwood. It has a nice back garden and overlooks a sea wall and inlet separating it from Stone Harbor.

There are fireworks every Friday evening in summer. Emblematic of a certain nostalgic flair, for over a century the beach at Wildwood has hosted the **National Marbles Tournament** – four days of thousands of competitive games in mid-June.

Atlantic City

TIME FROM CAPE MAY: **50 MINS**

The Loudest Sound in the World

Usually, when you say 'I can feel the music,' it's meant metaphorically. However, standing backstage next to **Boardwalk Hall's** 64ft-tall, 2300lb pipes, which make up the world's largest and loudest (unamplified) musical instrument, it takes on a literal meaning. (Boardwalk Hall, aka Jim Whelan Boardwalk Hall, was formerly the city's convention center.) To hear the pipe organ's 'lowest' stop of 138 decibels without blowing out your eardrums, keep your mouth closed, put in ear plugs and it will seem like the sound is passing through you. Built with mostly American-made parts, the pipe organ was

---

SURFING THE JERSEY SHORE

Chris Sciarra, co-owner of Kona Surf Shop. @konasurfcompany

Surfing culture on the Jersey Shore exploded during COVID-19. We have beginner-friendly waves that can get really good, even 10ft to 15ft during hurricane season. The lowest swell is during the summer season. Generally, the further north, the better and bigger the waves are, like around Belmar and other spots in Monmouth County. The area's best breaks are Cape May's Cove and Poverty beaches; in Wildwood at 10th and 2nd Sts in North Wildwood and at Diamond Beach south of Wildwood Crest.

Beginners should check out Jason Reagan's Cape May surf school, Randazzo surf school and camps in Margate and North Wildwood, Tim Kaye's Surftopia in Wildwood for rentals and lessons, and Elation surf camp in Avalon.

TOP SHORE TIPS

Heading 'down the shore' in the summer can be a nightmare. The traffic can be awful, parking impossible and the beaches overflowing. Come nighttime, large groups of rowdy teens can be a nuisance or worse. Often, it's a devil's bargain: relative quiet and space for sky-high parking, costly beach passes and accommodations, or more affordable options that include lugging beach gear for a quarter mile, tiny available slivers of sand and a run-down generic box to stay the night in. Pack your car the night before, leave at dawn, and if possible, come midweek. Early June or early September can be ideal. Make reservations as far in advance as possible and set junk-food and other expectations if you have kids in tow.

inaugurated in 1929, and was considered the only possible way of filling the massive Romanesque-style auditorium with sound. The barrel-vaulted ceiling is so high that in a promotional stunt in 1970, a helicopter was flown indoors. The Beatles played here three days after the 1964 Democratic National Convention (LBJ was nominated); the Rolling Stones, Bruce Springsteen, Madonna and Beyoncé have all performed at the hall. Mike Tyson as well as other big-name boxers have fought here and it continues to host A-list events. But it might be most associated with the long-running Miss America pageant, which ended its AC run for good in 2019.

However, besides a show, it's the pipe organ that should not be missed. From afar, the 16ft-high stage 'console,' where the organ is played, looks tiny, but up close it's an amazing sight, with rows and rows of keys, switches and pedals that can produce music that's as quiet as a lullaby or that's loud, bombastic and haunted sounding. Nearly every percussion sound is available, from the glockenspiel to the marimba and harp. There are free **tours**, with a live recital at noon Monday to Friday during the summer, and on Wednesdays, two-hour **curator's tours** take you 'inside' the organ, and include a concert. Reservations are required only for the latter and can be made on the organ's restoration committee website (boardwalkorgans.org). There's also a mid-July silent-film festival, with the pipe organ

EATING IN ATLANTIC CITY: OUR PICKS

Gilchrist: Breakfast and lunch spot overlooking the marina at Gardner's Bay that's known for hotcakes, smoothies and shakes. $	**Tennessee Ave Beer Hall:** This place has a menu of burgers, dogs, BBQ and more, plus DJs, cornhole, craft beers and cocktails. $$	**Cardinal:** The contemporary menu focuses on seasonal, local ingredients. There's an outdoor space with a fire pit and live music. $$	**Dock's Oyster House:** Dock's is an AC institution with a lively atmosphere, a full raw bar, the freshest seafood in town and great steaks. $$$

Atlantic City

CLASSIC SHORE TREATS

Shriver's Taffy:
In many people's opinion Shriver's has the best saltwater taffy: watch machines stretch and wrap it, and then fill a bag with all the flavors.

Country Kettle Fudge:
Long Beach Island's Beach Haven father-son institution churns out delicious handmade fudge.

Coney Waffle:
Half a dozen Shore locations, including on Asbury Park boardwalk, known for extravagant creations called 'sideshow shakes.'

LoPresti's Pizza & Grill:
Atlantic City boardwalk spot regarded as one of the best for funnel cake; also offers soft-serve ice cream and sausage and pepper subs.

Kohr Frozen Custard:
Nothing says summer like the traditional orange-and-vanilla swirl cone (frozen custard, not ice cream), a Shore favorite for 100 years.

providing the soundtrack, and other events throughout the year.

The organ has never fully recovered after serious flooding in the 1940s. There has been a long-running effort to restore it to its full capacity, with a hoped-for completion date of 2029.

Views: Aquatic & Panoramic

Atlantic dolphins aren't gambling when they come to AC. They migrate to the warm, shallow waters (too warm and too shallow for whales) from the end of April to early November before heading back to the Outer Banks of North Carolina. Captain Jeff, who runs and operates **Atlantic City Cruises** (two-plus hours, 1pm daily) out of the marina at Gardner's Basin, has been navigating these waters for over 35 years. And he's so sure of success spotting dolphins that he issues rain checks to every one of the 100 passengers aboard on the off chance of failure. It's often Captain Jeff's friends, either parasailing or fishing off a nearby pier, who radio in with the initial spot, somewhere between Brigantine to the north or south past the **Steel Pier**, the city's most iconic amusement park, built out over the Atlantic (its most infamous act involved diving horses; the show didn't stop until 1978). There are a couple hundred dolphins in the general area, but you can expect to see pods of around 20 to 40 porpoising and breaching close to your boat, including some identifiable by telltale markings that Captain Jeff has seen yearly for decades. After dolphin spotting, the cruise heads south along the AC shoreline for fantastic views of the gargantuan casino resorts that make everything else in the foreground appear like miniatures in a model toy train set.

For a land-based perspective on the northern end of the city, you need to climb the 228 steps of the **Absecon Lighthouse**, New Jersey's tallest at 171ft. Built in 1854, it's also the city's oldest building. It was decommissioned in 1933; these days its massive Fresnel lens is only turned on from sundown to 11pm

WHY I LOVE THE SHORE

Michael Grosberg, Lonely Planet writer

There's no better encapsulation of Shore summer days past than memories of leaving the beach to pack up the car, with a still-wet bathing suit, sandy, sandal-clad feet and smelling of cream applied post-sunburn. Then driving out to the Barnegat lighthouse at the northern tip of Long Beach Island and walking far out on the jetty to see if any of the people fishing have had good luck. And before braving the traffic home, stopping at a laid-back marina seafood shack for fried shrimp or oysters, followed by an ice-cream cone or frozen custard. And in the height of summer, at an old-fashioned roadside stand for fresh, seasonal berries on the way west, inland, back to the real world.

Absecon Lighthouse

daily. The lighthouse was once situated only 75ft from the water's edge, but in the 1880s engineers pushed back the continually eroding shoreline through a massive landfill project, including jetties and a seawall.

It's a never-ending battle; winter storms in 2024 were so strong that this northern end of the barrier islands' beach was narrowed dramatically. From the vertiginous panoramic views at the top, you can't miss the massive, all-glass Ocean Casino Resort, as well as the number of surrounding vacant lots, a legacy of Hurricane Sandy (and the cost of insurance required to rebuild). You can see south almost to the downtown AC neighborhood of 'Ducktown,' named for the Italian immigrants known to have fed the area's ducks, in lieu of the chickens they were accustomed to in the old country. Despite a number of prominent lighthouses built in the 19th century and a shoreline protected for long stretches by barrier islands, it might come as a surprise that the Jersey Shore is known as the 'Graveyard of the Atlantic,' with an estimated 4000 to 7000 shipwrecks.

Long Beach Island

TIME FROM CAPE MAY: **1 HR 45 MINS**

Shore Theater

The **Surflight Theatre** in Beach Haven has been staging Broadway-quality musical theater since the 1950s, from Gershwin's *Lady, Be Good!* to *The Million Dollar Quartet*, an infectious show featuring music by Elvis, Johnny Cash, Jerry Lee Lewis and Carl Perkins. Its season is long, beginning the week after Labor Day and running to New Year's, with periodic comedy nights, concerts and children's shows thrown into the mix.

Before a show, or to enliven up any summer night, especially with kids in tow, make a booking at the **Showplace Ice Cream Parlour** adjoining the Surflight. Owned and operated by the same team as the theater, here talented performers donning the costumes of an old-fashioned barber-shop quartet (matching the wallpaper) belt out tunes while also cajoling audience members into singing along to comedic ditties. Oh, and they're simultaneously the waitstaff delivering heaping sundaes and ice cream. It's an extremely popular experience, so reservations are recommended for the hour-long daily seatings (6pm, 7pm, 8pm and 9pm).

Get Your Sea Legs

Captain Steve Palmer, formerly of the Coast Guard, runs a mini fishing and cruising empire out of **Jingle's Bait & Tackle** on the main commercial road in Beach Haven. Just want to relax out on the bay with a drink in hand? Book a 1½-hour trip on the dry-grass-covered *Tiki Bar Boat* (sbbtikiboat.com); it's BYOB and can accommodate six (four trips daily in season, plus sunset and weekend brunch trips available). Want to try your hand at fishing? *Miss Beach Haven* (missbeachhaven.com) goes out twice daily (8am to noon and 1pm to 4pm) to a reef a few miles offshore. Passengers line the side decks and, with the aid of crew if needed, drop a line overboard (gear is provided). An early evening trip cruises out in the bay, south past the enormous vacation homes in Holgate and to the beginning of the Edwin B Forsythe National Wildlife Refuge. More serious-minded anglers can charter 36ft *Outer Limits* for offshore deep-sea fishing trips that run for around 30 hours (the season is from May 1 to mid-December).

Steve, with his son as first mate, can take you out to deepwater canyons that run anywhere from 1000 to 1400 fathoms, or nearer to shore to reefs and wrecks, trolling for black tuna, sea bass, tilefish and fluke. Any catch that meets the legal size limit can be filleted for cooking. If you have children in tow who lack the patience for angling, try out one of the 1½-hour interactive cruises with **Black Pearl Pirate Tours**, which combine piracy and a water fight; you shoot water cannons at an accompanying little boat that's meant to try to be boarding you. Adults can partake of the full bar.

Asbury Park

TIME FROM CAPE MAY: **1 HR 45 MINS**

Retro Fun

Asbury Park is known as the town that Bruce Springsteen built, and attracts music lovers from around the world. 'The Boss' is the most famous of a group of musicians who developed the Asbury Sound in the 1970s, with several of the musicians, including Steve Van Zandt, Garry Tallent, and the late Danny Federici and Clarence Clemons, forming Springsteen's

CHOWDA COOKOFF

One of the best off-season times to visit Beach Haven is in early October for the **Chowda Cookoff** (formerly known as the Chowda Fest). During this event, local restaurants go head to head, competing to have the best red or white chowder on Long Beach Island (or the best 'Jersey chowder,' a combo of red and white). There's also usually a 'most unique chowder' competitive category; one past noteworthy winner was a clam chowder ice cream, clearly not the most obviously refreshing taste for a warm-weather dessert. The opening and closing ceremonies bring out large crowds, and often it's the last weekend when summer-home owners head 'down the shore'.

EATING ON LONG BEACH ISLAND: OUR PICKS

| **Country Kettle Chowda:** Always a contender in LBI's chowder competition, this small shop doles it out with the option of a bread bowl. **$** | **Holiday Snack Bar:** Come for the homemade cakes and pies at this old-school beloved Beach Haven spot. **$** | **Creperie de la Mer:** Sweet and savory crepes, croissants and strong espressos are on offer at this quaint and charming Beach Haven spot. **$** | **Chicken or the Egg:** At this LBI classic you can get all-day breakfasts and delicious wings with 17 sauce choices. **$$** |

BEST BOOKS ON NEW JERSEY

The Meadowlands: Wilderness Adventures at the Edge of a City (1998; Robert Sullivan) Entertaining book on one man's travails by canoe through the Hackensack Delta.

The Pine Barrens (1967; John McPhee) A closely observed exploration of the history, ecology and culture of the region.

American Pastoral (1997; Philip Roth) This novel especially captures the political climate of late '60s Newark.

The Brief, Wondrous Life of Oscar Wao (2007; Junot Diaz) Partly set in Paterson, NJ, this is a tale of an immigrant teenager's complicated coming of age.

One for the Money (1994; Janet Evanovich) A series about a Trenton-based rookie bail bondswoman; it oozes Jersey attitude.

E Street Band. Grungy, seen-it-all clubs like the **Stone Pony** and **Wonder Bar** are still going strong and are great places to hear live music. Both are just off the boardwalk near the majestic if crumbling red-brick Paramount Theatre.

Generation Xers, especially, yearning for their long-ago teenage years when they scrounged around for quarters to play at the mall's arcade, might get teary-eyed and wistful stepping into the **Silverball Retro Arcade** on the boardwalk. There are over 160 pinball and arcade games (skee-ball too) restored to pristine condition, with the oldest a 'rotary merchandiser' from the 1930s. You not only play (all you can, for a single price; alas, no coins), but learn as well from the accompanying historical text above each machine. Pro pinball players come for tournaments in the off-season.

Ocean Grove

TIME FROM CAPE MAY: 1 HR 45 MINS

Time Warp

Known as 'God's Square Mile at the Jersey Shore,' Ocean Grove is separated from Asbury Park by a narrow lake, but decades apart by sensibility. Founded by Methodists in the 19th century as a revival camp, it's sober (no liquor), conservative and incredibly quaint. The Victorian architecture, especially the homes lining centrally situated Ocean Path Park, is covered in so much gingerbread trim that you may want to eat it. At the center of town is the **Great Auditorium**, a 6500-seat wooden theater with amazing acoustics and a historic pipe organ (with 11,000 pipes) that recall Utah's Mormon Tabernacle. Make sure to catch a recital or concert (Wednesday or Saturday during the summer; primarily religious themed) or one of the open-air services held in the boardwalk pavilion (May to September).

More than 100 quaint canvas tents, by the auditorium that made up the former revival camp, are now known as **Tent City**, and function as summer homes or cabanas for generations of families. It's an extremely tight-knit and tightly packed communal experience, with small kids roaming and playing freely, a world away from the massive, isolated Shore estates in other towns (Deal, to the north of Asbury Park, is perhaps the best example of the latter). After a legal challenge, Ocean's Grove beach opened to the public on Sundays in the summer of 2024 for the first time in 155 years.

EATING IN ASBURY PARK & OCEAN GROVE: OUR PICKS

Ada's Gojjo: An unusual combination of Dominican and Ethiopian in Asbury Park, with dishes from both cultures on the same menu. **$**

Starving Artist: Ocean Grove spot with an outdoor patio for breakfast, grilled fare and seafood; ice cream is available at the adjacent shop. **$**

Heirloom at The St Laurent: One of the Shore's best restaurants, with mouthwatering dishes combining flavors and ingredients. **$$$**

Moonstruck: Views of Wesley Lake, dividing Asbury and Ocean Grove, and an Italian-leaning menu. It's romantically lit up at night. **$$$**

Asbury Park

Sandy Hook
TIME FROM CAPE MAY: **2 HRS 10 MINS**

Perspectives: Historic & Panoramic

You can see New York City's skyline from nearly any spot along Sandy Hook's 7-mile-long sandy barrier beach at the entrance to New York Harbor. But, delightfully, the city feels much further away. The ocean side of the peninsula has wide beaches, including the state's only 'clothing optional' one at **Gunnison**, and an extensive system of bike trails. The bay side is for fishing, and wading for those who are allergic to waves of any size.

To get a sense of Sandy Hook's past, climb to the top of the **lighthouse**, the country's oldest. On most days, the southern tip of Manhattan is easily visible, as is Brooklyn's skyline, and across the Bay, the Atlantic Highlands in New Jersey. You can also scan the complex of former naval buildings, most being transformed into other uses; several house a school focused on marine sciences, others are labs, and there's a nice if overpriced restaurant and a B&B here too.

Pine Barrens
TIME FROM CAPE MAY: **1 HR 15 MINS**

Nature Lovers' Delights

The 50-mile **Batona Trail** (ie 'BAck TO NAture') cuts east–west, from Ong in the north to Quaker Bridge, Batsto, and ends in the southeast in the Bass River Reserve. You can grab some wild blueberries in midsummer. The route passes the **Apple Pie Hill Fire Tower**, giving a view over a veritable sea of forest from Atlantic City to Philadelphia. Call ahead (609-726-9010) to ensure the tower is open. A more manageable section (8.2 miles return) runs between the Apple Pie Hill Fire Tower and the **Emilio Carranza Memorial**, the site where the Mexican pilot, attempting to duplicate Charles Lindbergh's aviation feats, died in 1928 trying to find a place to land. The **Batsto Village** open-air museum is dedicated to the bog-iron

THE MAFIA ON THE SHORE

The state's shoreline attracts millions of beachgoers each summer, but in the late 1920s its coastal inlets, rivers and bays were ideal locales for rum-runners from Canada and abroad to get their liquor offloaded quickly, a phenomenon celebrated in the TV series *Boardwalk Empire*. The show was inspired by the real-life gangster Enoch 'Nucky' Johnson, who controlled and influenced politicians, businessmen and the heads of organized-crime families to such an extent that he hosted the Atlantic City Conference, a gathering of the heads of the most important crime syndicates, the first of its kind in the US. With the repeal of prohibition, AC's allure as a 'den of iniquity' and Johnson's power waned.

BEST ECO-CRUISES

Salt Marsh Safari:
Daily two-hour wetland birding boat trips out of Cape May from March to November.

Cape May Whale Watcher:
Wildlife-watching cruises (dolphins, whales, sea turtles, birds) led by marine biologists and naturalists, into the Delaware Bay and further offshore.

Seastreak:
Run out of the Atlantic Highlands on four winter Saturdays, on this tour a wildlife expert educates passengers on a variety of birds and seals.

Hackensack Riverkeeper:
Meadowlands pontoon boat trips tracing the history of the wetlands' pollution and reclamation efforts.

Atlantic City Cruises:
Daily dolphin-watching cruises with a money-back guarantee of success; the captain provides background and context on the behavior and health of the population.

Batsto Lake

industry (bog iron is an ore that was mined to produce cannonballs) and is worth a stop for the guided tour (11am, 1pm and 2pm Wednesday to Sunday March to October).

Another recommended route is the well-marked and scenic **White Trail Hike** that wends along narrow paths lined with bright-green moss. It begins and ends in Batsto Village (though it's a rough loop, and doesn't end in exactly the same spot). Take the time to observe ospreys, eagles and other birdlife in the early morning, and take a breather at the overlooks of Batsto Lake.

Ticks are common in the woods of New Jersey and can transmit Lyme disease, so wear long pants, a long shirt and high socks. The **Wharton State Forest** has nine different campgrounds of differing access and comfort levels. **Lower Forge Camp** and **Mullica River Camp** are accessible only by canoe or hiking. The small towns in Pine Barrens have basic chain restaurants, pizzerias and diners, and there are also a couple of sweet luncheonettes.

Bluegrass in the Barrens

A part of the Pine Barrens' cultural history, not to be confused with the Royal Albert Hall in London, is Waretown's **Albert Music Hall**. It packs a surprising punch, with high-quality smokin' live bluegrass, country music, and warmed-up sausage and meatball subs if you come hungry. Shows, with an average of five to six bands, are held every Saturday at 6pm. American folk legend Pete Seeger played two benefits here to raise money for the venue in the 1970s. It's really as far east as you can be in the Pine Barrens, a quarter-mile west of Rte 9, near Barnegat Township, almost at the Shore.

Places We Love to Stay

$ Budget $$ Midrange $$$ Top End

Princeton
MAP p154

Inn at Glencairn $$ Five serene rooms in a renovated Georgian manor with old-world style and modern amenities.

Nassau Inn $$$ In a prime location in an 18th-century building, Nassau has been updated with boutique luxury furnishings, though it's slightly frumpy (some may prefer the new wing).

Lambertville
MAP p156

Lambertville House $$ The rooms here creak with age, but the four-poster beds, immaculate wooden furniture and lobby bar make up for it. Located in the heart of town.

Lambertville Station Hotel $$$ Riverfront contemporary hotel, with most rooms having creek or bridge views. Rooms are nicely furnished, though riverside suites are an enormous step up in luxury.

Hoboken
MAP p156

W Hotel $$$ This riverfront high-rise has stunning vistas of the west side of Manhattan, as well as a stylish lounge and excellent on-site restaurant.

Cape May
MAP p161

The Hugh Inn $$ The eight individually designed rooms here have a mix of Victorian original detail and contemporary glam with bold colors. A sophisticated French bistro is attached.

Congress Hall $$$ Opened in 1816, the enormous Congress Hall is a local landmark, now suitably modernized with a spa and several recommended restaurants.

Wildwood
MAP p163

Pan American Hotel $$ Every room in this stylish retro air-travel-themed hotel has a balcony and sea views. There's a new restaurant, heated outdoor pool and fire pit.

Madison Resort Wildwood Crest $$ The newly opened, completely renovated Wildwood Crest beachfront hotel has pool-side cabanas and three restaurants. It's the largest property in the area.

Starlux (p163) $$ The thoroughly updated sea-green-and-white Starlux has a soaring profile, fake plastic palms and surfboard-shaped bed headboards, plus its own mini-golf course and ice-cream parlor.

Atlantic City
MAP p163

Borgata $$ A few steps up from most of the boardwalk hotels (metaphorically) and across town (literally), classy, 2000-room Borgata offers spas, salons, pools and concert venues.

Showboat Hotel $$ A good choice for families: in lieu of a casino there's an immaculately maintained indoor water park, indoor go-kart track and the state's largest arcade.

Long Beach Island
MAP p163

Spray Beach Oceanfront Hotel $$ Ideally situated on Beach Haven's oceanfront, with efficiently and sophisticatedly designed rooms, a nice heated pool, restaurant and bicycles, plus beach chairs for guests.

Daddy O $$ Brant Beach boutique with oversized surfing-themed photos in rooms, with rooftop and garden bars and restaurant, plus beach chairs and umbrellas.

Asbury Park
MAP p163

St Laurent Social Club $$ The stylish rooms here feature fold-down beds and designer surfboards. There's a pool and bar, and the restaurant is one of the best around.

Asbury Hotel $$ From the solarium to the rooftop bar, this large, eight-story hotel oozes style with a modern, industrial angle and loads of amenities.

Ocean Grove
MAP p163

Laingdon Hotel $$ This restored Victorian B&B (circa 1875) fronts the beach with ocean views and has cozy rooms with a variety of layouts.

Above: The Philadelphia skyline; Right: William Penn statue, City Hall (p192)

THE MAIN AREAS

OLD CITY & SOCIETY HILL
America's founding, great restaurants and class.
p178

CHINATOWN & THE GAYBORHOOD
Authentic Chinatown and flamboyant pride.
p185

RITTENHOUSE SQUARE & CENTER CITY WEST
Stately and elegant, great craft-cocktail culture. **p192**

LOGAN SQUARE & FAIRMOUNT
Incomparable art and science museums.
p196

Philadelphia

HISTORY, CULTURE, ART AND INCREDIBLE FOOD

Philadelphia consistently dazzles visitors with its stately museums, beautiful buildings, range of restaurants and exciting things to do.

Philadelphia is, in so many ways, America's most American city, be it for the incredible wealth of art and culture, the historic buildings and sites, or the melting pot of cultures and the melt-in-your-mouth cuisines. If any city deserves the label of a 'patchwork quilt,' it's Philadelphia. Founded in 1681 by William Penn, it was unique among America's first big cities in that it was planned from the outset, with plenty of parks and open space. Sure, New York gets the acclaim, but where else but Philly can you walk among dozens of museums that were so key to the founding of the nation and pick among five-star restaurants that encompass the flavors of the world, reflecting the multicultural mosaic that is, for all its faults, the America of today? Whether you come for a deep dive into the founding of the United States with Philly's dozens of historic houses and the incomparable Museum of the American Revolution, take your kids to see dinosaurs, seek out the creepy halls of the Eastern State Penitentiary, or marvel (or shudder!) at the exhibits of the macabre Mütter Museum, this city has incredible diversity.

Troubled genius Edgar Allan Poe spent six of his happiest years here, working on short stories that would spark a new genre and become a part of the canon of great American literature. Cocktail enthusiasts will head for the swanky speakeasies or homey dive bars, shoppers will find haute-fashion districts or gritty thrift stores in narrow alleyways. Philadelphia's districts and neighborhoods feel as distinct from each other as the city does from the rest of the US urban centers. The vibrant, flamboyant Gayborhood, the delicious flavors and aromas of Chinatown, the stately Rittenhouse district, the college-town feel of University City – they all add up to a city that's more than just the sum of its parts, a place that just about any visitor will enjoy, with a lot to see that's obvious but plenty more to discover as you spend additional time here.

FOTOSFORTHEFUTURE/SHUTTERSTOCK ©

FISHTOWN & NORTHERN LIBERTIES
Quirky events and funky bars.
p199

SOUTH PHILADELPHIA
Vibrant immigrant-driven restaurants and markets.
p204

UNIVERSITY CITY & WEST PHILADELPHIA
College-town feel with all the trimmings.
p208

Find Your Way

Philadelphia is a big city with a small-town feel, lots of parks and a variety of transportation options that make it easy to get around. Center City and the iconic City Hall are the nexus.

BICYCLE

The Indego bikeshare system is located around the city. You'll need a US-registered credit or debit card to rent bikes for the walk-up rate of $15 for 24 hours, with unlimited 60-minute rides.

BUS

Market St is the main artery – hop on buses here to cross the center, or go underground to take the trolley to University City. March to December, the PHLASH bus loops around major tourist sites.

Fishtown & Northern Liberties p199

Logan Square & Fairmount p196

Eastern State Penitentiary

Philadelphia Museum of Art

University City & West Philadelphia p208

Rail Park

Chinatown & the Gayborhood p185

Rittenhouse Square & Center City West p192

Reading Terminal Market

Independence Hall

Museum of the American Revolution

Independence National Historical Park

Old City & Society Hill p178

South Philadelphia p204

Schuylkill River

Bartram's Garden

Philadelphia International (5.5mi)

Delaware River

City Hall (p192)

Plan Your Days

Not everyone has time to wander. Make the most of your visit by hitting the spots in our convenient itineraries so you can dive right into the city.

Art & Culture

● Head to the **Pennsylvania Academy of the Fine Arts** (p193) for morning art viewing. Grab early lunch at **Kiddo** (p186) before a 12:30pm tour of **City Hall** (p192) with its giant statue of William Penn. Pose at the *LOVE* sculpture in **JFK Plaza** (p195) and finish the day with a drag-show performance in Philly's flamboyant **Gayborhood** (p185).

A Weekend Trip

● Start a fun weekend by heading out to the **Brandywine Valley** (p214) for its beautiful gardens and museums. Return to dine in town at the elegant **Gran Caffè L'Aquila** (p194) or at iconic **Zahav** (p181). Wake refreshed and stroll to **University City** (p208) before finishing the weekend with a meal in the **Gayborhood** (p186) and a beer at **Dirty Franks** (p189).

SEASONAL HIGHLIGHTS

SPRING
There's flowers everywhere – even the trees join in, with magnolias, cherries, and apples all in bloom.

SUMMER
Hot and humid, summer sees fountains on and children having fun. You may see umbrellas out – for shade, not rain.

AUTUMN
Beautiful fall colors grace the stately parks, and folks start to pull out the winter coats again. Bring layers, you'll need them.

WINTER
Mummers Parade on January 1 is a crazy, colorful bonanza that floods the streets. Snow makes sidewalks slippery.

Old City & Society Hill

HISTORIC AND STATELY

GETTING AROUND

Old City and Society Hill are walkable districts, but if you need some speed, the Indego bike-rental system has kiosks at convenient locations, making it easy to rent a bike in one place and return it to another. There are bus and metro routes that connect the district with other parts of the city as well.

If there's one place where visitors can find traces of the United States' Founding Fathers today, it's Philadelphia's Old City. A large L-shaped chunk of this neighborhood is Independence National Historical Park, where all the big names – including Washington, Jefferson and Franklin – crafted the grandest political experiment the world has ever known. Stroll along cobblestone streets lined with iconic landmarks such as Independence Hall, the Liberty Bell and the Betsy Ross House, and immerse yourself in the birthplace of US democracy. Museums, historic buildings, sites and statues make it easy to visualize these key events. If history tires, this neighborhood offers lots more to see. Across the sunken Delaware Expwy (I-95), old wharves have been transformed into the parks and skating rinks of Penn's Landing. South of Walnut St, largely residential Society Hill is one of Philadelphia's most stylish neighborhoods.

Discover World-Changing Documents at the National Constitution Center

Learn about the constitution

The **National Constitution Center** brings to life the potentially dry and dense US Constitution, starting with a dramatic theater-in-the-round presentation by a single actor explaining the evolution of the political experiment.

'The Story of We the People' exhibit narrates a captivating journey through the US Constitution. Interactive displays and multimedia presentations dive into detail about the founding document, from the Constitutional Convention of 1787 to contemporary debates. Temporary exhibits, covering topics such as Founding Father Alexander Hamilton or the challenges of Prohibition, invite visitors to grapple with modern and historical issues through the lens of constitutional principles, fostering a deeper understanding of citizenship.

Wander the halls and be reminded of the enduring power of this radical project. In the shadow of Independence Hall

☑ TOP TIP

All but two of Philadelphia's museums allow strollers, so don't be worried if you've got little ones. If you need a wheelchair, you can find loaners in the Independence Visitor Center. Many sights will be busy at peak times of day, with queues of 30 minutes to 1½ hours. Plan accordingly.

TOP SIGHTS
1. Independence Hall
2. Independence National Historical Park
3. Museum of the American Revolution

SIGHTS
4. Benjamin Franklin Museum
5. Betsy Ross House
6. Congress Hall
7. Franklin Court
8. Liberty Bell Center
9. National Constitution Center
10. President's House Site
11. Science History Institute

SLEEPING
12. Apple Hostels

EATING
13. Cafe Ole
14. Fork
15. Forsythia
16. High Street Philadelphia
17. Zahav

DRINKING & NIGHTLIFE
18. 48 Record Bar
19. La Colombe
20. Menagerie Coffee
21. National Mechanics
22. Olde Bar

YELLOW FEVER EPIDEMIC OF 1793

Soon after the euphoria of the birth of a new nation, the terrifying scourge of yellow fever hit Philadelphia. At the time, the outbreak had no known cause, and wild theories ranged from fumes of rotting waste to human-to-human contact. Cures, all ineffectual, were equally wild and included ingesting mercury and bloodletting. The knowledge that it was caused by the insidious mosquito was more than a century away.

Even upstanding citizens such as Samuel Powel died, one among the 50,000 who lost their lives in the epidemic. Close to 10 percent of Philadelphia's residents died in less than five months.

National Constitution Center

(p182), the National Constitution Center stands as a pilgrimage site for those who seek to understand democracy's roots and the challenges ahead.

Suffrage, the right to vote, is at the core of US democracy. The idealistic language of the Declaration of Independence is inspiring to read, but it ironically applied only to a small segment of the population when it was written: wealthy, landowning white men. Enslaved people, women, minorities, Indigenous people and non-landowners were not allowed to participate in this grand political experiment. Voting wouldn't be legal for these groups for centuries, and in some ways, the nation is still grappling with the problems of a country where people are legally equal but often not treated as such.

EATING & DRINKING IN THE OLD CITY

Cafe Ole: The sunshine-yellow decor makes the great muffins, pastries and sandwiches taste even better. Great coffees, lattes and teas as well. $$	**High Street Philadelphia:** Fancy mushroom bowls, nongrain pasta and other delicious fare. $$	**Menagerie Coffee:** A favorite go-to for its range of coffees and espressos, relaxed European vibe, snacks and sandwiches.	**La Colombe:** A Philly chain gone big, La Colombe offers great specialty coffees, a signature 'draft latte' and excellent indie vibes.
Olde Bar: Swanky spot featuring classic American seafood in a historic setting, with cocktails from Prohibition-era greats to unique new ones.	**National Mechanics:** In the former Mechanics National Bank, now plying liquid gold – cocktails.	**Panorama:** Wine-focused restaurant with an extensive list of Italian wines, craft cocktails, classic Italian dishes and gorgeous city views.	**48 Record Bar:** More casual than some of the Old City standbys, with a music-first vibe, friendly bartenders and creative cocktails.

Meet the Famous Flagmaker at Betsy Ross House
The woman behind the Stars and Stripes

Nestled along cobblestone pathways, the **Betsy Ross House** tells the story of one of the country's most enduring symbols: the Stars and Stripes, the first US flag. You get to meet 'Betsy Ross' herself (an actress in period clothing who stays in character); she's the prime attraction and a fun experience for visitors with kids. Ask her questions and watch her work on a flag while learning about the history of this icon. The modest rooms and cozy quarters offer a glimpse into the daily life of a Revolutionary-era upholsterer.

Most historians doubt that this house is actually where the first flag was made, and it's pretty certain that the house Ross lived in was next to this one. Even so, the Betsy Ross House is a highly popular tourist stop.

Put On Your Thinking Cap at the Science History Institute
Great for young scientists

The **Science History Institute** is a must-stop for scientists and young explorers. Step into this museum's hallowed halls to discover a treasure trove of artifacts, archives and exhibitions that offer a window into the minds of the world's greatest innovators and thinkers.

The institute's collections span centuries and continents, from rare manuscripts and laboratory equipment to chemical samples and scientific instruments. Among the relics of the past, you can trace the evolution of scientific thought and explore the interconnectedness of ideas across cultures and disciplines from ancient alchemy to modern chemistry. Learn about everything from how crayons get their colors to measuring the chemical composition of things in space.

HOP OVER TO CAMDEN, NEW JERSEY

Camden – directly across the Delaware River from Penn's Landing – has attractions, a pleasant waterside park and great views. **Battleship New Jersey**, the most decorated such vessel in the USA, has a 1½-hour guided tour on Saturdays and Sundays at 11am – you can even crawl in a 16in gun turret.

With more than 8500 aquatic creatures from sea turtles to zebra sharks, **Adventure Aquarium** is one of the country's largest. As well as myriad fish, you can also see a pair of 3000lb Nile hippos, Button and Genny, plus a flock of African penguins in their own outdoor park.

 EATING IN THE OLD CITY: FINE DINING

Fork: Locally sourced ingredients are crafted into innovative dishes and paired with a sophisticated atmosphere and excellent service. **$$$**

Forsythia: A French-inspired spot with plating as stunning to behold as it is to eat. Weekend brunch is sublime. **$$$**

Talula's Garden: Seasonal American cuisine using farm-to-table ingredients, with tables set in an elegant garden. **$$$**

Zahav: Modern Israeli cuisine featuring wood-fired dishes, mezze plates and innovative flavors in a sleek and stylish space. **$$$**

PRACTICALITIES

Scan this QR code for practical information and audio tours.

TOP SIGHT

Independence National Historical Park

Independence National Historical Park is a stunning, almost overwhelming collection of museums, exhibits and historic buildings that keeps alive the most important event in the history of the United States: its founding. Set aside a couple of days to see everything.

DON'T MISS

Independence Hall

Museum of the American Revolution

Liberty Bell Center

Congress Hall

Benjamin Franklin Museum

Franklin Court

President's House Site

Independence Hall

The most unmissable place at Independence National Historical Park is **Independence Hall**, where the Declaration of Independence was signed and the US Constitution was written, documents that enshrined the concept of democratic rule for the first time. Entry to this World Heritage Site, a Georgian building that also served as the Pennsylvania State House, is by tour only. Inside, you'll visit the **Supreme Court Chamber**, which has been restored to look much as it did in those hallowed days of the country's founding.

Across the hall is the **Assembly Room**, with its photogenic green felt tabletops and hardwood chairs, where most of the building's notable events took place. The Declaration of Independence was approved here on July 4, 1776. George Washington sat in the chair in the center, and Abraham Lincoln's body lay here in state for two days following his assassination in 1865.

Museum of the American Revolution

Enter this impressive, multimedia-rich **museum** and virtually 'participate' in the American Revolution through interactive dioramas and 3D experiences that take you from contentment with British rule to the eventual rejection of it. Learn about the events, people, cultures and religions that participated in one of the world's most important events. Lots of hands-on displays and video stories mean kids will have as much fun as adults. All entry tickets are timed; reserve them early online (amrevmuseum.org). A prime attraction is George Washington's battle tent, dramatically revealed after you watch a presentation about it. Actors dramatize period scenes as well, though the schedule and times vary. Check the website for details.

Liberty Bell Center

Originally called the State House Bell, the Liberty Bell was made in 1751 to commemorate the 50th anniversary of Pennsylvania's constitution. Mounted in Independence Hall, it tolled on the first public reading of the Declaration of Independence. The crack developed in the 19th century. The bell was retired in 1846 and now sits as the star attraction of the **Liberty Bell Center**.

Congress Hall

Near Independence Hall, **Congress Hall** served as the seat of the United States Congress from 1790 to 1800. It's where George Washington was inaugurated for his second term as president and John Adams took the oath of office as the nation's second president.

Franklin Court

The peaceful **Franklin Court**, accessible from Market and Chestnut Sts, is where Benjamin Franklin's home once stood. The house was demolished in 1812, but you can still get a good impression of its dimensions from the tubular steel 3D outline of the building designed by the architectural firm Venturi, Rauch and Scott Brown in 1976.

Benjamin Franklin Museum

The **Benjamin Franklin Museum** features a diverse collection of exhibits and artifacts related to his life and achievements. Explore interactive displays showcasing Franklin's inventions, scientific experiments and writings, including his famous Poor Richard's Almanack and contributions to the field of electricity. The exhibition, divided into five areas that focus on one of Franklin's traits, is cleverly laid out with interactive elements and plenty of famous quotations. In the courtyard, park rangers demonstrate the printing process Franklin would have used.

PRESIDENT'S HOUSE SITE

Across from the Liberty Bell Center, the President's House Site shows where the first two US presidents, George Washington and John Adams, had their presidential offices. Redbrick walls mark where the building once stood and frame exhibits and archaeological remains that offer a window into the lives of the enslaved people who lived and worked here.

TOP TIPS

- Time your visit carefully to avoid crowds; weekday mornings are best.
- Consider bringing games for kids as lines can be long, including those for bathrooms.
- Bring snacks and plenty of water.
- You will be walking a lot, both inside the buildings and from spot to spot.
- Some exhibits (such as George Washington's tent) are only viewable as part of hourly timed viewings (every hour on the hour), but general admission includes this opportunity.
- The National Park Service can provide wheelchairs for loan.
- Check nps.gov/inde for any alerts and information.

THE GUIDE

PHILADELPHIA OLD CITY & SOCIETY HILL

WALK THE OLD CITY

As you set out walking, prepare to be awed by what might otherwise seem uninspiring: wood. Incredible lathe-turned bowls, marquetry, nature photography and timber sculptures await you at the ❶ **Museum for Art in Wood**. The gallery puts on several exhibitions a year, and its museum collection has more than 1000 objects. The shop sells handcrafted pieces, and you may even be able to try your hand at crafting something. Swing by the ❷ **Fireman's Hall Museum** to peek at antique fire engines, see the tools and equipment that firefighters have used over the years and look inside an old brick building that was once the area's firehouse. Lined with brightly painted brick row houses fluttering with flags, photogenic, cobblestone ❸ **Elfreth's Alley** dates back to the 1720s, making it the US's oldest residential street. After sitting abandoned for decades, the early 20th-century municipal ❹ **Cherry St Pier** has been revamped as a mixed-use public space with a pop-up market, gardens, events and artists' studios. Within the old pier's shell, converted shipping containers make up the studios and market stalls. It's a perfect lunch stop. The ❺ **Independence Seaport Museum** offers a broad range of maritime-related exhibits and interactive displays. Check out the massive ship carpenter's screwdriver, which will change your views about what a simple tool can be. Some tickets include visiting the 1944 submarine USS *Becuna* and the distinguished 1892 USS *Olympia* moored alongside the main building. The summer-season ❻ **Spruce Street Park** is a great place to hang out by the river. Relax in a two-person hammock, play free games such as ping-pong and shuffleboard, or knock back craft beers and local eats from the many stalls.

Chinatown & the Gayborhood

HISTORY, FOOD & CULTURE

The star features of this central slice of Philly include a couple of amazing foodie destinations – the historic Reading Terminal Market and the fourth-largest Chinatown in the USA, both of which provide hungry visitors with an array of mouthwatering delights. But keep salivating, because there's tons of delicious food and great drinks awaiting just a few blocks away in the Gayborhood, which in no way is a neighborhood reserved just for LGBTIQ+ visitors. The rainbow-flag-flying Gayborhood, also known as Midtown Village, is a compact area roughly bounded by Walnut, Spruce, Broad and 11th Sts. Washington Sq West is a mostly residential area with a couple of large hospitals and Jewelry Row, but increasingly is seen as a food and drink destination. Did we mention the rainbow flags? They're not just flying from windows and rooftops – even the crosswalks are colorfully proud, and have been since 2015.

Ring in the Chinese New Year
Color, dance and fun
The US's fourth-largest Chinatown celebrates Asia's biggest holiday in January or February with exciting lion dances, a parade, and much eating and drinking. The streets fill with jubilant crowds, and wafts of special Chinese New Year foods

GETTING AROUND

SEPTA buses crisscross these neighborhoods. You can hop on the PHLASH bus along Market St. If you prefer the subway, the Market-Frankford Line stations include 15th, 13th and 8th Sts. Broad Street Line trains stop at City Hall, connecting with the trolley to 13th St. There's also train access on SEPTA Regional Rail lines at the underground Jefferson Station. The PATCO line has stations at 9th/10th St and 12/13th St. Electric-assisted bicycles rentable on Indego are ubiquitous. You can rent at one kiosk and return at another.

FAMOUS FRANKS

On the wall outside of the iconic **Dirty Franks** (p189) watering hole, the **Famous Franks** mural has faces of 19 people with 'Frank' in their names, from Aretha Franklin to Pope Francis and Frank Sinatra. Other notable Franks, all of which are connected in some way to either the painter or the city, include Frank Oz, Frank Zappa, a frankfurter, Frankenstein's monster and Frank Sherlock, a Dirty Franks employee and locally known poet. Two of the Franks – Pope Francis and Frank Sherlock – were added when the mural was restored in 2015.

Chinatown

like noodles, golden spring rolls, fish and buns delight the nostrils. Lion dances start at 10th and Race Sts and wind their way through the district, with firecrackers and festivities.

Chinese New Year is a time of togetherness. Families flood the restaurants, gather to pay respects to ancestors, exchange red envelopes for good luck, and dig into traditional dishes that symbolize prosperity and abundance. Many shops offer free gifts, and troupes of dancers parade from store to store, hoping for tips. Just about everything will be red and gold, colors that in China symbolize what the Lunar New Year is all about: hopes for wealth and prosperity to come.

Catch a Drag Show

Flamboyant, edgy and outlandish fun

Catching a drag show in the Gayborhood is a highlight of visiting Philly. They're big, brash, flamboyant and saucy, and audiences are often left in stitches. Beer and cocktails are on the menu, but what's really served are fun, fancy outfits, big hair and big booties. Each drag show is different. Some performers focus on dance numbers and show tunes, while others do standup or offer moving tales of their experiences. Many drag show performers are local celebrities, but others come from around the country, performing on tour. Don't think that if you've seen one show, you've seen them all.

☑ TOP TIP

Parking can be very challenging in this part of the city and meters run well into the night. Make things more relaxing by using a taxi, rideshare or walking if possible. You'll be glad you did.

 EATING IN CHINATOWN & THE GAYBORHOOD: BREAKFAST & BRUNCH

Dutch Eating Place: A great spot inside **Reading Terminal Market** (p190) to find Amish delicacies, breakfast, lunch and baked goods. **$**

Kiddo: Surprising flavor combinations turn brunch (often full of the familiar) into an exciting adventure that leaves you eager to return. **$$**

Sofi Corner: Delightful LGBTIQ+-friendly spot with a pretty patio and tables (often crowded) inside. The shakshuka is particularly good. **$$**

Green Eggs Cafe: All the traditional favorites, plus creative takes such as red velvet pancakes and birthday-cake French toast. Cash only. **$$**

CHINATOWN & THE GAYBORHOOD

TOP SIGHTS
1. Reading Terminal Market

SIGHTS
2. Famous Franks

ACTIVITIES, COURSES & TOURS
3. City Food Tours

SLEEPING
4. Alexander Inn

EATING
5. Barbuzzo
6. Dutch Eating Place
7. Green Eggs Cafe
8. Kiddo
9. Sofi Corner
10. Tom's Dim Sum
11. Vetri Cucina

DRINKING & NIGHTLIFE
12. Bike Stop
- see 2. Dirty Franks
13. McGillin's Olde Ale House
14. U Bar

ENTERTAINMENT
15. Franky Bradley's
16. Philly Pride
17. Wanamaker Organ

SHOPPING
18. Macy's

VISIT MACY'S WANAMAKER ORGAN CONCERT

Inside **Macy's** sits the beautiful **Wanamaker Organ**, installed by John Wanamaker, the building's first owner, in 1909 to host free concerts to delight shoppers and encourage them to linger. The tradition lives on, with classical and pop tunes filling the department store's central atrium at noon and 5:30pm. While you're hanging around Macy's Grand Court, check out *Eagle*, a 1904 bronze statue that's also a popular Philly meeting point. The department store also hosts the fun Christmas Light Show from Thanksgiving (late November) to New Year's Eve, when the Grand Court atrium is heavily decorated with trees, lights, candles and ornaments. The animated figures are a hit with kids.

Franky Bradley's is a Gayborhood standby, known for its 'dancing, DJs, and deviation,' as well as cheap beers and excellent food. **Bob & Barbara's Lounge** is a standby, with nightly drag shows, live music, burlesque and its famous 'Special,' a shot-and-beer combo at a ridiculously low price. (It's technically not in the official 'Gayborhood' but on nearby Broad St.)

Show Your True Colors at Philly Pride
Over-the-top, fun and flamboyant festival

The entire month of June features **Philly Pride** events in one of the city's biggest and most extravagant celebrations. The festivities kick off with a huge parade, which starts at 6th and Walnut Sts and ends in the Gayborhood. Because it takes place in warmer temperatures at the start of the summer season, clothing can be vastly more skimpy than on the

EATING IN CHINATOWN & THE GAYBORHOOD: OUR PICKS

Nan Zhou Hand Drawn Noodle House: Expect to wait for a table; everything is good, but the bowls of cut noodles in savory broth are best. **$**

Tom's Dim Sum: You can eat dim sum cheaply, but it's surprisingly easy to keep ordering as these morsels go down so easily. **$**

Barbuzzo: Packed restaurant with delicious Mediterranean dishes; expect small portions big on taste. **$$**

Vetri Cucina: One of Philly's priciest meals, this spot has a gourmet prix fixe that's divine. The wine pairings are highly recommended. **$$$**

Philly Pride

similarly festive Mummers Parade, which happens in January. Rainbows are everywhere, and revelers of all stripes – gay, straight and everything in between – pack the streets. It's a party for all, with hilarity, fun and a bit of the risqué. While the focus is on pride and the LGBTIQ+ community, everyone is welcome to take part.

Philly Pride features lots of food trucks, shows, events, buskers and performances. There are tributes to the Latinx LGBTIQ+ community, and speakers and events specifically promote this slice of the community to widen visibility.

In the 1980s, Philadelphia fought on the front lines of the AIDS/HIV epidemic, and its citizens were among the first to be diagnosed and shunned as fear of the disease gripped the country. In some ways, this history makes Philly Pride one of the city's most important celebrations.

PHILADELPHIA GAY MEN'S CHORUS

The Philadelphia Gay Men's Chorus (pgmc.org) has delivered engaging and thought-provoking performances to more than 100,000 listeners since 1982, when it began as a group of three gay men going door-to-door caroling at Christmas. The group is instrumental in raising LGBTIQ+ awareness and acceptance in Philadelphia and has several outreach programs to help the LGBTIQ+ community. The men have sung at many places, such as baseball stadiums, community centers and even City Hall, and their performances often include sing-alongs and audience participation.

 DRINKING IN CHINATOWN & THE GAYBORHOOD: GREAT BARS

Dirty Franks: Friendly neighborhood bar with cheap drinks, dartboards and even reverse BYOB – bring your own food to eat with a beer from the bar.

Bike Stop: At this leather-and-chains gay biker bar – a Philly icon – it's not uncommon to see someone walking around in a harness and little else.

U Bar: Popular gay bar with food and great pours. The vibe is quiet and conversational rather than frenetic.

McGillin's Olde Ale House: Come for the friendly welcome and the Irish-pub vibe rather than for the food.

TOP SIGHT

Reading Terminal Market

Keeping the balance right between food market and a dining destination, Reading Terminal Market dates from 1893 and is a city institution. The stalls provide strong flavors of Philly's cultural melting pot – from Pennsylvania Dutch to Asian cuisine – and attract visitors from billionaires to blue-collar workers.

PRACTICALITIES

Scan this QR code for opening hours and the vendor list.

DON'T MISS

- Bassetts
- Miller's Twist
- DiNic's
- Dutch Eating Place
- Hershel's East Side Deli
- Pearl's Oyster Bar
- Beiler's
- Sweet Nina's
- PA General Store

Take It All In

Visiting Reading Terminal Market is an adventure for the senses – a feast for the eyes as much as the taste buds. The atmosphere is electric, with vendors hawking fresh produce, artisanal cheeses, international cuisines and handmade crafts from crowded, bustling market stalls. The scent of aromatic spices and freshly baked goods wafts through the air, and the energy is palpable as locals and tourists weave through the chaos looking for that perfect treat on which to munch. Pick up Amish baked goods, handmade doughnuts, meats, cheeses, canned goods, preserves, soaps, clothing and more. Come back at different times of day because the vibe changes substantially from early morning to lunch to late afternoon.

Pick & Choose

Reading Terminal Market has nearly 100 stalls to check out, but you'll definitely want to try these top spots. Note that Amish and Mennonite stalls are closed on Sundays.

Bassetts The country's oldest ice-cream company, established in 1861.

Miller's Twist Known for its buttery pretzels.

DiNic's Dig into its succulent roast-pork sandwich.

Dutch Eating Place Amish delicacies, breakfasts, lunches and baked goods.

Hershel's East Side Deli Jewish favorites, including corned-beef sandwiches and kosher apple cake.

Pearl's Oyster Bar Freshly shucked oysters, spicy pepper pot and snapping turtle soup.

Beiler's Hot-from-the-fryer doughnuts and apple fritters, plus bread and barrels of pickles.

Sweet Nina's Incredibly tasty banana pudding.

PA General Store Stocks both food and nonfood items produced in the state.

Take a Tour

Snack and listen to Philly food lore during the 45-minute market visit with **City Food Tours** (phillysfoodtour.com). Tours begin at 10:30am and 2pm and kick off with a treat from a vendor and end with an additional something to savor. During the tour, you learn about the market, its history, the vendors and some interesting and colorful food-related stories.

A Bite of History

Philadelphia has always been a market city, but the markets weren't always indoors. Numerous outdoor markets grew organically (pun intended!) in various places around the city, to the point that, in the mid-1800s, they were becoming troublesome to city dwellers, who found them noisy and unsanitary. Because of this, the markets were either closed or moved to indoor locations. The current Reading Terminal Market is the combined descendent of two markets that were located on Market St's 1100 block. When the block was purchased by the Reading Railway, the merchants refused to leave, insisting they had a right to vend there. After many heated meetings with railway brass and merchant spokespeople, a compromise was reached that allowed the vendors to stay. For about a century the market served the citizens of Philadelphia, until a decline in the 1970s forced it to close. It was deemed too important to lose, however, and with the rise of interest in organic and farm-to-table produce that came in the '80s and '90s, the market again became relevant to city shoppers and travelers, who now can find a dizzying array of fresh, delicious foods and artisanal items.

ON-DEMAND DELIVERY

A fun fact about the Reading Terminal Market is that long before Amazon appeared, the market would send boys out with packages of whatever had been ordered. They delivered not just by foot or bicycle nearby, but even took trains to reach far-outlying areas. Items would be picked up by customers at the station.

TOP TIPS

- Come to the market hungry, and plan on eating something. (You'll want to, we promise!)
- Some vendors are cash only and even if they're not, using cash helps vendors keep 100% of the transaction; otherwise they pay bank transaction fees.
- Wander around the entire market before making a purchase.
- Plan two trips – one at breakfast time, one at lunch – to make the most of the food stalls.
- Use a variety of camera settings, as dim light and cavernous spaces make for difficult photos.
- Expect to wait in line for some of the most popular stalls.

THE GUIDE

PHILADELPHIA CHINATOWN & THE GAYBORHOOD

Rittenhouse Square & Center City West

STATELY AND SERENE

GETTING AROUND

SEPTA buses crisscross these neighborhoods. Access the PHLASH bus around City Hall. The Market-Frankford Line subway stations include 15th and 13th. Broad Street Line trains stop at City Hall, Walnut-Locust and Lombard-South. Rent a bike for an hour at a time using the Indego app (rideindego.com). Ride for up to an hour and then return it at one of the kiosks and rent another one if you need to.

Few US city centers are as magnificent as Philadelphia's, where the stunning, ornate City Hall is topped by an oversized William Penn statute and festive international flags greet people on Benjamin Franklin Parkway. In winter, City Hall has an outdoor skating rink, and the surrounding blocks are the engine of Philadelphia's economy: office buildings, big hotels, concert halls and restaurants.

Just a few blocks southwest, genteel Rittenhouse Sq is a quiet counterpoint, the center of an elegant residential district dotted with cafes and small restaurants. Between the two are the prime retail strips of Chestnut and Walnut Sts.

This area is both the prime attraction and also a bit rough and tumble. Bankers in three-piece suits pass by unhoused people napping on subway vents. Despite the disparity, it's a relatively calm neighborhood.

Say 'Eww!' at the Mütter Museum
Scientific and medical marvels

Maintained by the College of Physicians, the unique, only-in-Philadelphia **Mütter Museum** is an attraction dedicated to rare, odd and disturbing medical conditions. Want to see a life-size wax example of the stages of syphilis? You've come to the right place.

SIGHTS
1. Mütter Museum
2. Pennsylvania Academy of the Fine Arts
3. Schuylkill Banks

ACTIVITIES, COURSES & TOURS
4. Hidden River Outfitters

SLEEPING
5. Franklin on Rittenhouse
6. ROOST Rittenhouse

EATING
7. Cleavers
8. Dandelion
9. Dizengoff
10. Gran Caffè L'Aquila
11. Square 1682
12. The Love

DRINKING & NIGHTLIFE
13. Green Eggs Cafe
14. Harp & Crown
15. Metropolitan Cafe & Bakery
16. Monk's Cafe
17. Ranstead Room
18. Stir Lounge
19. Village Whiskey

Though the museum is not for the squeamish, it's not just here for shock value. Adults and budding junior scientists and physicians will find it educational, interesting and, sure, pretty gross. Exhibits include a saponified body, a conjoined female fetus, incredibly realistic wax models of medical conditions and skulls by the dozen, as well as descriptions of the now thoroughly debunked theory of phrenology, the pseudoscience that claimed (wrongly) that the size and shape of a person's skull dictated his or her abilities. Another exhibit explores the parallels between the 1918 Spanish Flu epidemic and COVID-19, with insightful history and analysis.

The museum is housed in a compact space, but its fascinating subject matter means you'll likely spend two to three hours here.

See the Pennsylvania Academy of the Fine Arts

Immerse yourself in fine art

The prestigious **Pennsylvania Academy of the Fine Arts**, an art school founded in 1805, occupies two buildings, including a masterwork of Victorian Gothic architecture designed by Frank Furness and George Hewitt.

☑ TOP TIP

Don't miss the chance to take a City Hall tour, where you'll get to ride on a centuries-old elevator and see the iconic statue of William Penn, whose legacy is seen throughout the city. You'll be able to look at him up close, and the views of the city are spectacular.

RACE MATTERS

Philadelphia is one of the most segregated cities in the USA, as well as one of the poorest. The geographical and economic divisions between ethnic groups in Philly are stark and controversial.

The Black Lives Matter movement upped the ante on such discussions. One of its targets was the statue of controversial former mayor Frank Rizzo, whose tough stance on crime led to deep divisions primarily along racial lines. Activist Asa Khalif voiced the feelings of the wider Black community when he said the statue represented decades of oppression and violence. In 2020, the statue was removed from its prominent location facing City Hall.

Start your tour of the museum's collection in that building (closed temporarily until fall 2025), where the interior design nearly – but not quite – overshadows the works on display. The sculptures are so lifelike they seem to watch as you tour the galleries, which feature famous works by Winslow Homer, Andy Warhol and Mary Cassatt.

Continuing education classes allow the public to dive in and experience art by making instead of viewing. Sculpture and painting classes and other workshops take place frequently, so check the calendar (pafa.org/museum/events).

Seek Out a Speakeasy
Prohibition fun

Some of Philadelphia's best bars can be found in this neighborhood, but they can be easy to overlook if you don't know better. **Ranstead Room** is one of several Philly speakeasies that hearken back to Prohibition. You won't find any signs outside, just a dim red lantern above a doorway next to some

 EATING IN RITTENHOUSE SQUARE & CENTER CITY WEST: BEST DINNERS

Dandelion: British-themed pub with great cocktails, a bar and excellent food, including Welsh rarebit and bangers and mash. **$$**	**The Love:** Fall in love with the menu at The Love, which ranges from fried chicken to a vegan platter. Desserts are sublime. **$$$**	**Dizengoff:** Incredible Israeli food by chef Mike Solomonov. Creamy, buttery takes on hummus and combinations of spices and flavors. **$$$**	**Gran Caffè L'Aquila:** Surprise and delight your taste buds with savory gelato (think cold sauces) and perfectly done Italian specials. **$$$**
Cleavers: Devour incredible cheesesteaks and a lot more at this popular sandwich spot that offers artisanal ingredients. **$$**	**Metropolitan Cafe & Bakery:** 'Power' muffins, croissants and bagel breakfast sandwiches to start a day; pizzas and sandwiches for lunch. **$$**	**Square 1682:** Inside Hotel Palomar, this restaurant has hearty breakfasts, tasty mains and nice drinks throughout the day. **$$**	**Green Eggs Cafe:** Mammoth portions make Green Eggs hard to beat, with exciting takes on French toast, eggs and waffles. **$$**

Schuylkill Banks

FIND LOVE AT JFK PLAZA

Officially called JFK Plaza, Love Park takes its nickname from Robert Indiana's iconic *LOVE* sculpture, which stacks the letters of the word in candy-apple red. In winter, the statue looks great when it's wearing a white coat of snow. In addition to the art, the plaza also has a fountain for cooling off in summer and orange chairs to sit in. Fun fact: the plaza was designed by architect and city planner Edmund Bacon, father of the actor Kevin Bacon.

dumpsters. All that clues you in that you're in the right place is the queue.

Wait in line to place your name on the reservations list for that night only (Ranstead Room doesn't take advance reservations). Once you've been given a time, you can leave to have dinner or drinks elsewhere until you get a text. Make sure your phone's volume is up because you have only a few minutes to reply. Hightail it over to be escorted into the swanky, dimly lit interior. It's a belabored process, but it adds to the evening's fun, and the drinks are sublime.

Schuylkill Banks
Kayak through the city

Schuylkill Banks (pronounced SKOOL-kill) is a wonderful outdoor recreation area that covers about eight miles of the Schuylkill River, mostly on the east bank below the Fairmount Dam through the heart of Philadelphia. It offers a fantastic wealth of outdoor fun in a surprising location: right in the center of the city. One of the best ways to enjoy this unique area is on a guided kayak tour. Set off with **Hidden River Outfitters** and paddle the river with an experienced guide, learning about the history and ecology of this riparian area. If you'd rather get on the water without the work, riverboat tours are also available. Check the Schuylkill Banks website (schuylkillbanks.org/events/riverboat-tours) for dates.

 DRINKING IN RITTENHOUSE SQUARE & CENTER CITY WEST: BEST BARS

Harp & Crown: This buzzing spot has a long horseshoe bar; downstairs is a two-lane bowling alley and gentleman's club-like space.	**Village Whiskey:** A perfect pub stop for an afternoon tipple, evening meal or nightcap, with a selection of about 200 world whiskeys.	**Stir Lounge:** Tiny and divey 'everyone's welcome' gay bar goes against the ritzy Rittenhouse vibe by just being a fun hangout.	**Monk's Cafe:** Hops fans crowd this mellow wood-paneled place for Belgian and American craft beers on tap – it has one of the best selections in the city.

Logan Square & Fairmount

PARADES, FLAGS AND GREAT MUSEUMS

GETTING AROUND

Useful SEPTA buses include 7, 27, 33, 38, 43, 48 and 49. The PHLASH bus also covers Benjamin Franklin Parkway to and from Logan Sq, Eastern State Penitentiary and (on a separate service) West Fairmount Park. Trolley route 15 connects with the Philadelphia Zoo. SEPTA Regional Rail lines serve Suburban station. Use East Falls and Wynnefield Ave stations for Fairmount Park.

☑ TOP TIP

On the first Sunday of each month, and Fridays after 5pm, Philadelphia Museum of Art has a pay-what-you-want policy, so you can save by visiting at these times and paying what you can afford. Otherwise, standard adult admission is $30, which is well worth it when you consider the priceless treasures inside.

Since its construction in the early 20th century, Benjamin Franklin Parkway has been the location of many of Philadelphia's most treasured cultural institutions, including the magnificent Philadelphia Museum of Art and 2000-acre Fairmount Park. This street is where the Mummers Parade festivities kick off, with groups gathering en masse before the parade begins. Logan Square and Fairmount are rich areas for art and science, and the Academy of Natural Sciences museum is a prime attraction. The neighborhood is full of interesting architecture, evocative streets and alleyways, and it's peppered with excellent spots to eat. The district's central location makes it a great hub for exploring almost anywhere in Philadelphia, but it remains quieter than spots such as Center City. You'll find that by 10pm there's not a lot happening on the streets, with most restaurants closing. A few bars stay open 'til the wee hours.

Philadelphia Museum of Art

World-class art museum

The **Philadelphia Museum of Art**, the city's premier cultural institution, occupies a Grecian temple-like building housing a superb collection of Asian art, Renaissance masterpieces, postimpressionist works and modern pieces. Especially notable are galleries filled with complete architectural ensembles, including a medieval cloister and a Japanese teahouse. The museum has a spectacular 12,000-piece collection of American art from colonial times to the modern day. Highlights to look for include *Portrait of Dr. Samuel D. Gross* (also known as *The Gross Clinic*) by Thomas Eakins, *The Life Line* by Winslow Homer, *Yarrow Mamout* by Charles Willson Peale and a teapot made by Paul Revere. Georgia O'Keefe fans will delight in seeing *Two Calla Lilies on Pink*, one of her many stunning works.

Appreciating contemporary art takes a bit more effort from the viewer, but the museum offers a depth and breadth unparalleled in its collection, which includes pieces by Andy Warhol, Edna Andrade, Bruce Nauman, Zoe Leonard and many others, with thousands of works in its collection that are not currently on display. Among hundreds of stunning works of ceramic art, silk scrolls and clothing is Sunkaraku, a real Japanese teahouse constructed in 1917 by Ōgi Rodō, his only work done outside Japan. The rooms display Japanese zen ideals, the concepts of simplicity and peacefulness, and harmony with the ceremony being performed. Many of the museum's tours, from in-depth looks at Rodin's hands to surveys of museum highlights and women in art, are free with your admission. Some tours are timed, so plan ahead if you want to join.

Tour Eastern State Penitentiary

Creepy prison museum

Tours of the eerie and fascinating **Eastern State Penitentiary**, a former prison, are a Philadelphia favorite year-round but especially at Halloween. A visit is more than a look into the past because exhibits explore issues that the country still grapples with today, such as racial prejudices and overcrowding. This prison was built like a giant asterisk, with all the structures originating from a point in the center. This design allowed one guard to stand in the center and easily monitor the entire prison by rotating around – he could check on all the hallways and respond quickly if problems arose. Other creative ways that guards kept tabs on inmates involved strategically placed mirrors so that it was easy to see around corners and check that nobody was hiding behind a wall.

When it opened in 1829, the Eastern State Penitentiary was seen as a paragon of modern incarceration, lauded by politicians, police and correctional institution directors. It offered something no other prison did at the time: solitary confinement, then seen as a miraculous solution to the unsafe practices of housing prisoners in dorms. But it was as costly as it was impressive, and as views on solitary confinement shifted, so too did the prison's fortunes.

Despite housing Al Capone and several other high-profile criminals, Eastern State Penitentiary began closing in 1960 and finally shuttered in 1971. Today, the beautiful decay of its eerie hallways, disused cells strewn with trash, peeling paint and rusted bars are a favorite for photographers. The prison has great spots for photos almost everywhere you look, and those with a fondness for urban exploration will find it easy to spend hours here.

THE BARNES FOUNDATION

In the first half of the 20th century, collector and educator Albert C Barnes amassed a remarkable trove of artwork by Cézanne, Degas, Matisse, Renoir, Van Gogh and other European stars. Alongside, he set beautiful pieces of folk art from Africa and the Americas, an artistic desegregation that was shocking at the time. Today's **Barnes Foundation** is a contemporary shell, inside which is a faithful reproduction of the galleries of Barnes' original mansion (still in the Philadelphia suburbs).

Admission is free on the first Sunday of the month. Tickets (only available at members.barnesfoundation.org/vip) are limited to four per person, and there's a focus on family activities.

EATING IN LOGAN SQUARE & FAIRMOUNT: BREAKFAST & BRUNCH

Cosmic Cafe & Ciderhouse: The view is the main course at this spot with sandwiches and all-day breakfasts overlooking the river. $$

Little Pete's: Come here for some of the finest Philly cheesesteaks in the city at reasonable prices in a spot near the Museum of Art. $

Sabrina's Cafe: This Philly mini-chain has several locations. This one on Callowhill St has giant breakfasts, friendly service and friendly vibe. $

Monkey & the Elephant: Special spot because it allows foster youth to gain valuable experience in the food industry. Great coffee and paninis. $$

TOP SIGHTS
1. Eastern State Penitentiary
2. Philadelphia Museum of Art

SIGHTS
3. Barnes Foundation
4. Rodin Museum

SLEEPING
5. Sheraton Philadelphia Downtown
6. Windsor Suites

EATING
7. Kansai
8. Little Pete's
9. Osteria
10. Stir Restaurant
11. Urban Farmer

DRINKING & NIGHTLIFE
12. Cosmic Cafe & Ciderhouse
13. Sabrina's Cafe

Rodin in Philadelphia

Get up close to the great sculpture

Walking through the incredible **Rodin Museum** is as close as you can get to meeting Auguste Rodin himself. You'll see not only versions of some of his most famous works but also many of the unknown, lesser works that give insights into his craft. Administered by the Philadelphia Museum of Art, this space is the only institution outside of Paris dedicated to the French sculptor, and its superb collection is based on works amassed by Jules E Mastbaum in the 1920s. The 140 sculptures from every part of Rodin's spectacular career include versions of *The Thinker* and *Burghers of Calais*. The museum's small garden is always open and free.

EATING IN LOGAN SQUARE & FAIRMOUNT: FINE DINING

Urban Farmer: More than 'just' a steakhouse, this spot on Logan Sq offers fantastic farm-to-table produce and pairing cocktails and wines. $$$

Stir Restaurant: This fine-dining spot in the Philadelphia Museum of Art looks as beautiful as the pieces that surround it. $$$

Osteria: Elevated Italian dining in a spacious glass-walled patio that is the perfect complement to al dente pasta and mains such as wild boar. $$$

Kansai: Artfully presented sushi rolls, sashimi and nigiri at a small, comfy spot near the Rodin Museum. $$$

Fishtown & Northern Liberties

HISTORY, DINING AND DIVES

This area is light on traditional sights but popular for eating, drinking, partying and shopping. Some of the world's (yes, the world's!) best restaurants are here. It also has a nice scene down at the shores of the Delaware River, with parks, casinos and distilleries to check out. Perhaps the most famous attraction is the Edgar Allan Poe house, where the macabre writer spent six of his happiest years penning some of his most successful stories and cementing his place in the American literary canon.

The gentrification that started a couple of decades ago in the former manufacturing district of Northern Liberties (nicknamed 'NoLibs') has since spread to Fishtown, so called because it's where the city's shad fishing industry was once based, and parts of Kensington. Northern Liberties was once its own city, separate from Philadelphia and one of America's ten largest cities. It was engulfed by Philadelphia in 1854.

Browse the Edgar Allan Poe National Historic Site

The famous author's Philly home

It's impossible to read Edgar Allan Poe's macabre tales without wondering what the author's own life was like. Similar to his characters, Poe was a troubled soul. He was an orphan and had financial problems, his wife was gravely ill, and for much of his life, his literary genius wasn't accepted or appreciated. Poe struggled for many years, but Philadelphia proved to be a respite. He had a decent job editing a respected literary magazine, he wrote some of his most popular tales in this house, and he is credited with inventing the modern detective story. He died at 40 under mysterious circumstances in Baltimore, Maryland.

This is a small **museum** and it's easy to see it all, but don't miss the cellar, which may have been the inspiration for his

GETTING AROUND

Walking this entire area would be tough, but it's a dense district and it's easy to walk between the hot spots. SEPTA buses 43 and 61 go along Spring Garden St; buses 5 and 25 are also useful north-south routes. Useful Market-Frankford Line subway stations include Spring Garden, Girard, Berks and York-Dauphin. The Broad Street Line also has Spring Garden and Girard stations. Trolley services run along Girard St from Frankford and Delaware.

☑ TOP TIP

Bar-hopping here is excellent, with so many beer halls, cocktail spots and dive bars. Start near the waterfront at the Casino or Philadelphia Distilling, then head (or stumble!) inland to spots such as Laser Wolf, Kung Fu Necktie or El Bar. Nondrinkers can nosh at Laser Wolf or La Colombe.

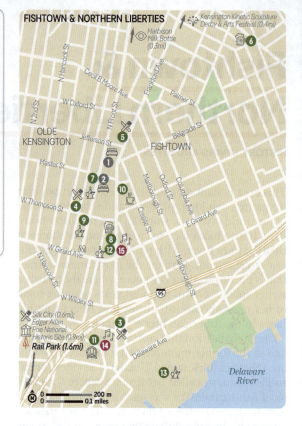

famous short story, *The Black Cat*. Rangers occasionally do dramatic (and hopefully scary!) readings of the famous story in the cellar.

Another top spot is the raven statue outside, an homage to Poe's famous poem of the same name. The garden has been planted with herbs and flowers that Poe describes in his works.

Creatives and readers should stop at the Reading Room, where you can bask in the ambience Poe himself described in his essay, 'The Philosophy of Furniture.' Perhaps it will inspire you to pen the next viral ghost story!

Get Messy at the Kensington Kinetic Sculpture Derby & Arts Festival

Craziness and muddy fun

Go wild and prepare for mud at the hilarious **Kensington Kinetic Sculpture Derby & Arts Festival** (kensington kineticarts.org), which takes place in early May. It features human-powered floats ranging from little more than bicycles to wildly extravagant creations, which do a 3-mile derby route through the area. Along the way, the creations must

The Fillmore

surmount various obstacles, including the Mud Pit, a massive pile of mud that must be traversed, often with comical fails, just before crossing the finish line.

This festival is the kind of crazy, fun-for-everyone event where the failures are as much fun as the successes. Enjoy lots of great music, vendors, food and shopping during the day. The event takes place rain or shine, so bring an umbrella (or just get wet).

Look for Fishtown's Iconic Sights
Familiar sights and fond memories

Boston has its famous Citgo sign, Hollywood has its hillside letters overlooking the city, and Fishtown has the **Harbison Milk Bottle**, an iconic water tower that has stood since the late 1800's advertising 'Harbison's Milk & Ice Cream.' A pioneer in the region's milk industry, Harbison's (with its trademark 'H') began producing milk before refrigeration and lasted a century before closing in the 1960s. The buildings below the water tower, and the tower itself, fell into disrepair, but luckily the Historical Commission has preserved them, and the tower now has a fresh coat of paint and its cheery red letters of old.

Another top sight (or venue, if you're in the mood for a show) is the **Fillmore**. It's large enough to bring in lots of big names while still retaining an industrial and intimate feel. The building was once a metal-works factory, and much

THE LA COLOMBE STORY

Coffee shop **La Colombe** has its flagship shop in Fishtown, and this business is as much a Philadelphia success story as the movie *Rocky*. It features two guys with a vision who slowly but surely grew their coffee shop – at a time when the big coffee chains had cornered the market – from a small store in Rittenhouse to multiple locations around Philly and then all over the country. Stop in at this clean, beautifully decorated store for any type of coffee or espresso. The signature Draft Latte helped the company rise to the top ranks.

EATING IN FISHTOWN & NORTHERN LIBERTIES: OUR PICKS

Suraya: Incredible Middle Eastern food, with lots of small Lebanese plates that make for one amazing meal. **$$**

Silk City: A fixture on Spring Garden St since the 1950s, with classic diner-style chrome-edged bar and booth layout. **$$**

Laser Wolf: One of the neighborhood's top dining experiences, with bold flavors and expertly crafted Middle Eastern dishes. *5-10pm* **$$$**

Elwood: Unique farm-to-table Pennsylvania Dutch dishes, such as shad roe, served on fine china. High tea on weekends. **$$$**

NOLIBS

It sounds like something a partisan radio personality might say, but in Philadelphia, it means something different: Northern Liberties gets shortened to NoLibs. Founded in 1803, it was originally one of the largest cities in the country for half a century from the late 1700s to the mid-1800s until it was absorbed into Philadelphia. Settlers were allowed to craft their own rules – hence the name. Northern Liberties is often called Philly's first suburb (though this honor is also claimed by a neighborhood in South Philly) and was the site for one of the country's most infamous red-light districts for decades.

of the design today reflects that heritage, including original chimneys and reclaimed wood used to build the bar. Something is happening almost nightly here, from comedy shows to live music. One feature that makes the venue popular is its open floor. Much like an outdoor venue, you're not confined to a particular seat and can weasel your way close to the stage (or arrive early and stake out space from the start). Recent stars to grace the stage include Jon Batiste and Margaret Cho.

Rail Park (therailpark.org) is a grand experiment to turn

DRINKING IN FISHTOWN & NORTHERN LIBERTIES: GREAT DIVES

El Bar: A hopping, fun spot with lively karaoke most nights (or other music performances), pool table and inexpensive beers.

Frankford Hall: Massive German beer garden with lots of German beers to choose from, plus ciders and non-alcoholic drinks.

Kung Fu Necktie: A dive bar with a reputation – it's not the spot for a quiet conversation; just get a drink and chill.

Johnny Brenda's: A hub of Philly's indie-rock scene, this is a great small venue with a balcony, plus a restaurant and bar with indie-minded beers.

Rail Park

an abandoned rail line into a multiuse public park with sitting and walking areas, performance spaces and nice elevated views of the city. Phase 1 of this multidecade project was completed in 2018, and it's a fun spot to bring a dog or walk with strollers or wheelchairs. The long, narrow paths are nicely paved, and the route has been landscaped with broadleaf trees and flowering plants and bushes. If you're a yoga fan, check out the schedulew of outdoor yoga classes on the Rail Park's website.

DRINKING & DINING AT SCHMIDT'S COMMONS

Schmidt's Commons has gone through many changes over the years and has had several different names. What was once the Schmidt's Beer building is now apartments, but the sign remains, overlooking the Piazza, named in honor of Italian public squares. Bars and restaurants are springing up, especially along the Liberties Walk, a narrow pedestrian avenue that snakes through several buildings, making it a great spot for small groups or families with kids who might want to window-shop for their meal before settling into a venue.

 DRINKING IN FISHTOWN & NORTHERN LIBERTIES: COCKTAIL PICKS

| **Cedar Point Bar & Kitchen:** Spacious bar, outdoor deck, good food and excellent creative cocktails – the pickletinis are a huge hit. | **Rivers Casino:** Has some unique craft cocktails (try the Ray of Sunshine, if you need help deciding), right on the water. *24hr* | **Philadelphia Distilling:** Drink and learn how to craft great cocktails at this distillery and teaching lab. | **R&D Cocktail Bar:** Great cocktails and tiki creations presented with flair in a setting that feels like the child of a spaceship bridge and a Hopper painting. |

South Philadelphia

MULTICULTURAL HUB WITH GREAT FOOD

GETTING AROUND

Rent a bike using the Indego app, picking up and dropping off at spots all over South Philadelphia, such as the Italian Market. SEPTA buses follow straight north–south routes through this district, making it easy to get around. The Broad Street Line subway is useful for accessing the area. It stops between Lombard-South and AT&T (the end of the line).

Sprawling, multicultural South Philadelphia appeals to visitors seeking diversity. A prime example is the historic South 9th Street Italian Market, the oldest outdoor market in the country and one of the best reasons to seek out this area. South Philly is a little hard-scrabble in some parts but gentrifying in others, so it will likely have something new any time you visit. This district covers Queen Village, which is home to Fabric Row, the hip gourmet strip of East Passyunk Ave, the repurposed, imposing Navy Yards, delightful, family-friendly FDR Park (bring a ball or Frisbee to toss) and the city's major sports stadiums. It's got green fields and leafy avenues and some delightful views of the river. Quirky activities range from visiting the Mummers Museum to finding Argentine tango studios. It's also home to some of the city's finest Philly cheesesteak spots, so whatever you do, come hungry.

Tantalize your Senses at the South 9th Street Italian Market

A world of tastes

In the late 19th century, Italian immigrants began settling in Philadelphia, mostly on 9th between Wharton and Fitzwater Sts. They brought with them their culinary traditions, including a love for fresh produce, meats and cheeses.

As the Italian community grew, so did the market, which became a hub for locals to purchase authentic Italian ingredients and goods. The market's fame expanded in the 1970s when it gained national attention through movies such as *Rocky* and *Philadelphia*. It's also expanded beyond Italian goods and now includes shops from around the world. It even has a section known as Little Vietnam.

Today, visitors to the **South 9th Street Italian Market** can explore historic streets lined with vendors selling fresh produce, seafood, meats, cheeses and pastries. It's not only a place to shop but also a community-gathering space where

☑ TOP TIP

Consider finding a Philly specialty: Wooder ice. Be sure not to call it 'water ice' (how gauche!) and never say 'shave ice' or you'll be laughed out of town. This delight is what you'd expect: shaved ice topped with flavored syrups in a cup or cone. Yum!

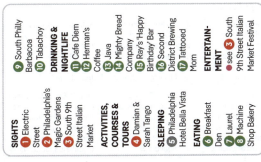

PHILADELPHIA SOUTH PHILADELPHIA

SIGHTS
1. Electric Street
2. Philadelphia's Magic Gardens
3. South 9th Street Italian Market

ACTIVITIES, COURSES & TOURS
4. Damian & Sarah Tango

SLEEPING
5. Philadelphia Hotel Bella Vista

EATING
6. Breakfast Den
7. Laurel
8. Machine Shop Bakery
9. South Philly Barbacoa
10. Tabachoy

DRINKING & NIGHTLIFE
11. Cafe Diem
12. Herman's Coffee
13. Java
14. Mighty Bread Company
15. Ray's Happy Birthday Bar
16. Second District Brewing
17. Tattooed Mom

ENTERTAINMENT
• see 3 South 9th Street Italian Market Festival

South 9th Street Italian Market Festival

FRANK RIZZO MURAL IS NO MORE

For more than two decades, a giant mural of former police commissioner and mayor Frank Rizzo (in office from 1972 to 1980) overlooked the corner of Montrose and 9th Sts. It was regularly vandalized, a reflection of Rizzo's controversial legacy of police brutality and widening racial tensions. After the 2020 Black Lives Matter protests, Mural Arts, an agency that funds and maintains the city's murals, said it was severing ties with the piece and no longer paying for its cleanup. It was painted over that year, just a few days after a Rizzo statue was removed outside City Hall.

people come together to experience the sights, sounds and flavors of South Philly's rich cultural heritage.

Laying claim to being Philly's largest block party, the citizens in and around the market throw the annual **South 9th Street Italian Market Festival**, a weekend party in mid-May. Highlights include the Procession of Saints, a half-ball tournament and team attempts at climbing a 30ft pole greased with lard, with treats and money at the top.

Learn to Tango

Discover the beautiful dance

Tucked into a quiet residence in South Philly is **Damian & Sarah Tango**, a wonderful studio run by a couple who've devoted their lives to performing and teaching this intoxicating form of dance. This isn't Buenos Aires, of course, but Philadelphia has a robust Argentine tango scene and is a fun place to give this beautiful art form a try.

Often called a dance that takes a lifetime to master, Argentine tango is essentially 'fancy walking,' so you may already

 EATING IN SOUTH PHILADELPHIA

Laurel: Fancy French doesn't get much better, with surprising menu options like black onion poached cod and duck with knotweed. $$$	**South Philly Barbacoa:** A delightful stop for *barbacoa* (shredded meat, often beef) tacos and other Mexican delights. Small menu, but popular. $	**John's Roast Pork:** As casual as it gets, this Beard Award–winning cheesesteak spot with cheery blue picnic tables is at a highway intersection. $	**Tabachoy:** Filipino favorites like pork *sisig* (meat with vinegar and spices) and *adobo* (a vinegar-soy combo) in a friendly spot. $$
Breakfast Den: With breakfasts like 'Kale It What You Want,' you're sure to giggle as you read the menu. Truly different from the normal fare. $$	**Cafe Diem:** If you're looking for Vietnamese food and don't mind a crowd, stop here for noodle soups and ice teas. Great for breakfast or lunch. $	**Herman's Coffee:** Has the feel of a European corner store, with shelves of jams, jellies, chocolates, condiments and liqueurs. $	**Mighty Bread Company:** Order to go and escape the throng by eating in nearby Columbus Square Park. The orange ricotta teacake is spectacular. $

have what it takes to begin – if you can walk, you can dance. Yet much like a language, tango takes practice and may take years to build up the 'vocabulary' for extended dances. It isn't a dance with memorized foot patterns; instead, it's a method where a leader learns to communicate to the follower, who in turn learns to listen for the leader's commands.

Damian & Sarah Tango offers instruction at all levels and can offer suggestions about where else to dance tango in Philadelphia.

Marvel at the Mosaics of Philadelphia's Magic Gardens
Amazing murals

The ongoing life's work of Philadelphia-based mosaic mural artist Isaiah Zagar, **Philadelphia's Magic Gardens** is a folk-art wonderland of mirror mosaics, bottle walls and quirky sculptures that will mystify, mesmerize and perhaps even baffle. The art has an ethereal, psychedelic and almost cosmic element, as if you're seeing things that aren't quite from this world.

Zagar's mosaic murals can be seen around the city, but visit the Magic Gardens first so you know what to look for. This spot also puts on small exhibitions of other artists' work, with a focus on those who are self-taught and making mosaics or folk art. Between November and March, site tours take place at 3pm on Saturdays and Sundays. Between April and October, walking tours around the area depart at 3pm Friday through Sunday.

See Vivid Neon at Electric Street
From dumped trash to a place of beauty

Los Angeles has Electric Ave but Philadelphia has **Electric St**, an otherwise unassuming alley with a nighttime surprise. Best visited at twilight when its neon colors stand out against an inky-blue-sky backdrop, this installation is a collaborative work by mural artist David Guinn and light artist Drew Billiau. It has transformed a crime-ridden alley where people illegally dumped trash into a place of beauty, and it's a testament to the healing power of art and imagination. Though not intended as a permanent installation, there are no immediate plans to remove it.

ACTIVITIES IN SOUTH PHILLY

Sarah Chung, Argentine tango dancer, names some of her not-to-miss South Philly activities. *damianandsarahtango.com*

South Philadelphia has lots of spots tourists often overlook. Check out the Bok Building, a converted school that now houses businesses and artists. Buy French pastries at **Machine Shop Bakery** downstairs, then go up to the rooftop to enjoy the breathtaking view.

Visit **FDR Park** – there's an amazing playground with the largest swing set in North America and cool climbing structures. There is also a lake, trails, picnic tables and Tinseltown, a holiday lights festival you can ice-skate through!

At night, step through the doorway of **Damian & Sarah Tango** to take your first class in Argentine tango.

 DRINKING IN SOUTH PHILADELPHIA: OUR PICKS

Java: Excellent espresso and coffees, European-style alfresco tables, fantastic rice pudding and Middle Eastern kebabs.	**Tattooed Mom:** Iconic dive bar with great food, creative cocktails, an artsy vibe downstairs and crazy graffiti in the upstairs pool bar.	**Second District Brewing:** Great beer selection with an old saloon vibe – dark rafters overhead, a long, laminated bar, and stool seats.	**Ray's 'Happy Birthday' Bar:** Come here for karaoke and to celebrate someone's birthday as if they were your best friend.

207

University City & West Philadelphia

ARTSY AND ACADEMIC

GETTING AROUND

SEPTA buses crisscross the area, and two LUCY bus services shuttle in a loop around University City, mostly serving student-to-classroom needs. The Market-Frankford Line subway and trolley stations include 30th & 34th Sts. Trolleys also stop at 30th St and 33rd before lines split into north and south branches. As elsewhere in the city, the Indego bikeshare app lets you rent for an hour at a time, picking up and dropping off at numerous locations close to the main neighborhood sights.

Across the Schuylkill River west of downtown Philly is the area that's home to both Drexel University and the Ivy League University of Pennsylvania (UPenn). The latter's leafy campus makes for a pleasant afternoon stroll and has an excellent museum and library. Further west, toward Spruce Hill, are the green spaces of Woodlands cemetery, Clark Park and Bartram's Garden. The Schuylkill River makes for relaxing strolls and bike rides, and there are lots of parks, playing fields and recreation areas that offer the sort of outdoor fun and exercise that are harder to find in other parts of the city. Delightful restaurants, bars, pubs, libraries, museums and historic monuments round out the experience of visiting University City and West Philadelphia, and it's all within an hour's walk of City Hall.

Step into History at 30th Street Station
Meander in the grandeur

Even if you're not catching a train, the grandness of the 1930s **30th Street Station** is worth seeing. The enormous neoclassical station's main concourse, with its marble-faced walls and 95ft-high coffered ceiling painted in red, gold and cream, is one of Philadelphia's most impressive public spaces. Corinthian columns support porte cochere (a roof over a driveway to shelter passengers getting out of vehicles) on the station's east

30th Street Station

☑ TOP TIP

Don't miss the quirky Cira Green, a grassy 1.25-acre park that's hidden in plain sight atop the Cira Centre South parking garage. It's a pleasant spot to relax and offers splendid views of the Schuylkill River and the city skyline beyond. Grab a bite to eat, or a latte or such, and enjoy.

and west sides. The east end of the concourse is overlooked by the giant bronze *Pennsylvania Railroad WWII Memorial* (aka *Angel of Resurrection*) statue, designed by Walter Hancock, who served in the US Army as one of the 'Monuments Men' who recovered art looted by the Nazis.

In a room off the concourse's north side, look for Karl Bitter's *Spirit of Transportation*, an 1895 sculptural frieze originally commissioned for the long-gone Broad St Station.

Immerse Yourself in Nature at Bartram's Garden

North Amercia's oldest botanic garden

Walking through **Bartram's Garden**, North America's oldest botanic garden, is a placid, pastoral diversion perfect for a balmy afternoon or sun-dappled morning. Founded by Quaker farmer John Bartram, the garden dates from 1728. The lovely 45-acre National Historic Landmark, which includes the sturdy stone Bartram Hall and the Sankofa Community Farm, is open year-round. Tours run Thursday through Sunday from April 1 to December 3. Garden tours are at 1pm and 3pm, and house tours are at noon and 2pm. Other activities and events that take place here include free kayaking and rowing on Saturday between 11am and 3pm from the end of April to the end of October.

EATING IN UNIVERSITY CITY & WEST PHILADELPHIA

Abyssinia: A farm-to-table Ethiopian experience with lots of creative lentil dishes, spiced meats and vegetarian options. **$$**

Walnut Street Cafe: Breakfast, brunch and lunch, with honey biscuits, fried chicken and a fun 'mimosa kit' to mix juice and champagne. **$$**

Honeysuckle Provisions: An impressive tasting menu and one of Philly's top breakfast sandwich spots. **$**

Fresh Donuts: These doughnuts, bagels and breakfasts always hit the spot, even in a city known for great doughnuts. **$**

UNIVERSITY CITY & WEST PHILADELPHIA

SIGHTS
1. 30th Street Station
2. Krishna P Singh Center for Nanotechnology
3. Penn Museum
4. Woodlands

ACTIVITIES, COURSES & TOURS
5. Penn Relays

SLEEPING
6. Cornerstone B&B
7. The Inn at Penn

EATING
8. Abyssinia
9. Don Barriga
10. Han Dynasty
11. Renata's Kitchen
12. White Dog Cafe

DRINKING & NIGHTLIFE
13. Fiume
14. Fresh Donuts
15. Green Line Cafe
16. New Deck Tavern
17. Smokey Joe's
18. Walnut Street Cafe

Bartram's Garden

When the Schuylkill River Trail bridges are completed in 2025, it will be possible to cycle, walk and jog directly from Center City to the garden. Check on updates and find entry points at schuylkillbanks.org.

Peek Back in Time at the Penn Museum
A magical mystery (art) tour

UPenn's magical **museum**, the largest of its type in the USA, contains archaeological treasures from ancient Egypt, Mesopotamia, the Mayan world and more. One of the museum's most well-respected archaeologists, Dr Simon Martin, was instrumental in deciphering the Maya language and regularly offers lectures about the Maya world and discoveries in the field. Stela 14 of Piedras Negras is a renowned work from the Maya that's part of the museum's collection. Other highlights to look for include the granite sphinx of Ramses II, a dazzling headdress worn by Queen Puabi of Ur and colorful textiles from Hawaii.

THE PENN RELAYS

Taking place over three days at the end of April, **Penn Relays** is the largest and oldest track-and-field meet in the USA, with more than 20,000 participants from across the country, as well as overseas. High-school and college events pack the UPenn stadiums, and in a sports-loving state like Pennsylvania, it's a festive, thrilling and fun time for participants and spectators. It's a rain-or-shine event, but umbrellas are not permitted, so bring wet-weather gear if the forecast doesn't cooperate.

DRINKING IN UNIVERSITY CITY & WEST PHILADELPHIA: OUR PICKS

Green Line Cafe: Named after the trolley line that passes outside, this is a relaxed place for organic coffee, loose-leaf tea or vegan soup.

New Deck Tavern: An Irish pub that could easily be the set for *How I Met Your Mother*, with great pours and a rounded menu of bar food and burgers.

Fiume: Upstairs at **Abyssinia** (p209), this dive bar has had a few names but is always friendly with a good selection of beer and cocktails.

Smokey Joe's: A venerable UPenn haunt that's been around since the 1930s, with cheap beer, pizzas, sandwiches and theme nights.

KRISHNA P SINGH CENTER FOR NANO-TECHNOLOGY

One of UPenn's most striking pieces of contemporary architecture is the **Krishna P Singh Center for Nanotechnology**, designed in 2013 by Weiss/Manfredi. A series of interlocking glass buildings set at angles includes a dramatic cantilevered box hanging three stories over the grassy courtyard. Below, on the lawn, you'll find Tony Smith's painted steel sculpture, *We Lost*.

The building itself is impressive, too. Take a moment to admire its eclectic 19th-century architecture and design, which includes a Japanese gate, Arts and Crafts–style brickwork, a rotunda, public gardens, sculptures by Alexander Stirling Calder and a koi pond. The Stoner Courtyard is the location for a series of outdoor summer concerts.

Wander Through a Hallowed Burial Spot
Final resting place of many notable figures

A National Historic Landmark, **Woodlands** is a 54-acre cemetery that was once the country seat of William Hamilton, who hailed from a family of wealthy colonial lawyers and politicians. Two of Hamilton's 18th-century buildings stand on the grounds surrounded by elaborate Victorian funerary monuments and shady trees he planted as part of his desire to craft an ideal English landscape. Many of Philadelphia's notable figures are buried here, including the artist Thomas Eakins and the surgeon Samuel David Gross, whom Eakins famously painted in *The Gross Clinic*.

 EATING IN UNIVERSITY CITY & WEST PHILADELPHIA: BEST DINNERS

White Dog Cafe: Amid dog-related ceramic kitsch, paintings and pillows, find farm-to-table food creatively prepared. **$$**

Han Dynasty: This west-side outpost of the local mini-empire offers sizzling Sichuan goodness in a shed-like space with some communal tables. **$$**

Don Barriga: Cheap, cheery and colorful in decor and the plating, Don Barriga has authentic Mexican tacos, salsas and guacamoles. **$**

Renata's Kitchen: Popular for its patio, with Middle Eastern food and American standards. Try the shakshuka, Moroccan carrots or a mocktail. **$**

Penn Museum (p211)

Beyond Philadelphia

The Brandywine Valley to the southwest and Bucks County to the north have picturesque countryside, gardens, museums and charming, quaint towns.

Places
Kennett Square p214
Chadds Ford p215
Valley Forge p215
Doylestown p216
New Hope p218

Covering relatively small swathes of Pennsylvania and Delaware southwest of Philadelphia, the Brandywine Valley is a patchwork of rolling, wooded hills, horse farms, historic villages, gardens, mansions and museums. Traditionally a rural escape and tony bedroom suburb of Philadelphia, it has the air of an ivy-cloaked, aristocratic enclave. Bucks County, to the north of Philly, with a similar bucolic feel, includes the charmingly compact museum-filled Doylestown and New Hope, which is connected to its sister city of Lambertville on the New Jersey side of the wide Delaware River by a pedestrian-friendly bridge. Besides a main street lined with idiosyncratic boutiques, cafes and restaurants, New Hope's action involves getting out on the river or cycling and walking along the Delaware Canal.

Kennett Square

TIME FROM PHILADELPHIA: 1 HR

Longwood Gardens' Flowers & Fountains

The choreographed water-fountain shows at **Longwood**, one of North America's largest and most spectacular gardens, blows even the Bellagio in Las Vegas away. Longwood occupies 1100 acres (400 open to the public) just outside the town of Kennett Square; its superlatives include having the largest tulip collection outside the Netherlands. Pierre du Pont, the great-grandson of the DuPont chemical-company founder, began designing this property in 1906 with the grand gardens of Europe in mind, especially those in France and Italy. He somehow mastered hydraulic engineering in his free time, and virtually every inch has been carefully sculpted into a display of horticultural magnificence. Whatever your mood, it can't help but be buoyed by the overwhelming variety of species showcasing nature's creativity.

'Longwood Reimagined,' a project costing nearly $300 million, is scheduled to open towards the end of 2024, and will add an additional 32,000 sq ft conservancy, the Mediterranean-inspired 'crystal palace.' It's designed to appear like it's floating on water, with island walks, canals, a relocated rainforest, and bonsai and water-lily displays.

During our visit, the century plant, misnamed since it in fact blooms every 20 to 30 years, not every 100, was about to

GETTING AROUND

You'll definitely need a car to explore this area fully, and given the flexibility that's needed, though bus services can transport you to Valley Forge from Philadelphia (90 minutes). The traffic can be notoriously bad, so it's best to plan your trip from Philly outside of rush hour. A SEPTA train runs as far as Doylestown (90 minutes), with a bus connecting from there to New Hope (30 minutes).

flower. With one of the world's largest greenhouses and 11,000 kinds of plants, something is always in bloom.

Even if you're only interested in horticulture and not exhibits about the du Ponts, you'll need a good two to three hours for a visit. Tickets don't allow you to leave and re-enter so grab snacks, drinks and meals at one of Longwood's eateries.

Chadds Ford

TIME FROM PHILADELPHIA: **1 HR**

The Wyeth Family Art Dynasty

The **Brandywine River Museum of Art**, a showcase of American art, includes the work of the Brandywine School: Howard Pyle, Maxfield Parrish and the Wyeths (NC, Andrew and Jamie). NC Wyeth's illustrations, for popular books such as *The Last of the Mohicans* and *Treasure Island,* are displayed along with rough sketches and finished paintings. The facility is a treat in and of itself, with tall glass windows and pleasant views onto the pretty countryside of the Brandywine Creek, a popular put-in spot for tubing, kayaking and canoeing.

Valley Forge

TIME FROM PHILADELPHIA: **1 HR 10 MINS**

Washington's War Refuge

Valley Forge National Historic Park commemorates not a battle but the 'birthplace of the Continental Army.' It is where, after the British occupation of Philadelphia, over the famously devastating winter of 1777–78, the rag-tag short-term militia of nearly 12,000 that Washington had whipped together was reconstituted and trained into a cohesive force. Marching and drills aside, Washington changed his recruitment strategy: he offered land and more money for those who'd commit to fight to the end.

It's now incongruously only minutes from King of Prussia, one of the largest malls in the area. Today, where 2000 continental soldiers died of exposure, the parks' 5.5 sq miles of rural beauty are bordered by paths popular with cyclists, runners and dog walkers, and symbolize Washington's endurance and leadership. Before taking to the paths or doing the self-guided audio tour, stop by the visitor center to learn about the historical context and importance of the place.

A 30-mile cycling path along the Schuylkill River connects Valley Forge to Philadelphia.

'SHROOM TOWN

That stink of putrefying organic matter you smell driving around the Kennett Square area smells like money to mushroom farmers. Essentially a liquified manure and compost mix, it's the fertilizer used to make the area the 'mushroom capital of the world' (and it accounts for 60% to 64% of the country's production annually). Locals say they get used to the smell, but, periodically, their complaints have led to campaigns to pressure the industry to make changes. Mushrooms are fungi, not plants, so they're not grown outside, but instead cultivated year-round inside 'mushroom houses.' The **Mushroom Cap**, a store in Kennett Square, sells locally produced mushrooms and mushroom-themed gifts and has an 'exhibit' with related mushroom-growing paraphernalia.

 EATING IN KENNETT SQUARE: OUR PICKS

La Michoacana: This place has been doling out homemade Mexican ice cream and popsicles for several decades. **$**

Market at Liberty Place: An excellent food court with Korean, Mediterranean, fried chicken and vegan offerings. **$**

Trattoria La Tavola: Exceptional Italian pastas, pizza and fish and meat mains, along with tasty mushroom soup, are all on offer here. **$$**

Talula's Table: This gourmet takeout cafe serves a sought-after eight-course tasting menu at dinnertime (booked out months in advance). **$$$**

PENNSYLVANIAN IMPRESSIONISM

Unsurprisingly, since the turn of the 20th century, painters have found inspiration in the area's bucolic scenery. So much so that it became a center of American impressionism and spawned its own identifiable style and collective called the 'New Hope School.' When Edward Redfield and William Langson Lathrop moved to New Hope in 1898–99, they established an artists colony that became associated with quick, moody landscapes done outside *(en plein air)*, no matter the weather conditions. Housed in a former prison in Doylestown is the **Michener Art Museum**, named after the prolific Pulitzer Prize–winning author whose philanthropy helped establish it. The museum has a gallery dedicated to this group, as well as top-flight rotating modern art exhibitions.

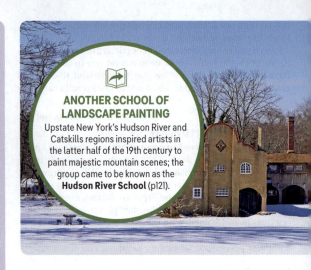

ANOTHER SCHOOL OF LANDSCAPE PAINTING

Upstate New York's Hudson River and Catskills regions inspired artists in the latter half of the 19th century to paint majestic mountain scenes; the group came to be known as the **Hudson River School** (p121).

Esherick Studio Tour

Wharton Esherick, known as the grandfather of the American studio furniture movement, designed and built his one-of-a-kind studio, now the **Wharton Esherick Museum**, just a few miles from Valley Forge. It's worth making a reservation for a guided tour if you're going to be in the area. Esherick (1887–1970) grew up in West Philly and, like other artists of his era, he sought nature as a refuge from urban living and lived a sort of proto-bohemian, hippie lifestyle. Every inch of the studio and living space, mostly organically shaped and curved wood designs, expresses Esherick's vision.

Doylestown

TIME FROM PHILADELPHIA: **1 HR 10 MINS**

From One Man's Eccentric Mind

Henry Mercer was an archaeologist, ceramicist, amateur historian, inveterate traveler and a polymath. He was also heir to his wealthy aunt's fortune, which allowed him to indulge his passions and leave a lasting, eccentric and utterly fascinating legacy in Doylestown. His idiosyncratic architectural vision led to the construction of the 19,000-sq-ft, 44-room Gothic-Romanesque-Byzantine **Fonthill Castle**, where Mercer lived as a bachelor for 18 years until his death in 1930. The hour-long guided house tours reveal how every feature reflects Mercer's obsessive scholarly mind: the 'main study' with four working desks positioned for various periods of the day; 4000-year-old Babylonian clay tablets embedded in a pillar; 800-year-old Chinese roof tiles; and pottery shards found in Switzerland dating to the late Paleolithic period suspended in chicken wire attached to the ceiling.

Next door, at the **Moravian Tile Factory**, is where Mercer established himself as 'America's foremost arts and crafts tile maker,' after fearing that pottery skills (and most others) were disappearing. The Spanish mission–style building houses a work-

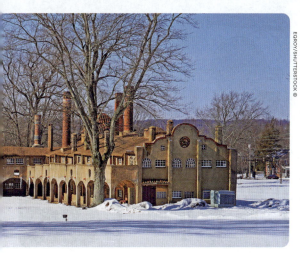

Moravian Tile Factory

ing workshop with apprenticeships and residencies. It's also opened to the public for enthusiastic tours, which are especially good for kids, who can try their hand at playing and molding clay. Come summer, there's often live music and picnicking in the grassy inner courtyard that feels like a European abbey. It also hosts Tile Fest in mid-May, the only tile festival in the US.

But it's the absolutely one-of-a-kind **Mercer Museum**, only a short drive away (across from the highly recommended **Michener Art Museum** that encapsulates Mercer's primary concern: post-industrial Americans were losing the knowledge and skills in how things were made and the meaningfulness that comes with this in what he described as a mass forgetting. Look up upon entering the main building's six-story light-filled central hall. It's like a vision out of a Dr Seuss story, with every manner of object hanging from the walls and ceiling, some upside down: according to Mercer, to better appreciate and see ordinary things from a different perspective. Keep an eye out for the whaling vessel, horse-drawn carriage and a treadmill for dogs. Throughout, niches dedicated to every imaginable craft, from candlemaking to gunsmithing to beekeeping, are filled with tools and explanatory text on the crafts' history and evolution. If you're a survivalist, there's no better resource than the Mercer to prepare for the end of civilization!

BEST WINERIES AROUND PHILADELPHIA

Penns Woods:
A family-run place for over 20 years, with European-style blends and tastings featuring artisanal cheeses and meats.

Chaddsford Winery:
Housed in a 17th-century dairy barn, it's festive outdoor scene on weekends. Close to Brandywine River Museum.

Va La Vineyards:
A highly regarded and small-batch artisanal producer with more than two dozen mostly Italian varietals, some fairly unique.

Wycombe Vineyards:
A family-owned farm since the 1920s, it's relatively new to winemaking and has friendly, personable attention during its tastings.

Bishop Estate Vineyard & Winery:
Charming farm/vineyard, with more than two dozen varieties offered at tastings; firepits and live music as well.

 EATING IN DOYLESTOWN AND NEW HOPE: OUR PICKS

Sprig & Vine: A New Hope all-vegan cafe with innovatively conceived dishes like an oyster mushroom po'boy wrap and jerk-grilled tofu. $$	**Hattery Stove & Grill:** Doylestown Inn's restaurant serves tacos, burgers, rack of lamb and a delicious pistachio-crusted salmon. $$	**Terrain Cafe:** Part of a Doylestown high-end garden center, Terrain offers a great daily 'brunch' and dinner. $$	**Bowman's Tavern:** This New Hope place has burgers and other pub grub, including fish and chips and *tamales oaxaqueños*, and live music. $$

BEST SHOPPING IN NEW HOPE

Peddler's Village:
Outdoor 'mall' with lovely grounds and walkways connecting more than 60 primarily locally owned boutiques and shops.

George Nakashima Woodworkers Studio:
There are guided tours and floor pieces for sale at this internationally renowned furniture designer/craftsman's workshop.

Rice's Market:
The county's oldest and largest flea market has indoor and outdoor spaces selling nearly everything, including antiques, clothing and fresh food.

Love Saves the Day:
This smorgasbord of secondhand clothing, one-of-a-kind objects and other ephemera was formerly an East Village, NYC mainstay.

Avigail Adam:
Magical fairy wonderland shop selling hand-crafted ornately designed whimsical 'goddess' jewelry.

New Hope

New Hope
Riverside Charm

TIME FROM PHILADELPHIA: **1 HR 15 MINS**

Like its sister town Lambertville, New Hope is a quaint, artsy town that's overrun with visitors gorging at its cafes, ice-cream shops and restaurants when the calendar flips over to May. An abundance of sophisticated B&Bs mean many make a weekend out of it. The former towpath that ran alongside the Delaware River has been converted into a 60-mile **walking and cycling path**. The old stone Locktender's House (145 S Main St) is the headquarters of Friends of the Delaware Canal, a nonprofit dedicated to preserving and improving the canal and its towpath; inside are some exhibits on the old towpath.

Places We Love to Stay

$ Budget $$ Midrange $$$ Top End

Old City & Society Hill   MAP p179

Apple Hostels $ The apple-green color scheme fits the name, but this Hosteling International–affiliated place is also strong on details such as kitchens, lounges and power outlets in lockers.

Penn's View Hotel $$ Great value for its location, Penn's View shows its age – mostly in a good way, as it's on the National Register of Historic Places. The rooms, some with fireplace or balcony, have a quaint style.

Chinatown & the Gayborhood   MAP p187

Alexander Inn $ Impeccably kept rooms have a subdued, slightly vintage style; some have old-fashioned half-size tubs. Original architectural details, including stained-glass windows, oak moldings and marble-tiled floors, add to the atmosphere.

Morris House Hotel $$ Morris House conjures colonial elegance without too much formality or frilliness. Beyond the 15 rooms, its finest asset is the courtyard garden (with a locally loved dinner restaurant), a true respite from the city.

Rittenhouse Square & Center City West   MAP p193

ROOST Rittenhouse $$ These luxe apartments have a great location on Chestnut St and are available in generous sizes, from studios to two bedrooms.

Franklin on Rittenhouse $$$ This 1911 mansion is a fine choice for small and local luxury. The place mixes old-world sophistication with contemporary touches, and its location can't be beat.

Logan Square & Fairmount   MAP p198

Windsor Suites $$ These perfectly situated suites aren't fancy, but they're clean, staff are polite and they're in walking distance of just about everywhere. On-site restaurants and bars make dining easy, too.

Sheraton Philadelphia Downtown $$$ Offers everything you'd expect from the brand, with spotless rooms, a business center, pool and several dining options.

Fishtown & Northern Liberties   MAP p200

Lokal Hotel Fishtown $$ Spotless, modern and chic, the Lokal offers reasonable prices and pretty snazzy accommodations, plus some common areas and a garden that make it possible to meet new friends.

Wm Mulherin's Sons $$$ In an 1890s building, this hotel features four super-stylish rooms with exposed brick walls, skylights, original architectural features, contemporary furniture, kitchens and gadgets such as record players.

South Philadelphia   p205

Courtyard by Marriott Philadelphia South at The Navy Yard $$ This contemporary business hotel is easy on the eye, offers comfortable rooms and is perfect if you have business in the Navy Yard complex or are attending an event at one of the nearby sports stadiums.

Philadelphia Hotel Bella Vista $$ A hotel with all the fancy bric-a-brac and trimmings of a cozy B&B. No two rooms are alike, and there's art on the walls that make some feel as if they're part of a museum.

University City & West Philadelphia   p208

Cornerstone B&B $$ Housed in an 1865 Victorian mansion, this family-run B&B is an appealing choice with six uniquely designed rooms. The garden/patio is a nice place for breakfast or to relax on a warm day, and the hosts are welcoming.

The Inn at Penn $$$ This Hilton hotel is a fail-safe option at the heart of University City. Rooms are comfortable, but it's a popular choice come graduation time so don't expect to find much room at the inn then.

Pennsylvania

FORESTED PARKS, LIVING HISTORY AND RIVER TOWNS

Outside vibrant Pittsburgh, much of Pennsylvania (PA) is a sparsely populated outdoor playground with charming pockets, including history-filled towns and east-coaster vacation spots.

More than 300 miles across, stretching from the East Coast to the edge of the Midwest, Pennsylvania contains multitudes. Philadelphia, once the heart of the British colonial empire, is very much a part of the east, a link to the Boston–Washington metro corridor. In the far west edge of the state, Pittsburgh, the state's only other large city and a long-ago staggeringly wealthy steel-manufacturing center, abounds with artistic energy and has a distinctive food culture.

Three wars and pivotal battles that determined the fate of empires and the future of the country were fought in Pennsylvania. Its coal, oil, timber and other natural resources drove the nation's economy and produced unimaginable riches. That legacy created great institutions, but also neglect. However, a culture of crafting and producing things locally is very much alive.

Outside Philadelphia's Main Line neighborhoods, things turn pastoral in Bucks County and Brandywine Valley. Further afield, the terrain is agricultural, emphasized by the Pennsylvania Dutch – Mennonite, Amish and others – who tend their farms by hand as if it were still the 18th century.

To the north, the Poconos Mountains beckon with outdoor adventures. West of here, the Appalachian Mountains begin, as do the so-called Pennsylvania Wilds, a sparsely populated region of deep forests and valleys bisected by snaking rivers. And south of Pittsburgh, the Laurel Highlands draws architecture fans and white-water enthusiasts alike.

THE MAIN AREAS

PITTSBURGH
Cultural capital of western PA.
p224

LAUREL HIGHLANDS
Iconic architecture; parkland for outdoor adventures.
p230

PA WILDS
Vast forests, gorges and isolation.
p235

Left: Amish buggy, Lancaster (p237); Above: Pittsburgh (p224)

THE POCONOS
Accessible nature and family holidays.
p239

LANCASTER & PA DUTCH COUNTRY
Gateway to Amish countryside.
p243

GETTYSBURG
Historic battlefield and charming town.
p247

Find Your Way

Pennsylvania is large, with an interior that feels remote and inaccessible without your own vehicle. You can easily fly to Pittsburgh or Philadelphia; Southern Airways Express can get you to smaller airports in the state.

TRAIN

Amtrak's daily Pennsylvanian train runs from NYC to Philadelphia, Harrisburg and Pittsburgh, passing through pretty scenery in parts, especially during the trip's western leg. Plans for a high-speed route between NYC and Scranton in the Poconos are moving forward.

CAR

Car-rental companies are found in large and medium-sized cities. GPS service can be sketchy away from major towns; a hard-copy map is a good backup. Gas-station chains (Sheetz, Wawa, Rutter's) might be your best bet for food in some parts.

PA Wilds, p235
An enormous swathe of forested parks and rivers, good for every manner of outdoor adventuring.

The Poconos, p239
Mountainous region with small towns, family resorts and beautiful natural scenery.

Pittsburgh, p224
Western PA's big city has its own proud personality and cuisine, with big-time museums to match.

Gettysburg, p247
Site of the pivotal Civil War battle and a lovely small town.

Lancaster & PA Dutch Country, p243
Historic town and gateway for bucolic rural countryside with Amish communities.

Laurel Highlands, p230
Iconic American architecture and cycling, hiking and white-water rafting.

Ohiopyle (p233)

Plan Your Time

There's so much to see and do in Pennsylvania, especially if you're interested in the outdoors. Tackle bite-sized regions one at a time or plan longer trips across the northern or southern parts.

Short on Time

- Head east on always backed-up I-76 from Philadelphia to Valley Forge for a primer on Revolutionary War history. Then travel directly east out to **Lancaster** (p243) for farmers markets and bucolic scenery, and take a buggy, bus or farm tour of Amish country. Or head further north up into the mountainous **Poconos** (p239) for hiking, waterfalls and family fun.

Southern Journey

- Plan for two or three full days in **Pittsburgh** (p224), hitting up the city's art and history museums, as well as the Strip for food. Get tickets for a game, for whatever sport that's on when you're in town. Head to the Laurel Highlands for a Frank Lloyd Wright tour: **Fallingwater** (p230) is a must, along with other spots too if time permits. Cycle, raft or hike at **Ohiopyle** (p233).

SEASONAL HIGHLIGHTS

SPRING
Shoulder season throughout forested federal, state and private parks means generally less crowds.

SUMMER
Attractions at popular holiday regions can feel mobbed and get booked far in advance. It's prime festival season as well.

FALL
Pennsylvania's forests take on spectacular coloring and roadways become packed with leaf peepers.

WINTER
Ski resorts in the Poconos are big draws and you can find deals everywhere, except during the holidays.

Pittsburgh

ART | HISTORY | FOOD

GETTING AROUND

Only two of 17 funicular inclines, the Dusquene and Monongahela, still operate. Downtown is walkable, and if based here you can walk to and from the Strip and the Heinz Center, as well as across the Roberto Clemente Bridge to the Andy Warhol Museum in the North Shore, being rebranded the Pop District. Otherwise, Pittsburgh's light-rail system, the 'T' is great for getting around downtown and to the North Shore (travel within downtown and the North Shore is free; there's a small fee to travel to neighborhoods on the south side).

☑ TOP TIP

Sports fans who can't make it to a Steelers (football), Pirates (baseball) or Penguins (hockey) game shouldn't overlook the city's soccer club, the Pittsburgh Riverhounds SC, who play at **Highmark Stadium**.

When driving into the city, it materializes fairly suddenly, especially at night when downtown's skyscrapers and steel bridges are lit up like a holiday-time toy train set. Pittsburgh boasts 90 distinctive neighborhoods, more bridges than Venice, impossibly steep hillsides that rival San Francisco's and world-class museums and cultural institutions. But it's the city's personality, its residents' pride in their Pittsburgh particularity – the slang, the food, the sports – that makes it uniquely interesting to visit.

The city was built at the confluence of the Ohio, Monongahela and Allegheny Rivers, its geographical positioning making it strategically vital to Native Americans long before the French and British started competing for territorial control in the late 1700s. Its evolution from 'Factory Belt' and headquarters for the country's largest companies to declining 'Rust Belt' city is primarily in the rear view. The ongoing transition visible today is to an identity associated with universities, tech and medicine, along with a relatively low cost of living.

Feasting on the Strip
Old-school specialty shops and signature sandwiches

Strolling the Strip is a don't-miss experience. Easily the liveliest neighborhood come the weekend, it's a 20-block stretch (3 blocks wide) just north of downtown, once dotted with funiculars (at the system's peak there were hundreds throughout the city) that transported residents between the hillsides and the Allegheny River. Newer developments like the **Novo Asian Food Hall** and **Aslin Brewery** are in converted warehouse spaces on Smallman St, one block north of Penn Ave.

One of the strip's anchor restaurants is **Primanti Bros**, whose signature contribution of adding fries to sandwiches has historic roots; you'll have little chance of grabbing a table here on any of the city's sports teams' game days.

PENNSYLVANIA PITTSBURGH

TOP SIGHTS
1. Andy Warhol Museum

SIGHTS
2. Carnegie Museums
3. Heinz History Center
4. Mattress Factory

ACTIVITIES, COURSES & TOURS
5. Highmark Stadium
6. Pittsburgh Glass Center

SLEEPING
7. Inn on Negley
8. Inn on the Mexican War Streets
9. Monaco

EATING
10. 40 North at Alphabet City
11. Carson Street Deli
12. Con Alma
13. Enrico Biscotti
14. Iron Born
15. Jimmy & Nino Sunseri Co
16. Kaya
17. Labad's Mediterranean Grocery
18. Novo Asian Food Hall
19. Pamela's Diner
20. Paris 66
21. Pigeon Bagels
22. Porch at Schenley
23. Primanti Bros
24. Square Café
25. Wholey Fish Market

DRINKING & NIGHTLIFE
26. Allegheny Wine Mixer
27. Aslin Brewery
28. Brillobox
29. Lefty's
30. Wigle Whiskey Distillery

ENTERTAINMENT
31. August Wilson Center

SHOPPING
32. Pennsylvania Macaroni Co

225

THAT'S SO PITTSBURGH

From its slang like 'jag-off' (idiot) and 'yinz' (you all), to its singular food culture, Pittsburgh is proudly and defiantly distinct. One of its most iconic food offerings is the Primanti sandwich: two pieces of Mancini Italian bread stuffed with pastrami or roast beef, french fries and coleslaw. Its origins are labor related: it was basically a way for truck and train drivers to grab a full meal on the go without stopping work, as it could be held and eaten with one hand.

And the Heinz legacy lives on in **Picklesburgh**, the city's downtown July festival dedicated to all things pickled, including pickle pizza, pickle beer and pickle doughnuts. Plastic vomit bags are kept on standby during the pickle-juice drinking contest.

Clayton House

Jimmy & Nino Sunseri Co, which boasts of having the best pepperoni roll in the city, gets so crowded in the warmer months that they're sold from racks out on the sidewalk (the 'atomic roll' is stuffed with peppers). Nearby **Iron Born** sells excellent Detroit-style pizza slices. **Pamela's Diner**, known for its fruit-flavored pancakes and a favorite of former President Obama, can be another place with a long wait on weekends.

The specialty markets are no less worth a look: **Wholey Fish Market** for every variety of seafood, plus soups, sandwiches and sushi; **Pennsylvania Macaroni Co** for Italian specialities and **Labad's Mediterranean Grocery** for Middle Eastern. One of the oldest businesses here, **Enrico Biscotti**, also offers cooking classes capped off with dinner (BYOB).

Iconic & Hands-On Art
The Andy Warhol Museum and more

There's more avant-garde art than steel now produced in Pittsburgh. And while Andy Warhol, the city's most notable prodigal artist son might not have imagined returning to the city he grew up in while alive, his 'return' after his death has helped spawn Pittsburgh's arts renaissance. (In an interesting juxtaposition, Warhol, born Warhola, dropped the 'a,' – Pittsburgh was known as 'Pittsburg' until an 'h' was added in 1911). Most people are familiar with Warhol's maxim that everyone in the future will have 15 minutes of fame, along with his screen prints of famous celebrities like Marilyn Monroe and Elvis Presley. But to realize how truly original and path-breaking he was, there's no better place in the world than the **Andy Warhol Museum**, dedicated solely to this single and singular artist.

Nearby, the **Mattress Factory**, so named because it's housed in a former Stearns & Foster mattress warehouse, is a warren of rooms given over to studio spaces for anything-goes art installations. The range is large: from 'permanent collection' highlights like Yayoi Kusama infinity rooms and James Turrell sensory-deprivation rooms to unsettling, even creepy stagings at one of the annex buildings.

If you're tired of passive viewing and want to create something of your own, head to the **Pittsburgh Glass Center** in the Friendship neighborhood, northeast of downtown. It's one of the best places to feel the city's thriving and welcoming arts community. It recently doubled in size, offering studio space for talented, experienced glassblowers. Workshops and quick classes are open to the public (they'll walk you through the art and science and help you produce your own ornament within a half hour or so). Every Friday evening its top-floor deck hosts drinks with special demonstrations, along with other studios on Penn Ave.

A Titan's House & the City's Story
Tour Henry Clay Frick's home

Andrew Carnegie's last words to Henry Clay Frick, reportedly, were 'Meet you in hell' (also the title of an excellent book about the two men). Some time between Frick's (steel-producing) coke monopoly merging with Carnegie's steel enterprise and this exchange of antipathy, they controlled an enormous chunk of the American economy and were two of the wealthiest people alive. Taking a guided tour of Frick's 24-room Gilded Age **Clayton House**, where he lived for 20 years, provides an enlightening and fascinating window onto not only Frick's complicated legacy but also the plight and travails of the ordinary workers who produced the steel. It's a tricky balance, handled with aplomb by talented guides who describe Frick's personal tragedies as well as his uncompromising opposition to organized labor, most notably in violently breaking up the Homestead Strike in 1892, during which 16 people were killed.

Frick's daughter Helen inherited everything upon Henry's death in 1919, becoming the richest heiress in the country. She moved back into her childhood room in 1980 at the age of 92 to help restore the house into the shape you see it in today.

The **Frick Art Museum**, on the same grounds as the Clayton House, is in and of itself one of the city's most prominent art institutions, with masterworks from the likes of Vermeer, Monet and Rembrandt.

BEST PITTSBURGH TOUR COMPANIES

Houser Talks:
Skyscraper rooftop tours led by a local journalist, a font of architectural and historic insight; only a few weekends in summer (housertalks.com).

Walk the Burgh Tours:
A wide variety of tours and themes, including films, history and whiskey, led by longtime locals (walktheburgh.com).

'Burgh Bits & Bites Food Tours:
Culinary walking tours of a number of 'hoods; the Strip is deservedly most popular (burghfoodtour.com/tours).

Rivers of Steel:
Offering a look at the city's past as a base for heavy industry and handcrafted manufacturing (riversofsteel.com/experiences/tours).

Free Pittsburgh Walking Tours:
Name your own price for walking tours tracing the history of downtown and the North Side (freepittsburgh.com).

 EATING IN PITTSBURGH: OUR PICKS

| **Pigeon Bagels:** Takeout kosher vegan bakery with tasty hand-rolled bagels and pastries, in the Squirrel Hill neighborhood. $ | **Carson Street Deli:** Some of the city's best sandwiches on the Southside, with especially good meats and cheese. $ | **Square Café:** East Liberty cafe with elevated diner food like brussels sprouts hash, banana foster waffles and strawberry Nutella crepes. $ | **Kaya:** Stand-out Strip restaurant with Caribbean-flavored specialties, including conch fritters, Jamaican jerk chicken and tropical paella. $$ |

HOW SMOKY WAS IT?

You can see the legacy of the now-defunct steel plants' pollution, and how omnipresent it was, in the strangely designed and placed 'Pittsburgh potties' that exist in unrenovated homes from the late 19th and early 20th centuries. They're situated just inside the basement or other entryways, with a bare shower spout, no walls and no curtain, so that working men could wash away grime and dust before entering the home proper. The city's tallest skyscraper, the rust-colored **USX Tower** (previously the US Steel Tower) once housed the world's most valuable company; as it aged, it too flaked off steel rust onto the sidewalk below. Streetlights often came on mid-morning due to the pollution. No wonder Pittsburgh was known as a 'two-shirt city.'

History & Culture: Local, Regional & Global
Wander the Carnegie and Heinz museums

In a city whose industrial wealth is synonymous with several family names, it's little surprise that the largest cultural institutions were established by their philanthropy. The **Carnegie Museum** and **Heinz History Center** deserve several hours each, or you can beeline for the galleries that serve your passions.

The eclectically organized art-museum wing of the Carnegie ranges wide, from one of the country's largest collections of Japanese prints to a massive art deco mural from the ballroom of the *Normandie*, a luxury ocean liner that sank in New York's harbor in 1942. Rothko and de Kooning masterpieces sit one gallery over from a room dedicated to newspaper photographs of Black life in Pittsburgh's Hill District. There's a hall of sculpture modeled after the Parthenon in Athens, with marble flooring harvested from the same quarry, and a gigantic space filled with plaster-cast facades of 12th-century French Romanesque and Gothic cathedrals.

 EATING IN PITTSBURGH: OUR PICKS

| **Con Alma:** Equally notable for its Latin-inspired menu and as a spot to hear top-flight jazz musicians while sipping excellent cocktails. **$$** | **Porch at Schenley:** Great local ingredients are served with flair in a casual yet chic environment with a mixed clientele. **$$** | **40 North at Alphabet City:** A seasonal, shifting menu of local ingredients is offered by a James Beard–nominated chef. **$$$** | **Paris 66:** Top-end rural French food (such as coq au vin and *steak frites*) in a cozy, bistro-style setting. **$$$** |

Carnegie Museum

Other wings are no less fascinating: an exhibition of globe-spanning gems and minerals; the skeleton of 'Dippy,' widely regarded to be the most famous dinosaur fossil in the world; an Ancient Egypt collection with ongoing conservation work of a funerary boat circa 1300 BCE; and an insect gallery with 12 million specimens (characters from the film *The Silence of the Lambs* were based on the butterfly and moth curators here).

Housed in a six-story former ice warehouse, the Smithsonian-affiliated Heinz History Center uncovers the city's and region's identities through a maze of fascinating galleries. Sports fans can head straight to the floor with displays of uniforms, memorabilia and artifacts from the Steelers', Penguins' and Pirates' glories and ignominies, interspersed with feats of local heroes from truly obscure 'sports' like marbles. There are fun, interactive exhibits for lovers of the iconic children's show *Mister Rogers*, which was filmed in Pittsburgh, and Heinz, the company. And the more serious-minded should take in the galleries tracing the French and Indian War or the newly installed ground-floor exhibit about prominent western Pennsylvania women and their struggles and accomplishments.

AUGUST WILSON

The prominent African American playwright August Wilson lived in the Hill District of Pittsburgh from his birth in 1945 to 1978, when he moved away, though he returned regularly. Only two of his plays, part of the Century Cycle, aka 'the Pittsburgh Cycle,' that documented the African American experience in Pittsburgh, were ever performed in Pittsburgh. Primarily an event space for the arts, downtown's **August Wilson Center** remarkably didn't have much space, if any, dedicated to Wilson until recently. Now you can walk through galleries dedicated to his most prominent plays, from *Joe Turner's Come and Gone* to *Two Trains Running*. There's also a replica of Eddie's Diner, where Wilson hung out.

 DRINKING IN PITTSBURGH: OUR PICKS

Lefty's: In the Strip, the city's dingiest dive bar has cupholders nailed to the wall. Crowds spill out onto the street in warm weather.

Allegheny Wine Mixer: This high-end Lawrenceville wine bar has a great list, smart staff and tasty nibbles.

Wigle Whiskey Distillery: North Side whiskey maker offering tastings and other craft drinks.

Brillobox: A Lawrenceville spot with live music, open-mic events and DJs, plus vegetarian-friendly food and a decent beer selection.

Beyond Pittsburgh

Not far south, the Laurel Highlands has iconic Frank Lloyd Wright homes, French and Indian War sites and rafting and hiking in Ohiopyle.

Places

Fallingwater, Kentuck Knob & Polymath Park p230

West Overton p231

Forts Necessity & Ligonier p232

Ohiopyle State Park p233

Where the Allegheny Mountains disperse into the emerald pastureland of lowland Pennsylvania, a hybrid landscape emerges, characterized by a quilt of small townships on the one hand and rolling, wooded hills on the other. This is the Laurel Highlands, a pretty slice of the state that shifts between fine stretches of pastoral loveliness and wild mountain ruggedness.

These forested foothills and mountains make for an excellent outdoors escape just a quick drive from Pittsburgh. Folks come here to take scenic drives, go on light hikes, ride on two wheels and generally grab some fresh air. Still, it's a human-built structure that constitutes the biggest draw: Fallingwater makes for a fascinating (if hurried) day trip from the urban jungle of Pittsburgh.

Fallingwater, Kentuck Knob & Polymath Park

TIME FROM PITTSBURGH: **1 HR 15 MINS**

Wright Central

Fallingwater is one of architect Frank Lloyd Wright's best-known creations, and was completed in 1938 when he was 70. It was the weekend retreat for the Kaufmanns, owners of the Pittsburgh department store, and Wright said the house should look like it grew there. However, it appears like a fantasy or dream. The genius of the design and features are too numerous to list. Ochre-painted concrete cantilevers appear as continuations of the rocky outcroppings over the waterfall that can be heard from every room. An ice-cold outdoor plunge pool, steps down from the main living room, sits in Bear Creek, one of Pennsylvania's most pristine trout streams. Standard guided tours last an hour and reservations should be made as far in advance as possible (closed January, February and the beginning of March). You can grab drinks, snacks and meals from the on-site cafe.

Kentuck Knob is another Wright house, located only around 7 miles southwest of Fallingwater (and only about 3 miles west of Ohiopyle). It's definitely worth visiting, even if less well-known and admittedly less remarkable. Designed in 1953 and built into the side of a rolling hill, it's especially notable for its natural materials, hexagonal design and honeycomb skylights. After a guided house tour, check out the breathtaking

GETTING AROUND

The majority of people drive here from elsewhere in the region or from Pittsburgh. However, United Express has daily flights from the Johnstown Airport (note: parking is free) to Dulles outside Washington, DC and Chicago O'Hare, and Spirit Airlines flies direct to Myrtle Beach and Orlando from the Latrobe Airport.

Cell-phone reception and GPS can be spotty in parts, especially along windy, rural roads.

Fallingwater

panoramic views of the Youghiogheny River gorge and take the woodland trail that passes by around 30 sculptural works, bought and installed by the British owner who opened the property to the public in 1996.

Maybe most remarkably for Wright aficionados, you can stay overnight in a Wright house, at family-owned **Polymath Park**. This collection of four homes was designed in Wright's distinctive and oft-imitated Usonian style; Mantyla, meaning 'among the pines' in Finnish (it was built in Minnesota by an all-Finnish work crew) is one of the two Wright originals. Birdwing, another Wright home, sits dismantled in a shipping container, waiting to be reconstructed. It's not a bad idea to share with other people as the price is steep and every house has multiple bedrooms (children under nine aren't allowed).

Tours of the homes are given to overnight guests and available to non-guests alike. Whether spending a night or not, Polymath probably has the Laurel Highland's best dining experience. If you go for the 'treehouse-style' dining at **Treetops Restaurant** (Thursday to Monday), you're greeted with champagne upon arrival followed by four-plus courses of a chef-driven menu, served in private cabanas set amidst the trees. 'Dinner' is early, with the last seating at 5:30pm. Other less-pricey options are available and an outdoor bar and pizza oven were in the works at the time of research.

West Overton

TIME FROM PITTSBURGH: **45 MINS**

Taste the region's spirit

Southwestern Pennsylvania was the birthplace of American whiskey and once synonymous with it (the same way Kentucky is to bourbon or champagne is to the region in France). The area is now undergoing a whiskey renaissance. In fact, the Whiskey Rebellion, a precursor to later rebellions against federal rule, originated from this area when residents responded

WRIGHT'S PITTSBURGH PLANS

Frank Lloyd Wright's drawings and blueprints for Pittsburgh buildings in the 1940s and '50s would have transformed the city. In one, a proposed civic center, purportedly large enough to house a sizeable percentage of the city's population, looks like a larger, more futuristic version of the Watergate building in Washington, DC, with more greenery and car ramps around the outside. Another shows a towering hillside apartment building. 'Frank Lloyd Wright's Southwestern Pennsylvania,' an exhibition originating from a partnership with Fallingwater and the Westmoreland Museum of American Art in Greensburg, PA, was held at the National Building Museum in DC in the summer of 2024, with many of the designs transformed into immersive 3D animated renderings, placed in their imagined environments.

BEST HIKES IN OHIOPYLE STATE PARK

Laurel Highlands Hiking Trail

Stretches 70 miles from Seward (near Johnstown) to Ohiopyle, with overnight shelters approximately every 10 miles.

Ferncliff Trail:

A short loop trail that's just over the bridge from Ohiopyle village, on the peninsula's and river's edge, with views of falls.

Great Gorge Trail:

Another popular loop easily accessible from Ohiopyle, partly along old train tracks, with river views and spring wildflowers.

Baughman & Sugarloaf Trail Loop:

Combining two routes and challenging because of the relatively steep ascent and descent; great views from the overlook.

Old Mitchell Loop:

A lesser-used meandering 2-plus miles through forests, past several waterfalls and meadows good for bird-watching.

---

with violence to a tax on their favorite beverage. The origins of PA rye whiskey or Monongahela rye (80% rye and 20% barley) can be traced to Mennonite farming communities. By 1810, there were an estimated 3600 distilleries in the area, the majority likely non-commercial, producing their own homemade moonshine versions. But the business boomed soon after, and by 1900 many dozens of operations were producing more than 7 million gallons annually.

Part of a larger complex of 19th-century buildings, the museum at **West Overton Village** (open to the public for tours and tastings from Thursday to Sunday between May and October) covers two floors of a converted barn and is dedicated to preserving whiskey's regional history. It's also an 'educational distillery' producing a few barrels of its own West Overton Distilling brand, sold only on-site.

Forts Necessity & Ligonier

TIME FROM PITTSBURGH (TO NECESSITY): **1 HR 20 MINS**

Visit historic battlesites

The first shots of the French and Indian War (aka 'the Seven Years' War,' which was fought in Europe and elsewhere) were fired in southwestern Pennsylvania. And those first shots were ordered by a Colonel George Washington, later Revolutionary War leader and first President of the United States. Washington's role in the battle at **Fort Necessity** near the present-day town of Farmington (only 15 minutes from Ohiopyle), in which he signed a document of surrender, and unwittingly accepted responsibility for 'assassinating' a French commander, is said to have haunted him for years. The story of Washington and the battle are told at the excellent visitor center, and you can stroll around a reconstructed fort in the meadow and the surrounding woods where the French and Indian fighters attacked. At the time they were accused of using uncivilized 'ambush' tactics: they did not announce their intent in advance.

But to get an even fuller picture of how this part of Pennsylvania, a frontier region in the mid- to late 1700s, was pivotal to the fate of empires and America's future, head to **Fort Ligonier**, in the small, charming town of the same name, an hour's drive north of Necessity. Galleries in the museum lay out the war's global battlefield sites, explain how various Native American nations (Shawnee, Delaware and Iroquois) chose who they allied with, and there are artifacts from the period, including the pair of pistols given to Washington by Marquis de Lafayette, who played a key role in the French Revolution and later fought on the colonists' side in the American Revolution. Outside, it's worth a stroll around the fort, which was attacked by the French in October, 1758, and has been entirely reconstructed from basic drawings, maps and archaeological finds.

Tens of thousands of people come to Ligonier on the second weekend in October to celebrate **Fort Ligonier Days**, with food vendors, battle reenactors and live music in closed-off streets.

> **MORE WRIGHT**
> New York City's **Guggenheim Museum** (p91), one of Wright's late-career iconic creations, didn't open until 16 years after he was commissioned and six months after his death.

Ohiopyle

Ohiopyle State Park

TIME FROM PITTSBURGH: **1 HR 15 MINS**

Pedaling & paddling between Ohiopyle & Confluence

One of the best ways of experiencing the area is combining cycling and rafting into a half day of cardio and lower- and upper-body workouts. You'll also get a chance to check out charming, if very different, small towns. The Great Allegheny Passage (GAP), a 150-mile trail (ideal for cross-country skiing in the winter) that runs between Pittsburgh and Cumberland, MD, has a 27-mile segment in Ohiopyle State Park. It's an easy 10-mile ride on the GAP, alongside the Youghiogheny River (pronounced 'yaw-ki-gay-nee') to the aptly named **Confluence**, where the Casselman River merges into the 'Yough' (pronounced 'yawk'). Timing's tight for lunch, but plan a return in the evening to the **River's Edge Cafe** (closed Mondays), housed in an 1890s clapboard home on a small isthmus overlooking the Yough, for an atmospheric candlelit dinner on the veranda. During the day, ride a few blocks east, over another bridge and grab sandwiches from **Mitch's Fuel & Food Restaurant**. Stop at **Tissue Farm** for good espresso drinks and a gander at their rotating art exhibits; Tissue Farm's owners also have a gourmet grocery a few blocks away and know what's going on around the village.

Ohiopyle Trading Post & River Tours in **Ohiopyle** can arrange the rentals and your day out, including electric bikes (you decide how much boost you want or need) and a three-hour rafting trip back on the Upper Yough on a shredder (a lightweight inflatable boat for two invented by a Ohiopyle native). They'll pick up the bikes and leave you the shredder, sans guide. Several class II rapids are easily navigated, but when in doubt stay right. You're not likely to capsize or get too wet, and the Upper Yough can be done before the prime

FLIGHT 93

On September 11, 2001, United Airlines Flight 93, on its way from Newark to San Francisco, was hijacked, as were the flights that hit the Twin Towers of the World Trade Center and the Pentagon. Flight 93 was pointed towards Washington, DC, the intended target. However, the passengers and crew heroically fought to wrest control of the plane and during the struggle the terrorists crashed the plane, killing everyone on board. A solemn and moving **memorial** was built at the crash site, a rural field in Somerset County, near Shanksville, just off Rte 30. Massive marble walls are aligned in the direction of the flight path. The visitor center lays out the timeline of that terrible day and the subsequent investigation.

Cucumber Falls

RAFTING THE YOUGHIOGHENY

Joel Means, owner of Ohiopyle Trading Post & River Tours. joelmeans@ohiopyletradingpost.com

The Youghiogheny River has the best white water in Pennsylvania, because of the consistency of the class III rapids on the Lower Yough, unusual for a river with this level of white water.

The rafting season runs from the spring through fall. Spring generally has higher water levels due to snowmelt and rains, but you're rafting in colder temperatures (both water and air) and need gear to keep you warm.

There are a lot of kayak competitions in the area, including an Upper Yough race, a few upstream races on the Loop (the first 1¼ miles of the Lower Yough), and the Falls Festival, where expert paddlers run the town's namesake 18ft falls.

---

white-water season begins. But if you're craving rapids, it's the more popular Lower Yough for you, and several long-running operations, including Ohiopyle Trading Post, can arrange trips.

If you're interested in tackling longer distances on the GAP with multiday group trips, check out **Wilderness Voyageurs**, a large operation that operates all over the country.

Make time to hang out around Ohiopyle, which comes out of its wintertime hibernation in a big way. Note that its year-round population of 36 explodes when the calendar ticks over to summer: access roads become clogged, and there are long lines and waits at the half dozen or so cafes and restaurants (always busy **Falls Market Restaurant** has good sandwiches and ice cream).

Check out the **Meadow Run**, a natural waterslide that's signposted along the road just before entering Ohiopyle. It's a narrow chute carved out of the river's rocky walls, ending in a deeper pool (popular for fly-fishing). When it's rushing through the channel at white-water speeds, no matter your risk tolerance, it's impossible to imagine not suffering severe injury. Nevertheless, people do it and survive unscathed; one pro's advice is to sit up and wear water shoes. But you can walk upstream in the river or via a path alongside the shore for pretty views.

Otherwise, if you're looking for a quick dip to cool off, try the pool at the base of nearby **Cucumber Falls**. There are also a few dozen hiking trails, as well as campgrounds, yurts and cottages, in the park.

PA Wilds

HIKING | STARGAZING | BOATING & BIKING

A region of over 3100 sq miles of deep forests, winding rivers and ancient mountains stretching from the New York border, the PA Wilds encompasses a patchwork of parks that for generations have balanced industry, conservation and recreation. Two of the largest rivers, the Susquehanna and Allegheny, and their tributaries that were graded, straightened and transformed as lumber 'highways,' are fly-fishing and kayaking dreamscapes. Native mountain lions and wolves were wiped out by hunting, while wildfires in the late 19th and early 20th centuries decimated some parts, but they've rebounded, as have elk that were reintroduced in the 1920s and are now the largest population in the northeast.

The legacy of self-sufficiency reigns and there are traces of the area's pioneering era and ethos. Isolated hunting and fishing cabins are commonplace. Major industries once thrived here, but now many small towns seem emptied out.

The Grand Canyon, in Pennsylvania
Take the gorge's trails

Pine Creek Gorge, around 800ft at its deepest, is undeniably worth seeing, the hyperbolic advertising notwithstanding. Views from behind the newly built visitor center at **Leonard Harrison State Park**, on the gorge's western side, are more panoramic and unobstructed compared those at **Colton Point State Park**, nearly directly across on the eastern side.

One of the better if more challenging hikes is the **Turkey Trail**, which begins just to the right of Leonard Harrison's visitor center. It descends to the valley floor, passing by several waterfalls. At the bottom of the gorge is the **Pine Creek Rail Trail**, a mostly flat 62-mile former railroad bed that's good for cycling, hiking and even a covered wagon ride – something for the kids. Stop by **Pine Creek Outfitters** on Rte 6, not far from the turnoff south to the park's visitor centers, for cycling, kayaking, canoeing and fishing gear and more: it's a one-stop shop for all outdoor needs.

GETTING AROUND

Towns, sights and parks are spread throughout a large region. Drives can be long between each, and GPS and cell service can be spotty. It's about two hours from Kane to Buffalo, and onward to Niagara Falls. There's no public transportation in the area. There's a regional airport in Bradford (Ace Rent a Car operates from here), just south of the New York border, with Southern Airway Express running daily flights to Pittsburgh and Washington, DC.

☑ TOP TIP

The only town worth considering as a base is Kane, towards the region's far western edge. Wellsboro, the largest town, is at the far eastern end. Both have several restaurants; in between, dining and grocery options are limited. Bringing groceries on a road trip isn't a bad option.

235

A PATCHWORK OF PARKS

Elk Country Visitor Center:
Interactive exhibits that are great for kids, with a viewing area and guided walks to spot elk.

Bald Eagle State Park:
Sliver of a park with a lake abutting a mountain; the valley is a prime spot for migrating birds.

Allegheny National Forest:
Pennsylvania's only national forest has campgrounds, cycling and hiking trails, and boating.

Cook Forest:
You'll find some of the northeast's tallest trees here; the Cook Forest Fire Tower has views of the Clarion River Valley.

Hyner View State Park:
One of the state's smallest parks, it's a popular destination for hang gliders, with astounding views.

Sinnemahoning State Park:
There are elk, eagles, wildflowers and an excellent wildlife center at this centrally located Appalachian Mountains park.

Dark Skies
Stargazing at Cherry Springs

On cloudless nights, especially in summer, hundreds of the astronomically inclined set up tents and telescopes and turn their gaze heavenward at **Cherry Springs State Park**, one of the best spots east of the Mississippi for looking up into space. Park educators are based in an amphitheater-like viewing area on many summer nights (often requiring registering in advance) and lead programs on constellations and other starry facts. It can feel fairly jubilant when crowded, in contrast to when it's empty under cloudy skies. The 82-acre mountaintop state park is surrounded by the Susquehannock State Forest and there's nothing but silence here. Flashlights, unless they have a red filter, are prohibited.

If staying at the **campsite** (no campfires) be sure to book well in advance in July and August, when the Milky Way is almost directly overhead. A few cabins are available for rent nearby; otherwise the closest recommended lodging is **Frosty Hollow Bed & Breakfast**. The burgers, chili and slices of pie at **Trails End at the Waldheim Bar**, 7 miles east, are the best you're going to do for an early dinner before heading to Cherry Springs.

Trees: What Are They Good For?
Educate yourself about the woods

The **Pennsylvania Lumber Museum**, outside Galeton, traces the lumber industry's evolution and its environmental and economic impact, as well as how forests have changed over time, through sophisticated, contemporary-style exhibits and galleries. Don't miss the coal-powered locomotive or what's likely the largest model toy train you've ever seen; it took 24 men 40 years to build. It's also worth planning a trip around the museum's July 4th Bark Peelers' Festival, when thousands turn up to cheer on lumberjacks competing in log rolling, greased pole climbing and other events. Pennsylvania produces and exports more hardwood than any state. So while lumberjacking skills aren't necessarily still practiced, logging and loggers remain vital to its economy.

The End of the Road
Kinzua's Sky Walk

When it was built in 1882, this 301ft-high **bridge** was the world's tallest and longest viaduct. Rebuilt in steel in 1900, it nevertheless couldn't withstand the power of the F1 tornado that hit in 2003. One end collapsed, leaving the remaining 624ft intact, which has been transformed into a sky walk with fantastic views of the snaking creek and gorge below. Step out onto a glass-covered square section near its terminus, an unnerving experience for those with a fear of heights. It's worth spending some time in the park's visitor center, which has exhibits explaining why it was such an engineering marvel.

General Kane Trail, an easy loop, begins south of the overflow parking lot and passes through some pretty forest scenery.

You can also cycle to and from Kinzua on the Knox & Kane Rail Trail (p238); the stretch between Kinzua and Lantz Corners is especially scenic.

SIGHTS
1. Cherry Springs State Park
2. Colton Point State Park
3. Kinzua Bridge Sky Walk
4. Leonard Harrison State Park
5. Pennsylvania Lumber Museum

ACTIVITIES, COURSES & TOURS
6. Pine Creek Outfitters

SLEEPING
- see 1 Cherry Springs State Park Campsite
7. Frosty Hollow Bed & Breakfast
8. Kane Manor Inn
9. Lodge at Glendorn
10. Penn Wells Hotel & Lodge
11. Rough Cut Lodge

EATING
12. Bell's Meat & Poultry
13. Flickerwood Wine Cellars
14. Table 105
15. Texas Hot Lunch
16. Trails End at the Waldheim Bar

DRINKING & NIGHTLIFE
17. Wilds Sonshine Factory

TRANSPORT
18. Kane Outfitters

Up-and-Coming Kane

Dining, drinking and a unique inn

The small town of Kane, at the Wilds' physical crossroads, appears as a laboratory for rejuvenation. It has no megastores and is all mom-and-pop shops, forward-thinking energy and collaboration between old-timers and newcomers. General Kane, credited with establishing the town just prior to the Civil War era, also built the Georgian Revival-style **Kane Manor Inn**, an 18,000-sq-ft, 26-room mansion that sits at the end of a block on 10 acres. The new owners, one formerly the chief chocolate scientist with Hershey and another a driving force behind developing cycling and kayaking in the area, have opened it as a charming B&B. They've also been lovingly restoring the manor's basement speakeasy with historic details intact; once opened, it promises to be a lively tavern. There's live music every Friday during summer and also drinks on the upstairs veranda.

The sunflower fields in the area are a joy to wander through. But it took creative minds to also see them as a source ingredient for making bottled spirits. And now, like champagne in France or scotch in Scotland, the PA Wilds holds the trademark on

---

THE FORESTS FOR THE TREES

Prior to the arrival of Europeans in the 1600s, Pennsylvania was nearly completely covered by forests. It was said that a squirrel could climb a tree in Philadelphia and emerge in Erie. What began as a cottage industry turned into the big business of lumber (and hemlock bark used in tanneries also made this region one of the biggest globally for leather). The trees were nearly depleted between the 1890s and 1930s.

FLY-FISHING THE PA WILDS RIVERS

Ralph Scherder, owner of Dark Skies Fly Fishing. *darkskiesflyfishing.com*

My favorite streams:

Spring Creek (Centre County) with over 5000 wild brown trout per mile, is considered our best trout stream; Little Juniata River (Blair County and Huntingdon Counties), another one with great mayfly; and Pine Creek (Tioga and Lycoming Counties), which has wild and native trout.

When to fish:

Early April through early June are best, when mayfliesy bring trout to the surface. But the limestone-influenced waters of central and southcentral Pennsylvania provide year-round opportunities. When visiting streams during summer, check water temperatures beforehand. Less than 68°F (20°C) is great for trout; above, focus on bass and panfish in lakes and ponds.

---

sunflower spirits because of the **Wilds Sonshine Factory**, the only place in the world to do this. The venture began as a way of rejuvenating abandoned farms in the area by planting sunflowers as a protein source for wildlife feed. Then eureka! Every piece of standard distillery equipment had to be modified to work with sunflowers or crafted from other parts, and everything, from the wood to the craftsmen to the ingredients, are all local. A visitor center describes how sustainability and natural-resource conservation guided this project. Stop by at night or weekends for a specialty cocktail at the beautiful bar and tasting room; the bar boasts the world's longest table made from a single piece of wood, appropriately enough from an Eastern hemlock, the Pennsylvania state tree. Ask to check out the nearby fields if you're here between mid-August and September, when the flowers are typically blooming. And the calendar is filled with festivals, live music and other outdoor performances.

The Allegheny: By Bicycle & Boat
Cycling rail trails and boating on the Allegheny

Cyclists who want to appreciate scenery without busting their quads should plan on riding a section of the primarily flat 47-mile-long trail between Mt Jewett and Marianne to the southwest, called the **Knox & Kane Rail Trail**; there's a trailhead in Kane just two blocks south of the Kane Manor Inn. Otherwise there's the more challenging **Jakes Rocks Overlook and Mountain Bike Trail**; the overlook segment has phenomenal views. **Kane Outfitters** rents high-end road and mountain bikes.

You can begin a kayaking and canoeing trip on the **Allegheny River and Reservoir**, known to boaters as the 'jewel in the forest,' not far from Kane. Kane Outfitters also rents kayaks, as does Allegheny Outfitters in Warren, PA, 28 miles northwest of Kane.

Welcome to Big Foot Country
Look out for the half-man, half-beast

Driving along the area's winding forested roads with hillsides stretching beyond the horizon and nary a person in sight, you might find yourself contemplating legends of half-man, half-beast creatures. So it shouldn't come as a surprise that one of the area's radio stations goes by 'Big Foot Country' or that Animal Planet's *Finding Bigfoot* show shot scenes in the region, or that there's a four-day **Big Foot Festival** in Marienville in early June, and a mid-July Squatch fest in Kane, which is basically a music festival. According to the official stats of the Bigfoot Field Researchers Organization (bfro.net), Pennsylvania has only 138 sightings, compared to Washington state, which has 708.

 EATING IN KANE: OUR PICKS

Texas Hot Lunch: A family-run place since 1914, with classic diner fare and Greek dishes like souvlaki and pita sandwiches. $

Bell's Meat & Poultry: At this market you can cobble together a lunch from a variety of cheeses and sausages, and maybe some Swedish specialties. $

Table 105: Upscale eatery, possibly the region's best, with pizza, juicy steaks and creatively conceived fish dishes. There's sushi on Wednesday nights. $$

Flickerwood Wine Cellars: There are Thursday pasta nights; otherwise appetizers, charcuterie and subs are served with their own wine. $$

The Poconos

RAFTING | HIKING | MOUNTAIN VIEWS

The Poconos region was once associated with cheesy TV ads featuring resorts with heart-shaped hot tubs for honeymooners. No longer. Today, the area's considerable outdoor charms are the main draw for tourists seeking a wilderness escape. The name comes from the Lenape for 'creek between two hills,' which rise in rocky crusts and folds across the northeast corner of Pennsylvania, where there are some 2400 sq miles of mountains, streams, waterfalls, lakes and forests. Bordered on the east by the Delaware Water Gap, to the west by coal country, and to the south by the Lehigh Valley, the region is easily accessible from Philadelphia and New York City.

Family Fun Poconos-Style
Rides, sweets and 'family camp'

Coal was king in the Poconos, fueling the country from the early 1800s to the early 1900s. Its legacy as a major coal-producing region, when the conundrum was how to get it out (canal, rail, then truck), can be experienced when riding the **Stourbridge Line**, a relaxing 1½-hour slow-moving train trip from Honesdale to Hawley and back. You pass through pretty scenery along the Lackawaxen River. While the tracks were built in the 1860s, the stately, comfortable Jersey Central Line cars are circa 1920s. You can also pay extra for the 'dinner' experience (served at lunchtime on regular Saturday or Sunday noon trips).

Coffee lovers and those with a sweet tooth should head over to the tasting room (Saturday 10am and 2pm) and the factory of **Moka Origins** (9am to 4pm), situated on the grounds of the **Himalayan Institute** (which runs highly recommended yoga and meditation retreats), only around 6 miles north of Honesdale. Their cacao beans are sourced directly from small farmers, primarily in several West African countries.

The film *Dirty Dancing* was set in an imaginary resort in the Catskills, a nearby region of New York. But those summer resorts didn't survive. Staying at **Woodloch Pines**, set on

GETTING AROUND

Greyhound buses run from Philadelphia to Stroudsburg and Mount Pocono. However, a car is a necessity once you're in the area. Uber and Lyft rideshare do operate here as well. Cell-phone and GPS service can be spotty. And winter driving, especially on partially plowed local roads, can be hazardous. A new Amtrak route connecting New York City and Scranton would be significant for opening up the region.

☑ TOP TIP

You can take a loop that avoids highways and instead passes through beautiful scenery. From Stroudsburg, take Rte 191 to Mount Pocono, then to Hawley (and up to the Honesdale area) on Rte 590; from there, take Rte 97 or Rte 6 to Milford. The road south to Stroudsburg on Rte 209 is especially scenic.

239

shimmering Lake Teedyuskung (near Honesdale and Hawley), is an opportunity to experience a slice of classic Americana. Families have been sharing the same dining-room tables for generations. Of course, facilities have been modernized and upgraded (including an adults-only separate lodge), but the daily smorgasbord of activities, like go-cart racing, family trivia, bingo, vaudeville-style performers, 'horseracing' and 'boomer storytime,' never gets old.

Scranton: Pizza Capital
A unique pizza style
Often trotted out as shorthand for President Joe Biden's working-class Pennsylvania roots, Scranton, the largest city in the Poconos region, is known to locals as, only somewhat tongue in cheek, the 'pizza capital of the world.' **Maroni's Pizza** in Scranton proper was reopened by the daughter of the original owners and is thriving once again. Some of the best, **Revello's**, **Salerno's** and **Arcaro & Genell** (their double-crusted white pizza is like a pizza-grilled cheese hybrid) are in Old Forge, considered the epicenter and just outside Scranton. Revello's pizzas can even be bought par-baked at grocery stores in the area or online. **Pizza L'Oven** and **Sabatini's Pizza**, in Exeter, a 20-minute drive from Scranton, offer two very different styles; Sabatini's is more traditional, with a slightly sweet sauce.

Alfredo's Cafe in Scranton is worth noting as a popular spot for travelers, not locals, as it's referenced as the 'good pizza place' in the TV show *The Office*, set in Scranton.

Whatever you do, don't ask for a 'pie,' but rather a 'tray' (they're cut into squares, not slices). And if you're craving a drink, keep in mind that Scranton is also a great place for cheap drinks. As the area has a large military veteran population, veterans clubs, which operate as non-profits, often sell draft beer and domestic bottles for less than $3. They do generally only admit members, but you can often sign-in as a guest, and events are occasionally open to the public.

Bird's-Eye Views of Big Majestic Birds
Climb Hawk Mountain
Southeast of the Poconos region proper, and part of the Kittatinny Ridge, **Hawk Mountain's** family-friendly hiking trails are distinguished from others in the region by the estimated 18,000 hawks, eagles, ospreys, kestrels and vultures that soar along windy updrafts, at eye level when viewed from the ridges' various lookout spots. While the large numbers of raptors stop here on their southern migration over the months of September, October and November, views of the soft-carpeted Appalachian hills below are available year-round. An enjoyable loop trail of medium difficulty involves clambering up and down boulder fields and stretches of forested canopy. You can also pick up the Appalachian Trail from here.

Floating at the Delaware Water Gap & Lehigh River
Leisurely tubing and white-water rafting
Tubing down the Delaware River is a big summertime activity – but bear in mind your peaceful idyll on the river may be broken by crowds of beer-chugging weekend tubers. The current can be slow, which means you'll have to be content with a lot of paddling. Tubing outfits like **Adventure Sports** and **Kittatinny Canoes** can drive you out to a river-access

WITH EVERY SEASON, TURN, TURN

Some of North America's oldest Native American communities, dating back 10,000 years, lived in the Stroudsburg area. Dutch, English and German settlers arrived in the 17th and 18th centuries, then the coal and resort industries boomed and came of age together; the former went bust, but the area remained a bona fide 'destination' through the 1960s, '70s and '80s. More recently, one-time vacation resorts have refashioned themselves into gated communities, some with prohibitions against short-term renting. COVID-19 only accelerated the dynamic, with New Yorkers, Philadelphians and others jumping at the chance for more space, fresh air and cheaper real estate. But as in the nearby Catskills region in New York, there's tension between newcomers, year-rounders and weekenders. More people, more problems…

WHY I LOVE THE POCONOS

Michael Grosberg, Lonely Planet writer

I've been coming up to the area for over 25 years with family and so there's a sepia-toned nostalgia to my memories: visits to horse and alpaca farms and to lessons with artists working out of ramshackle studios. One event, the week-long Wayne County Fair, has become a mid-August tradition. Now past its 160th year, and held on the grounds just outside Honesdale, it has a timeless charm. Once, my father-in-law accidentally bought a pig during a live animal auction because he waved his hand to get our attention (he 'returned' it after explaining the mishap). There are monster-truck shows, a demolition derby and live country and bluegrass music, a reminder of the area's rural roots even as development brings change and newcomers.

point in a rusty school bus, provide a tube and pick you up further downstream.

Plenty of outfitters either lead paddling tours up the river or rent out canoes and kayaks. Paddlers can **camp** alongside the river, a pretty memorable experience to do with a group of friends.

On the PA side of the river, several impressive waterfalls are easily accessible (Buttermilk Falls on the New Jersey side is worth checking out as well). We recommend **Dingmans Falls**, whose height (130ft) and scale only come into focus towards the end of a pleasant walk along a raised boardwalk through the forest. Raymondskill Falls is another 7 miles north, near Milford at the northern end of the Gap. Visiting privately owned Bushkill Falls, advertised as the 'Niagara Falls of PA,' for some might not be worth the fairly exorbitant cost of admission ($20 for adults).

The Lehigh River cuts a steep, dramatically arresting gorge through the uplands of northeast Pennsylvania. From May through August, the dam waters of the river are opened up (for four days in May and June, six in July and nine in August) to give an extra boost to loads of class II and III rapids for a fun day of rafting out of **Jim Thorpe**. **Pocono Whitewater** ends the day with a bonfire at their shop.

The main hiking attraction nearby is the 20-mile **Lehigh Gorge Trail**, which follows the river and an old railway cut. If you want a real challenge – with waterfall views as a payoff – attempt the steep climbs and rocky scrambles on the 3-mile **Glen Onoko Falls Trail**.

Jazz in the Gap

The oldest continually operating club

This isn't the West Village in NYC or the French Quarter of New Orleans. But a little street at the southern end of the Delaware Water Gap is home to the oldest continually operating jazz club in the country. Since the 1840s, when the **Deer Head Inn** opened up to New Yorkers and Philadelphians traveling to the Gap by train to stay at summertime resorts, it's been attracting top talent. Across the street, the Castle Inn, now home to several shops, was home base for Fred Waring and the Pennsylvanians, who together recorded the country's most popular musical radio show in the 1920s and prime-time TV show in the 1940s.

 EATING IN HONESDALE & HAWLEY: OUR PICKS

| **Cocoon Coffee House:** Located in Hawley, Cocoon serves Moka coffee, chocolate, house-made pastries, bread and gourmet sandwiches. **$** | **Scarfalloto's Town House Diner:** Honesdale place with classic diner menu, portions and decor, with a toy train running near the ceiling. **$** | **Dyberry Forks:** This chef-run bistro in Honesdale has a wide-ranging menu, from chicken parm and burgers to sushi and ramen. **$$** | **Glass:** Eat out on the deck for stunning waterfall views in Hawley while enjoying anything from a porterhouse to a variety of small dishes. **$$$** |

Lancaster & PA Dutch Country

FOOD | FARM STAYS | RURAL PANORAMAS

This is old country for the USA. Lancaster was founded as a market town by King James II, and a prominent Amish family, the Stoltfutz, bought their land 10 generations ago from the estate agent of Pennsylvania's founder William Penn for 5¢ an acre. Lancaster's age is revealed when walking through its red-brick historic district with buildings dating from the mid-1700s to late 1800s. The Lancaster Amish, the country's largest group at around 44,000, as well as Mennonite communities, turned the picturesque rolling hills into some of the most productive agricultural land in the country hundreds of years ago.

But Lancaster is also home to a small, thriving music and arts community, and the 'plain folk,' the Amish and Mennonite, coexist with the 'English,' anyone who isn't Amish. Chocolate lovers and roller-coaster enthusiasts should head to Hershey, the company town, and its amusement park, while boating and hiking opportunities abound along the Susquehanna riverfront.

Central Farmers Markets

Smorgasbords of good eats

Housed in a Romanesque revival–style building smack in the center of town, Lancaster's **central market** is equally noteworthy for its historical legacy as it is for its collection of stalls ranging from regional gastronomic delicacies – pretzels, whoopie pies, fresh horseradish and bottled jams – to West African, Thai and Middle Eastern specialties. Opened in 1730, it's the oldest continually run farmers market in the country. The building itself was renovated in the late 1980s, but notice how the floor slopes – designed for the runoff of melting ice blocks used before refrigeration.

Most every stall has a story: **Groff's Vegetables** has celebrated its 70th anniversary; **Kauffman Orchards** is run by the family's fourth generation; **Long's Horseradish** has used the same grinder since 1889; **S Clyde Weaver** won awards

---

GETTING AROUND

A car is the most practical way to get here. Amtrak serves the Lancaster train station, with frequent trains from Philadelphia (1¼ hours) and a once-daily service from Pittsburgh (6¼ hours). The town of Lancaster is walkable, but, elsewhere things are spread out. Bicycle rental is a possibility, though the terrain is hilly and road shoulders are thin or nonexistent. The Amish get around on horse-drawn buggies and several companies offer tours.

☑ TOP TIP

The simple life, with its picturesque horse-drawn buggies, ironically attracts busloads of visitors and has spawned a kitschy tourist industry. Get onto the back roads and you can appreciate the quiet pastoral serenity the religious orders here have preserved.

BEST ARTISANAL SHOPS IN PA DUTCH COUNTRY

Pennsylvania Guild of Craftsmen:
Real-deal well-curated PA Dutch artisanal goods in Lancaster, with furniture, home decor, fabrics and kitchen goods.

Dutchland Galleries:
High-quality original paintings by local artists and prints of more well-known ones, located in Intercourse's Kitchen Kettle Village.

Mount Hope Wine Gallery:
Tastings are available of their own products, including their Rumspringa craft beer and hard ciders.

Stoltzfus Meats:
This long-running shop produces and sells specialty smoked meats and sausages as well as homemade bakery items.

Old Country Store:
Stocking a great selection of handmade and local crafts (pillows, art, embroidery, quilts) as well as edibles such as jam and canned goods.

---

for the best cheddar at the 2023 World Cheese Championship in Norway; and a married couple started **Happiness is…Granola** in their garage during the COVID-19 pandemic.

Tuesday mornings might be the best, least-crowded time to visit. Saturdays get so crowded things sell out early. A **strawberry festival** in June features a strawberry pie eating contest.

Bird-in-Hand, one of the many delightfully named Amish towns, is known primarily for its **farmers market**, a one-stop shop of Dutch country food highlights that cardiologists might not approve. These include the scrapple (pork scraps mixed with cornmeal and wheat flour and fried) and shoofly pie (made with molasses or brown sugar and sprinkled with a crumbly mix of more brown sugar, flour and butter).

On & Off the Tracks
Train toys and steam engines

Train aficionados should make a beeline for this corner of bucolic countryside and the **Strasburg Railroad**, which has run the same route (at the same speed) to Paradise and back since 1832. It has gorgeously restored wooden train cars, with stained glass, shiny brass lamps and burgundy seats. Afterwards you can cross the street to the **Railroad Museum of Pennsylvania** to admire and climb aboard the nearly 100 gigantic mechanical marvels. Just up the road, appropriately enough, is the **National Toy Train Museum**. The walls are packed with many gleaming railcars and the push-button interactive dioramas will have you feeling like a kid again. It's next to the recommended Red Caboose Motel, where you can bed down in, yes, a train car (there's also a silo you can climb for panoramic views, out back next to the farm animals).

On the Farm
Get an up-close view of Amish life

The Amish are farmers, although tractors aren't used for plowing because they diminish connection to the land and Amish practices are essentially organic, in all but name. However, maintaining profitability, always challenging, means agriculture usually goes hand in hand with entrepreneurial endeavors, finding niches within the area's economy, whether its opening up properties to tourism, raising deer, making quilts or building buggies (they cost between $9500 and $14,000 and take around a year to complete). Especially good for kids is **Old Windmill Farm**, where they can pet farm animals, milk a cow, go on a hayride and jump around in a barn filled with corn, like a ball pit. Come in early spring when newly born kids (baby goats), lambs and piglets can be bottle-fed.

Amish Experience, a big operation along Old Philadelphia Pike in Bird-in-Hand, has a few options: there's a relaxing and

LANCASTER & PA DUTCH COUNTRY

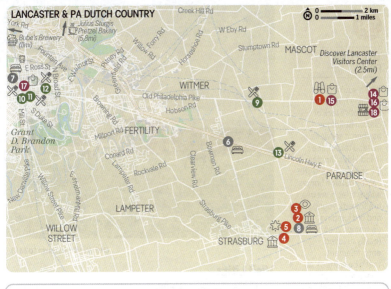

SIGHTS
1. Amish Experience
2. National Toy Train Museum
3. Old Windmill Farm
4. Railroad Museum of Pennsylvania

ACTIVITIES, COURSES & TOURS
5. Strasburg Railroad

SLEEPING
6. Fulton Steamboat Inn
7. Lancaster Arts Hotel
8. Red Caboose Motel

EATING
9. Bird-in-Hand Farmers Market
10. Central Market
11. Himalayan Curry
12. Horse Inn
13. Miller's Smorgasbord

SHOPPING
14. Dutchland Galleries
15. Mount Hope Wine Gallery
16. Old Country Store
17. Pennsylvania Guild of Craftsmen
18. Stoltzfus Meats

informative guided minibus tour along backcountry roads; a 'guided' walk through a recreated one-room schoolhouse and typical Amish home; and most recommended, a visit to a working farm and an Amish home for an opportunity to chat and ask questions unencumbered by phones and digital distractions.

Whatever your upbringing, late adolescence generally brings questioning and stirrings for more than what you've known. The Amish are no different. However, they've created an integral cultural tradition during this period and given it a name: rumspringa. At the age of 16, Amish youth are encouraged to experience the modern world, to literally 'run around.' An estimated 85% to 90% return to their communities, when they finally undergo baptism.

Divorce is prohibited, and they're excommunicated if they marry a non-Amish person. Perhaps surprisingly, many couples honeymoon in Florida, at an Amish community near Sarasota, traveling by train or 'Amish taxi,' basically a car driven by someone who isn't Amish. Most Amish are born in the home with a Mennonite midwife assisting.

THE 'PLAIN FOLK'

When you're here, you may notice the plain folk's lack of church buildings, as church services instead take place in individual homes; 'phone shanties' (little cabins outside homes where telephone use is allowed); young and old jumping on trampolines (easily enjoyed entertainment that's permitted); an absence of nursing homes for the elderly, but 'dotty houses' instead (annexes accommodating multi-generational families); many one-room schoolhouses (the average family has seven kids and schools can never be more than a mile away); graveyards with matching headstones, facing east because the Bible says the messiah will return from this direction; and men's pants with no belt buckles or zippers, as they're kept up by folding waistbands.

Old Windmill Farm (p238)

Visit Lititz
Pretzel making and strolling

Like other towns in Pennsylvania Dutch Country, Lititz was founded by a religious community from Europe, in this case Moravians who settled here in the 1740s. However, unlike the cloistered, austere feeling of other settlements like Ephrata, beyond its historic center Lititz was more outward looking and integrated with the world. Many of the original handsome stone and wood buildings line Lititz' streets. However, rather than feeling sealed in amber, the shops and cafes seem to relish their small-town character. There's an unusual effortlessness to the vibe, from the below-ground-floor hole-in-the-wall ice-cream shop where locals head on weekend nights to the English-style pub with tables spilling out onto the street during summer. Several newer developments, including a contemporary food hall, make it idyllic for an afternoon meander. And you can try your hand at rolling and shaping pretzels at the **Julius Sturgis Pretzel Bakery**, the oldest commercial pretzel factory in the country.

EATING IN LANCASTER & PA DUTCH COUNTRY: OUR PICKS

Himalayan Curry: Nepalese and Indian fare a block from Lancaster's central market, with good naan, lamb and cauliflower dishes. **$$**

Bube's Brewery: This 19th-century German brewery and restaurant complex contains several atmospheric bars and four dining rooms. **$$**

Miller's Smorgasbord: Anchoring a complex of shops, this restaurant, going for nearly a century, draws crowds for its buffet of Amish-style food. **$$**

Horse Inn: This gastropub has a great menu – one night you might nosh on Korean fried cauliflower, another on chicken with coconut milk and ginger. **$$**

Gettysburg

HISTORY | SCENERY | FOOD

This otherwise pretty, tranquil town surrounded by a gorgeous swathe of rolling hills is synonymous with one of the bloodiest battles of the Civil War, which occurred over three days in July 1863. The battle is considered by many as the turning point of the war and the high-water mark of the Confederacy's attempted rebellion, from which General Lee's army never recovered. Later that year, President Abraham Lincoln delivered one of his most eloquent and powerful speeches, forever after known as the 'Gettysburg Address' ('Four score and seven years ago…'), reinforcing the war's mission of equality and marking the 'new birth of the nation' on the country's birthday of July 4th. Every house in town that has existed since the battle is marked by a plaque, and some with holes from bullets fired during the battle.

The Battlefield

Get the big picture and the dark details

Tours of the battlefield last from two to three hours and are best done privately in your own car. The national-park guide drives and talks, telling a detailed story of the fighting. Other options are downloadable audio tours and bus tours with guides.

The museum at the **visitor center**, where tours begin, is a must-see, and to do it any justice you need a minimum of an hour or two (you can refresh with coffee and food at the cafe and restaurant on-site). Besides Gettysburg, galleries lay out the war, from its beginning to Lincoln's assassination and all the important moments in between. There's also the awe-inspiring **cyclorama** – a life-size, 360-degree painting – of Pickett's Charge, the especially deadly battle on the third, final day.

Interestingly, as soon as the battle ended, people, including photographers (some of the first to ever take war photos), flocked to the area to witness its aftermath. There's a photo of Lincoln consecrating the cemetery after his speech and a blurry one of him leaving by horseback.

Several free ranger-led activities, like a 'history hike' and a cemetery tour, are offered daily. Check out the digital board in the visitor center for the latest details.

GETTING AROUND

Gettysburg is closer to Baltimore and Washington, DC than Philadelphia. The only public transportation directly here is with Rabbit Transport, a commuter bus with several daily trips to/from Harrisburg (Amtrak runs trains here as well). The town itself is highly walkable, and you can rent bicycles or e-bikes to explore the area, including to get to the battlefield visitor center, only 1.5 miles from the southern edge of town.

☑ TOP TIP

Summer visits should be planned in advance, especially in July when the town is mobbed with battle reenactors. And once you've tackled the battlefield, get outside Gettysburg and explore the surrounding countryside, visiting quaint little towns like New Oxford for antiquing and Biglerville for apple picking, and Fairfield's inn, circa 1757.

SIGHTS
1. Children of Gettysburg 1863
2. Shriver House

ACTIVITIES, COURSES & TOURS
3. Gettysburg Ghost Tours

SLEEPING
4. Brickhouse Inn

EATING
6. Blessing
7. Dobbin House
8. Lincoln Social Food Hall

GETTYSBURG FESTIVALS

Gettysburg Festival of Races:
An April weekend of long-distance running through the battlefield's roads and fields.

Gettysburg Bluegrass Festival:
May and August weekends of top-flight contemporary and traditional bluegrass, in a farmland location.

Battle of Gettysburg Anniversary:
The first week of July sees book signings, talks and other events. Also called the 'Sacred Trust.'

National Apple Harvest Festival:
Held on the first two weekends in October, this biggie in Biglerville celebrates apples with great food and music.

Dedication Day, Remembrance Day:
There's a history reenactors parade, talks and more over November 18 and 19 on the anniversary of Lincoln's address.

Beyond the Battle
Interactive museums with other angles

Overlooked in descriptions of the tactical minutiae of the battle is what happened to the ordinary residents of Gettysburg, and how, amidst an occupation by the Confederate Army and all the fighting, including with artillery that could launch shells many miles, only one civilian, a woman named Jennie Wade, was killed. Led by a guide in period dress, a tour of the **Shriver House**, where you can learn how one family survived, helps fill in the holes. The house was built by the second-wealthiest family in the county, and its original walls and floors have been preserved. The owners, who originally intended to build a B&B, have furnished it with period antiques and recreated a mise-en-scène, as if the Confederate occupiers, including sharpshooters in the attic, have just fled. The tours, which are generally good for children as well, are offered every 45 minutes, daily from April through November, and from Christmas to New Year's. Families with younger children should head just a few blocks down to **Children of Gettysburg 1863**, a small museum with explanatory texts designed for kids and a few interactive exhibits and dress-up costumes.

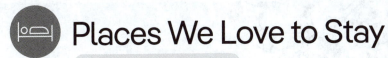

Places We Love to Stay

€ Budget €€ Midrange €€€ Top End

Pittsburgh MAP p225

Monaco $$ This good downtown choice has exceptionally stylish room decor and a recommended basement restaurant.

Inn on Negley $$ A Shadyside place with all the amenities and first-name-basis friendliness of a quiet B&B.

Inn on the Mexican War Streets $$ In a North Side mansion circa 1888, this hotel has hearty, homemade breakfasts and stunning antique furnishings.

Laurel Highlands MAP p230

Creek Haven $$ This large three-bedroom house situated by a burbling creek on a road named Dark Hollow has a Jacuzzi, deck and fully equipped kitchen.

Ohiopyle Hobbit House $$ A *Lord of the Rings*–themed three-story house in the woods with a massive outdoor space, including barbecue and firepit areas.

Smith House Inn $$ On a quiet street in Confluence, this four-room B&B offers a charming wraparound porch and delicious breakfasts.

PA Wilds MAP p237

Nature Inn at Bald Eagle $$ A state-park-managed eco-minded lodge, its rooms have all the creature comforts. There's a firepit and a board-game and puzzle room.

Rough Cut Lodge $$ Conveniently close to the PA 'Grand Canyon,' this place has homey room suites on one side of road and more lodge-style riverside options on the other.

Penn Wells Hotel & Lodge $$ This Wellsboro hotel is notable for its indoor pool and 1930s old-school, atmospheric annex building.

Lodge at Glendorn $$$ An enormous estate with a 'big house' and log cabins, this resort is one of the region's finest, with activities from skeet shooting to curling.

The Poconos MAP p240

The Darby $$ This stylish boutique lodging is located just over a bridge and the Delaware River from Narrowsburg, NY.

Ferncrest Campground $$ Glamping in dome tents, some with hot tubs and fireplaces, is available here, a few minutes' drive from Promised Land State Park.

Shawnee Inn $$$ A classic Federal-style grand-looking resort, Shawnee is known equally for its golf course and its spectacular riverside setting.

Lancaster & PA Dutch Country MAP p245

Fulton Steamboat Inn $$ This nautical-themed hotel is gimmicky, but the brass fixtures and flowery wallpaper are well kept, the rooms comfortable,w and there's an indoor pool.

Red Caboose Motel $$ A fun novelty hotel, the standard motel rooms here are wedged in a collection of caboose cars of every shape and color.

Lancaster Arts Hotel $$$ A member of the Historic Hotels of America, this hotel is housed in an old tobacco warehouse and features a cool, designer-hotel ambience.

Gettysburg MAP p248

Gettysburg Battlefield B&B $$ This atmospheric Civil War–era farmhouse has a wide variety of room configurations, morning 'history talks' and evening 'ghost talks.'

Brickhouse Inn $$ Set in two adjacent stately old houses (built in the 1800s), Brickhouse has charming rooms and a lovely back garden.

 EATING AROUND GETTYSBURG: OUR PICKS

Hollabaugh Bros: In Biglerville, this excellent farmers market has sandwiches, pastries and fresh produce. **$**

Blessing: This place offers comfy booths and a large menu of Mexican dishes, including especially juicy birria tacos. **$**

Lincoln Social Food Hall: A contemporary, light-filled spot near the battlefield, it serves artisanal pizza, BBQ, seafood and wings. **$$**

Dobbin House: Restaurant housed in Gettysburg's oldest building, and offers hefty portion sizes of crab cakes and strip steaks. **$$$**

WASHINGTON, DC

THE GUIDE

Above: Washington Monument (p262); Right: US Capitol Building (p276)

THE MAIN AREAS

THE WHITE HOUSE & FOGGY BOTTOM
The President's pad. **p256**

NATIONAL MALL
The nation's front lawn.
p261

PENN QUARTER & CHINATOWN
History, art and family museums.
p266

SOUTHWEST
Stadiums and waterfront living.
p269

CAPITOL HILL
Political epicenter and quirky art.
p273

Washington, DC

THE CAPITAL OF THE USA

The nation's capital may be small, but it's jam packed with history, art, nature museums and international culture.

Washington, DC is a small, diverse urban center that's easy to navigate, friendly and safe, and there's so much to do here. It's the United States' capital city, and was purpose built to be so more than 230 years ago. Both Maryland and Virginia donated land to the cause, with America's capital constructed on the banks of the Potomac and Anacostia Rivers.

The city grew over time, becoming a hub for freed slaves in the mid 1800s and eventually, thanks to immigration and international workers, the culturally diverse city that it is today. DC is also one of America's most LGBTIQ+-friendly cities, where same-sex marriages have been recognized since 2010 and transgender people can choose their gender identity both in public restrooms and on public documents. Yet as forward thinking as DC is, it's also a city of contrasts. The politically charged Washingtonians have only been allowed to vote in presidential elections since 1964, and they weren't even allowed their own mayor until 1973.

For cultural richness, however, DC can hardly be beat. In this small and action-packed city, it's easy to fill your days with all kinds of diverse activities that will make history buffs, foodies, culture and outdoors lovers swoon. You could visit DC just for the museums – the Smithsonian Institute alone has 17 free ones – or just to explore the history of the nation, its government and its majestic monuments. Do so, however, and you'd be missing out on all the gorgeous parks, too-cool live-music joints, incredible theater productions and amazing art (and brunches).

For all of its guise as a big city, Washington, DC feels more like a small town, a place where everyone is welcome and at home. It's a pretty quirky city, where neighborhood art projects and elementary-school kid lobbies get taken all too seriously (DC has an official dinosaur, thanks to those kids). Whether you're enjoying a picnic or a game of Frisbee on 'America's Front Lawn,' taking a paddle boat out on the Tidal Basin or catching a show at the Kennedy Center's iconic main stage, enjoy an immersion into international culture in this charming riverfront city.

FOMINA YAPHOTO/SHUTTERSTOCK ©

NORTHEAST	**ADAMS MORGAN & THE U STREET CORRIDOR**	**DOWNTOWN & DUPONT CIRCLE**	**GEORGETOWN**
Industrial and alternative. **p279**	Black history and nightlife. **p282**	Magnificent manors and chic brunches. **p288**	River walks, restaurants and retail therapy. **p292**

Find Your Way

DC is a small, walkable city with great public transportation and an expansive bikeshare program – which is great news, because it also has horrible rush-hour traffic you'll want to do everything you can to avoid.

Adams Morgan & the U Street Corridor
p282

Georgetown
p292

Downtown & Dupont Circle
p288

The White House & Foggy Bottom
p256

National Mall
p261

FROM THE AIRPORT
Whether you're coming into Reagan or Dulles airports, the best way to get into town is by Metro. If you have too much luggage to move easily, or arriving in the middle of the night (when the Metro is closed), you'll have to opt for a taxi.

METRO
The District's famous Metro system is really as good as it sounds. You can get cheaply and easily to nearly anywhere in the city, including to and from both airports, on comfortable, fully ADA-compliant trains.

DC CIRCULATOR BUS
The DC Circulator Bus (dccirculator.com) is a very underrated public-transportation option that takes you past most of DC's main sights – even those the Metro doesn't reach – for a flat $1 per trip. Check routes on its website.

252

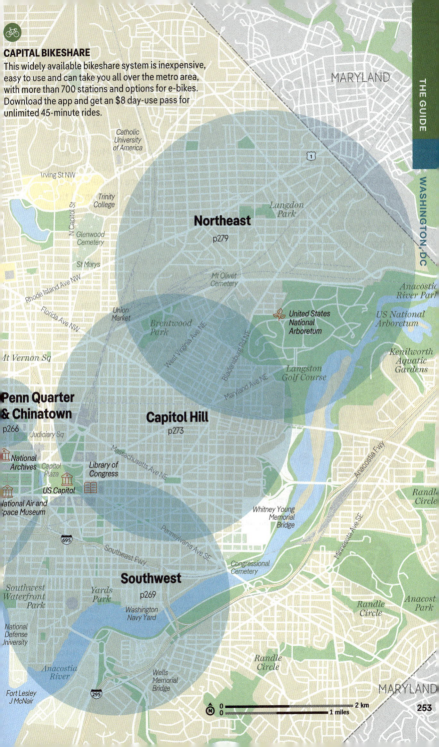

Plan Your Days

In such a small and action-packed city, it's easy to fill your days with all kinds of diverse adventures that will make history buffs, foodies, and culture and outdoors lovers swoon.

Recreation Pier (p272)

Day 1

Morning

● Start your day off at your Smithsonian museum of choice, be it the **National Museum of Natural History** (p261), **National Air and Space Museum** (p265) or the **National Museum of the American Indian** (p262).

Afternoon

● Take a walk along the **Wharf's waterfront** (p269), get your espionage fill at the **International Spy Museum** (p271), then grab lunch in the Navy Yard before heading to the **National Arboretum** (p280).

Evening

● Take a **DC Mural Tour** (p281), followed by dinner at **Union Market** (p279). Stay for some live music, or make your way over to **Echostage** (p281) for a late-night dance fest.

You'll Also Want to...

Skip the monuments and dive deeper into life in the nation's capital with a few local favorites.

CATCH A MATCH

Soccer fans can see **DC United** (p271) play at Audi Field or cheer on the women of the Washington Spirit, while baseball fans can root for the home team at Nationals Park.

HIT THE SHOPS

Head to chic and swanky **CityCenterDC**, or peruse the cool and quirky local stores around Union Market or the 14th St Corridor – perfect for thrifting favorites.

GET CRAFTY

Visit the **Renwick Gallery** (p260), with exhibits dedicated to American craft and decorative art from the 19th to 21st centuries – even art from Burning Man has been featured.

THE GUIDE

WASHINGTON, DC

Day 2

Morning
● Start your day with a run or walk along the Georgetown waterfront, or rent a kayak at the **Thompson Boat Center** (p295) for a serene paddle, before heading for brunch near **Dupont Circle** (p299).

Afternoon
● Head to the **Phillips Collection** (p288) for a modern-art immersion, followed by a languid afternoon spent on **Book Hill** (p292) or eating cupcakes in Georgetown.

Evening
● Grab a table at **Il Canale** (p294) for a pizza before taking in a free performance at the Kennedy Center's **Millennium Stage** (p256). If you've still got gas, hit up the bars on **U St** (p282) for a party, or simply head back to your hotel for a well-earned rest.

Day 3

Morning
● Grab your coffee to go and visit Oprah at the **National Portrait Gallery** (p268), followed by a stop at the **National Archives** (p266) to see the Charters of Freedom. Go dragon hunting at Chinatown's **Friendship Archway** (p266) before making your way to the **White House** (p258) for a tour.

Afternoon
● Spend a few hours on Capitol Hill, exploring the **US Capitol** (p276) building, wandering through **Eastern Market** (p274) and checking out the shops on **Barracks Row** (p274).

Evening
● Go for a stroll around **Black Broadway** (p284), grab some East African eats in **Little Ethiopia** (p282) before then catching a show at the iconic **9:30 Club** (p286).

PLAY WITH WORDS

Linguistics is the name of the game at **Planet Word** (p268), one of the city's newest museums, with interactive exhibits about language and its impact across the globe.

HIT THE MARKET

The farmers market, that is. Dupont Circle's **Farmers Market** (p290) is one of our (and the city's) favorites.

PROJECT YOURSELF

Visit the immersive **Artechouse** (p269), where installations, projections and exhibitions bring digital art and technology together to create immersive experiences.

GO GARGOYLE HUNTING

The most fun activity at the **Washington National Cathedral** (p294) is gargoyle spotting – look for the alligator, rattlesnake, raccoon and even Darth Vader.

255

The White House & Foggy Bottom

THE PRESIDENT'S PAD

GETTING AROUND

The main Metro stations in Foggy Bottom are Foggy Bottom and Farragut West, both of which lie on the orange, blue and silver lines. If you're going on a White House tour, it's better to get off at Federal Triangle, Metro Center or McPherson Sq, all of which are closer to the White House visitor entrance. The DC Circulator Bus also passes the White House. Rideshares are simple to arrange, and Capital Bikeshare stations are prevalent, however parking in this zone is not, though the Kennedy Center and GWU do have paid on-site garages.

☑ TOP TIP

Keep an eye on DC's social calendars (such as the *Washington Post's* Weekend section) to make the best out of some of the more famous sites, such as the White House, Kennedy Center and GWU.

Named after the whimsical fog rising off the Potomac River on cool mornings, the once-simple rural settlement of Foggy Bottom is now a scenic central DC neighborhood where academia, politics and culture intersect.

Foggy Bottom's recent history stretches back to 1763, when a German settler named Jacob Funck subdivided 130 acres near the intersection of Rock Creek and the Potomac River into what became the earliest European settlement in the District of Columbia. The settlement grew over the next century, eventually turning into a manufacturing hub, where breweries and glass factories thrived. These days, Foggy Bottom is home to the State Department, the Kennedy Center and the infamous Watergate Hotel. It's also a next-door neighbor to America's most well-known residence, 1600 Pennsylvania Ave NW. It's the perfect haunt for the politically minded, culture lovers and outdoor enthusiasts alike.

Performing Arts

Delve into the Kennedy Center

The **John F. Kennedy Center for the Performing Arts**, aka the Kennedy Center, is one of the United States' premier cultural institutions and is home to the National Symphony Orchestra, the National Opera and the National Ballet. The Kennedy Center also hosts symphonies, operas, ballets, theater and live-music shows by national and international artists. There are free daily performances on the smaller **Millennium Stage**, built with the aim of ensuring the arts are accessible to everyone, as well as a new permanent exhibit in the roof-level Atrium, celebrating the Kennedy family and their role in supporting the performing arts. Be sure to stop by the **Reach**, a 2019 addition to the center with huge multifunctional classroom, rehearsal and performance spaces, now directly accessible from the **Rock Creek Park trail** by a stylish pedestrian bridge.

THE GUIDE

WASHINGTON, DC THE WHITE HOUSE & FOGGY BOTTOM

TOP SIGHTS
1. John F. Kennedy Center for the Performing Arts
2. White House

SIGHTS
3. Black Lives Matter Plaza
4. Daughters of the American Revolution (DAR) Constitution Hall
5. Renwick Gallery
6. Textile Museum

SLEEPING
7. Hay-Adams Hotel
8. Hotel Hive
9. Mayflower Hotel
10. River Inn

EATING
11. Captain Cookie & the Milk Man
12. Founding Farmers
13. GW Delicatessen
14. Tonic at Quigley's

257

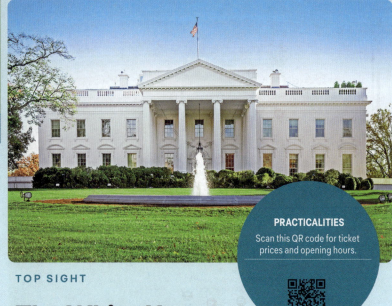

PRACTICALITIES

Scan this QR code for ticket prices and opening hours.

TOP SIGHT

The White House

A central piece of American identity, 1600 Pennsylvania Avenue NW is both the workplace and residence of the President of the United States of America. You can visit, though due to strict national-security measures, you'll need to do some (very) advanced planning. Getting to walk around this bucket-list site, however, is worth the effort.

DON'T MISS

Blue Room

China Room

Rose Garden

President's Park

National Christmas Tree Lighting Ceremony

White House Garden

Black Lives Matter Plaza

The White House Complex

The **White House** was designed by Irish-born architect James Hoban. Its construction took more than eight years, though President John Adams and his wife Abigail moved in in 1801, before it was complete. The North and South Porticoes were added in the 19th century, followed by the 2nd story and the West Wing in the early 1900s. In the 1950s, the entire 55,000-sq-ft building was remodeled to avert structural problems.

The White House complex of today is owned by the National Park Service, and includes a six-story Executive Residence, the West Wing (which holds the President's offices), the Eisenhower Executive Office Building (site of the staff offices) and the Blair House guest residence.

House Tours

White House tours take you through all the public rooms in the East Wing, including the Blue Room, Red Room, Green Room, State Dining Room and China Room, and also give you a view of the Rose Garden. While there are no official tour guides, there are Secret Service members posted in every room who can help to answer questions about the house's architecture and history.

To book a tour, US residents must submit a request through their Congress member between 21 and 90 days in advance – tours are subject to availability and security clearance. Foreign visitors should contact their country's embassy in DC. If your tour is confirmed, you'll get a scheduled time between 9:30am and 12:30pm, Tuesday to Saturday. The self-guided tours are free and last about 45 minutes. You'll need an ID card to enter (only valid US-issued ID cards or passports are accepted) and note that there are no restrooms available during the tour, so plan accordingly (especially if you're with kids).

There is a (very long) list of banned items, which can be found online. These include detachable-lens cameras, video cameras and tobacco products. There's no on-site storage, so your best bet is to leave your bag in your hotel before heading out.

Garden Tours & President's Park

Touring the White House Garden is another spectacular option, though a much rarer one. Garden tours only take place twice a year, in October and April, are announced only a week or two in advance, and last for just two consecutive days. Free tickets for the timed tours are distributed outside of the White House Visitor Center on the day, starting at 8:30am.

If you didn't manage to secure a garden tour, take a walk around the President's Park instead. This is an 18-acre natural setting surrounding the White House that's full of statues, memorials and other important structures. President's Park is open to the public for free.

Holiday Events

The White House hosts two truly special holidays events that are amazing to experience. The first is the Easter Egg Roll, which has been a tradition since 1878 (although it now takes place on the Monday after Easter). The second is the National Christmas Tree Lighting Ceremony, held in December since 1923. Tickets to both events are free, but are available by lottery only. Check recreation.gov for more info.

BLACK LIVES MATTER PLAZA

In June 2020, during the George Floyd protests, the MuralsDC program painted 16 bright-yellow letters on 16th St NW, just in front of the White House. The 35ft-tall letters spelled out 'Black Lives Matter' and, at the work's unveiling, Mayor Muriel Bowser declared the street would be renamed Black Lives Matter Plaza.

FUN FACTS

- It takes 570 gallons of paint to cover the outside surface of the White House.
- The White House became wheelchair accessible in the 1930s, during Franklin D Roosevelt's term.
- There is a movie theater, bowling alley, flower shop and dentist's office on the grounds.
- According to lore, Presidents Herbert Hoover and John Quincy Adams both kept pet alligators in the White House.
- The Briefing Room used to be a swimming pool.
- Franklin D Roosevelt hosted a toga party at the White House.
- The white house has 412 doors, 147 windows, 28 fireplaces, seven staircases and three elevators.

GWU TEXTILE MUSEUM

This hidden gem of a museum is the go-to if you love threads. Founded in 1925 on George Washington University's (GWU) campus, the **Textile Museum** *(museum. gwu.edu)* displays intricate textile artistry, as well as culturally significant threaded works from around the world. The permanent collection includes more than 21,000 examples of handmade textile art across five millennia and five continents, ranging from exquisite tapestries, costumes and clothing to woven artifacts. There's also a study collection as well as educational programs and workshops you can join – check its website for up-to-date details.

Renwick Gallery

American Craft
Decorative arts at the Renwick Gallery

The **Renwick Gallery**, located near the White House, is a museum dedicated to American crafts and decorative arts from the 19th century to the present. The museum, which is a branch of the Smithsonian American Art Museum, is generally devoted to exhibiting American craft art, though it tends to extend the definitions of craftsmanship and artistic expression, promoting innovative contemporary works that range from the 'Art of Burning Man' to 'Wonder', a large-scale sculptural exhibit designed to provoke exactly that.

Historic Hall
Catch a show at Constitution Hall

The **Daughters of the American Revolution (DAR) Constitution Hall** is one of DC's most important performance halls. This historic venue was built in 1929 by the DAR to house its annual conventions, though it soon became host to important events, lectures, concerts and ceremonies throughout the century. Designated a National Historical Landmark in 1985, Constitution Hall seats 3702 people in the tiers and the orchestra, and has 52 boxes (one for each state), plus one Presidential Box. As of 2024, every US president since Calvin Coolidge has attended at least one event at the hall while in office.

 EATING IN FOGGY BOTTOM: OUR PICKS

Founding Farmers: Farm-to-table eatery cooperatively owned by growers. One of the city's best brunch spots. $$	**Tonic at Quigley's:** Once a local drugstore and soda fountain, now a favorite for classic American cuisine. $	**GW Delicatessen:** Of all GWU's sandwich spots, only this one serves an absurd amount of bacon in your BLT. $	**Captain Cookie & the Milk Man:** Former food truck serving the best ice cream, cookies and milkshakes around. $

National Mall

THE NATION'S FRONT LAWN

Also known as America's Front Yard, the National Mall has more than 1000 acres of green space running from the Lincoln Memorial in the west to the US Capitol Building in the east. The sprawling park is lined by some of the Smithsonian Institute's most popular museums, and dappled with memorials of war veterans and past American leaders. The National Mall is also a hot spot for activist rallies, a space for festivals and events and a place to celebrate some of the nation's biggest holidays, such as the Fourth of July.

Marvel at the cherry blossoms along the Tidal Basin, gaze over the reflecting pool, or look out from the Lincoln Memorial at sunset – it's mesmerizing. Although the National Mall is the city's tourist hub, there's plenty of space to spread out and enjoy nature, history and the infinite educational opportunities the Mall offers.

Say Hi to Henry

And the butterflies, too

The free **National Museum of Natural History** is one of the most accoladed museums in the world and, with so much on offer, it's no wonder. Besides Henry, the giant African elephant greeting you in the Rotunda upon entry, museum highlights include rare gemstones and the Hope Diamond, the Hall of Fossils (think dinosaurs), the butterfly pavilion filled with living butterflies, and Egyptian mummies – and that's not even a quarter of it all. The museum is open 10am to 5:30pm.

From Africa to the World

African American history and culture

Opened in 2016, the **National Museum of African American History & Culture** is the only museum in the country dedicated to African American culture and history. The four-level museum, designed by Ghanaian-British architect

GETTING AROUND

The National Mall is quite large, so check which Metro stop is closest to where you want to start. L'Enfant Plaza, which runs all lines except red, gets you to the Air and Space and Hirshhorn museums, while Federal Triangle or the Smithsonian (blue, silver, orange) are closer to the Museum of Natural History and the Washington Monument. Archives (green, yellow) is closer to the National Art Gallery, while nothing is close to the Lincoln or FDR Memorials. Walk, cycle or take the DC Circulator bus's National Mall route.

☑ TOP TIP

The National Mall is bigger than it looks, and there are virtually no decent restaurants on the strip. With all the monuments and museums you'll want to see, it's best to start early, wear your walking shoes and pack a picnic.

NATIONAL MALL WASHINGTON, DC | THE GUIDE

SMITHSONIAN FOLKLIFE FESTIVAL

The Smithsonian Folklife Festival brings together artists, musicians, storytellers and chefs from around the world for a gathering and celebration on the National Mall. The two-week event includes song, dance, workshops, culinary performances, cultural food tents, narrative sessions, storytelling and other forms of cultural expression. Exhibitions are divided by country, region, state or theme, showcasing one to three cultures from around the world or across the nation, who are invited to showcase their living culture. Expect musical performances, local cuisine and plenty of family-friendly activities. More than a million people attend this free summer celebration each year, which has been a summer tradition since 1967.

David Adjaye, is often called the Blacksonian and includes exhibits on slavery and freedom, African American impact on sports, music and film, as well as the Power of Place, a powerful exhibition about belonging.

Get a Bird's-eye View
Ride 50 stories to the top

One of the city's iconic structures is the 555ft-tall Egyptian-style obelisk built to honor the first President of the United States, George Washington. The **Washington Monument** is the world's tallest freestanding stone structure and offers amazing views of the National Mall, Capitol Building and Lincoln Memorial. Reserve tickets in advance ($1) or get free same-day tickets for the minute-long elevator ride 50 stories up – expect lines in the summer. There's a small museum at the top, and on the two-minute ride down, look for the memorial stones gifted from different states on the monument's inner walls.

See the Cherry Blossoms in Bloom
Favorite spring festival

Cherry blossoms are some of DC's star attractions, and if you're visiting the city around March or April, you're likely to get to experience one of the District's favorite moments. Walk around the Tidal Basin and delight in the light-pink blooms all around you, then check out the events of the **National Cherry Blossom Festival**, such as live-music performances, outdoor markets and a parade. According to the festival's organizers, 'forecasting peak bloom is almost impossible more than 10 days in advance', and once the buds open, they only last about two weeks, so while seeing them on your visit is never guaranteed, it's a wonderful surprise when it does happen.

Indigenous Stylings
From indigenous communities to the world

The curvilinear, limestone building of the **National Museum of the American Indian** was designed entirely by Native American architects, and isn't just one of DC's most visually striking structures – it's also home to one-third of one of the world's largest collections of objects, archives and photographs of indigenous populations from the American continents.

 EATING IN THE NATIONAL MALL: MUSEUM CAFES

| **Sweet Home Café:** At the Blacksonian, this museum eatery serves soul and Southern food, grilled favorites and on-the-go sandwiches. **$$** | **Mitsitam Native Foods Cafe:** In the National Museum of the American Indian, serving dishes inspired by indigenous groups. **$$** | **America's Table:** Eatery in the National Museum of American History, serving burgers, hot dogs, barbecue, Tex-Mex and salads. **$$** | **Atrium Cafe:** The Natural History Museum's ground-floor cafe is a large, family-friendly affair with craft burgers and seasonal market specials. **$$** |

WASHINGTON, DC NATIONAL MALL

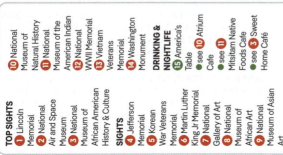

TOP SIGHTS
1. Lincoln Memorial
2. National Air and Space Museum
3. National Museum of African American History & Culture

SIGHTS
4. Jefferson Memorial
5. Korean War Veterans Memorial
6. Martin Luther King Jr Memorial
7. National Gallery of Art
8. National Museum of African Art
9. National Museum of Asian Art
10. National Museum of Natural History
11. National Museum of the American Indian
12. National WWII Memorial
13. Vietnam Veterans Memorial
14. Washington Monument

DRINKING & NIGHTLIFE
15. America's Table
 • see 10 Atrium Cafe
 • see 11 Mitsitam Native Foods Cafe
 • see 3 Sweet Home Café

263

TAKE A GALLERY TOUR

The National Mall's federally owned **National Gallery of Art** is home to a classical art collection with works by Miró, Mondrian, da Vinci, Monet, Kandinsky and more. The museum and its delightful sculpture garden are free and often host big events, such as the city's largest outdoor ice-skating rink in winter, or Jazz in the Garden on Friday evenings in summer. Also stop by the Smithsonian's **Hirshhorn Museum**, inside a 'brutalist donut' (as it's often lovingly called) – a 1960s construction by architect Gordon Bunshaf that's endowed with the contemporary and modern art collection of Joseph H Hirshhorn. The 60,000-sq-ft museum exhibits post-war art, with Picasso, Matisse, Cassatt, Pollock and Rothko featuring.

The Smithsonian museum covers indigenous populations across North and South America, and all of its exhibitions, landscaping and structures are designed in collaboration with tribes and communities.

President Lincoln's Memorial
Shrine to America's 16th President

You've seen it on the back of a penny or a $5 bill, but the **Lincoln Memorial** is something altogether different when seen in person. The neoclassical, Parthenon-like structure was idealized by architect Henry Bacon, while the 19ft-tall white-marble statue inside was designed by Daniel Chester French and carved by the Piccirilli brothers of New York. The memorial is full of symbology, such as the 36 columns that support the structure, each one representing a US state that existed at the date of Lincoln's death. Once inside, you'll find some of Lincoln's most famous words etched into the walls, including the entire 1863 Gettysburg Address.

Arrive from the east – entering across the Reflecting Pool best illuminates the scene – and after you've taken it all in, head around back to watch one of the city's best sunsets over the Potomac.

The Man Who Had a Dream
Monument to MLK

Along the Tidal Basin on 1964 Independence Ave SW (an address to honor the Civil Rights Act of 1964) is the fourth DC monument built in honor of a nonpresident, and the first for a nonwhite person. The **Martin Luther King Jr Memorial**'s centerpiece is a 30ft-high statue of Dr King himself, carved from the 'Stone of Hope,' which is emerging from two large boulders called the 'Mountain of Despair' – references from King's 'I Have a Dream' speech: "Out of the mountain of despair, a stone of hope." There is also a 450ft-long Inscription Wall with quotes from King's speeches and sermons.

From Asia to Africa
Explore art from around the world

For a global art immersion, start at the Smithsonian's **National Museum of Asian Art,** which is split between two galleries – the Freer Gallery of Art and the Arthur M. Sackler Gallery – situated in two separate but contiguous buildings. This century-old institution was the Smithsonian's first art museum and includes works from China, Korea, Japan, Southeast Asia, South Asia and the Middle East from as far back as the Neolithic period. Head also to the **National Museum of African Art,** which was originally located in Frederick Douglass' former townhouse before it was acquired by the Smithsonian and moved to a purpose-built building. The collection expanded beyond traditional sub-Saharan art to include modern works, becoming the first museum in America with a sustained focus on contemporary African art.

Let your Mind Soar
Fly high at the Air and Space Museum
It isn't just one of the most popular museums in the city – year after year, the Smithsonian's **National Air and Space Museum** is one of the most visited museums in the world. Exploring the planet's largest collection of aviation and space artifacts is true immersion into all things airborne. See the Wright Flyer that took the world's first successful flight in 1903, as well as the *Spirit of St Louis*, the first airplane to fly nonstop from New York to Paris. There are several adorable Mars Rovers on display, and even one of George Lucas' original X-wing fighters (a highlight for *Star Wars* fans).

Tomb of the Unknown Soldier
America's memorial resting place
Arlington National Cemetery is a 693-acre military cemetery managed by the US Army where over 400,000 people, including more than 300,000 veterans, lay at rest. The country's most famous ceremony isn't just a place to reflect or grieve – it's also a solemn but scenic walk through the nation's military history. Main sites include **Arlington House**, the former residence of Robert E Lee, as well as the **gravesite of President John F. Kennedy** and its eternal flame. The most notable site. however, is the **Tomb of the Unknown Soldier,** a tribute to the unknown fallen soldiers of the US's major wars. The neoclassical white-marble sarcophagus is guarded 24 hours a day.

Across the 38th Parallel and beyond
Remembering America's overseas wars
The **Korean War Veterans Memorial**, built in 1995, has two 164ft walls that come together like the point of a triangle over the reflecting Pool of Remembrance. In the middle, you'll find 19 stainless-steel statues from all branches of the armed forces. When they reflect against the shining granite walls, an optical illusion doubles them into 38 statues, the same number as the parallel that divides North and South Korea.

Dedicated in 2004, the **National WWII Memorial** is a circular, open-air construction with a central fountain surrounded by 56 columns (representing each of the states, territories and the District) and two 43ft-tall arches along the perimeter – one for the Atlantic, one for the Pacific. There are also two hidden inscriptions saying 'Kilroy was here,' a cartoon-like graffiti used by American troops during WWII to indicate that friendlies were in the area. Try finding them.

The two-acre **Vietnam Veterans Memorial** was less well received in its early days, due to American architect Maya Lin's somber design. The two black granite walls engraved with names of the fallen were called a 'nihilistic slab of stone,' yet, after some adaptations, the design was built and inaugurated in 1982.

JEFFERSON MEMORIAL

Thomas Jefferson wore many hats. He wrote the Declaration of Independence's first draft and was the US's Secretary of State and third President, along with being a scientist, linguist, diplomat, scholar and a farmer. His **memorial**, designed by John Russell Pope and constructed between 1939 and 1943, is meant to recall the Pantheon of Rome, and has a 19ft-high bronze statue of Jefferson inside (which was installed four years after the monument's inauguration).

The location of Jefferson's Memorial by the Tidal Basin was a controversial move, as it meant removing some cherry trees, which sparked a protest by some 50 local women that came to be known as the Cherry Tree Rebellion.

Penn Quarter & Chinatown

HISTORY, ART AND FAMILY MUSEUMS

GETTING AROUND

There are four main Metro stops in the area: Metro Center, McPherson Sq, Archives-Penn Quarter and Gallery Pl/Chinatown. The most central stop, with the most connecting lines, is Metro Center (red, blue, orange, silver), though McPherson Sq station (blue, orange, silver) is closer to many of the museums. Archives-Penn Quarter and Gallery Pl/Chinatown are both on the yellow/green line. There is also a Capital Bikeshare station on 7th and K St NW, though once you've arrived, walking is a very pleasant way to get around.

☑ TOP TIP

The courtyard of the Smithsonian American Art Museum is probably one of the best indoor oases in the city, whether you're out to escape the heat or the cold. The cafe is pretty so-so, so pack your own picnic.

First developed in the late 1800s as a commercial district, Penn Quarter was the city's market area throughout the 19th century. Chinatown was soon added to the fold, moved from its original Penn Ave location to H Street, where it is today. By the 1930's, both Chinatown and Penn's market quarter were thriving, and have continued to flourish. These days, the area is a splendid mix of culture, shopping, food and entertainment, with sites such as the Capital One Arena, the infamous Ford's Theater and the Smithsonian's National Portrait Gallery taking center stage.

Walk through Chinatown's Friendship Archway (the world's largest single-span archway), stop by *Ashes to Answers* (an adorable mini-monument to America's arson dogs), and say hello to the Lone Sailor at the United States Navy Memorial. Wherever you roam, these neighborhoods, with their array of restaurants, bars, theaters, museums and live-music venues, will keep you exploring ad infinitum.

Charters of Freedom
We hold these truths

The **National Archives** is home to the country's most significant documents – notably the Declaration of Independence, the Constitution and the Bill of Rights. Walk through the 40ft-high bronze doorway and into the 70ft-high main rotunda (all designed by architect John Russell Pope) to view the country's 'Charters of Freedom.'

Explore permanent and rotating exhibits, and the Public Vaults – just don't forget a sweater, as the building is kept quite cold to preserve the parchment. Visits are free and walk-ins are welcome, but do reserve timed-entry tickets online if you're coming in summer.

WASHINGTON, DC PENN QUARTER & CHINATOWN

TOP SIGHTS
1. National Archives

SIGHTS
2. Capital One Arena
3. Ford's Theatre
4. Museum of Illusions
5. National Building Museum
6. National Children's Museum
7. National Museum of Women in the Arts
8. New York Avenue Presbyterian Church
9. Planet Word
10. Smithsonian American Art Museum

SLEEPING
11. Kimpton Hotel Monaco DC
12. Motto by Hilton

EATING
13. China Boy
14. Zaytinya

DRINKING & NIGHTLIFE
15. Cuba Libre
    see 9 Immigrant Food

ENTERTAINMENT
16. National Theatre
17. Shakespeare Theatre Company
18. Warner Theatre
19. Woolly Mammoth Theatre Company

267

THEATERS & VENUES

The **Warner Theatre** has been hosting everything from concerts and comedy shows to Broadway favorites since 1924; the theater itself is a work of art.

The **National Theater** is one of America's oldest continually operating theaters (since 1835), and the oldest one still presenting Broadway productions.

The **Shakespeare Theatre Company** has two locations in Penn Quarter – both offer classic and contemporary takes on Will's writings.

Capital One Arena hosts everything from high-profile sporting events to headlining concerts, Cirque du Soleil shows, monster-truck rallies and NBA playoff games.

The **Woolly Mammoth Theatre Company** is known for its original, thought-provoking productions.

Child's Play
Best museums for kids and families

Some of the best museums for kids are in Penn Quarter, starting with **Planet Word**, an interactive language arts museum that compares languages and dialects from around the world, posing interesting questions about why we say things the way we do. If your kids aren't of reading age, take them to the **National Children's Museum**, an interactive play space that's intellectually stimulating and great for burning off excess energy. The **National Building Museum** is an underrated gem with exhibits that range from understandable architecture to LEGO structures (the outdoor frieze and the main courtyard are also aesthetic marvels). Finally, hit up the **Museum of Illusions**, a weird and wild no-holds-barred favorite for kids aged 3 to 73.

Art Abounds
Dive into American artistic heritage

Start your day at the **Smithsonian American Art Museum**, the extensive collection of which celebrates the US's rich artistic heritage from colonial era to modern day, with iconic American artists such as Louise Nevelson and Winslow Homer featuring. In the same building, you'll also find the **National Portrait Gallery**, with a permanent collection of American portraits that offer a unique look at the national identity from past and present (Oprah, Michelle Obama and Beyonce are all in there).

A few blocks north is the **National Museum of Women in the Arts**. The newly remodeled gallery focuses on the contributions of female artists and features pioneering works that challenge traditional narratives.

Till Death Do Us Part
The life and death of Abraham Lincoln

Penn Quarter was where President Abraham Lincoln lived his life and met his end. Visit the **New York Avenue Presbyterian Church**, where Lincoln worshipped during his time in office – the church even has an early draft he wrote of the Emancipation Proclamation – then head to **Ford's Theatre**, where he was assassinated. The onsite museum recounts the events leading up to Lincoln's death.

EATING IN PENN QUARTER & CHINATOWN: OUR PICKS

Zaytinya: Chic Greek-Turkish joint by renowned chef José Andrés with floor-to-ceiling windows. **$$$**	**Immigrant Food:** Adorable cafe below Planet Word serving global dishes and creative cocktails. **$$**	**China Boy:** No-frills, cash-only Chinese takeout that has never disappointed anyone, ever. **$**	**Cuba Libre:** Cuban cuisine and a rum bar in a Havana-style dining room; salsa nights are the true draw. **$$**

Southwest

STADIUMS AND WATERFRONT LIVING

There's nothing better than waterfront living, which makes it no surprise that following a huge, 21st-century urban-revival project, the Southwest Waterfront – made up of destinations such as the Wharf, the Yards and the Stadium District – became one of the city's most sought-after residential areas.

Once an industrial hub and bustling inland port, the Southwest Waterfront has become a leisure-lover's haven, chock-full of panoramic river views, spectacular ice-skating rinks, over-water outdoor movie shows, exciting sports games, vintage-boat rides, river cruises and more shops, restaurants and bars than you could possibly visit in a single stay. It's even got the East Coast's largest population of 'livea-boards' – boat enthusiasts who call their vessels home.

Southwest DC is the perfect mix of historic landmarks, innovative museums and modern developments, and its location – a convenient stone's throw from the National Mall – has put this spectacular collection of neighborhoods on everyone's radar.

Contemporary Culture

Art spaces sprout in SW

Contemporary art has found a home in Southwest DC, thanks to spots such as the **Rubell Museum** (rubellmuseum.org/dc), displaying pieces from one of the world's largest private collections of contemporary art (Keith Haring and Yayoi Kusama are on the list). Entrance is free for DC residents or members; Wednesday to Friday is 'pay what you wish'. The **Culture House DC** (culturehousedc.org) is an uber-colorful church-turned-cultural-center run on the principle that 'art is a catalyst for change.' Stop also at **Artechouse**, where digital art and technology come together to create truly immersive experiences – think colorful interactive projections, and installations that take you into someone's imagination. It's as cool for art lovers as it is for techies.

GETTING AROUND

If you're coming by Metro, take the green line to Waterfront station or the Navy Yard. To cross the Washington Channel, you can catch the free Wharf Jitney to East Potomac Park, or even hop on the free Southwest Shuttle Bus to the National Mall. Seasonal water taxis are available between the Wharf and Georgetown or Old Town Alexandria, while Capital Bikeshare stations are also prevalent in the area.

☑ TOP TIP

During the warmer months, the Southwest Waterfront comes alive with free outdoor movies, yoga and workout classes, while during the holiday season, you'll want to catch the Parade of Lighted Boats, a procession of brightly illuminated watercraft that run from Old Town Alexandria into the city.

SOUTHWEST WASHINGTON, DC

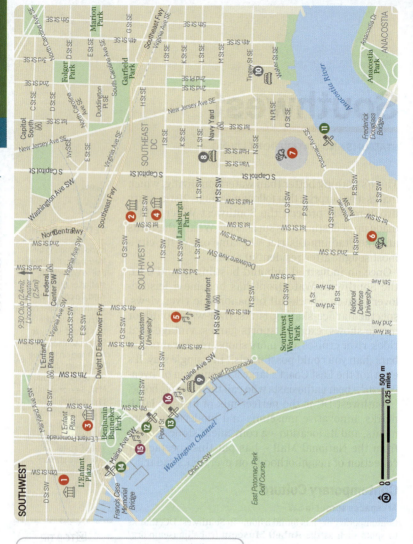

SIGHTS
1. Artechouse
2. Culture House DC
3. International Spy Museum
4. Rubell Museum
5. Westminster Presbyterian Church

ACTIVITIES, COURSES & TOURS
6. Audi Field
7. Nationals Park

SLEEPING
8. Coda on Half

9. Pendry Washington DC
10. Thompson Washington DC

EATING
11. All-Purpose Riverfront
12. Camp Wharf at the Firepit
13. Kaliwa
14. Officina

ENTERTAINMENT
15. Anthem
16. Pearl Street Warehouse
• see 16 Union Stage

Go Undercover
See what it takes to be a spy
Go undercover at the **International Spy Museum**, a longtime DC favorite that gives visitors an interactive and exciting peek into the world of espionage. Learn the art of codebreaking, understand why spies have to dress the part and find out why we have spies in the first place. The museum even confronts controversial topics such as counterfeiting, torture and secret surveillance in a multiperspective manner that sparks instant debate. Check out an immense collection of the coolest spy gadgets, or head to the 5th floor, where you'll find fascinating stories of the world's most famous spies.

Rock Out
Live music along the waterfront
Catch a show at the **Anthem**, a 57,000-sq-ft concert hall that stages everything from rock concerts and marquee performances to lectures, seminars and charity galas – we really recommend the rock shows. Just down the promenade, you'll find the **Pearl Street Warehouse**, where live-music gigs highlight the 'diversity of the American music experience' – it's ideal for date night). Its neighbor, **Union Stage** is an intimate, 450-person venue with a 16-brew taproom that's as much a draw as the laid-back live music. True music lovers shouldn't miss a stop at **Westminster Presbyterian Church**, where Fridays are for Jazz and Mondays are for blues. These super-popular live-music nights at a church that dates back to 1853 take place from 6pm to 9pm.

OUT TO A BALL GAME

DC natives are sports fans to the core, and two of the city's biggest teams have their home in the aptly named Stadium District. Baseball fans can root for the home team (the Nationals) at , where you can also take a non-game-day two-hour tour of the facilities, including the clubhouses, media box, bullpen and dugout. Pregame tours are also available, where you'll learn fun facts and history about the Nationals stadium and team. Next, hit up for a riveting DC United soccer match, or cheer on the women of the Washington Spirit. Audi Field is also home stadium for the DC Defenders UFL team.

ICONIC NIGHTLIFE
The Anthem is run by the same team behind some of the most iconic DC nightlife venues, including the **9:30 Club** (p286) and the **Lincoln Theatre** (p285).

EATING IN THE SOUTHWEST: TOP RESTAURANTS

Kaliwa: Eclectic Wharf restaurant focusing on Thai, Filipino and Korean cuisine with waterfront views. $$

Camp Wharf at the Firepit: Adorable Airstream trailer serving make-your-own S'mores kits in front of a wood-burning firepit. $

All-Purpose Riverfront: Italian-American artisanal pizzas; popular for its egg-topped breakfast pizzas on weekends. $

Officina: Three-story Italian Nirvana – cafe, bar, Italian market, 2nd-floor trattoria and rooftop terrace. $$

WALK THE WHARF

Completed in 2022, the Wharf DC quickly became the district's waterfront hot spot, where dining, shopping, leisure and live music come together. Start your tour at **① Recreation Pier**, where you can rent a kayak or stand-up paddleboard, then head over to **② Pearl St**, a live-music haven with a name that is a nod to the largest-known attempted slave escape in America – it took place in 1848 aboard a 65ft schooner called *The Pearl*. (The incident didn't end well for the 77 slaves, though it did inspire both Harriet Beecher Stowe and Abraham Lincoln to work towards ending slavery.)

Walk over to **③ Transit Pier**, a floating dock outside the Anthem theatre that's host to outdoor events, shows and markets along with the summer Sunset Cinema and the district's only over-water ice-skating rink in winter. Stop by the **④ Market Docks**, where you can hop on a boat and explore DC by water on a City Cruise lunch boat or monument tour, or on a beautifully restored (and retro-fitted with an electric motor) 1950s runabout from Retro Boat Rentals DC. Afterwards, refuel with delicious cooked crabs or fresh clam chowder from the **⑤ Municipal Fish Market**, the country's oldest continuously running open-air fish market. It's been in operation, without fail, since 1805. While here, take a gander at the **⑥ High Water Mark**, a public art installation that takes an honest look at the damage presented by climate change. Colorful buoys are suspended in the air, marking historic and possible future flood levels within DC's floodplain, as predicted by 2020 climate-change models. It's an important reminder of the impact humans are having on the natural world.

Capitol Hill

POLITICAL EPICENTER AND QUIRKY ART

They say that on seeing the project for the first US Capitol, Thomas Jefferson likened it to America's own Temple of Jupiter, like the one found on Capitoline Hill in Ancient Rome. The name stuck, and Capitol Hill grew to become the veritable heartbeat of America's government.

Capitol Hill is also one of the largest historic districts in the US, and beyond the grandeur of the government buildings, the neighborhood is home to an array of attractions and a vibrant community. Wander down tree-lined streets past historic row houses, let delicious flavors draw you into the artisanal food haven of Eastern Market, explore iconic secondhand book stores and join a neighborhood Art Walk in the community with perhaps the most art associations per capita in the city.

Capitol Hill is a genuinely down-to-earth, welcoming neighborhood where residents make you feel right at home, even while you're back-to-back with some of America's most poignant grandeur.

GETTING AROUND

If you're heading to the US Capitol Building, take the orange, silver or blue Metro lines to the Capitol South station, or stay on one more stop to get off at Eastern Market if the market or Barracks Rows is your final destination. If you're on the red line or a commuter train, Union Station is close enough to Capitol Hill to walk, and also has a paid parking facility, though coming by rideshare is preferable.

A Community of Artists

Art walks, workshops and festivals galore

Of all the (many) community-arts organizations in Capitol Hill, the longest running is the **Capitol Hill Arts Workshop** *(chaw.org)*, a community space that's been offering classes, workshops and educational opportunities for residents and visitors of all ages since 1972 (check its website to join in). Then there's the **Capitol Hill Art League**, a consortium of more than 100 metro-area artists that organizes seven juried exhibitions annually. The **Capitol Hill Arts District**, a collaborative of artists that runs the monthly **Capitol Hill Art Walk** (second Thursday of every month; check capitolhillartwalk.com for details on how to join), as well as helps produce the annual **Pride Festival** in June (spearheaded by the Capital Pride Alliance) and other community events.

☑ TOP TIP

If you can, organize your US Capitol Building tour through your (or a friend's) congressperson. You'll get a guided tour from one of their interns, have access to a few spots the general tours don't visit, and be in a smaller group – often just you and your travel buddies.

CAPITAL PRIDE

Capital Pride Alliance is a nonprofit organization serving DC's LGBTIQ+ community, though it's best known for organizing DC's annual Pride Parade and Festival, held every June on Pennsylvania Ave, aka America's Main Street. Capital Pride also puts together community events throughout the year, such as the Mr, Mx and Miss pageants and queer expression night, as well as smaller pride events such as DC Black Pride, DC Latinx Pride and DC Trans Pride. It also provides an extensive list of queer-owned and queer-friendly restaurants and bars across the city. Capital Pride Alliance will also be one of the co-hosting organizations for WorldPride DC 2025, which marks the 50th anniversary of Pride celebrations in Washington.

Eastern Market

Historic Culinary Hot Spots

Visit Eastern Market and Barracks Row

Eastern Market is as much a historic stop as it is a culinary one. Stop by the 19th-century brick building for all your meat, poultry, seafood, baked good, flower and deli needs, or visit one of the short-order spots for a meal (don't miss the Market Lunch's wildly popular crab cakes). Head also to **Barracks Row**, an olde-times main street full of shops, restaurants and cool sites. Stop by the birthplace of American composer John Philip Sousa, catch a flick at the **Miracle Theatre** and check out the artwork at the **Hill Center**, an art gallery in a renovated Civil War–era hospital, before catching the evening parade at the **Marine Barracks** (every Friday from May through August).

 EATING ON THE HILL: OUR PICKS

Art and Soul: Seasonal, locally sourced Southern comfort food with a view of the Capitol Dome. **$$**	**Pineapple & Pearls:** Fine dining with two Michelin stars, four courses, a disco-chic dress code and no disappointments. **$$$**	**Belga Cafe:** Belgian French brasserie serving savory waffles and stuffed truffle brie. **$$**	**Ted's Bulletin:** American eats done right, with homemade pop tarts and boozy milkshakes. **$**

CAPITOL HILL

TOP SIGHTS
1. Library of Congress
2. US Capitol

SIGHTS
3. Barracks Row
4. Capitol Hill Arts Workshop
5. Hill Center
6. Marine Barracks
7. Supreme Court
8. United States Botanic Garden

SLEEPING
9. Friends Place on Capitol Hill
10. Kimpton George Hotel
11. Phoenix Park Hotel
12. YOTEL Washington DC

EATING
13. Pineapple & Pearls
14. Ted's Bulletin

DRINKING & NIGHTLIFE
15. Belga Cafe

ENTERTAINMENT
16. Miracle Theatre

SHOPPING
17. Eastern Market

275

PRACTICALITIES

Scan this QR code for ticket prices and opening hours.

TOP SIGHT

Capitol Hill

The US Capitol complex is home to most of the government's major buildings. Built on Jenkins' Hill – now mostly referred to as Capitol Hill – it houses the Senate and House of Representatives buildings, the Library of Congress buildings, the Supreme Court, the 570 acres of the United States Botanical Gardens and, of course, the US Capitol Building itself.

DON'T MISS

Library of Congress' main reading room

Washington's tomb

Capitol Rotunda

Capitol Crypt

Whispering Gallery

US Capitol Building's meeting chambers

Supreme Court

The Capitol Building

The construction of the **US Capitol Building** began in 1793, and was completed in 1826, though it's been added to several times over the years.

The **Capitol Rotunda**, the large, circular room beneath the Capitol dome is 96ft in diameter and 180ft high at its tallest point. The neoclassical rotunda was intended to invoke the Pantheon of Ancient Rome, built primarily of sandstone and white marble, with Doric columns.

The most heavily visited area of the building is the **Capitol Crypt**, which is actually a brightly lit room one floor below the Rotunda. The neoclassical hall has 40 Doric columns and sandstone floors, and is centered on the exact spot where the city's (original) four quadrants meet.

The **National Statuary Hall**'s half-dome shape has some unique acoustics that have earned it the name 'Whispering Gallery.' There are some spots in which a person on the other side of the room can be heard more clearly than one next to you, meaning a whispered secret might be unintentionally heard across the room. In the same hall you'll find a **collection of 100 statues** of renowned citizens from across history, two from each US state (though only 12 are of women). The largest is a 15,000lb, 9ft-10in-tall statue of Hawaiian King Kamehameha I, donated by his island state.

Every visitor to the Capitol Building will inevitably pass through **Washington's tomb** – or rather, the tomb that wasn't. The area beneath the crypt was originally reserved for George Washington's remains, though his final wish was to be buried at his home in Mt Vernon, so the tomb remained empty.

You can also watch the government in session in the meeting chambers from the galleries, with a pass procured from your Senator or Representative or, for noncitizens, from the appointment desks on the upper level. Tours of the Capitol Building itself can also be organized through your congressperson (ideally), or through the US Capitol Visitor Center (visitthecapitol.gov). There are often walk-up tours available, though reservations are strongly recommended.

The Library of Congress

The **Library of Congress** is said to be the world's largest library, with approximately 173 million books, maps, photographs, films, recordings and manuscripts on file in more than 470 languages. Established in 1800, the library, which is housed in three separate buildings, functions primarily to research questions presented by Congress members through the Congressional Research Service.

In the Thomas Jefferson Building you'll find the **main reading room**, a grand research center that's the library's main attraction. See it from above on a self-guided tour (by appointment), or visit the main floor, which is open twice a day (Tuesday to Friday). Credentialed researchers can freely use the space and its resources.

Every Friday in July and August, movies from the National Film Registry are shown on the southeast lawn during the annual **Summer Movies on the Lawn** event.

Supreme Court

The **Supreme Court** (supremecourt.gov) building is home to the US's judicial branch of government and is the site where monumental, country-changing decisions are handed down. Download a PDF from the website and take a self-guided tour through the majestic Great Hall, past the ground floor's two self-supporting gold and marble spiral staircases, and into the courtroom, where you can sit-in on a case or listen to opinions being handed down (seating is first come, first served).

BOTANIC GARDENS

The United States Botanic Gardens is one of the oldest botanical gardens in North America, and inside its glass-encased Conservatory you'll find rare and endangered plants from around the world. Exhibits are thoughtfully divided by species or biome.

TOP TIPS

- If you're visiting around the holidays, stop by the popular Season's Greenings display at the Botanic Gardens, showcasing a giant Christmas tree and models of DC's major monuments made of plants.
- Many of the buildings on Capitol Hill are connected by underground passageways, some of which are open to visitors. Walk through the tunnel that connects the library's Thomas Jefferson Building to the Capitol Hill Visitor Center.
- There is an underground subway system for Congress members. Some Capitol Hill tours will take you on it, so ask your congressperson if it's possible.

CAPITOL HILL ALPHABET ANIMAL ART PROJECT

On street corners in Capitol Hill, whimsical animals hang from street signs. The Capitol Hill Alphabet Animal Art Project, a public installation, was idealized by a local resident while teaching his daughters the alphabet using street signs. Start this 2-mile walk at the corner on S Carolina Ave and 7th St, which is adorned with a forged-steel **1 spider web**, inspired by EB White's *Charlotte's Web*, with even the words 'Some Pig' appearing. Head to **2 Dog on D St**, where you'll find a big black dog leaping through a ring of fire – an expression of overcoming fear, perseverance and transcendence – while on N Carolina Ave and 2nd St, you'll find a **3 narwhal pod** swimming up the signpost. On F St is a **4 Falcarius Chasing a Capitalsaurus**, which is DC's official dinosaur. After the first fossil of this species was found in the district in 1898, it remained unidentified for decades, until one paleontologist declared it a new species – Capitalsaurus – in 1980. While not adopted by the scientific community at large, the Capitalsaurus became a part of DC's history when, in 1998, local elementary students lobbied for it to become the city's official dinosaur. See Evan Reed's **5 Ibis on I St**, made from old license plates, followed by **6 Ladybug On L St**, which artist Sue Champney made of almost entirely recycled materials, including a CD boom box, barbecue skewers and four Frisbees she found on the beach. Say hi to **7 Emu on E St**, which artist Beth Baldwin designed based on an art-deco brooch she found thrifting, and finally visit artist Carolina Mayorga's **8 Grasshopper on G St**, affectionately named CHAWmper in honor of its location in front of the CHAW building,

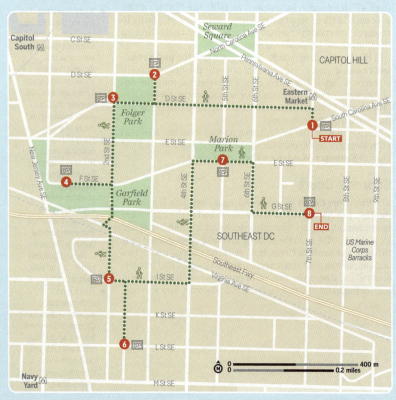

Northeast

INDUSTRIAL AND ALTERNATIVE

Northeast DC is a constantly changing creative space, colored by beautiful street murals, lined with live-music venues and anchored by the best food halls, breweries and distilleries in town. It's also home to some exceptional under-the-radar national parks, as well as iconic heritage architecture.

Formed by the boroughs of Ivy City, Union Market, NoMa and the H Street Corridor (aka the Atlas District), Northeast counts itself as one of the fastest-growing areas in the DC area – and, like most revitalized industrial zones, it's also one of the coolest. Northeast's unique blend of innovation, independent retailers and community spaces defines what has become one of the most sought-after destinations for those in the know.

Whether you're into shopping, dining, art, parks or just hanging out on incredible rooftops, take a gander at the once-overlooked neighborhood that has everything to offer.

DC's Coolest Food Court

Dig in at Union Market

Union Market (unionmarketdc.com) is a bustling food hall that attracts culinary lovers from across the metro area. Located inside a revitalized industrial space from the 1930s, when it was an indoor/outdoor farmers market, Union Market had all but fallen into ruin until 2012, when it was renovated into the food hall, event hub and retail space that it remains today. Union Market is a DC darling, with more than 40 permanent vendors and one of the largest rooftops in the city. It's also a de facto neighborhood association, holding concerts, dance nights, drive-in movies, farmers markets, fitness classes and more. Check the website's events calendar for details.

GETTING AROUND

Northeast is primarily accessible by the red-line Metro or by car, though there is also a recently reopened light-rail line called the DC Streetcar that runs up H St. The street car runs from Union Station (where you'll also find the Metro, commercial buses, Amtrak, MARC, VRE and Capital Bikeshare stations) to Oklahoma Ave NE and Benning Rd NE, near RFK Stadium, where there's also a Capital Bikeshare station.

☑ TOP TIP

Northeast DC's old industrial buildings hide most of the city's distilleries and breweries – check out Republic Restoratives, an all-female-owned distillery with small-batch bottles that are often named after famous DC ladies (eg Rodham Rye), and Red Bear Brewing Co, a gay-owned brewery known for its craft bottles and game nights.

279

SIGHTS	SLEEPING	EATING	ENTERTAINMENT
1 Art Alley	4 citizenM	6 La Cosecha	8 Atlas Performing
2 Gallery O on H	5 Hotel Nell	7 Union Market	Arts Center
3 Mehari Sequar Gallery			

Latinx Lovin' at La Cosecha

The spicy little sister

Two blocks down from Union Market, you'll find its little sister, a spicy Latino food hall called **La Cosecha**. This 20,000-sq-ft contemporary Latin American marketplace serves up Latino cuisine and culture, with retail spaces, artist works and culinary stylings on display. Dig into some made-to-order pupusas and sip on Panamanian coffee while breathing in the delectable scents of vegan Bolivian fare and chic Mexican dishes being prepared nearby.

MURALSDC

The MuralsDC program is responsible for the realization of 141 murals across the city, each depicting themes important or relevant to their local area, such as the **Black Lives Matter Plaza** (p259) near the White House.

Tree Spotting

Azaleas, bonzai and Corinthian columns

Established in 1927, the 450-acre **United States National Arboretum** is a the perfect DC escape into nature. Wander along the 9 miles of parkland roads, stopping to visit attractions such as the National Bonsai and Penjing Museum (a collection of the legendary minute Japanese and Chinese trees), the National Herb Garden, the Gotelli Conifer Collection, the azalea collection and Flowering Tree Walk.

Then there are the columns – 22 huge Corinthian sandstone columns that somewhat awkwardly supported the US

Capitol's frieze from 1828 until 1958, when the building was renovated and the columns were replaced. In the 1980s, the ousted columns were cleverly reassembled in the Ellipse Meadow of the National Arboretum, where they became a favorite (and very Instagram-worthy) tourist attraction.

Water Gardens
Water-loving plant paradise

On the east bank of the Anacostia River is a true hidden gem. The **Kenilworth Aquatic Gardens** is the only national park in the country focusing on aquatic and semi-aquatic plants. Stroll around the park's 45 ponds or along the boardwalks over the marshlands, spotting busy beavers and lazy turtles, along with egrets, dragonflies and butterflies. This living garden (free entry) is as much a conservation zone as it is a classroom for ecology, hydrology and zoology. The water lilies, one of the park's main attractions, bloom from late May until mid-September, while the colorful wildflowers remain in bloom through the fall.

Art on H Street
Gallery hopping galore

The H Street Corridor's revitalization can be credited to art, so it's no wonder the neighborhood has galleries galore. Stop by Linden Court Alley, aka **Art Alley**, where you'll find a collection of murals commissioned to celebrate the 15th anniversary of the MuralsDC initiative, then head over to **Mehari Sequar Gallery**, an independent art gallery focused on contemporary African and African American female and BIPOC artists (only open during exhibitions). **Gallery O on H** is a unique event and exhibition space with a gallery that features exhibitions by intuitive (aka self-taught) artists, while the **Atlas Performing Arts Center**, which was renovated and repurposed in 2006, is considered to be the cornerstone of the neighborhood's wave of revitalization. Get tickets for the annual **Intersections Festival** (February/March), a performing-arts event aimed to inspire and connect the community

Take a Street-art Tour
The ever-changing artistic landscape

Explore the ever-changing artistic landscape in the Union Market and NoMa neighborhoods on a DC Mural Tour. These two-hour jaunts take you past dozens of new and old murals, such as the heart-filled work created in 2015 by LA-based graffiti artist Mr Brainwash in honor of International Women's Day (even Michelle Obama had her picture taken in front of it) and Yoko Ono's text-based design made in partnership with the Smithsonian's Hirshhorn Museum. Version one, starting at 11am Thursday to Saturday, is a late-morning outing to 20-plus murals, while option two (5:30pm Thursday and 2pm Saturday) takes you to 15 works, with a craft-beer bar crawl added on.

DANCE THE NIGHT AWAY

Echostage is a must for nightlife lovers. Opened in 2012, this 30,000-sq-ft, 3000-person capacity nightclub cum music venue was quickly voted best live music spot in the US – in 2021, *DJ Magazine* called it the best live-music venue in the world (after being in the top ten since 2017). Echostage specializes in EDM (electronic dance music) and has hosted names such as Calvin Harris, Avicii, David Guetta, Armin van Buuren and Tiesto. Although it's located well out of the city center (in a rather sketchy part of Langdon, DC, if we're being honest), it's well worth the trek to get there. Arrive and leave by taxi or rideshare.

Adams Morgan & the U Street Corridor

BLACK HISTORY AND NIGHTLIFE

GETTING AROUND

Woodley Park-Zoo/Adams Morgan station takes you to, well, the National Zoo and Adams Morgan along the red line. Otherwise, you can walk up from Dupont Circle (also on the red line), or across from the U St station, located on the green line. U St visitors can also get off at the Shaw-Howard University station. There is also a DC Circulator bus that goes from Franklin Park up 14th St, across U St and through Adams Morgan to the National Zoo.

☑ TOP TIP

Every Sunday at Meridian Hill/Malcolm X Park, residents host an afternoon drum circle – its a 40-year-plus tradition that has become a community centerpiece, bringing together people from all walks of life for a weekly celebration of drumming and dancing.

Known for an eclectic mix of restaurants and bars, Adams Morgan and the U Street Corridor have some of the most diverse, creative communities – and excellent nightlife – in the city. These neighborhoods are also brimming with history, especially for African Americans and immigrant groups.

Once called 'Black Broadway,' the U Street Corridor was ground zero for what was once the most important African American urban community in the country, while Adams Morgan's history began when the communities around a predominantly white school and a predominantly Black one joined forces, creating a catalyst for an ongoing neighborhood renaissance that continues to this day. Colorful murals, neighborhood festivals, mouthwatering Ethiopian food and iconic live-music venues are daily delights for visitors and residents alike in what might just be some of the coolest 'hoods in the district.

Ethiopian Eats
No forks required

DC is home to one of the largest Ethiopian populations outside of Ethiopia, their presence shining in Adams Morgan and along a stretch of U St (near 9th) locally known as **Little Ethiopia**. Both spots are perfect for trying some of this East African nation's unique cuisine. Adams Morgan's **Tsehay**, which opened as an homage to owner Selam Gossa's late mother's Addis Ababa cafe, is a crowd favorite. Gossa sources many important ingredients directly from Ethiopia and hand-grinds her own spices (just like her mother taught her). Another spot that summons is the Michelin-recommended **Chercher,** in a townhouse just outside of Little Ethiopia. The menu is mouthwatering enough, but it's the off-the-menu dishes that have Ethiopian expats swooning. Dig into deeply flavorful stews and traditional vegetarian fare, all served on the squishy, fermented injera flatbread, which also doubles as your utensils.

WASHINGTON, DC ADAMS MORGAN & THE U STREET CORRIDOR

SIGHTS
1. African American Civil War Memorial
2. Duke Ellington Statue
3. Howard University
4. Langston Hughes Residence
5. Meridian Hill Park
6. Old Whitelaw Hotel
7. Thurgood Marshall Center

SLEEPING
8. American Guest House
9. HighRoad Hostel
10. Line Hotel DC

EATING
11. Ben's Chili Bowl
12. Chercher
13. Compass Rose
14. Rita Loco
15. Tsehay

DRINKING & NIGHTLIFE
16. Alice DC
17. Bunker
18. Busboys & Poets
19. Colada Shop
20. Convivial
21. Dirty Goose
22. Dram & Grain
23. Kiki
24. Number Nine
25. Shakers
26. Solly's
27. Trade

ENTERTAINMENT
28. 9:30 Club
29. Howard Theatre
30. Lincoln Theatre
31. U Street Music Hall

283

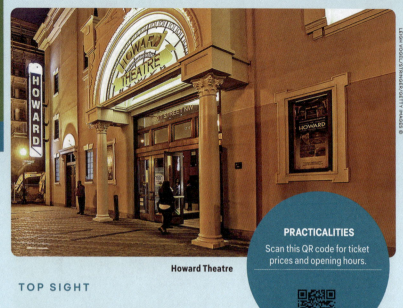

Howard Theatre

TOP SIGHT

Black Broadway

Until NYC's Harlem took over in 1920, DC was the cultural and social capital of Black America, boasting the largest urban Black population in the country. A strong society of Black-owned and run businesses, newspapers, civic groups and churches sprouted up along the U Street Corridor, along with the country's first Black University, transforming DC into a Black cultural and intellectual epicenter.

PRACTICALITIES

Scan this QR code for ticket prices and opening hours.

DON'T MISS

- Howard University
- Howard Theatre
- Lincoln Theatre
- Dunbar High School
- Duke Ellington's Statue
- Ben's Chili Bowl
- Meridian Hill Park

Howard University

The country's first African American **research university** opened in 1867 and quickly became a magnet for Black intellectuals from around the country. Howard University was an anchor for the community that would become the country's largest and most prosperous Black middle class of its time.

Howard Theatre

When the **Howard Theatre** opened in 1910, it was dubbed the largest colored theater in the world, and received all the greats of the era – Louis Armstrong, Billie Holliday, Ella Fitzgerald, Duke Ellington and Nat King Cole all graced the stage. The theater remained a hot spot for Black American culture until the 1980s, when it was neglected and shuttered, before being reborn in 2012 as the cultural powerhouse it remains today.

Lincoln Theatre

Shortly after it was opened more than 100 years ago, the **Lincoln Theatre** became the epicenter of Black Broadway. The theater had a 1600-seat auditorium and movie theater backed by the Lincoln Colonnade, a big-band dance hall that became the place to meet on U St.

Dunbar High School

The first high school for African Americans in the nation, **Dunbar High School**, opened in 1870, had such an incredible reputation that families from all over the country shipped their children to DC to study. Teachers often had doctorate degrees and were some of the highest-paid African Americans in the country, as the federal government paid Black and white teachers in the District the same wages. High percentages of the student graduates went onto college, an extreme rarity at the time.

Duke Ellington's Statue

Before becoming famous in Harlem, the king of jazz, Edward Kennedy 'Duke' Ellington, was born and raised in Washington, DC, where he quickly became a well-known musician. A **statue**, entitled *Encore*, sits outside the Howard Theatre in honor of the hometown hero.

Langston Hughes Residence

From 1924 to 1926, poet Langston Hughes lived in a small **house** on S St while working odd jobs to help support his family. His first book of poems was published after his time at the DC residence (now a private home) and the rest, as they say, is history.

Thurgood Marshall Center

Located on the site of the 12th St YMCA, which was the first YMCA established in the nation for 'colored men and boys.' The original 1853 structure was designed by William Sidney Pittman, one of the nation's earliest Black architects, and poet Langston Hughes once had a room here. The building was fully restored and renamed the **Thurgood Marshall Center**, a community center with some historical displays inside.

Old Whitelaw Hotel

The **Old Whitelaw Hotel** was a community masterpiece. Funded by Black investors and built by Black entrepreneurs and craftsmen, the gray-brick hotel was named for its builder, John Whitelaw Lewis (and not for the 'white laws' that segregated the city). In its heyday, the Whitelaw attracted Washington's Black elite, though it deteriorated into a drug den in the 1960s and '70's, before being fully restored into apartment buildings in the early '90s, which it remains today.

A BOWL OF CHILI

A late addition to the scene is the area's most important culinary landmark: Ben's Chili Bowl. Opened in 1958 by Virginia and Ben Ali, Ben's quickly became a watering hole for Washington's Black community and, with the Lincoln Theatre next door, for entertainers as well. Some good old chili lore?

TOP TIPS

● When you're ready for a rest, stop at the corner of 10th and U Sts and contemplate the **African American Civil War Memorial**, a monument designed by Ed Hamilton. Its centerpiece depicts a sailor and a soldier going off to war while loved ones wave them away.

● Read through the **Wall of Honor**, where you'll find the names of the 209,145 colored servicemen who served in the Civil War.

● Head to **Meridian Hill Park** (aka Malcom X Park), a 12-acre park with cascading waterfalls and a sculpture garden. The park was ground zero during segregation – white DC lay to the west, while Black DC lay to the east.

PAINTING STORIES

In 2007, DC's Department of Public Works started a Murals Program, aimed to beautify walls in every part of the city. The initiative has resulted in 141 murals across the district, each depicting or supporting important themes from the area, including a handful of murals that memorialize DC's Black history and immigrant stories around the U St area. Some favorites include *The Wailin' Mailman: A Portrait of Buck Hill* by Joe Pagac (a masterpiece more than 70ft high) and *The Torch*, in which Aniekan Udofia tells the story of 'the torchbearers who illuminate the way', including Harriet Tubman, Muhammed Ali and the Obamas (it's located on the alley wall of Ben's Chili Bowl).

A Night on the Town
DC's nonstop nightlife

While DC isn't quite a 24-hour city, the nightlife around U St will nearly get you to sunrise. Start off with a cocktail at the low-key, chic **Dram & Grain**; get a colada and an empanada at the colorful Cuban **Colada Shop**; dive into the surreal and whimsical **Alice DC**, unabashedly mixing pho, arcade games and hip-hop beats; or head to **Solly's** for a straight-forward dive-bar experience. The LGBTIQ+ crowd converges on laid-back bars such as **Kiki**, the **Dirty Goose** and **Trade**, before heading to a drag show at **Shakers** (aka 'the little gay pub') then over to dance it out at the two-story martini-swinging **Number Nine**. Opt for a concert at the **Howard Theater** (p284), the ever-iconic **9:30 Club** or the **U Street Music Hall**. If you've still got some gas, it's on to a late-night fiesta at one of the LGBTIQ+ hot spots of **Bunker** or **Green Lantern.**

Furry Friends
A menagerie at the National Zoo

Established in 1889, DC's 163-acre **Smithsonian National Zoo,** just north of Adams Morgan in Rock Creek Park, is home to more than 2100 animals of nearly 400 different species – elephants and sea lions to sloth bears, bison and orangutans.

 EATING IN ADAMS MORGAN & THE U STREET CORRIDOR: OUR PICKS

Rita Loco: Counter-service burritos, tacos and cocktails with a popular upstairs patio. $	**Busboys & Poets:** Bookshop, coffee shop and world-food cafe, serving as a neighborhood cultural hub. $	**Convivial:** Hip French-American bistro with craft cocktails and lovely patio. $$	**Compass Rose:** Eclectic international restaurant in a brick townhouse with a cool bar. $$

Smithsonian National Zoo

The lovely meandering pathways take you through regional exhibits, such as the American Trail, where California sea lions, North American beavers and red wolves live; the Great Ape House, where you'll find gorillas and orangutans (a highwire trail allows them to travel over the heads of visitors to their second home at the 'Think Tank'); and the Africa Trail, where you can spot cheetahs, zebras, warthogs, gazelles, lesser kudu and ostriches. As with all Smithsonian Institutions, entrance is free.

Festival Day

Celebrate Adams Morgan Day

DC's longest-running neighborhood festival is a vibrant celebration of community and culture. Adams Morgan Day has been held on 18th St on the second Sunday in September for the past 45 years, showcasing the area's food, music, art and music. You'll find local artist and international cuisine lining the street, and for entertainment, expect everything from drag-queen story time, reggae bands and gospel miming to go-go fitness, flag football clinics and dance collectives. There's also live music and DJ performances, and a dedicated kids zone with activities for the little ones.

The festival, organized entirely by volunteers, welcomes residents and visitors alike to meet the neighborhood's businesses and enjoy the local offerings – but mostly to celebrate living in one of DC's most diverse neighborhoods.

ZOO LIGHTS

Zoo Lights is a beloved holiday tradition at the National Zoo that's not to be missed if you're wintering in DC. The entire zoo is turned into a dazzling light display for six weeks in which 500,000 environmentally friendly bulbs illuminate seemingly every branch in sight. Enjoy immersive lantern displays, live music performances and delicious holiday treats, all with your favorite furry friends nearby – do note, however, that animals are not part of the show as they need to get their beauty rest. For its first 14 years, the event was free, but due to increasing costs (and popularity), entrance has been ticketed since 2023.

Downtown & Dupont Circle

MAGNIFICENT MANORS AND CHIC BRUNCHES

GETTING AROUND

Dupont Circle has its own Metro station on the red line, though you can also take the orange, blue and silver lines to Farragut West or McPherson Sq and walk up through Downtown. There are parking lots and metered parking around, but both are expensive – taking a rideshare or using a Capital bikeshare bike is preferable. A few different lines on the DC Circulator bus pass through, or you can lace up your sneakers – these neighborhoods are also only a 20-minute walk (max) from the White House, or a half-hour stroll to the National Mall.

☑ TOP TIP

DC's most queer-centric neighborhoods, with a host of LGBTIQ+-owned spots – to get a rundown on the best, visit the Capital Pride Alliance's website *(capitalpride.org/life-in-dc-2)*.

Downtown is DC's commercial center, where swanky hotels and broker bars attract lobbyists by the droves, while Dupont Circle's trendy boutiques, historic mansions and embassies make it the epicenter of sophistication in the city. The Venn diagram of these neighboring 'hoods does overlap, however, especially if you're an art lover, foodie or keen on nightlife.

While Downtown is a place of fancy hotels, a chic shopping stop and the headquarters for some of the nation's coolest organizations (even National Geographic has its base camp here), Dupont is known for its tree-lined streets and bucolic charm, where hot spots such as the Dupont Underground and events like the Dupont ArtWalk create a vibrant cultural scene. Explore embassies, hit up a farmers market, peruse art galleries and admire monuments, or maybe just enjoy some of the best brunches in the city. Whatever you're after, these two districts have exactly what you're looking for.

Modern Art, Storied History
America's first modern-art museum

Founded in 1921 by Duncan Phillips, the **Phillips Collection** is widely considered to be America's first modern-art museum, founded on the pioneering idea of (in Phillips' words) 'a museum where one could encounter the art of the past and the present on equal terms.' Featuring works by renowned artists such as O'Keeffe, Van Gogh and Renoir, the Phillips Collection combines modern and contemporary artistic endeavors in thought-provoking, highly curated exhibitions.

The intimate and experiential museum, inside a historic mansion in Dupont Circle, aims to provide a space where visitors can connect deeply with each piece of art on display, and is an inspiring stop for art lovers of all ages. Reserving tickets in advance is encouraged, although walk-ins are welcome.

WASHINGTON, DC DOWNTOWN & DUPONT CIRCLE

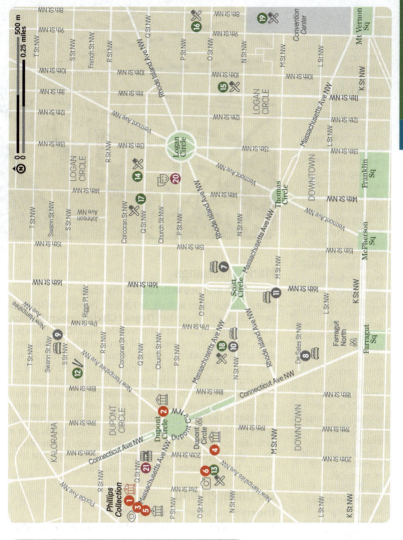

TOP SIGHTS
1. Phillips Collection

SIGHTS
2. Dupont Underground
3. Embassy Row
4. Heurich House
5. Larz Anderson House
6. Mansion on O Street

SLEEPING
7. The Darcy
8. Mayflower Hotel
9. Swann House
10. Tabard Inn
11. The Jefferson

EATING
12. Anju
13. Firefly
14. Le Diplomate
15. Nina May
16. Oyster Oyster
17. Pearl Dive Oyster Palace
18. Tabard Inn
19. Unconventional Diner

ENTERTAINMENT
20. Studio Theatre

SHOPPING
21. Dupont Circle Farmers Market

STUDIO THEATRE

Studio Theatre is a nonprofit theater company whose 1978 creation was a catalyst for the Logan Circle neighborhood's revitalization. The company, which began in a former warehouse, now has a multimillion-dollar building (renovated in 2021–22) spanning half a city block. Its thought-provoking, contemporary shows feature national and international players, and the troupe also offers apprenticeships, in-house residencies, student-priced matinees and myriad community-engagement programs. It also has some of the most accessible offerings of any DC theater, with wheelchair-accessible areas in all its theaters, as well as free assistive-listening devices and regularly scheduled sign-language-interpreted and audio-description performances.

Market Mornings
Farm-fresh produce with community vibes

Every Sunday from 8:30am to 1:30pm, Dupont Circle transforms into the lively outdoor **Dupont Circle Farmers Market**, where colorful stalls offer a diverse selection of farm-fresh produce, locally sourced meats and cheeses, fresh-baked goods and artisanal products. In peak season, more than 50 vendors make up what the *Financial Times* called 'one of the top farmers markets in the country.' This beloved community gathering began in 1997 and has become a weekend staple for locals and visitors alike, who come not just for shopping but also for the friendly, community atmosphere. Arrive early to get the best produce, but stay later to try goods such as artisanal bourbon or to get a fresh-made meal on site. Even if you're not buying, the market is worth a wadner – just leave Fido at home, as dogs are strongly discouraged.

Go Underground
Underground art with a social mission

In 2005, an organization of local artists took over an abandoned underground streetcar station, transforming 15,000 sq ft of empty space into a socially conscious art gallery aiming to amplify the voice of independent, BIPOC and upcoming artists in the DC area.

 EATING IN DOWNTOWN & DUPONT CIRCLE: BEST RESTAURANTS

| **Tabard Inn:** DC's oldest restaurant, with a Michelin Star–studded chef in a Civil War-era-style dining room. $$$ | **Oyster Oyster:** Chic, carefully source plant-based cuisine with a sustainability ethos. $$$ | **Le Diplomate:** Old-style French cafe with Hemingway-in-Paris vibes and an excellent brunch. $$$ | **Anju:** Homey Korean joint with comfy seating and comfort food to match. $$ |

Dupont Circle Metro Station

COOLEST HISTORIC BUILDINGS

The Hotel of Presidents:
The 1925 Mayflower Hotel has been host to countless prominent people and events.

A Brewer's Castle:
The mansion turned museum of Heurich House was built for German immigrant Christian Heurich, whose brewery was once DC's second-largest employer.

Row-house Mansion:
Four historic row houses stuck together, the Mansion on O Street is a black hole of oddities and memorabilia.

The Gilded Age Lives:
Larz Anderson House (now museum) is a 1905 beaux-arts Gilded Age mansion.

All In a Row:
Many of Massachusetts Ave NW's chic residences were converted into embassies and social clubs after the Great Depression, giving birth to Embassy Row.

Dupont Underground, however, became so much more, as it grew into a space that could showcase different aspects of DC's cultural identity as well as connect the local art community with the world. Rotating exhibits highlight diverse artistic talents in painting, photography, sculpture and multimedia, curated around themes such as environmental consciousness, identity and social justice. The space closes in winter and in extreme weather, but is generally open 10am to 6pm Tuesday to Saturday (March to November).

Discover New Culture

An ambassador's life for me

DC is the nation's capital, which means it also plays host to all the foreign embassies. The embassies return the hospitality by hosting events that allow residents and visitors to immerse themselves in unique cultural experiences from the embassies' home countries. From foreign-film screenings to culinary festivals, art exhibitions and musical performances, each embassy event is meant to highlight unique traditions or customs – think a traditional tea ceremony at the Japanese embassy, or a wine-tasting night with the Chilean ambassador.

Although some events carry a small fee, most are free but require that you RSVP in advance – check embassy websites for more info.

 EATING IN DOWNTOWN & DUPONT CIRCLE: BRUNCH IT UP

| **Nina May:** Hyper-local, farm-to-table American cuisine with outdoor seating and weekend brunch. $$ | **Firefly:** American comfort food served around a large indoor tree, boasting one of the area's best brunches. $$ | **Unconventional Diner:** Contemporary-chic New American diner with a nod from Michelin, serving brunch until late afternoon. $$ | **Pearl Dive Oyster Palace:** Southern-inspired oyster house serving lip-licking seafood. $$ |

Georgetown

RIVER WALKS, RESTAURANTS AND RETAIL THERAPY

GETTING AROUND

Georgetown is a very walkable neighborhood, which is lucky, as it has no Metro stations to call its own. The Foggy Bottom-GWU Metro station (blue, orange and silver lines) is about a 15-minute walk from Georgetown, though the DC Circulator bus will take you in. Capital Bikeshare stations are found primarily along the waterfront, and during the summer season, you can even get a water taxi from the Southwest Waterfront or Old Town Alexandria in Virginia.

☑ TOP TIP

Georgetown is best explored on foot – there are so many shops, galleries and bakeries that you'll miss some gems if you're moving too fast. The area is also rather small and it's rare that it's more than a 15-minute walk to anywhere.

Established in 1751 as a busy port town, DC's oldest neighborhood was once home to textile, paper and flour mills. Georgetown's location along the Potomac River provided both cultural and commercial benefits, further amplified by the construction of the C&O Canal in the early 1800s.

In the 19th century, however, the boom went bust, causing an exodus from the area, and an insurge of African Americans, who took advantage of the falling prices. In the 1930s and '40s, however, it was all to change. The Old Georgetown Act of 1950 was introduced as a government gentrification effort, designating the area as a historic district and catalyzing Georgetown's transformation into an upscale neighborhood. Which is how it stands today. Georgetown is the epicenter of preppy culture, with a charming collection of tree-lined streets, historic row houses, high-end shops and mouthwatering restaurants, plus enough bakeries to keep you cupcake-full till the end of time.

Spend a Day on Book Hill
Hilltop stop for intellectuals and artists

Start your day at Book Hill's namesake attraction, perusing the shelves of independent booksellers such as **Bridge Street Books**, or used and rare-edition treasure trove, the **Lantern Bookshop**. Next, wander in and out of some of the numerous art galleries lining Wisconsin Ave, such as the **Washington Printmakers Gallery**, **Addison/Ripley Fine Art**, or **Gallery Article 15** for vibrant Congolese art. More into antiquing? Stop by **David Bell Antiques**, Georgetown's go-to for unique furniture.

After browsing the shops, it's time to refuel. Grab some noodles at the colorful and quirky **Oki Bowl Ramen,** followed by a creamy cone from old-school ice-cream shop **Thomas Sweet,** a mouthwatering pastry from **Boulangerie Christophe** or a cookie from Oprah's favorite French bakery, **Maman**.

WASHINGTON, DC GEORGETOWN

TOP SIGHTS
1. Georgetown University
2. Volta Laboratory and Bureau

ACTIVITIES, COURSES & TOURS
3. Key Bridge Boathouse
4. Meridian Health and Relaxation
5. Thompson Boat Center

SLEEPING
6. Graham Georgetown
7. Rosewood Washington, DC

EATING
8. Bluefin Sushi
9. Chaia
10. Good Stuff Eatery
11. Il Canale
12. Oki Bowl Ramen
13. Thomas Sweet

DRINKING & NIGHTLIFE
14. Boulangerie Christophe
15. Clydes
16. El Centro D.F.
17. Maman
18. Mr. Smith's
19. Sovereign

ENTERTAINMENT
20. Blues Alley

SHOPPING
21. Addison/Ripley Fine Art
22. Bridge Street Books
23. David Bell Antiques
24. Gallery Article 15
25. Lantern Bookshop
26. Shop Made in DC

● see ④ Washington Printmakers Gallery

293

GEORGETOWN UNIVERSITY

Founded in 1789 as Georgetown College, **Georgetown University** is a beautiful riverfront campus that exudes historic and intellectual charm (and the collegiate Gothic-style buildings of which give off serious Harry Potter vibes). The country's oldest Jesuit university has seen plenty of history – during the Civil War, many of the buildings were turned into hospitals, and Georgetown's gray and blue colors were chosen in honour of the soldiers' uniforms. Noteworthy alumni include former President Bill Clinton and former Associate Justice of the Supreme Court Antonin Gregory Scalia. It's worth stopping by to see the architecture and the bucolic grounds – get a takeaway picnic to enjoy on the lawn for a relaxing afternoon.

Washington National Cathedral

Still feeling stressed? Locals rave about the affordable acupressure and massages at **Meridian Health and Relaxation**, located at the top of Book Hill. Think 30-minute massages for less than $30.

May the Force be with You
Gargoyle hunting at the National Cathedral

Officially named the Cathedral Church of St Peter and St Paul, the neo-Gothic **Washington National Cathedral** is just north of Georgetown. From the day the cornerstone was laid in 1907, the cathedral took 83 years to complete, and is the sixth-largest cathedral in the world. It has 215 stained-glass windows – standouts include the Space Window, which contains a rock from the moon, and the Rose Window, made of more than 10,500 pieces of glass. The grounds are home to one of the few remaining old-growth forests in the city, but the most fun activity at the cathedral is gargoyle spotting. Among the 112 gargoyles on its exterior are an alligator, an American rattlesnake, a raccoon and even Darth Vader.

EATING IN GEORGETOWN: OUR PICKS

Il Canale: Thin-crust, wood-fired pizza done to perfection from a place named one of the US's Top 100 pizza spots. **$$**	**Bluefin Sushi:** Serving high-grade sushi and sashimi in a tiny canalfront dining room (plus takeaway) for nearly 30 years. **$$**	**Good Stuff Eatery:** Nothing but burgers, fries and shakes served just right by Spike Mendelsohn of Top Chef fame. **$**	**Chaia:** The chic vegan and vegetarian tacos of farmer's market fame found an adorable red-brick-and-mortar location. **$**

Embrace your Inner Artist
Wine and watercolor time

Shop Made in DC isn't just one of our favorite shops in the city. This cozy Georgetown boutique (with sister locations near Union Market, at the Wharf and on Embassy Row) is also a space where you can connect with your creative side. Every month the shop launches an extensive list of classes and workshops open to everyone – no art experience required. Reserve your space for an ever-popular wine and watercolor evening (5pm to 7pm Friday) at the shop's upstairs studio, where you'll discover your inner artist while making new friends. Tickets are on Eventbrite for $25, with all materials and two glasses of wine included.

Scientific Discoveries
Historic laboratories and observatories

Nestled among Georgetown's quiet streets, and a short walk from each other, are two important scientific sites. The first is Alexander Graham Bell's research center, the **Volta Laboratory and Bureau**. Build in 1893, after Bell won 50,000 francs from the French government for his invention of the telephone, the Volta Bureau was dedicated to the 'increase and diffusion of knowledge relating to the deaf,' a cause Bell took on for his mother, who was nearly deaf, and his wife, Mabel Gardiner Hubbard, who was deaf. The building is open to the public with prior reservation.

The second site, the **Georgetown University Astronomical Observatory**, is the third-oldest observatory in the United States, dating back to 1844. One of the observatory's most notable researchers was Vera Rubin, a National Medal of Science winner whose work revealed the evidence of dark matter. Rubin was a mother of two in her 20s when she received her PhD in astronomy from Georgetown. Although now closed, the building is still beautiful to view if you're walking around the campus.

Paddle the Potomac
A wetter way to explore DC

The Potomac River is a renowned rowing and kayaking spot, and if you're keen to join in, the **Thompson Boat Center** and the **Key Bridge Boathouse** are the two main spots to rent watercraft. Whether you're a master kayaker or looking simply to cruise, either of these boating centers will help you find the best way to get on the water. Both locations provide paddling and safety instructions and gear, and offer introductory classes for those who've never paddled. At Thompson, you can even learn to row a skull, or rent one if you're already a rower.

NIGHTLIFE IN GEORGETOWN

Blues Alley: This landmark jazz supper club has hosted all the greats, from Ella Fitzgerald and Count Basie to Dizzy Gillespie and Tony Bennett.

Sovereign: This Belgian resto-bar has more than 50 beers on tap as well as 300 bottles and rare brews to boot.

El Centro D.F.: Authentic Mexican fare and mezcal served in a two-story space with a happening back patio.

Mr. Smith's: Georgetown's favorite karaoke piano bar since 1965, with American-style fare and classic decor.

Clydes: This well-loved saloon still serves cold beers in the location in which it first opened in 1963.

Mayflower Hotel

Places We Love to Stay

$ Budget $$ Midrange $$$ Top End

The White House & Foggy Bottom   MAP p257

Hotel Hive $$ Affordable, friendly and convenient (albeit with small rooms), with a bar and rooftop.

River Inn $$ Although not on the river, this quiet hotel near the Kennedy Center offers well-appointed suites and kitchenettes.

Mayflower Hotel $$$ Nicknamed the Hotel of Presidents for good reason – expect service worthy of a head of state.

Hay-Adams Hotel $$$ Expect old-school elegance at this luxurious heritage hotel with White House views.

Penn Quarter & Chinatown   MAP p267

Motto By Hilton $$ The Motto offers 245 small, clean rooms in a great location with a rooftop bar.

Morrison-Clark Historic Inn & Restaurant $$$ Filling two 1864 Victorian houses, this historic 114-room hotel mixes Gilded Age and Asian decor with graceful success.

Kimpton Hotel Monaco DC $$$ Art-deco-inspired hotel inside a landmark 1839 neoclassical building where the cool kids hang.

Southwest   MAP p270

Pendry Washington DC $$$ European-inspired sensibility combines with modern hospitality at this hotel-spa with river views.

Coda on Half $$$ Stylish apartment hotel that's a perfect option for longer stays, or for those preferring apartment-style amenities.

Thompson Washington DC $$$ Clean and cozy boutique-style hotel by Hyatt with good amenities and a central Navy Yard address.

Capitol Hill   MAP p275

Friends Place on Capitol Hill $ This Quaker guesthouse is possibly the friendliest and most affordable hostel in the city.

Phoenix Park Hotel $$ Clean rooms, respectable amenities and solid service close to Union Station and Capitol Hill.

YOTEL Washington DC $$ Four-star contemporary business hotel with a rooftop pool and cool outdoor terrace, steps from Capitol Hill.

Kimpton George Hotel $$$ Creamy-white rooms adorned with presidential pop art located near Union Station. Kid and pet friendly.

Northeast   MAP p280

citizenM $$ Small but super-high-tech rooms and thoughtfully decorated common areas – perfect for single travelers.

Hotel Nell $$ Industrial-chic hotel with a cool rooftop. Rooms are on the small side, but the location is perfect for nightlife lovers.

Adams Morgan & the U Street Corridor   MAP p283

HighRoad Hotel $ One of the city's better hostel options, with clean rooms and stylish decor in the heart of Adams Morgan.

American Guest House $$ Twelve-bedroom B&B in a home-style environment with comfortable rooms, friendly staff and great breakfast.

Line Hotel DC $$$ Stylish, vintage-chic hotel in a converted 1900s church with a hip cafe/bar on the ground floor.

Downtown & Dupont Circle   MAP p289

Swann House $$ Historic B&B with spacious rooms, aesthetically pleasing minimalist decor, impeccable service and a seasonally open outdoor swimming pool.

The Darcy $$$ Cosmopolitan boutique hotel with free bicycle use, daily cocktail tastings and an acclaimed restaurant.

The Jefferson $$$ This elegant, two-winged 1923 mansion regularly places near the top of Washington's best-hotel lists. The cocktail bar is perfect for a piano-soundtracked nightcap.

Georgetown   MAP p293

Graham Georgetown $$$ Modernist boutique hotel in the middle of Georgetown with contemporary decor and rooftop lounge that's perfect for sundowners.

Rosewood Washington, DC $$$ This five-star canal-front hotel falls blissfully under the radar, so you can enjoy the rooftop, infinity pool and impeccable service without the hype.

Delaware

BEACHES, ART AND HISTORY

Discover the nation's second-smallest state, filled with surf and sand, blooming gardens and centuries-old buildings.

In just two hours you can drive from Delaware's southern beaches to its countryside estates in the Brandywine Valley bordering Pennsylvania, bypassing historic towns and nature reserves en route. Its diminutive size has earned it a few nicknames, including 'small wonder' and the Diamond State. Local legend says the latter originated with Thomas Jefferson, who compared it to the jewel because it was small and valuable. Delaware's precious rivers, bays and ocean access attracted European colonists, and it played an integral role in shaping US history. It was the first state to ratify the US Constitution in 1787, which had a domino effect on the other 12.

Delaware's commitment to preserving its history is evident throughout the state, with numerous museums and walking tours featuring costumed reenactors. A significant milestone was reached in 2013 when President Barack Obama designated six historic Delaware sites in Wilmington, New Castle and Dover as the First State National Historical Park, the state's first national monument.

Historical attractions also recount the arduous struggle for African American residents. The 'first state' was among the last to ratify the 13th Amendment (in 1901) abolishing slavery, and many of its critical political figures enslaved people. The state was an essential conduit for the Underground Railroad. Harriet Tubman and other abolitionists relied on its safe houses and forests to secure freedom as they escaped north.

THE MAIN AREAS

WILMINGTON
Mansions, museums and a lively waterfront.
p302

DOVER
History and shopping in the capital.
p307

REHOBOTH
Beaches and other natural wonders.
p310

Left: Delaware Legislative Hall (p307); Above: Rehoboth Beach (p310)

Find Your Way

Delaware stretches 120 miles from the southern beach town of Fenwick to the northern city of Wilmington and the surrounding Brandywine Valley, with the capital city of Dover sandwiched between the two.

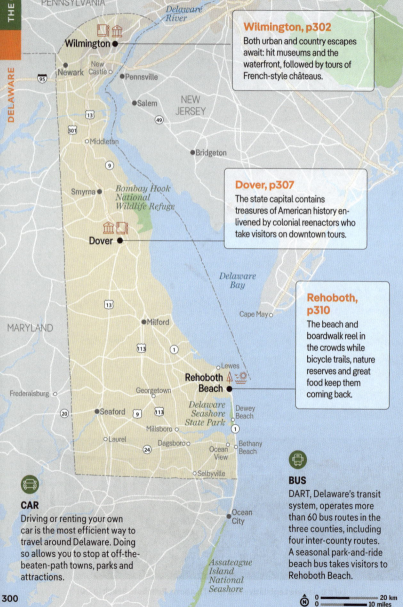

Wilmington, p302
Both urban and country escapes await: hit museums and the waterfront, followed by tours of French-style châteaus.

Dover, p307
The state capital contains treasures of American history enlivened by colonial reenactors who take visitors on downtown tours.

Rehoboth, p310
The beach and boardwalk reel in the crowds while bicycle trails, nature reserves and great food keep them coming back.

CAR
Driving or renting your own car is the most efficient way to travel around Delaware. Doing so allows you to stop at off-the-beaten-path towns, parks and attractions.

BUS
DART, Delaware's transit system, operates more than 60 bus routes in the three counties, including four inter-county routes. A seasonal park-and-ride beach bus takes visitors to Rehoboth Beach.

Wilmington (p302)

Plan Your Time

Beach lovers should head straight to Delaware's southern end to soak up the joy of being surrounded by surf, sand and saltwater taffy.

Pressed for Time

● Grab a spot in the sand in Rehoboth, followed by a stroll on its **boardwalk** (p310) and a spin at the games at the amusement park **Funland** (p310). Then drive to Delaware's **Brandywine Valley** (p306) to marvel at the mansions, stopping at historic attractions and museums in **Dover** (p307), the historic town of **Milford** (p308) and the **Riverfront Wilmington** (p302).

A Week-Long Stay

● Spend three days exploring the **beach towns** (p312) beyond Rehoboth: Dewey for its party atmosphere, Bethany for a quieter experience and Lewes if you're a history buff. Make time to indulge in beach eats, from fries to farm-to-table fare. Spend a day in **Dover** (p307) to refresh your knowledge of colonial history before heading to the museums, parks and mansions of **Wilmington** (p302).

SEASONAL HIGHLIGHTS

SPRING
The two-day **Dover Days** (p307) festival features costumed reenactors, fireworks and hot-air balloon rides.

SUMMER
Vacationers arrive in droves, especially during holidays like July 4, when fireworks erupt over **Rehoboth** (p310).

FALL
This is a good time to view waterfowl and listen to musicians during the **Rehoboth Beach Jazz Festival**.

WINTER
The majestic mansions and gardens in Kent County's **Brandywine Valley** (p306) brim with yuletide joy.

Wilmington

COUNTRY CHÂTEAUS | WALKABLE WATERFRONT | ENGAGING MUSEUMS

GETTING AROUND

Wilmington is easily accessible by **Amtrak** from the East Coast – ask President Joe Biden, who famously commuted by train from his hometown to Washington, DC. Delaware is one of the most bicycle-friendly states, and trails allow you to reach attractions along the Brandywine Valley and the historic town of New Castle, connected to the Wilmington Riverfront by the 5.5-mile **Jack A Markell Trail**. Non-cyclists can drive or use ride-hailing apps Uber and Lyft to the Brandywine Valley and other attractions outside the city center. Drivers to Wilmington can leave their cars at their hotel or garage to explore the waterfront and city center on foot.

The Lenni Lenape Native American tribe were the first inhabitants of Wilmington, followed by the Dutch, Swedes, and the British, who strategically set up near the waterways – the Delaware, Brandywine, and Christina Rivers – that enabled favorable trade routes. Wilmington's location remains an asset today. Its proximity to Philadelphia (40 minutes) and New York (two hours) and its business-friendly climate have prompted nearly two-thirds of Fortune 500 companies to incorporate here.

The city's newer attractions have made it alluring to travelers. The waterfront has been transformed into a recreational destination, and the Delaware History Museum expanded in 2019 to include exhibits highlighting African American history. It's also home to new and refreshed hotel properties: the Quoin Hotel, a boutique property that opened in a former bank, adding Wilmington's only rooftop bar, while its premier luxury property, the Hotel du Pont, renovated its restaurant and lobby. Travelers will also find new food halls, speakeasies and Black-owned and James Beard–nominated restaurants.

A River Runs Through It
Explore Wilmington's riverfront

Once the site of thriving shipbuilding businesses, Wilmington's Christina River continues to benefit the city today as a prime recreational spot. The Riverfront Wilmington area features an accessible boardwalk with restaurants, museums and parks. You'll find joggers, rowers and cyclists, as well as folks enjoying more leisurely activities like playing cornhole at the seasonal beer garden or just gazing at the water at one of the Adirondack chairs.

On the north end, the 1.3-mile stretch begins at the **Du Pont Environmental Education Center,** whose elevation provides a bird's-eye view of the 212-acre tidal marsh and

SIGHTS
1. Delaware Children's Museum
2. Delaware History Museum
3. LaFate Gallery
4. Tubman Garrett Riverfront Park

SLEEPING
5. Hotel du Pont
6. The Quoin Hotel & Restaurant

EATING
7. Bardea Food & Drink
8. DECO Wilmington
9. Oath 84
10. Riverfront Market

DRINKING & NIGHTLIFE
11. Constitution Yards
12. Merchant Bar
13. Torbert Street Social

ENTERTAINMENT
14. Delaware Theatre Company
15. The Grand Opera House
16. The Playhouse on Rodney Square
17. The Queen

TRANSPORTATION
18. Joseph R Biden Jr Railroad Station

---

wildlife refuge below. The abundance of trees and cool breeze here make it a good respite on warmer days.

Walk south on the riverfront path for an impressive view of the city skyline, passing minor league baseball venue **Frawley Stadium**, **Delaware Children's Museum** and food stalls in a restored warehouse at **Riverfront Market**. Just across Market St lies **Tubman Garrett Riverfront Park**, a popular spot for city festivals anchored by a moving statue depicting abolitionists Thomas Garrett and Harriet Tubman guiding the enslaved through the Underground Railroad.

Scandinavian Legacy
Tour a Swedish ship and church

A mile north of Tubman Garrett Riverfront Park, the Kalmar Nyckel Shipyard features a replica of a Dutch tall ship that brought Swedish and Finnish settlers to Wilmington in 1638 and laid the foundation for the city's robust shipbuilding business. The site's **Copeland Maritime Center** highlights the area's first European settlement and the city's maritime history with educational videos, artifacts, model ships and a

☑ TOP TIP

From 5K races to a summer Shakespeare festival, the Brandywine Valley hosts numerous events. Check visitwilmingtonde.com/events for the schedule and visitwilmingtonde.com/savings for discounts.

BEST FOR MUSIC & ART LOVERS

The Queen: This historic venue features two concert stages and a bar hosting live music.

Grand Opera House: Built in 1871, the ornate Grand hosts Broadway shows, concerts and opera in its two performance halls.

Playhouse on Rodney Square: Located in the Hotel du Pont, the Grand operates this nearby hall exhibiting plays and concerts in the city's historic district.

Delaware Theatre Company: New and classic off-Broadway shows and a traveling improv comedy teams shine at this Riverfront Wilmington venue.

Delaware Art Museum: An outdoor sculpture garden, American masters' works and a renowned collection of Pre-Raphaelite art make this a must-visit museum.

log cabin replica. Check the schedule for free deck tours and ticketed sailings in Wilmington or New Castle, and don't forget to step out on the museum balcony for a prime view of the river and boat when it's docked.

Scandinavians buried their dead and worshipped at the church and cemetery at **Old Swedes Historic Site** down the street. Enter through Hendrickson House, a 1722 stone home owned by a Swedish American family that was moved from its original location in Pennsylvania. Old Swedes is one of the oldest Protestant churches in North America; its sparkle comes from crushed oyster shells from the Christina River that builders added to the mortar. Inside, white pews contrast with colorful stained-glass windows. Guests get to try their hand at pulling the heavy church bell during their tours.

DRINKING IN WILMINGTON: OUR PICKS

Constitution Yards: Riverfront beer garden with cornhole, axe throwing, live music, draft beers and ciders.

Torbert Street Social: Dimly lit speakeasy with creative cocktails and shareable plates in a repurposed building.

Merchant Bar: Friendly cocktail bar and gastropub where the bartender adjusts drinks according to preference.

Wilmington Brew Works: Enjoy food along with the ciders and beers brewed on-site.

Wilmington

A Window to the Past
View exhibits on Delaware history

The **Delaware History Museum and Mitchell Center for African American Heritage** chronicle the state's journey over hundreds of years, starting with the earliest residents, the Lenni Lenape Native American tribe, and continuing with the fight for freedom faced by African Americans. Permanent exhibits reside in an art deco former Woolworth building connected to the brick-covered Old Town Hall, Delaware's first government building, completed in 1799. It features temporary works on the 2nd floor.

Delaware held enslaved people during the Civil War and was among the last of the states to ratify the 13th Amendment abolishing slavery, so the road to freedom and equality here was an arduous one for African Americans. That struggle is chronicled here, from the Underground Railroad's route through Delaware to ending segregation in public schools to the role of churches – depicted in an exhibit with stained-glass panels and piped-in gospel music.

MUSIC CITY

Eunice LaFate, local artist and owner of LaFate Gallery. @lafategallery

Bob Marley's family is establishing a museum to honor him, his Jamaican heritage and reggae music. He lived here in the 1960s and early '70s. He and I are from the same place in Jamaica, St Ann Parish. There is a park in Wilmington called **One Love Park** (named after the Marley song) at W 24th and N Tatnall Sts. I have a permanent wall in my gallery for Bob Marley. The annual People's Festival Tribute to Bob Marley features music, storytelling and food. Music fans should also visit during the annual Clifford Brown Jazz Festival in June. Thousands of people come from all over. It's big.

 EATING IN WILMINGTON: OUR PICKS

| **Bardea Food & Drink:** Italian James Beard–nominated eatery serving pizza, pasta and seafood, with a seasonal garden and steakhouse. **$$** | **DECO Wilmington:** A food hall with vegan comfort food, pizza, chicken and waffles, livened-up with art markets, karaoke and trivia. **$** | **Oath 84:** Black-owned New American restaurant carrying creative meat and seafood small plates. **$$** | **Jessop's Tavern:** Colonial-era decor, pub fare and Belgian beer in a 350-year-old building in historic New Castle. **$$** |

TOUR THE BRANDYWINE VALLEY'S ESTATES

The French-style sprawling estates in the Brandywine Valley – known as château country – are a testament to the outsized legacy of the industrialists and philanthropists of Delaware's du Pont family. If you have a day, begin the first tour at 10am, or spend two covering the hundreds of acres. Start at **1 Nemours Estate**, a 15-minute drive north of Wilmington, flanked by towering black-and-gold iron gates – one hailing from Wimbledon Manor and the other with the initials of Catherine the Great. Helpful blue-shirted staff guide visitors through the bedrooms and elaborate reception hall outfitted with 18th- and 19th-century paintings, wall tapestries and du Pont family portraits. There are a 25-minute tours of the 200-acre garden filled with statues, a pool and a maze of evergreen trees. It's a 10-minute drive to the indoor-outdoor **2 Hagley Museum & Library,** which features dozens of stone structures, waterwheels and a coal-fired steam engine that whisks you back to the 19th-century gunpowder factory founded by EI du Pont. One highlight is a booming black powder explosion demonstration. Then, drive slowly along the narrow winding roads to the **3 Mt Cuba Center**. This botanical garden blooms with various native plants and habitats along the newly ADA-accessible, fragrant garden paths. Set out on one of the trails or take a horticultural class. After this, it's five minutes to **4 Winterthur Museum, Garden & Library**, whose tens of thousands of furniture items, porcelain and other decorative objects are spread throughout rooms in the former home of Henry Francis du Pont in two buildings. One building resembles the original mansion and the other a conventional museum. Signs show what's in bloom each month in the garden, which can be viewed via a tram.

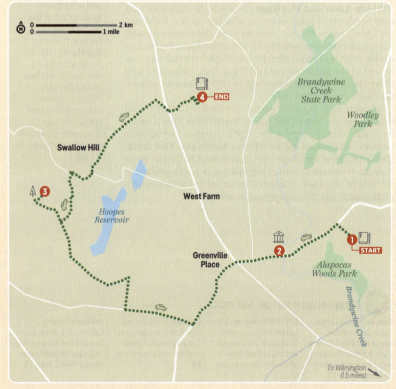

Dover

AMERICAN HISTORY | CHARMING STREETS | UNDERRATED MUSEUMS

Travelers heading from Wilmington to the beaches might forget about Dover unless they head to the casino to gamble. However, the town holds significance as the state capital and for its role in US history. Local tour guides will tell you about hometown hero Caesar Rodney, an oft-forgotten revolutionary who rode 80 miles in a storm to Philadelphia to make the tie-breaking Delaware vote for independence in 1776. Dover is also where the state delegates ratified the US Constitution at the Golden Fleece Tavern (now an art gallery and souvenir shop), earning Delaware the 'first state' nickname.

The town capitalizes on this important history by offering walking tours, lantern tours and various events, including an 18th-century Colonial Market Fair held in the fall and the annual Dover Days heritage celebration, a two-day event in May with fireworks, reenactors, tethered hot-air balloon rides and a parade.

Step Back in Time
Relive history in downtown Dover

Downtown Dover's half-acre, tree-filled lawn surrounded by historic buildings, known as the **Dover Green**, holds most of the town's treasures. It is where suffragettes demanded the right to vote and legislators voted to ratify the US Constitution. First State Heritage Park storytellers dressed in 18th-century garb recount these pivotal moments during walking tours held Wednesday through Saturday.

Visitors can also tour the former and current homes of the Delaware General Assembly. Built in 1791, the Georgian-style **Old State House** features an exhibit on free Black man Samuel D Burris, who was tried and convicted for helping the enslaved escape. Members of the State House and Senate, where a commanding George Washington portrait hangs, met in the two chambers upstairs until 1933, when the new Legislative Hall was built. Ten murals depicting scenes from Delaware history painted by artist John Lewis were added to the chambers of the **Delaware Legislative Hall** in 1987 to memorialize the 200th anniversary of Delaware signing the US Constitution.

GETTING AROUND

While long-haul buses stop in Dover, most visitors arrive by car and use it to get around Dover and Kent County. But cyclists can ride the 4.5-mile Capital City Trail connecting downtown attractions, parks, government offices and Dover Air Force Base. Bike trails like the Mispillion River Greenway, which runs through the historic town of Milford, let you enjoy the green spaces without a car. Delaware's transit system, DART First State, operates buses to 10 stops. Intercounty buses also run between Dover, Wilmington and the beach.

☑ TOP TIP

Kent County's agricultural bounty is on display at its country stores. History buffs won't want to miss downtown Dover's free walking tours.

DOVER'S BEST MUSEUMS

Biggs Museum of American Art: The decorative and fine art collection features paintings, sculptures and furniture from the 1600s to the present.

Air Mobility Command Museum: A must-visit museum for military-aviation enthusiasts, with 30-plus aircraft and wartime-airlift exhibits.

John Bell House: First State Heritage Park walking tours start at Dover's oldest wooden-frame house, built in the mid-1700s.

John Dickinson Plantation: Tours guide visitors through the home of a US Constitution signer who granted freedom to the enslaved here after inheriting it in 1785.

Delaware Agricultural Museum: A general store, farmhouse and gristmill are some of the features of this site that recounts Delaware's agricultural history.

Musical Marvel
Tour the Johnson Victrola Museum

Antique phonographs made during the early 20th century by the Victor Talking Machine Co are displayed at the **Johnson Victrola Museum**. Tour guides explain the evolution of the company, founded by Dover native Eldridge Reeves 'ER' Johnson, and play records that let you hear some of the earliest music devices. Photos, artifacts and images of Nipper, the recognizable fox-bull terrier company mascot, accompany the exhibits of the two-story museum.

Doughnuts and Dishware
Dive into Spence's flea market

The Dover area is home to several Amish markets, but locals favor **Spence's Bazaar, Auction and Flea Market** for the breadth of offerings here. Open Tuesdays, Fridays and Saturdays, the site consists of two buildings: one containing bakery treats, meats and snacks, and the other holding one big garage sale with multiple vendors. Doughnuts, cinnamon sticky buns, soft pretzels stuffed with egg and cheese, a deli and a variety of pickles are just some of the offerings in the Amish food hall. Bring your best bargaining skills to purchase purses, records, dishware, jewelry and other items in the flea market, which extends outside when the weather is favorable. Note that some vendors only take cash.

A Charming Main Street
Wander through quaint Milford

With several attractive buildings and a scenic riverwalk, Milford has Main Street charm in spades. It straddles Kent and Sussex Counties (home of Rehoboth), and a line at the base of the riverwalk marks that fact. Dog walkers and cyclists roam the waterfront path that weaves through parks and has several miniature painted small boats that remind visitors of the town's shipbuilding history. Spring through fall, the downtown attracts a crowd with food trucks, live music on the first Friday of the month and a seasonal ice-cream stand, **North Pole Creamery**.

S Walnut St contains art galleries, restaurants, a theater and some newer tenants: **Farmacy Market**, which sells locally made foods, soaps and candies, and honey-wine producer **WTF What to Ferment Meadery**. A couple of blocks away, the Milford Museum's exhibits detail the town's past, including its role as a shipbuilding hub and stories of Black students who fought to integrate its high school.

EATING IN KENT COUNTY: OUR PICKS

The Cured Plate Libations & Lounge: This speakeasy serves creative cocktails and charcuterie. **$$**

Rail Haus: A Black-owned brewery restaurant with an outdoor beer garden, cornhole, German-inspired food and beers on draft. **$**

Stonerail Market: This women-owned wine bar and market offers salads, sandwiches and small plates. **$**

Elizabeth Esther Cafe: An organic, made-from-scratch menu is available inside this manor built in 1868; it's open for lunch, brunch and dinner. **$$**

A Charming Main Street
Wander through quaint Milford

Kent County is home to six sites associated with Harriet Tubman, whose journeys rescued 70 enslaved individuals. Tubman relied on a network of safe houses, trails and waterways (the Underground Railroad) in Maryland and Delaware before arriving at the free state of Pennsylvania. The 6000-acre **Blackbird State Forest** is said to be one of her landmarks during her passages, while the Quaker church **Camden Friends Meeting** and **Star Hill AME Church** provided shelter to those escaping slavery. A historical marker at the **Norman G Wilder Wildlife Area** tells the story of freed African American Samuel D Burris, who helped others escape slavery and was tried and convicted in the Old State House.

SIGHTS
1. Air Mobility Command Museum
2. Biggs Museum of American Art
3. Blackbird State Forest
4. Camden Friends Meeting
5. Delaware Agricultural Museum
6. Delaware Legislative Hall
7. Dover Green
8. Harvest Ridge Winery
9. John Bell House
10. John Dickinson Plantation
11. Johnson Victrola Museum
12. Norman G Wilder Wildlife Area
13. Old State House
14. Star Hill AME Church
15. WTF What to Ferment Meadery

SLEEPING
16. Hilton Garden Inn Dover
17. Home2 Suites by Hilton
18. SpringHill Suites by Marriott
19. State Street Inn

EATING
20. Elizabeth Esther Cafe
● see 15 North Pole Creamery
21. Rail Haus
22. Stonerail Market
● see 15 The Cured Plate Libations & Lounge

DRINKING & NIGHTLIFE
23. Easy Speak Spirits
24. Mispillion River Brewing

SHOPPING
● see 15 Farmacy Market
25. Spence's Bazaar, Auction & Flea Market

 DRINKING IN KENT COUNTY: OUR PICKS

Mispillion River Brewing: IPAs and sours are on offer here, along with live music, food trucks and outdoor space.

Easy Speak Spirits: Easy Speak has house-made vodka, gin, rum and bourbon, plus arcade games and a ping-pong table.

WTF What To Ferment Meadery: This pirate-themed tasting room serves honey wine, beer and canned cocktails. BYO food.

Harvest Ridge Winery: Wine tastings, food trucks and Sunday brunch are all available at this off-the-beaten-path winery.

Rehoboth

TOP BEACHES | UNSPOILED NATURE | EXCEPTIONAL EATS

GETTING AROUND

Most tourists who aren't part of a group tour arrive by car, and there are no Amtrak or Greyhound stops. In the summer a bicycle comes in handy as you can ride to the beach towns without feeding parking meters. Exercise caution on the busy stretch of Rte 1 between Lewes and Rehoboth, where numerous bike fatalities have occurred. Delaware's transit system, DART, operates a seasonal bus route from Wilmington to Lewes and another from Dover to Lewes, with additional buses connecting the various beach towns. It also runs seasonal buses from park-and-ride stops on Coastal Hwy (SR1) to Rehoboth Beach.

☑ TOP TIP

Agriculture is one of the top industries in Sussex County, and the backroads are filled with markets and seasonal pop-up stands selling locally grown food.

Native Americans were the first settlers in Rehoboth Beach, later established as a seaside town by a Methodist minister in 1873. Since then, it has become one of the top Mid-Atlantic beaches, prized for its mile-long boardwalk, unique assortment of stores and restaurants and clean waters. The family- and LGBTIQ-friendly town retains its Main Street appeal by maintaining building-height restrictions that prevent towering condos and hotels from blocking the Atlantic Ocean views. While most visitors come in the summer, Rehoboth and its neighboring beach towns have become a year-round destination, aided by the post-pandemic remote-work boom.

While the sand and surf are Sussex County's strongest selling points, its natural beauty extends beyond the beach, with cycling trails, birdwatching spots and botanical gardens all within easy reach. Its agricultural bounty has also propelled it to become a leading farm-to-table culinary destination, prompting the county's tourism bureau to anoint it 'the Culinary Coast.'

Boardwalk, Beaches and Boutiques
Shop and stroll in Rehoboth

Strolling the mile-long Rehoboth Beach boardwalk is a favorite summer pastime when visitors cover every inch of it, often with **Thrasher's French Fries** or Kohr Bros Frozen Custard in hand. Music from the bandstand plays at the end of the main drag, Rehoboth Ave, near the Atlantic Ocean beach. Riding the Haunted Mansion and trying your luck at Skee-Ball at the seasonal amusement park **Funland** is another rite of passage while on vacation here.

Arrive early to grab a parking spot and plop your umbrella on the beach before sunbathers and swimmers swallow every available space. It's worth venturing past the souvenir shops near the beach to peruse the assortment of

SIGHTS
1. Cape Henlopen State Park
2. Charles W Cullen Bridge
3. Delaware Seashore State Park
4. Lavender Fields at Warrington Manor
5. Lewes Canalfront Park
6. Lewes Historical Society
7. Lightship Overfalls
8. Prime Hook National Wildlife Refuge
9. Rehoboth Art League
10. Ryves Holt House
11. Salted Vines Vineyard
12. Savannah Beach
13. Zwaanendael Museum

ACTIVITIES, COURSES & TOURS
14. Cape May-Lewes Ferry
15. Coastal Kayak
16. Gordons Pond Trail

EATING
see 2 Big Chill Beach Club
17. Cafe Azafran
18. Cafe Papillon
19. Confucius Chinese Cuisine
20. Fish On
21. Henlopen City Oyster House
22. Off the Hook
23. One Coastal
24. Raas
25. Rusty Rudder
26. The Blue Hen
27. The Starboard
28. Thrasher's French Fries

DRINKING & NIGHTLIFE
29. Aqua Bar & Grill
30. Blue Moon
31. Dewey Beer Co
32. Diego's Bar & Nightclub
33. Dogfish Head Milton Brewery
34. The Brimming Horn Meadery
35. The Pines American Bistro

ENTERTAINMENT
36. Bottle & Cork
37. Cinema Art Theater
38. Clayton Theatre
39. Clear Space Theatre Company
40. Funland
41. Milton Theatre

SHOPPING
42. Browseabout Books
43. Buddhas and Beads
44. Penny Lane Mall

TRANSPORTATION
45. Georgetown-Lewes Trail

NATURE SPOTS BEYOND THE BEACH

Lavender Fields at Warrington Manor: The lavender fields are the main attraction but don't skip the native-plant gardens and the shop selling lavender products.

Delaware Seashore State Park: With 6 miles of oceanfront and 20 miles of bay shoreline, this is a prime spot for all water activities.

Georgetown–Lewes Trail: This bicycle and pedestrian trail will add its final leg in fall 2025, making it 17 miles to connect Lewes and Georgetown.

Gordons Pond Trail: The loop traverses its namesake saltwater lagoon and Cape Henlopen State Park, where you'll see sand dunes and remnants of the former WWII military base.

Prime Hook National Wildlife Refuge: At this migratory bird sanctuary you might spot bald eagles, ospreys or waterfowl.

independent stores. Longstanding **Browseabout Books** features author signings, while **Buddhas and Beads** sells crystals, jewelry and antiques. Venture down the storybook-like alleyway **Penny Lane Mall** to grab a sweet crepe or savory croissant from **Cafe Papillon**.

Beach-Hopping

Explore the Delaware beach towns

While Rehoboth commands the most name recognition, Sussex County contains a cluster of waterside hamlets stretching 24 miles along the Coastal Hwy from Lewes to Fenwick Island, passing through Dewey Beach and Bethany Beach. Explore each for a few hours or days.

Filled with remarkably well-preserved historic homes and blooming gardens, Lewes looks like it's been plucked from the English countryside. After driving past Rehoboth, the road turns narrow, with the rushing Atlantic Ocean waves on one side and serene bay waters on the other. Party hot spots and live-music venues like **The Starboard**, **Bottle & Cork**, and **Rusty Rudder** overflow with singles in the summer. The 15-minute drive to Bethany Beach takes you across the **Charles W Cullen Bridge**, whose slanted pylons

DRINKING AROUND REHOBOTH: OUR PICKS

Dogfish Head Milton Brewery: The Milton headquarters of the iconic beer brand has brewery tours, beer tastings and a steampunk treehouse.

The Brimming Horn Meadery: This Viking-themed meadery features ciders and honey wines on tap.

Salted Vines Vineyard & Winery: A hidden treasure with vineyard views, live music and red, white and rosé wine tastings.

Dewey Beer Co: The original Dewey Beach location serves IPAs, fruity sours and a sizeable food menu.

Bethany Beach

resemble a ship's sails and are lit up an ocean-blue color. Stop in **Delaware Seashore State Park** or the restaurant **Big Chill Beach Club** for a prime bridge view.

Collectively called 'the quiet resorts,' Bethany Beach and Fenwick Island have a tranquil atmosphere that draws families. The half-mile boardwalk in Bethany contains a couple of arcades, souvenir shops and restaurants with beach views, while mini golf and a water park are the highlights of Fenwick's small boardwalk. The gentle waters of Assawoman Bay make an excellent spot for beginners to rent kayaks, paddle boards and sailboats at **Coastal Kayak**.

Go Dutch

Walk through historic Lewes

The picturesque town of Lewes packs five centuries of architecture into its historic district, which contains a mishmash of styles from colonial to Federal and Victorian. The Dutch settled here in 1631, making it the first settlement and earning Lewes the 'first town in the first state' moniker. Its Dutch history is on display at the free **Zwaanendael Museum**, whose striking red-and-white shutters take after a town hall in the Netherlands.

BEST FOR FILM & ART LOVERS

Cinema Art Theater:
The Rehoboth Beach Film Society operates this two-screen movie hall showcasing foreign and independent movies from emerging filmmakers.

Rehoboth Art League:
With exhibits, lectures and festivals, this nonprofit continuously hosts events for art lovers.

Clear Space Theatre Company:
Featuring plays and Broadway musicals, this regional theater company also holds acting classes for all ages.

Milton Theatre:
Live bands, musical theater and a Pride festival are just some of the events held at this two-story building built in 1910.

Clayton Theatre:
Classic and first-run movies are shown at this single-screen movie theater, with its retro marquee lit at night.

 DRINKING IN REHOBOTH: LGBTIQ+-FRIENDLY BARS, RESTAURANTS & CLUBS

The Pines American Bistro: Convivial hangout with Sunday drag brunch and a stylish lounge with a tree in the center.	**Blue Moon:** An upscale restaurant serving meat and seafood that turns into a gay bar after supper.	**Diego's Bar & Nightclub:** Popular dance club with a food truck, happy-hour specials and a patio.	**Aqua Bar & Grill:** Hosts live music and parties, with a patio that turns into a lively scene in the summer.

WHY I LOVE LEWES

Julekha Dash, Lonely Planet writer

My husband and I visit Lewes at least every other month. While the highway traffic and businesses have quadrupled in the last 20 years, the heart of Lewes is unchanged. The calm waters of **Savannah Beach** appeal to a nervous ocean swimmer like me, and even during high season you can find a stretch of sand to call your own. I've spent many afternoons at **Cape Henlopen State Park** walking the three-mile loop past sand dunes, wetlands and the point where the Delaware Bay meets the Atlantic Ocean. I love taking visitors on boat tours from the Lewes Canal to the Delaware Bay to spot dolphins, waterfowl and lighthouses, or on the **Cape May–Lewes Ferry**.

Park your car or bicycle and explore the town on a walking tour with **Lewes Historical Society** (see historiclewes. org for times). Engaging storytellers in period costumes take you past landmarks, including the **Ryves Holt House**, Delaware's oldest building and one of the many small museums the society operates. You can also pop into the 18th- and 19th-century buildings at the organization's main Shipcarpenter St campus, including a former school, doctor's office and a tavern, which sells cocktails made from colonial-era recipes on the first Friday of each month.

Lewes' main thoroughfare, 2nd St, houses an eclectic assortment of independent stores selling antiques, vintage jewelry and art, women's clothes and books. A leisurely walk toward the water leads to the picturesque **Lewes Canalfront Park**, where you can tour the last lighthouse boat made for the US Lighthouse Service, the **Lightship Overfalls**.

Flower Power
Wander through botanical gardens

It's worth the detour to the **Delaware Botanic Gardens at Pepper Creek**, whose central 2-acre meadow was crafted by New York Highline designer Piet Oudolf and filled with native plants that change throughout the year. Shaped like a figure eight, the meadow's center houses an elevated grassy knoll in the middle, offering an ideal spot to survey the entirety. The trail through the 12.5-acre woodland gardens takes you through a canopied forest with whimsical sculptures made of natural materials that serve a dual purpose as art installations and as hotels for insects, bees and reptiles. The cool breeze from Pepper Creek and the natural shade make it a good escape on a hot day.

 EATING IN SUSSEX COUNTY: OUR PICKS

Henlopen City Oyster House: Arrive early to this popular no-reservations eatery offering a wide fish selection and a raw bar. $$$	**Cafe Azafran:** Garlic shrimp, ratatouille and other Mediterranean dishes are on offer here, with a sister cafe in Lewes. Check for specials. $$$	**Confucius Chinese Cuisine:** Longstanding Chinese spot with shareable Hunan dishes, including salt-and-pepper shrimp and Peking duck. $$	**The Blue Hen:** A woman-owned hotel restaurant with a daily-changing menu, weekly specials and good happy-hour specials. $$$
Fish On: One of a dozen restaurants under local SoDel Concepts' domain, with a happy hour and seafood specials daily. $$	**Raas:** Indian cuisine served in a 125-year-old Victorian home with traditional and unique fare, including chili olive naan and a street-fare menu. $$	**One Coastal:** A James Beard–nominated chef here sources ingredients from local farms and waters to deliver standout meat and seafood dishes. $$$	**Off the Hook:** Standout farm-to-table small plates and seafood dishes with a daily happy hour and weekday specials. $$$

Places We Love to Stay

$ Budget $$ Midrange $$$ Top End

Wilmington MAP p303

The Quoin Hotel $$$ Former bank building turned into a 24-room boutique property with a rooftop bar and speakeasy.

Hotel du Pont $$$ Luxury property with a spa, opulent lobby and food court in the Italian Renaissance building that debuted in 1913.

Hyatt Place Wilmington Riverfront $$$ This suite hotel has a weekday happy hour, free breakfasts and a riverfront patio.

Brandywine Valley MAP p306

Homewood Suites by Hilton Wilmington-Brandywine Valley $$$ A suite hotel 10 minutes from Winterthur Museum Garden & Library, with an outdoor pool and free breakfasts.

The Inn at Montchanin Village & Spa $$$ This historic inn has a spa and a restaurant in a former blacksmith shop.

Dover MAP p309

Home2 Suites by Hilton $$ A suite hotel within walking distance of downtown Dover attractions, with free breakfasts and an indoor pool.

Hilton Garden Inn Dover $$ This place is close to the casino, with an indoor pool and rooms with microwaves and mini fridges.

State Street Inn $$$ In a Tudor-style, early-20th-century home, this B&B is close to downtown Dover sights.

SpringHill Suites by Marriott $$$ An all-suite hotel in Frederica with an indoor pool and free breakfasts, near Kent County beaches and a sports complex.

Milford MAP p309

Causey Mansion Bed & Breakfast $$ This landmark 18th-century building set on a 3-acre property is sprinkled with art, fountains and antique period details.

Rehoboth MAP p311

Avenue Inn & Spa $$$ Located one block from the beach, with a spa and James Beard semi-finalist restaurant The Blue Hen.

Boardwalk Plaza Hotel $$$ Pink Victorian charmer with a waterside patio facing the ocean, rooms with balconies and a heated soaking pool.

The Bellmoor Inn & Spa $$$ This hotel two blocks from the beach is decorated with cozy, coastal-chic furnishings and has a premier spa.

Hotel Rehoboth $$$ An indoor pool, daily wine-and-cheese happy hours and a complimentary beach shuttle with chairs and towels are on offer here.

Dewey Beach MAP p311

Atlantic View Hotel $$$ This hotel has ocean-facing rooms and a sundeck, an outdoor pool, and wine, cheese and cookies in the evening.

Bethany Beach MAP p311

Bethany Beach Ocean Suites Residence Inn $$$ This oceanfront property has an indoor-outdoor pool, kitchenette suites and an on-site Italian restaurant.

Lewes MAP p311

Hotel Rodney $$ Located in downtown historic Lewes, this historic hotel has fun furnishings and a British-style gastropub.

The INN at Canal Square $$$ This waterfront property with Nantucket-style cedar shingles and free breakfasts is within walking distance of the beach.

Hyatt House Lewes/Rehoboth Beach $$$ Hyatt House, an all-suite hotel with free breakfasts and an indoor pool, is nearby to several restaurants.

Dogfish Inn $$$ This pup-friendly inn from the Dogfish Head beer makers has e-bikes and beer-cooler carts available for rent.

Above: Baltimore (p331); Inner Harbor (p331)

THE MAIN AREAS

ANNAPOLIS
Maryland's historic, waterside capital.
p320

EASTERN SHORE
Islands, inlets and crabbing.
p325

OCEAN CITY
Boardwalk, barrier island and wild horses.
p329

Maryland

AMERICA IN MINIATURE

Maryland is packed with attractions: discover its long history and diverse landscapes, from tidal marshes and a dune-lined barrier island to quiet coves and forested mountains.

Straddling the historical divide between north and south and the topographical divide between east and west, Maryland mixes southern charm with northern savvy and an eastern shoreline with its western highlands. Wild horses wander amidst the dunes and coastal grasses on Assateague Island. Spring redbuds and fall foliage brighten the slopes of the Allegheny Mountains. Watermen ply their trade amidst the coves and waterways of Chesapeake Bay, whose bounty has been a source of livelihood for generations. Nineteenth-century drum rolls and battle cries seem to echo across the now-peaceful expanses of Maryland's Civil War battlefields around Frederick, recalling the state's pivotal border position between the Union and the Confederacy. In Baltimore, Maryland's commercial hub, creative chefs dish up some of the Mid-Atlantic's most exciting cuisine, while in Annapolis, the picturesque waterside capital, a fine collection of 18th-century buildings set the backdrop for museums, eateries and international-class boat shows. In Maryland's western panhandle, lively mountain towns, Deep Creek Lake, waterfalls and rivers offer year-round outdoor fun. Wherever you go, you'll find something for every taste and budget, all wrapped up in a small-enough package that you'll be able to sample everything with ease.

JAY YUAN/SHUTTERSTOCK ©

BALTIMORE
Art museums, historic ships and local culture.
p331

FREDERICK
Antique shops, mountain hikes and Civil War battlefields.
p336

WESTERN MARYLAND
C&O Canal, hiking and waterfalls.
p340

Find Your Way

Maryland is small enough that you can drive from one side to the other in a day, but so full of attractions that you'll likely want to allow considerably longer.

Annapolis, p320
Maryland's charming capital offers a wealth of 18th-century buildings, cobbled streets, a waterside setting and a sailing vibe.

Ocean City, p329
Walk for hours along the beach, enjoy the Ocean City boardwalk or camp on nearby Assateague Island with its wild horses.

Baltimore, p331
Grit meets sophistication in this rough-and-ready port city with its seafaring roots, fine museums and 'Bawlmer' culture.

Eastern Shore, p325
Immerse yourself in the watermen's way of life amid the islands, inlets and small towns of Chesapeake Bay's Eastern Shore.

Frederick, p336
Browse the art galleries and antique shops, hike at Catoctin Mountain and explore Civil War battlefields.

Western Maryland, p340
Hike, snow-tube and ski around Deep Creek Lake, cycle along the C&O Canal or take a scenic train ride around Cumberland.

CAR & BUS
Check visitmaryland.org for scenic byway routes. Bay Runner Shuttle links Baltimore and BWI Airport with Ocean City, Cambridge, Frederick and Cumberland. Flixbus connects Washington, DC and Annapolis. Maryland Transit Administration (mta. maryland.gov) has commuter bus info to/from Baltimore.

TRAIN
MARC commuter trains link Washington, DC with Baltimore and Frederick. Amtrak's Capitol Limited runs between Washington, DC and Cumberland. Check the Maryland Transit Administration for all connections. The **Western Maryland Scenic Railroad (p340)** links Cumberland with Frostburg.

Swallow Falls State Park (p342)

Plan Your Time

Annapolis and the Eastern Shore are unique, and make an ideal focus if you only have a day or two in the state. With more time, linger along the coast or enjoy the western mountains.

If You Do One Thing

- After exploring **Annapolis** (p320), cross the Bay Bridge and make your way to the area around the charming towns of St Michaels, Bellevue and Oxford, using the seasonal ferry to make a loop. If time permits, extend your journey south to take in Cambridge, the **Harriet Tubman Underground Railroad Visitor Center** (p325) and **Blackwater National Wildlife Refuge** (p326).

One Week or More

- Expand the other itinerary to spend more time on the Eastern Shore before heading to **Assateague Island National Seashore** (p329) and the coast. Then recross the Bay Bridge and detour to **Historic St Mary's City** (p323) before visiting **Baltimore** (p331) and around **Frederick** (p336). Continue onto **Cumberland** (p340) and **Deep Creek Lake** (p341).

SEASONAL HIGHLIGHTS

SPRING
Crab season begins with May's first full moon. Annapolis celebrates May Day with flowers, and horse-racing culminates.

SUMMER
Hot days, thunderstorms and black-eyed Susans (Maryland's state flower). It's also peak season for plates of blue crabs.

FALL
Late September and early October bring glorious foliage, especially around Frederick and Western Maryland.

WINTER
It's easy to forget Maryland's winter weather when the snow decides to fall, bringing snow-tubing and cross-country ski.

Annapolis

HISTORIC BUILDINGS | WATERSIDE DINING | SAILING CAPITAL

GETTING AROUND

Walking is the best way to get around. Nothing is too far away and there's plenty to discover. There are also buses, a **water taxi** linking the City Dock with Eastport, and the Free Downtown Shuttle (Magenta Shuttle) linking parking areas with downtown. During the warmer months, the Annapolis–Eastport drawbridge (Compromise Bridge) opens up every 30 minutes outside of rush hour to let boat traffic through.

☑ TOP TIP

If you're interested in sailing, time your visit to catch a boat show *(annapolisboatshows. com)*. For a profusion of blooms, visit in early May, when Annapolis homes and shops are decorated with baskets of May Day flowers. In April, don't miss the **Annapolis Cup croquet** match between students at the US Naval Academy and St John's College.

With its cobbled central area, 18th-century architecture, sailing and waterside setting, Annapolis easily ranks as one of the Mid-Atlantic's most charming capitals. It's a walkable place, with quaint streets radiating from its City Dock. Wherever you wander, Chesapeake Bay, with its whitecaps and circling gulls, is never far away. Get a feel for things in a day or two, taking in the daily parade of boats on Ego Alley, rubbing shoulders with the well-heeled at one of Annapolis' annual sailboat shows and mingling with midshipmen from the US Naval Academy. Across Spa Creek from the City Dock is Eastport, which is part of Annapolis, though there's a long-standing, albeit lighthearted, rivalry between the two towns, culminating in 1998 when Eastport declared its 'independence.'

Sailboats & Duck Decoys

America's largest estuary

Maryland is almost split in two by the massive Chesapeake Bay, the largest estuary in the US. Starting near the Pennsylvania border, it extends about 200 miles into southern Virginia. Its 11,000-mile-plus shoreline takes in countless secluded coves and quiet peninsulas and provides a habitat for ospreys, blue herons and many other birds and animals, while its waters, with their abundant crabs, oysters and other marine life, have provided a livelihood for generations. The bay also offers some of the state's most sublime scenery, with quiet sunrises, blazing sunsets, picturesque waterside towns and a handful of islands. Annapolis is an ideal jumping-off point for exploring, with **Schooner Woodwind** (schoonerwoodwind.com) and **Watermark** (watermarkjourney.com) offering cruises from the City Dock.

At the bay's northernmost end, is the pretty town of **Havre de Grace**. This is the self-proclaimed 'decoy capital of the world,' where the waterfowl hunter's staple skill of decoy carving has been elevated to an art form. Stop in at the **Havre de Grace Decoy Museum** to open doors onto the area's rich history of decoy carving.

ACTIVITIES, COURSES & TOURS
1 Schooner Woodwind

SLEEPING
2 Capital Hotel
3 Historic Inns of Annapolis
4 Inn on Main

EATING
● see 4 Chick & Ruth's Delly
5 Osteria 177
6 Reynold's Tavern

DRINKING & NIGHTLIFE
7 Dry 85

ENTERTAINMENT
8 Annapolis Cup Croquet

TRANSPORT
9 Water Taxi

Maryland's Native American Heritage
A rich tapestry of history

Chesapeake, Choptank, Patuxent, Potomac – these and other Maryland place names hint at the rich array of Algonquian-speaking peoples who once inhabited eastern North America. In 1666, Maryland colonists signed the Articles of Peace and Amity with representatives of a dozen indigenous nations. To discover Native American heritage, past and present, visit the Woodland Indian Hamlet at **Historic St Mary's City** (p323), the **Nanticoke River Discovery Center** in Vienna, the **Baltimore American Indian Center**, or paddle some of the Nanticoke River Water Trail around Vienna.

 EATING & DRINKING IN ANNAPOLIS: OUR PICKS

Chick & Ruth's Delly: This informal eatery is an Annapolis institution, featuring hugely portioned sandwiches and all-day breakfasts. $	**Osteria 177:** This popular place draws in guests with a convenient Main St location, authentic Italian cuisine and chilled but welcoming vibe. $$	**Reynold's Tavern:** Ambience is key at this 18th-century tavern, whether in the cozy 1747 Pub, the upper tearoom or the beer garden.	**Forward Brewing:** In Eastport, with sidewalk seating, an airy taproom, good food and good beer brewed on-site.
Vin 909: An intimate, casual ambience, seasonal neo-American cuisine and a pleasant Eastport setting make this a perennial favorite. $$	**Jimmy Cantler's Riverside Inn:** This longstanding place still delivers if you're looking for a typical Maryland seafood meal. $$	**The Point Crab House & Grill:** Fresh seafood and a waterside setting draw the crowds. It's north of Annapolis in Arnold. $$	**Dry 85:** A speakeasy-style place known also for its homestyle gourmet food and Sunday bacon brunches.

ANNAPOLIS WALKING TOUR

Dating to the late 18th century, Maryland's ❶ **State House** is the oldest state capitol in continuous legislative. Atop its dome is an upside-down acorn symbolizing wisdom. The building is open daily for self-guided tours (with photo ID). Just beyond is Church Circle, with ❷ **St Anne's Episcopal church** (1692). Continue down Franklin St to the ❸ **Banneker-Douglass-Tubman Museum**, highlighting the achievements of Marylanders of African American ancestry. It's named after Frederick Douglass, Harriet Tubman and Benjamin Banneker, a notable astronomer and mathematician. The statue in front was created by Dr Joyce Scott to honor Tubman. Return past Church Circle before turning southeast on ❹ **Main St** At its eastern end is ❺ **City Dock** and the ❻ **Kunta Kinte–Alex Haley Memorial**, commemorating Kunta Kinte's 1767 arrival at this spot. The surrounding Story Wall has quotes on reconciliation and healing. Just beyond is the boat-turnaround channel known as ❼ **Ego Alley**, and bordering is Compromise St, leading over Spa Creek to Eastport and the ❽ **Annapolis Maritime Museum**. Back at City Dock, you'll pass ❾ **Market Sq** as you make your way to the ❿ **US Naval Academy**, where you can arrange walking or driving tours (in one of the academy's electric vehicles). Diagonally opposite is ⓫ **St John's College**, one of the US's oldest post-secondary institutions. From here, it's about 2 miles (but worth it) across the Severn River bridge to the ⓬ **WWII and Gold Star Families Memorial**, set on a rise overlooking the Severn. The spot is serene and moving, with beautiful river views and has the names of 6000-plus Marylanders who lost their lives during the war.

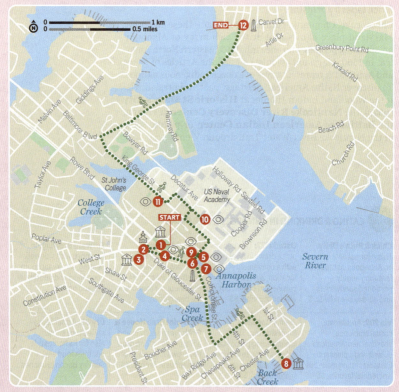

Beyond Annapolis

From Annapolis, almost all roads lead to the bay. Most visitors head across the 4-mile Bay Bridge to Ocean City. For something quieter, travel south to discover colonial Maryland's roots.

If you're caught in rush-hour traffic, it can feel like a bit of a slog to get down to southern Maryland, the mostly rural peninsula south of Annapolis that is framed by the Potomac River to the west and Chesapeake Bay to the east. Yet, once you get past the congestion, things quieten down, landscapes open up and glimpses of the surrounding water become more frequent. This is the historic heart of the state, ancestral home of the indigenous Piscataway and Yaocomico and site of modern Maryland's first settlement. The vibe is down-to-earth and authentic, without the city-weekender feel of some destinations closer in to Annapolis, and roots run deep.

Places

Southern Maryland
p323

Southern Maryland

TIME FROM ANNAPOLIS: **2 HOURS**

Colonial-ra Life in Historic St Mary's City

On March 23, 1634, the Yaocomico people living in what is now southern Maryland were surprised by the arrival of a 40-ton-capacity English ship, the *Dove*, which – together with its larger sister ship, *Ark* – tied up at St Clement's Island after several months at sea. The Yaocomico welcomed the new arrivals, who – in exchange for cloth, tools and other items – were given permission to settle on land around 15 miles southeast, on a low cliff overlooking St Mary's River. With significant help from the Yaocomico, they began settling in and constructing what was to become Maryland's first capital. Life in the early years of the settlement is commemorated at the **Historic St Mary's City** open-air site. You can walk around and into reconstructions of many of the original buildings, including the 1676 State House and some personal dwellings, and read detailed descriptions of life here during the colony's early days. There's also the Woodland Indian Hamlet, which aims to portray the daily life of the Yaocomico.

GETTING AROUND

Public transportation to and within southern Maryland is scarce. Having your own vehicle is definitely the best way to get around. From Annapolis, follow Rte 4 across the Governor Thomas Johnson Bridge from Solomons, a popular stop-off for a seafood meal. For the return journey, mix things up by taking Rte 5 north to Leonardtown.

323

Point Lookout State Park

JOUSTING

How cool is it to have jousting as your state sport? Jousting in Maryland traces its earliest roots to the 17th century, though it wasn't until the 19th century that it began to gain in popularity, with ring jousting tournaments – where a rider on a cantering horse aims to spear a series of successively smaller rings – being held on country estates. Jousting was named Maryland's official sport in 1962 (a title it's struggling to hold onto against its team-sport rival, lacrosse) and though much diminished in recent years, it still has loyal followers. Check with the Maryland Jousting Tournament Association (marylandjousting.com) for upcoming events.

Anchored in the river down below is a life-sized replica of the *Dove*, which you can board and tour. While visiting, watch for the nationally ranked St Mary's College sailing team training offshore.

About 10 miles south of St Mary's City, where the Potomac River flows into Chesapeake Bay, is **Point Lookout State Park**, the site of a medical center for wounded Union soldiers during the Civil War and now a quiet area of pines and marshes. Its camping area is currently closed for renovations, but the setting is peaceful and, in season, there's a half-day ferry excursion to and from Smith Island (p328), which lies about two hours southeast of Point Lookout in the bay.

EATING IN SOUTHERN MARYLAND: OUR PICKS

Courtney's Seafood Restaurant: This fish shack doesn't look like much, but the freshly caught crabs and rockfish are delicious. **$**

Front Porch: Southern coastal cuisine in Leonardtown, with Maryland favorites such as house-smoked pork belly and crab cakes. **$$**

The Pier: For waterside views, you can't go wrong at the Pier, overlooking the Patuxent River with prime sunset seating. **$$**

CD Cafe: A pleasant place with a creative fusion menu and an emphasis on seafood. It's along Solomons Island Rd. *hours vary* **$$**

Eastern Shore

CRABS | WATERWAYS | UNDERGROUND RAILROAD

Until the opening of the first Chesapeake Bay Bridge in 1952, the Eastern Shore remained a place set apart, shaped by the moods and seasons of the bay and seldom visited by outsiders, except for holidaymakers en route to Ocean City. Today, the area has most definitely been discovered, but despite the influxes of weekend and summer crowds, its small crabbing and oystering communities have managed to maintain their traditional way of life. As the birthplace of underground railroad heroine Harriet Tubman and abolitionist Frederick Douglass, and home to Civil Rights leader Gloria Richardson Dandridge, the Eastern Shore also has long historical roots, and is an ideal spot to immerse yourself in Maryland's African American heritage.

Plan on at least several days to explore, visiting picturesque towns such as St Michaels and Oxford, calling in at the county hub of Easton, learning about the waterman's life in Crisfield, following the Harriet Tubman Byway and taking in the birdlife around Blackwater National Wildlife Refuge.

The Underground Railroad
Suffering and heroism in the search for freedom

The underground railroad was a secret network of people and safe houses that offered support and assistance to enslaved people who were trying to escape bondage by fleeing north or into Canada. During the early to mid-19th century, hundreds of mostly unsung heroes, Black and white, helped what is estimated to be thousands of enslaved people to reach freedom. One of the most famous 'conductors' of the underground railroad was Harriet Tubman (1822–1913), who was born and lived in the rural area around Cambridge before managing to escape. Later, she travelled back repeatedly to the Eastern Shore to help her family and friends to safety. Her story is movingly portrayed in the excellent **Harriet Tubman Underground Railroad Visitor Center**, about 10 miles south of Cambridge on the edge of the Blackwater National Wildlife Refuge. Start here, or in the smaller

GETTING AROUND

Once away from Rte 50, many of the Eastern Shore's backroads are quiet, scenic and ideal for cycling, although only a handful have shoulders. Bikes can be rented in Easton, St Michaels and Cambridge, with advance bookings advised throughout. For public transportation, the MUST bus has a handful of routes, including between Easton, Cambridge and St Michaels, while Shore Transit links Salisbury (which is served by Greyhound and the Bay Runner Shuttle) with Crisfield, Berlin and Ocean City.

☑ TOP TIP

Eastern Shore destinations can get crowded during summer weekends, with traffic on the Bay Bridge extending for miles. Visit offseason or during the week to better experience the area's charm.

TOP SIGHTS
1. Blackwater National Wildlife Refuge

SIGHTS
2. Chesapeake Bay Maritime Museum
3. Harriet Tubman Museum & Education Center
4. Harriet Tubman Underground Railroad Visitor Center
5. Nanticoke River Discovery Center

ACTIVITIES, COURSES & TOURS
6. Blackwater Adventures

SLEEPING
7. Black Walnut Point Inn
8. Old Brick Inn
9. Robert Morris Inn
10. Whitehaven Hotel

EATING
11. 4 Sisters Kabob & Curry
- see 11 Bas Rouge
- see 8 Bistro St Michaels
- see 3 Carmela's Cucina
12. Old Salty's
- see 11 Out of the Fire
- see 3 RaR Brewing
- see 9 Scottish Highland Creamery

TRUE BLUE CRAB

Throughout Maryland, you can be sure you're eating crab meat from real Maryland crabs by watching for the True Blue logo on restaurants. This certifies that the majority of the crab meat served is locally sourced. Not many restaurants participate in this voluntary program, but when you do find one, it's worth supporting.

Harriet Tubman Museum & Education Center in Cambridge, to learn about Tubman's life and work. Afterwards, embark (with your own transport) on the Harriet Tubman Underground Railroad Byway (harriettubmanbyway.org), a 125-mile, self-guided driving tour taking you north from Cambridge, roughly following the course of the Choptank River into Delaware and on to Philadelphia, where Tubman settled after reaching freedom. En route are 45 stops, with markers describing the significance of each site. You can also pick up a comprehensive Driving Tour Guide from the visitor center. Even doing part of the byway offers an excellent immersion into the conditions faced along the way by early 'passengers,' as the escaping enslaved people were called in coded language.

Marshlands & Bird-Filled Skies at Blackwater
Year-round birding

One of the Eastern Shore's lesser-known attractions is **Blackwater National Wildlife Refuge**, which was established in 1933 to protect feeding and resting areas for migrating birds along the Atlantic Flyway – one of the USA's four major migratory bird flyways – that stretches at its extremes from Greenland into South

Blackwater National Wildlife Refuge

America. Blackwater is a serene spot that's worth visiting at any time, but is at its peak in late fall, when ducks, geese and tundra swans arrive by the thousands from points north, joined by bald and golden eagles. The area of the refuge open for exploration is relatively small, but beautiful. If the weather is inclement, head indoors to the visitor center, where you can look out over the marshes and (depending on the season) watch live camera footage of bald eagle hatchlings and eaglets, or of nesting ospreys. In the warmer months, you can rent kayaks or bicycles from **Blackwater Adventures**' (blackwateradventuresmd.com) on-site shop and ride one of the mapped 20- to 25-mile cycling routes, or paddle along the waterways spreading out just south of the visitor center. There are also short (less than 1 mile) walking trails and a 4-mile mapped wildlife drive. While there's no camping at the refuge, it's possible to get a taste of its nighttime serenity by booking one of the monthly (weather-dependent) night-sky tours offered by **Friends of Blackwater** (friendsofblackwater.org).

ATTRACTIONS FOR KIDS

Take a **sightseeing cruise** in Annapolis or Baltimore (watermarkjourney.com).

Watch a boat being constructed at the **Chesapeake Bay Maritime Museum**.

Visit Baltimore's **Port Discovery Children's Museum** (younger kids) or the **Maryland Science Center** (all ages).

Call in at the **Harriet Tubman Underground Railroad Visitor Center** or the **Fort McHenry National Monument and Historic Shrine**.

Hike, ski or swim at **Deep Creek Lake** (p341).

Spend time at the beach at **Ocean City** (p329) and see the wild horses at **Assateague**.

Cycle on the trails around **Cumberland** (340), or take a ride on the scenic **railroad**.

EATING ON THE EASTERN SHORE: OUR PICKS

Scottish Highland Creamery: In Oxford, and an essential stop for ice-cream lovers, with premium homemade flavors. **$**	**4 Sisters Kabob & Curry:** Maryland has one of the highest rates of foreign-born residents, meaning delicious ethnic cuisine, like this Easton food truck. **$**	**Carmela's Cucina:** Carmela's is the place to go in Cambridge for tasty pizza and homestyle Italian-American cuisine. **$$**	**Old Salty's:** Pull up by boat or vehicle for hearty, homestyle crab and meat dishes and to catch up on local gossip. **$$**
RaR Brewing: Craft brews and American pub-style dining in Cambridge. **$$**	**Bas Rouge:** European-style fine dining in Easton, prepared by 2024 James Beard award-winning chef Harley Peet. **$$$**	**Bistro St Michaels:** Eastern Shore dining with a French touch, including multicourse menus and a delicious seafood gumbo. **$$$**	**Out of the Fire:** Sustainable, farm-to-table dining in Easton, with a global array of dishes. **$$$**

EASTERN SHORE DRIVING TOUR

Follow Rte 50 from Annapolis to historic ❶ **Easton** and then Rte 33 to ❷ **St Michaels**, with its shop-and-eatery-lined main street and the Chesapeake Bay Maritime Museum. Continue towards tiny ❸ **Bellevue** and catch the seasonal vehicle ferry (dating to 1683) across the Tred Avon River to ❹ **Oxford**, also dating to 1683 and one of Maryland's oldest towns. Continue southeast towards ❺ **Cambridge**. Although the town's entry is uninspiring, its historic center has plenty to offer, including the Choptank River lighthouse, a replica of the original 1870s structure. Continue along Rtes 16 and 335, detouring to quiet ❻ **Hooper's Island** for a slice of local life. Return on Rte 335 to ❼ **Blackwater National Wildlife Refuge** (p326) and the neighboring ❽ **Harriet Tubman Underground Railroad Visitor Center** (p325) before rejoining Rte 50 near Vienna to the fledgling ❾ **Nanticoke River Discovery Center.** Leave Rte 50 at Salisbury towards ❿ **Crisfield**, a working watermen's town known for its September crab festivals – the Hard Crab Derby (nationalhardcrabderby.com) and the Tawes Crab and Clam Bake. Crisfield is the departure point for boats to ⓫ **Smith Island**, 7 miles offshore. The ferry can be booked at Captain Tyler Motel near the dock; alternatively, enquire about local boats doing the crossing. Smith Island is known for its distinctive old English accent, its multilayered Smith Island cake and its traditional way of life. Day trips are possible, but an overnight stay is better to get a feel for local life. Back on the mainland, spend a few days around ⓬ **Ocean City** and ⓭ **Assateague Island**, where you can arrange kayaking with Ayers Creek Adventures (ayerscreekadventures.com) or Assateague Outfitters (assateagueoutfitters.com).

Ocean City

SEA BREEZES | BOARDWALK | ASSATEAGUE ISLAND

Especially in August, it can seem as if the population of the Washington, DC metropolitan area has descended on Ocean City. But don't let that dissuade you. In the offseason, you'll have the long, wide beach almost to yourself, and even in season, the sea air, surf and cooler temperatures are a balm. If you're a fan of boardwalks, Ocean City's two-mile-plus boardwalk is one of the region's best, with a wheelchair-friendly surface (beach wheelchair rentals are also available), the Giant (Ferris) Wheel, arcades, rides, waterslides and amusements. Tiny Berlin (pronounced BUR-lin), about nine miles inland, has an eminently walkable historic town center. About 10 miles south of Ocean City is Assateague Island, with low dunes, long stretches of sand and surf and a population of wild horses that dates back more than 300 years.

The Wild Horses of Assateague

Dunes, seascapes and free-roaming horses

The alluring image of wild horses galloping free across the sand is true – or almost true – on Assateague Island, a 37-mile-long narrow barrier island stretching from just south of Ocean City into Virginia. Its population of wild horses, currently estimated to number about 80 on the Maryland side, is thought to be descended from domesticated horses brought to the area in the 17th century. While they may not be galloping on the beach, you'll almost certainly see them during your time on the island. They are beautiful, though visitors have been bitten and injured, so keep your distance.

Horses aren't the island's only attraction. Especially in summer, you may see dolphins playing in the sea just offshore, and egrets and herons are frequently spotted, especially on the bay side. To get the most out of your Assateague stay, stop in at the excellent **National Seashore Visitor Center** before crossing the bridge to the island. Its displays about the island and its ecosystems are highly informative. Once on the island, there are two sections: **Assateague Island State Park** to the north, and the larger **Assateague Island National Seashore** to the south. During the warmer months, you can rent bicycles and kayaks in the park with **Assateague Outfitters** (assateagueoutfitters.com),

GETTING AROUND

Ocean City has ride-hailing services (Uber and Lyft) and the Ocean City Beach Bus runs along the Coastal Hwy to 144th St (no winter service). In summer season, there's also the Boardwalk Tram. There's a **Park & Ride** lot in West Ocean City, with free shuttle service to/from South Division St, at the boardwalk's southern end. To Assateague, it's a flat, easy bike ride from Ocean City. Once on the island, there's a paved 4-mile out-and-back trail.

☑ TOP TIP

For camping at Assateague Island, make bookings up to six months in advance, especially for weekends; spots fill quickly. Note that backcountry (walk-in) campsites can't be reserved; it's first-come, first-served only. If you're camping in summer, be prepared for mosquitoes and other biting insects. Repellent and/or protective clothing is essential.

OCEAN CITY MARYLAND

THE GUIDE

TOP SIGHTS
1. Assateague Island National Seashore

SIGHTS
2. Assateague Island State Park
3. Henry Hotel
4. Ocean City Life-Saving Station Museum

SLEEPING
5. Assateague Island Campground
6. Atlantic Hotel
7. Days Inn Ocean City Oceanfront
8. Holland House
9. King Charles Hotel

EATING
10. Berlin Farmers Market
11. Blacksmith Restaurant & Bar
12. Blue Fish
13. Hobbit Restaurant
14. Island Creamery
15. Ripieno's Italian Bistro
16. Sunset Grille

DRINKING & NIGHTLIFE
17. Burley Oak Brewing Co

ENTERTAINMENT
18. Jolly Roger at the Pier
19. Trimper Rides

INFORMATION
20. Assateague Island National Seashore Visitor Center

TRANSPORT
21. Assateague Outfitters
22. Park & Ride

and hiking is possible year-round. There are campsites on both the bay and ocean sides, including rustic walk-in (or kayak-in) sites. While winter visits are for the hardy, the island's magic and serenity are easier to feel with fewer visitors around. Summer brings warmth and crowds, while spring and fall are both lovely, with fewer visitors and insects.

EATING & DRINKING AROUND OCEAN CITY: OUR PICKS

Berlin Farmers Market: The emphasis is on fresh, homemade and artisanal. $	**Island Creamery:** Try flavors such as Java Jolt and Key Lime Pie – all homemade at the Chincoteague (Virginia) main shop. $$	**Blacksmith Restaurant & Bar:** A Berlin favorite, with craft beer, well-prepared farm-to-table dishes and a laid-back vibe. $$	**Blue Fish:** Sushi and Asian-fusion cuisine along Ocean City's main drag. $$
Ripieno's Italian Bistro: Probably Ocean City's best (and biggest) pizzas. Also has sandwiches, subs and platters. $$	**Sunset Grille:** This sprawling West Ocean City place packs in the crowds with bay views and weekend live entertainment. $$	**Burley Oak Brewing Co:** Berlin microbrewery with live music and hearty fare, such as pulled-beef sandwiches and Chesapeake crab melts.	**Hobbit Restaurant:** Long-standing Ocean City restaurant with views over Assawoman Bay and a creative seafood-oriented menu. $$$

Baltimore

MUSEUMS | GREAT DINING | FORT MCHENRY

'Welcome to Bawlmer, Hon.' Maryland's largest city and major port and commercial hub is a mix of grit and sophistication, with a down-to-earth vibe and its own unique twist on the English language. It offers much to do, whatever your tastes and budget. Surround yourself with art at world-class museums and dine on some of Maryland's best cuisine. Learn about the stars and unearth dinosaur fossils at the Maryland Science Center and Davis Planetarium. Take a water taxi to Fort McHenry and relive the night that inspired Francis Scott Key to compose what is now the US national anthem. Step aboard the USS *Constellation*. See marine life galore at the National Aquarium and go pub-hopping at Fells Point, one of the city's oldest neighborhoods. Whatever you choose, embrace Baltimore's spirit, accept its congestion and settle in to discover its endless layers. Soon you, too, will be ending your sentences with 'hon' and speaking Bawlmerese like a Baltimorean.

A Day Around the Inner Harbor

Historic ships, aquarium and Fells Point

The Inner Harbor is Baltimore's tourist hub and a convenient jumping-off point for exploring the city. If it's a clear day, start with a bird's-eye view of the city from the **Top of the World observation deck** at the Baltimore World Trade Center before choosing between the nearby **National Aquarium**, considered to be one of the best in the US, or a visit to the Inner Harbor's **historic ships**. In addition to the USS *Constellation* – the US Navy's last sail-only warship, notable also for its role in working to halt the foreign slave trade – these include the USS *Torsk* submarine, the lightship *Chesapeake* and US Coast Guard Cutter 37, all of which you can board and tour.

Continuing around the west side of the Inner Harbor, you'll reach the **Maryland Science Center** and Davis Planetarium, which are particularly good stops if you're travelling with kids. There's also an adventure playground next door.

GETTING AROUND

Baltimore's light rail runs from **BWI airport** to Lexington Market and Mt Vernon/Center St (for Penn Station) and MARC commuter trains run between BWI, **Penn Station** and Washington, DC. For schedules and fares, see mta.maryland.gov. In good weather, the Baltimore Water Taxi (baltimorewatertaxi.com) is a great option, with free connector service around the Inner Harbor and a paid route to Fort McHenry. There's also the free Charm City Circulator bus, serving downtown neighborhoods, plus regular metro buses, taxis, Uber and Lyft.

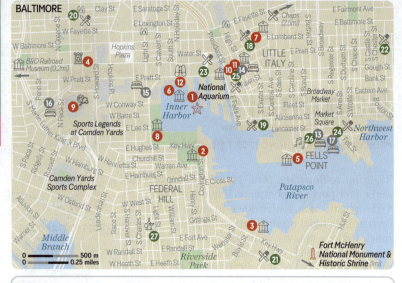

TOP SIGHTS
1. National Aquarium

SIGHTS
2. American Visionary Art Museum
3. Baltimore Museum of Industry
4. Bromo Seltzer Tower
5. Frederick Douglass-Isaac Meyers Maritime Park
6. Historic Ships in Baltimore
7. Jewish Museum of Maryland
8. Maryland Science Center
9. Oriole Park at Camden Yards
10. Reginald F Lewis Museum
11. Star-Spangled Banner Flag House
12. Top of the World Observation Deck

SLEEPING
13. Admiral Fell Inn
14. BlancNoir
15. Hyatt Regency Baltimore Inner Harbor
16. Rachael's Dowry B&B
17. Sagamore Pendry

EATING
18. Attman's Deli
19. Charleston
20. Faidley Seafood
● see 20 Lexington Market
21. Locust Point Steamers
22. Marta
23. Mt Everest
24. Thames Street Oyster House
25. Vaccaro's Italian Pastry

DRINKING & NIGHTLIFE
26. Horse You Came In On
27. Muir's Tavern

☑ TOP TIP

As enjoyable as Baltimore's Inner Harbor is, don't limit your visit to this area. It's well worth exploring further afield to really get a feel for the city. A number of Baltimore museums are closed on Monday and/or Tuesday, so plan accordingly.

Just beyond is Baltimore's Federal Hill neighborhood, and the community-oriented **American Visionary Art Museum**. Featuring the work of self-taught artists, including homemade robots and matchstick models, this place will challenge your ideas of both museums and art. Just beyond is the **Baltimore Museum of Industry**, a fascinating place focused on the city's entrepreneurs and inventors, with live demos and hands-on activities. Once finished, head around to the harbor's east side, past cruise operators and paddle boats, to the mostly open-air **Frederick Douglass-Isaac Meyers Maritime Park** and to **Fells Point**, a former shipbuilding hub known for its ethnic neighborhoods, cobbled streets, restaurants and pubs. In the evenings, Fells Point is as good as it gets around the Inner Harbor. Another option is to catch an Orioles game at nearby **Oriole Park at Camden Yards** stadium.

Frederick Douglass-Isaac Meyers Maritime Park

Museum Round-Up
From railroad memorabilia to art

Baltimore has enough museums to keep you busy for months. The city's art museums are a highlight, starting with the free **Baltimore Museum of Art**, known for its superb Matisse collection and its important collection of African art. About 3 miles south of here, in the Mt Vernon neighborhood, is the equally wonderful, and also free, **Walters Art Museum**, with permanent collections that span continents and millennia, from ancient Egypt to Renaissance Europe, illustrated Islamic manuscripts and an impressive collection of medieval arms and armor. From here, it's about 1.5 miles southeast to the edge of the Little Italy neighborhood – well worth a stroll, if only to sample a pastry at **Vaccaro's Italian Pastry** – and the **Reginald F Lewis Museum** of African American history and culture. For more on African American history,

FREDERICK DOUGLASS

Frederick Douglass, the famed abolitionist, writer, orator and civil-rights activist, was born around 40 miles east of Annapolis on the Eastern Shore, near Tuckahoe Creek, but came to Baltimore for five years as a child to work in the shipyards at Fells Point, and again when he was 18. It was from Baltimore that he escaped by train to Pennsylvania and freedom, although he remained proud of his Eastern Shore roots throughout his life.

EATING & DRINKING IN BALTIMORE: BEST FOR AMBIENCE

Mt Everest: Large portions of tasty Nepali and Indian dishes near the Inner Harbor. $	**Clavel Mezcaleria and Taqueria:** Known for its mescals, Clavel also has top-notch, traditional-style tacos, expertly simmered and seasoned. $$	**La Cuchara:** Well-prepared Basque cuisine in an atmospheric setting. $$	**WC Harlan:** Vintage, speakeasy-style cocktail bar in Remington neighborhood.
Thames Street Oyster House: Get your fill of oysters and other seafood at this iconic Fells Point eatery. $$	**Woodberry Tavern:** Small but elegant dinner and Sunday brunch menus featuring local produce, seafood and meats. $$$	**Charleston:** Take advantage of the small-plate approach here to maximize your culinary experience. $$$	**Helmand:** A Baltimore institution serving Afghan cuisine, such as *kaddo borwani* (pumpkin in yoghurt-garlic sauce) and *aush* (soup). $$$

333

BALTIMORE INSIDER TIPS

Jon Patrick Leary, a Baltimorean, recommends the following. *facebook.com/jon.p.leary*

Attman's Deli:
It's 100-plus years of age and like delis in NYC.

Club Charles:
Come for cocktails. Blondie, Johnny Depp, and more have visited.

Bromo Seltzer Tower:
You can get behind the big clock face.

Lexington Market:
One of the country's oldest markets.

Schultz's Crab House:
An old-school rarity; it's about 10 miles from Baltimore in Essex.

Koco's Pub:
Best crab cakes around.

Ash Bar:
Think velvet bar stools and a mirrored ceiling.

Baltimore Museum of Industry:
A tourist destination, but still well worth a visit.

Muir's Tavern:
A real dive bar, but not one you'll find on any list of dive bars.

also check out the simple but thought-provoking **National Great Blacks in Wax Museum**, spotlighting famous figures such as Jackie Robinson as well as lesser-known figures such as Maryland-born explorer Matthew Henson. For more niche interests, try the **B&O Railroad Museum** with its old locomotives and roundhouse, or the **Evergreen Museum**, offering glimpses into upper-class Baltimore life during the 1800s. Surrounding it are expansive, landscaped grounds and the campuses of several universities. The **Jewish Museum of Maryland**, under renovation at the time of writing, offers tours of two well-preserved synagogues that open doors into the history of Jewish Baltimore.

Fort McHenry

O say can you see, by the dawn's early light...

On a dark, rainy night in September 1814, American lawyer Francis Scott Key found himself stuck on a ship in the Patapsco River, watching as the British attacked Fort McHenry

EATING IN BALTIMORE: RELIABLE CHOICES

Faidley Seafood: This long-standing place at Lexington Market is famous for its crab cakes and other seafood. **$$**

Alma Cocina Latina: Creatively prepared and beautifully presented Latin American cuisine, with a focus on Venezuelan dishes. **$$**

Dukem: A branch of the Washington, DC restaurant, featuring well-seasoned Ethiopian cuisine, with vegetarian and non-veg options. **$$**

Marta: Creative, intimate and upmarket Italian dining in an early 20th-century building in the Butchers Hill neighborhood. **$$$**

Fort McHenry

during the War of 1812 as part of their efforts to seize control of Baltimore. When dawn finally came, Key's incredulity, joy, pride and gratitude at seeing the giant (30ft by 42ft) American flag still waving over the fort, despite the heavy shelling, prompted him to pen the stanzas of a poem, which he called *The Defense of Fort M'Henry*. The poem's title was later changed to *The Star-Spangled Banner* and, in 1931, its words became the US national anthem. The whole series of events is commemorated at the **Fort McHenry National Monument and Historic Shrine**, starting with a short but moving film that concludes with a stirring rendition of the anthem, followed by time to wander the grounds and take in the views over the harbor. In town, at the **Star-Spangled Banner Flag House**, you can visit the house where seamstress Mary Pickersgill made the original Fort McHenry flag (which is now on display in the Smithsonian's **National Museum of American History** in Washington, DC).

CHARLES STREET

If you could pick one Baltimore street that encapsulates all the city has to offer, it would likely be Charles St, which runs north from the Inner Harbor for about 5 miles. En route, it takes you through the Bromo and Station North arts districts, historic Mt Vernon with its 178ft **Washington Monument** (climb to the top for views), several historic churches, including the neoclassical **Basilica of the Assumption**, the **Walters Art Museum** (p333) and the **Baltimore Museum of Art** (p333) before coming to the **Johns Hopkins University** campus. Just west of campus is **Hampden**, known for its hipster-creative working-class vibe and the vintage shops and eateries lining 'The Avenue' (W 36th St).

 EATING & DRINKING IN BALTIMORE: BEST FOR LOCAL FLAVOR

| **Horse You Came In On:** Live music, cowboy-saddle bar stools and the distinction of being one of Baltimore's oldest bars. | **R House:** This sleek food hall in Remington offers an array of cuisines, including Egyptian, Korean and Italian. **$** | **Chaps:** The go-to stop for pit beef (grilled, sliced top-round on a kaiser roll with 'tiger sauce' and onion slice). **$** | **Locust Point Steamers:** A classic Baltimore crab house, with a hometown vibe and tasty seafood. **$$** |

Frederick

CIVIL WAR HISTORY | AUTUMN FOLIAGE | MOUNTAIN HIKES

GETTING AROUND

There is commuter rail and bus service to Frederick, and free public bus service within Frederick town. However, there is no public transportation from Frederick to Catoctin Mountain Park, nor to Antietam or Monocacy battlefields. The rolling farm country around Frederick is laced with mapped bike routes (mostly on roads), including a scenic, 40-mile covered bridges route.

Heading northwest from Baltimore, you'll soon reach fertile, open country with orchards, pick-your-own pumpkins, cornfield mazes, wide valleys and rolling hills. Spend time in the historic hub of Frederick, which served briefly as Maryland's capital and which, during the height of the Civil War, was memorialized by abolitionist poet John Greenleaf Whittier in 'Barbara Frietchie':

Up from the meadows rich with corn,
Clear in the cool September morn,
The clustered spires of Frederick stand
Green-walled by the hills of Maryland.
Round about them orchards sweep,
Apple- and peach-tree fruited deep...

Today, Frederick is popular as a getaway from Baltimore and Washington, DC and as a jumping-off point for day hikes in the nearby Catoctin Mountain section of the Appalachians. Given Frederick's proximity to the Mason–Dixon line (the town lies about 20 miles south of the Pennsylvania border), the area is also rich in Civil War history, with the peacefulness of the grassy fields of Antietam and Monocacy belying a tragic past.

Antique Shops & Mountain Hikes
Exploring Frederick and Catoctin Mountain

Central Frederick's flat, orderly streets are ideal for exploring on foot. Boutiques, art galleries and antique shops line the old Market St, and music groups enliven the waterside promenade at **Carroll Creek Park**. Stop in at the visitor

TOP SIGHTS
1. Antietam National Battlefield

SIGHTS
2. Black Ankle Vineyards
3. Burnside Bridge
4. Carroll Creek Park
5. Catoctin Mountain Park
   • see 1 Dunker Church
6. Linganore Wine Cellars
7. Monocacy National Battlefield
8. National Museum of Civil War Medicine
   see 1 Observation Tower

EATING
9. Bentztown

10. The Ordinary Hen
11. Wine Kitchen

DRINKING & NIGHTLIFE
12. Carroll Creek Breweries

center at the eastern edge of town for an orientation, and then head a few blocks west towards Market St for shopping and dining. Along the way, watch for the **National Museum of Civil War Medicine**, which is particularly recommended if you'll also be visiting nearby Antietam National Battlefield (p338). On the first Saturday of the month, many of downtown Frederick's shops, galleries and eateries stay open late, with special exhibits, tastings and other events.

About 20 miles north of Frederick is **Catoctin Mountain Park**, home to the US presidential retreat, Camp David (though this entire area is closed to the public). The mountain is a popular destination for hikers, especially in spring, when pink-hued redbud blossoms and cascading greenery blanket the hillsides, and in fall, when the hills are ablaze with orange, yellow and red foliage. There are several short hiking trails at Catoctin that can be linked into circuits, including one approximately 4-mile loop (classified by the park service as 'semi-strenuous') taking in the 1419ft **Chimney Rock viewpoint**. In addition to camping or overnight cabins, you can also sleep at the primitive Adirondack Shelters, which are in Catoctin's northwestern corner and a 3-mile hike-in from the nearest car park.

☑ TOP TIP

Each July, Frederick is home to one of the US's few (perhaps the only) high-wheeled bike races *(highwheelrace.com)*. Watch the fun or, if you own one of these penny farthings, think about competing. For more modern velocipedes, there's the annual Tour de Frederick *(tourdefrederick.com)* in June.

GLEN ECHO CAROUSEL

If you're heading to Frederick from Washington, DC, take time for a detour to Maryland's **Glen Echo Park**. Its historic (and still operational) carousel – at its best on the park's annual Carousel Day in late April – became a focal point for the Civil Rights movement in 1960, when Black and white protesters joined forces and picketed for several months against Glen Echo's segregationist policies, until the park's owners finally announced that Glen Echo would be open to all visitors. The 2024 documentary film, *Ain't No Back to a Merry-Go-Round*, tells the story in detail.

Civil War History at Antietam
Hear the echoes of the Civil War

In the open, rolling farm country on the edge of Sharpsburg, about 25 miles northwest of Frederick, is **Antietam National Battlefield** (pronounced (an-TEE-tum), where an estimated 23,000 people were killed or injured in what is considered the bloodiest single-day conflict in US history. The battle marked the end of the southern attack aimed at Maryland and Washington, DC. It was also a significant turning point in the Civil War, and served as a springboard for Abraham Lincoln's Emancipation Proclamation. Today, surrounded by the battlefield's bucolic expanses, it's difficult to imagine the battle's carnage and suffering. To relive some of the

 EATING & DRINKING IN FREDERICK: CREATIVE CUISINE & CRAFT BEER

| **Carroll Creek Breweries:** Get introduced to Frederick's craft-beer culture at this cluster of breweries around Carroll Creek's eastern side. | **The Ordinary Hen:** Enjoy cornbread, squash-and-dumplings and other Appalachian cuisine, plus live music Fridays at the outdoor Shed. **$$** | **Wine Kitchen:** Local beef cuts of distinction, plus seafood and vegetarian options and curated wine pairings. **$$** | **Bentztown:** Southern cuisine goes upmarket at this place, where music is as much a draw as the menu. **$$** |

Monocacy National Battlefield

history and learn more about Antietam, start out at the visitor center, where there is an informative welcome film. It's then easy to explore the battlefield on a self-drive, self-guided tour, taking advantage of informative plaques at each of the designated stops. Alternatively, you can arrange in advance to take a guided tour. However you visit, don't miss the **Dunker Church**, **Burnside Bridge** and the **Observation Tower**, with wide views over the surrounding area. If you want to immerse yourself even more in Civil War history, the smaller **Monocacy National Battlefield**, site of a decisive battle for the national capital, is about 25 miles southeast of Antietam on Frederick's southeastern outskirts, and also well worth a stop. It has short walking trails and a similar self-guided-drive setup as Antietam.

BEST MARYLAND FESTIVALS

Maryland Renaissance Festival:
Weekends from August to October, Annapolis (*rennfest.com*).

Kunta Kinte Heritage Festival:
Commemorates Maryland's African and African American heritage (September, *kuntakinte.org*).

Baltimore Pride:
Takes place in June, with the Pride parade at its center (*baltimorepride.org*).

Annapolis Boat Show:
There are several, but October's remains one of the best (*annapolisboatshows.com*).

Deal Island Skipjack:
Race At Deal Island, with skipjack races and a parade (September).

Watermen Appreciation Day:
At Chesapeake Bay Maritime Museum, with seafood and a boat-docking contest (August).

Maryland Crab Cake Festival:
Sample Maryland's best crab cakes at Carroll County Farm Museum (October).

 DRINKING IN MARYLAND: WINERIES

| **Crow Vineyard:** Stay at the onsite B&B and sample the rosés at this scenic working farm; it's about 55 miles from Annapolis. | **Linganore Wine Cellars:** Notable for its Seventh Rosé, sustainability initiatives and vineyard tours; about 15 miles east of Frederick. | **Black Ankle Vineyards:** Enjoy the sustainably grown syrah and albariño; it's near Frederick. | **Boordy Vineyards:** Maryland's oldest winery, known for its dry and semi-dry wines; it's near Baltimore. |

Western Maryland

DEEP CREEK LAKE | SKIING | SCENIC RAILWAY

GETTING AROUND

The Bay Runner Shuttle will get you from Baltimore to Cumberland, but once there, car is the best way to get around and is the only practical way to reach Deep Creek Lake and other attractions west of Cumberland. Cumberland itself is easily walkable, especially its pedestrian-friendly historic central area, on and around Baltimore St. This area was being rehabilitated at the time of research, but is planned to soon reopen with bike racks and a lane accommodating bicycles and limited vehicle traffic. The **Western Maryland Scenic Railway** (p340) links Cumberland with Frostburg.

Maryland's western panhandle is mountain country, with low peaks, forested slopes, deep valleys, rivers, waterfalls and small rural towns. Thanks in part to the elevation, which averages about 2400ft near the West Virginia border, temperatures are markedly cooler and the air is fresh. Historically, this was a transit hub, especially around Cumberland, which marked the terminus of the C&O Canal and the start of the 19th-century National Road westwards towards Illinois. Today, Western Maryland is known for its year-round outdoor activities, especially around Deep Creek Lake. Spend days hiking and exploring around Swallow Falls and Herrington Manor State Parks, rafting on the upper Youghiogheny or skiing and snow-tubing at Wisp, Maryland's only ski resort. In the evenings, snuggle up against the chill in front of a warm fireplace and enjoy the stillness. Whatever you do, once you've acclimated, you're sure to love your time in this part of the state.

A Weekend in Cumberland

Crossroads of America

While tiny Cumberland's historical designation as 'Crossroads of America' might seem an exaggeration, the more you delve into the area's rich history, the more apt the name becomes. Start at the **Allegany Museum**, where the Crossroads of America exhibit covers everything from Cumberland's earliest inhabitants to its pivotal transportation position during the French and Indian War to the development of the C&O Canal and the B&O Railroad. From here, make your way over to the **Crossroads of America mural**, which stretches for 200ft along the wall in front of the train station. The plaza just beyond the mural marks the starting point for cycling both the C&O Canal towpath to Washington, DC and the **Great Allegheny Passage** trail to Pittsburgh, Pennsylvania. Back at the train station, check out the **Cumberland Visitor Center & Museum**, before taking the **Western Maryland Scenic**

SIGHTS
1. Allegany Museum
2. Crossroads of America Mural
3. Cumberland Visitor Center & Museum
4. Herrington Manor State Park
5. Swallow Falls State Park

ACTIVITIES, COURSES & TOURS
● see 3 Western Maryland Scenic Railroad

SLEEPING
6. Garrett Inn
7. Lakefront Lodge

EATING
8. Archie's Barbeque

9. Brenda's Pizzeria
10. Crabby Pig
11. Curtis' Coney Island Famous Wieners
12. Ristorante Ottaviani

DRINKING & NIGHTLIFE
● see 7 Canoe on the Run Cafe

13. Caporale's Bakery
14. Mountain State Brewing Co

TRANSPORT
15. Wheelz Up Adventures

Railroad – these days, a historic diesel train – to Frostburg (4½ hours return, including about 1½ hours in Frostburg). Finish up back in Cumberland with a walk around the historic central pedestrian area focused around Baltimore and Center Sts. It's lined with late-19th-century buildings and, especially in the summer, serves as Cumberland's town hub, with a farmers market and frequent sidewalk festivities.

Outdoor Adventures at Deep Creek Lake
Skiing, hiking, snow-tubing and river rafting

Maryland's westernmost corner is open, rural land, with wide valleys, low mountains and crisp country air with just a hint of pine. The focal point in these parts is the beautiful,

☑ TOP TIP

Life in Western Maryland seems to revolve around local festivals. Check out the event listings at garrettheritage.com. If you're around in October, don't miss the annual Autumn Glory Festival *(autumnglory.com)* in Oakland, about 8 miles southwest of Deep Creek Lake.

 EATING & DRINKING AROUND DEEP CREEK LAKE: OUR PICKS

Brenda's Pizzeria: Efficient service, tasty pizzas sold by the slice or whole and lake views. **$**

Mountain State Brewing Co: Wash down wood-fired flatbreads with a craft ale at this popular microbrewery.

Canoe on the Run Cafe: Popular breakfast spot near Wisp Resort with granola, oatmeal, chili omelets and more. Sit outdoors or in. **$**

Archie's Barbeque: Local-style place featuring a wide selection of smoked and barbecued meat. **$**

Swallow Falls State Park

CYCLING THE C&O CANAL

One of the Mid-Atlantic's great cycling trails runs between Washington, DC and Pittsburgh, first following the C&O Canal (184 miles) and then the Great Allegheny Passage (GAP; 149 miles). Cumberland's Canal Pl is the meeting point of the two. The three-season ride can be done in either direction, is mostly flat (with some gradual ascents/ descents around Cumberland) and is a great mix of nature and scenery. En route, there's rustic but free trail camping and a mix of public and private campgrounds. Alternatively, you can detour into nearby towns to stay at a hotel. Many cyclists do the trail independently, but if you want to arrange a tour, **Wheelz Up Adventures** in Cumberland can help with bike rentals and tours.

6-sq-mile **Deep Creek Lake**, with year-round activities and a low-key, family-oriented vibe. If the snow is falling, cross-country ski at **Herrington Manor State Park** (which has ski rentals; confirm in advance) or ski and snow-tube at Wisp Resort. In late spring (continuing until early fall), there's challenging rafting on the Upper Youghiogheny River around Friendsville. In summer, swim, SUP, boat and fish in the lake, and in any season hike at **Swallow Falls State Park**, where the shaded, 1.25-mile Canyon Trail will take you past stands of hemlock and Maryland's highest single-drop waterfall, **Muddy Creek Falls**, which is about 52ft high and wheelchair accessible. Don't expect roads lined with hotels and malls at Deep Creek Lake. Everything is low-key and subdued, with private-home rental generally the best accommodation option. There's a supermarket in tiny McHenry town, plus several small grocery shops and a handful of cozy restaurants. Fun fact: none of Maryland's lakes are natural. All, including Deep Creek Lake, were made by damming rivers.

 EATING IN CUMBERLAND: LOCAL STANDBYS

| **Caporale's Bakery:** Don't miss the pepperoni rolls, ramp rolls and other delicacies at this old-style Cumberland institution. $ | **Curtis' Coney Island Famous Wieners:** Serving hot dogs, burgers and its signature Coney Island sauce to a loyal clientele for over a century. $ | **Crabby Pig:** Crab cakes, cream of crab soup, pulled pork sandwiches and other seafood and meat dishes. $ | **Ristorante Ottaviani:** Enjoy wine tastings and well-prepared Italian-American cuisine in downtown Cumberland. $$ |

Places We Love to Stay

$ Budget $$ Midrange $$$ Top End

Annapolis   MAP p321

Inn on Main $$ In a central Main St location above **Chick & Ruth's Delly** (p321), with small, homey rooms. Breakfast included.

Historic Inns of Annapolis $$ Enjoy Annapolis' 18th-century architectural heritage at these three historic inns: Maryland Inn, Governor Calvert House and the Robert Johnson House.

Capital Hotel $$ A slick, six-room boutique hotel with contactless check-in, the Parley Room cocktail bar and two restaurants.

Eastern Shore   MAP p326

Whitehaven Hotel $$ This early 19th-century house overlooks the Wicomico River near Blackwater National Wildlife Refuge.

Black Walnut Point Inn $$$ Set serenely on its own at the tip of Tilghman Island, near St Michaels, with rooms, cabins and water views.

Robert Morris Inn $$$ In an early 18th-century building, this Oxford classic lays claim to the title of America's oldest full-service inn. Several rooms have views over the Tred Avon River, and there's an in-house restaurant.

Old Brick Inn $$$ A charming inn in St Michaels. Rooms have been impeccably renovated and some have a Jacuzzi.

Ocean City & Assateague Island   p330

Assateague Island Campground $ Basic facilities and sometimes-crowded camping, but you'll wake to unobstructed views of the sea or bay.

Days Inn Ocean City Oceanfront $ A good beachfront location at the northern end of the boardwalk and helpful staff. The beach-facing rooms are worth the extra money.

King Charles Hotel $ This aging but functional hotel is near the Ocean City boardwalk.

Holland House $$ Turn-of-the-20th-century property offering a central Berlin location and B&B-style accommodation. No children under 10.

Atlantic Hotel $$ This Ocean City classic has rooms of varying sizes, all decorated in period style, and the Bistro Bar restaurant.

Baltimore   p332

Rachael's Dowry B&B $$ Spacious rooms in a restored historic house near Camden Yards.

BlancNoir $$ In Little Italy and easy walking distance from the Inner Harbor, with spotless, comfortable rooms.

Hotel Revival $$ Well-located in the heart of trendy Mt Vernon, and billing itself as Baltimore's only boutique art hotel. There's also a rooftop restaurant.

Admiral Fell Inn $$ For a convenient Fells Point location with a smattering of nautical touches, consider staying at this old sailors' hotel. Rooms fronting Thames St can be loud late at night, when Fells Point is in full party mode.

Hyatt Regency Baltimore Inner Harbor $$ Popular family choice, with harbor views (request when booking), reasonable rates and a convenient Inner Harbor location.

Sagamore Pendry $$$ Directly overlooking the water in Fells Point, this place embraces Baltimore's history and culture, with local art on the walls and nautical and equestrian touches in the common areas.

Frederick   p337

Stayinfrederick.com $$ Manages three restored historic homes in downtown Frederick.

Western Maryland   p341

Garrett Inn $ This good-value place is conveniently located between Deep Creek Lake and Swallow Falls State Park. Most rooms come with two large beds.

Lakefront Lodge $$ Overlooking a small cove at the northern end of Deep Creek Lake. Rooms have water views and some have fireplaces.

Inn on Decatur $$ This biker-friendly B&B is near the trails in Cumberland. Management also runs the nearby budget- and cyclist-friendly 9 Decatur Guest House.

343

Virginia

A TIME-TESTED, EVER-EVOLVING 'OLD DOMINION'

This is Virginia, where mountain, ocean and historic city landscapes intertwine, storied pasts are told and a vibrant new chapter is being written.

'Virginia, my home sweet home, I wanna give you a kiss.' It's a famous line from the musical *Hamilton*, as Thomas Jefferson celebrates returning home from France in the late 1700s. Anyone who spends any time exploring Virginia's geographic wizardry, interacting with its centuries of classic American lore and engaging with Southern-charm-filled locals will wanna give the state a kiss, too.

Nestled on the East Coast, Virginia is a mix of vivid Mid-Atlantic landscapes and rich American history. From the misty peaks of the Blue Ridge Mountains to the serene ripples of Chesapeake Bay, the state offers an array of natural beauty. Virginia's past is as varied as its geography: it's the birthplace of America where the first English settlement of Jamestown was established, and a state where crucial Civil War battles were fought. Bustling urban epicenters, from the capital of Richmond to the DC-adjacent Arlington, brim with architectural landmarks, while Virginia's coastal towns exude a nautical heritage that's a mix of quaint and captivating. Whether you're tracing the footsteps of founding fathers, savoring concoctions in the statewide wine country, or exploring the rugged trails of Appalachia, Virginia offers plenty of adventure and discovery and will enchant you with its stories and scenery.

THE MAIN AREAS

RICHMOND
Edgy and historic, with capital vibes.
p348

WILLIAMSBURG
Carriage rides and colonial charm.
p353

CHARLOTTESVILLE
A small town and a big university mingle.
p359

ROANOKE
A Southwest Virginia star (literally) within mountains.
p362

HARRISONBURG
Skyline Drive and Shenandoah National Park bliss.
p366

Left: Chincoteague National Wildlife Refuge (p372); Above: Shenandoah National Park (p366)

VIRGINIA BEACH	**ARLINGTON**	**FREDERICKSBURG**	**ALEXANDRIA**
Virginia's biggest city and longest boardwalk.	DC's diverse, monument-filled neighbor.	Bursting with boutiques and history.	Preserved cobblestone strolls on the Potomac.
p369	**p373**	**p376**	**p380**

Find Your Way

Northern Virginia, where nearly 40% of the population resides, bustles with urban landscapes. South and west are more rural and smaller-town vibes, with Richmond and Virginia Beach being the major exceptions.

TRAIN

Amtrak connects the entire state, from Roanoke and Danville in the southwest to Norfolk in the southeast and Alexandria in the north. The trains connect with Virginia systems, including Virginia Railway Express and Metro.

CAR

Renting a car is the easiest way to navigate the state's entirety. Take note, particularly in Northern Virginia and along major highways, of HOV lanes (often requiring two or more passengers per vehicle) and snag an E-Z Pass toll pass to navigate rush-hour traffic.

Alexandria, p380
A historic square awaits with the country's oldest farmers market held at the one site.

Fredericksburg, p376
Once known for its place in Civil War history, now blossoming as a lively destination.

Arlington, p373
An urban retreat on the Potomac River, with a diverse collection of dynamic neighborhoods.

Harrisonburg, p366
More than a college town, with a quaint local scene tucked into the Shenandoah Valley.

Roanoke, p362
Small mountain city where art, culture and an outdoors-loving spirit mesh.

Charlottesville, p359
Nestled in rolling foothills, teeming with pedestrian friendly hubs and with wine to match any palette.

Virginia Beach, p369
The world's 'longest stretch of pleasure beach' bustling with a vibrant nightlife.

Richmond, p348
A true capital city, beaming with museums, breweries, cobblestone streets and a progressive edge.

Williamsburg, p353
The first capital of the colony of Virginia, now with a preserved epicenter with friendly reenactors.

Williamsburg (p353)

Plan Your Time

Plan a few days in each region – the coastal plains and Virginia Beach, central Piedmont and Richmond, the Blue Ridge Mountains and points west – to experience Virginia's unique zing.

An Action-Packed Week

- Explore a triangle of history, urban wonder and mountains. Start with a day each of history in **Arlington** (p373), **Alexandria** (p380) and **Fredericksburg** (p376). Zip to **Richmond** (p340) to e-bike along the James River and saunter through museums. Venture to **Roanoke** (p362) for two days of Blue Ridge Mountain vistas, a drive along the **Blue Ridge Parkway** (p363 and a stop in **Harrisonburg** (p366).

Long Weekend Lounging

- Start in **Virginia Beach** (p369) on a Friday, strolling its boardwalk and plopping on its white sands for relaxation. When adventure beckons, climb one of the oldest lighthouses in the country at **Fort Story** (p369). On Saturday, venture to **Richmond** (p340), less than two hours west. For a Sunday stroll, explore **Colonial Williamsburg** (p353) and hitch a wagon ride for a walking reprieve.

SEASONAL HIGHLIGHTS

SPRING
Temperatures hover in the mid-70s, making for perfect daytime and early-evening strolls.

SUMMER
Virginians swarm to water as the heat sizzles, with Virginia Beach and Piedmont lakes being favorites.

FALL
Oranges and yellows swirl among the treetops along some of Virginia's most scenic roads.

WINTER
It's the season to bundle up fireside, unless you're braving cold temps and embarking on a skiing trip.

Richmond

HOPPY BREWS | STATE MUSEUMS | CREATIVE HUBS

GETTING AROUND

Richmond is a walkable yet spread-out city. For a break from walking, the RVA Bike Share has 20 stations throughout town. The Greater Richmond Transit Company (GRTC) is the local bus company, with the GRTC Pulse bus serving most tourist routes. It's free to ride on the bus, which passes every 15 or 30 minutes. If arriving or departing RVA via plane, the airport is approximately 10 miles outside of town.

☑ TOP TIP

From the strollable boutiques of Carytown to the seemingly endless breweries in Scott's Addition, each neighborhood has its own ambience and flair. If you're looking to 'hop' to similar types of bars, shops, galleries and establishments, there may be a neighborhood with everything right there without having to venture beyond.

Richmond soars along the banks of the James River, wearing its history like a badge of honor, yet pulsing with a vibrant, modern beat. Founded in 1737, 'River City' served as the backdrop to pivotal chapters in American history, notably as the capital of the Confederacy during the Civil War. Its streets echo with the footsteps of revolutionaries, presidents and visionaries, yet are visibly bubbling with a progressive vibe. Today, RVA, as it's locally known (an abbreviation for Richmond, Virginia), is a mosaic of parks, rapid waters, towering architecture and a burgeoning creative scene. In its coolest neighborhoods, such as Carytown and the Fan, prepare to take in vibrant graffiti art, seasonally flavored lattes and galleries upon galleries from local artisans. It's a city where history and progress have found balance, yet are ever-evolving. This gateway to the American South is an essential stop for any traveler seeking to understand the heart and soul of Virginia.

Get Crafty with Your Brews

Exploring the Richmond Beer Trail

There are more than 30 craft breweries to explore within greater Richmond's confines. Amid the beer boom, the local tourism bureau recently created a Richmond Beer Trail, with a printable map taking folks as far north as the dog-friendly, pinball-machine-haven **Center of the Universe Brewing Co** in Ashland, and south to **Dancing Kilt Brewery** in Chester with its banana-infused Hefeweizen. In between are some key breweries (and beers).

A little-known fact: Richmond has a Historic German Brewing District. Start your journey there at **Hardywood Park**, which has a super-strong 12% Bourbon Barrel Cru available year-round and, come winter, a gingerbread stout that cheers the palate right up. Its Virginia Roots series has true local flavor, incorporating state-grown ingredients into seasonal brews that have spanned a peach tripel with Crozet-grown peaches

THE GUIDE

VIRGINIA RICHMOND

TOP SIGHTS
1. Poe Museum
2. Virginia Museum of Fine Arts

SIGHTS
3. American Civil War Museum
4. Branch Museum of Architecture and Design
5. Hollywood Cemetery
6. Institute for Contemporary Art
7. James River Park
8. Science Museum of Virginia

SLEEPING
9. Linden Row Inn
10. Quirk Hotel
11. The Jefferson Hotel

EATING
12. Hot for Pizza
13. LunchSUPPER!
14. Stella's
15. Tobacco Company

DRINKING & NIGHTLIFE
16. Black Hand Coffee Company
17. Blanchard's Coffee
18. Byrdhouse at Graduate
19. Capital Ale House
20. Hardywood Park
21. Harry's at Hofheimer
22. Ironclad
23. Kabana Rooftop
24. Lift Coffee Shop
- see 10 Q Rooftop Bar
25. The Camel
26. Väsen Brewing Company

ENTERTAINMENT
27. Altria Theater
28. Canal Club
- see 19 Richmond Music Hall at Capital Ale House
29. Richmond Triangle Players
30. The National

SHOPPING
31. 17th Street Market

TRANSPORT
32. Riverside Cycling

349

17th St Market

LIVE-MUSIC VENUES IN RICHMOND

The National: Has large capacity, an intimate feel, stunning architecture and a state-of-the-art sound system.

The Camel: Catch up-and-coming local talent in a cozy setting, with yummy smashburgers, too.

Canal Club: Industrial chic, adjacent to Canal Walk, with indoor and outdoor performance spaces.

Richmond Music Hall at Capital Ale House: Mid-size venue with a big sound that's attached to a craft-beer haven.

Altria Theater: Historic space with opulent features and arguably the best sight lines and acoustics in town.

and a juicy IPA with honey from Charlottesville farms. **Väsen Brewing Company** is a comparative newcomer – opening in 2017 – that's carved a niche in the sour-ale space...and it holds periodic yoga sessions, too. In Lakeside, **Final Gravity Brewing Co** has risen from home-brew supply shop to brewing and selling its own concoctions. Beyond its ever-rotating takes on IPAs, you'll find more than 20 taps with brews from across the US.

Museum Hop Downtown
Collections of art, science and in-between

Richmond's museum scene offers a treasure trove of experiences, from grand art to gripping science. Begin your journey at the **Virginia Museum of Fine Arts**, where the collections span continents and centuries – don't miss the permanent Fabergé and Russian Decorative Arts exhibit, with nearly 300 gold and precious-metal-draped objects to be mesmerized by. Hit also the **Institute for Contemporary Art** (ICA) at Richmond's inner-city university, Virginia Commonwealth University (VCU). The free ICA is one of the city's newer museums, opening in 2018 with a modern sculpture garden.

DRINKING IN RICHMOND: COFFEE SHOPS

Blanchard's Coffee: A sleek contemporary spot known for its own roasts and fun-flavored lattes.

Ironclad: Specialty coffee meticulously sourced, roasted, ground and brewed on-site with friendly vibes.

Lift Coffee Shop: Locally roasted organic coffee nestled in the Art District. Complement that brew with freshly baked goods.

Black Hand Coffee Company: Cute brick-draped spot with indoor/outdoor seating, brewing sustainably sourced beans roasted in-house.

The **Branch Museum of Architecture and Design** surprises visitors from first glance – it's housed in a stately, brick castle of sorts on Monument Ave that was completed in 1919. Its rotating exhibits focus on anything from how Richmond's cityscapes came to life to international women's-rights posters at a given time. For a hands-on experience, the **Science Museum of Virginia** captivates curious minds of all ages. You can generate tornadoes or test your reflexes against the speed of light in interactive science labs. The **American Civil War Museum** includes personal artifacts and narratives conveying the various characters throughout the 1861–65 war. Its exhibits often focus on one of three perspectives – the north, south or African American. The museum is housed in the former Tredegar Iron Works building, which has some history itself – cannons made on its grounds fired the first shots at Fort Sumter in South Carolina to kick off the Civil War.

Stroll the Cobblestoned Shockoe Bottom
Dabble in Poe and tobacco history

From the first step on Shockoe Bottom's cobblestones, you know the streets have been a setting for the extraordinary through the centuries. This is where George Washington mapped out a national system of transportation canals, laying the groundwork for America's infrastructure. It's where Thomas Jefferson signed the Virginia Statute for Religious Freedom, a cornerstone of American civil liberties. And it's where Abraham Lincoln famously arrived by canoe to witness the historic fall of the Confederacy. Knowing Shockoe Bottom's lore makes it magical to take in.

The neighborhood's hub is **17th St Market**, which regularly hosts art shows as well as a bimonthly farmers market. A communal favorite is the Richmond Night Market (second Saturday of every month), with an artisan village, live art activations and jam sessions from local bands. The **Tobacco Company** is a three-level, charm-filled restaurant that was once a – you guessed it – tobacco warehouse. The pecan-crusted lollipop lamb chops, brass elevator and central walnut staircase dazzle 'round the clock. The **Poe Museum** is a living homage to famed Richmond resident, Edgar Allan Poe, offering insights into his enigmatic life and the theories surrounding his demise.

The courtyard space – dubbed the Enchanted Garden, which was inspired by Poe's 'To One in Paradise' poem – is a quiet oasis and regularly hosts 'UnHappy Hours' sponsored by local breweries.

EDGAR ALLAN POE'S RICHMOND

Baltimore often claims Edgar Allan Poe's legacy, yet Richmond is his origin story. Orphaned at two years of age, Poe was raised in Richmond by a tobacco merchant. As editor of the local *Southern Literary Messenger*, he published his early tales. His first thriller, *Bernice*, was a success, but its horror led to his firing. After stints in Philadelphia and Baltimore, he returned with intentions to settle down. His time was spent reciting and discussing poetry around town. Poe met his demise nine days after boarding a steamboat for some out-of-town business, sparking mystery around his final days.

DRINKING IN RICHMOND: ROOFTOP BARS

Byrdhouse at Graduate:	Kabana Rooftop:	Harry's at Hofheimer:	Q Rooftop Bar:
Lively cocktail haven with a playful twist featuring booze-infused slushes, refreshing cocktails and downtown views.	Trendy eatery transforms into a late-night lounge offering classic cocktails, DJ sets and weekend brunch.	Atop the historic Hofheimer, craft beer, cocktails and live music blend polished vibes with casual charm.	Savor sweeping skyline views with elevated street food and a dynamic bar menu featuring local craft-beer favorites.

351

THEATER IN RICHMOND

Maggie Bavolack, long-standing Richmond theater artist, dishes on her top theater finds. @maggersyeah

Richmond Shakespeare Festival at Agecroft Hall:
A unique theater experience. Sit outdoors while gazing upon the backdrop of the 16th-century manor. Where else in North America can you get that experience?

Yes, And! Theatrical Company:
Yes, And! produces evocative and exciting experiences. With its Cover to Cover series and Ghost Light After Party, there are many ways to engage with the stage.

Richmond Triangle Players:
Since 1993, RTP has been producing works rooted in the LGBTIQ+ experience. Its intimate venue in Scott's Addition is the perfect place to enjoy a cabaret and sip a filthy martini.

Biking, James River

Bike Along the James River
Unwind as you cruise landmarks

There are multiple trail systems connected to the James River's banks, making it perfect for exploring by bike. As you pedal, expect lush greenery, a tranquil yet muddy riverside and, on a lucky day, perhaps even a bald eagle soaring overhead. For bike rentals, head to **Riverside Cycling**. Make your first stop at Belle Isle along the southern bank, accessible via a pedestrian bridge. Once a Civil War prison camp, this island now offers scenic trails for walkers and bikers alike. There are flat gravel trails and a rock- and mound-filled skills area. If you're looking to take things to another outdoorsy level, there's a small granite cliff for rock climbing, too.

Cruise to **James River Park**. The 600-acre park has more than 22 miles of bike trails. Continue to sprawling **Hollywood Cemetery**, the final resting place of notable figures, including presidents James Monroe and John Tyler. The cemetery is also home to the 'Richmond Vampire' legend, involving a mysterious and reported shadow figure said to roam the grounds at night.

 EATING IN RICHMOND: OUR PICKS

Stella's: Intimate Greek eatery with authentic flavors evoking a homemade charm in every bite. Reservation recommended. $$$	**Lunch.SUPPER!:** Southern fare featuring local ingredients. You can't miss the deer-antler chandelier and ornate decorations. $$	**Pho Tay Do:** Vietnamese cuisine in a quirky house setting, with authentic pho and Vietnamese dishes. Cash only. $$	**Hot for Pizza:** A divey den, boasting drink deals and a lineup of pies with ingredients like fennel sausage and oyster mushrooms. $$

Williamsburg

COLONIAL OPULENCE | REVOLUTIONARY RAVINES | BOUNTIFUL LANDMARKS

Williamsburg is a walk back in time, where echoes of 1776 greet you at each carefully restored and reconstructed building. This was Virginia's capital during the American Revolution and, today, you'll find a historic district – Colonial Williamsburg – where you can deep-dive into early American life. Former US presidents James Monroe, Thomas Jefferson and John Tyler studied in town and Patrick Henry, of 'Give me liberty, or give me death' speech fame, served as the first governor of post-colonial Virginia. Beyond historic goodness, the city is home to the esteemed College of William & Mary and two famed parks on different extremes of the thrills spectrum. Busch Gardens Williamsburg is a region-wide favorite with a hoppin' waterpark – Water Country USA – come summertime. Freedom Park is a 600-acre oasis with walking and mountain-bike trails that's also home to one of the first free Black settlements in America, dating back to 1803.

Roll Slowly through Time
Hitch a wagon ride in Colonial Williamsburg

Colonial Williamsburg is a living time capsule that transports locals and visitors alike to the 1700s. Throughout the 300-plus-acre area, which is beloved by families, historical reenactors with powdered wigs and tricorn hats wander about as horse-drawn carriages coast by. For a carriage ride, head to the **Colonial Williamsburg Visitor Center**, where rides start from $10.

By wagon or foot, prioritize a stop at the **Governor's Palace**. Amid its three-story brick grandeur, note all the pineapple accents – an emblem of hospitality and wealth in the mansion's 1700s heyday and beyond. From the palace, head just west to the **Capitol Building** – this is where the House of Burgesses initially proposed US independence from the British in 1776. A final stop is the **Public Gaol**. At the prison, learn about colonial-era crime and punishments. Take note of

GETTING AROUND

At approximately 9 square miles, Williamsburg is compact and largely walkable. Colonial Williamsburg is particularly easy to stroll, with wide, pedestrian-friendly expanses. Beyond its colonial core, the Williamsburg Area Transit Authority (WATA) serves key tourist attractions such as Jamestown, Busch Gardens and the College of William & Mary. WATA has an all-day pass for $3 and is particularly handy for venturing beyond Colonial Williamsburg. Pay cash for the all-day pass on the bus (credit cards are not accepted).

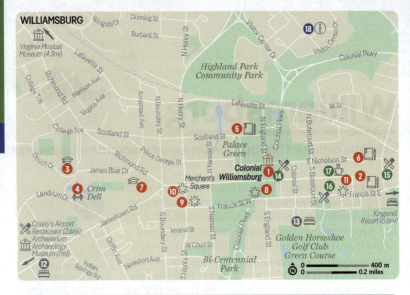

TOP SIGHTS
1. Colonial Williamsburg

SIGHTS
2. Capitol Building
3. College of William & Mary
4. Crim Dell Bridge
5. Governor's Palace
6. Public Gaol
7. Wren Building

ACTIVITIES, COURSES & TOURS
8. Haunted Williamsburg
9. Murder Tour and Pub Crawl
10. Taste of Williamsburg
11. Ultimate Pirate Tour
● see 10 We Shall Overcome

SLEEPING
12. The Cedars of Williamsburg B&B Inn
13. Williamsburg Inn

EATING
14. Chowning's Garden Bar
15. Christiana Campbell's Tavern
16. King's Arms Tavern

DRINKING & NIGHTLIFE
17. Raleigh Tavern Bakery

INFORMATION
18. Colonial Williamsburg Visitor Center

the historic pillory, a wooden structure with slots for criminals' heads and hands. It was common for passersby to hurl tomatoes and other objects at criminals, so come to this photo opp – and the other pillories scattered about Colonial Williamsburg – creatively.

Unexpected Historic Pizzazz

Spend a day exploring quirky history

Don't let Williamsburg's generally refined vibe fool you – there's some quirkiness to explore here. Hit the **Virginia Musical Museum**, which celebrates the state's musical heritage through a collection of rare musical instruments and memorabilia celebrating Virginia-bred icons. Learn all about the likes of country-pop legend Patsy Cline and the 'Queen of Jazz', Ella Fitzgerald. Among the more unique items is the country's first talking doll and a 1790 Joshua Shudi harpsichord – one of two in existence today. The **College of William & Mary** is the US's second-oldest institution of higher education (Harvard is the oldest). Stop at the **Crim Dell Bridge** – local lore promises eternal love to those who kiss

☑ TOP TIP

There's a fee to enter buildings and experience educational programming in Colonial Williamsburg. Odds are that you may want to pair your visit with a Yorktown trek, a Busch Gardens trip or more, and a variety of discounted packages are available at colonialwilliamsburg.org.

Crim Dell Bridge

atop its burgundy-and-gold-railed steps and, if you cross the bridge alone, well, you're doomed to solitude. While at William & Mary, check out the **Wren Building**, which has survived three major fires since its 1700 inception and is the oldest college building still in use in the country.

When hunger inevitably beckons, **Charly's Airport Restaurant** is a quirky and unexpected find. Situated at Williamsburg Jamestown Airport, watch smaller and sometimes vintage aircraft depart and land as you nosh on homestyle plates. Round out a day of the unordinary at the **Archaearium**, an archaeology museum dedicated to America's first English colony, Jamestown. The museum has more than 2,000 artifacts, including tobacco pipes bearing the names of prominent settlers and Native American arrowheads.

WALKING TOURS

Ultimate Pirate Tour: All-ages tour that delves into the history of pirates and their impact on early colonies.

Murder Tour and Pub Crawl: Learn about the seedy, murderous history of the town while sipping on a libation at each pub.

Haunted Williamsburg: Candlelight tour in which you get to enter historic buildings in Colonial Williamsburg.

We Shall Overcome: Hear inspiring stories of African Americans while visiting the Williamsburg landmarks connected to their stories.

Taste of Williamsburg: Williamsburg's best bites and craft drinks are the focus of this tasty tour.

 EATING IN WILLIAMSBURG: HISTORIC TAVERNS

King's Arms Tavern: Authentic colonial dining, blending 18th-century recipes with modern flavors. $$$

Christiana Campbell's Tavern: George Washington's favorite local seafood spot. Come for the crab cakes, stay for the balladeers. $$$

Chowning's Garden Bar: Relaxed open-air dining with a colonial twist, offering classics such as burgers and hot dogs. $$

Raleigh Tavern Bakery: Fresh ginger cake, sandwiches and baked treats from this bakery with wood-fire ovens. $

HELP ME PICK:

Scenic Drives

Virginia consists of five geographical regions. Combine that with its deep historical roots and it makes Virginia a top-tier destination for a road trip (or five). From east to west, travelers can experience Tidewater's coastal plains and historic ports, Piedmont's rolling hills and agricultural landscapes, Blue Ridge Mountains' views, Valley and Ridge's parallel valleys and ridges, and the Appalachian Plateau's rugged terrain, gorges and coal-mining heritage. Virginia's vibrant yet distinct regions each offer a unique driving experience.

Where to Cruise if You Love...

Mountains

Skyline Drive 105 miles of mountain bliss, this public road through Shenandoah National Park provides awe-inspiring views from the crest of the Blue Ridge Mountains. There is no shortage of opportunities for snapping photos, with 75 overlooks along the way.

Goshen Pass This byway winds 14 miles along the Maury River. It offers panoramic views of the gorge and surrounding forests and is known for wildlife sightings, including bald eagles and river otters. At its upstream end, find a swinging footbridge spanning the river for more views.

History

The Crooked Road Virginia's Heritage Music Trail. A 333-mile route links 60 sites celebrating Appalachian and bluegrass music, offering an authentic Virginian pastime. Explore museums, music centers, country stores and theaters amid the beauty of Southwest Virginia, immersing yourself in the sights and sounds of the region's rich heritage.

Journey Through Hallowed Ground This drive is a build-your-own adventure in a chunk of the state that oozes Virginian history. Explore Revolutionary and Civil War battlefields, homes of US presidents and charming small-town main streets.

An Urban Sanctuary

George Washington Memorial Parkway Discover an oasis amid Northern Virginia's hustle and bustle. Pause to witness Great Falls flow into Mather Gorge, visit the US Marine Corps Memorial and explore Jones Point Lighthouse. This 25-mile drive offers myriad experiences in a short stretch.

Unexpected Surprises

Icons of Virginia's Western Highlands Soak in the Jefferson Pools hot springs, look up in awe at Falling Springs Falls, pop into the Omni for libations and soak in some Civil War history. The rolling ridges of the Allegheny Mountains provide delights around every corner along the drive's 100 miles.

Eastern Shore Embark on a journey across the modern marvel of the Chesapeake Bay Bridge-Tunnel, a 17-mile structure alternating between bridge and tunnel across Chesapeake Bay. Arrive at the Eastern Shore engrossed with coastal wilderness, with the wild ponies of Assateague Island as the highlight.

Skyline Drive

--- HOW TO ---

When to go Visit spring to fall for optimal road conditions. Each season offers unique beauty – vibrant blooms in spring, bright skies in summer and colorful foliage in fall.

Utilize online resources Stay informed by checking area conditions and entrance fees and downloading free audio guides and maps. GPS is not always dependable.

Budget your time Allow time for stops at scenic overlooks, short walks and hikes, souvenir shopping and more along the way.

Look out for wildlife While it's exciting to witness wildlife in its natural habitat, remember that the animals are wild and unpredictable. Maintain distance and avoid feeding.

Preparing for a Smooth Ride

Even for the most seasoned driver, embarking on a scenic drive takes some preparation to make the most of the experience. Some of the drives are rural in nature, so make sure all systems are in good working order and your gas is topped up. Consider packing snacks, water, sunscreen and, depending on the season, weather-appropriate gear. Some of the drives won't have many places to stop for gas or sustenance. Weather conditions will vary depending on the time of year and region. Always check the forecast to ensure a smooth journey, as the Virginia heat can radiate in summer and snow can accumulate in mountainous areas in winter. Ask park rangers about weather conditions on any of the drives that take you through parks. They are seasoned experts who can provide deeper insight to the day's outlook. GPS is often unreliable, so pack a map, which will ensure access to your route plan and directions even with spotty reception in some rural areas. Leave no trace wherever you go – whether it's a stop at a scenic overlook or a more involved walk or hike along the way, you should never leave behind any evidence you were there. Keeping a garbage bag in the car will stave off the temptation to dump garbage outside of proper receptacles and ultimately keep Virginia beautiful.

DRIVE THROUGH WARTIME & COLONIAL HISTORY

Begin at ❶ **Yorktown Battlefield** to soak in Revolutionary War history that is quite literally seeped into the ground. This 1781 battle was a turning point in the war, leading to its end and the USA's independence from Great Britain. Make your way towards ❷ **Nelson House**, the one-time residence of Thomas Nelson Jr, a signatory of the Declaration of Independence. Most features in the Georgian home are original. If you visit when enough staff are present, a tour of the interior is possible. Wind your way through the streets of ❸ **Yorktown's historic waterfront**, where restored 18th-century homes line the streets. Water St will lead you to the ❹ **French Memorial**, where you can pay tribute to the French soldiers who lost their lives in battles in and around Yorktown. Hop on the ❺ **Colonial Parkway** from here. This 23-mile scenic drive weaves its way through pine and hardwood forests, tidal estuaries along the James and York Rivers and through Williamsburg on its way to Jamestown. Overlooks dot the parkway, providing a chance to take in the greenery. Head to Jamestown Island where you'll find the ❻ **Jamestown Settlement**. Exhibits and outdoor re-creations tell the story of America's beginnings, including its indigenous people and the arrival of English colonists in 1607. Just around the corner from the settlement you'll find ❼ **Jamestown Glasshouse.** Here, modern glassblowers hold demonstrations while utilizing tools and techniques similar to those used in the 17th century. Just a bit further and you can cruise the ❽ **Historic Jamestowne Island Loop** and discover the beauty of the island's marshy landscape.

Charlottesville

BOW-TIE HAVEN | COLLEGIATE SPIRIT | FOOTHILL FARMS

Along the foothills of the Blue Ridge Mountains, Charlottesville is equally as ahhhh-worthy visually as it is historically. It is famously home to the University of Virginia (UVA), which was founded by Thomas Jefferson in 1819 and remains a centerpiece of the city's architectural and cultural story. The university's Rotunda and vast lawn are quintessential landmarks, embodying Jefferson's vision of an 'academical village.' President James Monroe's home, Highland, is notably in Charlottesville as well. Beyond its walkable college campus, the city's Downtown Mall is also a pedestrian-friendly hot spot. Friendly is truly the vibe here, with oft bow-tie-wearing dudes and pastel-summer-dress-wearing gals adding much to the Southern charm. Pair it all with a wine-producing region, farm-to-table restaurants aplenty and specialty clothiers (yes, you can buy a bow-tie, too) and you should feel right at home in Charlottesville.

A Different Type of Mall
Shop and stroll the pedestrian-friendly downtown

Oh, the charm of a stroll through downtown Charlottesville. It's a brick- and column-draped experience with pops of energy coming in the form of buzzing breweries, the facade of the ever-glowing **Paramount Theater** and more. The **Downtown Mall** is a seven-block stretch, with the Ting Pavilion and Omni Charlottesville Hotel as its east and west anchors. Between them, hit **Lone Light Coffee** for a coffee concoction or sweet treats such as bourbon vanilla-infused ice cream.

Along the drag are three used bookstores: **Blue Whale Books**, **2nd Act Books** and **Daedalus Bookshop**. Among the trendier shops is **Beautiful Idea**, which dubs itself 'a radical community hub,' with goods from the town's queer and trans artists. On a rainy day – or when you're tired of strolling – **Violet Crown Theater** is an intimate, locally owned cinema showing a mix of independent and classic flicks.

GETTING AROUND

Charlottesville is walkable, bikeable and scooterable. VEO is the city's dockless scooter and bike program, with its own app. Charlottesville Area Transit operates buses serving the city and surrounding Albemarle County from 6am to 10:30pm daily except Sundays. The Charlottesville Free Trolley offers free trips between the University of Virginia and Downtown Mall area. For regional travel, Charlottesville has an Amtrak station, with routes that stem out of state. You may periodically see the Piedmont Express and Afton Express publicized – these are airport and commuter buses, respectively.

SLEEPING
1 Graduate Charlottesville

DRINKING & NIGHTLIFE
2 Kardinal Hall
• see 12 Lone Light Coffee
3 Random Row Brewing
4 Rockfish Brewing
5 Starr Hill
6 SuperFly

ENTERTAINMENT
7 Paramount Theater
8 Violet Crown Theater

SHOPPING
9 2nd Act Books
10 Beautiful Idea
11 Blue Whale Books
12 Daedalus Bookshop
13 Downtown Mall

☑ TOP TIP

The University of Virginia is Charlottesville's lifeblood – when big events are in town (namely football games), traffic and hotel rates can be heightened. Keep an eye on UVA events at virginia.edu and plan accordingly.

A quick stroll from the Downtown Mall, Preston Ave has four breweries in a four-block stretch: **SuperFly**, **Rockfish Brewing**, **Random Row Brewing** and **Starr Hill**. The last is one of Virginia's most famous independent craft breweries – in 2005 it moved its beer production to nearby Crozet. **Kardinal Hall** is another community favorite, housed in a retro Coca-Cola facility. Nowadays it's an Alpine-inspired beer hall with two outdoor bocce courts and a hearty selection of board games.

It's Wine O'Clock

Uncork Virginia's wine wonderland

Charlottesville wasn't named Wine Enthusiast's Wine Region of the Year in recent times for no reason. The city and Albemarle County are home to more than 40 wineries, producing everything from the heartiest of merlots to light hybrids. Companies such as **Central Virginia Wine Tours** offer transportation and winery hops. If you're plotting your own wine adventure, start at **Blenheim Vineyards**. The property dates to 1730 and was started as a sustainable winery by world-renowned musician and local icon Dave Matthews.

Monticello, former home of Thomas Jefferson

From there, hit **King Family Vineyards** – situated on a former thoroughbred horse farm, its deep and complex Meritage always delights. **Pippin Hill** is a rolling hills staple with farm-to-table dinners and estate tours. **Jefferson Vineyards** is on the land where Thomas Jefferson and his close friend and Italian winemaker, Philip Mazzei, grew grapes together more than 250 years ago. Today, the winery has an expansive portfolio and is owned by the Monticello estate, which is just to the north. Try Jefferson's take on Virginia's flagship varietal, viognier.

PROFESSOR O'KEEFFE

We can thank the hallowed halls of the University of Virginia for inspiring Georgia O'Keeffe to be the artist we recognize today. O'Keeffe spent summers at UVA studying art, eventually teaching some courses herself. It was under her teachers' mentorship that she began exploring the abstract, drawing inspiration from the Blue Ridge Mountains and campus life. O'Keeffe endured many trials over those years, including her mother's death, but it was camping trips in the mountains near Charlottesville that reinvigorated her, allowing her painting to flourish again. UVA and Charlottesville provided the foundation from which O'Keeffe's art blossomed, leaving a mark on the art world.

 DRINKING IN CHARLOTTESVILLE: CIDERIES

| Bold Rock Carter Mountain: Views of the Charlottesville valley plus a blend of barn and country-store aesthetics and local flavors. | Potter's Craft Cider: Century-old stone church turned cidery, offering crisp, tart ciders, including the bold-flavored Bloom series. | Albemarle CiderWorks: A diverse selection of high-ABV ciders crafted from various apples (predominantly dry) in scenic country surrounds. | Castle Hill Cider: Sip cider crafted using the ancient qvevri fermentation method amid the rustic elegance of a vast farm estate. |

Roanoke

QUAINT NEIGHBORHOODS | HILLY STROLLS | MOUNTAINOUS DRIVES

GETTING AROUND

Roanoke is a hilly town with neighborhoods far and wide. If you're going to rent a car to explore a Virginian city and its broader region, this is it. Roanoke is easily connected to the Blue Ridge Parkway, with scenic lookouts aplenty. Another stellar option is renting an e-bike – Roanoke's streets are bike-friendly, and there's the central greenway for longer bike rides. Scooters are sparsely available, too. For public transportation, Valley Metro is the local service, with 20-plus routes. Its Star Line Trolley is free and makes stops downtown on weekdays from 7am to 7pm.

Nestled in a region known for rolling farmlands, winding rural roads and farms-upon-farms, Roanoke is Southwest Virginia's city hub. It's known as the 'Star City of the South' because of the Mill Mountain Star – the world's largest human-made star at nearly 90ft tall – looming over the city from a nearby peak. The city itself sparkles on many levels, ranging from a regionally beloved farmers market downtown, an expansive greenway for running and biking along the Roanoke River and small neighborhoods, such as Grandin and Wasena, each with their own Southern flair. Considered by many to be the mountain-biking capital of Virginia, if not the entire East Coast, it's common to see folks on bikes in all forms zipping around Roanoke. Beyond its modernized buzz, it's steeped in Virginian history, which is showcased by museums, including the Virginia Museum of Transportation and the Taubman Museum of Art, which regularly exhibits international and regional artists alike.

Just What the Doctor Ordered
Explore Roanoke's quirky history with Dr Pepper

What in the world does Roanoke have in common with the Texas-bred soda icon, Dr Pepper? Quite a bit, actually. Roanoke was the site of Dr Pepper's first bottling plant in Virginia. It opened in 1936 and, from 1957 through 1961 (with the exception of 1960), Roanoke locals consumed more Dr Pepper per capita than anywhere else on Earth. Today, you'll see homages to this special relationship throughout town. Notably, there's a circular, vintage, illuminated **Dr Pepper sign** atop a brick building downtown on Williamson Rd. It has the numbers 10, 2 and 4 on it, which related to the beverage's slogan way back to encourage folks to drink Dr Pepper as a pick-me-up at 10am, 2pm and 4pm. There's also **Dr Pepper Park at the Bridges**, an outdoor concert venue that comes alive during the summer. Perhaps most charming, the

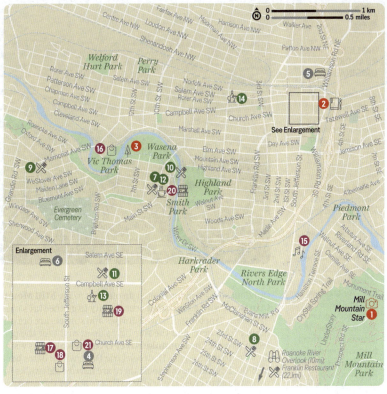

TOP SIGHTS
1. Mill Mountain Star

SIGHTS
2. Dr Pepper Sign
3. Wasena Park

SLEEPING
4. Fire Station One
5. Hotel Roanoke
6. The Liberty Trust

EATING
7. Bloom Restaurant & Wine Bar
8. River and Rail
9. Scratch Biscuit Company
10. The Green Goat
11. The Hatch

DRINKING & NIGHTLIFE
- see 5 1882 at the Pine Room
12. Roasters Next Door
13. Six and Sky Rooftop Grille
- see 4 Stock Café & Bar
14. The Front Row
- see 20 Wasena City Tap Room & Grill

ENTERTAINMENT
15. Dr Pepper Park at the Bridges

SHOPPING
16. Black Dog Salvage
17. Crafteria
18. Mast General Store
19. Roanoke Farmers Market
20. Roanoke Mountain Adventures
21. TXTUR

city celebrates Dr Pepper Day on October 24 each year, with commemorative T-shirts and freebies. The date – 10-24 – honors the aforementioned sign.

Rolling Greens upon Rolling Greens
Cruising the Blue Ridge Parkway

The Blue Ridge Parkway runs 469 miles through Western Virginia and North Carolina. It's accessed less than a 10-minute drive from downtown Roanoke, and has a handful of

✅ TOP TIP

Roanoke is the principal city within 'Virginia's Blue Ridge,' encompassing nearby towns and a trio of counties. Its website, visitroanokeva.com, is comprehensive in outlining the small-town-Virginia experiences nearby.

363

BIG LICK: ROANOKE'S ORIGINAL NAME

Wandering around Roanoke, you'll see names of businesses and slogans with 'Big Lick' in them. That was the name given to the town when it was established in 1874, due to the fact that it was loaded with salt licks, which attracted deer, elk and buffalo, which indigenous locals and settlers alike hunted. In 1881, Big Lick was officially renamed Roanoke, taking on the same name as the surrounding county and nearby river. The name is derived from a similar-sounding Indigenous word, Rawrenock, which are beads that Native Americans wore and traded.

standout stops. Among them is an offshoot to the **Mill Mountain Star**, with a viewpoint over the city from the star's base – it's open 7am to 11pm daily. Sunrises and sunsets are breathtaking from here, and the star lights up at night for the perfect photo op. The **Roanoke River Overlook** also has vistas down onto the Niagara Hydroelectric Dam, which dates back to 1906. Beyond the overlook, there are narrow sidewalks for pedestrians to cross the bridge itself. It's not for the woozy or faint of heart, as the guardrails are somewhat low. However, if you can stomach reaching the middle, the views down to the rocky, tree-lined river are well worthwhile. The Blue Ridge Parkway is free to access, and its speed limit is typically 45mph. Parkway regulars say mid to late October is the best time to drive it, thanks to its vivid foliage. However, with its springtime pops of flowers and the snowcapped mountain vistas in winter, it's a visual treat year-round.

A Wasena Wander

Explore one of Roanoke's quaint neighborhoods

Between the Old Southwest, Grandin Village and others, Roanoke is full of quaint neighborhoods with main-street charm. Wasena is tucked along Roanoke's greenway and is buzzing

EATING IN ROANOKE: BEST SOUTHERN FARE

Scratch Biscuit Company: Grandparents' recipes provide flavorful takes on biscuits, gravy and home cookin'. **$**

River and Rail: Produce sourced from area farms, fresh cuts from the butcher next door and intricate cocktails. **$$$**

The Hatch: Downtown lunch destination for piled-high fried-chicken sandwiches, plus a waffle-loaded weekend brunch. **$$**

Franklin Restaurant: No-frills, family-vibed restaurant with a brick interior and a weekend buffet with fried favorites. **$**

Mill Mountain Star

all day long. Fuel your neighborhood visit at **Roasters Next Door,** a small-batch coffee roaster with outside seating for people-watching – odds are a friendly Roanoker will want a chat. The same can be said about **Bloom Restaurant & Wine Bar** across the street, which is a seasonal, fare-driven hot spot. Adjacent to the greenway is **Roanoke Mountain Adventures**, which is the city's go-to for outdoor-related rentals. Among its offering are e-bikes, mountain bikes, tubes and kayaks. Opt for a daily rental to cruise the paved greenway, or sign up for one of its tours, such as an e-bike adventure through town with stops at various breweries. Its shop has an expansive consignment section, with some excellent deals on used outdoor equipment and clothing.

Once you've wrapped up your outdoor ventures, wind down at **Wasena City Tap Room & Grill**. Beyond craft brews, the expansive spot has a competitive weekly trivia night (Monday) and a tap takeover from regional breweries every Wednesday. To grab a quiet moment, head to **Wasena Park** – there are picnic tables along the greenway and benches for taking in the green surroundings. If you didn't pack picnic fare, **The Green Goat** is in the park, has a full menu and an ample outdoor space with picnic tables under strung bistro lights.

ROANOKE SHOPS

Black Dog Salvage: Reality-TV-famous spot with an on-site shop for crafting one-of-a-kind wares and furniture. Say hello to the friendly black dogs wandering around.

Crafteria: Crafts from hundreds of local artisans under one roof, including stationary, sauces and more. Check out the record shop's vinyl selection.

Roanoke Farmers Market: Permanent stalls come to life daily with flowers, baked goods and produce in front of the city market. Weekends are busiest.

Mast General Store: Massive store loaded with outdoor apparel and gear, as well as penny-priced candy in barrels.

TXTUR: Locally made furniture that's totally customizable and globally renowned. Smaller keepsakes (coffee mugs, candles etc) are also scattered about.

 DRINKING IN ROANOKE: OUR PICKS

Six and Sky Rooftop Grille: Roanoke's only rooftop bar, with skyline views, a firepit and upscale cocktail concoctions.

The Front Row: Quintessential dive bar with a killer food menu from ramen to a Philly cheesesteak quesadilla.

1882 at The Pine Room: Circular bar inside Roanoke's most historic hotel, with an astrological ceiling that has a story of its own.

Stock Café & Bar: Nordic- and Scandinavian-inspired fare and libations, tucked inside a furniture store you can lounge in.

Harrisonburg

FRIENDLY FOLKS | COLLEGIATE ROARS | SHENANDOAH MISTS

GETTING AROUND

The Harrisonburg Department of Transportation has a bus system with five different routes, connecting James Madison University with the city. It also operates a bus, known as the Inner Campus Shuttle, that hits a dozen-or-so different stops on campus. Otherwise, Harrisonburg is pedestrian-friendly, with seamless walkability. Ridesharing apps Lyft and Uber are available for quick trips and longer jaunts. The city has an extensive network of biking trails, though there is no current bikeshare program. Shenandoah Bicycle Company is the town's heavyweight for rentals, though it's closed on Sundays.

Harrisonburg is named the 'Friendly City' for a reason, and between the smiling townies, strollable downtown lined with art galleries and bistros, and the majestic Blue Ridge Mountains looming at every turn, you'll feel that sense of welcome. The city dates back to 1780 and is named after early English settler Thomas Harrison. Historically, Harrisonburg and the Shenandoah Valley were vital in providing livestock and grain to American troops, earning it a reputation as a breadbasket. In 1862, during the Civil War, it was the site of a notable success in General Thomas 'Stonewall' Jackson's Valley campaign. Today, it's a vibrant city of 50,000 people – a population that exponentially comes alive, as do its mom-and-pop restaurants, bars and quaint shops, when James Madison University (JMU) is in session. If the stars align, you'll want to catch a JMU basketball or football game, as the buzz around JMU's teams has been growing in recent years.

A Shenandoah Summit
'Park it' in a nearby natural legend

Shenandoah National Park spans more than 310 sq miles of soaring forests, wildflower-dotted meadows and trinkling waterfalls. A good portion of it is within a 45-minute drive of Harrisonburg's downtown. A highlight of the park, and one of the most popular hikes in the region, is **Old Rag Mountain**. You'll need to snag a day-use ticket in advance during peak season (March 1 through November 30). Allow seven hours for the hike – there are two different routes you can take, amassing approximately 2500ft in elevation. Along the way, count on some rock scrambles and boulder hiking. On

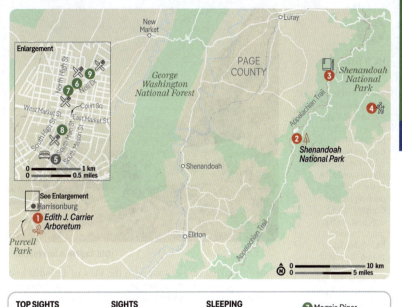

TOP SIGHTS	SIGHTS	SLEEPING	⑦ Magpie Diner
① Edith J. Carrier Arboretum	③ Massanutten Lodge	⑤ Hotel Madison	⑧ Rocktown Kitchen
② Shenandoah National Park	**ACTIVITIES, COURSES & TOURS**	**EATING**	⑨ The Little Grill
	④ Old Rag Mountain	⑥ Local Chop & Grill House	

completion, you'll be rewarded with 360-degree views of the valley, which glows yellow and orange during the fall foliage season.

For a more relaxing experience, tour **Massanutten Lodge**. Once a Civilian Conservation Corps project during the Great Depression, its living room has morphed to reflect the 1915 style of its then-owners, Addie and George. The lodge also has a Women of Skyland exhibition, showcasing the lives of various women who frequented the building – once a resort – in the 1920s.

Pops of Color

Saunter through the arboretum at JMU

You don't find a botanical garden on every college campus, let alone an arboretum, but there's both at James Madison University, in the form of the **Edith J. Carrier Arboretum**. Nestled on the campus's southeast edge, it's a 125-acre wooded and blossoming oasis with nearly 4 miles of trails. It's open 365 days a year from dawn to dusk and is free to visit. In 2024, the university unveiled a StoryWalk trail in the park, with 16 stops – or bookmarks – showcasing different pages along the way. By the end of the walk, you'll have read an entire book,

☑ TOP TIP

Downtown aside, pack for an adventure (or prepare for equipment rental) in Harrisonburg. Fishing, wild caving, rock climbing and more are popular in the broader region.

HE'S THE JM IN JMU

James Madison, born in Virginia in 1751 and nicknamed 'Father of the Constitution,' helped write the US Constitution and the Bill of Rights. Madison also co-wrote the Federalist Papers, pushing for the Constitution's approval. As the fourth president, he led the nation during the War of 1812 and helped negotiate the Treaty of Ghent. Back home in Virginia, he was involved in founding the University of Virginia and served in the state's House of Delegates and the US House of Representatives. His legacy is closely tied to Virginia's history and politics. Today, Harrisonburg's own James Madison University bears his name as tribute.

Old Rag Mountain (p366)

under a soaring tree canopy with the likes of daffodils and dwarf iris species blooming beside you. There are approximately 20 different areas and points of interest to explore within the arboretum, from a herb garden to a wood wildflower garden that especially pops come springtime. The Monarch Waystation is a must-see that's loaded with nectar-filled plants, purposefully planted to attract masses of monarch butterflies come summertime. The Bodkin Oak-Hickory Forest features a straight tract of soaring hickories that will make you feel a world apart from Harrisonburg, or any other town.

EATING IN HARRISONBURG: FARM-TO-TABLE RESTAURANTS

Rocktown Kitchen:	Local Chop & Grill House:	Magpie Diner:	The Little Grill:
Locally sourced, seasonal American cuisine in an elevated yet casual dining venue. $$$	Organic ingredients from neighborhood farms nestled in the historic City Produce Exchange building. $$$	1950s service station turned diner, with locally roasted coffee and craft cocktails alongside seasonally inspired classic dishes. $$	Cozy spot offering a menu for vegetarians and those seeking locally sourced organic-meat options. $

Virginia Beach

SOFT WAVES | BOOMING BOARDWALK | VAST CITYSCAPES

There's a reason you'll see so many Quebec license plates in Virginia Beach come summertime – it's absolutely worth the trek folks make near and far. Its three-mile-long boardwalk is its main attraction, lined with mid-rise hotels, bars and seafood spots. And yes, the oft-tranquil Atlantic Ocean is right there, too, making it prime for a stroll or to rent a surrey bike to pedal with loved ones. Amid the tranquility, Virginia Beach is also Virginia's largest city and home to the Virginia Aquarium, Marine Science Center, which has a world-class sea turtle rehab center, and the Military Aviation Museum, which has retired WWI and WWII warbird planes aplenty. As for history, nearby Jamestown gets a lot of love for being the first English Settlement in the US, but the first English colonists actually stopped at Cape Henry in Virginia Beach in 1607 before venturing west.

A Non-bored Walk

Marvel at monuments along the coastline

This much is certain: you might be on vacation, but you'll still want to wake early, plop it on the **Virginia Beach Boardwalk** adjacent to white sands and take in a sunrise. Beyond that, there is so much to explore along the boardwalk. Starting in the south at 2nd St and running north to 40th St, it spans three miles and is nearly 30ft wide in most spots. Among its quirkier highlights, just north of 30th St, is **Neptune's Park**, where you'll find a large, Instagrammable statue of the Roman god. At 38th St is the **Navy Seal Monument** and at 25th St is the **Norwegian Lady** statue, commemorating a nearby shipwreck. For bird enthusiasts, the **Atlantic Wildfowl Heritage Museum** is housed in a small cottage near 12th St.

A Brick Ascent

Climb Cape Henry Lighthouse

There are many firsts pertaining to the 90ft-tall, red and tan-bricked **Cape Henry Lighthouse**. Beyond being near the first landing site of English settlers in the US, the lighthouse also marks

GETTING AROUND

If you're sticking to the beach, strolls and a periodic rideshare (Uber and Lyft both operate in Virginia Beach) will do the trick. Hampton Roads Transit operates an Atlantic Ave trolley that runs parallel to the boardwalk. If you plan to bounce around from the beach to museums or downtown, the VB Wave trolley system has nearly 10 distinct routes. There are plenty of touristy bike shops along the boardwalk area with hourly rentals as well as daily packages in the $40 range.

☑ TOP TIP

Coupon books are everywhere in Virginia Beach – hotel lobbies, coffee shops, gas stations; they all have 'em. Peruse them for on-the-fly inspiration and deals that often extend well beyond tourist traps.

369

VIRGINIA BEACH

TOP SIGHTS
1. Virginia Beach Boardwalk

SIGHTS
2. Atlantic Wildfowl Heritage Museum
3. Navy Seal Monument
4. Neptune's Park
5. Norwegian Lady

SLEEPING
6. Hilton Virginia Beach Oceanfront

DRINKING & NIGHTLIFE
7. Chix on the Beach
8. The Shack on 8th
9. Waterman's Surfside Grille

SURF'S UP, DUDE

Virginia Beach is home to the world's oldest continuously run surfing competition, the Coastal Edge East Coast Surfing Championship, known as ECSC. For more than 60 years, surfers have flocked to the area to claim their place on the podium, creating an event that has morphed into much more. The week-long festival, held in August, delights with showcases in longboard, shortboard and stand-up paddleboarding. Through the years, other beach-favorite activities and live music have been added.

the first public works project of the US government, overseen by Alexander Hamilton. The lighthouse is on the Fort Story military base, meaning there are some special steps that must be taken to access it – you'll need to provide ID at the base's gate and then shuttles take non-military civilians directly to the lighthouse.

There are 191 steps to climb, but at the top, you're treated to 360-degree coastal views from its cozy lantern room. On-site, you'll notice another lighthouse, which, in stark contrast, is striped in white and black. That has been the functional lighthouse here since 1881.

 DRINKING IN VIRGINIA BEACH: ORANGE CRUSHES

Waterman's Surfside Grille: The OG – Waterman's vodka, fresh OJ, a splash of Sprite, enjoyed at the beach.	The Shack on 8th: Crush on Classic Orange to Honey Habanero among patio vibes with firepits and yard games.	The Back Deck: Indulge in refreshing crush variations at this laid-back bayside waterfront venue.	Chix on the Beach: Beachfront crushes with the personal touch of lime and cranberry.

Beyond Virginia Beach

Water in so many blissful forms – Chesapeake Bay, James River, Atlantic Ocean – awaits a short drive from Virginia Beach, as do distinctly Virginian adventures.

After spending time along Virginia Beach's glistening sands and perusing its beachy shops, it's time to take in some different coastal landscapes. Detached from the mainland of Virginia, and part of what's known as the Delmarva Peninsula, these comparatively quiet surrounds feel like a different world. Upon arrival, find horses roaming and swimming in the wild in Chincoteague and the freshest of oysters star on local menus in and around Cape Charles. Closer to Virginia Beach, and also nautical in nature, is Norfolk, which has a number of homages to life involving the sea, including the world's largest naval base and a museum on a warship.

Places
Norfolk p371
Cape Charles p371
Chincoteague p372

Norfolk
TIME FROM VIRGINIA BEACH: **20 MINUTES**

Explore naval history
It's only appropriate that Norfolk has a naval museum on a ship. Part of the **Nauticus** maritime discovery center, the *Battleship Wisconsin* includes interactive spaces that you can stroll through, including an on-ship hospital with a surgery center, barber shop and even a brig where misbehaving sailors were temporarily jailed. There's also a sailing center on-site where you can take a craft for a guided spin on the water, with a unique perspective on downtown Norfolk's skyline. For a more relaxed time on the water, **Half Moone Cruise** and **Victory Rover Naval Base Cruises** are next door and offer narrated cruises of the city's coastline.

Cape Charles
TIME FROM VIRGINIA BEACH: **1 HOUR**

A historic-district saunter
It's a walk worth a photo outing to a **Neptune statue** at the north end of Cape Charles' quiet beach. It's resemblant of the statue on Virginia Beach's boardwalk. At the southern end of the beachfront, and also worth a pic, is an art installation of the word **LOVE**, made of kayaks, tires and other outdoorsy components. Tucked within the colonial locale, **Cape Charles Museum** features exhibits on the town – arguably the wildest exhibit covers how the town was the center of a massive crater 35 million years ago. The museum is open daily mid-April through November.

GETTING AROUND

Rent a car for your ventures beyond Virginia Beach. Norfolk is an east–west straight shot along Interstate 264. The drive to Virginia's Eastern Shore has at its core a 17-plus-mile journey across the Chesapeake Bay Bridge-Tunnel. Within the over-under-water stretch, there are two 1-mile sections of tunnel. There's a $22 fee (round trip) on the Bridge-Tunnel, which is best navigated with an E-Z Pass.

371

A HIP-HOP HAVEN

New York City may be the birthplace of hip-hop, but the Hampton Roads region (Virginia Beach and its surrounding confines) is also rich with hip-hop history and a culture all its own. The region has produced major names in the biz such as Missy Elliot, Timbaland, Pharrell Williams, Commonwealth, Clipse and Nottz. Local venues, such as **The NorVa** in Norfolk, host regular showcases for emerging artists to grow and make their own impact on the genre. The library at the **College of William & Mary** (p354), a 75-minute drive from Virginia Beach, houses a comprehensive, special collection dedicated to Virginia's hip-hop culture and history.

Chincoteague National Wildlife Refuge

Chincoteague
TIME FROM VIRGINIA BEACH: **2 HOURS**

Horsing around on the Eastern Shore

It's an otherworldly scene – wild horses roaming, chomping on marsh grasses and slurping up water from ponds. It's a common scene in and around Chincoteague Island. **Chincoteague National Wildlife Refuge**, on neighboring Assateague Island, is the epicenter of the action. The lower third of the island is in Virginia, whereas the upper two-thirds is in Maryland. On the Virginia side, nearly 300 ponies wander through the park's forests and prairies, and it's not uncommon to see colorful shorebirds and bald eagles soaring in the sky. **Assateague Explorer** has a Pony Express Nature Cruise, which lasts about two hours and coasts safely up to the horses. Perhaps the most unique pony spectacle in the region, held on the last consecutive Wednesday and Thursday in July, is the annual **Pony Swim**, where the area's ponies are guided to swim across the Assateague Channel to Chincoteague Island, where select foals are auctioned off. This sale helps to humanely control the pony population and proceeds benefit veterinary care for the herd. Visually, it's about as cute as it gets, with the ponies' heads bobbing above water before reaching the coast.

 EATING IN CAPE CHARLES: OYSTERS

Oyster Farm Seafood Eatery: Raw and steamed offerings, with a deck overlooking Chesapeake Bay. **$$$**

The Shanty: Cottage vibe with local oyster selections, rice bowls and orange miso-glazed calamari. **$$**

Hook @ Harvey: Open for dinner, with a bistro setting, rotating fare and ever-fresh seafood catches. **$$$**

Coach House Tavern: Tucked in a golf community, this neighborhood restaurant has fresh oysters served on the half shell. **$$**

Arlington

RIVER OVERLOOKS | GOVERNMENT VIBES | REFLECTIVE SPACES

That white needle and dome you see looming in the distance? Why, yes, that's the Washington Monument and US Capitol. Arlington is Washington DC's bustling neighbor to the west and south, nestled just across the Potomac River. Whereas Washington, DC has height restrictions on its buildings – nothing can be taller than the Capitol – Arlington is lined with skyscrapers, towering monuments and the most modern of condo towers. Arlington is unique in that it's a county with no cities. There are just a lot of neighborhoods – more than 60 – each with their own unique vibes. Rosslyn is a corporate haven that's home to government contractors. Clarendon is the young professionals' haven, bumping with fitness studios and late-night bars. Crystal City is Amazon's new East Coast home and has a small-town strip of restaurants with fare from across the international spectrum. The bottom line: Arlington and all its tall stature was built for wandering.

Honor 400,000 Heroic Souls
Pay respects at the National Cemetery

If seeing the multitude of white marble headstones at **Arlington National Cemetery** doesn't give you the chills, what will? This graveyard spans more than 600 acres, with more than 400,000 servicepeople buried within its confines. Among the notables are two presidents (Taft and Kennedy), Jacqueline Kennedy, astronaut John Glenn and Army General John Pershing. The grounds are walkable, with trails having occasional small hills. Beyond the graves, there are dozens of other memorials honoring key American moments such as the Spanish-American War and 1986 Space Challenger Shuttle explosion.

To find a specific grave or memorial, download the ANC Explorer app, which has maps and photos down to individual tombstones. There is a blue-line Metro station at the cemetery. Inside the cemetery, make sure to speak softly, respect funeral services that may be in progress and take note of no-photo areas.

GETTING AROUND

The underground Metro has 11 stations throughout Arlington. The orange, yellow, silver and blue lines zip through Arlington, but stay cognizant of connections at the Pentagon and Rosslyn stations or you might end up in DC or Maryland. WMATA, which operates the Metro, also has more than a dozen bus routes that weave throughout the county, in addition to Arlington Transit buses. Arlington's neighborhoods are primarily walkable, though you might want to hop on a Capital Rideshare bike or hail an Uber/Lyft when venturing beyond a mile or so, to avoid crossing over major roads.

URBAN TRAILS

Washington & Old Dominion Trail:
A 45-mile, multi-use paved path. The Arlington portion intersects other trails, with parks along the way for extra exploration.

Mount Vernon Trail:
An easy 18-mile paved path following the Potomac. Take in scenery from Rosslyn to **Mount Vernon** (p381).

Four Mile Run Trail:
A 10-mile paved path adjacent to Four Mile Run stream creates an easy-to-moderate bike ride or walk surrounded by ample greenery.

Custis Trail:
Moderate 5-mile hilly paved trail with nearby parks. Make a pit stop in Ballston for a snack and some shopping.

Gulf Branch Park:
This park has a 1.4-mile moderate-to-difficult walking trail – visit the nature center, traipse along the stream, or peep the blacksmith shop.

Look to the sky and you might spot three 200ft-plus spires seemingly touching the sky. Completed in 2006, the **Air Force Memorial** commemorates accomplishments and advancements in flight, paying homage to pioneers such as Orville Wright and his first flight, through to heroes of today. The memorial features many spaces for reflection. The Parade Ground leads to granite walls inscribed with names of Medal of Honor recipients. A glass wall with an engraved image honors missing Air Force members. The memorial and grounds were finely crafted to provide a space for contemplation and remembrance, inviting visitors to pause and reflect on the sacrifices made in service to the nation.

Prepare for Landing
Watch planes land at Gravelly Point Park

Among the world's more memorable spots to watch planes land is **Gravelly Point Park**, just north of Reagan National Airport, which you can access from George Washington Memorial Parkway – there's ample parking on-site and it's free to enter. The skies are the attraction here, with planes soaring a few hundred feet above your head. Making it that much more picturesque is the Washington Monument and Potomac River in the background.

For some, it may be a 30-minute experience easily done from behind the wheel of a car or seated at one of the few picnic tables on-site. Others will want to pack a picnic lunch or explore more of the riverside expanse on the **Mount Vernon Trail**, which runs through the park itself.

The Pentagon's Five Captivating Points
Tour the US's largest office building

It's the headquarters of the United States Department of Defense and a setting for some of your favorite DC-set shows, from *The West Wing* to *24*. The **Pentagon** is such a cultural icon that it can be easy to forget it's actually an office building where 25,000-plus people work daily. To explore it, you'll need to book a tour two weeks in advance through the defense.gov website. As the building protects US secrets, there are some security checks on-site – you must be at least 18 years of age, and you have to pass through an airport-like scanner. Once you're in, it's a 1.5-mile stroll past portraits of Founding Fathers and a 'Hall of Heroes' recognizing Medal of Honor recipients. While here, make sure to visit the two-acre National 9/11 Pentagon Memorial, which includes reflection pools – unlike inside the Pentagon, you can take photos at the memorial.

DRINKING IN ARLINGTON: BEST COCKTAIL BARS

Salt: Warm and intimate space pouring seasonally inspired twists on classic cocktails.

The Board Room: Beyond a brewery, with craft cocktails and a vast board-game library creating a lively, entertaining atmosphere.

Ms. Peacock's Champagne Lounge: Evoking a bygone era with a speakeasy vibe, offering classic and champagne-inspired cocktails.

Brass Rabbit Public House: Innovative cocktails paired with healthy fare for a refined pub experience.

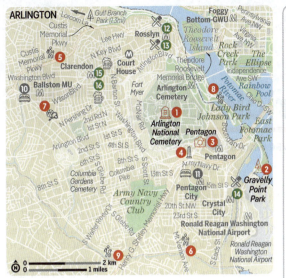

TOP SIGHTS
1 Arlington National Cemetery
2 Gravelly Point Park
3 Pentagon

SIGHTS
4 Air Force Memorial

ACTIVITIES, COURSES & TOURS
5 Custis Trail
6 Four Mile Run Trail
7 MedStar Capitals Iceplex
8 Mt Vernon Trail
9 Washington & Old Dominion Trail

SLEEPING
10 Placemakr Marymount Ballston
11 Ritz-Carlton Pentagon City

EATING
12 Happy Eatery
13 Upside on Moore
14 Water Park

DRINKING & NIGHTLIFE
15 Brass Rabbit Public House
16 The Board Room
see 16 Ms. Peacock's Champagne Lounge
see 13 Salt

Deck the Halls

Local eats at Arlington's food halls

Compared to some of the more outwardly vibrant Virginia cities such as Richmond or Virginia Beach, parts of Arlington can feel sterile. If you're getting that vibe, hit one of the county's food halls for a literal taste of color. **Upside on Moore** opened in early 2024 above the Rosslyn Metro station, featuring nearly a dozen different vendors. A favorite is Ghostburger, where you can top fresh-sizzled burgers with everything from aged cheddar to a house-made 'spooky sauce.' Less than a block away, **Happy Eatery** is a two-level, mini-food-hall of sorts with a teahouse, fast-casual Vietnamese spot and a pho counter under one roof.

Water Park in Crystal City is a newcomer in the modern, shopping-filled National Landing area. It's more of a park with food stalls, art installation nooks and a stage for local bands. Among its vendors are NY-style slice purveyor Crush Pizza and DC Dosa. Half the fun after you've snagged your grub is parking it on a grassy space and watching the water features and waterfall walls.

Ice, Ice Baby

Skate where the Washington Capitals practice

The Washington Capitals hockey team is arguably the region's favorite sporting franchise, particularly after winning the Stanley Cup in 2018. While the team plays its home games at Capital One Arena in DC, its practice facility – the **MedStar Capitals Iceplex** – is in Arlington's Ballston neighborhood. During hockey season (October through April), the Capitals typically post their practice schedule at the beginning of the week – practices are open to the public. Beyond hockey season, the complex hosts open skate sessions, lessons and, for the daring, pick-up hockey games. If you don't have skates, there's a pro shop with rentals.

✅ TOP TIP

Take note of restaurant and boutique hours on weekends. As some neighborhoods in Arlington – namely Rosslyn, Pentagon City and Crystal City – are primarily business and government focused, they may have extremely limited hours on weekends, if any.

Fredericksburg

BOUTIQUE BLISS | RIVER WALKS | FAMOUS FOOTSTEPS

GETTING AROUND

Downtown Fredericksburg has an Amtrak train station that doubles as a Virginia Railway Express (VRE) station. The VRE primarily serves as a straight-shot option for Northern Virginia and DC commuters and is not for hopping around town. For exploring downtown and the surrounding Stafford and Spotsylvania counties, there is a tan FRED bus with nearly 20 different routes. Otherwise, Fredericksburg is made for pleasant strolling, with periodic hills on William St and around the University of Mary Washington campus.

☑ TOP TIP

The Fredericksburg Visitor Center osells an XPass, offering admission to eight historic sites at a deep discount. The passes begin at $24 for 24 hours, stretching to $48 for 365 days.

Long the 'midpoint between Washington, DC and Richmond,' beautifully preserved, heritage-filled Fredericksburg has truly made a name for itself. It has history in the form of four area battlefields, as well as some downtown residences that date back to the early 1700s. It's the site of George Washington's boyhood home (from age six through his 20s), where he allegedly threw a coin across a 275ft span of the Rappahannock River, and it's the final resting place of some 15,000 Union troops in Fredericksburg National Cemetery. Its Caroline and William St main drags are home to some of Virginia's buzziest restaurants and, in 2022, the single-A affiliate of Major League Baseball's Washington Nationals chose Fredericksburg as its home. With a liberal-arts-driven college (the University of Mary Washington), quaint-yet-bustling downtown and culture aplenty, it's a happy medium of so much Virginia wonder.

A Slow Float

Tube the Rappahannock River

You'll see the Rappahannock River and its general muddiness running north-south along downtown Fredericksburg's eastern edge. The Rappahannock runs approximately 200 miles and feeds into Chesapeake Bay. In Fredericksburg, it's been the setting for a vicious Civil War battle, and was arguably a long-time boundary between the Union and Confederacy during the war. Today in Fredericksburg, the river is a recreation haven, with the new **Riverfront Park** – with a stellar playground – downtown along its banks, and **Old Mill Park** for picnics and water adventures aplenty. For the latter, head to **Virginia Outdoor Center**, which has canoe, kayak and tube rentals. The center provides equipment (including lifejackets) and curates journeys down the river – anything from two to 14 hours. The current is typically smooth with bursts of rushes – you'll want to wear shoes in the river as its bed, when touchable, is quite rocky.

SIGHTS
1. Chatham Manor
2. Kenmore
3. Mary Washington House
4. Riverfront Park

SLEEPING
5. Courtyard by Marriott Historic District
6. Ironclad Inn
7. Richard Johnston Inn & 1890 Caroline House

EATING
8. Billiken's Smokehouse
9. Casey's
10. Fahrenheit 132
11. Foode + Mercantile
12. Rebellion Bourbon Bar & Kitchen
13. Sammy T's

SHOPPING
14. Blue Shark Antiques
15. Card Cellar
16. Caroline Square
17. Fredericksburg Antique Mall & Clock Shop
18. LibertyTown Arts Workshop
19. Made in Virginia
20. Monkee's
21. PONSHOP Studio
22. River Rock Outfitter
23. Wildflower Collective

INFORMATION
24. Fredericksburg Visitor Center

Finds Old & New

Antique and boutique shopping on Caroline St

Fredericksburg offers plenty of shopping relics, from Civil War bullets to one-of-a-kind lamps and treasured art pieces. Caroline St is a long-time favorite for antique shopping, with the **Fredericksburg Antique Mall & Clock Shop** being among the larger stops, with dozens of stalls from local vendors. **Blue Shark Antiques** and **Caroline Square** are also solid, with similar set-ups. The latter has a sports-collectables space (Mike's Sports Memorabilia) with rare action figures. For sports lovers, the **Card Cellar** has rare baseball and

WHY I LOVE FREDERICKSBURG

Jesse Scott, Lonely Planet writer

Consider me one of those dudes that's ultra-proud to be where he's from. Hint: it's Fredericksburg. In my 37 years, I've seen this town blossom from a sleepy Civil War town to one with a rockin' culinary scene, a broadminded and artsy vibe and rad public spaces. Rte 3 is now nuts with shopping and there's even a baseball team. Who woulda thought? Hurkamp Park has the giant word LOVE to take photos with – it's painted a different vibe each season. This town is full of love – people say hi to you on the streets, and generations want to tell you how proud they are to be from 'the 'Burg. I don't blame them.

sports cards as well as quirky socks, jewelry and keepsakes. For a Fredericksburg-branded souvenir, **Made in Virginia** is a Caroline St staple, selling T-shirts and Virginia products from ham to peanuts. On the clothing front, **River Rock Outfitter** has men's and women's outdoorsy attire, **Wildflower Collective** is a haven for vintage finds and **Monkee's** is a chic boutique for women's wear with a southern flair.

Caroline St is dotted with art galleries as well. Among the hipper galleries, **PONSHOP Studio** has poppy, painted skateboards and periodic Fredericksburg-inspired shirts and prints for sale. A bonus art stop is **LibertyTown Arts Workshop**, which is home to dozens of local artists' studios and regular classes for all ages, including glass, pottery, drawing and painting.

A couple of storefronts south of PONSHOP, the **Fredericksburg Visitor Center** is a great starting point for any Fredericksburg visit, with helpful staff, maps, on-site educational movie theater and unique 'Burg swag.

Revolutionary Residences
Take a historic-house hop

Look closely at some of the better preserved homes in downtown Fredericksburg and you'll notice bronze markers

---

 EATING IN FREDERICKSBURG: BEST BREAKFASTS

| **Mason-Dixon Cafe:** Tastes of the north meet south at this beloved local gem with a relaxed, inviting ambience. $$ | **Casey's:** Vibrant brunch destination infusing bold flair into beloved classics; perfect weekend indulgence. $$ | **Battlefield Restaurant:** The comforting nostalgia of a home-cooked meal served with genuine hospitality in a cozy dive setting. $ | **Foode + Mercantile:** In a former bank, with a chic vibrance and locally inspired ingredients in the heart of downtown. $$ |

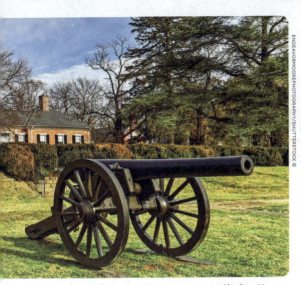

Chatham Manor

SAUCY ORIGINS

Move over Civil War: Fredericksburg has another claim to fame – the beloved Chick-fil-A sauce was invented here. Before you could simply ask for packets of Chick-fil-A with any meal, the finger-licking concoction was only found being whipped up in-house at the Spotsylvania Mall store. It all started in the 1980s, after an employee accidentally mixed barbecue sauce with the owner's special-recipe honey mustard. It wasn't until 2008 that the sauce became available nationwide. Ask the OG locals and they'll tell you that they used to do whatever they could to get their fix, such as bringing Mason jars to the store to fill up.

beside their front doors. These are some of the town's oldest and most significant homes, some of which are open to the public and host regular tours. **Chatham Manor** looms over the Rappahannock River and dates back to 1771. During the Civil War, it was a hospital and Union headquarters, with famous visitors such as Abraham Lincoln and Walt Whitman. There are free walking tours of the grounds, including a stop with views of Fredericksburg's steeple-filled skyline. **Mary Washington House** is a larger, white-paneled downtown home where George Washington's mother lived toward the end of her life (1772–89). Today, it's an homage to colonial life. Beyond rooms set up to replicate Mary's lifestyle, the lush-yet-quaint gardens offer a lovely and colorful stroll, particularly in springtime.

Kenmore is another standout residence, constructed in 1775 by Fielding Lewis and his wife Betty, who was George Washington's sister. At the time of its construction, it was an architectural marvel for its ornate plasterwork and ceilings, which have been tastefully restored through the years. Stop at the Crowninshield Building, which has an art gallery and exhibit detailing its past inhabitants and garden-infused grounds. If you plan to visit Kenmore and Mary Washington House, there is a combo ticket you can buy at Kenmore for discounted entry.

 EATING IN FREDERICKSBURG: OUR PICKS

| **Rebellion Bourbon Bar & Kitchen:** Bourbon-inspired, local menu with a cocktail bar nestled within the walls of a former armory. $$ | **Sammy T's:** American cuisine in a welcoming, snug setting with many vegetarian- and vegan-friendly choices. $$ | **Fahrenheit 132:** Cutting-edge steakhouse with a regularly evolving menu, showcasing the freshest regional ingredients and cuts. $$$ | **Billiken's Smokehouse:** A barbecue smokehouse, bar, outdoor venue and historic home all in one – try the spectrum of sauces. $$ |

Alexandria

HISTORIC WATERFRONT | COBBLESTONE STROLLS | SHOPPING STRETCH

GETTING AROUND

Alexandria slopes slightly down to the waterfront, making for easy walks. As some sidewalks are cobblestone or bricked, watch your steps. Scooter companies Lime, Bird and Spin are prevalent throughout town and operate at a reduced speed in blocks near the waterfront. There are four Metro stations in town, along the yellow and blue lines – to get to the core of Old Town, there's the King St Trolley that travels from the Metro station to City Hall.

☑ TOP TIP

Alexandria is beautiful from the water. City Cruises Alexandria has a water taxi that offers unique vistas of the town's skyline as well as trips to nearby Georgetown in Washington, DC and National Harbor in Maryland.

Adjacent to Arlington, Alexandria is known for its Old Town with its cobblestone streets and 18th-century buildings that culminate at the Potomac River. The riverfront is often swirling with activities aplenty – rowers coasting by, locals strolling with their leashed pups in quaint parks and plenty of spots for an often seafood-focused treat. The broader landscape features a mix of homes donning gas lamps and some of the hottest boutiques and watering holes in the region. Alexandria is very much a favorite of DC commuters and those seeking a reprieve from the big city. It's only 15 sq miles in area but carries a memorable punch. As with so much of Virginia, Alexandria was the stomping ground of Founding Fathers and household names – it was the hometown of George Washington, Robert E Lee and, more recently, Jim Morrison, lead singer of The Doors. It was also the setting for many episodes of *The West Wing*, so prepare to find a bit of familiarity if you're a fan of the show.

A Walk Fit for a King
Roam King St to the Potomac banks

Old Town Alexandria is a nationally designated historic district and its core, King St, puts so much of its zest on display, particularly between the **King St Metro station** and the Potomac River waterfront. Among the highlights along this strollable stretch is **Torpedo Factory Art Center**, a former munitions plant that celebrated its 50th year as an art gallery in 2024. Inside, you can weave through the galleries of 70-plus local artists. For Alexandria-themed tchotchkes, **The Old Town Shop** has Americana-inspired ornaments, puzzles and charms. The **Alexandria Visitor Center** has some fun keepsakes, too, including an ever-evolving collection of history-themed candles inspired by past events and Virginian towns.

Eastward, King St culminates at a **waterfront park** with views of DC's skyline. Within it, you'll find some photogenic

art installations (eg a larger-than-life 'I Love You' sign) in addition to surrounding restaurants. Just north of the waterfront park is **Founders Park**, which turns on quite the cherry-blossom spectacle come March and April.

By George!

Walk in Washington's footsteps at Mount Vernon

Mount Vernon is right up there on the list of Virginia's most famous residences. This was George Washington's most famous home, built by his dad in 1734. George and wife Martha lived here for 40-plus years, with George dying here in 1799. What once covered 8000 acres along the banks of the Potomac is now 500 acres of interactive experiences. To enter the grounds, you'll need to purchase a ground pass, with an additional fee to access the main mansion. There are a number of add-ons available from there – the best are a 45-minute boat excursion on the Potomac River and, for *Hamilton* lovers, a look at how Washington's life correlated with the famed Broadway show's songs.

Highlights in the mansion include Washington's cozy private study and the majestic New Room, the home's largest

THE GUIDE

ALEXANDRIA VIRGINIA

COBBLE, COBBLE

Embracing the historical whimsy of Old Town's cobblestone streets is no challenge. It's like stepping straight back in time. This style of paving wasn't chosen for its charm – during construction, cobblestones were affordable and readily available as merchant ships used river-rounded rocks as ballast in Alexandria. However, their durability posed challenges. Alignment issues and erosion meant ongoing maintenance, which eventually became unsustainable. Cobblestones eventually became a thing of the past in Alexandria as brick and other sturdier materials became more common. Ongoing preservation efforts, including the repaving of some cobblestones in 1979, have contributed to local conservation.

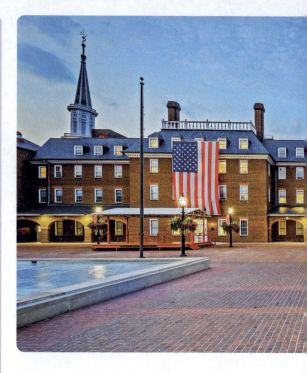

room. You'll also want to check out the 4-acre farm space, with costumed interpreters depicting how Mount Vernon's workers sheared sheep, harvested crops and more. There's also a working replica of Washington's distillery, which at one point was one of the largest distilleries in the US. Today, it's open to visitors on weekends from April through October, with tastings on select Saturdays. Mount Vernon was also once home to hundreds of slaves – 317, to be exact upon, Washington's passing – and among the more moving moments at the mansion is a small, replica slave cabin.

Making a Mark on Market Square
Peruse the farmers market and surroundings

A quiet square six days of the week, Market Sq comes alive on Saturdays (7am to noon) for the **Old Town Farmers Market**. Dozens of local artists and farmers showcase their

---

 EATING IN ALEXANDRIA: BEST RIVER VIEWS

Vola's Dockside: Riverfront dining, with seafood, tacos, classics and a midcentury-modern throwback in the Hi-Tide Lounge. **$$$**	**Ada's on the River:** Seafood and steaks surrounding a custom wood-burning oven with views of the Potomac. **$$$**	**BARCA:** Mediterranean fare, tapas and a wine bar situated on a pier. **$$**	**Jula's on the Potomac:** American classics on the 4th floor, with a terrace overlooking the river. **$$$**

Market Square and City Hall

ALEXANDRIA'S VIBRANT NEIGHBORHOODS

Old Town typically gets most recognition among Alexandria's neighborhoods, but wander beyond its cobblestone streets and you'll find many bustling neighborhoods to explore. Soak in the small-town, main-street vibes of Del Ray, where local boutiques, shops and bountiful food options line the main drag. Hop over to Arlandria for diverse cuisines, public art and to catch a show at the legendary music hall. Dive into Alexandria's burgeoning craft-beer scene in the West End, the city's fastest-growing neighborhood, and explore the more contemporary energy of Carlyle and Eisenhower, the county's hub of science and innovation.

latest offerings, and this is where many Alexandrians come to load up on their weekly essentials, including fresh fish, farm-raised meats and local dairy and produce.

At any time of week, the square's surrounding confines are among the city's most historic. The brick, chimney-dotted **City Hall** lines its northern edge. **Carlyle House**, a lux 1753 manor home, is also right there. Beyond its light stone facade, the house's interior gardens include a quaint gazebo that's primed for tranquil moments. **Gadsby's Tavern**, a late-1700s tavern and hotel, makes for a lively stop, too. This is where early American deals and discussions went down, attracting the likes of John Adams and James Monroe. Today it's a fine-dining establishment with stately wooden furniture, retrospective art and colonial actors adding to the vibe. There's an attached museum with grounds tours for taking in even more of the tavern.

 EATING IN ALEXANDRIA: BEST RAW BARS

| **The Wharf:** Rooftop dining in Old Town with an oyster happy hour. $$$ | **Whiskey & Oyster:** Local Virginian oysters, sandwiches and a rare-whiskey menu. $$$ | **BARCA:** Fine seafood dining for 500-plus years, with the coziest historical vibes. Indoor and outdoor seating. $$$ | **Clyde's at Market Center:** Sustainable ingredients are front and center in an eclectic atmosphere with a replica boathouse. $$$ |

ALEXANDRIA **VIRGINIA** | THE GUIDE

The Jefferson Hotel

Places We Love to Stay

$ Budget $$ Midrange $$$ Top End

Richmond MAP p349

Linden Row Inn $$ Victorian style with modern comforts. Enjoy the terrace and garden before making your way on foot to bustling Broad St.

Quirk Hotel $$$ Boutique hotel using Richmond's rich art scene as inspiration, complete with a gallery featuring local artists.

The Jefferson Hotel $$$ A century of tradition, history, luxury and elegance downtown, more reminiscent of an apartment than a hotel room.

Williamsburg MAP p354

The Cedars of Williamsburg B&B Inn $$ Georgian architecture, cozy rooms, friendly service and walkable to downtown.

Kingsmill Resort $$$ Elegant riverfront resort with stunning water views, a golf course and a variety of accommodations.

Williamsburg Inn $$$ Sophisticated, refined resort with picturesque outdoor spaces against a backdrop of colonial-revival architecture and a history of notable guests.

Charlottesville MAP p360

Graduate Charlottesville $$$ Channeling Charlottesville and UVA college charm and nostalgia for a quirky and creatively inspired ambience.

Keswick Hall $$$ Grand, contemporary luxury resort rooted in wellness experiences and nature, surrounded by Blue Ridge vistas.

Boar's Head Resort $$$ Modern amenities and outdoor activities with a classic appeal, surrounded by the rolling foothills of the Blue Ridge Mountains.

Roanoke MAP p363

The Liberty Trust $$ Restored downtown bank incorporating original features such as a tasting room in the original vault.

Fire Station One $$$ Renovated 1907 fire station with stunning architecture, large, open common spaces and each room boasting a unique style.

Hotel Roanoke $$$ Newly renovated for modern, stylish comfort within a Tudor exterior that seems to come from another country.

Harrisonburg MAP p367

Hotel Madison $$ Comfortable accommodations with refined touches close to downtown. Catch views of the city or the mountains and nods to James Madison.

Virginia Beach MAP p370

Cavalier Hotel & Beach Club $$$ Stately oceanfront stay with a lot of history and modern comfort.

Hilton Virginia Beach Oceanfront $$$ Private balconies, panoramic ocean views, prime boardwalk location and a rooftop pool and bar.

Arlington MAP p375

Placemakr Marymount Ballston $$$ Sleek apartment-style rooms and state-of-the-art amenities make this feel more like modern-city living than a hotel stay.

Ritz-Carlton Pentagon City $$$ Ritz-level comfort with a convenient location. Walkable to dining and shopping, and a quick drive to Arlington National Cemetery.

Fredericksburg MAP p377

Ironclad Inn $$ Historic residence turned inn walkable to downtown, with an Ironclad Distillery bourbon-tasting room.

Richard Johnston Inn & 1890 Caroline House $$ Two historic properties with big stories located on the main downtown drag.

Courtyard by Marriott Historic District $$ Comfortable accommodations, indoor pool and a central downtown location.

Alexandria MAP p381

Hotel Indigo Old Town $$$ Chic, modern style against a Potomac backdrop, a short walk from the cobblestone streets of Old Town.

Hotel AKA Alexandria $$$ Residential-style accommodations with an elevated urban design, including fun architectural touches for the ultimate Old Town retreat.

Above: Base jumper, New River Gorge Bridge (p394); Right: State Capitol Building, Charleston (p393)

THE MAIN AREAS

CHARLESTON
West Virginia's low-key capital.
p390

NEW RIVER GORGE
Fifty-three miles of outdoor adventure.
p394

MORGANTOWN
A sports town with a college habit.
p398

West Virginia
THE ENDURING HEART OF APPALACHIA

Lose yourself in the forests and small towns of this resilient state.

'The sun doesn't always shine on West Virginia,' President John F Kennedy once said, 'but the people do.'

Kennedy wasn't alone in his affection for the Mountain State. 'Take Me Home, Country Roads' is one of John Denver's most enduring ballads, and countless native writers have waxed poetic on this wild and wonderful land. Yes, West Virginia has seen plenty of drama over the years, from the Hatfield-and-McCoy blood feud to the complicated legacy of coal mining. But open-minded visitors will find the best of Appalachia in these textured highlands. Nearly 80% of West Virginia is blanketed in forest, and its six national parks are a paradise for temperate wildlife – as well as birders, hikers and anglers in search of nature. West Virginia is a constellation of farms and small towns; the largest city has only 47,000 residents.

Folks here also take pride in their rebellious spirit: The state broke away from Virginia in 1863 to reject slavery and ally with the Union. Grit and determination have helped these communities weather tough times, and the state continues to reinvent itself as an outdoors playground and incubator for small businesses. West Virginia's reputation for hospitality is well earned, and locals tend to wear their hearts on their sleeves. As you fall into its down-home rhythms, you'll likely find yourself shining, too.

HARPERS FERRY
An antebellum
town frozen in time.
p400

BERKELEY SPRINGS
Thermal waters fit
for a president.
p401

THE NORTHERN PANHANDLE
A quirky frontier
between states.
p402

WEST VIRGINIA

THE GUIDE

Find Your Way

With its odd shape and rolling topography, West Virginia is best explored one mile at a time. Drives can be long and service stations scattered, so keep an eye on that fuel gauge.

CAR

West Virginia's curving motorways are ideal for road trips; you'll marvel at the rich wooded landscape. But there's a reason many residents drive pickups – potholes plague pavements, and many back roads are gravel.

BUS

As a last resort, Greyhound connects most major towns. Tickets aren't cheap, though, and the winding routes may burn time – a Greyhound ride from Morgantown to Charleston takes nearly 10 hours.

Morgantown, p398

West Virginia's consummate college town is a friendly riverside community with a diehard love for football and craft beer.

Charleston, p390

This modest state capital is steeped in history, and the old downtown area has recently come alive with dining and nightlife options.

PENNSYLVANIA

Harrisburg

Hagerstown

Frederick

Rockville

MARYLAND

WASHINGTON, DC

Charles Town

Martinsburg

Berkeley Springs

Romney

Keyser

Moorefield

Spruce Knob-Seneca Rocks National Recreation Area

Franklin

George Washington National Forest

Lexington

VIRGINIA

Roanoke

Pittsburgh

Morgantown

Grafton

Bridgeport

Elkins

Weston

Holly River State Park

Monongahela National Forest

Summersville

Watoga State Park

Lewisburg

Fayetteville

Wheeling

Parkersburg

Spencer

Charleston

New River Gorge National River

Princeton

Bervina Lake Wildlife Management Area

OHIO

Wayne National Forest

Huntington

KENTUCKY

Dayton

Cincinnati

79

70

50

16

14

33

77

35

54

119

77

75

119

19

19

60

64

220

39

33

64

81

68

0   50 miles
0   100 km

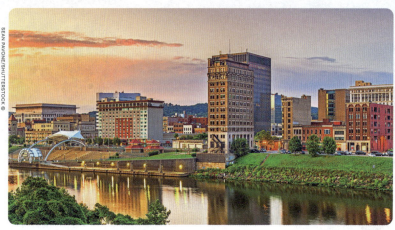

Charleston (p390)

Plan Your Time

West Virginia is made for outdoor enthusiasts, no matter the season. History buffs will also find plenty of landmarks to track down.

Beeline to New River Gorge

- Thousands of tourists drive to West Virginia to play around in **New River Gorge** (p394). The national park caters to a wide range of backwoods activities and levels of experience, occupying a single day or a whole week. Stick around **Fayetteville** (p395) for a local cabin or campground, or head to **Charleston** (p390) for a comfy hotel. Spend a day roaming the surrounding byways.

A Drive Through the Past

- From Virginia, you can explore West Virginia's history in roughly chronological order: Start in **Berkeley Springs** (p401), then **Harpers Ferry** (p400) for a lesson in abolitionism, or **Morgantown** (p398) and the **Northern Panhandle** (p402) for the Industrial Revolution. Hike the **Ivy Branch trail system** to follow Hatfield and McCoy. Then there's **Charleston** (p390), the capital that almost wasn't.

SEASONAL HIGHLIGHTS

SPRING
The warmer months kick off with blossoming trees and perfect temperatures. Expect motorcycles and mountain bikes.

SUMMER
Pitch a tent, raft the rivers, cast a line – summer is West Virginia's active season.

FALL
Leaf-peepers go wild for the colorful foliage. This is the high season for both hikers and hunters.

WINTER
With so many hills, it's no surprise that this state has four ski resorts. The trails are ripe for snowshoeing and cross-country.

Charleston

COOL NIGHTLIFE | INTERACTIVE MUSEUMS | LOCAL ARTS

GETTING AROUND

Most of Charleston is flat and stretched along the river. If time is no issue, the Kanawha Valley Regional Transportation Authority has bus stops around every major destination. Downtown Charleston is easy to navigate on foot or in a wheelchair. Charleston doesn't have a bikeshare program at the moment, but travelers bringing their own bikes might have the easiest time of all. The vast majority of visitors arrive by car.

Charleston stands at the confluence of two rivers, the Elk and Kanawha, and it's hours from any major city. This unique location has put the town at the forefront of industry and politics since its founding. Charleston moguls made their fortunes on salt, coal and the first-ever natural gas well. During the Civil War, Charleston was torn between the Union and Confederacy, and rival armies captured and recaptured the city. The wane of manufacturing has left its mark, and the population today has nearly halved since 1950.

Like many industrial towns, Charleston is on the upswing. The revitalizing downtown area is busy with new pubs and restaurants, and the city hosts numerous festivals throughout the year. Charleston's pro baseball team, the Dirty Birds, plays all summer at the GoMart Ballpark. West Virginia's capital can feel a little underutilized, but exciting developments are afoot.

Party Down in Downtown
A dusty district turned hip

Capitol St is a tree-lined commercial strip with vintage storefronts and brick-paved sidewalks, and it has become the go-to stomping ground for visitors to Charleston. Its few blocks are thick with brewpubs and restaurants, and most thrum with patrons any night of the week. You can amble across downtown Charleston in no time, but the neighborhood is rich in historic architecture and commemorative plaques. The most recent addition is **Slack Plaza**, a beautiful pedestrian concourse, playground and splash-pad. Two whimsical sculptures of fiddling musicians welcome you to the plaza, and real-life instrumentalists play here in the warmer months. Downtown Charleston is best enjoyed in the

SIGHTS
1. Booker T Washington Memorial
2. Capitol Street Clock
3. Clay Center for the Arts and Sciences
4. Coal Miner Sculpture
5. Former Capitol Site
6. Homeless Jesus
7. Slack Plaza
8. State Capitol Building
9. The Block Sign
10. West Virginia State Museum

SLEEPING
11. Brass Pineapple Inn

EATING
12. Adelphia Sports Bar
13. Black Sheep Burrito & Brews
14. Hale House

DRINKING & NIGHTLIFE
15. Bar 101

16. Fife Street Brewing
17. Red Carpet Lounge
18. The ROQ
19. Vino's Bar & Grill

SHOPPING
20. Capitol Market
21. Taylor Books

summer, when the streets are busy and food trucks are out, but Slack Plaza also has a skating rink in the winter.

Learn What This Town Is Made Of
Multisensory schooling at two museums

A theater, an art museum and a planetarium – it's hard to believe how much the **Clay Center for the Arts and Sciences** packs into a single downtown facility. This 240,000-sq-ft complex is geared especially to families and kids: the Maier Foundation Music Studio is a hands-on acoustic workshop, and the Discovery Center has a fern-like climbable sculpture that rises three stories above the main floor. The Maier Foundation Performance Hall seats more than 1800 people and hosts concerts, dance recitals and touring Broadway shows.

Around the corner from the Capitol stands a monolithic concrete building, and you'd never guess that the maze-like **West Virginia State Museum** is housed in its basement. Visitors are treated to dioramas, vintage newsreels and framed

✓ TOP TIP

For such a small and low-traffic town, Charleston's layout can confuse first-time visitors. Many of the main avenues are one-way, and drivers have to circle back through streets to face the right direction. Parking is also fierce – within city limits, Charleston is a minefield of meters, paid lots and no-parking signs.

OVERLOOKED CHARLESTON MONUMENTS

Capitol Street Clock: This handsome freestanding clock is Capitol St's unofficial mascot.

Former Capitol Site: This tiny, pie-shaped park marks the location of the old Capitol building before it burned down.

Homeless Jesus: Timothy Schmalz's bronze sculpture of Jesus sleeping on a park bench will make you look twice.

The Block Sign: Directly east of downtown, a sign commemorates 'The Block,' a former nucleus of Charleston's African American community.

Coal Miner Sculpture: Burl Jones' realistic sculpture of a miner in hard hat stands in a plaza near the Capitol.

Booker T Washington Memorial: The African American leader was born in what's now West Virginia; a bust and plaque stand near the capitol.

'paintings' that come to life and talk to each other. These multimedia exhibits take you on a journey through West Virginian history, from Paleolithic settlement to the Battle of Blair Mountain labor uprising. Originally opened in 1976 as the West Virginia Science and Culture Center, this museum remains impressive – and admission is free.

Browse Local Merchants
Shopping local in the capital's heart

Yes, **Taylor Books** is a bookstore, and its shelves offer a nice range of bestsellers, used volumes and titles by local authors, but this Capitol St institution quadruples as a bookseller, coffee house, art gallery and music venue. You could easily spend

EATING & DRINKING IN CHARLESTON: HIP STOPS

Adelphia Sports Bar: Bustling bar and dining room with a diverse pub menu and lot of TVs. **$$**

Black Sheep Burritos & Brews: Upmarket Mexican fusion restaurant with reasonable prices, plus cocktails. **$$**

Hale House: Refined bistro with a brick dining room and menu of 240 varieties of bourbon. Head downstairs to the Volstead speakeasy. **$$**

Fife Street Brewing: Lively taproom with high ceilings and big windows, on a lively pedestrian walkway.

Clay Center for the Arts and Sciences

a whole afternoon sipping java and chatting up literary locals, and there's even a screening room in the basement for watching art films with new friends. Visit in the evening for a rotating lineup of singer-songwriters.

Similar in spirit is **Capitol Market**, a turn-of-the-century train station that has served as a small-business bazaar and community hangout since 1997. Residents shop here year-round for fresh produce and handmade gifts, and rows of stalls are also set up outside during the warmer months. Unlike many traditional farmers markets, this location is open almost every day of the week. Capitol Market's 'culinary ambassador' is chef Paul Smith, the state's first finalist for a James Beard Award. He hosts live cooking demonstrations on the third Thursday of every month.

A CAPITOL AFFAIR

West Virginia's **State Capitol Building** is a beautiful Palladian structure with a central dome and gold-leaf trim, but until its construction in 1932, the state legislature seemed cursed. The designation of 'state capital' was volleyed between Charleston and Wheeling for 22 years. The government finally settled on Charleston, and the city razed the previous building in order to construct an imposing Italianate capitol in 1885. This second capitol accidentally caught fire in 1921, detonating a cache of ammunition inside. As if to distance itself from all the bad luck, a new capitol was erected in its current location, nearly 2 miles from Capitol St. The complex is nested among plazas and other government buildings – and the curse appears to be broken.

DRINKING IN CHARLESTON: LOCAL HAUNTS

Red Carpet Lounge: Local favorite, with a sizable patio out back and bargain prices.	**Bar 101:** Busy bar with craft beer, pub menu, regular DJs and throbbing dance floor.	**The ROQ:** Atmospheric lounge specializing in cocktails, live music and salsa dancing. Thoughtful menu, including flatbreads.	**Vino's Bar & Grill:** Upstairs is a West Virginia lounge with a Manhattan streak; downstairs is a casual hangout. DJs, pool and pinball.

Beyond Charleston

The forests around Charleston abound with historic tales and outdoor opportunities. This is West Virginia at its wildest and most wonderful.

Places

New River Gorge p394
Hatfield-McCoy Trails p396
Point Pleasant p396
Sutton p397

Part of Charleston's appeal is its remoteness. Even second-tier cities such as Columbus and Pittsburgh are located across state lines and take hours to reach. What lies between is an ocean of rolling hills and deciduous forest, small towns and hidden valleys, all ripe for exploration. Charleston is a great place to begin or end a journey, and you can base yourself in one of many hotels as you drive figure-eights through surrounding counties.

For outdoors people, the options for hiking and water sports are nearly endless. Bumper stickers may reveal strong political persuasions, but almost everyone around here is united in their love for fresh air. A taste for bourbon may also score you points.

GETTING AROUND

A car is necessary to really explore southern West Virginia, and the tougher your vehicle, the better – there's a reason you'll see so many pickup trucks on the road. Highways are well maintained and connect major towns, but secondary roads have their share of potholes, especially in spring, and you don't have to stray too far to hit gravel and severe inclines. If you're visiting in the winter, snow tires are a smart precaution.

New River Gorge

TIME FROM CHARLESTON: **70 MINUTES**

Admire the Bridge

The steel **bridge** that arcs over New River Gorge is one of the most resplendent sights in West Virginia, and its image has been recreated on every canvas, T-shirt and mug imaginable. The architectural masterpiece was completed in 1977 and, at 3030ft in length, it remains the longest single-span arch bridge in the Western Hemisphere. Speeding across in a car, you may barely notice the one-minute journey over the bridge, but before its construction, driving across the canyon took at least 40 minutes. No visit to Fayette County is complete without stopping at the visitor center – on the eastern side – and admiring those maroon beams from two designated platforms. The bridge is a fitting gateway to the **New River Gorge National Park and Preserve**, a wooded wonderland covering 70,000 acres. The walls of the canyon are heavily forested and slide dramatically into the river, and it's easily the most photographed panorama in the state.

Hit the Trails. And Rocks. And Water.

The national park is a magnet for hikers, campers, rock climbers and mountain bikers, especially in summer. Motor activities are also common here, with routes for ATVs and snowmobiles.

New River Gorge

After a good winter storm, snowshoers and cross-country skiers take over the trails. A typical year will bring in more than 1.5 million visitors, making it one of the most popular destinations in the state. But even in the busiest months, you can find peace and solitude among the corrugated hills.

The New River itself extends 53 miles through the protected landscape, with waters that range from calm and glassy to frothing class III rapids. The waterway's length attracts kayakers and white-water rafters from around the world, and the varying conditions appeal to both newbies and veterans. If you love to paddle, you will find something to love in New River Gorge. Many tour operators are based in Fayette County, but the largest and most dynamic is **Adventures on the Gorge** (adventuresonthegorge.com), based in Lansing. This outfit can arrange class-V rafting trips, family ziplining and accommodations in its luxury cabins.

Unwind in Fayetteville

The best place to base yourself is Fayetteville, a tiny historic town on the western side of New River Gorge, just a mile from the bridge. Court St is lined with bistros, outfitters and antebellum houses, and visitors typically stop here to grab lunch and get their bearings. The town is ringed with hotels, lodges and campgrounds, and plenty of visitors bed down in Fayetteville while spending daylight hours in the park.

TOP ONE-DAY ACTIVITIES

Fayette Station Road: This one-way road spirals 8 miles through the gorge. The 40-minute drive includes a trestle bridge over the New River.

Endless Wall Trail: The hiking is tame; the views are epic. This popular 2.4-mile walk skirts a spectacular series of cliffs.

Bridge Walk: Join this tour (bridgewalk.com) to conquer acrophobia and cross the New River Gorge Bridge on a narrow catwalk. Don't worry: you're safely clipped in.

Cathedral Falls: Twenty minutes' drive from the bridge, this waterfall makes for a spectacular selfie. Park in the lot and you're steps away.

Bridge Day: Mark your calendars: the bridge is closed to motor traffic on the third Saturday of October. Pedestrians, vendors and BASE jumpers rejoice.

EATING IN FAYETTEVILLE: BEST GRUB

The Stache: Come for the toys and knickknacks, stay for the eclectic ice cream and candy. $

Wanderlust Creativefoods: Sophisticated plates served in a cozy setting, with decor highlighted with woodwork. $$

Southside Junction Tap House: LGBTIQ+-friendly corner bar in an old brick building. Craft beers, burgers and live music. $$

Pies & Pints: Funky pizzas and a dizzying range of beers on tap in a polished modernist venue. $$

YARNS SPUN ABOUT THE HATFIELD-MCCOY FEUD

Blood Feud: The Hatfields & McCoys: Novelist Lisa Alther presents an authoritative nonfiction biography of the Hatfields and McCoys and their multigenerational feud.

The Feud: The Hatfields & McCoys: Prolific nonfiction writer Dean King describes the peaceful coexistence between the two families before the Civil War wrenched them apart.

The McCoys Before the Feud: A Western Novel: This fictional account by author Thomas A McCoy imagines his ancestors' less-known exploits in the American West.

The Coffin Quilt: Ann Rinaldi's YA novel illustrates life in 1870s Appalachia through the eyes of young Fanny McCoy.

Hatfields & McCoys: Kevin Costner and Bill Paxton star as rival patriarchs in this action-packed History Channel miniseries.

Hatfield-McCoy Trails

TIME FROM CHARLESTON: **30 MINUTES**

Hike Through History

It's strange to think that these peaceful paths were once the backdrop for a bitter blood feud, and members of the Hatfield and McCoy clans spent 28 years treading these very routes in their quest for shotgun justice. What started as an argument over land rights in the 1860s ballooned into an interfamilial conflict, and at least 20 lives were lost in West Virginia's woodlands before its ceasefire in 1891. Founded in 2000, the Hatfield-McCoy Trails extend more than 1000 miles through the southwestern quarter of the state, spanning nine counties.

Such a vast network has plenty of segments and trailheads, but the closest to Charleston is the **Ivy Branch trail system** (p389). An entry point in the town of Julian stands about a half-hour drive from the capital, and you'll find a sizable parking lot and welcome center. From here, you can access 60 miles of rugged, wending paths.

Start Your Engines

The Ivy Branch makes fertile ground for ATVs and dirt bikes, and the woods regularly rumble with motors. Many of these 'trails' are basically unpaved backroads, and plenty of riders like to test their suspension by plowing through rocky terrain and careening around tight turns. The Hatfield-McCoy system is also a magnet for mountain bikers of all abilities.

You can rent high-quality ATVs from the **Ivy Branch ATV Resort** in nearby Sunerco. The resort specializes in Ivy Branch tourism and also has ATV-friendly cabins and grounds.

Point Pleasant

TIME FROM CHARLESTON: **1 HOUR**

The World's Only Mothman Museum

West Virginia has many folk heroes, but none of them excites the imagination like the Mothman. This insect-human hybrid made its debut in *The Mothman Prophecies*, a 1975 memoir by John A Keel, which takes place in the small riverside town of Point Pleasant. The Mothman has gone on to win worldwide attention among cryptozoologists, and many a local has claimed to spot this winged, 10ft-tall critter in the wild. The legend inspired a 2002 feature film, *The Mothman Prophecies*, starring Richard Gere; a year later, a Mothman statue was

The World's Only Mothman Museum

unveiled in the middle of Point Pleasant. The statue stands directly in front of **The World's Only Mothman Museum**, a small storefront that houses newspaper clippings, artwork and other ephemera.

Sutton

TIME FROM CHARLES: **1 HOURS**

Flatwoods Monster Museum

Learn about West Virginia's less-famous supernatural sighting at the **Flatwoods Monster Museum**, a former soda fountain in the town of Sutton. The museum's mascot is the Flatwoods Monster, a 10ft-tall extraterrestrial with a red face and flowing gown that locals claimed to have spotted in 1952. The town embraces this strange episode, with a sign that reads 'Home of the Green Monster,' a reference to the creature's green outfit.

West Virginia Bigfoot Museum

Sutton is also home to the **West Virginia Bigfoot Museum**, a roomy exhibition space dedicated to all things Sasquatch. This newest addition opened in 2021 and displays art, artifacts and testimonials from Bigfoot lore.

OUTDOOR EXCURSIONS IN NEW RIVER GORGE

Bill Chouinard, pilot, vacation-rental operator and owner of Wild Blue Adventure Co. *wildblueadventurecompany.com*

Mark my words, Fayette County is the epicenter of multisport days anywhere in the US. I moved here nearly 30 years ago, dropping out of college with $300 and a one-way ticket, and heading for the world-class climbing at New River Gorge.

I've spent almost three decades climbing, kayaking, mountain biking, running, paragliding, BASE jumping and now flying here. This place is more than just our home. It's fuel for daily inspiration, exploration and adventure. The thing that really makes this place stand out is the people – an incredible mix of locals and transplants drawn here by a common interest in the outdoors and everything it offers.

Morgantown

COLLEGE TOWN | PARTY DISTRICT | OUTDOORS LAUNCHPAD

GETTING AROUND

Despite the hills, Morgantown is compact and easy to get around on foot. The best sights, including restaurants, a waterfront path and WVU campus, are tucked into a single square mile. Mountain Line Transit (busride.org) connects much of the county by bus, and you'll spot sheltered stops along the main arteries. Most visitors prefer the freedom of a car, especially if staying in one of the many chain hotels on the town's outskirts. Parking can get competitive when school is in session.

☑ TOP TIP

Morgantown has an active rideshare network, which can be a literal lifesaver on boozy weekends. Between the party-town rep and the winding roads, late-night return trips are always safer with a designated driver.

The underlying spirit of Morgantown is best illustrated by a mural, painted by an unknown artist on a brick wall off Chestnut St. In this idyllic landscape, residents smile among pastel-colored storefronts, while a cyclist pedals past and a ballerina practices her twirls. Modern Morgantown doesn't quite match that shiny image, but this hilly college community retains a neighborly vibe. The former coal capital is made up of craftsman houses and brick commercial buildings, which crowd along the Monongahela River. Morgantown is best known as the home of West Virginia University (WVU), a campus that enrolls nearly 27,000 students. The downtown area is infused with breweries, global restaurants and sporty pastimes, and this 'big small town' makes for a perfect overnight stop on West Virginia road trips. On game days, the sleepy streets blow up, and the Mountaineers – WVU's beloved football team – draw up to 60,000 spectators to Milan Puskar Stadium.

Stroll High Street

A cultural oasis in town

Most of the culture and nightlife in Morgantown is squeezed into High St, a long commercial corridor just east of the Monongahela River. On the north end, WVU campus crowns a hilltop with stately brick buildings, and students trickle down steep walkways to the restaurants, bars and galleries below. Weekends can get rowdy, as WVU has a long-standing party-school rep. One exception is First Friday, a family-friendly showcase of local artists and gourmands. The lynchpin of First Friday is the **Monongalia Arts Center**, or MAC, a historic gallery and performance venue.

The **Metropolitan Theatre** is an active show-space for concerts, plays and comedians. Each year, some 35,000 theatergoers travel from across the tristate area, most to catch touring musicians. The auditorium dates back to 1924, when it served as a vaudeville stage. Nearby stands a statue of TV star Don Knotts, a beloved native son. Morgantown is named after its tough-as-nails founder, Colonel Zackquill Morgan, who was born in Wales

SIGHTS
1 Monongalia Arts Center

ACTIVITIES, COURSES & TOURS
2 Morgantown Adventure Outfitters

SLEEPING
3 Hotel Morgan

DRINKING & NIGHTLIFE
4 Apothecary Ale House & Cafe
5 Gibbie's Pub & Eatery
6 Metropolitan Billiard Parlor
7 Sports Page

ENTERTAINMENT
8 Metropolitan Theatre

THE GUIDE

WEST VIRGINIA MORGANTOWN

and fought in both the French and Indian War and the American Revolution. Morgan and his wife, Catherine Garretson, weren't just early settlers in the region; they were the first known colonists to build a home in the land that would become West Virginia. In his postwar life, Morgan commissioned a courthouse and public square, and he personally opened the town's first tavern. In 2016, some 221 years after his death, a statue of Morgan was unveiled on Spruce St. It was sculpted by artist Jamie Lester, who also created the Don Knotts monument around the block.

Explore the River

Fun by the banks

The Monongahela River – the 'Mon' – has always been the lifeblood of Morgantown, first for industry and now for recreation. The Mon River Trail is a multiuse path that snakes along the river for 19.5 miles, arriving at last in the town of Reedsville. This patchwork of pavement and crushed limestone is a blessing for cyclists and joggers.

For a more intimate view of the river, rent a kayak or stand-up paddleboard from **Morgantown Adventure Outfitters**. There's a boat launch just across the path from this little brick building, and visitors can paddle the gentle waters – and take in a gorgeous skyline – from April to October.

 DRINKING IN MORGANTOWN: BEST BARS

| **Gibbie's Pub & Eatery:** Deep hangout with multiple bars, an impressive local beer selection and generous patio. Lots of regulars. | **Apothecary Ale House & Cafe:** Hip pub with vintage interior and wide selection of brews on tap. | **Metropolitan Billiard Parlor:** Basement pool hall with a small bar and lots of vintage decorations. A local institution since prohibition. | **Sports Page:** Immensely popular sports bar with TVs, wings baskets and a locally famous iced tea. |

Beyond Morgantown

Learn the story of the state, one town at a time.

Places

Harpers Ferry p400
Berkeley Springs p401
The Northern Panhandle p402

Few US states are as oddly shaped as West Virginia – its outline has been compared to a leaping frog or a galloping turkey. The borders are most erratic in the northern half, which has two distinct 'panhandles.' The Eastern Panhandle is wedged between Maryland and Virginia, while the Northern Panhandle thrusts itself between Ohio and Pennsylvania. Morgantown stands roughly in the middle, making it a handy base camp.

Many motorists have driven along this jagged frontier and felt as though they were traveling through time. These scattered towns reflect important moments in American history, and a parade of famous people trudged through here, from presidents to freedom fighters. Traces of their passage are everywhere.

Harpers Ferry

TIME FROM MORGANTOWN: **3 HOURS**

Explore a Blue Ridge Paradise

To call Harpers Ferry a special place is a serious understatement. Here, the beloved Shenandoah River merges with the Potomac on its journey to Chesapeake Bay. Three states – Maryland, Virginia and West Virginia – huddle together as well, and you can hopscotch across multiple borders without breaking a sweat. This valley has received more than its share of natural and structural beauty, thanks to rolling hills, soaring cliffs and two railroad bridges that span the wide waters. Even its architecture excels: the Historic District's stone houses, federalist brick facades and cobbled streets look virtually unchanged since hoop skirts were in fashion.

Harpers Ferry was also the backdrop for John Brown's final standoff. In 1859, the radical abolitionist attempted to attack the town, raid its armory and free enslaved people across the region. Instead, Brown's men embedded themselves in a local engine house and clashed with the US Army. Brown was tried and executed, but he became a hero of the antislavery movement.

You can see this story in three dimensions at the **John Brown Wax Museum**, which vividly brings this final struggle to life. The center of the action was **John Brown's Fort**, the name given to the little brick firehouse he used as a stronghold. The 'fort' has been moved slightly from its original location, but visitors can still tour the structure, and Harpers

GETTING AROUND

Greyhound buses require superhuman patience in these parts, which is why almost everyone traveling here drives a car. There is no single highway that connects one panhandle to the other, and most drivers use Interstates 68, 70 and 79, taking shortcuts through Maryland and Pennsylvania. Whether you prefer highways or those famous country roads, get comfy: the fastest route from Harpers Ferry to Wheeling takes four hours.

400

Berkeley Springs State Park

WHY I LOVE WEST VIRGINIA

Robert Isenberg, Lonely Planet writer

For years, I've proclaimed that 'wild, wonderful' is America's most fitting state slogan. Yes, West Virginia can be wild – I've seen rifles mounted over beer taps, teens jumping off trestles and junkers who had no business being on the road. I've heard tall tales from chain-smoking strangers that were just weird enough to be true. Meanwhile, the state is also wonderful: friends, old and new, ache to show me the best view, the most storied pub and the most swimmable 'crick'. Locals expect me to dress casual and speak plain, and I'm always happy to oblige. Another famous slogan is 'Almost Heaven,' and when I hike those hills, I believe it.

Ferry is packed with other historic monuments from the era. The town was literally designed for walking, but note that some streets are steep and not ideal for wheelchairs.

Berkeley Springs

DISTANCE FROM MORGANTOWN: **2 HOURS**

Soak in Waters Fit for a President

Not only did George Washington sleep here, he also bathed in Berkeley Springs – indeed, he was such a fan of the area, he bought up much of its real estate. Travelers have flocked to the town's 74°F thermal pools since colonial times, and indigenous people likely enjoyed the mineral-rich waters long before that. Berkeley Springs is a long drive from Morgantown, but the mineral baths and quaint downtown are well worth the trip.

The town has two full-service retreats: **Atasia Spa** and Renaissance Spa at the **Country Inn**. You can also find warm waters in **Berkeley Springs State Park**, home to the Old Roman Bath House. This historic brick structure contains a 750-gallon private mineral bath, where four adults can soak for up to an hour. All facilities offer a complete menu of facials, massages and other wellness services.

 EATING IN BERKELEY SPRINGS: BEST BITES & DRINKS

Mary's Vegetarian Cafe: A cozy converted house with a cornucopia of plant-based bowls, salads and noodle dishes. **$$**	**Naked Olive Lounge:** This olive-oil tasting room triples as a gourmet food market and LGBTIQ+-friendly cocktail lounge. **$$**	**Cacapon Mountain Brewing:** Follow your spa session with a craft beer in an upbeat taproom. Kitchen window available for bites. **$$**	**Lot 12 Public House:** Savor chef Damien Heath's masterful dishes and thoughtful wine pairings in a century-old converted house. **$$$**

OUTDOOR ACTIVITIES AROUND HARPERS FERRY

Ziplining:
Fly along seven ziplines through the canopy, or walk an elevated skybridge, at **Harpers Ferry Adventure Center** (harpersferry adventurecenter.com).

Maryland Heights Trail:
This 6.5-mile trail has some tough climbs, but hikers are rewarded with unparalleled views of the town and valley.

River Tubing:
The lazy currents are ideal for floating downriver in an inflatable tube. Come summer, make arrangements with **River Riders** (riverriders.com).

C&O Canal Towpath:
This segment of rail trail is composed of limestone and is part of a 333-mile bike route between Pittsburgh and DC.

Bolivar Heights Battlefield:
These peaceful meadows and forest were hotly contested during the Civil War.

The town's main drag is naturally named Washington St, and its handful of shops and restaurants should occupy most visitors for an afternoon or two.

The Northern Panhandle

TIME FROM MORGANTOWN: **70-90 MIN**

Monuments in Moundsville

Moundsville is named after the massive burial mounds created by the Adena people two millennia ago. Many of the mounds were removed by settlers, but the **Grave Creek Mound** still stands and visitors can ascend a walkway to the 62ft-high summit. Grave Creek also has a small museum, which chronicles the region's prehistoric past and displays a full-size mammoth skeleton.

Cross Jefferson Ave to visit the **West Virginia Penitentiary**, a medieval-looking compound that once incarcerated as many as 2000 inmates. The eerie site now hosts a 1½-hour tour, paranormal visits and even an escape-room challenge.

EATING IN HARPERS FERRY: UNIQUE VENUES

| **Rabbit Hole Gastropub:** Craft cocktails and gourmet dining in a discerning country-charm setting. Beautiful porch and stone walls. **$$** | **Kelley Farm Kitchen:** West Virginia's first plant-based restaurant, set in a farmhouse. Riffs on traditional entrees and great ramen. **$$$** | **Barn of Harpers Ferry:** Converted barn with regular live concerts and creative libations. Food served on Fridays and Saturdays. **$$** | **Yatai Hibachi Food Trailer:** Pan-Asian food truck. Watch chef Made Sudira work the hibachi and claim a picnic table. **$$** |

West Virginia Penitentiary

Gamble on Wheeling

Wheeling is the Panhandle's largest town and once served as the state capital. It's no longer famous for producing iron nails, and Main St has seen better days, but the downtown still boasts an amazing suspension bridge over the river and, on the opposite bank, card sharps can try their hand at the **Wheeling Island Casino and Racetrack**. The casino has more than 1100 slot machines, and the live entertainment attracts patrons from across the tristate area.

Become One with New Vrindaban

The Panhandle's most peculiar attraction is the **New Vrindaban** community, a spiritual estate founded by Hare Krishna guru Srila Prabhupada in 1968. The central complex is known as the Palace of Gold, with ornamented walls and curved roofs that would look perfectly at home in rural India. Guests are invited to roam the grassy grounds, interact with peacocks and cows and enjoy a spice-infused vegetarian meal at Govinda's Restaurant.

TOP SKI RESORTS OF WEST VIRGINIA

Canaan Valley:
This state park has a sizable lodge, cabins and tent sites. There are 47 ski trails in the winter, plus an 18-hole golf course in summer. canaanresort.com

Snowshoe Mountain Resort:
A beloved resort modeled on Alpine villages. The mountain boasts 14 lifts and 60 ski trails. Fire-tower visits and mountain biking are popular in summer. snowshoemtn.com

Winterplace Ski Resort:
An intimate four-season resort in southern West Virginia, with 28 trails, nine lifts and 16 lanes of snow tubing. winterplace.com

Timberline Mountain:
A great place for beginners and crowd-shy skiers. Timberline has 37 easygoing trails and a 20-room boutique hotel. timberlinemountain.com

---

 EATING IN THE PANHANDLE: HIPPEST LITTLE JOINTS

| **Avenue Eats:** Slick Wheeling eatery with a canoe fastened to the brick wall. Inventive burgers and ice cream. *11am-9pm Tue-Sat* $$ | **Later Alligator:** Crepes, wraps and fun salads in a Wheeling storefront. Eclectic pictures on the walls and patio seating on warm days. $$ | **Prima Marina:** Riverside restaurant in Moundsville serves up hoagies, freshwater-fish platters and beautiful Ohio River sunsets. $$ | **Oh Briens Tavern:** Casual Fallansbee bar serving pub food, drinks, karaoke and sports. $ |

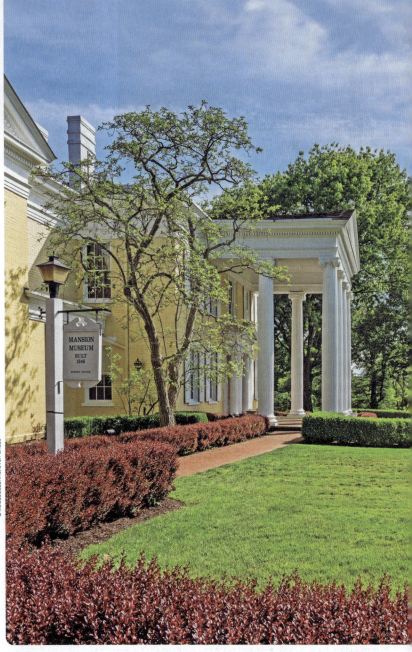

Oglebay Resort

Places We Love to Stay

€ Budget €€ Midrange €€€ Top End

Charleston MAP p391

Brass Pineapple Inn $$ This century-old inn was formerly a private home, and rooms retain an Edwardian hominess. Some have claw-foot tubs; room service on silver trays.

Fayette County MAP p394

The Outpost $ Cabins, tent platforms and RV hookups – The Outpost is ready for almost any kind of outdoors enthusiast. Regular fireside jams for music fans.

Glen Ferris Inn $$ A lovely way station for travelers for nearly two centuries, just a stone's throw from photogenic Kanawha Falls. Home-style restaurant.

Bear Mountain Cabins & Campground $$$ Amish-style log cabins with air conditioning and fully equipped kitchens. A range of tent sites also available.

The Historic Morris Harvey House $$$ Elegant turn-of-the-century inn with gardens, seven fireplaces and claw-foot tubs. Grab a cocktail at Rosa's Speakeasy.

Opossum Creek Retreat $$$ The modern cabins are comfortable, and the Farmhouse and Ayres House are even comfier. Great getaway for families and groups.

Morgantown MAP p399

Hotel Morgan $$$ Distinguished flagship hotel in the middle of town, fully renovated in 2020. Anvil + Ax is a gorgeous cocktail lounge on the 1st floor.

The Cranberry $$$ Luxury escape on nearby Cheat Lake. Immaculate rooms, plus restaurant and bar, right next to Lakeview Golf Resort & Spa.

Harpers Ferry MAP p400

Stonehouse B&B $$$ True to its name, a handsome 1839 stone residence with gorgeous views, tasteful rooms and a doily-free environment.

1799 Inn $$$ When the Harpers Ferry armory was being built in 1799, workers stayed in this very house. The beautiful rooms thoughtfully blend old and new.

Light Horse Inn $$$ Once known as the Keyes Inn, this stately brick house has welcomed guests since the 1780s. Suites with creative decor.

Cantuta Inn $$$ Historic B&B owned by a Peruvian artist and National Geographic associate. Snug rooms with country-charm aesthetic.

Berkeley Springs MAP p400

Country Inn (p401) **$$** Built in 1933, this Greek Revival–style estate is the town's keystone. Two restaurants, live music and a firepit.

Mendenhall 1884 $$ Victorian house recast as an inn with thematic rooms. On-site massages and cruiser bicycles for rent.

Maria's Garden & Inn $$ Pleasant former house with a brick patio and tons of Catholic imagery. Operated by the deeply religious Perry family.

Wheeling MAP p390

McLure Hotel $$ This modern-looking hotel actually dates to 1852. Rooms have been beautifully renovated, and an 8000-sq-ft ballroom hosts all kinds of events.

Wheeling Island Casino (p403) **$$** Games, live entertainment and upmarket accommodations on a small river island. Fridays bring stand-up comics to the Comedy Club.

Palace Lodge $$ Stay overnight at New Vrindaban, where comfortable rooms, a cow reserve and yoga sessions await the spiritual seeker.

Oglebay Resort $$$ Golf, lake views, festivals and outdoor adventure – since the 1920s, Oglebay has been a 2000-acre recreational wonderland. Splendid, family-friendly rooms.

Point Pleasant MAP p394

Lowe Hotel $$ Stately brick hotel in continuous operation since 1901. Well-preserved interior and perfect central location – it nearly casts a shadow over the Mothman statue.

Sutton MAP p394

Elk River Hotel & Cafe $$ Traditional and romantic rooms, with geodesic glamping domes outside on manicured grounds. Bar, breakfast and EV charger on-site.

TOOLKIT

The chapters in this section cover the most important topics you'll need to know about in New York and the Mid-Atlantic. They're full of nuts-and-bolts information and valuable insights to help you understand and navigate New York and the Mid-Atlantic and get the most out of your trip.

Arriving
p408

Getting Around
p409

Money
p410

Accommodations
p411

Family Travel
p412

Health & Safe Travel
p413

Food, Drink & Nightlife
p414

Responsible Travel
p416

LGBTiQ+ Travelers
p418

Accessible Travel
p419

Nuts & Bolts
p421

US Capitol Building (p276)
PANDORA PICTURES/SHUTTERSTOCK ©

Arriving

Most travelers flying to the Mid-Atlantic will pass through its busiest airports, located in NYC, Philadelphia, Baltimore and Washington, DC. In major metropoles, public transportation easily ushers visitors from airports to urban centers. Upon arrival, the cheapest way to travel between cities is via bus or train. Smaller towns often require a rental car, available for pick-up at airports.

Airports
Smaller regional airports may be closer to your intended destination, and renting cars from these hubs is usually cheaper than options in cities with higher demand. The downsides: fewer flight options and potential delays.

To the City Center
If you're staying in a city and don't need a rental car, taking public transit (bus and/or train) from the airport is often cheaper than taking a cab – and sometimes just as fast.

By Train
Amtrak's Acela and Northeastern Regional trains travel between NYC and Washington, DC, with stops in major cities like Philadelphia and Baltimore. Acela is slightly comfier and quicker – book in advance for ticket deals.

By Bus
Networks of bus routes offered by companies like Greyhound and Megabus link all major cities and many smaller towns throughout the region. Purchase Megabus tickets in advance for steep discounts.

Travel Times

	From	To	Duration
TRAIN	New York City	Philadelphia	1½ hours
TRAIN	New York City	Washington DC	3½ hours
TRAIN	Washington DC	Philadelphia	2 hours
CAR	Philadelphia	Pittsburgh	5 hours

SAY NO TO THAT RIDE

Keen on taking a rideshare or taxi from the airport to the city center? Ensure you're hopping in a certified cab, Uber or Lyft. In major urban airports around NYC and Philadelphia, you may be greeted by friendly faces offering rides without the hassle of waiting in a taxi line. Don't fall for it: these are scammers who charge significantly more for their service. Rideshare and taxi drivers will always pick up passengers from designated locations. Follow signs in the airport and say no to solicitors. Licensed cabs in big cities like NYC, DC and Philly have metered fares that passengers can see.

Getting Around

Transportation options change drastically based on your location. Urban areas are great for walking, cycling and public transit, while remote, rural areas require a car.

TRAVEL COSTS

NYC's subway/bus
$2.90/ride

DC's Capital Bikeshare
$8/day

Philadelphia car rental
From $35/day

Tank of gas in New Jersey
Approx $3.55/ gallon

Go Far By Car

Driving a car is often the only way to reach tiny villages and most outdoor adventures. Watch out for speed traps – ticket-touting officers regularly police sudden speed-limit changes, frequently found at town entrances. New Jersey is the only state in the US where it's illegal to pump your own fuel – wait for an attendant at gas stations. Forgo driving in NYC and Washington, DC – the traffic is a nightmare.

Trains Between Towns

Mid-Atlantic cities boast rail networks with frequent services to suburbs and smaller towns, making it possible to visit a list of destinations sans car. In NYC, the Long Island Railroad provides service out to Montauk, the NJ Transit travels along the Jersey Shore and Metro-North Railroad stops in Beacon and beyond. In DC it's easy to connect to Baltimore, Wilmington, Harpers Ferry and towns throughout Virginia.

TIP

Google Maps is the ubiquitous navigation tool, but Citymapper is even more comprehensive for NYC, Philadelphia and DC, accounting for all possible modes of transport beyond roads, public transit and bicycle routes.

FERRY FUN

Consider trading highways for breezy boat rides throughout parts of NYC, New Jersey, Maryland and DC. It isn't always the most efficient option, but riding the ferry can be a way to experience local sites. In NYC, ride the Staten Island Ferry and NYC Ferry to waterfront neighborhoods; the Seastreak Ferry sails to Sandy Hook, NJ. DC's Potomac Water Taxi travels between the Wharf and Mount Vernon, VA.

Taxis & Rideshares

Taxis are easy to find in all major metropoles. You can hail them streetside in NYC, Philadelphia and DC or use the Curb app. Rideshare apps Uber and Lyft are also available – but the further you get from city centers, the more difficult it is to find drivers. Don't assume you can take the train to far-flung destinations and rely on local chauffeurs.

Subway & Public Transit

NYC's subway, Philadelphia's SEPTA and Washington, DC's Metro are cheap ways to get around town. To pay for subway and bus rides in NYC, use OMNY, which charges the digital wallet on a smartphone. In Philly, use a smartphone or cash, or buy tickets at kiosks. The DC Metro uses SmarTrip.

Cities for Cycling

Cycling in Mid-Atlantic cities is thriving thanks to bike-share programs and miles of bike lanes. Renting a set of wheels can be a fast, fun way to explore town. NYC uses Citi Bike; Philadelphia has Indego; Washington, DC, rolls with Capital Bikeshare. Download the apps and obey traffic laws. If you're a novice, stick to bike lanes.

DRIVING ESSENTIALS

Drive on the right-hand side of the road.

Pass in the left-hand lane on highways.

Speed limits vary: the maximum speed on interstates is often 65–70mph, 55mph in urban areas and 15–45mph in rural and residential areas.

Money

CURRENCY: US DOLLAR ($)

Pay What You Can

If the entry fee for a museum is 'pay what you wish,' it means exactly that – pay whatever you desire, no questions asked. But if you make an advance reservation online, you'll usually have to pony up the suggested fee. Spontaneity works in your favor: show up sans reservation to save some dough.

Tax Town

NYC is the most expensive city in the US. On top of having the highest sales tax in the Mid-Atlantic (8.875%), housing expenses are 4.8 times the national average. Delaware, meanwhile, is one of only five US states without a sales tax: save your big shopping spree for Wilmington.

Cash or Credit?

Always carry a little bit of cash along with a credit card. Some businesses – especially street vendors and mom-and-pop restaurants – only accept cash, while new businesses are increasingly card-only. ATMs are widely available at airports, banks, gas stations and grocery stores. Some smaller establishments don't accept $100 bills – carry $20s.

HOW MUCH

Museum entry
Free-$25

Broadway show
$30-200+

Highway tolls between NYC and DC
$20-25

Parking garage in DC
$10-30

HOW TO...

Tip

Tips aren't appreciated – they're expected. Although it often isn't mandatory, gratuity is factored into the wages of service-industry professionals. Receiving tips from customers is an essential part of their income. For restaurants, tip 18% to 25% – unless service is terrible. At bars, start with $1 to $2 a drink, more for speciality cocktails, or 15% to 20% overall. Give taxi drivers a 10% to 20% tip and put aside $2 to $5 per day for hotel maids.

MORE FOR LESS

CityPASS (citypass.com) offers discounts to museums in NYC and Philadelphia. Buy admission for three to five major tourist attractions and save around 40% on prices – just ensure you want to see what's offered.

INFLATION NATION

The COVID-19 pandemic did a number on the US economy. Blame supply-chain hiccups, spend-happy shoppers, labor shortages, fuel hikes and Uncle Sam's stimulus spending for those higher-than-average prices. Although inflation is down from its 2022 peak, the outlook isn't great. In 2024, groceries cost over 25% more than they did in 2019, so you'll definitely feel the burn at restaurants. Pinching pennies? Get your fill at farmers markets and food trucks – the food costs less, there's no table service to tip and you'll still get to taste local flavors.

Accommodations

Go Camping or Glamping

Pitching tents and nursing bonfires is a beloved summer pastime along the East Coast. DIY campsites range from remote Adirondacks islands to communal sites with bathrooms and pools. Glamping (glamorous camping) is increasingly common, with rustic resorts featuring snug cabins, safari-style tents or vintage Airstream trailers – all creature comforts included. Sustainability and digital disconnection are usually central to the experience.

Stay in Historic Buildings

Expect architectural intrigue, museum-worthy interiors and goosebump-inducing ghost stories. Preservationists have turned some of the region's historic buildings into sensational (and usually pricey) stays – like the 18th-century **Inn at Montchanin Village** (p315) and the 19th-century homes around **Inns of Aurora** (p149). You can even snooze in famous shadows: JFK stayed at NYC's **Carlyle** (p101) and Queen Elizabeth II caught Zs at Virginia's **Williamsburg Inn** (p385).

Get Cozy at B&Bs

It's difficult finding B&Bs (bed and breakfasts) in big cities, but these privately owned affairs with local flair delight in rural villages and their outskirts. Accommodations range from snug rooms with shared bathrooms (less expensive) to swanky settings akin to boutique hotels (more expensive). Anticipate cheery customer service and chatty guests: you'll likely share a table over breakfast.

Choose Rustic Resorts

A resort revival around the Catskills and Adirondacks waxes nostalgic for the days of *Dirty Dancing*, when the hotel was the destination. Be it the **DeBruce** (p149) or the **Lodge at Schroon Lake** (p149), these boutique compounds ply visitors with plenty of on-site activities, inviting guests to park their cars and kick back. Expect hiking trails, nightly bonfires, spectacular restaurants and occasional entertainment.

HOW MUCH FOR A NIGHT AT A...

Bare-bones campsite
$15-35

Rural B&B
$100-300

High-end hotel
From $350

Park it at Motels

'Motor hotels' – modest roadside accommodations with mid-century-modern appeal – surged in popularity during the pandemic. A lynchpin of 1960s American road-trip travel, these often affordable digs are getting rediscovered by a new generation that appreciates pulling front bumpers up to their front door. Recently renovated and remodeled motels attract stylish sightseers seeking budget-friendly rooms and retro kitsch.

AIRBNB VS NYC

Short-term rentals on Airbnb and Vrbo are common throughout the Mid-Atlantic, with plenty of stays on sprawling properties, at reasonable prices and in private locations far from hotels. But if you're looking for an Airbnb in NYC, you're likely out of luck. In 2023 city officials implemented a law prohibiting rentals under 30 days when a host isn't present on the property. Roughly 80% of NYC's Airbnb units immediately vanished. NYC's argument? Airbnb hosts contributed to the city's housing crisis by distorting the value of rents, displacing locals and upending communities.

Family Travel

The East Coast has activities for all ages. Soon-to-be city slickers, mountaineers in the making, budding academics and sand-castle connoisseurs will appreciate the variety of youth-geared entertainment, interactive museums and parks. Cities are fantastic for endless options, while rural areas provide more space for kids to explore the animal within. No matter the destination, no one's getting bored.

Best for Kids in NYC

Bop around your choice of 1000 playgrounds – there are 21 in **Central Park** (p94) alone, and you can glide down the city's tallest slide on **Governors Island** (p54). Ride **Jane's Carousel** (p98) beneath the Brooklyn Bridge. Inspect dinosaur bones at the American Museum of Natural History. Visit the world's largest Harry Potter–themed store. Applaud a Disney musical on Broadway.

Best for Kids in DC

Inquisitive minds go bonkers for DC's kid-friendly museums – most are free. Crawl through a lifesize termite mound at the **National Museum of Natural History** (p261) or stroll through planets at the **National Air and Space Museum** (p265). Go undercover at the **International Spy Museum** (p271) or wave to pandas at the **National Zoo** (p286). Ride slides at the **National Children's Museum** (p268).

TRAIN & PLANE TRAVEL

Children aged two to 12 can ride most Amtrak trains at 50% of the adult fare; infants under two ride for free, as long as they're in an adult's lap. In NYC, kids under 44in tall ride the subway for free with a fare-paying adult; in DC, up to two children under the age of five ride for free with each paying adult. All infants two and under can ride domestic US flights for free.

Beach Day

The Jersey Shore should be on every sand-bucket list during summer. In Asbury Park, chew on saltwater taffy from the Fun House, build sandcastles by the boardwalk then become a pinball wizard at the **Silverball Retro Arcade** (p170).

Mountain Time

Of all Mid-Atlantic parks, the Adirondacks calls loudest. Float down the Hudson River with **Tubby Tubes River Co** (p132) or cruise **Lake George** (p129). Meet the goats at **Kemp Sanctuary** (p132), nosh maple candies and experience history at Revolutionary War forts.

DINING WITH KIDS

Mid-Atlantic restaurants regularly cater to families. Most diners and chains offer children's menus with smaller portions and lower prices, and if you need a high chair or booster seat there's likely one available. Establishments without children's menus don't necessarily discourage kids, though you should think twice before bringing a picky palate to a Michelin-starred hot spot. Luckily, the Mid-Atlantic excels at cooking up what kids crave: cheesy pizzas, buttered bagels, mayonnaise-glazed lobster rolls and more. If you'd rather dine outdoors with messy eaters, stop by one of the area's ubiquitous farmers markets: pick out fruits, cheeses and sweets and voilà – a DIY picnic.

Health & Safe Travel

STORMY WEATHER

The East Coast's hurricane season runs from June to late November, but it reaches its peak from mid-August to mid-October. Snow storms tend to hit northeastern states like New York hardest between January and February. Keep abreast of weather forecasts so you can plan and reroute your itinerary if necessary.

Tick Watch

If you go hiking – or frequent any wooded, grassy region where wild animals roam – lookout for ticks. These little bloodsuckers are most active in warm months but live throughout the Mid-Atlantic year-round – and some carry Lyme disease. To protect yourself, wear closed-toed shoes, long socks, pants and tick repellent – and always do a full-body tick check after spending time outside.

Wildlife

Heading into the wild comes with inherent risks. You're encroaching on animal territory, and though most creatures aren't interested in humans, a few will get aggressive when provoked. Cottonmouths, copperheads and timber rattlesnakes all have venomous bites, as do black widow spiders. Sharks lurk along shorelines; black bears live among forests. Attacks are rare.

MARIJUANA

Recreational use of marijuana is legal for adults 21 and over in most Mid-Atlantic states, aside from Pennsylvania and West Virginia.

OCEAN SAFETY

Green Flag Calm conditions – exercise caution

Yellow Flag Waters might be rough – use extreme caution

Red Flag Hazardous conditions – high surf or strong current

Double Red Flag Danger: do not enter the water

Purple and Blue Flags Dangerous marine life (sharks, jellyfish) spotted

Public Transit in Cities

While waiting for NYC's subway or DC's Metro, stand away from the platform edge. Avoid empty cars – there's often a stinky reason why there's no one else inside. Don't engage with aggressive riders. If something makes you uncomfortable, change cars at the next stop. NYC's subway runs 24/7, but if it's after midnight and you're alone, consider a cab.

INSURANCE & MEDICATIONS

If you're a foreign visitor, consider buying travel insurance. Medical care and prescription drugs can be shockingly expensive in the US – and emergency-room visits without insurance can cost thousands of dollars. Travel-insurance policies may also cover theft-related expenses, lost luggage or delayed travel. For over-the-counter medications, head to a pharmacy like CVS or Walgreens.

Food, Drink & Nightlife

When to Eat

Breakfast (7am to 11am) Ranges from on-the-go grub to eggs and bacon.

Brunch (11am to 2pm) Usually replaces breakfast on weekends with fancier fare.

Lunch (noon to 2pm) Everything from sandwiches to three-course meals.

Happy Hour (5pm to 7pm) Some places serve reduced-price snacks and drinks.

Dinner (5pm to 10pm) Two to three courses: appetizer, main, dessert.

Where to Eat

Cafes Pastries and light meals until noon.

Diners Casual greasy-spoon haunts specializing in breakfast fare and sandwiches, with comically long menus.

Farmers markets Growers and artisanal makers selling local fare at outdoor pop-ups, often on Saturdays or Sundays.

Food halls Groups of indoor food counters plating a variety of cuisines, usually at reasonable prices.

Food trucks Carts or trucks serving handheld street food to the urban eater: tacos, dosas, hot dogs and more.

Restaurants Full sit-down meals for lunch and/or dinner.

MENU DECODER

BEC Bacon, egg and cheese sandwich: NYC's bodega staple.

Buffalo wings Deep-fried chicken wings doused in spicy sauce, usually dipped in bleu cheese dressing. Invented in Buffalo, NY.

Cheesesteak Steak-and-cheese sandwich with Philly roots. Gooey cheese tops chopped or sliced beef on a hoagie roll or baguette. Fried onions add tang.

Crab cake Crab meat bound by breadcrumbs, egg, mayo, seasonings and maybe mustard, served with tartar sauce. Popular along the Chesapeake Bay.

Manhattan Bourbon- or rye-based cocktail with sweet vermouth and bitters. Garnished with a maraschino cherry or orange peel.

Orange crush Vodka, orange liqueur, lemon-lime soda and OJ: Maryland's invention, Virginia's summer signature.

Scrapple Loaf of pig parts mixed with cornmeal and flour, sliced and served on bread. A Pennsylvania Dutch classic.

HOW TO... Taste Wine

Grapevine trellises line the Finger Lakes and Long Island's North Fork, and a few standout vineyards plant themselves throughout the lower Mid-Atlantic – many of which warrant slow sipping. If you show up for a tasting, use the '5 Ss' (see, swirl, sniff, sip and savor) to sample and talk about wine with a sommelier's zest. Start by 'seeing' the color: is it pale, dark or deeply saturated? Next, 'swirl' the wine to release aromas and reveal its complexities. Don't be afraid to stick your nose inside the glass while 'sniffing' to note the bouquet. When it's time to 'sip,' swish the wine, ensuring it hits all parts of your mouth. It might be sweet, acidic, floral, fruity, spicy or oaky; maybe like rubber tires, baked bread or cat's pee. The flavor potential is infinite. Finally, 'savor' it. The taste might disappear quickly or linger (a 'long finish'). Rinse and repeat.

HOW MUCH FOR A...

Bagel
$1.75

Plain pizza slice
$3-5

Bodega BEC
$4.50-6

Philly cheesesteak
$14-18

Coffee
$2-4

Pint of beer
$4-12

Glass of wine
$10-20

Craft cocktail
$10-22

HOW TO...

Eat Oysters

Long before pizza became the cheap-eat treat for famished New Yorkers, this salty sea candy reigned supreme on NYC's streets. Thick beds of the decadent aphrodisiacs lined the city's estuaries, plucked by the indigenous Lenape, then pillaged by European colonizers. The same was true along the Chesapeake Bay, where John Smith said oysters 'lay as thick as stones' while sailing up the waterway in 1608.

NYC earned a reputation as the world's oyster capital, and some biologists estimate that New York Harbor contained half the world's supply. Ellis Island was called 'Oyster Island.' Pearl St was once paved with their shells. But by 1927 pollution and overharvesting had killed masses of the meaty mollusks.

Eaters now consider oysters a fine dining delicacy – and they're enthusiastically slurped down throughout the Mid-Atlantic. Coastal Maryland, Virginia and parts of Long Island are particularly proud of their briny bivalve bounty.

Treat oyster eating like wine tasting – let it luxuriate on your tongue. Restaurants often serve oysters on a half shell – no shucking (removing the shell) involved. Use a small fork, usually provided, to loosen the meat, then tip the shell to your mouth. Rather than gulping it down, take a bite to appreciate how the oyster's flavor reflects its *merroir* (a portmanteau of the French words for 'sea' and 'earth,' referencing the habitat where the oyster was raised). Savoring oysters should be like traveling with your taste buds.

TIME TO PARTY

A night out in the Mid-Atlantic is defined by the destination. In big cities you might see a live performance at 7pm or 8pm, sip cocktails until midnight and step-touch until dawn. In rural areas, you might try beer flights at local breweries around 5pm and spend the rest of your evening stargazing beside a bonfire.

When it comes to small towns, don't expect late-night shenanigans. On weekdays you'll be hard-pressed to find restaurants open past 8:30pm, and most bars close by 10pm. Most breweries close shortly after sundown, so if you want to sample local suds, plan an excursion in the late afternoon or early evening. Weekends tend to get rowdier, with the occasional dive bar blaring jukebox tunes until 1am.

If you're looking for a rager, stick to cities. On weekends in NYC, 10pm is too early to hit the dance floor and 2am is too late (bars will be closing at 4am). Try to hit the sweet spot somewhere in between: 11pm means shorter lines, while 1am means rowdier crowds.

Dance clubs and music venues often require a cover at the door (bring cash), and in populated areas it's wise to pre-purchase tickets. Events with well-known DJs regularly sell out. If you can't snag a ticket, try queuing early to get in.

Use the Dice app to search for upcoming parties and live performances. If you prefer electronic music, check out the Resident Advisor app, which allows users to find events in various regions and secure tickets.

Responsible Travel

Climate Change & Travel

It's impossible to ignore the impact we have when travelling; Lonely Planet urges all travellers to engage with their travel carbon footprint, which will mainly come from air travel. While there often isn't an alternative, travellers can look to minimise the number of flights they take, opt for newer aircrafts and use cleaner ground transport, such as trains. One proposed solution—purchasing carbon offsets—unfortunately does not cancel out the impact of individual flights. While most destinations will depend on air travel for the foreseeable future, for now, pursuing ground-based travel where possible is the best course of action.

The **UN Carbon Offset Calculator** shows how flying impacts a household's emissions

The **ICAO's carbon emissions calculator** allows visitors to analyse the CO2 generated by point-to-point journeys

Join the Clean Plate Club

Champion zero-waste goals at restaurants like Brooklyn's **Rhodora Wine Bar** and Philly's **McGillin's Olde Ale House** (p189; possibly the greenest Irish pub in America), where owners work hard to recycle, reuse and eliminate waste.

Drink Responsibly

Beeline for bud-to-bottle operations like **Channing Daughters** (p114; a member of the Long Island Sustainable Winegrowers), where protecting local ecology is crucial to producing exceptional wines.

High-Five a Farmer

Pluck organic apples at **Fishkill Farms** (p120) in the Hudson Valley or bottle feed baby goats at **Amish Experience** (p238) in rural Pennsylvania. Can't make it to the farmstead? Meet farmers at NYC's 50 **greenmarkets** (p79).

Try Meat-Free Meals

Reduce greenhouse gas emissions by ordering plant-based dishes. Dig into vegetarian fare at Ithaca's plant-based stalwart **Moosewood** (p139), going strong since the 1970s, or make it a vegan Michelin-star memory at NYC's **Eleven Madison Park**.

The original stewards of America's landscape hold the keys to protecting its ecology. Support indigenous communities at Delaware's **Nanticoke Indian Museum** or learn about native ancestors at NYC's **National Museum of the American Indian**.

Ignite your passion for the natural world at the **Wild Center** (p132), an interactive indoor-outdoor Adirondacks museum dedicated to finding climate solutions, or at science-centered natural-history museums in DC, NYC and Pittsburgh.

Set Sail Sustainably

Forget gas-powered boats: paddle your way to a cleaner planet by kayaking Virginia's Roanoke River with **Roanoke Mountain Adventures** (p365) or by hopping on the Maid of the Mist, the electric cruiser that sails into **Niagara Falls** (p160).

Roll & Stroll

Minimize your carbon footprint by choosing transportation alternatives to taxis and cars. Join the zero-emission pedal party with bike-share programs in DC, Philadelphia and NYC, or hit Main Streets from Morgantown, WV, to Beacon, NY.

Upcycle Your Style

Turn sustainability into your aesthetic by sporting ecofriendly fashion designed by Brooklyn's **Zero Waste Daniel**, buying upcycled, gender-neutral pieces from Pittsburgh's **Flux Bene** or styling your home with reused T-shirt chairs from Hudson's **LikeMindedObjects** (p119).

Choose the Train

Reduce fuel usage by zipping between cities on Amtrak trains or taking regional railroads to villages and towns. It's possible to go from DC to Philly and on to NYC and beyond without pressing a gas pedal.

Pitch a Tent

Forgo electricity by falling asleep under starlight at **The Outpost** (p405) – a campsite within New River Gorge National Park – or wake up with the sun on a private island on **Lake George** (p129).

Tap water in the Mid-Atlantic is safe to drink: carry a reusable water bottle.

Delaware and New York have banned single-use plastic bags: carry a tote or use a backpack.

Future of Flooding

The Mid-Atlantic is at the front lines of human-caused climate change, with sea levels and eroding coastlines threatening beloved destinations. Scientists predict Baltimore's port will spend 65 days a year underwater by 2050, compared to 3 in 2023.

RESOURCES

Go foraging on an NYC park tour
wildmanstevebrill.com

Follow Leave No Trace's outdoor guidelines
lnt.org

Learn about sustainable practices
nps.gov/subjects/sustainability/index.htm

LGBTIQ+ Travelers

NYC gave birth to Pride at Stonewall. Washington, DC boasts the nation's highest percentage of LGBTIQ+ residents. Archipelagos of queer life dot Philadelphia, Pittsburgh and Baltimore; tiny Cherry Grove is considered 'America's first gay and lesbian town.' While some rural regions may seem conservative and unwelcoming, they represent the minority.

Out in NYC

NYC's historic LGBTIQ+ epicenter is the West Village, where queer life erupted after wordsmith Walt Whitman downed pints here in the 19th century. The **Stonewall Inn** (p75) is its heart, with bars **Julius'**, **Pieces** and lesbian bar **Cubbyhole** (p75) nearby. Other Manhattan gayborhoods include Chelsea (home of daddies), Hell's Kitchen (pretty-boy posturing) and the East Village (alternative edge). Williamsburg and Bushwick are Brooklyn's LGBTIQ+ hot spots, anchored by **3 Dollar Bill** (p100; a sprawling club), **Exley** (laidback cocktails) and **Mary's** (women-forward).

SUMMER ESCAPES

From May to September, it's all about the beach. In NYC, there's **Jacob Riis** or nude beach **Gunnsion** at Sandy Hook. **Cherry Grove** and **Fire Island Pines** (p113), and sbury Park (p170) on the Jersey Shore. Delaware plants its flag at **Rehoboth Beach** (p310). Tent-pitching pros, try **The Woods**, PA, or **Roseland Resort and Campground**, WV.

DC's Gayborhoods

LGBTIQ+ residents colonized DuPont Circle in the 1970s, home to bars like **Larry's Lounge** (a neighborhood pub). Today, there are several gayborhoods, including Logan Circle (home base for LGBTIQ+ publication *Washington Blade* and low-key bar **Little Gay Pub**), Adams Morgan (with lesbian bar **A League of Her Own**) and Capitol Hill.

PHILADELPHIA & PITTSBURGH

Philly lovingly refers to a slice of Midtown Village as the **Gayborhood** (p185) – the 13th St corridor, sprinkled with LGBTIQ+ bars and other businesses. Pittsburgh doesn't have a formal gayborhood, but there are a sprinkling of LGBTIQ-owned businesses throughout the city, especially around Shadyside and the North Side. Consult online resource qburgh.com.

ANNUAL FESTIVALS

Pride celebrations start in early June, with the **Philadelphia Pride Festival** and DC's **Capital Pride** leading the charge. NYC celebrates all month long; events culminate in a massive parade on June's last Sunday – one of the world's largest LGBTIQ+ events. For EDM festivals with Burning Man flair, join campers at **Honcho** – a week-long August dance fete in rural Pennsylvania. For dynamo drag, don't miss NYC's **Bushwig** in September.

Watch & Read

Tune into LGBTIQ+ culture with documentary *Paris is Burning*, miniseries *Fellow Travelers* and rom-com film *Fire Island*. Torrey Peters' novel *Detransition, Baby*.

Accessible Travel

Navigating the Mid-Atlantic with physical or cognitive impairments can be tricky. Call ahead to ensure hotels, restaurants and activities provide necessary accommodations.

Outdoors for All

Letchworth State Park (p145), New York's 'Grand Canyon of the East,' made a splash in 2021 by opening the Autism Nature Trail – a 1-mile route designed specifically for hikers on the autism spectrum.

Airport

US airlines must legally provide travelers with disabilities guided assistance while boarding, deplaning or connecting to other flights. Call your airline's special assistance phone line to ensure additional requests can be met. Damage to power wheelchairs is devastatingly common.

Accommodation

All US hotels constructed after 1993 must include accessibility features for people with disabilities: bathtubs with grab bars and a seat, roll-in showers with a seat, and communication equipment for those with hearing and vision impairments.

WHEELCHAIRS IN WASHINGTON, DC

The capital's 17 Smithsonian museums set the standard for access, with tactile or visual-description tours and sign-language interpretation available at most sites. All museums offer manual wheelchairs and at least one accessible entrance.

DC'S PUBLIC TRANSPORTATION

DC's Metro is one of the most wheelchair-friendly subway systems worldwide, featuring elevators, oversize fare gates and gap reducers at all 91 stations. Travelers with disabilities who can't ride the train use door-to-door paratransit service MetroAccess.

Food for Thought

In the US, 80% of adults with cognitive disabilities are unemployed. Hungry for change? Grab a bite at NYC's **Café Joyeux**, lowering the statistic one employee at a time.

Accessible NYC Experiences

The Autism Friendly Performances series with **TDF** revamps Broadway shows for people with sensory sensitivities. Peruvian restaurant **Contento** bakes wheelchair accessibility into its design. At **the Met** (p88), folks can join multisensory workshops.

RESOURCES

The America the Beautiful pass waves entrance fees at federal recreation sites and national parks for US citizens with permanent disabilities (nps.gov/planyourvisit/passes.htm).

Tourism boards round up accessibility info for NYC (nyctourism.com/accessible-nyc), Washington, DC (washington.org/accessibility), and Philadelphia (visitphilly.com/features/accessible-philadelphia).

Power-wheelchair user Cory Lee blogs about his adventures, including stops throughout the Mid-Atlantic (curbfreewithcorylee.com).

Buses

Buses – the cheapest, easiest way for wheelchair users to get around town – are equipped with wheelchair lifts and designated seating. Trains are tough – only 25% have accessible elevators, and they aren't always operational. Order accessible taxi cabs on the Curb app.

Brooklyn Bridge (p55)

Nuts & Bolts

OPENING HOURS

Hours remain consistent year-round in cities, but vary in rural areas based on seasons. Many small-town establishments have truncated hours throughout winter.

Banks 9am–6pm, Monday–Friday. Some also 9am-noon Saturday.

Cafes 7am–4pm in small towns; to 7pm in large cities.

Restaurants Breakfast 7–11am, lunch noon to 3pm, dinner 5–10pm. Weekend brunch 10am–4pm.

Bars Normally 5pm–2am; to 1am in Delaware; to 4am in NYC & Buffalo (some bars open earlier/later).

Clubs 10pm–2am; to 4am in NYC.

Shops 10am–7pm weekdays, 11am–8pm Saturday. Hours vary Sunday.

Grocery stores 8am–9pm

Measures & Weights

The US uses the Imperial system. Distance is measured in miles, weight is measured in pounds.

Internet Access

Coverage is good in cities but unreliable in rural areas. Many establishments offer wi-fi access.

Public Toilets

Public bathrooms are shamefully scarce.

GOOD TO KNOW

Time zone
Eastern Standard Time (UTC/GMT minus five hours)

Country calling code +1

Emergency number
911

Population
60.1 million (Mid-Atlantic)

Electricity
Type A 120V/60Hz

Type A
120V/60Hz

PUBLIC HOLIDAYS

The Mid-Atlantic observes over a dozen public holidays, and while many businesses remain open, hours are subject to change. Expect peak hotel prices and packed venues; plan travel around these dates well in advance.

New Year's Day January 1

Martin Luther King Jr Day Third Monday in January

Presidents Day Third Monday in February

Memorial Day Last Monday in May

Juneteenth June 19

Independence Day July 4

Labor Day First Monday in September

Columbus Day Second Monday in October

Veterans Day November 11

Thanksgiving Fourth Thursday in November

Christmas Day December 25

STORYBOOK

STORYBOOK

Our writers delve deep into different aspects of
New York and the Mid-Atlantic life

A History of New York & the Mid-Atlantic in 15 Places

The story of the region is a crash course in US history

John Garry

p424

Meet the East Coasters

The Mid-Atlantic is a mix of big-city riches and small-town simplicity

John Garry

p428

The Birth of America's Summer Vacation

How stories about the Adirondacks became a prototype for guidebooks.

John Garry

p430

Mid-Atlantic Wines

One of the country's most interesting wine-growing regions.

Michael Grosberg

p433

Captain John Smith statue, Jamestown Settlement (p358)
STEVE HEAP/SHUTTERSTOCK ©

STORYBOOK

A HISTORY OF NEW YORK & THE MID-ATLANTIC IN
15 PLACES

The story of the Mid-Atlantic is a crash course in US history. Almost all the essential plot points from the nation's narrative happened here. Stitching together its tales of indigenous tribes, determined colonists, bloody wars and industrial dynamism reveals a collage of America's complex, never-ending quest for liberty. By John Garry

LOOK AT THE Mid-Atlantic's most climactic moments since the 1600s and a theme emerges – water plays a supporting role. With seaside ports and boat-friendly waterways, coastal cities and riverfront towns became international trading epicenters, shaped by the exchange of goods, ideas and people passing through.

When European colonizers established coastal settlements in the 17th century, native groups already populated the land. The Iroquois Confederacy lived around the Great Lakes and the Mohicans called the Hudson River Valley home. Lenape communities spread along the Atlantic Ocean from southern New York to northern Delaware. Algonquin-speaking tribes thrived near the Chesapeake Bay – including the Powhatan Confederacy, who British colonists encountered while building their first permanent American outpost.

Over the next few centuries, these tribes nearly vanished as a new nation spread across the continent. British, Dutch and French forces vied for control first, colonists demanded dominance by winning the American Revolution, and since then, the Mid-Atlantic has seen it all: slavery, civil war, business booms, economic collapse, natural disasters and deadly attacks. This is where millions of immigrants entered the US and social movements exploded, investigating the realities behind America's promise that all are 'created equal.' Get ready to sail through 400 years of history – it's a bumpy ride.

1. Broadway, New York
INDIGENOUS ORIGINS UNDERFOOT

Centuries before NYC became a concrete jungle, the Wickquasgeck Trail wound its way through what the indigenous Lenape called 'Manahatta' – an island of old-growth forests, wetlands and rolling hills. Native people traded goods along this route, crisscrossed by wildlife. This is what the landscape explorer Giovanni da Verrazzano would have seen from his ship in 1524, followed by Henry Hudson in 1609 – when an estimated 15,000 Lenape lived in and around the region. Contact with Europeans began the displacement and genocide of America's indigenous population, but the Wickquasgeck Trail remains. Today, it's called Broadway.

For more on Manhattan's Lenape history, see the walking tour on p80.

2. Historic Jamestown
LAYING THE GROUNDWORK

When the British established an American settlement at Jamestown, Virginia, in 1607, it wasn't clear its inhabitants would survive, with sickness, starvation and clashes with the indigenous Powhatan Confederacy. But the colony flourished: the new arrivals planted seeds for the Protestant religion to prosper and, in 1619, introduced British America's first representative government, a precursor to US democracy. That same year, the colony received a boatload of over 20 enslaved Africans – the beginning of an evil institution that lasted two centuries, forging a framework for racial inequality that still reverberates around the nation.

For more on Jamestown, see p258.

3. Independence Hall
BUILDING A NEW NATION

The US took its first small step inside Philadelphia's steepled Georgian civic center in 1776 as the Second Continental Congress signed the Declaration of Independence – a condemnation of British tyranny and a manifesto of American ideals, proclaiming 'all men are created equal.' Eleven years later, the government signed the US Constitution inside the same room. Much like the Declaration's unmet ideals, the building's history is rife with contradictions: from 1850–54, African American freedom seekers accused of being 'fugitive slaves' were put on trial inside Independence Hall and, in some cases, forced back into bondage.

For more on Independence Hall, see p178.

Witt Clinton set sail from Buffalo (at what's now called Canalside) along the Erie Canal – a new artificial waterway linking Lake Erie to the Hudson River. When he reached NYC, his final destination, he dumped two casks filled with Lake Erie water into the Atlantic. This 'Wedding of the Waters' became a profitable marriage. Trade along the route transformed NYC into America's commerce king, with money and knowledge flowing freely along the waterway through Buffalo and into the Midwest. Railroads eventually took the canal's place; today, the waterway is primarily recreational.

For more on Canalside, see p143.

6. Seneca Falls
REVOLUTIONARY WOMEN ROAR

In 1848, a sleepy street in Seneca Falls, New York, boomed with the voice of Elizabeth Cady Stanton, who read the Declaration of Sentiments before a congregation of 300 at Wesleyan Chapel. Her speech, modeled after the Declaration of Independence, demanded rights for women and sparked an ongoing fight for gender equality. Among Stanton's requests was: suffrage for women, not granted until Congress passed the 19th Amendment in 1919. The Women's Rights National Historical Park, spread across several buildings, tells the story of the groundbreaking 1848 convention and the social revolution that followed.

For more on the Women's Rights National Historical Park, see 140.

7. Gettysburg
CIVIL WAR TRAGEDY

There were over 50,000 casualties during the 1863 Battle of Gettysburg – a three-day snapshot of the Civil War's brutality and the bloodiest conflict in American history. From 1861 to 1865, the US fractured in two along the Mason–Dixon Line – a Maryland–Pennsylvania boundary symbolizing the ideological split between agrarian, enslaved-holding southern states and the industrial, abolitionist north. The fratricidal in-fighting ultimately ended slavery and claimed over 620,000 lives. Its haunting memory is palpable among the meadows and monuments, where Lincoln declared in the battle's aftermath, 'that this nation, under God, shall have a new birth of freedom.'

For more on Gettysburg, see p241.

Jamestown (p258)

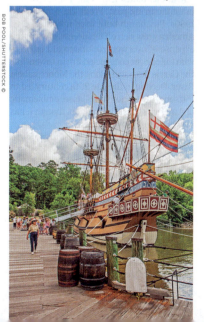

8. Ellis Island
AMERICA'S IMMIGRANT ORIGINS

America owes its image as an international melting pot to Ellis Island: from 1892 to 1954, roughly 12 million immigrants entered the US at this site. Hopefuls who passed through the island's 'Golden Gate' went on to make significant cultural contributions to the nation, including a who's who of notable New Yorkers like anarchist Emma Goldman, filmmaker Elia Kazan and songwriter Irving Berlin. Today, over 100 million Americans can trace their ancestry to this immigration depot, where newcomers once waded through a conveyor belt of exams to gain admittance and build a new life.

For more on Ellis Island, see p58.

9. Shenandoah National Park
CONSERVATION AND DISPLACEMENT

Virginia's wild west epitomizes preservation's costs and benefits. After establishing Shenandoah in 1935, the US employed around 5000 Civilian Conservation Corps workers to develop the land – part of a New Deal project that helped young Americans find work during the Great Depression. The 200,000-acre park now protects over 50 mammal species and 1400 types of plants. But hike the park's trails and you'll notice abandoned barns and forgotten cemeteries. To create Shenandoah, over 2000 residents were displaced under 'eminent domain' – the act of seizing private property for public use, a practice disproportionately impacting and economically undercutting poor US residents.

For more on Shenandoah National Park, see p366.

10. Lincoln Memorial
FREEDOM FIGHTERS

America's aspirational quest for equality takes the form of a temple along the western side of Washington, DC's National Mall, with 36 Doric columns surrounding a 19ft marble-clad Abraham Lincoln. Lincoln's statue has witnessed countless presidential inaugurations, concerts and demonstrations since its completion in 1922 – though none echo louder through history than Dr Martin Luther King Jr's 1963 'I Have a Dream' speech, delivered 18 steps below the president's stone feet. King's call for racial justice, coming a century after Lincoln signed the Emancipation Proclamation, paved the way for landmark legislation like the Civil Rights Act of 1964.

For more on the Lincoln Memorial, see p264.

11. Stonewall Inn
EPICENTER OF LGBTIQ+ LIBERATION

Going to a gay bar in 1960s NYC came with potential consequences, including police raids and arrests – which is exactly what officers planned to inflict during a routine shakedown at the Stonewall Inn on June 28, 1969. But visitors to this Greenwich Village pub – mostly marginalized members from the LGBTIQ+ community, including gender- non-conforming drag queens and people of color – decided to revolt. There are contradictory accounts about who threw the first mythic brick at police and how long the uprising lasted, but one thing is certain: the events at Stonewall galvanized LGBTIQ+ people worldwide to fight for their rights.

For more on Stonewall, see p75.

12. Carrie Blast Furnaces National Historic Landmark
INDUSTRIAL BOOM AND BUST

Remnants from the US Steel company's heyday act as mausoleums for Pennsylvania's manufacturing past. From the 1870s to the 1980s, Pittsburgh built itself into Steel City. America grew rich off its success, often at the expense of overworked, underpaid laborers who toiled over coal-fueled fire in towers like the Carrie Furnaces along the Monongahela River. Decline in the late 20th century led to Pittsburgh's economic collapse, emblematic of America's 'Rust Belt' region, though it has slowly risen from its demise.

For more on industrial Pittsburgh, join a Rivers of Steel tour, p221.

13. One World Trade Center
A SKYLINE ALTERED, A NATION TRANSFORMED

Soaring 1776ft into the sky like a phoenix since 2014, One World Trade Center is a testament to American strength and New York's unwavering spirit. The glassy skyscraper overlooks the site where the Twin Towers stood until September 11, 2001, when two planes hijacked by Al Qaeda terrorists were flown into

Manhattan (p48)

the buildings. A third plane hit the Pentagon outside Washington, DC; a fourth crashed in Shanksville, PA. Nearly 3000 people died – the deadliest attack on US soil – launching the nation's contentious 'global war on terror.' A somber memorial beneath the skyscraper honors those who were lost.

For more on One World Trade Center, see p60.

14. The Jersey Shore
FIGHTING CLIMATE CHANGE

As Hurricane Sandy crashed along the East Coast in October 2012, it claimed the lives of over 100 people in the US and destroyed over 600,000 homes. Damages cost upwards of $70 billion, devastating swathes of New Jersey and New York. The superstorm forced city planners and politicians to wake up: the hypothetical horrors of climate change were now bleak reality. In the coming years, coastal areas like Atlantic City and Cape May reshaped themselves with new seawalls, restored oyster beds and improved drainage systems – attempts to thwart rising sea levels and fight the next inevitable storm.

For more on Cape May, see p160.

15. New River Gorge National Park
NATURE'S RECLAMATION

'New' might seem like a misnomer for North America's oldest river, which some geologists estimate to be 320 million years old. Its prehistoric stones have seen Cherokee tribes come and go, followed by railroads and coal-mining towns, nearly 50 of which erupted along the West Virginia waterway in the late 1800s to mine for 'black gold.' But in 2020, this 70,000-acre expanse became the US's newest national park, where coal-fueled ghost towns have been reclaimed by green vines, and forests once logged are now fully regrown. It's exciting headway for a nation attempting to heal industrial scars.

For more on New River Gorge National Park, see p394.

MEET THE EAST COASTERS

The Mid-Atlantic is a mix of big-city riches and small-town simplicity, with a population as diverse as its seashores, mountains and skyscraper-strewn landscapes. John Garry introduces his people.

'TEMPERAMENTAL AND UNINHIBITED' – that's how demographers labeled the Mid-Atlantic region in a 2013 study published in the *Journal of Personality and Social Psychology*, which makes me want to say, in a thick 'New Yawk' accent, 'You talkin' to me?'

My gut response – reactionary and confrontational, originally ad-libbed by Robert de Niro as a Manhattan cabby in Martin Scorsese's *Taxi Driver* – reinforces the results.

Researchers suggest people here are 'reserved, aloof, impulsive, irritable and inquisitive' – exactly how someone might describe the characters on Seinfeld, an NYC-based sitcom following four irreverent friends through their lives in Manhattan. It's also how I act while riding NYC's subway – slightly guarded, endlessly intrigued. I tend to exude a wary wonder – a necessary shield to survive cramped quarters around the country's most populous metropole.

According to the study, the Mid-Atlantic is also 'passionate' (ask New Jersey residents about their favorite son, singer Bruce Springsteen), 'competitive' (evidenced while watching Philly crowds cheer at an Eagles football game) and often 'liberal.' This last trait doesn't ring true for the entire region but showcases a divide frequently felt between life in urban and rural areas.

Philadelphia, Pennsylvania's largest city, regularly votes for liberal candidates in elections (the mayors have been a Democrat since 1952), while rural counties keep a conservative edge, prioritizing Republican ideals. The same pattern exists in nearly all Mid-Atlantic

America's Melting Pot

Roughly 18% of all Americans call the Mid-Atlantic home, with immigrants making up over a fifth of the population in New Jersey (23.2%) and New York (22.6%), along with a substantial portion of Maryland (15.67%).

states – a sociopolitical divide that creates cultural canyons deeper than the gorge at Niagara Falls.

Urban/rural demographics are similarly split. Washington, DC is racially diverse (roughly 40.9% Black, 38% white, 11.3% Latino and 9.8% identifying as something else), with the nation's highest percentage of same-sex-couple households (7%). Pastoral West Virginia is predominantly white (90%) and straight (only 1.5% are same-sex-couple households). Then there's money: Maryland and New Jersey are two of the nation's wealthiest states (median incomes top $75,000), while West Virginia is one of the poorest (the median income hovers around $53,000).

The East Coast's eclectic soundtrack includes Jay-Z hyping NYC's concrete jungle in 'Empire State of Mind' and John Denver crooning about rural Appalachia in 'Take Me Home, Country Roads.' Comparing much of the region is like comparing the Big Apple and the pawpaw (West Virginia's 'banana'). They might both be fruits, but they've got different flavors.

Despite these differences, the Mid-Atlantic defines America's cultural melting pot, much like the stew that defines the classic 'New Yawk' accent. It's equal parts Italian, Irish, Puerto Rican and Jamaican, peppered with Yiddish slang and decorated by hip-hop poetry. It's the sound of someone who came here to prove something; an immigrant reaching for the American Dream. It might sound gruff – there's no time for nonsense here – but it's backed with heapings of heart.

I LIVE ON THE EAST COAST

I was born in the Catskills, where white-tailed deer outnumber people, and refined in NYC over the past 14 years. Like much of New York, I'm a transplant, though my family's city history goes back several generations. My paternal great grandmother immigrated to America aboard the *Titanic* (a 3rd Class passenger; she survived) – one of the estimated 4.5 million Irish people who arrived in America between 1820 and 1930. She planted herself in Manhattan, but like many New Yorkers, spent summers in the Catskills, where my parents fell in love and raised a family.

I now reside in Brooklyn with my partner, whose Jewish Ukrainian grandfather found refuge in the US during Russia's early-20th-century pogroms. We're two of NYC's 700,000 LGBTIQ+ residents – the nation's largest queer population.

I see our lineage all over the city: Irish pubs, Jewish delis, gay bars like Julius', where trailblazers fought for equality, and in the stories of NYC's newest immigrants, numbering over 3 million people.

429

Lake George (p129)
DEBRA MILLET/SHUTTERSTOCK ©

THE BIRTH OF AMERICA'S SUMMER VACATION

A series of 19th-century stories about New York's wild Adirondacks became a prototype for the modern guidebook and a passport to freedom. By John Garry

FOR MANY WATERFRONT destinations throughout the Mid-Atlantic, summer is more than a season – it's the most exciting time of year. Populations boom with vacationers who leave behind their cities and look forward to letting loose. The tradition may seem old hat, but it's relatively new. These are its origins.

Summer Arrives

Memorial Day sets off an East Coast alarm bell. Tiny waterfront towns that hibernated from October through April spring back to life by the last Monday of May. Summer has arrived. Vacationers are coming.

The wake-up call is particularly pronounced in Lake George – an Adirondack Mountains village where the population can swell from roughly 1000 to 50,000 throughout summer. When it comes to preparing for the incoming deluge, Lake George is a well-oiled machine. Mini-golf courses polish their fiberglass sculptures and fudge shops set out chunks of sweet treats. Marinas fill up their rental boats with gas. Campgrounds clean up winter's debris.

The entire region simmers with the splendor of summer vacation until Labor Day, when the season's enchantment disappears. But for those few precious months, the Adirondacks ace the art of escapism. This is, after all, where the American vacation was born.

Rise of the Vacation Class

In the early 19th century, traveling for leisure was a privilege reserved for the rich. In New York, the well-heeled went to spa towns like Saratoga Springs, where 'taking the waters' supposedly cured various ailments, while newlyweds traveled to Niagara Falls to sojourn with the sublime. But the average American had no concept of 'vacation.' The word wasn't even used in common parlance.

All that changed after the Civil War. Rapid industrialization transformed America's demographics: urban factories gave rise to an affluent middle class, and Puritan prejudice against 'idle hands' was countered with arguments about relaxation's benefits.

With time to kill and money to burn, the number of Americans traveling for rest and recreation began growing, aided by railroads. The nation was becoming an open book. The only thing nascent travelers needed was a guide.

STORYBOOK

America's Proto-Travel Guide

In the mid-1860s, a young clergyman named William HH Murray took his first trip to the Adirondacks – a vast wilderness known mostly by indigenous inhabitants and rugged outdoorsmen. Murray fell in love with the landscape and began writing about his off-the-radar adventures. By 1869, he published a book – *Adventures in the Wilderness; or, Camp-Life in the Adirondacks*.

Much like the poetic ponderings of his academic contemporaries Henry David Thoreau and Ralph Waldo Emerson, Murray persuasively preached the physical and spiritual benefits of connecting with nature. He argued that the pine-scented mountains could be the antidote to urban ailments, writing, 'no portion of our country surpasses, if indeed any equals, in health-giving qualities, the Adirondack Wilderness.'

His writing was simple and straightforward, and laid out plenty of practical information. This easy-to-follow advice – what to pack, where to stay, who to hire as a guide, how much money to spend – gave novice nature lovers confidence to rough it in the woods. Murray also attempted to democratize the Adirondack experience by appealing to a group often left out of outdoor exploration – women. A section of the guide focused solely on what they should wear. He noted that 'none enjoy the experiences more than ladies, and certain it is that none are more benefited by it.'

While critical reviews of Murray's work were mixed, the public ate it up. Within months, New York's mountains erupted with stampedes of urbanites, who streamed in from NYC, Boston and beyond, clutching Murray's words like their wilderness Bible.

But the summer of '69 wasn't exactly the Edenic destination Murray described. Locusts of black flies left visitors bug-bitten and bloody. Rain came down in torrents. Lodges became overwhelmed. Untrained wilderness guides led groups astray. Even with Murray's instructions, travelers were ill-prepared. Critics of Murray's disgruntled disciples derided them as 'Murray's Fools.'

Still, many readers remained undeterred. Some even waxed poetic about their experiences. Journalist and lecturer Kate Field, who spent that summer camping with three pioneering female companions among the mountains, summed up the region's unflagging magnetism best: 'The moral of the Adirondacks is freedom.'

Signs of Overtourism

The promise of freedom continued luring masses to the Adirondacks in 1870, and as crowds multiplied, businesses sprang up to meet their demands. By the end of the century, hotels, railroads, steamboats and wagon roads dotted the wilds, ready to make a buck off the bucket-list destination.

NYC blue bloods like the Vanderbilts and Rockefellers joined their ranks, purchasing private lakeside properties where they could 'vacate' the city's heat for cool mountain air. Their sprawling estates became the sites of 'Great Camps' – Gilded Age fortresses constructed with logs, covered in tree bark and decorated with taxidermy.

At the same time, local farming and logging reached its feverish peak. In 1885, maps commissioned by New York State's legislature showed that an estimated 27.8% of what's now Adirondack Park had been cleared. Murray's work presented a paradox, a dilemma plaguing sites from Machu Picchu to Venice today: extolling the virtues of the pristine Adirondacks inadvertently played a role in their decay.

Paradise Found

Thanks to state legislation and environmental activism, fortunately the story of the Adirondacks doesn't end in destruction. By 1885 New York's governor established a law ensuring the Adirondacks would be 'forever kept as wild forest lands.'

As America marched into the 20th century and the nation's final frontiers vanished, no destination would quite match what Murray described in 1869. Still, plenty of other East Coast utopias emerged as getaway hot spots. New Jersey's Atlantic City and Brooklyn's Coney Island became blue-collar escapes for work-weary travelers. Jewish summer resorts took root in New York's Catskills. African Americans found relaxation at Maryland's Highland Beach. The country's first gay and lesbian summer community spread its wings in Cherry Grove.

More travel guides soon filled the shelves of bookstores while Murray's musings faded into obscurity, but an idea he planted permanently lodged itself in the American psyche: now and then, everyone deserves a vacation.

Wölffer Estate (p114)

MID-ATLANTIC WINES

One of the country's most productive, vital and interesting wine-growing regions. By Michael Grosberg

NEW YORK IS the area's big wine producer, followed by Virginia and Pennsylvania, with Maryland and New Jersey establishing their own contemporary bona fides. Like grape-cultivating areas the world over, the scenery, whether it's the Finger Lakes' rolling hills or the Shenandoah Valley's mountainous backdrop, plays a close second fiddle to the wine.

New York

From Long Islands' sandy soils, to the Hudson Valley's geologically complex slopes and the Finger Lakes' steeply angled mineral-filled ones, there's a winery and vintage for every palate. Seneca is best known for its German-style rieslings, but there are over 130 wineries in the area, most with picturesque views hugging Seneca, Cayuga and Keuka Lakes; Dr Konstantin Frank Winery, on Keuka Lake, started the New York wine revolution in 1962 and is currently the state's most award-winning. Long Island's North Fork is younger, starting on a potato farm in 1973. But like Long Island as a whole, its oenophile credentials look nothing like they did back then, and its Bordeaux-style terroir developed to include over 60 vineyards, including pioneering Borghese and award-winning Paumanok Vineyards. But even New York City has played a role. Prince Family Nurseries in Flushing, Queens, experimented with, cultivated and catalogued North American grapes in the late 1700s, and standardized the varieties in a system still used by American grape growers today. And urban winery Rooftop Reds in Brooklyn's Navy Yard produces its own wines with grapes grown on its rooftop.

Virginia

TextVirginia has over 300 wineries, and its wine-growing roots go way back, all the way to 1619. The 'New World's first legislative assembly' passed a law requiring every man to plant 10 vines of grapes to make wine. And Virginian Thomas Jefferson, Founding Father and third US president, was also a passionate wine connoisseur who attempted to cultivate his own vineyard adjacent to Monticello. But it wasn't until the 1970s that a prominent Italian wine-industry family expanded to a farm near Charlottesville to create Barboursville Vineyards, which today makes world-class wines, especially viognier and cabernet franc. There's a fair bit of quality and some new wineries here trying new things, like King Family, and Veritas in the Charlottesville and Monticello areas; the Trump family owns a vineyard nearby. Virginia's varied rural geography, such as the Blue Ridge Mountains, Appalachia and low-lying Eastern Shore, means the majority of estates are set amidst beautiful surroundings.

Pennsylvania

One of Pennsylvania's advantages, besides Philadelphia's burgeoning wine-bar scene at sophisticated places like Bloomsday in Queen Village, is its very old and very large agro-economy. In fact, one of the first American attempts at viticulture was by William Penn, the founder of Pennsylvania in 1683, at a property along the Schuylkill River; however, all of his French and Spanish vines died. The majority of vineyards, former fruit orchards (of peaches, apples, pears, cherries, and yes, grapes) in the eastern half of the state, have long histories of sustainable, low-impact farming. And because they're relatively small, they tend to be more nimbly experimental, always looking for an edge. Vox Vineti in the Lancaster area takes terroir and 'minimalism' seriously; call ahead for a tasting in the 300-year-old farmhouse or outdoor gazebo. Seventh- and eighth-generation

Barboursville Vineyards

family-owned Galen Glen near Jim Thorpe enters its rieslings and grüner veltliners into European competitions; its modern tasting room has beautiful 360-degree views of the property. And fourth-generation-owned Va La Vineyards in Chester County grows a hodgepodge of Italian peninsula varietals; there are views into the cellar from the tasting room and live music on Friday nights in summer.

New Jersey

New Jersey is unfairly maligned as all highways and sprawl – its 'Garden State' moniker isn't unfounded. There's space left over for plenty of forests, parks, farms and grape growing. And uniquely, all 56 Jersey wineries are family owned, with a reputation for down-to-earth on-site owners. The state's only survivor of the Prohibition era, Renault Winery is not far north of Atlantic City and is one of the country's oldest; it sold a kind of 'wine tonic' marketed for medicinal purposes with the government's approval. Fifth-generation-owned Tomasello Winery in the Pine Barrens is the state's largest. Nearby, in the Outer Coastal region, whose terroir resembles that found in Bordeaux, France, is one of New Jersey's oldest post-Prohibition vineyards, the proudly traditional Amalthea Cellars Farm Winery. Beneduce Vineyards, only 60 miles east of the Holland Tunnel into Manhattan, is helmed by a young, fourth-generation farmer and produces small-batch low-impact world-class wines. Others to check out are Hawk Haven in Cape May and seventh-generation family-owned William Heritage Winery in Mullica Hill, just over the Delaware River from Philadelphia. And Darryl Mack, one of the founders of legendary hip-hop group Run DMC, collaborated with York Cellars in central New Jersey to produce and sell his own branded and labeled wines.

Tomasello Winery

MARK MAKELA/CORBIS/GETTY IMAGES ©

DARRYL MACK, ONE OF THE FOUNDERS OF LEGENDARY HIP-HOP GROUP RUN DMC, COLLABORATED WITH YORK CELLARS IN CENTRAL NEW JERSEY TO PRODUCE AND SELL HIS OWN BRANDED AND LABELED WINES

Maryland

As with the other Mid-Atlantic states, the viticulture history of Maryland goes back to early colonial times. However, its post-Prohibition commercial operations didn't get going until 1945, with Boordy Vineyards north of Baltimore. While the state is compact, it's blessed with a variety of microclimates, all encouraging experimentation and significant yearly differences in taste from the same grapes planted on the same terroir. The vidal blanc from Crow Vineyards in the Chesapeake Bay region can be best appreciated with a meal of locally harvested oysters. You can enjoy beautiful vineyard views from the patio of Black Ankle in Mt Airy while enjoying excellent grüner veltliner. Family-owned Old Westminster, on a farm in northern Maryland, besides producing highly regarded reds and whites, also sells Farm Fizz, a canned sparkling wine you can find in stores out of state.

INDEX

accessible travel 419
accommodations 411, *see also individual locations*
activities 20-1, 42-5, 409, **44-5**
　Maryland 327, 341
　New Jersey 158
　New York State 124, 132, 145
　Pennsylvania 233, 242
　Philiadelphia 207
　West Virginia 395, 399, 402
Adams, John 383
Adams Morgan & the U Street Corridor 282-7, **283**
　accommodations 285
　food 282, 286
　nightlife 286
African American culture 145, 284-5, 325, 334
Airbnb 411
air pollution 228
airports 408
Alexandria 380-3, **381**
　accommodations 385
　food 382, 383
Allentown 142
Amish community 22
Amish culture 244, 246
animals, *see individual species*
Annapolis 320-2, **321, 322**
　accommodations 343
　beyond Annapolis 323-4
　drinking 321
　food 321
　walking tour 322, **322**
antiques 292, 377
Appalachia 30

Map Pages **000**

436

architecture
　Frank Lloyd Wright 230
　New York City 76, 80, 83, 86, 92, 96
　New York State 121, 134, 142
　Philadelphia 192
　Pittsburgh 228
　Virginia 382
　West Virginia 393
Arlington 373-5, **375**
　accommodations 385
　food 375
arriving 408
art 63, 206, 216, 281, 286, *see also* museums & galleries
Asbury Park 33, 170
　accommodations 173
Assateague Island 328, 329, 356
Atlantic City 165, 427
　accommodations 173
Aurora 141

B&Bs 411
Baltimore 27, 331-5, **332**
　accommodations 343
　drinking 333, 334, 335
　food 333, 334, 335
base jumping 397
basics 36-7
beaches 18, 32-3, 412, 430
　Bethany Beach 312
　Cape May 160
　Dewey Beach 312
　Ditch Plains Beach 108
　Fenwick Island 312
　Gansevoort Peninsula 77
　Jessup's Neck 112
　Kirk Park Beach 109
　Lewes 312
　Long Beach Island 169
　Million Dollar Beach 133
　New Jersey 166
　nudist 171
　Rehoboth Beach 19, 310
　Savannah Beach 314
　South Edison Beach 110
　Virginia Beach 15, 32, 369
Beacon 28, 116-21, **117**

accommodations 149
drinking 119, 121
food 118, 120
beer 40, 99, 128, 348
Berkeley Springs 401
　accommodations 405
Bethany Beach 312
　accommodations 315
Bethel 127
Big Foot 238, 397
bird-watching 42, 161, 326
Black Broadway 284-5
Black Lives Matter 194, 206
Bloomingdale's 67
blue crabs 326
boat travel 18, 60, 85, 97, 167, 172, 181, 409
　Delaware 314
　Maryland 320, 327, 328
　New York City 85
　New York State 113, 133, 145
　Pennsylvania 238
　Virginia 352, 371
　Washington, DC 272, 295
books 37, 110, 124, 155, 170, 292, 312, 359
Brandywine Valley 306
　accommodations 315
Broadway 62, 81, 424, *see also* theaters
Brooklyn 15, 97-100, **98**
　accommodations 101
　drinking 99, 100
　food 98, 99
　nightlife 100
Brooklyn Bridge 55
budgeting 34, 410
Buffalo & Niagara Falls 29, 142-8, 425, **144**
　accommodations 149
　drinking 145
　food 143
business hours 421
bus travel 408

Cady Stanton, Elizabeth 425
Callicoon 128
Cambridge 328
camping 411

New York State 133
Pennsylvania 236, 239, 242
Canalside 143, 425
canoeing, *see* kayaking
Cape Charles 371
Cape May 19, 32, 160-2, 427, **161**
　accommodations 173
　beyond Cape May 163-72
　food 162
Capitol Hill 273-8, **275, 278**
　accommodations 285
　food 274
　walking tour 278, **278**
car travel, 409 *see also* driving, driving tours
casinos 165, 168, 203, 403
Center City West, *see* Rittenhouse Square & Center City West 19
Central Park Zoo 94
Chadds Ford 215
Charleston 390-3, **391**
　accommodations 405
　beyond Charleston 394-7
　drinking 392-3
　food 392
　nightlife 391
　shopping 393
Charlottesville 359-61, **360**
　accommodations 385
　drinking 361
　shopping 359
Chelsea, *see* West Village & Chelsea
Chesapeake Bay 320, 356
children, traveling with, *see* family travel
Chinatown (New York City), *see* SoHo, Chinatown, Nolita & Little Italy
Chinatown (Philadelphia) & the Gayborhood 185-91, 219, **187**
　drinking 189
　food 186, 188
Chinatown (Washington, DC), *see* Penn Quarter & Chinatown
Chincoteague 372
Chrysler Building 81
churches & cathedrals

Basilica of St Patrick's Old Cathedral 67
Basilica of the Assumption 335
Camden Friends Meeting 309
Dunker Church 339
New York Avenue Presbyterian Church 268
St Anne's Episcopal church 322
Star Hill AME 309
Washington National Cathedral 294
Westminster Presbyterian Church 271
cider 361
cinema, 37, 69, 110, 277, 313
climate change 416, 427
clothes 36
coffee 201
Colonial Parkway 358
Colonial Williamsburg 353
comedy 76
Coney Island 19, 99
costs 410, 411, 415
crafts, *see also* shopping
credit cards 410
Crim Dell Bridge 354-5
cycling 409
 Buffalo 145
 Delaware 312
 Maryland 342
 New Jersey 157
 New York City 54-5, 60
 Pennsylvania 233, 238, 239
 Philadelphia 218
 Virginia 352, 374
 West Virginia 402

dancing 206
de Niro, Robert 428
Deep Creek Lake 341
deer 126
Delaware 298-315, **300**
 accommodations 315
 itineraries 301
Dewey Beach 312
 accommodations 315
Dimes Sq 72
dirt bikes 396
disabilities, travelers with, *see* accessible travel
Douglass, Frederick 333
Dove, 11, 323
Dover 307-9, **309**
 accommodations 315
 drinking 309
 food 308

Downtown & Dupont Circle 23, 288-91, **289**
 accommodations 2-285
 food 290, 291
Doyers St 65
Doylestown 216
Dr Pepper 362
drinking 15, 38-43, 237, 414-15, *see also individual locations*
driving 409
driving tours 16-17
 Brandywine Valley 306
 Catskills, The 128
 Delaware 306
 Eastern Shore 328
 Virginia 356-8, 363-4
drugs 413
Dupont Circle, *see* Downtown & Dupont Circle
Du Pont Environmental Education Center 302-3
Dutch Country, *see* Lancaster & PA Dutch Country

Eastern Shore 325-8, **326**
 accommodations 343
 driving tour 328, **328**
 food 327
Easton 328
East Village & the Lower East Side 68-72, **70-1**
 drinking 69, 72
 food 69, 72
electricity 421
emergencies 421
Emerson Kaleidoscope 125
Empire State Building 81
etiquette 36
events, *see* festivals & events

Fairmount, *see* Logan Square & Fairmount
family travel 43, 412
 Delaware 310
 Maryland 327, 331, 338
 New Jersey 164
 New York City 67, 94, 99
 New York State 124, 129
 Pennsylvania 236, 239, 244
 Philadelphia 181, 207
 Washington, DC 268, 278, 286
 West Virginia 395, 402
Famous Franks 186

farms 22-3, 39
 Fishkill Farms 120
 Kelder's Farm 125-6
 Kemp Sanctuary 132
 Old Windmill Farm 244
 Sunset View Creamery 137
 Tissue Farm 233
fashion 75
Fayette County 395
 accommodations 405
Fells Point 332
ferries, *see* boat travel
festivals & events 35
 Maryland 339
 New Jersey 158
 New York State 120, 127
 Pennsylvania 238, 244, 248
 Philadelphia 200, 206
 Virginia 352
 Washington, DC 262, 281, 287
Fillmore, the 201
film 37, 110, 277, 313
Financial District & Lower Manhattan 54-62, **56-7, 62**
 drinking 61
 food 60
 walking tour 62, **62**
Fire Island 113
fishing 42
 New Jersey 169
 Pennsylvania 238
Fishtown & Northern Liberties 199-203, **200**
 accommodations 219
 drinking 202, 203
 food 201
Foggy Bottom, *see* White House, the, & Foggy Bottom
food 22-3, 38-43, 167, 169, 179, 414-15, *see also individual locations*
Franklin, Benjamin 183, 192
Frawley Stadium 303
Frederick 23, 336-9, **337**
 accommodations 343
 drinking 338
 food 338
 shopping 336
Fredericksburg 376-9, **377**
 accommodations 385
 food 378, 379
 shopping 377
Frick, Henry Clay 227

galleries, *see* museums & galleries
gay travelers, see LGBTIQ+

travelers Gayborhood, the, *see* Chinatown & the Gayborhood
George Washington Memorial Parkway 356
Georgetown 292-5, **293**
 accommodations 285
 food 292, 294
 nightlife 295
 shopping 295
Georgetown University 294
Germantown 91
Gettysburg 247-8, **248**
 accommodations 249
 food 249
Grand Central Terminal 83
Great Allegheny Passage 340

Hamilton 381
Hampden 335
Hamptons, the 112
Hare Krishna 403
Harpers Ferry 400
Harrison, Thomas 366
Harrisonburg 31, 366-8, **367**
 accommodations 385
 food 368
Havre de Grace 320
health 357, 413
Heinz 226
hiking, *see also* walking tours
 Delaware 312
 Maryland 336, 341
 New Jersey 172
 New York State 119, 124, 137, 145
 Pennsylvania 232, 235, 236, 241
 Philadelphia 218
 Virginia 374
 West Virginia 396, 402
historic buildings & sites
 30th Street Station 208-9
 Antietam National Battlefield 338
 Arlington National Cemetery 265, 373
 Battery Maritime Building 55
 Battleship New Jersey 181
 Brewer's Castle, a 291
 Brooklyn Bridge Park 97
 Capitol Building 353
 Capitol Crypt 276
 Capitol Rotunda 276
 Carlyle House 383
 Carrie Blast Furnaces National Historic Landmark 426

437

Castle Clinton 58
Castle Williams 55
Chatham Manor 379
City Hall 383
College of William & Mary 354
Dakota building 96
Delaware Legislative Hall 307
Dunbar High School 285
Ellis Island 58-9, 426
Emlen Physick Estate 161
Fallingwater 230
Fonthill Castle 216
Ford's Theatre 268
Fort Jay 55
Fort Ligonier 232
Fort McHenry 11, 334
Fort McHenry National Monument 425
Fort Necessity 232
Gadsby's Tavern 383
Georgetown University Astronomical Observatory 295
Gettysburg 247-8, 426
Governors Island 54
Governor's Palace 353
Harbison Milk Bottle 201
Historic St Mary's City 323
Hollywood Cemetery 352
Hotel of Presidents, the 291
Howard University 284
Independence Hall 425
Jamestown Settlement 358
John Brown's Fort 11, 400-1
John Hand Black & White House 161
Kenmore 379
Kentuck Knob 230
Langston Hughes Residence 285
Library of Congress 277
Lovelace Tavern 62
Mary Washington House 379
Monocacy National Battlefield 339
Mount Vernon 381
National September 11 Memorial 61

Map Pages **000**

National Statuary Hall 276
Nelson House 358
Old Dutch Church 125
Old State House 307
Old Whitelaw Hotel 285
One World Trade Center 61, 427
Opus 40 126
Polymath Park 231
Public Gaol 353
Reading Terminal Market 190-1
Senate House State Historic Site 125
St John's College 322
State Capitol Building 393
State House 322
Statue of Liberty 58-9
Stonewall Inn 426
Supreme Court 277
Thomas Cole National Historic Site 121
Ulster County Courthouse 125
US Capitol Building 276
White House, the 258-9
Woodlands cemetary 212
Wren Building 355
Yorktown Battlefield 358
history 10-11, 424-7
 African American 145
 American Revolution 78, 356
 Baltimore 331, 335
 Civil War 11, 155, 247-8, 336, 338, 356, 402, 426
 colonial 62, 129, 323, 358
 Constitution, the 368
 Declaration of Independence 266, 425
 enslaved people 62, 325
 Hatfield & McCoy clans 396
 immigration 59, 68, 426
 LGBTIQ+ 75, 426
 New York City 61, 65, 87
 Pennsylvania 237, 241
 Philadelphia 178, 180, 202
 Prohibition 194
 racial 338-9
 Scandinavian 303
 Virginia 364
 War of Idependence 215
 women's rights 140, 425
Hoboken 158-9
 accommodations 173
holidays 421
Hooper's Island 328
horses 324, 329, 372
hot springs 356
Hudson 28, 119
Hughes, Langston 285

Hurricane Sandy 427

ice skating 42,
 New York City 94
 New York State 145
 Virginia 375
insurance 413
internet access 421
Irving, Washington 121
Ithaca 11, 29, 136-41, **138**
 accommodations 149
 drinking 140, 141
 food 137, 139, 141
itineraries 26-33, see also *individual locations*

Jacqueline Kennedy Onassis Reservoir 95
Jamestown 424
Jay-Z 428
Jefferson, Thomas 133, 273
Jewish culture 43, 91, 125, 432
Johns Hopkins University 335
jousting 324

Kane 237
Katz's Delicatessen 68
kayaking
 Delaware 313
 Maryland 327
 New Jersey 158, 172
 New York City 85
 New York State 124, 133
 Pennsylvania 233
 Philadelphia 195
 Virginia 376
 West Virginia 395, 399
Kennedy, John F 256, 265
Kennett Square 214
Kent Country 308
Key, Francis Scott 425
King, Dr Martin Luther 426
Kingston 124
Krishna P Singh Center for Nanotechnology 212

Lake George 28, 129-35, **130-1**
 accommodations 149
 drinking 133
 food 132, 134
Lake Placid 20, 135

lakes 18, see *individual lakes*
Lambertville 157
 accommodations 173
Lancaster & PA Dutch Country 243-6, **245**
 accommodations 249
 food 246
language 37
Laurel Highlands
 accommodations 249
Lee, Robert E 380
Lennon, John 95
lesbian travelers, see LGBTIQ+ travelers
Lewes 313
 accommodations 315
LGBTIQ+ travelers 418
 Delaware 313
 New York City 75
 Philadelphia 185-91
 Washington, DC 273, 274, 286
lighthouses 110, 165, 168, 171, 314, 369
Lincoln, Abraham 247, 264, 268, 426
Little Italy, see SoHo, Chinatown, Nolita & Little Italy
Livingston Manor 128
Logan Square & Fairmount 196-8, **198**
 food 197, 198
 accommodations 219
Long Beach Island 164
 accommodations 173
Long Island 23, 110
Lower East Side, see East Village & the Lower East Side
Lower Manhattan, see Financial District & Lower Manhattan
Lyme disease 172

Mack, Darryl 435
Macy's 188
Madison, James 368
Madison Square Garden 83
Mafia, the 171
markets
 Baltimore 334
 Brooklyn 98
 Delaware 303, 308
 Lancaster & PA Dutch Country 243
 New Jersey 157
 New York City 67, 75, 79
 Philadelphia 190, 204
 Virginia 351, 365, 382
 Washington, DC 272,

279, 290
West Virginia 393
Maryland 317-43, **318**
 accommodations 343
 itineraries 319
measures 421
Midtown 80-5, **82**
 accommodations 101
 food 83, 84, 85
 nightlife 81
Milford 308
 accommodations 315
Mill Mountain Star 13, 364
money 410
Monroe, James 383
Montauk 33, 108-15, **109**, **111**
 accommodations 149
 drinking 110
 food 110, 112, 113
monuments
 African American Civil
  War Memorial 285
 African Burial Ground
  National Monument 62
 Air Force Memorial 374
 Block Sign, the 392
 Booker T Washington
  Memorial 392
 Capitol Street Clock 392
 Coal Miner Sculpture 392
 Duke Ellington's Statue
  285
 Flight 93 233
 Former Capitol Site 392
 Homeless Jesus 392
 Jefferson Memorial 265
 Korean War Veterans
  Memorial 265
 Kunta Kintte-Alex Haley
  Memorial 322
 Lincoln Memorial 264,
  426
 Martin Luther King Jr
  Memorial 264
 National WWII Memorial
  265
 Navy Seal Monument 369
 Neptune statue 371
 Norwegian Lady 369
 Stonewall National
  Monument 75
 Vietnam Veterans
  Memorial 265
 Washington Monument
  262, 335
 Washington's tomb 277
 WWII & Gold Star
  Families Memorial 322
Morgantown 30, 398-9, **399**
 accommodations 405
 beyond Morgantown
  400-3
 drinking 399
mountains 12-13, 412

Adirondacks, the 133, 432
Allegheny Mountains 356
Appalachian 12
Blue Ridge Mountains
 12, 356
Buck Mountain 13
Catoctin Mountain 336
Catskill Mountains 12,
 126-8
Hawk Mountain 241
Hunter Mountain 21, 124
Indian Head 132
Mt Beacon 118
Old Rag Mountain 366-7
Overlook Mountain 124
Prospect Mountain 132
Shawangunk Ridge 124
Snowshoe Mountain 21
Storm King Mountain 119
Whiteface Mountain 21,
 132, 135
Mulberry St 66
museums & galleries
 1914 mansion 86
 Abby Aldrich Rockefeller
  Sculpture Garden 83
 Addison/Ripley Fine
  Art 292
 Air Mobility Comm &
  Museum 308
 AKC Museum of the
  Dog 83
 Allegany Museum 340
 American Civil War
  Museum 351
 American Folk Art
  Museum 96
 American Museum of
  Natural History 92
 American Visionary Art
  Museum 332
 Andy Warhol Museum
  226
 Annapolis Maritime
  Museum 322
 Archaearium 355
 Art Alley 281
 Artechouse 269
 Art Omi 118
 Asia Society & Museum 91
 Atlantic Wildfowl
  Heritage Museum 369
 August Wilson Center
  229
 B&O Railroad Museum
  334
 Baltimore American
  Indian Center 321
 Baltimore Museum of
  Art 333
 Baltimore Museum of
  Industry 332, 334
 Banneker-Douglass-
  Tubman Museum 322

Barnes Foundation 197
Benjamin Franklin
 Museum 183
Bethel Woods Center for
 the Arts 127
Betsy Ross House 181
Biggs Museum of
 American Art 308
B&O Railroad Museum
 334
Boscobel House &
 Gardens 118
Branch Museum of
 Architecture & Design
 351
Brunel Sculpture Garden
 125
Buffalo AKG Art Museum
 143
Buffalo History Museum
 143
Buffalo Transportation
 Pierce-Arrow Museum
 143
Burchfield Penney Art
 Center 143
Cape Charles Museum
 371
Capitol Hill Art League
 273
Capitol Hill Arts District
 273
Capitol Hill Arts
 Workshop 273
Carnegie Museums 228
Catskill Fly Fishing
 Center and Museum 127
Chesapeake Bay
 Maritime Museum
 327, 328
City Reliquary 99
Clay Center for the Arts &
 Sciences 392
Clayton House 227
Copeland Maritime
 Center 303
Corning Museum of
 Glass 141
Culture House DC 269
Cumberland Visitor
 Center & Museum 340
Delaware Agricultural
 Museum 308
Delaware Art Museum
 304
Delaware Children's
 Museum 303
Delaware History
 Museum & Mitchell
 Center for African
 American Heritage 305
Dia Beacon 116
Dia Bridgehampton 112
Dia Chelsea 79

Dupont Underground 291
Eastern State
 Penitentiary 197
Edgar Allan Poe National
 Historic Site 199
Evergreen Museum 334
Fabulous Furniture 125
Fireman's Hall Museum
 184
Flatwoods Monster
 Museum 397
Fort McHenry National
 Monument and Historic
 Shrine 327, 335
Fort Ticonderoga 132
Fort William Henry
 Museum 132
Frick Art Museum 227
Frick Collection 91
Gagosian 79
Gallery Article 15 292
Gallery O on H 281
Gilded Age Lives, the 291
Grounds for Sculpture
 154
Guggenheim Museum 91
Hagley Museum & Library
 306
Harriet Tubman Museum
 & Education Center 326
Harriet Tubman
 Underground Railroad
 Visitor Center 325-6
Havre de Grace Decoy
 Museum 320
Heinz History Center 228
High Line Nine 79
Hill Center 274
Hole 69
Hudson River Maritime
 Museum 125
Hyde Collection 134
Independence National
 Historical Park 182
Independence Seaport
 Museum 184
Institute for
 Contemporary Art 350
International Center of
 Photography 69
International Spy
 Museum 271
Intrepid Sea, Air & Space
 Museum 85
Jamestown Glasshouse
 358
Jewish Museum 91
Jewish Museum of
 Maryland 334
John Bell House 308
Johnson Victrola
 Museum 308
Judd Foundation 67
Kensington Kinetic

439

INDEX

M-M

INDEX

M–N

Sculpture Derby & Arts Festival 200
KuBe Art Center 118
Kykuit 118
Lake Placid Olympic Museum 135
Leslie-Lohman Museum of Art 63
Liberty Island 58
Magazzino Italian Art 118
Maryland Science Center 327, 331
Mattress Factory 226
Mehari Sequar Gallery 281
Mercer Museum 217
Merchant's House Museum 67
Metropolitan Museum of Art 88-90
Michener Art Museum 216, 217
Military Aviation Museum 369
Monongalia Arts Center 398
Moravian Tile Factory 216
Museum for Art in Wood 184
Museum of Broadway 81
Museum of Illusions 268
Museum of Modern Art 83
Museum of the City of New York 87
Mütter Museum 192
Nanticoke River Discovery Center 321, 328
National Air & Space Museum 265
National Archives 266
National Building Museum 268
National Children's Museum 268
National Constitution Center 178
National Great Blacks in Wax Museum 334
National Museum of African American History & Culture 261
National Museum of

African Art 264
National Museum of American History 335
National Museum of Asian Art 264
National Museum of Civil War Medicine 337
National Museum of Natural History 261
National Museum of the American Indian 262
National Museum of Women in the Arts 268
National Portrait Gallery 268
National Toy Train Museum 244
Nauticus 371
New Museum 69
New York City Fire Museum 67
New York Earth Room 65
New-York Historical Society 96
Nicholas Roerich Museum 96
Pace Gallery 79
Park Avenue Armory 91
Paula Cooper Gallery 79
Penn Museum 211
Pennsylvania Academy of the Fine Arts 193
Pennsylvania Lumber Museum 236
Philadelphia Museum of Art 196
Philadelphia's Magic Gardens 207
Phillips Collection 288
Pittsburgh Glass Center 227
Planet Word 268
Pollock-Krasner House 112
Port Discovery Children's Museum 327
Princeton 155
Railroad Museum of Pennsylvania 244
Reginald F Lewis Museum 333
Rehoboth Art League 313
Renwick Gallery 260
Rockwell Museum of Western Art 141
Rodin Museum 198
Row-house Mansion 291
Rubell Museum 269
Ryves Holt House 314
Sag Harbor Whaling & Historical Museum 110
Science History Institute

181
Science Museum of Virginia 351
Smithsonian American Art Museum 268
Smithsonian museums 10
South Street Seaport Museum 60
Star-Spangled Banner Flag House 335
Storm King Art Center 118
Sunnyside 121
Tenement Museum 68
Textile Museum 260
Thurgood Marshall Center 285
Valley Forge National Historic Park 215
Virginia Museum of Fine Arts 350
Virginia Musical Museum 354
Volta Laboratory & Bureau 295
Walters Art Museum 333
Washington Printmakers Gallery 292
West Virginia Bigfoot Museum 397
West Virginia State Museum 392
Wharton Esherick Museum 215
Whispering Gallery 276
Whitney Museum of American Art 73
Wild Center 132
Winterthur Museum, Garden & Library 306
World's Only Mothman Museum, the 396
Zwaanendael Museum 313
music 37, 428
Delaware 304, 305, 312
New Jersey 163, 172
New York City 69, 76
New York State 127, 145
Pennsylvania 237, 242
Philadelphia 188, 201
Virginia 350, 356, 372
Washington, DC 271, 281, 286, 295

N

Narrowsburg 128
National Aquarium 331
National Mall 261-5, **263**
food 262

national & state parks & reserves, *see also* parks & gardens
Adirondack Park 12, 133
Allegheny National Forest 236
Assateague Island National Seashore 329
Assateague Island State Park 329
Bald Eagle State Park 236
Berkeley Springs State Park 401
Blackbird State Forest 309
Blackwater National Wildlife Refuge 326
Buttermilk Falls State Park 136
Camp Hero State Park 110
Cape Henlopen State Park 312, 314
Cape May Point State Park 162
Catoctin Mountain Park 337
Cheesequake State Park 157
Cherry Springs State Park 13, 236
Chincoteague National Wildlife Refuge 372
Colton Point State Park 235
Cook Forest 236
Delaware Park 142
Delaware Seashore State Park 312, 313
Elizabeth A Morton National Wildlife Refuge 112
Elk Country Visitor Center 236
Herrington Manor State Park 342
High Point State Park 157
Hither Hills State Park 109
Hyner View State Park 236
Kittatinny Valley State Park 157
Leonard Harrison State Park 235
Letchworth State Park 145
Montauk Point State Park 110
National Seashore Visitor Center 329
New River Gorge National Park &

Map Pages **000**

440

Preserve 13, 30, 394, 427
Norman G Wilder Wildlife Area 309
Norvin Green State Forest 157
Ohiopyle State Park 19, 233
Pine Creek Gorge 235
Point Lookout State Park 324
Prime Hook National Wildlife Refuge 312
Princeton Battlefield State Park 154
Robert H Treman State Park 136
Shadmoor State Park 112
Shenandoah National Park 356, 366, 426
Sinnemahoning State Park 236
Sourland Mountain Preserve 154
Swallow Falls State Park 342
Watkins Glen State Park 136
West Virginia Penitentiary 402
Wharton State Forest 157, 172
Wild Birds Nature Trail 112
Women's Rights National Historical Park 140
Native American culture 10, 59, 129, 135, 159, 241, 262, 302, 321
New Hope 218
New Jersey 150-73, **152**
 accommodations 173
 itineraries 153
New River Gorge 394
New Vrindaban 403
New York City 26, 48-101, 78, **50-1**
 accommodations 101
 food 38
 itineraries 52-3
New York State 28, 103-49, **104-5**
 accommodations 149
 itineraries 106-7
Newark 157
Niagara Falls, see Buffalo & Niagara Falls, waterfalls
nightlife, 15, 414-15, see also individual locations
Nolita, see SoHo, Chinatown, Nolita & Little Italy

Norfolk 371
North Fork 113-15
Northeast 279-81, **280**
 accommodations 285
 food 279, 280
 nightlife 281
Northern Liberties, see Fishtown & Northern Liberties 199
Northern Panhandle, the 402

Ocean City 32, 164, 328, 329-30, **330**
 accommodations 343
 food 330
Ocean Grove 170
 accommodations 173
O'Keeffe, Georgia 361
Old City & Society Hill 15, 178-84, **179**, **184**
 accommodations 219
 drinking 180
 food 180, 181
 walking tour 184, **184**
Oxford 328

PA Wilds 235-8, **237**
 accommodations 249
 food 238
parks & gardens, see also national & state parks & reserves
 Bartram's Garden 209
 Battery 60
 Bryant Park 84
 Carl Schurz Park 91
 Carroll Creek Park 336
 Central Park 94-5
 Delaware Botanic Gardens at Pepper Creek 314
 Dover Green 307
 Elizabeth St Garden 66
 Founders Park 381
 Glen Echo Park 338
 Gravelly Point Park 374
 High Line 75
 Hudson River Park 77
 Institute Woods 154
 James River Park 352
 Kenilworth Aquatic Gardens 281
 Lavender Fields at Warrington Manor 312
 Little Island 75
 Longwood 214
 LongHouse Reserve 112
 Meridian Hill Park 285

 Mt Cuba Center 306
 Nemours Estate 306
 Neptune's Park 369
 Old Mill Park 376
 One Love Park 305
 Riverfront Park 376
 Riverside Park 96
 Rock Creek Park trail 256
 Schuylkill Banks 195
 Spruce Street Park 184
 Tubman Garrett Riverfront Park 303
 Union Sq 79
 United States National Arboretum 280
 Virginia Outdoor Center 376
 Washington Square Park 78-9
Pearl St 62
Penn Quarter & Chinatown 266-8, **267**
 accommodations 285
 food 268
Penn Relays 211
Penn, William 192, 243
Penn Yan 141
Pennsylvania 220-49, **222**
 accommodations 249
 itineraries 223
Penn, William 192, 243
Penn Yan 141
Pentagon, the 374
people 428-9
Philadelphia 10, 26, 175-219, **176**
 accommodations 219
 beyond Philadelphia 214-18
 itineraries 177
 shopping 190
Pine Barrens 171
Pittsburgh 30, 224-9, **225**
 accommodations 249
 beyond Pittsburgh 230-4
 drinking 229
 food 224, 227, 228
Poconos, the 10, 239-42, **240**
 accommodations 249
 food 241, 242
Poe, Edgar Allan 199, 351
Point Pleasant 164, 396
 accommodations 405
population 421
Prabhupada, Srila 403
Princeton 154-5, **155**
 accommodations 173
 beyond Princeton 156
 food 155
public transportation 409, 413

public holidays 421

rafting 43
 Maryland 341
 Pennsylvania 234, 241
 West Virginia 395
Rehoboth 310-14, **311**
 accommodations 315
 drinking 312, 313
 food 310, 314
 shopping 312
responsible travel 416-17
Richmond 348-52, **349**
 accommodations 385
 drinking 350, 351
 food 351, 352
rideshares 408, 409
Rittenhouse Square & Center City West 192-5, **193**
 accommodations 219
 drinking 195
 food 194
rivers
 Anacostia River 281
 Casselman River 233
 Choptank River 326
 Christina River 302
 Delaware River 124, 126
 Elk River 390
 Kanawha River 390
 Monongahela River 399
 New River 395
 Potomac River 295, 373, 380
 Rappahannock River 376
 Roanoke River 364
 Schuylkill River 195
Rizzo, Frank 206
Roanoke 13, 31, 362-5, **363**
 accommodations 385
 drinking 365
 food 364
 shopping 365
Robbinsville 156
Rockefeller Plaza 80
Rockefellers, the 432
Rocky 201, 204
Ross, Betsy 181
Run DMC 435
running 211, 374

safe travel 357, 413
Sag Harbor 110
Sandy Hook 171
Sardi's 81
Scorsese, Martin 428
Scranton 241
Seaside Heights 164

Seeger, Pete 120
Seneca Falls 425
sharks 18
Shockoe Bottom 351
shopping 218, 244, *see also individual locations*
Skaneateles 141
skiing 20-1, 43
  Maryland 341
  New York State 135
  West Virginia 403
Slide Hill 54
Smith Island 328
Smithsonian National Zoo 286
Society Hill, *see* Old City & Society Hill
SoHo, Chinatown, Nolita & Little Italy 63, **64**
  drinking 67
  food 65, 66
  shopping 67
Southern Maryland 323
South Philadelphia 204-7, **205**
  accommodations 219
  nightlife 207
Southwest 269-72, **270**, **272**
  accommodations 285
  food 271
spas 69, 294, 401
sports 211, 271, 303, 324, 332, 375, 428
Springsteen, Bruce 428
star-gazing 236, 295
St Michaels 328
Stone St 62
subways 409
surfing 43
  Montauk 108
  New Jersey 165
  Virginia Beach 370
Sussex County 308, 314
Sutton 397
  accommodations 405
swimming 124, 413

Taxi Driver 428
taxi travel 408, 409
telephones 421
theaters

Map Pages **000**

442

Agecroft Hall 352
Atlantic Theater Company 76
Atlas Performing Arts Center 281
Capital One Arena 268
Cherry Grove Community House & Theater 113
Cinema Art Theater 313
Clayton Theatre 313
Clear Space Theatre Company 313
Comedy Cellar 76
Daughters of the American Revolution (DAR) Constitution Hall 260
Delaware Theatre Company 304
drag shows 186
Grand Opera House 304
Howard Theatre 284
Joe's Pub 66
John F. Kennedy Center for the Performing Arts 256
Lincoln Center 96
Lincoln Theatre 285
Lucille Lortel Theatre 76
Metropolitan Theatre 398-9
Milton Theatre 313
National Theater 268
Playhouse on Rodney Square 304
Playwrights Horizons 83
Public 66
Radio City Music Hall 83
Queen, The 304
Richmond Triangle Players 352
Shakespeare Theatre Company 268
Slipper Room 69
Studio Theatre 290
Village Vanguard 76
Violet Crown Theater 359
Warner Theatre 268
Woolly Mammoth Theatre Company 268
Yes, And! Theatrical Company 352
ticks 172, 413
time zones 421
Times Square 80, 84
tipping 410
TKTS booth 81
toilets 421
Top of the Rock 80
tours, *see also* driving tours, walking tours
  Buffalo 143

Cape May 160
New Jersey 172
New York City 85
Philadelphia 191
Pittsburgh 227
Star Trek Original Series Set Tour 132
Valley Forge 215
Washington, DC 264, 281
wine 360
train travel 408, 409
  Maryland 327, 340
  Pennsylvania 244
Trumansburg 141
tubing
  Maryland 341
  New York State 124, 132
  Pennsylvania 241
  Virginia 376
  West Virginia 402
Tubman, Harriet 325-6

U Street Corridor, the, *see* Adams Morgan & the U Street Corridor
Underground Railroad, the 325
United Nations 83
University City & West Philadelphia 208-13, **210**
  accommodations 219
  drinking 211
  food 209, 212
Upper East Side 86-91, **87**
  accommodations 101
  drinking 91
  food 91
Upper West Side 92-6, **93**
  accommodations 101
  food 96
US Naval Academy 322

vacations 430-2
Valley Forge 215
Vanderbilts, the 432
vineyards
  Delaware 306
  Maryland 339, 433
  New Jersey 162, 433
  New York State 114-15, 139, 433
  Pennsylvania 433
  Philadelphia 217
  Virginia 360, 433
Virginia 344-85, **346**
  accommodations 385
  itineraries 347
Virginia Beach 369-70, **370**
  accommodations 385
  beyond Virginia Beach 371-2
  drinking 370
von Furstenberg, Diane 76-7

walking 14
walking tours
  Alexandria 380
  Annapolis 322, **322**
  Delaware 314
  Financial District & Lower Manhattan 62, **62**
  Philadelphia 184, **184**
  Pittsburgh 227
  Virginia 355
  Washington, DC 272, 273, 278, **272**, **278**
Wall St 62
Washington, DC 15, 27, 251-285, **252-3**
  accommodations 285
  itineraries 254-5
Washington, George 11, 379, 381
waterfalls
  Bastion Falls 124
  Cucumber Falls 234
  Dingmans Falls 242
  Falling Springs Falls 356
  Ithaca Falls 137
  Kaaterskill Falls 121, 122
  Lucifer Falls 139
  Meadow Run 234
  Muddy Creek Falls 342
  Niagara Falls 19, 146-8
  Taughannock Falls 136
  Watkins Glen 141
weather 34-5
weights 421
West Overton 231
West Philadelphia, *see* University City & West Philadelphia
West Village & Chelsea 73-79, **74**
  accommodations 101
  drinking 75, 76
  food 75, 77
  shopping 75
West Virginia 387-405, **388**
  accommodations 405
  hiking 394
  itineraries 389
Wharf DC 272
Western Maryland 340-342, **341**
  accommodations 343
  food 342

Wheeling 403
  accommodations 405
whiskey 40, 231
White House, the & Foggy
  Bottom 256-60, **257**
  accommodations 285
  food 260
wildlife 413, *see also*
  individual species
  Delaware 302, 309, 312
  Maryland 320, 325,
    326, 329
  New Jersey 161, 172
  New York State 126
  Virginia 372
Wildwood 163
  accommodations 173
Williamsburg 353-58,
  354, **358**
  accommodations 385
  driving tours 356-58
  food 355
Wilmington 26, 302-06,
  303, **306**
  accommodations 315
  drinking 304
  food 305
  walking tour 306, **306**
Wilson, August 229
wine 23, 40, *see also*
  vineyards
Winter Olympics 20, 135
Woodstock 122-28,
  123, **128**
  accommodations 149
  drinking 125
  food 124, 126
Wright, Frank Lloyd 230

yoga 156
Yorktown 358

Z

ziplining 135, 395, 402

NOTES

NOTES

445

NOTES

NOTES

"Take a bite of the Big Apple and you'll barely scratch the surface – spend a lifetime in New York City and you'll still find yourself surprised."
– JOHN GARRY

"For all of its guise as a big city, Washington, DC feels more like a small town, a place where everyone is welcome and at home."
– MARISA PASKA

All rights reserved. No part of this publication may be copied, stored in a retrieval system, or transmitted in any form by any means, electronic, mechanical, recording or otherwise, except brief extracts for the purpose of review, and no part of this publication may be sold or hired, without the written permission of the publisher. Lonely Planet and the Lonely Planet logo are trademarks of Lonely Planet and are registered in the US Patent and Trademark Office and in other countries. Lonely Planet does not allow its name or logo to be appropriated by commercial establishments, such as retailers, restaurants or hotels. Please let us know of any misuses: lonelyplanet.com/legal/intellectual-property.

Mapping data sources:
© Lonely Planet
© OpenStreetMap http://openstreetmap.org/copyright

THIS BOOK

Destination Editor
Caroline Trefler

Production Editor
Graham O'Neill

Book Designer
Megan Cassidy

Cartographer
Valentina Kremenchutskaya

Assisting Editors
Andrew Bain, Imogen Bannister, Nigel Chin, Charles Rawlings-Way, Maja Vatrić

Cover Researcher
Marc Backwell

Thanks Ronan Abayawickrema, Melanie Dankel, Karen Henderson, Alison Killilea, Katerina Pavkova

FROM LEFT: ROMANISLAVIK.COM/SHUTTERSTOCK ©, LUNAMARINA/SHUTTERSTOCK ©

MIX
Paper | Supporting responsible forestry
FSC™ C021741
www.fsc.org

Paper in this book is certified against the Forest Stewardship Council™ standards. FSC™ promotes environmentally responsible, socially beneficial and economically viable management of the world's forests.

Published by Lonely Planet Global Limited
CRN 554153
3rd edition – Jan 2025
ISBN 978 1 83758 491 8
© Lonely Planet 2025 Photographs © as indicated 2025
10 9 8 7 6 5 4 3 2 1
Printed in China